INTERNATIONAL
WORLD ORDER

SECOND EDITION

In *International Law and World Order*, B. S. Chimni articulates an Integrated Marxist Approach to International Law (IMAIL) combining the insights of Marxism, socialist feminism and postcolonial theory. The book uses IMAIL to systematically and critically examine the most influential contemporary theories of international law including new, feminist, realist and policy-oriented approaches. In doing so, it discusses a range of themes relating to the history, structure and process of international law. The book also considers crucial world order issues and problems that the international legal process has to contend with, including the welfare of weak groups and nations, the ecological crisis and the role of human rights. This extensively revised second edition provides an invaluable, in-depth and updated review of the key literature and scholarship within this field of study. It will be of particular interest to students and scholars of international law, international relations, international politics and global studies.

B. S. CHIMNI is Professor of International Law at the School of International Studies, Jawaharlal Nehru University, India.

INTERNATIONAL LAW AND WORLD ORDER

A Critique of Contemporary Approaches

SECOND EDITION

B. S. CHIMNI
Jawaharlal Nehru University

CAMBRIDGE
UNIVERSITY PRESS

CAMBRIDGE
UNIVERSITY PRESS

University Printing House, Cambridge CB2 8BS, United Kingdom

One Liberty Plaza, 20th Floor, New York, NY 10006, USA

477 Williamstown Road, Port Melbourne, VIC 3207, Australia

314-321, 3rd Floor, Plot 3, Splendor Forum, Jasola District Centre, New Delhi - 110025, India

79 Anson Road, #06-04/06, Singapore 079906

Cambridge University Press is part of the University of Cambridge.

It furthers the University's mission by disseminating knowledge in the pursuit of education, learning and research at the highest international levels of excellence.

www.cambridge.org
Information on this title: www.cambridge.org/9781107692220
DOI: 10.1017/9781107588196

© B. S. Chimni 2017

First edition published by Sage (New Delhi) in 1993
Second edition 2017
First paperback edition 2018

A catalogue record for this publication is available from the British Library

Library of Congress Cataloging in Publication data
Names: Chimni, B. S., 1952– author.
Title: International law and world order: a critique of contemporary approaches /
B. S. Chimni, Jawaharlal Nehru University.
Description: Second edition. | New York : Cambridge University Press, 2017. |
Includes bibliographical references and index.
Identifiers: LCCN 2016059343 | ISBN 9781107065260 (hardback)
Subjects: LCSH: International law.
Classification: LCC KZ3405.C45 A35 2017 | DDC 341–dc23
LC record available at https://lccn.loc.gov/2016059343

ISBN 978-1-107-06526-0 Hardback
ISBN 978-1-107-69222-0 Paperback

CONTENTS

PREFACE TO THE SECOND EDITION

The second edition is more *a new book* than a new edition. The different chapters of the first edition have been substantially revised. New chapters have been added on New Approaches to International Law (NAIL) and Feminist Approaches to International Law (FtAIL). A new theoretical framework has also been advanced incorporating the insights of Marxism, socialist feminism and postcolonial theory. In this light, a chapter on an Integrated Marxist Approach to International Law (IMAIL) replaces the earlier chapter on a Marxist theory of international law.

It is hoped that the new edition will be useful for students of international law and international relations who wish to have a deeper understanding of both disciplines. For between them these approaches raise the most vital epistemological and ontological questions that must concern anyone attempting to explain and understand contemporary international law and world order. Indeed, these approaches question, albeit from different standpoints, every single assumption and belief pertaining to the history, structure and process of international law and world order. They also engage with and discuss the central issues of our times. Therefore, there is no gain in saying that some familiarity with them will be rewarding. While the chapters on individual approaches can be read as standalone chapters, these are also intended to clarify the IMAIL perspective on different themes and issues dealt with by them. Thus, in an important sense the entire book may be read as devoted to the elucidation and elaboration of IMAIL.

I believe that the geographical location of an author has an important influence on how different theories of international law and world order are received and evaluated. It is therefore perhaps worth mentioning that I have had all my formal education in India where I have lived and taught all my life. It colours the way I approach and look at issues of international law and also write about them. I would request the readers to bear this in mind.

In the writing of this edition of the book, I have incurred a great number of debts. It is my pleasant duty to acknowledge them. Above all I wish to acknowledge the enormous debt of gratitude I owe to the Third World Approaches to International Law (TWAIL) movement. It has been an absolute privilege and honour to be part of the TWAIL project which has shaped in fundamental ways my thinking on international law and world order. I wish to especially thank fellow travellers Antony Anghie, James Gathii, Usha Natarajan, Obiora Okafor, Karin Mickelson, Vasuki Nesiah, Balakrishnan Rajagopal and Hani Syed for their friendship. I also wish to thank the pioneers of TWAIL scholarship, especially Georges Abi-Saab, R. P. Anand, Mohammed Bedjaoui, T. E. Elias, Muthuswamy Sornarajah and Christopher Weeramantry for giving me the confidence to chalk out my own path.

There are several individuals who helped in the writing of this edition. Antony Anghie not only commented on the introduction and the chapter on NAIL but also provided moral support throughout the writing of the book. I have turned to him for advice on countless occasions. Prabha Kotiswaran, Vasuki Nesiah and Dianne Otto read and commented on the chapter on feminist approaches to international law, and Siddharth Malvarappu reviewed the chapter on classical realism. I wish to express my heartfelt thanks to all of them.

I would also like to take this opportunity to thank José Alvarej, Hilary Charlesworth, Michael Fakhri, Richard Falk, David Kennedy, Benedict Kingsbury, Susan Marks, Gregor Noll, Yasuaki Onuma, Anne Orford, Akbar Rasulov, Siddharth Malvarappu and Thomas Skouteris for their encouragement and support over the years.

I would be failing in my duty if I did not thank the two anonymous reviewers who recommended the publication of this edition to the Cambridge University Press. Their suggestions on how to improve the first edition were very helpful. I would also like to thank Finola O'Sullivan of Cambridge University Press for her help and guidance in producing this edition. Needless to add, I alone remain responsible for the shortcomings of the book.

Last but not the least I wish to thank my family for their love and affection without which this book would not have come to fruition.

ACKNOWLEDGEMENTS TO THE FIRST EDITION

This study captures and incarcerates the moment of self-clarification. If it has assumed the form of a book it is because of the felt absence of any work, written in the developing world, which critically explores the principal contemporary approaches to international law and world order. I am deeply grateful to Professor Richard Falk for agreeing to contribute a foreword. It is my regret that the critical nature of the work prevented me from recording at length the empathy and solidarity he has shown in his writings with the cause of the developing world. He has been for me, as I am sure for many others, an inspirational figure. I would also like to thank Dr Sudipta Kaviraj for the discussions I had with him on a wide range of issues. Finally, I would like to thank my wife for the constant encouragement I received. Needless to add, I alone am responsible for the errors and infelicities.

FOREWORD TO THE FIRST EDITION

There has, of course, been significant work done by non-Western international law specialists in the several decades since the collapse of the colonial order. But virtually all of this work, even the most explicitly anti-Western, has relied on Western approaches in a relatively uncritical manner. On reflection, this reliance is not surprising. There was a strong tendency for Third World students to receive their advanced graduate training in law, especially international law, from leading universities in Europe and North America. Further, the received scholarship was dominated by Western authors.

As a consequence, the emergence of distinctive modes of thought and analysis failed to accompany the process of decolonisation, or even to follow upon it. Oddly, also, even where intellectual fashions were strongly influenced by Marxist currents of thinking, almost all international law writing emanating from the Third World tried to avoid any ideological imprint. Here again, it is not difficult to find an explanation. International legal work automatically aspired to be scientific in a Western sense, a pattern evident even in the better work of Soviet international lawyers in the period after Stalin. This Soviet work, including that of Grigory Tunkin and Rein Mullerson, relied almost exclusively on non-Marxist scholarship even when intent on defending Soviet policy positions and attacking those of the United States. It was pragmatically oriented towards enabling Soviet bloc participation in the prevailing debates in Western international law circles.

What makes the work of B. S. Chimni so exciting and exceptional is that it clears the way for a jail-break from such lingering intellectual hegemony. His *International Law and World Order; A Critique of Contemporary Approaches* is a double achievement. It is an explicit critique of Western non-Marxist thinking, but it also lays the basis for a genuinely Marxist approach rooted in the realities and projects of the Third World. Chimni displays a real mastery over the complex and diverse material that he discusses, and is impressively fair in presenting criticism, taking real account of the most serious efforts by the scholars whom he criticises. As one of those, I can report that reading Chimni's book is a learning experience, and does not tempt me to evade criticism with the retort, 'He has got me wrong'. His readings of the work of others is careful and his interpretations illuminating.

Let me try briefly to explain why Chimni seems successfully embarked on a long journey of scholarly liberation. Unlike others who have criticised substance, doctrine, and history, Chimni concentrates on the modes of theorising, pointing to their inadequacies. As such, his book opens the way for new modes, including his own prescriptions for a Marxist jurisprudence informed by and distinct from the sort of statist distortions and polemical imperatives that were characteristic of the Soviet era. Such an orientation strikes me as promising, but by no means exclusive; there are other orientations toward law-in-the-world that do not draw their primary inspiration from the Marxist tradition, yet offer a basis for a progressive and coherent approach to international law and world order. For instance, I continue to work toward the formulation of such a perspective without nearly as explicit affinities as Chimni, while at the same time acknowledging Marxist influences.

Among Chimni's many virtues is his persuasive rehabilitation of Marxist thought as the foundation for a progressive theory of international law. The timing of publication is intriguing. At the very moment when much of the West is celebrating 'the end of history', Chimni is convincingly demonstrating that not only does history persist – really, a rather banal conclusion – but that Marxism, properly regarded, continues to offer the preferred vehicle for its most beneficial embodiment. What Chimni means by Marxism is a rich, varied, and humanist tradition of thought that encompasses the young Marx, Gramsci, Laclau, Poulantzas, and Wallerstein. This Marxist orientation offers the socio-economic grounding for a new jurisprudence.

There is another reason to celebrate the publication of Chimni's book. By taking the trouble to emphasise theoretical approaches, Chimni is implicitly confirming the importance of international law for progressive politics at this time. That is, international law is not reduced to a tool of foreign offices or as a technical area of expertise that has a bearing upon the organisation of international life. For Chimni, international law provides part of the foundation of world order, and as such, needs to be rooted in fundamental thought about society and the state. Such an outlook is particularly responsive to increasing complexity and intensifying environmental hazards of global scope. Without a normatively self-aware perspective, international law would again certainly become an instrument for legitimising the oppressive features of the current world order, a role historically played to fullest extent during the period of colonial rule and capitalist expansion beyond Europe.

In these early post–Cold War years there is already evident a strong and conscious disposition to appropriate international law as a hegemonic instrument of the North, especially the United States. During the 1990 build-up to the Gulf War, George Bush repeatedly insisted that a prime motive for reversing Iraq's aggression against Kuwait was the importance of strengthening international law. Taken in isolation such an assertion is plausible, but if accompanied by the most minimal recall of the United States' own recourse to force on a unilateral basis (for instance, the military intervention in Panama just months earlier) or of the refusal to bring pressure on Israel to withdraw from the occupied territories of West Bank, Gaza, and East Jerusalem or on Indonesia to quit East Timor or West Papua, then the level of hypocrisy is crass. Yet what is more disturbing, than the American project to appropriate international law on behalf of a comprehensive framework of double standards is the acquiescence of the rest of the world, especially countries in the South. Such acquiescence undoubtedly reflects a mood of demoralisation, including the conviction that the United States is in unchallengeably firm control of the institutional and normative structures of international political and economic life, possibly sharing such control, to the extent necessary, with other centres of capital in the North, especially Japan and Europe.

Fortunately, there are alternative lines of response that create a more hopeful and far less deterministic prospect for the future. One such line, about which Chimni is helpfully critical, is the realisation by transnational political and social forces that international law can be used counter-hegemonically. An illustration of this effort to democratise the application of international law goes back to Bertrand Russell's idea of constituting a tribunal of prominent citizens to assess the charges of war crimes being made in the late 1960s against US political and military leaders during the Vietnam War. International law in such an arena becomes a valuable instrument of critical pedagogy and delegitimation. The attempt of such enactments is not to indict and punish the individuals charged in any substantive sense, but to give structure and substance to progressive and symbolic attacks on contested international policies and practices. The Permanent Peoples Tribunal, centred in Rome, has regularly, since 1976, held sessions that assessed and condemned interventions by the North in the South and the use of the IMF and World Bank in oppressive roles.

A recent instance of reliance on international law in the service of radical politics has been the Gulf War Crimes Tribunal constituted in 1992 under the inspirational leadership of Ramsey Clark. In short, these events suggest that peoples as well as states can invoke international law, and have been doing so with particular effectiveness in such areas as the protection of human rights and of environmental quality.

Chimni's progressive jurisprudence is a second line of defence against new hegemonic designs. It opens the way for a comprehensive rethinking of the substance and role of international law, including a critique and repudiation of any legal claims that are not based on mutuality. It cuts through mystifications, and calls for the articulation of a liberation jurisprudence (in this regard, curiously, legal thought has lagged behind even theology!), that is, a framework of laws and procedures dedicated to human well-being, including the enterprise of restructuring the world economy.

It is only fair to acknowledge that Chimni has started the job that now needs to be carried further, hopefully by himself, but also by others. After critique comes construction. This book achieves clarity at the critical level, but it is still enmeshed in Western narratives about the state of the world and the place of international law and international lawyers in it. There is, of course, a continuing need for critical discourse of both a specific and general nature, especially to identify and discredit attempts to impose regimes of double standards on behalf of Western interests: a good current challenge would be a critical account of the US-led effort to insist selectively on non-proliferation of nuclear weaponry without being willing itself to accept even such minimal constraints on its own nuclearism as a Comprehensive Test Ban or a No First Use Pledge, But possibly even more important than criticism at this stage would be a jurisprudential account of international law and world order that carried out positively the critical mandate that Chimni brilliantly fulfils in this book. Hence, as we read this book with appreciation and admiration, we await his next in a spirit of expectation, and given the tormented condition of much of humanity, of urgency.

Richard Falk
Princeton, New Jersey
1992

Introduction

I. Objectives

This book has been written in the belief that much disagreement in international legal discourse is theoretical. As Steven Ratner and Anne-Marie Slaughter observe in their introduction to the volume *The Methods of International Law* 'beneath the surface of much scholarship … are a host of unanswered questions about presuppositions, conceptions, and missions, all of which influence … analysis of an issue and … conclusions and recommendations for decision makers'.[1] There are few occasions to clarify the 'presuppositions, conceptions, and missions' because explicit theorization is still the exception and unspoken theory tends to occlude arguments pertaining to the underlying epistemological and ontological premises.[2] It is not as if there are not enough theories of, or about, international law. But these are not subjects of sustained debate and reflection. A focus on theory is also necessitated today by the growing 'specialization and fragmentation' of the field of international law.[3] In the absence of a theoretical framework it is difficult to explain and evaluate a range of disparate developments that are taking place. The ultimate justification for doing theory is, of course, the desire to transform the world into a place where individuals can live with dignity in harmony with Nature. However, these twin goals cannot be realized without a good understanding of how the present system of world order is constituted, the reasons why it produces inequality and injustice, the role of international law in it and the ways to move forward.

---

[1] Steven R. Ratner and Anne-Marie Slaughter, 'Introduction' in Ratner and Slaughter (eds.) *The Methods of International Law* (Washington DC: The American Society of International Law, 2004), p. 2.

[2] It is another matter that the "empirical" itself has not received sufficient attention. See however Gregory Schaffer and Tom Ginsburg, 'The Empirical Turn in International Legal Scholarship', 106 (2012) *American Journal of International Law*, pp. 1–46.

[3] See ibid., p. 1.

In the backdrop of the felt need for explicit theory, this book sets itself three broad objectives. The first objective is to articulate an Integrated Marxist Approach to International Law (IMAIL), combining the insights of Marxism, socialist feminism and postcolonial theory. The plain justification for this theoretical eclecticism is the recognition that theories overly focused on some social logics (e.g., the 'logic of capital') or on some social categories (e.g., 'class' or 'gender') or on some geographical spaces (e.g., the west) fail to develop a systematic and comprehensive understanding of extant world order, as also the history, nature and character of international law. In contrast, IMAIL enables an accurate diagnosis of the ills that afflict current world order and the role international law and international lawyers can play in addressing them. But it has been well observed that while theoretical eclecticism is not in itself problematic, there is an 'obligation to establish the compatibility of the theoretical elements that are combined', for theories often 'exhibit specific incompatibilities which makes simple appropriation or fusion of distinct theories impossible'.[4] IMAIL is advanced on the assumption that Marxism, socialist feminism and postcolonialism or more accurately *particular versions of each* are not only congruent but helpfully complement each other. It is readily acknowledged that it is possible to offer an interpretation of the three theoretical traditions that place them in opposition to each other.[5] Thus, for example, postcolonial theory may be counterposed to versions of Marxism that subscribe to a linear theory of evolution of society. But IMAIL proceeds on the understanding that the diversity postcolonial theory celebrates is compatible with an interpretation of Marxism that draws on Marx's historicist work.[6] In so far as socialist feminism is concerned,

---

[4] Alan Hunt, 'The Theory of Critical Legal Studies' in Costas Douzinas and Colin Perrin (eds.) *Critical Legal Theory* (London: Routledge, 2012), Volume I pp. 243–286 at pp. 244–245.

[5] For instance, as Sankaran Krishna notes of the works of Hamza Alavi and Robert Young, 'both regard Marxism as the critical tradition that is indispensable for postcolonial thought ... Young and Alavi regard Marx's legacy as complex and contradictory but always indispensable to the politics of resistance that animates postcolonial thought'. Sankaran Krishna, *Globalization and Postcolonialism: Hegemony and Resistance in the Twenty-First Century* (Lanham, MD: Rowman & Littlefield Publishers, Inc., 2009), p. 68.

[6] It is no accident that non-Western thinkers such as Aimé Césaire, Frantz Fanon, Walter Rodney, Amilcar Cabral and C. L. R. James are claimed by both Marxist and postcolonial theoretical traditions. It is unfortunate that, as Benita Parry notes, postcolonial theorists such as Edward Said embraced them 'as comrades ... while omitting to identify them as Marxists'. Benita Parry, 'Edward Said and Third World Marxism', 40 (2013), *College Literature: A Journal of Critical Literary Studies*, pp. 105–136 at pp. 105–106. See also Bart Moore-Gilbert, 'Marxism and Postcolonialism Reconsidered', 7 (2001) *Hungarian Journal*

the influence of Marxism is more apparent albeit the category 'gender' rather than 'class' occupies the pride of place in it. But both the traditions imbibe the other in ways that allow them to come together. Later in the chapter, something more will be said on the nature of borrowings from Marxism, socialist feminism and postcolonial theory.

The second objective of the book is to critically examine the most insightful and influential contemporary approaches to international law from an IMAIL perspective. These are the classical realist approach of Hans Morgenthau, the policy-oriented approach of Myres McDougal and Harold Lasswell, the world order model approach of Richard Falk, the feminist approach of Hilary Charlesworth and Christine Chinkin, and the 'new approaches' of David Kennedy and Martti Koskenneimi. To each of these approaches an independent chapter is devoted. While the book concludes with a separate chapter on IMAIL, it is in vital ways articulated through a critique of these approaches. It is, however, important to stress that the critical moment in the volume does not seek to simply counter-pose IMAIL to different approaches but attempts to examine each of them on its own merit. It is believed that criticism in order to be effective has to proceed at two levels: before proceeding to demonstrate that an alternative perspective can offer more persuasive responses to the questions that are asked or issues that are raised, it must seek to identify the problems, discrepancies and limits of a theory on the basis of its premises and its stated ambitions. Such a procedure helps avoid the tendency of being dismissive of an approach simply because it is different from the preferred approach, both in terms of method and its aspirations. In other words, there must be an internal and external moment of critique – the former identifying the inner tensions and contradictions in an approach and the latter offering ways of addressing or transcending them. This dual mode of critique, at once empathetic and oppositional, not only does justice to individual approaches considered but also yields valuable insights that can be productively incorporated in the favoured approach.

This book does not deal separately with two other leading contemporary approaches to international law, viz., the dominant Positivist Approach to International Law (PAIL) and the influential Third World Approaches to International Law (TWAIL). The reasons for this are discussed presently. The book also does not examine the transnational legal process and the law and economics approaches as these do not as yet have a larger or global appeal.[7] The new international relations-international law (IR-IL) approach is discussed, albeit in the chapter on classical realist approach. On the other hand, the constructive Global Administrative Law (GAL) initiative is not examined as it only offers a partial approach to international law, focused as it is primarily on addressing democratic deficit in the functioning of international bodies.[8] It may be argued that some of the approaches receiving extensive treatment (e.g., the policy-oriented approach) have lost their appeal over time. Even if this were to be the case, these approaches invite study because they rely on assumptions or advance concepts and constructs that continue to inform contemporary writings on international law. An acquaintance with them helps avoid hubris about the novelty of any proposed new approach to international law. Thus, for example, the policy-oriented approach anticipated in many ways the views of 'new approaches' advanced by Kennedy and Koskenneimi. For instance, it centrally raised the issue of indeterminacy of rules long before New Approaches to International Law (NAIL), even as it stressed semantic indeterminacy of rules as against structural indeterminacy emphasized by 'new approaches'. There is also intrinsic value in understanding why any approach was influential at a particular time in history and has much to tell us about why particular approaches matter today.[9] In that limited sense, the present book can be considered as offering a fragment of an intellectual history of the discipline of international law in the post–Second World War period.[10]

---

[7] For a brief discussion of these approaches see Ratner and Slaughter, *Methods of International Law*, pp. 211–239 and 79–109, respectively.

[8] On GAL, see Benedict Kingsbury, Nico Krisch and Richard B. Stewart, 'The Emergence of Global Administrative Law', 68 (2005) *Law and Contemporary Problems*, pp. 15–63. For a critique of GAL, see B. S. Chimni, 'Cooption and Resistance: Two Faces of Global Administrative Law' 37 (2005) *New York University Journal of Law and Politics*, pp. 799–827.

[9] The idea also being to 'try to reconstruct the intellectual contexts in and for which their texts were originally written'. Interview with Quentin Skinner, (2001) 'On Encountering the Past', p. 44. Accessed on 25 May 2015 at www.jyu.fi/yhtfil/redescriptions/Yearbook%20 2002/Skinner_Interview_2002.pdf

[10] There are, of course, many ways in which this history can be told. The different examples of intellectual history can include the story Antony Anghie tells of the relationship of the colonial project to the emergence of positivism in the nineteenth century, David Kennedy's history of the discipline of international law in the United States in the post–Second World War era and Martti Koskenniemi's history of the work and vision of European international lawyers in the nineteenth and twentieth centuries. See Antony Anghie, *Imperialism, Sovereignty and the Making of International Law* (Cambridge: Cambridge University Press, 2003); David Kennedy, 'When Renewal Repeats: Thinking Against the Box' 32 (2000)

The third objective of the book is to consider crucial world order issues and problems that the international legal process has to grapple with. These inter alia include the welfare of weak groups and nations, the ecological crisis, the role of human rights and the absence of democratic structures in the international system. The overall aim of engagement with world order concerns is to arrive at a better understanding of them, and in its light think of global legal and institutional arrangements that can help advance human freedom.[11] Such an ambition anticipates the deployment of what Edward Said termed 'secular criticism', that is, 'a criticism freed from the restrictions of intellectual specialization'.[12] It calls for transgressing disciplinary boundaries to produce knowledge that is life enhancing. The 'secular criticism' is articulated in this book in the matrix of five separate but overlapping and intersecting logics that co-constitute 'world order' viz., the 'logic of capital', the 'logic of territory', the 'logic of nature', the 'logic of culture' and the 'logic of law'. Some bare reflections on the meaning of 'world order' (and 'global governance') and the different logics are offered later in the chapter.

At first, however, something needs to be said on (i) the significance of the fields of origin and reception for assessing contemporary approaches to international law and world order; (ii) the reasons for excluding PAIL and TWAIL from detailed treatment (while offering thumbnail sketches of them) and (iii) the traditions of Marxism, socialist feminism and postcolonial theory that are combined to articulate IMAIL – postcolonial theory receives a little more space as it is not explicitly discussed further in the chapters to follow. The remarks on these themes, especially the inclusion of outlines of PAIL and TWAIL, make this introductory chapter somewhat unusual and protracted. It is, however, hoped that the clarifications and elaborations will help set the stage for the subsequent chapters.

New York Journal of International Law and Politics, p. 335; David Kennedy, 'The Disciplines of International Law and Policy', 1 (1999) *Leiden Journal of International Law*, pp. 9–133; Martti Koskenniemi, *The Gentle Civilizer of Nations: The Rise and Fall of International Law 1870–1960* (Cambridge: Cambridge University Press, 2004).

[11] The broad function of criticism is to be 'life-enhancing and constitutively opposed to every form of tyranny, domination, and abuse; its social goals are noncoercive knowledge produced in the interests of human freedom'. Edward Said, *The World, the Text and the Critic* (Cambridge, MA: Harvard University, Press, 1983), p. 29.

[12] Bill Ashcroft and Pal Ahluwalia, *Edward Said* (London: Routledge, 1999), p. 15, pp. 30ff. According to Ashcroft and Ahluwalia, Said 'introduces the disarming, not to say disconcerting, idea of the critic as "amateur", by which he means that the critic must refuse to be locked into narrow professional specializations which produce their own arcane vocabulary and speak only to other specialists'. See ibid., p. 35.

II.   Fields of Origin and Reception

Since a principal objective of the book is the critique of contemporary approaches to international law which happen to have been articulated in the West, and whereas their critique is being advanced from a location in the non-West i.e., India, it is useful to keep in mind in this regard the distinction Pierre Bourdieu draws between the 'field of origin' and the 'field of reception'.[13] This is an intricate subject that calls for much greater consideration than can be given here. What follows is a mere observation or two on the subject with the sole purpose of alerting readers to the complexities of advancing a critique of approaches that have originated in 'fields of origin' different from that in which these are received, interpreted and understood.[14]

The 'field of origin' is of critical relevance in international exchanges as 'texts circulate without their context'.[15] If particular texts are read without situating these in 'forms of life' in which they have germinated, these can be easily misconstrued. To take the 'field of origin' into account entails that a theoretical approach be read and assessed after locating it in the spatial and temporal contexts in which it assumes life and evolves, including the past approaches to which it is a response.[16] A crucial reason for making the latter move is that concepts and arguments are most often used as 'weapons' in ongoing conversations on a subject in the 'field of origin'.[17] A new approach is also advanced in order to address the perceived inadequacies of existing approaches in a field. From this standpoint it is significant that many of the approaches to international law discussed in the

[13] Pierre Bourdieu, 'The Social Conditions of the International Circulation of Ideas' in Richard Schusterman (ed.) *Bourdieu: A Critical Reader* (Oxford: Blackwell Publishers, 1999), pp. 220–228 at p. 221. It is this distinction that perhaps made Said note that what he was doing in his book *Culture and Imperialism* is 'rethinking geography'. Edward Said, 'Response' in Bruce Robbins, Mary Louise Pratt, Jonathan Arac, R. Radhakrishnan and Edward Said, 'Edward Said's Culture and Imperialism: A Symposium', 40 (1994) *Social Text*, pp. 1–24 at p. 21. It may, however, be noted that the distinction between the 'field of origin' and 'field of reception' equally applies in the West and non-West.
[14] Some of these observations are also valid in the instance of the theories used to articulate IMAIL. But this point is made later through the discussion of the value of postcolonial theory. See infra, pp. 22–30.
[15] Bourdieu, 'The Social Conditions', p. 221.
[16] See ibid. Postcolonial theory is in an important sense all about how literature in the 'field of origin' imagined and portrayed the non-Western world. It is also about how work in the 'field of origin' is received and translated in the 'field of reception'. See Chapter 6, pp. 371, 379.
[17] See generally Quentin Skinner, *Visions of Politics Volume I: Regarding Method* (Cambridge: Cambridge University Press, 2002), p. 177.

book have been articulated by US scholars. These approaches naturally tend to explore theoretical and practical issues that are prominent in legal and public discourse in the United States at a particular time reacting to or building upon prior approaches that have been advanced. Thus, for example, the policy-oriented approach of McDougal and Lasswell was a response to the classical realist and formalist or positivist approaches to international law, as these were not seen as possessing the requisite theoretical and conceptual tools to adequately address issues arising out of the Cold War. Similarly, the intermediate approach of Falk was advanced in relation to the policy-oriented approach in order to affirm a position of relative neutrality during the Cold War. Falk wished to sustain the relationship between law and politics without collapsing the one into the other in the manner of McDougal. He, therefore, sought to occupy the middle ground between McDougal's policy-oriented approach and Hans Kelsen's pure theory of law with its emphasis on the autonomy of law. The different approaches in the 'field of origin' may, despite their divergence, often draw upon common intellectual sources. Thus, for instance, both the policy-oriented approach and NAIL have derived inspiration from American legal realism. Albeit, in moving beyond American legal realism, the two approaches draw upon vastly different intellectual sources: one relying on the conceptual apparatus of Lasswell and the other on a heady mix of linguistic, deconstructive, Weberian, post-structural and post-Marxist theories.[18]

From the perspective of the Global South, the 'field of origin' of contemporary approaches to international law has a broader significance. The fact that most of these have been articulated in the Global North, and further that this state of affairs is reflective of intellectual production in the field of international law in general, has meant that much of scholarship is characterized by lack of sufficient familiarity with the non-Western world. It has also meant that non-Western scholarship has been submerged under a torrent of writings emerging from the Global North. At least one outcome of this situation is that the decolonization of international law scholarship is yet to be accomplished. The academia in the Global North continues to set the intellectual agenda and prescribe the standards and protocols of good scholarship allowing it to, among other things, decide

---

[18] It may be noted that while the pioneers of the liberal feminist approach to international law come from outside the United States, both Charlesworth and Chinkin have degrees from a US university and draw upon feminist scholarship done there. Thus, the work of Catherine MacKinnon has influenced their writings even as they are critical of radical feminism. See Chapter 6.

which critical tradition is valuable. It is this troubling scenario among others that postcolonial theory seeks to address. In recent years the situation has begun to change, albeit at glacial pace, with TWAIL gaining ground.[19] It is perhaps important to clarify here that the point being made is not about the existence of distinctive knowledge systems in the Global South or to in any way recommend a nativist turn. It is rather about the domination of the field of international law by scholarship that does not engage with the history and realities of the Global South or displays relatively poor understanding and knowledge of it. This is unfortunately as true of critical as of the mainstream scholarship.

The problem of understanding different theoretical approaches to international law is not just about knowledge of the 'field of origin'. As Bourdieu notes, 'the sense and function of a foreign work is determined not simply by the field of origin, but in at least equal proportion by the field of reception'.[20] The 'field of reception' has a critical bearing on how theories are received and the transmutations they undergo in the process. In other words, 'the recipients, who are themselves in a different field of production, re-interpret the texts in accordance with the structure of the field of reception'.[21] The field of reception in the non-Western world is constituted, above all, by their different histories and flowing from them multiple traditions of doing international law, both national and regional.[22] Thus, arguably there is a Mexican, Kenyan or an Indian approach to international law or more broadly Latin American, African and Asian approaches to international law.[23] To be sure, those who do international law deploy concepts, doctrines and practices on which there is a degree of intersubjective understanding permitting communication.

---

[19] The slow process of change should not come as a surprise. As Karl Marx and Frederick Engels explained long ago, the ruling ideas of an age are most often the ideas of dominant social forces in society, in this case ideas that have been advanced by legal elites in advanced capitalist states. Karl Marx and Frederick Engels, *Selected Works* vol. 1 (Moscow: Progress Publishers, 1973), p. 47.

[20] Bourdieu, 'The Social Conditions', p. 222.

[21] See ibid., p. 221.

[22] It is true that we can also speak of the 'field of origin' and 'field of reception' in the Western world, but it is believed that the 'contexts' in which different approaches to international law are advanced and received are for historical reasons not as different in the instance of the Western as in the case of the non-Western world.

[23] See generally Bardo Fassbender and Anne Peters (eds.), *The Oxford Handbook of the History of International Law* (Oxford: Oxford University Press, 2012) Part III: Regions, pp. 383–813; B. S. Chimni, 'Is There an Asian Approach to International Law: Questions, Theses, and Reflections', 14 (2008) *Asian Yearbook of International Law*, pp. 249–265.

But flowing from the location and situation of nations and regions, and the way in which the discipline has evolved within them, there are diverse approaches to the history, doctrines and development of international law, amidst which different approaches to international law are received and examined. Matters are further complicated by the fact that the national or regional approaches are not monolithic approaches but comprise of different theoretical traditions and sensibilities that are shaped by particular understandings of the history of the nation and the region.[24] These factors explain, including fortuitous ones, why each local tradition is more receptive to some approaches to international law than others and in distinct ways.[25] To speak of an accidental factor, the policy-oriented approach has had some resonance in the international law academia in India as a number of Indian scholars, which include B. S. Murthy, R. P. Anand and P. Sreenivasa Rao, went to Yale Law School in the 1960s and 1970s to take their doctoral degrees. While only some of them later used the complex methodology and vocabulary of the New Haven approach, its Cold War orientation ensured that a left approach to international law was not explored despite the strong presence of the Marxist tradition in social sciences in India.[26] To put it differently, IMAIL is being articulated amidst a complex constellation of factors that impact the 'field of reception'. These inter alia account for its weak or strong reactions to particular formulations advanced by different approaches to international law. It is important to underscore this point as these responses can be misunderstood if not read in the context of the field of reception.

Finally, it may be noted that the hermeneutic complexities introduced by the 'field of origin' and 'field of reception' acquire critical significance also because intellectual life is very often 'home to nationalism and imperialism'.[27] Therefore, as Bourdieu observes, 'a truly scientific internationalism, which ... is the only possible ground on which internationalism of any sort is going to be built, is not going to happen of its own

---

[24] The distinct approaches are also interpreted by an individual scholar given his or her own life experiences and theoretical orientation.

[25] Each of the different contemporary approaches has therefore a different presence in countries of the Global South.

[26] The influence of the New Haven approach has waned over time, especially with the passing away of the key figure of B. S. Murthy. It is also perhaps the case that elements of the New Haven approach have been incorporated in 'new' approaches that have a more current appeal. See Chapter 5 for discussion of 'new' approaches.

[27] Bourdieu, 'The Social Conditions', p. 220.

accord'.[28] It can come about only through a cooperative search for 'truth'. It is in that spirit that the present book undertakes a critical review of different approaches to international law.[29]

III. Omission of Positivist Approach: Reasons and Sketch

It was noted that this book does not deal separately with PAIL which remains since the nineteenth century the most influential approach to international law. The principal reason for this exclusion is that most of the other approaches discussed in the book engage with it, albeit these admittedly are focused on a critique of positivism or its variants.[30] But devoting an independent chapter to PAIL would have involved unnecessary repetition as it would inevitably involve reviewing its critique by other approaches to international law. However, for the very reason, a few words on the positivist approach and its strengths are in order here. Ratner and Slaughter describe the positivist approach as follows:

> Positivism summarizes a range of theories that focus upon describing the law as it is, backed by effective sanctions, with reference to formal criteria, independently of moral or ethical considerations. For positivists, international law is no more or less than the rules to which states have agreed through treaties, custom, and perhaps other forms of consent. In the absence of such evidence of the will of states, positivists will assume that states remain at liberty to undertake whatever actions they please. Positivism also tends to view states as the only subjects of international law, thereby discounting the role of nonstate actors. It remains the lingua franca of most international lawyers, especially in continental Europe.[31]

Two adherents of PAIL, Bruno Simma and Andreas Paulus, distinguish between 'classical positivism' and 'modern positivism' which encompasses

[28] See ibid.
[29] While it is written by someone educated in the history, tradition and practices of international law in India and whose thinking has been critically shaped by the left academia, the author aspires to be a participant in the collaborative search for 'truth'.
[30] See for instance Chapter 2, pp. 65–70 for Morgenthau's views on positivism or MILS; Chapter 3, pp. 113–116 for McDougal and Lasswell's critique of positivism; Chapter 4, pp. 183–191 for Falk's views on positivism; Chapter 5, pp. 259–271 for Kennedy's critique of positivism; Chapter 6, pp. 409ff for the Charlesworth and Chinkin critique of positivism; and finally Chapter 7, pp. 449ff for the Marxist critique of positivism.
[31] Ratner and Slaughter, *Methods of International Law*, p. 5. The Austro-Marxist Karl Renner describes 'positive legal analysis' as follows: 'Positive legal analysis has no other task than to ascertain all the legal norms relevant to the facts and to apply them in the case in hand. This exhausts the function of positive legal analysis.' Karl Renner, *The Institutions of Private Law and Their Social Functions* (London: Routledge and Kegan Paul, 1949), p. 48.

an 'enlightened view of positivism'.[32] Simma and Paulus summarize classical positivism thus:

> Law is regarded as a unified system of rules that, according to most vari-
> ants, emanate from state will. This system of rules is an 'objective' reality
> and needs to be distinguished from law 'as it should be'. Classic positiv-
> ism demands rigorous tests for legal validity. Extralegal arguments, e.g.,
> arguments that have no textual, systemic or historical basis, are deemed
> irrelevant to legal analysis; there is only hard law, no soft law. For some,
> the unity of the legal system will provide one correct answer for any legal
> problem; for others, even if law is 'open-textured' it still provides deter-
> minate guidance for officials and individuals.[33]

Simma and Paulus then proceed to 'modify classic positivism' in light of
recent developments and criticisms advanced against it. Thus, for instance,
they recognize that 'other actors than states are assuming importance'.[34]
Simma and Paulus also concede that there may not be, as presumed
by classical positivists, 'only one correct answer to any legal problem'.[35]
However, they do not for that reason 'give up the claim to normativity
and the prescriptive force of law'.[36] Instead, they propose an enlightened
conception of positivism:

> enlightened positivism is identical neither with formalism nor with volun-
> tarism. Both custom and general principles cannot simply be reduced to
> instances of state will. So-called soft law is an important device for the attri-
> bution of meaning to rules and for the perception of legal change. Moral
> and political considerations are not alien to law but part of it. However,
> formal sources remain the core of international legal discourse. Without
> them, there is no 'law properly so-called'. Only when linked to formal
> sources recognized as binding by the international community does law
> serve the decision maker in the search for a balance between idealism and
> realism, common values and ideological neutrality, apology and utopia.[37]

---

[32] Bruno Simma and Andreas L. Paulus, 'The Responsibility of Individuals for Human
Rights Abuses in Internal Conflicts: A Positivist View', in Ratner and Slaughter, *Methods
of International Law*, pp. 23–47 at pp. 25ff. See also J. d'Aspremont, *Formalism and the
Sources of International Law: A Theory of the Ascertainment of Legal Rules* (Oxford: Oxford
University Press 2013); J. d'Aspremont and J. Kammerhofer, *International Legal Positivism
in a Post-modern World* (Cambridge: Cambridge University Press, 2014); Sahib Singh,
'Narrative and Theory: Formalism's Recurrent Return', 84 (2014) *The British Yearbook of
International Law*, pp. 304–343
[33] See Simma and Paulus, 'The Responsibility of Individuals', pp. 26–27.
[34] See ibid., p. 29.
[35] See ibid., p. 31.
[36] See ibid.
[37] See ibid., pp. 31–32.

Simma and Paulus claim that 'the vision of an international law more amenable to the realization of global values' is 'compatible with the regime of traditional sources'.[38] They however hasten to add that this would be true only if the global values find 'sufficient expression in the legal form'.[39] It is clear from even this cursory statement that the positivist method has evolved over time. Its essentials were articulated in the nineteenth century when it helped legitimize colonialism.[40] It has assumed more sophisticated forms today. The different variants of the positivist approach together constitute what may be called mainstream international law scholarship (MILS).

Broadly speaking, two types of critique of MILS are advanced. These may be categorized after the distinction made earlier as the internal and external critiques. The basic thrust of internal critique is that MILS has been unable to recognize the tensions and contradictions that characterize the doctrines and rules of international law. It allows states, in particular powerful states, to justify their acts of omission and commission. The internal critique is most effectively advanced by NAIL even as other approaches like the New Haven approach and TWAIL have made prior and important contributions to its articulation. The external critique points to the troubling distributive outcomes that cannot be either adequately taken cognizance of or addressed by MILS. Indeed, by delinking the analysis of the legal sphere from deep structures MILS is unable to come to terms with the fact that international law facilitates the exploitation and oppression of subaltern groups, peoples and nations. It is therefore overly sanguine about the prospects of contemporary international law contributing to ushering in a peaceful and just world order. TWAIL and Feminist Approaches to International Law (FtAIL) are at the forefront of advancing this critique.

If the positivist approach yet remains the dominant approach to international law, it is because its historical pre-eminence has meant that scholars and state officials, including from weak nations, come to be socialized in its understanding of the workings of international law and institutions.Furthermore, in view of the intimate association of positivist method with the history and development of modern international law, MILS seamlessly speaks for both. In other words, MILS is able to cope with the critique of the positivist approach to international law with a variety of arguments, pertaining to history, method, process, and outcomes,

[38] See ibid., p. 46.
[39] See ibid.
[40] Anghie, *Imperialism*, pp. 32–114.

even if with different degrees of persuasiveness.[41] It is worth listing *a mix* of these arguments schematically leaving their critical assessment to subsequent chapters. First, MILS claims that the positive method and its variants provide the most accurate and economical understanding of the functioning of the international legal process. By keeping out non-legal or extraneous considerations, especially in the process of interpreting and applying a rule, it lends stability to the international legal system. Second, MILS contends that since international law is no longer Eurocentric in its orientation but broadly multi-civilizational in its approach, the use of the positivist method does not bias it against postcolonial nations. In this view the very diversity of nations that subscribe to the idea of international law today demonstrates that it is sensitive to the concerns of the non-Western world. Third, MILS successfully naturalizes a narrative of progress and claims that all states gain, even if differentially, from the working of contemporary international laws and institutions. Fourth, MILS challenges the contention of critics of the continuing relationship between imperialism and international law through drawing attention to the fact that powerful states in the third world (such as Brazil, China and India) are committed to the liberal international order. Fifth, MILS notes that the positivist approach allows pragmatic responses to be shaped to the problems of international community in a bid to realize a peaceful and just world order. Sixth, MILS uses the rapid development of international human rights law to contend that contemporary international law is truly concerned with the welfare of individuals and subaltern groups in the international system. The adoption of separate human rights conventions on the rights of subaltern groups (workers, women, children, disabled, refugees, indigenous peoples etc.) is offered as evidence of the engagement of international law with the concerns of the most marginal and oppressed groups in international society. Seventh, MILS traces the wrong doings in the world of international law and institutions to mistaken interpretations by actors of relevant rules or depicts them as unlawful practices that are a function of parochial national interests pursued by nations. It contends that these situations can be adequately addressed through, inter alia, promoting a shared understanding of rules, the idea of common good and

---

[41] Jason A. Beckett, 'Faith and Resignation: A Journey through International Law' in Matthew Stone, Illan rua Wall and Costas Douzinas (eds.) *New Critical Thinking: Law and the Political* (New York: Routledge, 2012), pp. 145–167. See also Benedict Kingsbury, 'Legal Positivism as Normative Politics: International Society, Balance of Power and Lassa Oppenheim's Positive International Law', 13 (2002) *European Journal of International Law,* pp. 401–436; José E. Alvarez, 'Contemporary International Law: An "Empire of Law" or the "Law of Empire"', 24 (2009) *American University International Law Review,* pp. 811–842.

a repertoire of measures and remedies to deal with violations of international law. Eighth, MILS contends that the uneven implementation of
international laws in particular areas (e.g., international criminal law) will
be corrected over time. For instance, it is said that the leaders of powerful
states will eventually become answerable to the International Criminal
Court (ICC). Ninth, MILS points to the proliferation of international tribunals in recent decades as evidence that international law is capable of
creating legal and institutional mechanisms for peaceful and equitable
resolution of disputes in different areas of international life. Finally, MILS
claims that the faith in the reformist impulse of international law is not
misplaced, as human history shows that a revolutionary legal order cannot be established at even the national level without being accompanied
by oppressive violence.

In sum, MILS contends that since imperialism is a thing of the past,
and the contemporary world order is an egalitarian order, means that
international law can address the ills of the world and make it a place
where all nations can flourish and individuals live with dignity. In this
view, the positivist approach has never proved a hurdle in this process and
therefore never lost its attraction, so much so that even critical approaches
often reveal an ambivalent attitude towards it.[42] Its continuing influence
is a useful reminder that functional explanations are not sufficient to
explain why particular approaches become dominant and remain so for
long periods of time. On the other hand, the burden of the argument of
nearly all the critical approaches considered in the book is that the different variants of the positivist approach or MILS neither accurately depicts
the structure and process of international law nor possesses the conceptual and theoretical resources to contribute to the realization of a peaceful and just world order. Some critical approaches like TWAIL, NAIL
and FtAIL go further in contending that the positive approach assists in
sustaining the domination of powerful states in the international system
through actively contributing to the mystification and legitimization of an
unfair and exclusionary international legal process.

IV. Omission of TWAIL: IMAIL Is TWAIL

Among the contemporary approaches that are not discussed in the book,
the omission of TWAIL is also glaring. However, the omission is more

---

[42] Thus, for example, Martti Koskenneimi invokes a 'culture of formalism' to advance a 'progressive' agenda. For a discussion of the notion of 'culture of formalism' see Chapter 5, pp. 333–344.

apparent than real as IMAIL is a version of TWAIL. It is important to remind here that TWAIL is a loose network of third world scholars who articulate a critique of the history, structure and process of contemporary international law from the standpoint of third world peoples, in particular its marginal and oppressed groups. The critique is advanced using a range of social and political theories that include liberal, Marxist, feminist, post-colonial and postmodern theories. In the instance of IMAIL, Marxism is combined with elements of postcolonial theory and feminism to evaluate the role of international law, both past and present.[43] It, however, deserves emphasis that while encompassing diverse theoretical orientations TWAIL scholarship is united by the presence of certain common features. Before listing these, a distinction may be usefully drawn between two different phases of TWAIL scholarship that have come to be classified as TWAIL I and TWAIL II respectively. TWAIL I was articulated by a first generation of postcolonial scholars in Asia and Africa, and was therefore often called in the beginning an Asian-African approach to international law.[44] The prominent names associated with TWAIL I include Georges Abi-Saab, R. P. Anand, Mohammed Bedjaoui, T. O. Elias, Nagendra Singh, J. J. G. Syatauw and Christopher Weeramantry. TWAIL II has been advanced by a second generation of third world scholars that include Antony Anghie, B.S.Chimni, James Gathii, Karin Mickelson, Vasuki Nesiah, Obiora Okafor and Balakrishnan Rajagopal.

Each generation of TWAIL scholarship is characterized by certain distinctive features. The central features that constitute TWAIL II, of which IMAIL is a part, reflect both elements of continuity and discontinuity.[45] At least four of these may be mentioned:

First, the category 'third world' is used to refer to both a geographical space and a political project. In so far as it is a geographical construct TWAIL II believes that despite the myriad differences that separate

---

[43] It could be equally christened TWAIL (Marxist-Feminist). If the proposed approach is termed IMAIL, it is to signal its primarily materialist orientation, as also its discomfort with aspects of postcolonial theory.

[44] See for instance R. P. Anand, 'Attitude of the Asian-African States toward Certain Provisions of International Law', 15 (1966) *The International and Comparative Law Quarterly*, pp. 55–75. The Asian-African Legal Consultative Organization (AALCO), established in 1958, can be viewed as an expression of the Asian-African approach to international law. See AALCO at www.aalco.int/scripts/view-posting.asp?recordid=1

[45] For an elaboration of the differences between TWAIL I and TWAIL II see Antony Anghie and B. S. Chimni, 'Third World Approaches to International Law and Individual Responsibility in Internal Conflict' in Ratner and Slaughter, *Methods of International Law*, pp. 185–211; B. S. Chimni, 'Towards a Radical Third World Approach to Contemporary

third world countries they are united by the history of colonialism. In as much as it is a political project, TWAIL II is about a politics of emancipation which is alert to the fact that there is a third world in the first world and a first world in the third world. The geographical and political meanings of the term 'third world' intersect in complex ways depending, inter alia, on the subject under consideration.

Second, TWAIL II subscribes to the view that the conceptual and doctrinal apparatus used to justify colonialism continues to frame contemporary international law in a variety of ways.[46] It believes that the reality of universalizing capitalism or imperialism continues to define the relationship between the Global North and the Global South. While there is no necessary agreement on the understanding of the concept of 'imperialism' among TWAIL II scholars, there is a consensus that its manifestation is the systemic bias of international law against subaltern states and peoples.[47] TWAIL II attempts to demonstrate this reality in relation to different international law regimes be it international economic law or international environmental law. In doing so it lays great store by the genealogical or the historical method.[48]

Third, TWAIL II is wedded to the idea of 'global cognitive justice' and therefore challenges Eurocentrism in all its forms.[49] In writing the history of international law, TWAIL II proceeds on the assumption that a reliable history of international law cannot be written without taking into account the narratives emanating from nations that were the objects of colonial

---

International Law', 5 (2002) *ICCLP Review* (Tokyo University School of Law Publication), pp. 16–30.

[46] Anghie, *Imperialism*, p. 3. See also James Thuo Gathii, 'Neoliberalism, Colonialism and International Governance: Decentering the International Law of Governmental Legitimacy', 98 (2000) *Michigan Law Review*, pp. 1996–2055 at p. 2000.

[47] Gathii, for example, is critical of Lenin's theory of imperialism even as the present author is more sympathetic to it. James Thuo Gathii, 'Imperialism, Colonialism, and International Law', 54 (2007) *Buffalo Law Review*, pp. 1013–1066 at p. 1018.

[48] This approach contrasts with that of MILS best reflected in standard textbooks of international law that either begin without a word on the history of international law or narrate a sanitized history which assign, if at all, secondary significance to colonialism in the shaping of modern international law. An instance of the former is Ian Brownlie, *Principles of Public International Law* (Oxford: Clarendon Press, 1990), 4th edn. An example of sanitized history is Malcolm Shaw, *International Law* (Cambridge: Cambridge University Press, 2008) 6th edition, pp. 13–42.

[49] The phrase 'global cognitive justice' is borrowed from Boaventura de Sousa Santos, *Epistemologies of the South: Justice against Epistemicide* (Boulder, CO: Paradigm Publishers, 2014), p. viii. He writes that there can be 'no global social justice without global cognitive justice'. See ibid.

oppression. It involves among other things recognition of the contribution of the non-West to the evolution and development of international law.

Fourth, TWAIL II attaches methodological significance to the response of subaltern groups, classes, and nations to different international law regimes. The mere compliance with positive procedure is not seen as sufficient to confer validity or legitimacy on rules of international law. In this regard the factor of resistance is seen as a significant factor to be taken into account.

Beyond these common features TWAIL II 'is not fixed and established'.[50] TWAIL II scholars willingly 'acknowledge the fluidity and multiplicity of the stories' that can be told about it.[51] There is in fact an 'exciting diversity within TWAIL'.[52] Indeed, even the differences between TWAIL I and TWAIL II cannot be neatly captured. Broadly speaking, TWAIL I has been critiqued for its identification of imperialism with colonialism, the absence of a class or gender or indigenous critique of international law, and the lack of attention to issues such as indeterminacy of rules. But there are also continuities between TWAIL I and TWAIL II. Speaking from the perspective of IMAIL, the writings of Mohammed Bedjaoui, who in generational terms belongs to TWAIL I, also deployed the materialist method to analyse the international legal system. In his classic work *Towards a new international economic order* Bedjaoui wrote that 'the development of international law appears to result from a series of factors encompassed in what economists call the production mode. Socio-economic phenomena are themselves the product of a series of interactions between them and the institutions of international law'.[53] The statement plainly echoes Marx's famous preface to *A Contribution to the Critique of Political Economy* whose methodological spirit also informs IMAIL.[54] To put it differently, the idea of talking about distinct phases in TWAIL is not necessarily to signal a clean break from the past. In the final analysis the differences between TWAIL I and TWAIL II are about

---

[50] Antony Anghie, 'TWAIL: Past and Future', 10 (2008) *International Community Law Review*, pp. 479–482 at p. 480.

[51] Karin Mickelson, 'Taking Stock of TWAIL Histories', 10 (2008) *International Community Law Review*, pp. 355–362 at p. 355.

[52] Chinedu Obiora Okafor, 'Critical Third World Approaches to International Law (TWAIL): Theory, Methodology, or Both?', 10 (2008) *International Community Law Review*, pp. 371–378 at p. 375.

[53] Mohammed Bedjaoui, *Towards a new international economic order* (New York: Holmes & Meir Publishers Inc., 1979), p. 249.

[54] For statement and discussion, see Chapter 7, pp. 449–455.

the nature of scholarship and the accompanying political project and not about the generation to which an individual scholar belongs. The hypothesis of continuity also helps subsume the work of nineteenth-century jurists like Calvo and Drago under the banner of TWAIL.[55]

V.   A Word on Marxism and Socialist Feminism

A few words need to be said on both staying the course with Marxism and the nature of borrowings from socialist feminism and postcolonial theory in articulating IMAIL.

In the aftermath of the collapse of 'actually existing socialism' Marxism faced the most serious crisis of its long career.[56] In view of the historic failure of Soviet Union and other socialist states to build the promised democratic and egalitarian societies, and given the weaknesses in Marxist thought identified over a century and half of debates, serious doubts were expressed as to the continuing value in subscribing to its tenets.[57] It is, however, not possible to retrieve Marxism from its critics without undertaking a long detour that would distract from the essential tasks the book sets itself. Instead, it is hoped that the materialist critique of contemporary approaches to international law and the case for IMAIL is able to demonstrate the abiding usefulness of Marxist method and sociology. However, three bare overlapping methodological points may yet be made in the context of elaborating IMAIL. First, all dogmatic versions of Marxism that are marked by an 'excess of coherence',[58] including its formulaic application to non-Western societies, are rejected. Second, it is believed that Marxism as an intellectual paradigm is capacious enough to address many of the theoretical lapses and gaps in its oeuvre, including those revealed by the past and present practices of 'actually existing socialism'.[59] Third, while Marxism facilitates a systematic and wide-ranging understanding of social phenomena, it has to be leavened, enriched, and where

[55] James Thuo Gathii, 'War's Legacy in International Investment Law', 11 (2009) *International Community Law Review,* pp. 353–386 at p. 353.
[56] Terry Eagleton, 'Introduction Part 1', in Terry Eagleton and Drew Milne (eds.) *Marxist Literary Theory: A Reader* (Oxford: Blackwell Publishing, 1996), pp. 1–15 at p. 1.
[57] See ibid.
[58] Bruno Latour, *Reassembling the Social: An Introduction to Actor-Network Theory* (Oxford: Oxford University Press.2002), p. 188. See also William E. Connolly, *The Fragility of Things: Self-organizing processes, Neo-liberal Fantasies, and Democratic Activism* (Durham, N.C: Duke University Press, 2013). Connolly rightly cautions that 'perfect answers are suspect'. See ibid., p.182.
[59] Perry Anderson, *In the Tracks of Historical Materialism* (London: Verso, 1984), p. 105.

necessary reframed using the insights of other critical theories. Two such critical theories that IMAIL turns to are postcolonial theory and socialist feminism, the one helping to better explain and understand non-Western societies and the other to effectively fill the gender gap in Marxism. At the level of political principles two deserve to be strongly stated from the standpoint of IMAIL. First, learning from the experience of building socialism over the past century, IMAIL makes a non-negotiable commitment to democratic forms of governance in thinking about alternative futures. As will be noted in the chapter on IMAIL, key Marxist figures like Karl Kautsky and Rosa Luxemburg had always argued that democracy was absolutely essential to the building of socialist societies.[60] Second, IMAIL departs from those Marxist traditions that endorse the use of violence in bringing about radical social transformation.[61] It contends that the principle of non-violence must inform all efforts to create a more egalitarian and just society. It draws in this regard from the thought of Mohandas Karamchand Gandhi and the experiences of the Indian freedom struggle. In short, the Marxism embraced in the book is non-doctrinaire and conscious of the need to reconfigure it for present times.

If the Marxist tradition does not have a serious presence in the literature on international law and world order studies, it is not merely because of the experience of 'actually existing socialism', or the problems with Marxist theory, but also because of the hostility to the Marxist tradition in Western social science academia, especially in the United States, the 'field of origin' of most contemporary approaches to international law and world order. Robert Cox has observed of the United States that 'Marxism appears to thinkers in the mainstream as a manifestation of dissidence, obstinate ignorance, even treachery'.[62] The dominance of US academia in international relations and international law scholarship has ensured the general discrediting of an openly Marxist mode of analysis. Yet, since the

---

[60] See Chapter 7, pp. 544–545. On the other hand, it is worth noting that the association between capitalism and democracy is tenuous. As Milton Friedman conceded, you can 'have economic arrangements that are fundamentally capitalist and political arrangements that are not free'. After all, as he noted, 'Fascist Italy and Fascist Spain, Germany at various times . . . Japan before World Wars I and II, tsarist Russia in the decades before World War I – are all societies that cannot conceivably be described as politically free. Yet, in each, private enterprise was the dominant form of economic organization.' Milton Friedman, *Capitalism and Freedom* (Chicago: University of Chicago Press, 1962), p. 10.

[61] See generally Alain Badiou, 'The Communist Idea and the Question of Terror' in Slavoj Zizek (ed.) *The Idea of Communism* Volume 2 (London: Verso, 2013), pp. 1–13.

[62] Robert Cox, 'The "British School" in the Global Context', 14 (2009) *New Political Economy*, pp. 315–328 at p. 322.

first edition of this book was published, many scholars have joined the effort to articulate in different ways a Marxist approach to international law, including Bill Bowring, Claire Cutler, Robert Knox, Susan Marks and China Miéville.[63] However, it cannot be said even today that Marxist scholarship on international law is acceptable in mainstream academic circles. But that is a price that critical theories in general have to pay for contesting dominant ideas and approaches. They have to constantly confront the 'subtle censorship of academic decorum'.[64] Therefore, the fate of other critical theories such as TWAIL, FtAIL or NAIL has only been a shade better. Indeed, all critical theories are sought to be marginalized by MILS. But that is only to be expected as critical theories are ranged against the interests of dominant national and international social forces, and therefore often portrayed by the mainstream as unacceptable forms of academic dissent. To be sure, the claim of Marxist or other critics is not that they alone have the welfare of humankind or the global poor or oppressed in view. The issue is not about intent at all. Mainstream scholars are as concerned as the critics in this regard. The differences arise over the realistic evaluation of methods and outcomes, precisely the kind of critique directed against Marxists. The point is that MILS may mean well but the legal and institutional structures it supports belie its best intentions, as testified to by historical experience. The question then is about which approach to international law has learnt the lessons of history better and is willing to undertake course correction.[65] Insofar as IMAIL is concerned it seeks to borrow from the best in other critical traditions. As noted earlier, one such tradition is feminism. It helps IMAIL takes theoretical account of the lament of feminist legal scholars that Marxism tends to relegate 'gender' issues to the margins. This was, for instance, the complaint of Catherine MacKinnon in her famous essay on radical feminism.[66] From an IMAIL perspective the socialist feminist tradition is

---

[63] See China Miéville, *Between Equal Rights: A Marxist Theory of International Law* (Leiden: Brill, 2005); Susan Marks, *International Law on the Left* (Cambridge: Cambridge University Press, 2004).

[64] Pierre Bourdieu, Gisele Sapiro and Brian McHale, 'Fourth Lecture. Universal Corporatism: The Role of Intellectuals in the Modern World', 12 (1991) *Poetics Today*, pp. 655–669 at p. 662.

[65] To put it differently, the contest today is between transformed MILS (for example, 'enlightened positivism') and critical traditions. It is not a new battle, but is playing itself out in a new era. These contests eventually rest on the belief of critical scholars that 'another world is possible' and that the search for 'alternative futures' remains an urgent mission even after the demise of 'actually existing socialism'.

[66] Catharine A. MacKinnon, 'Feminism, Marxism, Method, and the State: An Agenda for Theory', 7 (1982) *Signs*, pp. 515–544. It has been observed that, 'many of the founders of

the most persuasive among feminist theories.[67] The fact that socialist feminism recognizes that the criticism of social relations can proceed from different standpoints such as class, gender and race, including the ways in which these intersect, both within and across nation states, helps bring the traditions of Marxism and socialist feminism together. Both crucially acknowledge that while the journey of criticism may begin using a particular standpoint, it may travel beyond to address different forms of inequality, subordination and marginalization. There are, of course, complex questions that arise in the process including whether beginning with a particular standpoint controls the ways in which other social fractures are addressed. Is it the same to begin with the category 'gender' or 'class' or for that matter 'race' and move towards the others through using some form of intersectional analysis? Are different critical theories based on such contrasting or conflicting assumptions that it is impossible to achieve integration? IMAIL considers that Marxism and versions of socialist feminism can be meaningfully combined.[68] From an IMAIL standpoint many of the apparent theoretical tensions between the two are effectively resolvable in the world of praxis.[69] It contends that rather than a priori privilege the category 'class' or 'gender', it is important to bear both in mind even as one of them is assigned priority in a concrete situation in shaping a social, political or legal strategy. In the final analysis the idea of bringing Marxism and socialist feminism together is to supplement and enrich both the traditions in different ways. For instance, while Marxists have successfully articulated a general theory of law, socialist feminists have yet to do so. A materialist theory of law can, therefore,

radical feminism were socialists frustrated by the refusal of men on the Left to address patriarchal systems of power'. Rosemary Hennessy and Chrys Ingraham, *Materialist Feminism: A Reader in Class, Difference, and Women's Lives* (New York: Routledge, 1997), pp. 1–14 at p. 6.

[67] It is also the most compatible with the Marxist tradition even as not all socialist feminists subscribe to Marxism. In putting together a reader on materialist-feminism (often a synonym for socialist feminism) after the end of the Cold War, Hennessy and Ingraham wrote: 'feminists have continued to find in historical materialism a powerful theoretical and political resource. The tradition of feminist engagement with marxism emphasizes a perspective on social life that refuses to separate the materiality of meaning, identity, the body, state, or nation from the requisite division of labor that undergirds the scramble for profits in capitalism's global system'. Hennessy and Ingraham, *Materialist Feminism*, p. 1. For discussion of socialist feminism see Chapter 6, pp. 400–409.

[68] Thus, Hennessy and Ingraham write: '*historical materialism* is *emancipatory* critical knowledge. Historical materialism offers a systemic way of making sense of social life under capitalism that simultaneously serves as an agent for changing it'. See ibid., p. 4. Emphasis in original.

[69] Since there is a separate chapter devoted to FtAIL the idea of socialist feminism will be further clarified there. See Chapter 6, pp. 400–409.

assist socialist feminists to articulate a more profound critique of law and
the legal sphere, even as they recast it to theoretically reflect the implications of taking gender seriously.

VI.   Uses and Limits of Postcolonial Theory

The crisis in Marxism in recent decades has been matched by the growing
popularity of postcolonial theory among those doing critical scholarship.
It is neither possible here nor necessary to go into the intricate debates on
the principal ideas of postcolonial theory, including the meaning of the
term 'postcolonial' or 'postcolonialism'.[70] It will suffice to spotlight two
overlapping tenets of postcolonial theory and its uses and limits. The first
canon is succinctly captured in the observation of Dipesh Chakrabarty
that while 'for generations now, philosophers and thinkers shaping the
nature of social science have produced theories embracing the entirety of
humanity ... these statements have been produced in relative, and sometimes, absolute, ignorance of the majority of humankind – that is, those
living in non-Western cultures'.[71] Second, in contrast to Marxism which
is seen as stressing the roles of universalizing forces of capitalism and
European modernity in shaping third world societies, postcolonial theory
raises questions with regard to:

> the supposedly universal status of the European experience – the uni-
> versalizing function of its capital, the universality of its reason, and the
> complicity of capital and reason in elevating the broad brand of European
> modernity to a universal model valid for all continents of mankind – in

[70] Leela Gandhi has observed that 'there is little consensus regarding the proper content,
scope and relevance of postcolonial studies'. Leela Gandhi, *Postcolonial Theory: A Critical
Introduction* (St. Leonards: Allen and Unwin, 1998), p. 3. Others have noted that the term
'postcolonialism' is 'a slippery term' that is 'notoriously difficult to define'. Vivek Mishra
and Bob Hodge, 'What Was Postcolonialism?', 36 (2005) *New Literary History*, pp. 375–
402 at p. 377. See also Peter Childs and R. J. Patrick Williams, 'Introduction: Points of
Departure' in Peter Childs and R. J. Patrick Williams (eds.) *An Introduction to Post-Colonial
Theory* (London: Prentice Hall, 1997), pp. 1–25; Bill Ashcroft, Gareth Griffiths and Helen
Tiffin, *The Post-Colonial Studies Reader* (New York: Routledge, 1995), p. xv and 'General
Introduction', pp. 1–4; Arif Dirlik, 'The Postcolonial Aura: Third World Criticism in the
Age of Global Capitalism', 20 (1994) *Critical Inquiry*, pp. 328–356; Krishna, *Globalization
and Postcolonialism,* chapter 3. On postcolonial approach to law, see Eve Darian-Smith,
'Postcolonial Theories of Law' in Reza Banakar and Max Travers (eds.) *An Introduction to
Law and Social Theory* 2nd edn (Oxford: Hart, 2013), pp. 247–264.

[71] Dipesh Chakrabarty, 'Postcoloniality and the Artifice of History: Who Speaks for "Indian"
Pasts?' in Ranajit Guha (ed.) *A Subaltern Studies Reader 1986–1995* (New Delhi: Oxford
University Press, 1997), pp. 263–294 at p. 265.

short, questions that cast doubt on the presumption of what is European and modern as paradigmatically metropolitan and on the elevation of its history, a bundle of national and regional specificities like any other history, to Universal History.[72]

According to postcolonial theory any determining role for universalizing capitalism and European modernity goes to deny all contingency from the historical development of non-Western societies.[73] At the same time, the call for 'provincializing Europe' is not to be seen as an attempt to argue the case for cultural relativism or nativist histories.[74] The demand is only for a history and a present in which 'the world may once again be imagined as radically heterogeneous'.[75] The meaning and practice of what constitutes the middle ground between universalism and nativism is left to each non-Western society to evolve. The only thing that can be said with certainty is that it anticipates a non-imperial world in which alone the idea of radical heterogeneity can come into play. Indeed, postcolonial theory is in a central way a response to the ever-present reality of imperialism in the non-Western world since the sixteenth century.

The general strength and weaknesses of postcolonial theory in relation to these tenets may be assessed from the limited perspective of articulating IMAIL. The principal attractions of postcolonial theory for IMAIL are fourfold. First, postcolonial theory places at the heart of humanities and social sciences the goal of liberating humankind from imperialism.[76] As the influence of Marxism declined, it is postcolonial theory that helped sustain the idea of envisioning 'human experience in non-imperialist terms'.[77] In view of the intimate relationship between imperialism and the evolution and development of modern international law, postcolonial theory is of obvious value. Second, postcolonial theory has helped underscore the problem of Eurocentrism in humanities and social sciences.[78] It has successfully demonstrated that the phenomenon

---

[72] Ranajit Guha, 'Introduction' in Ranajit Guha (ed.) *A Subaltern Studies Reader 1986–1995* (New Delhi: Oxford University Press, 1997), pp. ix–xxii at p. xxi.
[73] Vivek Chibber, 'Capitalism, Class and Universalism: Escaping the Cul-de-Sac of Postcolonial Theory', (2014) *Socialist Register*, pp. 63–79 at p. 68.
[74] Chakrabarty, 'Postocolonial and the Artifice', p. 290. p. 290.
[75] See ibid. The idea is 'to write into the history of modernity the ambivalences, the contradictions, the use of force, and the tragedies and the ironies that attend it'. See ibid., p. 288; or as Guha put it in the context of 'Indian history' there is a need for 'Indianizing the idioms of modernity imported by the Raj'. Guha, 'Introduction', pp. ix–xxii at p. xx.
[76] Edward W. Said, *Culture and Imperialism* (London: Chatto & Windus, 1993), pp. 331, 333.
[77] See ibid., p. 333; Chibber, 'Capitalism', p. 77.
[78] Chibber, 'Capitalism', p. 77.

of universalizing capitalism does not mean the obliteration of differences between the West and the non-West. In fact postcolonial theory has compelled Western social sciences to come to terms with the idea of multiple or alternative modernities that arises not only from different ways in which separate elements of modernity assemble or are historically sequenced but also from 'initial conditions' in which elements of modernity are embedded in the non-Western world.[79] It would not be wrong to say that it is the success of postcolonial theory in challenging Eurocentrism in social sciences and humanities that has made it possible for TWAIL to get a serious hearing in the Western international law academia.[80] It has in turn helped expand the pool of 'regional' social and cultural resources available to democratize and strengthen the fabric of international law.[81] Thus, for example, Judge Christopher Weeramantry in his dissenting judgment in the *Nuclear Weapons* case drew attention to the historical prevalence of laws of war in non-Western countries in order to enrich and reinforce them.[82] Third, postcolonial theory frees critical scholarship from the bind of a singular imagination where alternative futures are concerned. The institutional features of envisioned post capitalist societies that are to be constructed as authentically democratic and egalitarian may differ from nation to nation. The preferred futures may also come to be established through a variety of means. Thus, for example,

---

[79] As Kaviraj points out: 'When we are talking about modernity, we are talking about a number of processes of social change which can be studied or analyzed independently of each other – such as, capitalist industrialization, the increasing centrality of the state in the social order (Foucault's "governmentality"), urbanization, sociological individuation, secularization in politics and ethics, the creation of a new order of knowledge, vast changes in the organization of family and intimacy, and changes in the fields of artistic and literary culture.' Sudipta Kaviraj, 'An Outline of a Revisionist Theory of Modernity', 46 (2005) *European Journal of Sociology*, pp. 497–526 at p. 508.

[80] See generally Lorca, Arnulf Becker, 'Eurocentrism in the History of International Law' in Fassbender and Peters, *The Oxford*, pp. 1034–1058.

[81] See ibid.; and Antony Anghie, 'Identifying Regions in the History of International Law' in Fassbender and Peters, *The Oxford*, pp. 1058–1081.

[82] Dissenting Opinion of Judge Weeramantry in Advisory Opinion on *Legality of the Threat or Use of Nuclear Weapons, 1996*, available at www.icj-cij.org/docket/files/95/7521.pdf. The Indian concept of 'composite culture', with its accent on syncretism, is another idea that can be explored to address the cultural tensions prevalent in the domain of international law. See B. S. Chimni, 'Legitimating International Rule of Law' in James Crawford and Martti Koskenneimi (eds.) *Cambridge Companion to International Law* (Cambridge: Cambridge University Press, 2012), pp. 290–309 at pp. 305–306. Postcolonial theory has also helped appreciate the need to study the variance in and implications of the interface between international law and national and local laws in order to devise appropriate modes of compliance with rules of international law.

the idea of non-violent resistance with a strong emphasis on work on the self that Mahatma Gandhi advanced in the course of the freedom struggle in India is in many ways unique, that is, as against the idea of non-violent resistance per se.[83] For IMAIL it is important that different ways of imagining and realizing alternative futures be kept in mind. Fourth, from the standpoint of IMAIL what appeals in postcolonial theory is its 'anti-anti-Marxism'.[84] Thus, for example, those scholars who identify as TWAIL II are most often not Marxists, but are willing to go along with explanations that have a Marxist tone and colour.

Many as the achievements of postcolonial theory are, these come at a price. First, there is the near abandonment of the concept of universalism.[85]: postcolonial theory tends to underplay the historical reality that the 'logic of capital' or universalizing capitalism has since the sixteenth century penetrated and impacted all third world nations. In fact, since the dawn of the colonial era, as Vivek Chibber aptly notes, 'both parts of the globe [i.e., the Global North and the Global South] are subject to *the same basic forces* and are therefore part of *the same basic history*'.[86] This reality is testified to by colonial international law that has shaped in crucial ways not only the relationship between the Global North and the Global South but also influenced the ways in which metropolitan and postcolonial societies have been imagined and shaped. The universal thrust of capitalism is today promoted by a neocolonial international law which is in the process of creating a borderless global economic space in which uniform global standards apply.[87] In this regard, postcolonial theory does not adequately recognize that universalizing capitalism does not require the destruction of all differences for the 'universal' is not the equivalent of 'homogeneous'.[88] In the literature of international law, this has come to be

---

[83] B. S. Chimni, 'The Self, Modern Civilization and International Law: Learning from Mohandas Karmchand Gandhi's *Hind Swaraj*', 23 (2012) *European Journal of International Law*, pp. 1159–1173.

[84] Stephen Howe, 'Edward Said: Anxieties of Influence', 67 (2007) *Cultural Critique*, pp. 50–87 at p. 79.

[85] Chibber, 'Capitalism', p. 77. For a summary of a broad materialist critique of postcolonial theory see Krishna, *Globalization and Postcolonialism*, pp. 109ff.

[86] Vivek Chibber, *Post Colonial Theory and the Specter of Capital* (New Delhi: Navayana Publishing Pvt. Ltd, 2013)p. 291; emphasis in original.

[87] It is worth noting here that postcolonial theorists like Said used a 'narrow and flawed definition of imperialism' treating it 'as coterminous with colonialism' leading to a lack of engagement with contemporary forms of imperialism and with the internal relationship between capitalism and imperialism. Parry, 'Edward Said', pp. 106–107.

[88] Chibber, *Post Colonial Theory*, p. 150.

slowly accepted in debates relating to the interpretation and enforcement of international human rights law.[89] In fact, the prevalence of differences amidst universalizing capitalism is precisely the reason why there has been so much discussion within Marxism about the specificities of capitalism in the third world.[90] It is true that dogmatic Marxists are reluctant to recognize that differences between the West and the non-West can impact the deployment of even essential categories like 'class', as is the case in India where it is partially displaced by the category 'caste'.[91] Therefore, the project of provincializing Europe is undoubtedly important. It helps challenge the use of unmodified universal categories to understand the non-West, and from this perspective stress the view that when theories travel they must connect to local realities (the 'field of reception') if they have to retain their relevance or edge.[92] But the need for bringing the local context in does not necessarily justify the rejection of any form of universalism or the charge of Eurocentrism against Marxism.[93] In so far as the latter

[89] Sally Engle Merry, *Human Rights and Gender Violence: Translating International Law into Local Justice* (Chicago, IL: University of Chicago Press, 2006). The issue of cultural diversity has today also come to be addressed by international covenants like the UN Convention on the Protection and Promotion of the Diversity of Cultural Exception that was adopted in 2005.

[90] As Chibber observes, '*The history of Marxian analysis in the twentieth century is the history of doing just this – understanding the specificity of the East*'. He goes on to write: 'There is probably no project to which Marxist theorists have devoted more energy and time since the first Russian Revolution of 1905 than to understand the peculiar effects of capitalist development in the non-West ... If we draw up a list of the main theoretical innovations to come out of the Marxist tradition after Marx's death, we see that many of them are attempts to theorize capitalism in backward settings: in the first half of the century, there was Lenin's theory of imperialism and the "weakest link", his analysis of agrarian class differentiation, Kautsky's work on the agrarian question, Trotsky's theory of uneven and combined development, Mao's theory of New Democracy, Gramsci's distinction between state legitimacy in Eastern and Western Europe. All of these were attempts to understand social reproduction in parts of the world where capitalism was *not* working in exactly the way Marx described it in *Capital*. In the years of the New Left, there came dependency theory, world-systems theory, Cabral's work on the African revolutionary path, the theory of the articulation of modes of production, the Indian "modes of production" debate – and the list goes on.' Chibber, *Post Colonial Theory*, pp. 291–292.

[91] Sudipta Kaviraj, 'Marxism in Translation: Critical Reflections on Radical Indian Thought' in Richard Rourke and Raymond Guess (eds.) *Political Judgment: Essays for John Dunn* (Cambridge: Cambridge University Press, 2009), pp. 172–201. Kaviraj offers 'some observations on the characteristic problems that have beset the "translation" of radical socialist ideas into an Indian context'. See ibid., p. 177. For a brief discussion see Chapter 7, pp. 446–447.

[92] Raymond Duvall and Latha Varadarajan, 'Travelling in Paradox: Edward Said and Critical International Relations', 36 (2007) *Millennium: Journal of International Studies*, pp. 83–99 at pp. 91–92.

[93] Chibber, *Post Colonial Theory*, p. 285. See also Crystal Bartolovich, 'Introduction: Marxism, Modernity, and Postcolonial Studies' in C. Bartolovich and Neil Lazarus (eds.) *Marxism,*

is concerned all that need be said is that Marxists can readily accept the Chakrabarty critique of universalism as an integral part of their critique of cultural imperialism.[94] On the other hand, in discussing the themes of alternative or multiple modernities in the non-Western world, postcolonial theory needs to acknowledge that 'the only satisfactory semantic meaning of modernity lies in its association with capitalism.'[95]

Second, postcolonial theory confines its concerns primarily to the cultural sphere.[96] At least one reason for this trend is that Edward Said, a key figure of postcolonial theory, self-consciously eschewed examination of the political economy of imperialism, leaving it for others to study.[97] However, the fact that he limited himself to the cultural sphere impacted the work of those who disregarding his conscious delimitation of the subject of study applied his mode of analysis in other fields. These scholars tend to remain in the realm of cultural explanation, ignoring the centrality of critique of the political economy of imperialism.[98] For instance, TWAIL scholars who rely on postcolonial theory to narrate the history of international law overlook the significance of political economy, at best making passing or general reference to economic phenomena. This lapse characterizes the historical work of even a leading TWAIL scholar like

Modernity and Postcolonial Studies (Cambridge: Cambridge University Press, 2002), pp. 1–21 at pp. 10–11; and Kolja Lindner, 'Marx's Eurocentrism. Postcolonial Studies and Marx Scholarship', (2010) *Radical Philosophy*, pp. 27–41; Irfan Habib, 'Introduction: Marx's Perception of India' in Iqbal Hussain (ed.) *Karl Marx on India* (New Delhi: Tulika, 2006), pp. ix–liv; Prabhat Patnaik, 'Appreciation: The Other Marx', in Hussain, *Karl Marx on India*, pp. Iv–Ixviii.

[94] Dipesh Chakrabarty, *Provincializing Europe* (Princeton, NJ: Princeton University Press, 2007), 2nd edn, p. 95.

[95] Fredric Jameson, *A Singular Modernity: Essay on the Ontology of the Present* (London: Verso, 2002), p. 13.

[96] It raises the question 'whether the quest for cultural identity seeks also to resolve issues of social justice and democracy, or is made into an end in itself oblivious to those issues, in which case its claims to alterity are deeply compromised by its complicity in the existing system, substituting illusory promises of identity in return for compliance in social inequality and political injustice'. Arif Dirlik, 'Thinking Modernity Historically: Is "Alternative Modernity" the Answer?', 1 (2013) *Asian Review of World Histories*, pp. 5–34 at p. 8.

[97] In his own words, Said concerned himself with 'the processes of imperialism ... beyond the level of economic laws and political decision'. Said, *Culture and Imperialism*, pp. 12, 3.

[98] Bartolovich, 'Introduction', p. 10. Speaking of scholars who rely on Said, Barkawi writes that 'much of this work, concerned to elucidate the culturally constructed character of world politics, failed to build in a sustained way on Marxian-inspired analyses of political economy, imperialism and dependency'. Tarak Barkawi 'Empire and Order in International Relations and Security Studies' in Robert A. Denemark (ed.), *The International Studies Encyclopedia* (Blackwell Publishing), Blackwell reference online; *The International Studies Encyclopedia*, vol. III (Chichester: Wiley-Blackwell, 2010), pp. 1360–1379 (available online), p. 14.

Antony Anghie. It is, therefore, not incorrect to point out Anghie's lack of engagement with the 'empire of private rights' in his work on imperialism and international law.[99]

Third, postcolonial theory does not advance in a systematic way a theory of law. It essentially uses the idea of 'legal orientalism' to show how Europe discursively constructed legal systems in colonial territories as its deficient and flawed Other.[100] But postcolonial theory fails to go further and offer a reliable and persuasive understanding of the relationships between distinct social and legal formations, not even as an inverted grand theory that celebrates singularity but offers a coherent account of how it came to be constituted. Therefore, postcolonial theory at best offers an orientation, a weak method, to understand how legal structures, processes and practices in colonized territories were depicted and transformed. To put it differently, like socialist feminism, postcolonial theory does not possess a general theory of law, but provides an important corrective to those theories of law that claim strong universal validity such as Marxist theories of law. In so far as postcolonial approach to international law is concerned it ably shows how doctrines and practices in the modern era evolved to justify colonialism and continue to play a determining role today. This explains why, as Darian-Smith notes, 'there is considerable overlap between scholars who talk about legal orientalism and the intellectual movement associated with TWAIL'.[101] But, because postcolonial scholarship on international law is relatively inattentive to the political economy of imperialism, it does not offer a credible theoretical account of the relationship between universalizing capitalism and international law over the centuries. It is therefore unable to identify the social forces that drive imperialism in different eras and the need for different strategies of resistance in each phase. All in all, as Darian-Smith aptly observes, 'postcolonial theories of law do not form a coherent field of inquiry'.[102]

Fourth, postcolonial theory does not adequately recognize that the idea of heterogeneity does not prevent groups divided along class, gender,

---

[99] Martti Koskenniemi, 'Empire and International Law: the Real Spanish Contribution', 61 (2011) *University of Toronto Law Journal*, pp. 1–36 at p. 31.

[100] Darian-Smith notes that the most obvious purpose 'legal orientalism' served was that 'declaring non-Western legal systems inferior helped to justify European law and culture as a superior civilization, worthy of world leadership and dominance'. E. Darian-Smith, 'Postcolonial Law' in James D. Wright (editor-in-chief), *International Encyclopedia of the Social & Behavioral Sciences*, 2nd edn, vol. 18 (Oxford: Elsevier, 2015), pp. 647–651 a t pp. 650.

[101] Eve Darian-Smith, 'Postcolonial Theories of Law', p. 260.

[102] See ibid., p. 248.

race, ethnicity, caste and other lines to adopt forms of resistance prevalent in the West even as these may come to display cultural peculiarities. This possibility is overlooked because postcolonial theorists do not subscribe to the idea that objective interests drive the world of universalizing capitalism and bear upon the lifeworld of its subjects. Thus, for instance, the struggles of the working classes are seen as local struggles rather than as a reflection of universal basic needs.[103] In other words, postcolonial theory cannot productively theorize postcolonial forms of resistance. On the other hand, Marxists do not sufficiently appreciate the distinctive forms of resistance that each culture and different groups within a culture may throw up. IMAIL, however, recognizes that it is only a combination of diverse forms of resistance that can help transform the character of contemporary international law. Thus, it not only accepts that 'the new emancipatory politics' will be the act of 'an explosive combination of different agents',[104] but also that it will manifest different cultural forms of resistance.

To sum up, IMAIL accepts the legitimate concerns of postcolonial theory but believes that what is necessary is 'to break the impasse between a colonizing Marxism and an overelaborated postcolonialism'.[105] IMAIL works with the hypothesis that in order to retain its relevance postcolonial theory needs to be embedded in Marxism even as the latter needs to theoretically internalize its insights.[106] The sensibility of postcolonial theory assists IMAIL in identifying troubling gaps in the different approaches to international law considered in the book, including that of Marxist scholars like Miéville. Indeed, most of the approaches considered pay little attention to peoples and nations in the Global South. Their proponents either rarely engage with its realities, as in the case of Morgenthau and McDougal, or like Charlesworth, Chinkin, Kennedy, Koskenneimi, and Miéville display inadequate understanding of the non-Western world

---

[103] As Chibber writes, 'whereas Marxists have understood resistance from below as an expression of the real interests of laboring groups, postcolonial theory typically shies away from any talk of objective, universal interests. The sources of struggle are taken to be local, specific to the culture of the laboring groups, a product of their very particular location and history – and not the expression of interests linked to certain universal basic needs'. Chibber, 'Capitalism', p. 73.

[104] Slavoz Zizek, 'How to Begin From the Beginning', 57 (2009) *New Left Review*, pp. 43–55 at p. 55.

[105] Vijay Mishra and Bod Hodge, 'What was Postcolonialism?', 36 (2005) *New Literary History* pp. 375–402 at p. 391.

[106] As Mishra and Hodge put it, 'unless postcolonialism can reestablish vital links with Marxism it will not survive nor deserve to survive long into the twenty-first century'. See ibid., p. 388; emphasis deleted.

leading to a deficient view of the nature, character and role of contemporary international law.

VII.   Meaning of World Order: Integrating Five Logics

While the book is arranged with reference to most influential approaches to international law, it also provides occasion to consider a wide range of world order issues that these address. The individual approaches examined in this book may be varyingly comprehensive in their coverage of relevant world order issues, but these together respond to the central questions of our times. Since their views are critiqued from an IMAIL perspective, it is important to indicate the particular understanding of 'world order' it deploys for this purpose.

Over the years the term 'world order' has been assigned a variety of meaning by scholars. Nearly five decades ago, Stanley Hoffman identified five different ways in which the term 'world order' was being used. He noted that two of the meanings were 'purely descriptive: order as any arrangement of reality, order as the relation between the parts', two other meanings were 'analytical – partly descriptive, partly normative: order as the minimum conditions for existence, order as the minimum conditions for coexistence', and a final conception as a 'purely normative order as the conditions for the good life'.[107] A spectrum of definitions of 'world order' have been offered since, privileging one meaning over another or combining them in different ways. Thus, for instance, Hedley Bull combined analytical and normative conceptions to offer a generic definition of 'world order' as 'those patterns or dispositions of human activity that sustain the elementary or primary goals of social life among mankind as a whole'.[108] Falk has offered a more elaborate understanding of 'world order':

> My approach to world order combines analytic, empirical, ideological, and normative concerns in its definition. Such a conception of world order involves studying the extent to which a given past, present, or future arrangement of power and authority is able to realize a set of human values that are affirmed as beneficial for all people and apply to the whole world and that have some objectivity by their connection with a conception of basic needs, as required for the healthy development of the human person.[109]

---

[107] Stanley Hoffman, 'Report of the Conference on Conditions of World Order-June 12–19, 1965, Villa Serbelloni, Bellagio, Italy', 95 (Spring 1966) *Daedalus*, pp. 455–478 at p. 456.
[108] Hedley Bull, *The Anarchical Society: A Study of Order in World Politics* (New York: Columbia University Press, 1977), p. 20.
[109] Richard Falk, *The End of World Order: Essays on Normative International Relations* (New York: Holmes and Meier, 1983), p. 45. Mohammed Bedjaoui writes that the term

Henry Kissinger has recently offered a cultural understanding of 'world order' defining it as 'the concept held by a region or civilization about the nature of just arrangements and the distribution of power thought to be applicable to the entire world'.[110] The Kissinger definition envisages contending visions of world order that are in tension with each other.

IMAIL for its part adopts a comprehensive understanding of the term 'world order' on the lines advanced by Falk but theorizes its meaning, content and scope in terms of 'five logics' and their complex interrelationships that constitute the bourgeois world order that is in place since the seventeenth century. These logics are the 'logic of capital', the 'logic of territory', the 'logic of nature', the 'logic of culture' and the 'logic of law'. The relationship of the different logics is dynamic and complex and evolves over time. While the five 'logics' together co-constitute 'world order', each of the logics has its own inner structure, dynamics and rituals. In other words, while each of the logics represents 'a rich totality of many determinations and relations'[111] no logic is reducible to other logics. However, in this composite framework of intersecting logics, IMAIL assigns relative priority to the 'logic of capital' as the other four logics operate within the boundaries drawn by it in different phases of history, even as its map and workings come to be influenced and modified by other logics. This intricate matrix of intersecting logics is the template on the basis of which the critique of contemporary approaches to international law and world order is articulated. It may be noted that the term 'world order' is used interchangeably with that of 'global governance' in this book, the latter being principally used to speak of the workings of the capitalist world order in the era of accelerated globalization.[112] Generally speaking, it can be said

---

'order' 'should be understood in its legal connotation, i.e., as simply implying a system of norms governing a society, regardless of any overall cohesion, but above all as not making any value judgment about such a system'. Mohammed Bedjaoui, *Towards a new international economic order* (New York: Holmes & Meir Publishers Inc., 1979), p. 19.

[110] Henry Kissinger, *World Order: Reflections on the Character of Nations and the Course of History* (London: Allen Lane/Penguin, 2014), p. 9. On the limitations of Kissinger's conception of 'world order' see Andrew Hurrell, 'Kissinger and World Order', 44 (2015) *Millennium*, pp. 165–172.

[111] Karl Marx, *Grundrisse: Foundations of the Critique of Political Economy (Rough Draft)*, translated with a Foreword by Martin Nicolaus (Middlesex: Pelican Books, 1973), p. 100.

[112] The term 'global governance' has been defined as 'the sum of the many ways individuals and institutions, public and private, manage their common affairs' at the global level. Commission on Global Governance, *Our Global Neighborhood* (Oxford: Oxford University Press, 1995), p. 2. The term inter alia indicates the greater density of actors, processes and institutions in contemporary international life. For different ways of conceptualizing 'global governance' see James N. Rosenau, 'Governance in the Twenty-First Century', 1 (1995) *Global Governance*, p. 14; James N. Rosenau and Ernst-Otto

that what is common to most non-IMAIL approaches to international law and world order is a tendency to neglect the 'logic of capital' which is at best assigned secondary significance. But the focus on the 'logic of capital' in the instance of IMAIL does not mean that 'small causes and their larger effects' are neglected;[113] or for that matter the role of individuals in the making and working of world order.[114] IMAIL not only accepts the need to take all logics into account but also both macro and micro global processes.

A few words more may be said on each of the logics beginning with the 'logic of capital'. To begin with, it is worth noting that there is no single definition of 'capitalism'. In his well-known book, *Capitalism and Freedom*, Milton Friedman defined capitalism as the 'organization of the bulk of economic activity through private enterprise operating in a free market'.[115] On the other hand, following Marx, the British economist Maurice Dobb defined capitalism as follows:

> Capitalism was not simply a system of production for the market – a system of commodity production as Marx termed it – but a system under which labour power had 'itself become a commodity' and was bought and

Czempiel (eds.), *Governance without Government: Order and Change in World Politics* (Cambridge: Cambridge University Press, 1992); Thomas G. Weiss, 'Governance, Good Governance, and Global Governance: Conceptual and Actual Challenges', 21 (2000) *Third World Quarterly*, pp. 795–814; Rodney Bruce Hall and Thomas J. Biersteker, *The Emergence of Private Authority in Global Governance* (Cambridge: Cambridge University Press, 2002); Klaus Dingwerth and Phillip Pattberg, 'Global Governance as a Perspective on World Politics', 12 (2006) *Global Governance*, pp. 185–203; Nico Krisch and Benedict Kingsbury, 'Introduction: Global Governance and Global Administrative Law in the International Legal Order', 17 (2006) *The European Journal of International Law*, pp. 1–13; David Kennedy, *A World of Struggle: How Power, Law, and Expertise Shape Global Political Economy* (Princeton, NJ: Princeton University Press, 2016).

[113] Bruno Latour, *We Have Never been Modern* (Cambridge, MA: Harvard University Press, 1993), translated by Catherine Porter, p. 125. On the other hand, it needs to be emphasized that no strategy of critique involves an approach to totality that Latour appears to be mocking in observing: 'Every totalization, even if it is critical, helps totalitarianism. We need not add total domination to real domination. Let us not add power to force. We need not grant total imperialism to real imperialism. We need not add absolute deterritorialization to capitalism, which is also quite real enough. Similarly, we do not need to credit scientific truth and technological efficacity with transcendence, also total, and rationality, also absolute. With misdeeds as with domination, with capitalisms as with sciences, what we need to understand is the ordinary dimension: the small causes and their large effects ... totalization participates, in devious ways, in what it claims to abolish. It renders its practitioners powerless in the face of the enemy, whom it endows with fantastic properties.' See ibid.

[114] For a discussion of the idea of 'methodological individualism', see Chapter 5, pp. 276–282.

[115] Friedman, *Capitalism and Freedom*, p. 4.

sold on the market like any other object of exchange. Its historical prerequisite was the concentration of ownership of the means of production
in the hands of a class, consisting of only a minor section of society, and
the consequent emergence of a propertyless class for whom the sale of
their labour power was their only source of livelihood.[116]

Any reference to capitalism or the use of the term 'deep structures' in the
text is primarily to the Dobb understanding of capitalism.[117] Capitalism,
it is also important to stress, is not uniform in its materialization. There
are a variety of capitalisms that can indicate different levels and forms of
capitalist development.[118] In the case of nations of the Global South, capitalism often coexists with other modes of production. Yet IMAIL assigns
priority to the 'logic of capital' because, as Marx explained, 'in all forms of
society there is one specific kind of production which predominates over
the rest, whose relations thus assign and rank and influence to others.
It is a general illumination which bathes all the other colors and modi-
fies their particularity'.[119] Since the colonial era, capitalism has travelled
to other nations on the back of imperialism making it the dominant global mode of production. In fact, IMAIL posits an internal relationship
between capitalism and imperialism, a relationship recognized by Rosa
Luxemburg more than Marx.[120] But this relationship is repressed in the
case of capitalist nations of the Global South as these are 'dependent and
dominated social formation(s)' with asymmetric relationship to advanced
capitalist formations.[121] However, even as IMAIL deploys the categories

---

[116] Maurice Dobb, *Studies in the Development of Capitalism* (London: Routledge and Kegan
Paul, 1947), p. 7. Likewise, according to Sweezy, 'the buying and selling of labor power is
the *differentia specifica* of capitalism'. Paul M. Sweezy, *The Theory of Capitalist Development*
(New York: Modern Reader Paperbacks, 1968), p. 56. For Marx's definition, see Karl Marx,
Capital: A Critique of Political Economy, vol. 3 (Moscow: Progress Publishers, 1977),
pp. 879–880. It is cited in Chapter 7, fn 81.

[117] However, the definition offered by Friedman will serve as a convenient shorthand expression in particular contexts.

[118] Thus, for instance, according to Antonio Negri 'immaterial production' (as against industrial production) is today coming to play a critical role in advanced capitalist countries.
Negri contends that in the last three decades 'there is an emergent hegemony of immaterial production compared with other forms of production', replacing 'the previous hegemony of industrial production'. In this form of production 'labor that creates immaterial
products: knowledge, information, communications, linguistic and emotional relations'
is coming to dominate the global economy. These products can be accessible to all if not
made the subject of exclusionary intellectual property rights. Antonio Negri, *Empire and
Beyond*, translated by Ed Emery (Cambridge: Polity, 2006), pp. 127–128.

[119] Marx, *Grundrisse*, pp. 106–107.

[120] See Chapter 2, pp. 61–62, Chapter 7, pp. 490–492.

[121] Nicos Poulantzas, *Classes in Contemporary Capitalism* (London: Verso, 1978), pp. 43–44.

of the Global North and the Global South or first and third worlds, it contends that a transnational capitalist class (TCC) is emerging in the era of accelerated globalization which is constituted of the transnational fractions of the capitalist classes in the nations of the Global North and the Global South.[122] In other words, IMAIL simultaneously explores difference, fluidity and contingency in understanding universalizing capital and the inevitable consequences that flow from its extension to nations of the Global South.

The 'logic of territory' is of fundamental significance because international relations and international law are not about a single state but a states system.[123] In the past, Marxists have not paid adequate attention to this fact, privileging the 'logic of capital' in understanding international relations and international law. In contrast, IMAIL assigns a critical role to the 'logic of territory' in the evolution and development of international law even as it closely looks at the interface between the 'logic of capital' and the 'logic of territory'. It additionally recognizes that non-state actors, professional networks and informal processes and institutions are increasingly coming to play an important role in global governance, pointing to the limits of the 'logic of territory' in contemporary times. It can be said that a combination of coalescing trends driven by factors ranging from the information and communication revolution to the imperatives of roving capitalism is slowly leading to the emergence of an incipient global social formation presided over by a nascent world state. But for the present the international system remains an inter-state system.

The 'logic of nature' refers to the totality of man–nature relationship that today calls for urgent rethinking.[124] As the ecological crisis deepens and threatens life on planet earth the future of man–nature relationship has to be reimagined so that nature is not treated as the Other of humankind. The extent to which this task is accomplished will have a critical bearing on the survival of both. From the IMAIL standpoint the 'logic of capital' is the key to understanding the 'logic of nature' even as it is significantly influenced by the other logics. The intersecting logics are coming to have a bearing upon, among other things, social and political relationships within nation states. For instance, it is said that the nature of democracy is coming to be transformed as a result of the ecological crisis.[125]

---

[122] For a detailed discussion, see Chapter 7, pp. 507–509.

[123] For a discussion, see Chapter 7, pp. 504–506.

[124] For a detailed discussion of man–nature relationship see Chapter 4, pp. 202–211.

[125] According to Latour, 'the very notion of a representative government, or representative democracy, now includes the highly complex set up that represents non-humans as well

The 'logic of culture' encompasses the world of ideas and ideology that shape perspectives on capital, territory, market, democracy, nature, language, law, ethics, democracy, arts and aesthetics and above all the state. The 'logic of culture' shapes among other things the meaning and role of such key ideas as nationalism, development and security.[126] These deeply impact the quotidian lives of individuals and groups within and across nations. The 'logic of culture' also influences the modes of resistance that are used to protest inegalitarian and oppressive practices. In other words, the influence of 'logic of culture' is deep and profound.

Finally, there is the 'logic of law' which is intimately related to the workings of the other four logics. Of these the 'logic of capital' and the 'logic of territory', and their interface, determine in a primary way the form and content of international law. But the other logics also play a crucial role in its evolution and development. The 'logic of culture' for instance explains why international law matters are discussed in characteristic vocabulary in the matrix of a distinctive history that manifests in a continuity of issues and preoccupation with problems uniquely related to its genesis and evolution, influencing the manner in which the other four logics are approached. This inclusive view of the logic of international law explains the rejection by IMAIL of both positivism and the instrumentalist Marxist theory of law.[127] While arguing that contemporary international law principally reflects the interests of dominant social forces and states, IMAIL recognizes that the international legal system also serves the general interests of the international community of states.

VIII.   Final Words on Form and Content

A few final words need to be said on the form and content of the book. First, there is no separate chapter containing the conclusions of the book. It ends with the chapter on IMAIL. While an attempt has been made therein to draw the threads together, only a separate tome can do justice to the effort of articulating IMAIL as part of a seamless discussion on different subjects. At this point only the promise of such a volume can be

---

as humans'. Bruno Latour, 'Politics of Nature: East and West Perspectives', 4 (2011) *Ethics and Global Politics*, pp. 1–10 at p. 2.

[126] For a critique of the modern state, see the brief but incisive essay of Ashish Nandy, 'The State: The Fate of a Concept' in *The Romance of the State: And the Fate of Dissent in the Tropics* (New Delhi: Oxford University Press, 2003), pp. 1–15.

[127] For a detailed discussion of the rejection of a dogmatic Marxist approach to law, see Chapter 7, pp. 449–462.

held out. Meanwhile, readers may keep in mind that the *IMAIL emerges in the book as a whole*.[128] The different chapters clarify the IMAIL position with regard to crucial themes and issues pertaining to the articulation of a theory of international law and world order.[129] The separate chapter on IMAIL only addresses a set of core topics that are not dealt with in the other chapters but are critical to the exposition of IMAIL. These include a Marxist theory of law and international law, a materialist history of international law, the nature, character and features of contemporary international law, a materialist theory of interpretation, the Marxist view of human rights and reflections on alternative futures.[130]

Second, the effort to arrange the materials in a clear fashion has led on many occasions to their schematic presentation. Further, reliance is often placed on the words of the proponents in presenting the different approaches. This is done not only in order to validate the reading of their work but also to offer a flavour of the original approach. Such a method is on occasions also necessitated by the fact that views are articulated in language that is relatively inaccessible or open-ended allowing the authors to distance themselves from unanticipated interpretations and critiques.[131] It is useful in such instances to know what the author(s) have written. These procedures may at times not make for elegant reading but ensures that a particular approach is expressed with as much fidelity and clarity as possible. The indulgence of readers is solicited in these regards. It is, of course, for them to judge whether these ways of assembling materials are helpful.

Finally, the book is written with both the students of international law and international relations in mind, even as the former is without doubt its primary subject. There is increasingly a felt need for greater interaction between the disciplines of international law and international relations

---

[128] It may also be worth noting that some issues or themes have been dealt with in many chapters. For example, the issue of indeterminacy of international legal rules is grappled with in nearly all chapters with the exception of FtAIL. Those interested in it would greatly benefit from reading the detailed discussion on indeterminacy in the other chapters.

[129] These include the subjects of concept of law, fragmentation of social sciences, capitalism, colonialism, postcolonialism, imperialism, feminism, socialism, anarchism, theory of state, human nature, power, national interest, indeterminacy of rules, human rights, global civil society, development, ecological crisis, function of world court, role of international lawyers, the relevance of international morality, that state of international community and the emergence of a world state.

[130] This was the only way to advance a critique of distinct approaches to international law and also elaborate IMAIL without extensive repetition.

[131] See generally Jean D'aspremont, 'Wording in International Law', 25 (2012)*Leiden Journal of International Law*, pp. 575–602.

in order to better understand and respond to the complexities that are coming to inform international life. While IMAIL is critical of the liberal international relations-international law (IR-IL) approach articulated by Anne Marie Slaughter, Kenneth Abbott and others, pioneers of contemporary IR-IL approach, it shares the underlying sentiment that there must be closer interaction between the two disciplines.[132]

---

[132] For a discussion of the liberal IR-IL approach, see Chapter 2, pp. 93–101.

2

The Classical Realist Approach to International Law: The World of Hans Morgenthau

I. Introduction

It has been observed that classical realism 'remains the single most important approach for understanding international politics.'[1] One of its most distinguished proponents, Hans Joachim Morgenthau, has been described as among 'the most important political thinkers of the 20th century and one of the greatest realist thinkers of all times.'[2] His classic work *Politics among Nations* is certain to have an enduring place in the history of ideas.[3] However, its immense influence in the first decades after the Second World War can be traced primarily to the fact that it was 'a quintessential cold war text.'[4] It explains why in the wake of Morgenthau's opposition to the Vietnam War the influence of classical realism began to wane in the United States.[5] The realist emphasis on the idea of prudence

---

[1] Keir A. Lieber, 'Introduction: The Enduring Relevance of International Political Realism' in Keir A. Lieber (ed.) *War, Peace, and International Political Realism: Perspectives from The Review of Politics* (Notre Dame, IN: University of Notre Dame Press, 2009), p. 25.

[2] John Mearsheimer, 'Hans Morgenthau and the Iraq War: Realism versus Neo-conservatism', openDemocracy, (19 May 2005), p. 1, available at www.opendemocracy.net/democracy-americanpower/morgenthau_2522.jsp

[3] Hans J. Morgenthau, *Politics among Nations: The Struggle for Power and Peace*, 4th edn (New York: Alfred A. Knopf, 1967).

[4] Richard Little, *The Balance of Power in International Relations: Metaphors, Myths and Models* (Cambridge: Cambridge University Press, 2007), p. 2. The 'political realist' view was the most widely taught approach to international relations in the fifties and sixties. Olsen and Onuf, after reviewing the literature in the area, reported that *Politics among Nations* is 'the most influential textbook of the early post-war period'. William Olson and Nicholas Onuf, 'The Growth of a Discipline Reviewed' in Steve Smith (ed.), *International Relations: British and American Perspectives* (Oxford: Oxford University Press, 1985), pp. 1–28 at p. 20. In so far as the developing countries were concerned, Korany had noted that 'the power paradigm has been presented as the most valid, since *Politics Among Nations* has been translated into such languages as Arabic, Chinese, Turkish and Swahili'. B. Korany, 'Strategic Studies and the Third World: A Critical Evaluation', 110 (1986) *International Social Science Journal*, pp. 546–562 at p. 549.

[5] In the seventies Rosenau et al. concluded that 'the primary reliance on Morgenthau's text has come to an end, but ... it [is] no less clear that the influence of realist thinking continues

38

and an ethic of consequences was perceived as a concession to the enemy. It slowly came to be challenged in the international relations academia at first by neorealism and later by liberal, feminist, constructivist and post-structuralist approaches.[6] In the world of international law, classical realism came to be contested at first by the policy-oriented approach of Myres McDougal and Harold Lasswell and then from a different direction by the world-order model approach of Richard Falk.[7]

But recent years have seen a renewed interest in the classical realist approach to international politics, especially in the work of Morgenthau.[8] There are several reasons that account for this revival of interest. At least three may be mentioned. First, to critics of US foreign policy, classical realism offered incisive arguments for opposing the wars against Afghanistan and Iraq. It provided 'an effective language for criticizing the moral crusades of neoconservatives and the aggressive idealism of

---

to prevail'. James N. Rosenau et al., 'Of Syllabi, Texts, Students, and Scholarships in International Relations: Some Data and Interpretations on the State of a Burgeoning Field', 29 (1976–77) *World Politics,* pp. 263–340 at p. 330. On Morgenthau's views on the Vietnam War, see Hans J Morgenthau, *Truth and Power: Essays of a Decade, 1960–70* (London: Pall Mall Press, 1970).

[6] Mark A. Pollack, 'Is International Relations Corrosive of International Law?: A Reply to Martti Koskenniemi', 27 (2013) *Temple International & Comparative Law Quarterly,* pp. 339–376 at pp. 358ff.

[7] See Chapter 3, pp. 112–113, Chapter 4, pp. 194–202, 211–212.

[8] Michael C. Williams, 'Introduction' in Michael C. Williams (ed.) *Realism Reconsidered: The Legacy of Hans J. Morgenthau in International Relations* (New York: Oxford University Press, 2007), pp. 1–17 at p. 1. This renewed interest is reflected in the burgeoning literature on classical realism and Morgenthau. See Nicolas Guilhot (ed.) *The Invention of International Relations Theory: Realism, the Rockefeller Foundation and the 1954 Conference on Theory* (New York: University of Columbia Press, 2011); Lorenzo Zambernardi, 'The Impotence of Power: Morgenthau's Critique of American Intervention in Vietnam', 37 (2011) *Review of International Studies,* pp. 1335–1356; Oliver Jütersonke, *Morgenthau, Law and Realism* (Cambridge: Cambridge University Press, 2010); Lieber, *War Peace and International Political Realism*; Muriel Cozette, 'Reclaiming the Critical Dimension of Realism: Hans J. Morgenthau on the Ethics of scholarship', 34 (2008) *Review of International Studies,* pp. 5–27; Michael C. Williams, *The Realist Tradition and the Limits of International Relations* (Cambridge: Cambridge University Press, 2005); Anthony F. Lang, *Political Theory and International Affairs: Hans J. Morgenthau on Aristotle's The Politics* (Greenwood, CT: Praeger, 2004); G. O. Mazur (ed.) *One Hundred Year Commemoration to the Life of Hans Morgenthau (1904–2004)* (New York: Semenenko Foundation, 2004); Campbell Craig, *Glimmer of a New Leviathan: Total War in the Realism of Niebuhr, Morgenthau and Waltz* (New York: Columbia University Press, 2003); Christopher Frei, *Hans J. Morgenthau: An Intellectual Biography* (Baton Rouge: Louisiana State University Press, 2001); Jack Donnelly, *Realism and International Relations* (Cambridge: Cambridge University Press, 2000).

militarized democracy promotion.[9] Morgenthau had always warned against the use of force to spread democracy, as it would inevitably run up against the ideological and political force of nationalism.[10] He had also cautioned against the tendency of states to present national ethics as universal ethics. Morgenthau had equally advised against substituting force for diplomacy. The resulting stress on the value of prudence contrasted sharply with the lack of self-restraint in US foreign policy under the George W. Bush administration. The fact that in his life time Morgenthau never hesitated to speak 'truth to power' enhanced the appeal of classical realism.[11] The idea of 'the scholar as a heroic figure' ready to sacrifice everything to his mission has a certain draw in troubled times. International relations scholars drew inspiration from the Morgenthau view that 'a political science that is true to its moral commitment ought at the very least to face the risk of unpopularity'.[12]

Second, the end of the Cold War did not turn out to be the 'end of history', making students of international relations look for answers to endemic conflicts. In this endeavour classical realism was appealing since it sought answers in 'the timeless philosophical questions about the nature of man, society, and politics'.[13] Its stress on objective forces of history rooted in a dark and unchanging human nature was particularly attractive at a time when theorizing was becoming 'an innocuous pastime ... without effect upon political reality and unaffected by it'.[14] In retrospect, Morgenthau seemed right to observe that 'novelty is not necessarily a virtue in political theory, nor is old age a defect'.[15] At the same time, the hermeneutic element in classical realism, which requires critical concepts like 'national interest' be given meaning in changing historical circumstances, left space for creative thinking.

Third, ongoing attempts to encourage collaboration between the disciplines of international relations (IR) and international law (IL) made scholars from both domains to return to Morgenthau to understand the reasons for divorce.[16] It may be recalled that in the inter-war era of the last

[9] Nicolas Guilhot, 'Introduction: One Discipline, Many Histories' in Nicolas Guilhot (ed.), *The Invention of International Relations Theory*, pp. 1–33 at p. 5; Williams, *Realist Tradition*, pp. 197ff.
[10] See Guilhot, 'Introduction', pp. 5–6. See also Mearsheimer, 'Hans Morgenthau', pp. 5–6.
[11] Morgenthau, *Truth and Power*, pp. 13–29.
[12] Cozette, 'Reclaiming the Critical', p. 14.
[13] Lieber, 'Introduction', pp. 2, 4.
[14] Cozzette, 'Reclaiming the Critical', p. 23.
[15] Morgenthau, *Politics among Nations*, p. 4.
[16] See Martti Koskenniemi, *The Gentle Civilizer of Nations: The Rise and Fall of International Law 1870–1960* (Cambridge: Cambridge University Press, 2005), pp. 436ff.

century 'the disciplines of international law and international relations overlapped substantially'.[17] The era of 'disciplinary convergence', however, ended with the Second World War. Over the next decades the disciplines of IR and IL 'developed along separate and rarely intersecting tracks'.[18] The separation of the two disciplines is usually traced to the dominance of classical realism in the international relations academia with its deep scepticism about the role of international law in international politics. Therefore, both the advocates and critics of what is termed the IR-IL approach sought to revisit Morgenthau's views, especially in the backdrop of his sustained reflections on international law in the early years of his intellectual life in Europe to which attention had been drawn in recent years.[19] Written in the inter-war years, Morgenthau's doctoral thesis was on 'The judicial function in the international realm, the nature of its organs and the limits of its application; in particular, the concept of the political in international law', later published under the title 'The Judicial Function in the International Realm, its Nature and its Limits'.[20] His other writings on international law in the period included 'Limitations of the International Judicial Function' (1929), 'The Reality of the League of Nations' (1933), 'The Collapse of Ethics' (1935) and *La Realite des Normes* (1934).[21] He retained many of the ideas from these writings in *Politics among Nations*. In fact it has been argued that 'his engagement with questions of law, and with the relationship between law and politics as a whole, contributed to his understanding of IR and the development of his realism'.[22] Indeed, there is little doubt that Morgenthau's theory of international politics owed much to his thinking on international law.[23] Since it also accounted for the neglect of international law by the international relations academia, this called for fresh engagement with classical realism.

---

[17] Jeffrey L. Dunoff and Mark A. Pollack, 'International Law and International Relations: Introducing an Interdisciplinary Dialogue' in Jeffrey L. Dunoff and Mark A. Pollack (eds.) *Interdisciplinary Perspectives on International Law and International Relations* (Cambridge: Cambridge University Press, 2013), pp. 3–35 at p. 5.

[18] See ibid., pp. 5 and 4.

[19] See, for instance, Jütersonke, *Morgenthau*.

[20] Hans Morgenthau, *The Judicial Function in the International Realm, Its Nature and Its Limits* (Leipzig: Noske, 1929). See ibid., p. 52 fn 65. For discussion, see Jütersonke, *Morgenthau*, pp. 51–57.

[21] Frei, *Hans J. Morgenthau*, p. 134. For discussion of his early ideas on international law see pp. 138–141.

[22] Williams, 'Introduction', p. 7.

[23] For instance, Jütersonke points out that 'the chapter on judicial settlement [in *Politics among Nations*] is taken straight from his doctorate: an analysis of international conflict

While these factors account for the renewed interest in classical realism, those who turned to it for guidance had to deal with conventional wisdom that it rests on simplistic assumptions about the nature of man, society and politics. There was a realization that if the classical realist tradition had to be revived it had to be enriched to deal with the growing complexity in international relations. In view of the rich intellectual lineage of Morgenthau, of which he himself left a brief account, this did not prove a difficult task.[24] To put it differently, the turn to 'intellectual lineage' was driven by the 'intriguing puzzle' that someone who was influenced by a range of first rate minds (which included Karl Marx, Friedrich Nietzsche, Sigmund Freud and Max Weber) could advance a simplistic view of politics.[25] It is now suggested that when read carefully and in context the realist theory emerges 'as a sophisticated, self-conscious, and highly political interrogation of the relationship between power and politics'.[26] In fact it is said that Morgenthau deliberately ignored 'the complexity of the concept of "the political," ' as a 'part of a sophisticated intellectual strategy seeking to address the centrality of power in politics'.[27]

Most writings that explore Morgenthau's intellectual roots have turned to Freud, Nietzsche and Weber to give depth to the classical realist approach.[28] The influence of each of these figures on Morgenthau's scholarship is, however, often underscored and contested. Thus, for example,

needed to distinguish between disputes (i.e., legally formulated conflicts) and tensions (or 'unformulated conflicts of power')'. Jütersonke, *Morgenthau*, p. 69.

[24] Hans J. Morgenthau, 'An Intellectual Autobiography', (1978 Jan-Feb) *Society*, pp. 63–68.

[25] Michael C. Williams, 'Why Ideas Matter in International Relations: Hans Morgenthau, Classical Realism, and the Moral Construction of Power Politics', 58 (2004) *International Organization*, pp. 633–665 at p. 636; emphasis added.

[26] See ibid., p. 634; emphasis added.

[27] See ibid., p. 637.

[28] Carl Schmitt is also mentioned even though his association with the Nazi regime discredited him in the eyes of Morgenthau. In fact after meeting him, the only time the two met, Morgenthau described Schmitt as the most evil person alive. For a discussion of the relationship between the thinking of Schmitt and Morgenthau see William Scheuerman, *Carl Schmitt: The End of Law* (New York: Rowan and Littlefield, 1999); Williams, *Realist Tradition*, pp. 84ff; Koskenniemi, *The Gentle Civilizer*, pp. 459–465. The other figures mentioned are Reinhold Niebuhr and lesser known individuals like Hugo Sinzheimer. See G. O. Mazur, 'Introduction' in G. O. Mazur (ed.), *One Hundred Year*, pp. 1–10 at p. 5. In his intellectual biography of Morgenthau, Frei also refers to the 'Red Castle', that is, the Frankfurt Institute for Social Research where 'he met Max Horkheimer, Franz Oppenheimer, Karl Mannheim, Theodor Wiesengrund (Adorno), Herbert Marcuse, Friedrich Pollock, Karl Landeur, and Erich Fromm'. Frei, *Hans J. Morgenthau*, p. 39. Researchers often identify different primary influences. For instance, according to Rice, Niebuhr and Nietzsche had a major impact. Daniel Rice, 'Reinhold Niebuhr and Hans Morgenthau: A Friendship with Contrasting Shades of Realism', 42 (2008) *Journal of American Studies*, pp. 255–291.

while it has been contended that Morgenthau was 'methodologically, a Weberian',[29] it has also been argued that Morgenthau throws 'the Weberian limitations on the objectivity of the social sciences overboard and indulges in absolute statements'.[30] There is also debate on whose influence was most dominant. His biographer Frei believes that 'Nietzsche's influence has been nothing less than profound',[31] noting that the phrase Morgenthau himself used in the context was 'most powerful and decisive influence'.[32] In contrast, Jütersonke claims that the writings of the jurist Hans Kelsen were most influential (along with the critique of Morgenthau's work by Hersch Lauterpacht).[33] In his view, the revival of Morgenthau's thought 'is neither particularly interesting nor an added value to the disciplinary history of International Relations if it continues to occlude the law debates within which his ideas were shaped'.[34] It would appear from these cogitations that different scholars are emphasizing those influences that help sustain a preferred view of international relations.

From the perspective of an Integrated Marxist Approach to International Law (IMAIL) it is surprising that in all the effort to consider the intellectual lineage of Morgenthau, not much is made of his observation that 'modern sociology is inconceivable without Marx'.[35] While there is much that divides Morgenthau and Marx the two appear to be united by realist philosophy.[36] To be sure, Morgenthau's realism was opposed to the realism of Marx, but it was realism nevertheless. Morgenthau was inspired among other things by Marx's 'analysis of the gap between legal and social reality'.[37] The reason Morgenthau turned away from Marxism was primarily its reductionist orientation.[38] But, it is then good to remember that he

[29] Stephen Turner and George Mazur, 'Morgenthau as a Weberian Methodologist', 15 (2009) *European Journal of International Relations*, pp. 477–504 at p. 478.
[30] Hans-Karl Pichler, 'The Godfathers of 'truth': Max Weber and Carl Schmitt in Morgenthau's Theory of Power Politics', 24 (1998) *Review of International Studies*, pp. 185–200 at p. 185.
[31] Frei, *Hans J Morgenthau*, p. 108.
[32] See ibid.
[33] Jütersonke notes that Morgenthau owed to Hans Kelsen the award of his *Habilitation*. Jütersonke, *Morgenthau*, pp. 48–49.
[34] See ibid., pp. ix-x.
[35] Morgenthau, 'Intellectual Autobiography', p. 66.
[36] Noting the affinity of classical realism with historical materialism Leiter observes that 'Marx can agree with the Classical Realist appraisal of human beings in every respect except one: human beings must necessarily and always be this way'. Brian Leiter, 'Classical Realism', 11 (2001) *Social, Political, and Legal Philosophy*, pp. 244–267 at p. 254.
[37] William E. Scheuerman, 'Realism and the Left: The Case of Hans J. Morgenthau', 34 (2008) *Review of International Studies*, pp. 29–51 at p. 41.
[38] Morgenthau, 'Intellectual Autobiography', p. 67. He was also concerned about its claim of 'infallibility, that is, the monopolistic possession of the truth about men and society'. Hans

also found psychoanalysis (or Freud) reductionist.[39] In his words, 'what defeats a psychoanalytical theory of politics is what has defeated a Marxist theory of politics: the impossibility of accounting for the complexities and varieties of political experience with the simplicities of a reductionist theory, economic or psychological'.[40] Yet, Freud is repeatedly invoked by commentators to lend depth to classical realism.[41] In assessing the complicated debates on particular influences on Morgenthau, it is perhaps best to go along with the observation of Turner and Mazur that where 'several thinkers are a source for another, there is usually a problem of overdetermination'.[42] Since it is not easy to separate the various influences, an effort should be made to see that the exercise does not 'degenerate into a highly subjective exercise of finding and alleging similarities between texts'.[43] Be that as it may, the debate on his intellectual lineage remains relevant as it helps focus on the epistemological and ontological assumptions that form the basis of the realist theory of international politics. Indeed, their discussion is absolutely necessary if a serious review of the realist approach to international politics and international law is to be undertaken.

In the backdrop of these introductory remarks, this chapter proceeds as follows. Section II schematically presents the fundamental principles of the realist theory of international politics. Section III goes on to examine the 'realism of realism' by critically analysing, often in telegraphic language, key premises, such as an unchanging human nature and the existence of an autonomous political sphere, and central realist concepts such as 'power', 'national interest' and 'imperialism'.[44] The larger aim of this section is to contrast the assumptions of classical realism with those that inform IMAIL. It is contended that human nature is not innate but determined in fundamental ways by an ensemble of social relations, even as there are elements that are shaped by biology. Likewise, it is

---

J. Morgenthau, *Truth and Power*, p. 356. It may be worth adding that his critique was more focused on the practices of socialist societies than on Marxist theory.

[39] See ibid.

[40] See ibid.

[41] Morgenthau, 'Intellectual Autobiography', p. 67. One may note here that the 'critical theory' initiated by the Frankfurt School in the 1930s was largely concentrated on 'study of superstructures'. Perry Anderson, *Considerations on Western Marxism* (London: New Left Books, 1976), p. 75.

[42] Turner and Mazur, 'Morgenthau as a Weberian', p. 479.

[43] See ibid., p. 480.

[44] One scholar has argued that realism is not defined by 'an explicit set of assumptions and propositions' but by 'a general orientation'. Donnelly, *Realism*, p. 6. But Morgenthau's 'six principles of realism' which are discussed presently may be seen as a statement of assumptions and propositions of the realist approach to international politics.

suggested that the idea of the autonomy of the political sphere is mis-construed and exaggerated. The section also contests the restrictive real-ist view of power and endorses in its place a multidimensional concept of 'power'; points out the limitations of the concept of 'national inter-est' used by realism; and rejects its political definition of the concept of imperialism by pointing to its internal relationship with capitalism. It notes in the latter context how, given Morgenthau's concern with great power politics, he never seriously engaged with the world of weak non-Western nations making it particularly susceptible to the critique of postcolonial theory.

Section IV offers a detailed statement and critique of the realist approach to international law. The broad argument is that while clas-sical realisms' scepticism of the role of international law in international politics is shared by other critical approaches, the nature and sources of their scepticism go beyond biological realism and power politics. More specifically, it contends that a fundamental problem with the realist approach is that, given its assumption of the autonomy of the political sphere, it only takes into account the 'logic of territory' to the neglect of the 'logic of capital'. This deficiency pervades all aspects of its understanding of international law including its nature, charac-ter and effectiveness. In contrast to the classical realist approach of Morgenthau, IMAIL attaches critical importance to the 'logic of capital' and is therefore able to offer a richer analysis of the structure and pro-cess of international law.

Section V touches on the realist understanding of the relationship between international morality and international law. It argues that while the classical realist critique of moralism is valuable, and something can be said for the principle of prudence and 'ethic of consequences', it does not sufficiently appreciate the intricate linkages between international ethics and international law. While many of these linkages serve the interests of powerful social forces and states, there are others that help defend weak states.

Section VI examines Morgenthau's views on the possible emergence of a world state, the creation of which is seen as a precondition for bringing about world peace. It is contended that the prospect of the emergence of a world state is tied to a flawed theory of functionalism advanced by David Mitrany. Since Morgenthau ignores the 'logic of capital' in thinking about the materialization of a world state he does not recognize the crucial role of universalizing capitalism in engendering a 'global social formation' that will constitute its sociological basis. He, therefore, also did not appreciate that given the 'logic of capital' such a world state would necessarily have an imperial character.

Section VII explores the ongoing debate on the relationship between the disciplines of IR and IL. As mentioned earlier, it has not been sufficiently noticed, if at all, that the renewed interest in the realist approach coincides with growing pitch in the United States for collaboration between IR-IL scholars. The renewal of the relationship between IR and IL is called for in the backdrop of the increasing 'legalization' and 'judicialization' of international politics and the enhanced role of non-state actors in law-making and law observance. The new IR-IL approach does not, however, seek a renewal of the idealist or utopian schools that Morgenthau (and E. H. Carr) criticized. It proposes an entirely different basis for collaboration between IR and IL. It is argued that while the new IR-IL approach is welcome it is dominated by the liberal approach to IR that in collaboration with hospitable IL approaches hopes to advance US national interests. In contrast, IMAIL envisages collaboration with critical theories that help focus on the interests of subaltern peoples and nations.

Section VIII contains some final reflections on the realist approach to international politics and international law.

II.   The Realist Theory of International Politics

It is important to begin with a systematic statement of the classical realist approach to international relations which rests on a certain understanding of the place of politics in society.[45] That is to say, it is on classical realism's general understanding of politics that a theory of international politics is based. In this view international politics does not have a distinctive essence. It merely deals with a peculiar subject matter. But Morgenthau concedes that there may be a need 'to reformulate, modify and qualify' the general principles of politics in this light.[46] His basic understanding of politics is stated and extended to international politics in the famous six principles of realism added to the second edition of *Politics among Nations*. It may be useful to summarize these principles as the realist approach of Morgenthau is more often invoked than read.

First, according to the realist approach, politics 'is governed by objective laws that have roots in human nature'.[47] Morgenthau speaks of politics

---

[45] See generally Hans J. Morgenthau, *Scientific Man versus Power Politics* (Chicago, IL: University of Chicago Press, 1965).

[46] Morgenthau, *Dilemmas of Politics*, pp. 47–48.

[47] Morgenthau, *Politics among Nations*, p. 4.

being a 'result of forces inherent in human nature' which has remained unchanged from times immemorial.[48] The timeless elements of human nature that he identifies are 'the drives to live, to propagate, and to dominate' and in general the desire for power. The drive to dominate – posited as an element of all human associations, family through state – explains why all politics is a struggle for power. Morgenthau contrasted his view with those who assume 'the essential goodness and infinite malleability of human nature'.[49]

Second, the realist approach sees politics 'as an autonomous sphere of thought and action'[50] and following it distinguishes 'between political and nonpolitical facts'.[51] Having made that distinction, Morgenthau identifies 'power' as the 'central concept' to explain political facts.[52] It does not mean that 'none but power relations control political action'.[53] But accepting the centrality of power to political action 'allows the observer to distinguish the field of politics from other social spheres'.[54] By power Morgenthau means 'man's control over the minds and actions of other men'.[55] The meaning of 'political power' is 'the mutual relations of control among holders of public authority and between the latter and the people at large'.[56] It expresses 'a psychological relation between those who exercise it and those over whom it is exercised'.[57]

Third, in the realist view 'international politics, like all politics, is a struggle for power. Whatever the ultimate aims of international politics, power is always the immediate aim'.[58] According to Morgenthau, 'the struggle for power is universal in time and space and is an undeniable fact of experience'.[59] Therefore 'international politics is of necessity power politics'.[60] The struggle for power is not an historic accident. Rather, irrespective of how society is structured, it is its eternal essence. However, it is important to note that Morgenthau defines the scope of international

---

[48] See ibid., pp. 3–4.
[49] See ibid., p. 3. See also Morgenthau, *Dilemmas of Politics*, p. 55.
[50] Hans Morgenthau, *The Decline of Democratic Politics* (Chicago, IL: Chicago University Press, 1962), p. 3.
[51] Morgenthau, *Politics among Nations*, p. 5.
[52] Morgenthau, *Decline of Democratic Politics*, p. 48.
[53] See ibid.
[54] See ibid., p. 5.
[55] Morgenthau, *Politics among Nations*, p. 26.
[56] See ibid.
[57] See ibid., p. 27.
[58] See ibid., p. 25.
[59] See ibid., p. 31.
[60] See ibid., p. 29.

politics narrowly. He observes that 'not every action that a nation per-
forms with respect to another nation is of a political nature'.[61] Thus, for
instance, Morgenthau terms the employment of international organizations as a 'nonpolitical' means of achieving ends.[62] He also excludes from
the ambit of international politics all international economic relations
unless they have a bearing on power.[63] Most significantly, according to
Morgenthau, 'not all nations are at all times to the same extent involved
in international politics'.[64] His concern was narrowly with high politics
or 'power politics', politics that captured the central contradiction of the
times. This understanding ruled out almost by definition the concern of
classical realism with the fate of subaltern nations and peoples.

Fourth, a central tenet of realism 'is the concept of interest defined in
terms of power'.[65] According to Morgenthau, in international politics the
statesman must 'think and act in terms of national interest'.[66] The meaning of 'national interest' is, however, not permanently fixed.[67] It depends
upon 'the political and cultural context within which foreign policy is
formulated'.[68] In fact, the goals that may be pursued by nations 'can run
the whole gamut of objectives any nation has ever pursued or might possibly pursue'.[69] However, there is a 'hard core' of national interest that all
nations pursue with survival of the nation as an 'irreducible minimum'.[70]
All nations 'protect their physical, political, and cultural identity against
encroachments by other nations'.[71] Besides there are 'the variable elements
of the national interest' to which scientific analysis can only make a limited contribution.[72] These are shaped by 'group interests' (both 'ethnic and
economic groups') with no one interest independently determining the
course of foreign policy of a nation.[73]

Fifth, in the realist view 'political science is not interested in any
legal subject per se', but has 'a vital interest in the interrelations between
law and politics. It looks at law not as a self-contained system of rules

[61] See ibid., p. 25.
[62] See ibid.
[63] See ibid., p. 26.
[64] See ibid.
[65] See ibid., p. 5.
[66] See ibid., p. 7.
[67] See ibid., p. 8.
[68] See ibid., p. 9.
[69] See ibid.
[70] Morgenthau, *Dilemmas of Politics*, p. 66.
[71] See ibid.
[72] See ibid., pp. 69–70.
[73] See ibid., p. 70.

of conduct, but rather as both the creation and the creator of political forces'.[74] Therefore, realism rejects a legalistic approach to politics.[75] This rejection is pointed in the case of international politics because of the decentralized nature of international society resulting in the lack of an effective system of enforcement. However, this rejection does not signal a disregard for international law. Morgenthau's plea is that international law should be assigned its 'proper sphere and function'.[76] Likewise, the task of the lawyer should be confined to asking whether a particular policy is in accord with rules of law.[77]

Sixth, the realist view rejects a moralistic approach to politics. Instead, it regards prudence as the highest virtue in international politics. Indeed, Morgenthau speaks of 'the moral precept of prudence'.[78] A politics of prudence requires 'the weighing of the consequences of alternative actions – to be the supreme virtue in politics'.[79] The exercise of prudence helps minimize risks and maximize benefits.[80] The stress on the value of prudence explains why, while Morgenthau does not reject the role of morals or ethics in international politics, he insists that 'they must be filtered through the concrete circumstances of time and place'.[81] His concern was that in the era of nationalism each state would be inclined to treat its particular ethics as universal ethics. He, therefore, called for the 'moderation of moral judgment'.[82]

Seventh, the realist theory places great emphasis on the concept of 'balance of power'. It treats it as a 'universal concept' with particular applications in international politics.[83] Among other things, balance of power ensures 'the freedom of one nation from domination by another'.[84] Morgenthau even explains colonialism in terms of a period in which 'the balance of power was quantitatively and qualitatively circumscribed by geographical limits'.[85] In the realist view, the effectiveness of international law also often depends on the prevailing balance of power.[86]

[74] See ibid., p. 50.
[75] See ibid., p. 11.
[76] See ibid., p. 13.
[77] See ibid., p. 11.
[78] Morgenthau, *Politics among Nations*, p. 7.
[79] See ibid., p. 10.
[80] See ibid., p. 7.
[81] See ibid., p. 10.
[82] See ibid., p. 11.
[83] See ibid., pp. 161ff.
[84] See ibid., p. 168.
[85] See ibid., p. 343.
[86] See ibid., p. 284.

Finally, realism does not rule out the future possibility of the nation state being 'replaced by larger units of a quite different character, more in keeping with the technical potentialities and the moral requirements of the contemporary world'.[87] While Morgenthau did not see the emergence of a world state in the near future, it remained for him a long run possibility and a precondition for establishing world peace.

III.   The Realism of Realism

If the entire history of political thought were to be described as a quest for political realism, then the claim whether a particular theory is realist has to be judged not by the name it bears but with reference to the nature of realism advanced.[88] Therefore, in order to arrive at any judgment about the realism of classical realism it is vital to undertake a critical review of Morgenthau's fundamental assumptions with regard to human nature and the autonomy of the political sphere and his understanding of the critical concepts of power, national interest and imperialism. The lack of realism in any of these respects would tend to undermine the realist theory of international politics and international law.

A.   On Human Nature

It was noted that the work of Sigmund Freud greatly influenced Morgenthau. In fact Robert Schuett contends that 'Freud is one of Morgenthau's intellectual fathers'[89] and that his realism was 'founded upon Freud's insights into human nature'.[90] He points out how in his book *Scientific Man vs. Power Politics* Morgenthau 'applauds' Freud for having 'rediscovered the autonomy of the dark and evil forces which, as manifestations of the unconscious, determine the fate of man'.[91] Schuett argues that Morgenthau derived 'his instinct of self-preservation from Freud's ego instinct and his instinct of self-assertion from Freud's sexual instinct',[92] and further that 'Freud's conception of identification and

---

[87] See ibid., p. 9.
[88] See generally, R. N. Berki, *On Political Realism* (London: J. M. Dent and Sons, 1981).
[89] Robert Schuett, 'Freudian Roots of Political Realism: The Importance of Sigmund Freud to Hans J. Morgenthau's Theory of International Power Politics', 20 (2007) *History of the Human Sciences*, pp. 53–78 at p. 66. The unpublished manuscript was titled 'On the Derivation of the Political from the Nature of Man'. See ibid., p. 55.
[90] See ibid., p. 54.
[91] See ibid., p. 58.
[92] See ibid., p. 60.

his group psychology are essential ingredients to Morgenthau's international thought'.[93] These were used by him to understand among other things the basis and power of nationalism.[94] If Morgenthau did not explicitly acknowledge his debt to Freud, it is perhaps because of extraneous reasons such as trying to conceal his German intellectual roots.[95] He was also somewhat uncomfortable with the reductionist nature of psychoanalysis.[96] But there is little doubt that Morgenthau relied heavily on Freud for his innate and pessimistic conception of human nature.

From an IMAIL perspective, Morgenthau's timeless conception of human nature can be usefully compared and contrasted with that of Karl Marx who noted in his sixth thesis on Ludwig Feurbach that 'the essence of man is no abstraction inherent in each single individual. In its reality it is the ensemble of the social relations'.[97] This view is commonly understood to mean a negation of a biological conception of human nature. It was in fact associated by Morgenthau with the idea of 'infinite malleability' of human nature[98]. It is, therefore, important to clarify that to challenge biological realism does not involve the rejection of all of its elements. As has been aptly observed, 'to declare of anything that it changes does not commit one to the view that *everything* about it changes or that it has *no* enduring features'.[99] What is problematic about classical

---

[93] See ibid., p. 57.

[94] Thus, for instance, Morgenthau writes that: 'The growing insecurity of the individual in Western societies, especially in the lower strata, and the atomization of Western society in general have magnified enormously the frustration of individual power drives. This, in turn, has given rise to an increased desire for compensatory identification with the collective national aspirations for power'. Morgenthau, *Politics among Nations*, p. 100.

[95] Schuett, 'Freudian Roots', p. 58. This may have been the case because as Koskenniemi observes that despite that act of distancing 'the notion of power remains psychologically grounded: the limits of law and rationality remain set by what Morgenthau continues to assume as the existential condition off an unending quest for power'. Koskenniemi, *The Gentle Civilizer*, p. 449.

[96] According to Morgenthau, 'what defeated a psychoanalytical theory of politics is what has defeated a Marxist theory of politics: the impossibility of accounting for the complexities and varieties of political experience with the simplicities of a reductionist theory, economic or psychological'. Morgenthau, 'Intellectual Autobiography', p. 67.

[97] Karl Marx and Friedrich Engels, *The German Ideology* (Moscow: Progress Publishers, 1977), p. 616.

[98] Morgenthau writes that 'according to Marx, the lust for power and its political manifestations are a mere by-product of the class division of society. In the classless society, the domination of man by man will be replaced by the administration of things'. Hans Morgenthau, *The Restoration of American Politics* (Chicago, IL: University of Chicago Press, 1962), p. 7.

[99] Norman Geras, *Marx and Human Nature: Refutation of a Legend* (London: Verso, 1983), p. 90; emphasis in original.

realism is not that it draws on biology to arrive at its conception of human nature, but that certain attributes such as the eternal drive to dominate are traced to it. Otherwise, it can hardly be denied that biology contributes to the formation of human nature.[100] The real issue is the extent to which biology determines human nature as opposed to social relations, practices and institutions. The IMAIL view is not that the latter alone have shaped human nature, and thereby the content of politics over centuries, but rather that it is shaped by a dialectic between biology and sociology. The nature of politics is neither to be viewed as 'epiphenomena of structures'[101] nor as a mere manifestation of the individual psyche.[102] While social structures determine human nature in a significant way, there is always a biological surplus that escapes their boundaries. But to suggest that social transformations cannot impact human nature is to naturalize it for all times. An unintended consequence of such a position is the support for status quo in social arrangements. For as has been pointed out 'if the status quo is an extension of natural, then any major change, if possible at all, must inflict an enormous cost – psychological for individuals, or economic for society – in forcing people into unnatural arrangements'.[103] It also leads to tracing the causes of all social divides to simply the drive to dominate. In the process the responsibility of deep structures to engendering social conflicts and wars is neglected.[104] Morgenthau followed this path by ignoring the responsibility of the 'logic of capital' in events leading up to the First and Second World Wars. On the other hand, Morgenthau's biological realism also made him overlook historical evidence of the social traits of solidarity and mutual aid required for the functioning of any society.[105] Finally, it never allowed him to take into

---

[100] In the words of Cohen, 'the contribution of biology will have to be acknowledged'. G. A. Cohen, *Karl Marx's Theory of History: A Defence* (Oxford: Oxford University Press 1978), p. 152.

[101] The phrase is that of Pierre Bourdieu cited in Keith Topper, *The Disorder of Political Inquiry* (Harvard, MA: Harvard University Press, 2005), p. 163.

[102] Morgenthau did acknowledge anthropological literature which noted that 'certain primitive peoples seem to be free from the desire for power', but sought escape in the argument that not enough is known about these societies, and that it is impossible to reproduce parallel conditions on a world scale. Morgenthau felt that those who would free themselves first from the desire for power would fall victims to those who do not; it is improbable that the desire for power could be abolished at one stroke. Morgenthau, *Politics among Nations*, p. 31.

[103] Stephen Jay Gould, *The Mismeasure of Man* (Middlesex: Penguin, 1981), p. 21.

[104] B. S. Chimni, 'Peace through Law: Lessons of 1914', 3 (2015) *London Review of International Law*, pp. 245–265.

[105] As Waltz queried of the realists, 'what about the counter-evidence provided by acts of charity, love and self-sacrifice'. Kenneth N. Waltz, *Man, the State and War: A Theoretical*

account the possibility of transforming human nature through work on the self. In fact he had 'a deep distrust for solution to real world problems that were based on a plan to fix men's souls'.[106] But political leaders like Mahatma Gandhi wished to do precisely that. For classical realists there is a need to 'reconcile what is morally desirable with what is politically possible'.[107] Gandhi understood this. His was also 'a practical morality' but of a different sort.[108] But, classical realists and their successors have had little interest in the experiences of individuals and groups who have used soul power to transform themselves and the world. It explains why Gandhi's idea of non-violence or 'soul power', and its implications for a theory of international politics, is not a part of the realist oeuvre.

In sum, it can be said that there is an element of truth in all three approaches to human nature, that of biological realism, social relations realism and soul power realism. Freud, Marx and Gandhi are the rich sources to draw upon to reach an understanding about human nature and its relationship to politics. But by neglecting Marx and Gandhi, Morgenthau articulated an impoverished theory of human nature and therefore also of international politics and international law.

B.   On Autonomy of the Political Sphere

It was seen that a fundamental assumption of classical realism is the autonomy of the political sphere.[109] It implies, first, that the political sphere has to be differentiated from and cannot be reduced to the economic, moral or legal spheres.[110] Second, it means that the rules for acting in the political sphere are different from that in other spheres. Once you enter the political sphere all decisions must be taken in keeping with its logic.[111] The principal feature of the logic of the political sphere is that it 'has no

---

Analysis (New York: Columbia University Press, 1959), p. 28. See generally, Emile Capouya and Keith Tomkins (eds.), *The Essential Kropotkin* (London: Macmillan, 1976).

[106] Lieber, 'Introduction', p. 11.

[107] See ibid., p. 19.

[108] B. S. Chimni, 'The Self, Modern Civilization and International Law: Learning from Mohandas Karmchand Gandhi's *Hind Swaraj*', 23 (2012) *European Journal of International Law*, pp. 1159–1173.

[109] Morgenthau, *Politics among Nations*, p. 11.

[110] Morgenthau wrote that 'when we refer to international relations as a distinct object of human action and understanding, we have in mind only those collective or individual actions, transcending national boundaries, which affect the position of nations vis-à-vis each other. International relations are in this sense political relations'. Hans Morgenthau, *Restoration*, p. 167.

[111] Turner and Mazur, 'Morgenthau as a Weberian', p. 494.

intrinsic object of interest; it is lacking in any concrete "interest" except the pursuit of power.[112]

The notion of the autonomy of the political sphere is misleading because among other things, as Stanley Hoffman has observed, 'politics divorced from economics, law, or ethics becomes a kind of "pure game" that is played by nobody, for the simple reason that it would be a game without either cards or stakes.'[113] It has been argued in defence of Morgenthau that 'the essential emptiness of politics also represents its promise and positive potential' as it allows 'a *strategy* to maximize the promise of politics and limits its perils.'[114] The strategy is that of 'balancing social spheres and interests against one another in order to limit the reach of politics while also limiting the influence of other spheres on the political.'[115] But what Morgenthau and his sophisticated defenders fail to see is that the real challenge lies in explaining how the political sphere is constituted in the first place. While there is certainly an internal logic that informs the working of the political sphere, the fact that it is co-constituted by the functioning of other logics leaves its mark. In reality, there are only intersecting social spheres that co-constitute each other, including the political sphere, assigning it distinct content in different phases of history. While no sphere is reducible to the other, none is also entirely independent of the other. To borrow the words of Hans Gadamer, while 'nothing exists entirely for the sake of something else, nothing is entirely identical with the reality of something else ... but still a deep inner coherence penetrates everywhere.'[116] In the case of Marx the 'deep inner coherence' was provided by the productive activities of man.

The disregard of the relationship of the political and other social spheres prevents Morgenthau from looking at deep structures beyond biological realism that can explain international politics. He confined himself to the political sphere which was in his view constituted at the international level by the 'logic of territory'. Morgenthau, therefore, did not pay attention to the fact that since the dawn of the age of capital, there are two distinct but intersecting logics at work in shaping international politics: the 'logic of capital' and the 'logic of territory'. He left out of purview the 'logic

---

[112] Williams, *Realist Tradition*, p. 115.
[113] Stanley Hoffman, *Janus and Minerva: Essays in the Theory and Practice of International Politics* (Boulder, CO: Westview, 1987), p. 72.
[114] Williams, *Realist Tradition*, p. 117.
[115] See ibid., p. 121.
[116] Hans–Georg Gadamer, *Truth and Method*, 2nd revised edn (London: Continuum, 2005), First South Asian Edition, p. 202.

of capital' in the same way as Marxists have tended to ignore the 'logic of territory'. A few words need to be said on the latter failing, as it not only provides a necessary corrective to the Marxist view but also brings out the strength of the Morgenthau approach. In the past, Marxists have not adequately theorized 'the question of the political' in international relations'.[117] According to Alex Callinicos, Marxists have therefore been rightly reproached for 'failing to see the kind of competition specific to inter-state systems as a transhistorical phenomenon governed by a logic irreducible to that of class exploitation'.[118] This is despite the fact that 'there is, necessarily, a realist moment in any Marxist analysis of international relations and conjunctures' as the territorial logic has always had a bearing on the 'logic of capital'.[119] At issue is both the explanation for the historical emergence of the states system and the extent to which the logics of territory and capital define the nature and character of the international system. Callinicos believes that he and David Harvey have found an appropriate answer through developing an understanding of international politics 'as constituted by the intersection of, respectively, capitalist and territorial logics of power and economic and geopolitical competition'.[120] The advantage of such an approach is that it does not 'reduce the geopolitical strategies of states to economic interests'.[121] However, as Callinicos goes on to note, 'to assert that the two logics intersect or interact tells us nothing about the relative causal primacy of one over the other'.[122] But, perhaps the issue is not that of assigning a priori 'primacy' to a particular logic but of understanding the relationship between the two logics in a particular historical conjuncture. There is a dialectical relationship between the 'logic of territory' and the 'logic of capital' that sees universalizing capitalism and the states system evolving together in particular ways in different periods of history. But while the modern states system has an intimate relationship with capitalism, the relationship between states is not always determined by the logic of capital. On the other hand, it is worth reiterating that classical realists like Morgenthau failed to recognize that 'there can be no predictive theory of the goings-on in a 'sphere' in any

---

[117] Andrew Davenport, 'Marxism in IR: Condemned to a Realist Fate', 19 (2011) *European Journal of International Relations*, pp. 27–48 at p. 27.
[118] Alex Callinicos, 'Does Capitalism Need the State System?', 20 (2007) *Cambridge Review of International Affairs*, pp. 533–549 at p. 538.
[119] See ibid., p. 542.
[120] See ibid., p. 539.
[121] See ibid.
[122] See ibid., p. 540.

strict sense, because people will act 'in' the sphere for reasons that arise from other spheres'.[123] In other words, by arriving at a 'sphere-relevant intelligible core', all that can be achieved is a degree of 'intelligibility' or understanding of the political sphere.[124] But to make this claim is different from asserting the autonomy of the political sphere. At best it implies the relative autonomy of the political sphere from other social spheres, a view IMAIL adopts.

C. On Power, National Interest and State

It was noted that the concept of power is central to a realist theory of politics which is defined essentially as a 'psychological relation' between individuals. Morgenthau explicitly excluded from the concept of power the concern with 'man's power over nature ... or over the means of production or consumption'.[125] Thus, in arriving at his concept of power he once again failed to allocate conceptual space for the 'logic of capital'.[126] As a consequence, the realist view cannot see that power is in a critical sense 'the capacity of a social class to realize its specific objective class interests'.[127] Historically, every class that seeks to win and thereafter retain political power represents its own interest as the common interest of society. It is precisely the task of political science to determine the groups or classes whose interests are safeguarded by the exercise of state power in particular social formations, including in the sphere of international politics. Morgenthau saved himself from performing this task by abstracting from the production process.[128] He therefore spoke of group interests without locating them in a particular mode of production.[129]

In view of Morgenthau's restrictive view of power it is not surprising that he did not identify the different ways in which power manifests itself at the international level. The critics of the classical realist approach have offered in its place a multidimensional and complex understanding of

---

[123] See ibid., p. 494.

[124] See ibid., pp. 494–495.

[125] Morgenthau, *Politics among Nations*, p. 26.

[126] In viewing political power as a mere 'psychological relation', Morgenthau overlooks the fact that it is in reality 'the official expression of antagonism in civil society'. Karl Marx, *The Poverty of Philosophy* (Moscow: Progress Publishers, 1975), p. 101.

[127] Nicos Poulantzas, *Political Power and Social Classes* (London: Verso, 1978), p. 104.

[128] See Karl Marx and Friedrich Engels, *The Individual and Society* (Moscow: Progress Publishers, 1984), pp. 143–155 and 162–163.

[129] Since he ignored the 'logic of capital' both at the domestic and international levels, he also paid no attention to the relationship of capitalism with nature and its implications for international politics.

power. Such a concept of power takes into account both 'power over' and 'power to' formulations of the concept of 'power'.[130] Thus, for instance, Michael Barnett and Raymond Duvall identify four forms of power at work in international politics viz., compulsory power, institutional power, structural power and productive power[131]:

> *Compulsory power* refers to relations of interaction that allow one actor to have direct control over another. It operates, for example, when one state threatens another and says, 'change your policies, or else'. *Institutional power* is in effect when actors exercise indirect control over others, such as when states design international institutions in ways that work to their long-term advantage and to the disadvantage of others. *Structural power* concerns the constitution of social capacities and interests of actors in direct relation to one another. One expression of this form of power is the workings of the capitalist world-economy in producing social positions of capital and labor with their respective differential abilities and to alter their circumstances and fortunes. *Productive power* is the socially diffuse production of subjectivity in systems of meaning and signification.[132]

The taxonomy of 'power' that Barnett and Duvall advance is helpful in explaining and understanding the different modes of exercise of power in international politics. For instance, by including the role of 'structural power' they allow cognizance to be taken of the role of particular classes in shaping the foreign policy of states. But even the classification they offer is incomplete. Thus, for example, while they do refer to 'productive' power, they do not explicitly take on board the feminist critique that the classical realist approach is 'embedded in a masculine perspective' that 'works with the [limiting] notion of "power as domination"'.[133]

---

[130] Michael Barnett and Raymond Duvall, 'Power in Global Governance' in Michael Barnett and Raymond Duvall (eds.), *Power in Global Governance* (Cambridge: Cambridge University Press, 2005), pp. 1–33 at p. 10. It is now also accepted in the literature on power that the meaning of power is not theory or context neutral. Thus, for instance, power can be conceptualized as both 'power over' and 'power to' depending on the theoretical apparatus it is part of. Steven Lukes, *Power: A Radical View*, 2nd edn (Basingstoke: Palgrave Macmillan, 2005). Peter Morriss, 'Steven Lukes on the Concept of Power' in Mark Haugaard and Stewart R. Clegg (eds.), *Power and Politics*, vol. 1 (London: Sage, 2012), pp. 231–242.

[131] Barnett and Duvall emphasize that the concept of power 'cannot be captured by a single formulation' for 'power does not have a single expression or form'. See Barnett and Duvall, 'Power', pp. 2–3.

[132] See ibid., p. 3. For a similar classification see Emile M. Hafner-Burton, David G. Victor and Yonatan Lupu, 'Political Science Research on International Law: The State of the Field', 106 (2012) *The American Journal of International Law*, pp. 47–97 at p. 52.

[133] J. Ann Tickner, 'Hans Morgenthau's Principles of Political Realism: A Feminist Reformulation', 17 (1988) *Millennium – Journal of International Studies*, pp. 429–440 at p. 430.

As a consequence, Morgenthau neglected the elements of 'cooperation and regeneration' in international relations.[134] In contrast, Ann Tickner flags definitions of power given by women thinkers that include 'acting in concert' or 'power as persuasion' or 'power as a relationship of mutual enablement'.[135] While she concedes that 'power as domination is a pervasive reality in international relations',[136] Tickner argues that the feminist view helps focus on the potential of power to enable different forms of cooperation to address troubling outcomes that flow from interactions between states and with other actors. In this view women tend to 'see issues in contextual rather than in abstract terms'[137] and value 'ambiguity and difference'.[138] Tickner, therefore, calls for 'a feminist epistemology of international relations'.[139] Whether one agrees with Tickner about there being a distinct feminist epistemology or not,[140] she along with critics like Barnett and Duvall demonstrate how classical realists like Morgenthau underestimated the sources and role of power in international politics.[141] Some authors have attempted to argue that Morgenthau in fact advanced a 'multiple, fluid, and relational view of power' in as much as he does not equate it with material power but also refers to charismatic power and the role of ideologies.[142] But, this interpretation clashes with that advanced by the inheritors of realism with their emphasis on 'material' structures.[143]

The one-dimensional notion of power in Morgenthau is accompanied by an empty concept of 'national interest' which is essentially defined in terms of accumulation of power. It may suffice to say that by ubiquitously defining 'national interest' as the seeking of power, both as means and as an end, Morgenthau advanced a concept that offers scant theoretical or practical guidance.[144] It has, however, been contended that his intent was

---

[134] See ibid., p. 432.
[135] See ibid.
[136] See ibid.
[137] See ibid., p. 433.
[138] See ibid., p. 437.
[139] See ibid., p. 436.
[140] See generally in this regard Nancy Holmstrom, 'A Marxist Theory of Women's Nature' in Nancy Holmstrom (ed.), The Socialist Feminist Project: A Contemporary Reader in Theory and Politics (Delhi: Aakar, 2011), pp. 360–377.
[141] Barnett and Duvall, 'Power', p. 2.
[142] Williams, Realist Tradition, p. 110.
[143] See, for instance, John Mearsheimer, 'The False Promise of International Institutions', 19 (1994–95) International Security, pp. 5–49.
[144] But Williams concedes that defining interest in terms of power 'seems strangely amorphous and ill defined' and 'completely lacking in content', but seeks to explain it by noting

to construct the concept of 'national interest' as 'a critical category seeking to foster public discourse and reflection' in the matrix of a philosophy of limits.[145] Even if one were to accept this understanding, the need to identify concrete interests around which the debate on acting responsibly must necessarily take place will not go away. It was seen that Morgenthau does speak of 'necessary' and 'variable' elements of the national interest of states, with 'necessary' interest being state survival embedded in the 'logic of territory'. But, when it came to variable interests Morgenthau candidly admitted that only limited contribution could be made by political science in clarifying them. Instead of exploring, in this context, the 'logic of capital', he was satisfied noting that in a liberal democracy 'variable' interests are determined by competing interests. In this connection, he did mention economic group interests but saw them as simply one set of interests that a state took into account.[146] At the end of the day, Morgenthau confessed to the 'elusiveness' of the concept of 'national interest' and 'its susceptibility to interpretations' but argued that it did not invalidate its usefulness.[147]

In view of his neglect of variable interests, Morgenthau did not see the 'state' as having dynamic link with the interests of particular groups and classes in society. Instead, following Weber, Morgenthau viewed the 'state' as 'another name for the compulsory organization of society – for the legal order that determines the conditions under which society may employ its monopoly of organized violence for the preservation of order and peace'.[148] While he conceded that 'the legal order it [i.e., the state] enforces is not completely neutral and cannot help favoring the status quo to which it owes its existence',[149] he did not share the view that it is biased against any particular group, that is, that it is 'in favor of any particular status quo'.[150] Since Morgenthau did not lift the veil over the state he failed to see how domestic social and economic structures matter in shaping the legal order and determining national interests.[151] This lapse explains why critics of all hues 'are largely united in the conviction that a concern

that this indeterminacy allows politics to balance values and interests that materialize in other spheres. Williams, *Realist Tradition*, pp. 113ff.

[145] See ibid., pp. 187, 175.
[146] Since Morgenthau rarely spoke of capitalism or its universalizing nature, he had little to say about variable interests of contemporary Western states.
[147] Morgenthau, *Dilemmas of Politics*, p. 65.
[148] Morgenthau, *Politics among Nations*, p. 489.
[149] See ibid., p. 488.
[150] See ibid.
[151] Morgenthau, *Dilemma of Politics*, p. 69.

with political economy, the impact of domestic structures, or the influence of culture and identity, all appear remarkably marginal (or at best inadequately developed and unsystematically theorized) within "classical" realism'.[152] In the view of critics what is required is a 'more sociologically and institutionally rigorous theory of the structure, dynamics, and multiple determinants of politics at the domestic level' for the further development of realist theory of international politics.[153]

D. On Imperialism

In keeping with his assumption of the autonomy of the political sphere Morgenthau defines the term 'imperialism' in political terms 'as a policy that aims at the overthrow of the status quo'.[154] It leads him to the conclusion that 'the *preservation* of an empire' is not imperialism.[155] He then predictably rejects Lenin's theory of imperialism as an economic theory of imperialism that is in any case not supported by historical evidence.[156] In his view, Lenin's theory fails to recognize the 'primacy of politics over economics'.[157] On his part, Morgenthau explains even colonialism in the vocabulary of power politics by speaking of 'the existence of weak states' whose territories were acquired by European powers.[158] He talks of 'the politically empty spaces of Africa and Asia',[159] that is, of 'so much political no-man's-land'.[160] Morgenthau explicates that this is 'a negative way of saying that during that [colonial] period the balance of power was quantitatively and qualitatively circumscribed by geographical limits'.[161] Once all external spaces were exhausted, the struggle for power returned to the familiar surroundings of Europe. However, at one point he concedes that

---

[152] Williams, 'Why Ideas Matter', p. 635.
[153] See ibid.
[154] Morgenthau, *Politics among Nations*, p. 42. He notes that 'a nation whose foreign policy aims at acquiring more power than it actually has, through a reversal of power relations – whose foreign policy, in other words, seeks a favorable change in power status – pursues a policy of imperialism'. See ibid., p. 37.
[155] See ibid., p. 42. Emphasis added.
[156] See ibid., p. 48.
[157] See ibid., p. 46.
[158] Morgenthau, *Politics among Nations*, p. 52. He later writes: 'Nations in that period [i.e., the colonial era] sought power through the acquisition of territory, then considered the symbol and substance of national power. Taking land away from a powerful neighbor was one method of gaining power'. See ibid., p. 340.
[159] See ibid., p. 342.
[160] See ibid..
[161] See ibid., p. 343.

the British Empire was of a kind that gave the idea of imperialism 'an economic connotation.'[162] But no theoretical significance is attached to it.

Morgenthau also admits that a few wars were fought for economic objectives but contends that 'the two world wars were certainly political wars, whose stake was the domination of Europe, if not of the world.'[163] The economic advantages and losses were only 'by-products' of the political consequences of success or defeat.[164] In other words, power and not economic gain were at issue in the two world wars. He therefore concludes that economic imperialism should merely be viewed as a 'rational method of gaining power.'[165] In the event, he dismisses the view that 'the end of capitalism would signify the end of imperialism as well.'[166] The Morgenthau view may be contrasted with that of German thinker Rosa Luxemburg (1871–1919) who argued in her book *The Accumulation of Capital* (published in 1913) that imperialism is linked to the very survival of capitalism.[167] She recognized the historical fact that 'the extension of capitalism into new territories was the mainspring of ... the "vast secular boom" between the 17th and the 19th centuries.'[168] But, she also understood the dialectics between the political and economic spheres in stating that 'imperialism is the *political expression* of the accumulation of capital in its competitive struggle for what remains still open of the non-capitalist environment.'[169] To put it differently, Luxemburg understood the significance of 'logic of territory', but did not view it in isolation from the 'logic of capital'. She grasped the essence of imperialism by recognizing its internal relations with capitalism and tracing the cause of the First World War to competitive colonialism.[170] In fact, she was among the first to link

---

[162] See ibid., p. 44.

[163] See ibid., p. 47.

[164] See ibid.

[165] See ibid., p. 56.

[166] Morgenthau, *Decline of Democratic Politics*, p. 10.

[167] Morgenthau mentions Rosa Luxemburg in a footnote but her work is not considered. See Morgenthau, *Politics among Nations*, p. 45 fn. 7.

[168] Joan Robinson, 'Introduction' to Rosa Luxemburg, *The Accumulation of Capital* (London: Routledge and Kegan Paul, 1951), p. 28.

[169] Luxemburg, *Accumulation of Capital*, p. 446; emphasis added.

[170] In a powerful and insightful passage she wrote (and I quote): 'The events that bore the present war did not begin in July 1914 but reach back for decades. Thread by thread they have been woven together on the loom of an inexorable natural development until the firm net of imperialist world politics has encircled five continents. It is a huge historical complex of events, whose roots reach deep down into the Plutonic deeps of economic creation, whose outermost branches spread out and point away into a dimly dawning new world, events before whose all-embracing immensity, the conception of guilt and retribution, of defense

the growth of armaments industry (in modern parlance the military-industrial complex) to the problem of accumulation of capital, eventually leading to 'lawlessness and violence' in international relations.[171] Lenin had also noted with acute insight that 'politically, imperialism is, in general, a striving towards violence and reaction'.[172] The history of the twentieth century testifies to the truth of this statement. It was also Lenin who in the course of a debate with Trotsky and Bukharin observed that 'politics must take precedence over economics. To argue otherwise is to forget the ABC of Marxism'.[173] In fact, the relationship between the economic and political is also best captured in Lenin's dictum that 'politics is a concentrated expression of economics'. To therefore characterize Lenin's theory of imperialism as 'economic' theory of imperialism is a gross distortion.[174] What is more, the Luxemburg-Lenin thesis that 'imperialism belonged inseparably to capitalism',[175] and is at the same time its political expression, has stood the test of times even in the postcolonial era.

It is interesting that while Morgenthau defines 'imperialism' in political terms he speaks of 'economic imperialism' in discussing the 'methods of imperialism'. Morgenthau aptly defines 'economic imperialism' 'as an unobtrusive, indirect, but fairly effective method of gaining and maintaining domination over other nations'.[176] He recognizes that economic imperialism involves a change in power relations between the imperialist nation and 'others' 'not through the control of territory but by way of economic control'.[177] Thus, he notes that in his times the Central American republics were subject to US imperialism.[178] In fact, he goes on to observe

and offence, sink into pale nothingness'. Rosa Luxemburg, *The Crisis in German Social-Democracy: (The 'Junius' Pamphlet)* (The Socialist Publication Society, 1919), p. 97. She then went on to note how capitalist nations 'were competing in their expansion toward the non-capitalist countries and zones of the world'. See ibid., p. 34. She referred to the 'strong tendency toward colonial expansion' and detailed the efforts of England, France, Russia, Germany and the United States in this direction. See ibid., pp. 34–35. An edition of 'The Junius Pamphlet' is available at *Marxists Internet Archive*, accessed at www.marxists.org/archive/luxemburg/1915/junius/ (last visited 29 June 2015). The pamphlet is said to have been written between February and April 1915 from her prison cell. Luxemburg was incarcerated for opposing the war. The essay contains exceedingly rich analysis of the times.

[171] Luxemburg, *Accumulation of Capital*, p. 446.
[172] V. I. Lenin, *Selected Works* (Moscow: Progress Publishers, 1975) vol. 1, pp. 702–703.
[173] V. I. Lenin, *On Dialectics* (Moscow: Progress Publishers, 1980), p. 83.
[174] Morgenthau, *Politics among Nations*, p. 45.
[175] V. G. Kiernan, *Marxism and Imperialism* (London: Edward Arnold, 1974), p. 22.
[176] Morgenthau, *Politics among Nations*, p. 56.
[177] See ibid.
[178] See ibid.

that 'the share of economic and cultural imperialism in the overall international activities of governments has greatly increased since the mid-fifties',[179] defining 'cultural imperialism' as 'the conquest and control of minds of men'.[180] Morgenthau also admits that economic and cultural imperialism impacts the relative power of nations. But, as a result of the theoretical separation of the political from other social spheres, he could not proceed to offer an integrated definition of imperialism. In other words, Morgenthau failed to make the internal connections between the logics of capital, territory and culture. Marxist thinkers like Luxemburg were able to do so as they understood that the political sphere was co-constituted by economic and cultural spheres. Albeit, as already noted, Marxists need to pay greater heed to the 'logic of territory' and also successfully integrate the phenomenon of cultural domination with a theory of imperialism in the manner of postcolonial thinkers such as Edward Said and Dipesh Chakrabarty.[181] For the rest, Marxists agree with Morgenthau that the real intentions of imperialist states are disguised behind progressive rhetoric.[182] They are also sceptical about the progressive role of international law in world politics. But, as would be evident by now, their sources of scepticism are different from that of classical realism.

IV.   The Realist Theory of International Law

Scepticism about international law has a long history. Quincy Wright cites Grotius as observing that 'there is no lack of men who view this branch of law with contempt as having no reality outside of an empty frame'.[183] In view of the decentralized character of international law this trend has persisted over the centuries. Writing in the inter-war period, the German historian Friedrich Meinecke observed that, 'in many ways, international law is performing a labor of Sisyphus by struggling with raison d'êtat' as it was not possible 'to confine the behavior of States to one another within legal bounds'.[184] Morgenthau shared this

---

[179] See ibid., p. 60.
[180] See ibid., p. 57.
[181] Edward W. Said, *Culture and Imperialism* (London: Chatto & Windus, 1993); Dipesh Chakrabarty, *Provincializing Europe* (Princeton, NJ: Princeton University Press, 2007) 2nd edn. See also Chapter 1, pp. 22–30.
[182] Morgenthau, *Politics among Nations*, pp. 67–68.
[183] Quincy Wright, *The Strengthening of International Law* (Leyden: A. W. Sijthoff, 1960), p. 262.
[184] Friedrich Meinecke, *Machiavellism: The Doctrine of Raison d'etat and Its Place in Modern History* (Boulder, CO: Westview Press, 1984), pp. 208, 209.

understanding.[185] His lack of faith in international law had its basis in the failure of the dominant legalistic-moralistic approach to prevent the Second World War. In order to appreciate Morgenthau's standpoint it is necessary to savour the atmosphere of those heady days when international law was offered as a panacea for the ills of the world. Josef Kunz, who was often in Geneva between 1920 and 1932, has described the then prevailing spirit admirably:

> In all the dealings of the League, international law was at the heart of the discussion. Idealistic approach, optimism, emphasis on international law created the 'Geneva atmosphere'... One must have been there in order to evaluate the impression, the genuine enthusiasm all around, when Aristide Briand made his famous speech: 'Plus de mitrailleuses'. The legal department of the League played a great role; the Permanent Court of International Justice was frequently resorted to. The Mandates Commission was primarily moved by legal considerations. Legal arguments were the core of every debate; every delegate knew that he must justify his attitude legally. Hence, greatest importance was given to international law in the foreign offices. Many a delegate travelled to Geneva with a whole library of international law and always well accompanied by legal advisers.[186]

Those in the academic community who subscribed to the panacea thesis often refused to take cognizance of harsh realities. Thus, as Kunz went on to point out, 'fancy interpretations of the Kellogg [-Briand] Pact were put forward; the more "collective security" was shown to be non-existent, the more the utopian writers emphasized it. The more the facts were in contradictions to their writings, the more lyrical they grew'.[187] It was all this and more that prompted E. H. Carr to write *The Twenty Years' Crisis* in which he launched an effective assault on the idealist approach to international politics. Morgenthau too believed that a legalistic-moralistic approach led to utopian schemes in which wishful thinking replaced serious understanding of the social forces which shaped international politics.

---

[185] This scepticism is expressed in much of the work that he did in the inter-war years. For an overview of this work see Koskenniemi, *The Gentle Civilizer*, pp. 440ff; Oliver Jütersonke, 'The Image of Law in *Politics among Nations*' in Michael C. Williams (ed.) *Realism Reconsidered: The Legacy of Hans J. Morgenthau in International Relations* (Oxford: Oxford University Press, 2007), pp. 93–117.

[186] Josef L. Kunz, *The Changing Law of Nations: Essays on International Law* (Athens, OH: Ohio University Press, 1968), p. 127.

[187] See ibid., p. 128. The reference is to the Kellogg-Briand Pact of 1928 that outlawed war as an instrument of national policy.

In 1940, he published an important essay on the science of international law in which he attempted to identify the problems of the legalistic-moralistic approach.[188] He wrote of the 'retarded stage of scientific development' of the discipline of international law which he traced to the 'determining influence' of positivism which had 'not developed a criterion to distinguish, in an objective way, between *seemingly* and *actually* valid rules of international law'.[189] This problem arose because positivism proceeded 'on the assumption that the law, as it really is, can be understood without the normative and social context in which it actually stands'.[190] In contrast, Morgenthau argued that 'the foundation of the binding force of "positive" law can only be found, not in this "positive" law itself, but only outside it'.[191] His critique of positivism extended to traditional rules of interpretation of treaties which did not require changing political realities to be taken into account. Morgenthau pointed out that the traditional civil law technique of interpretation was completely inadequate to the task as the real meaning of a treaty is often disguised.[192] Indeed, he felt that 'no branch of the traditional science of international law is more in need of reform than the doctrine of interpretation'.[193] He concluded his critique of positivism with the observation that 'the fundamental weakness of the positivist doctrine of international law lies in its inadequacy to international law as it really is'.[194] Morgenthau called his own approach 'a functional theory of international law'.[195] He argued that a theory rooted in the real world must 'search for the psychological, social, political and economic forces which determine the actual content and working of legal rules and which, in turn are determined by them'.[196] In the absence of such a functionalist approach 'grandiose legalistic schemes purporting to solve the ills of the world replaced the less spectacular, painstaking search for the actual laws and the facts underlying them'.[197]

Martti Koskenniemi has observed that the 1940 essay 'was written as a prelude for anti-formalist jurisprudence that would hark back to

---

[188] Hans Morgenthau, 'Positivism, Functionalism and International Law', 34 (1940) *American Journal of International Law*, pp. 260–284 at pp. 260–261.

[189] See ibid., pp. 264, 263 and 266; emphasis in original.

[190] See ibid., p. 267.

[191] See ibid., p. 269.

[192] See ibid., p. 282.

[193] See ibid., p. 281.

[194] See ibid., p. 273.

[195] See ibid.

[196] See ibid., pp. 273–274.

[197] See ibid., p. 283.

sociology and ethics'.[198] In a sense this is correct, albeit it is important to recognize that the kind of anti-formalist jurisprudence Morgenthau had in mind did not represent a plea for 'interdisciplinarity' in the ordinary sense of the term.[199] In view of his assumption of the autonomy of different social spheres the proposed anti-formalist jurisprudence had to do its work within the bounds of the legal sphere; Morgenthau did not wish in any way to subvert the autonomy of the legal sphere.[200] A helpful distinction can be made in this respect between what may be termed internal and external interdisciplinarity. Morgenthau was recommending the former. He merely wanted international lawyers to appreciate the conditions necessary for the continuing validity of rules of international law. Interdisciplinarity for Morgenthau did not mean assessing the justice of the rules of international law. He was not interested for instance in exploring the links between economic imperialism and international law to consider the nature of universalism (false or genuine) that was being promoted. He simply wanted to replace idealistic with realistic formalism. In other words, what Morgenthau was proposing was an anti-formalist jurisprudence of a different kind. He did not later change his views in *Politics among Nations*. In this regard, Jütersonke is right in noting the continuity of Morgenthau's views from the time he wrote his doctoral dissertation. He had come to believe that international law was not 'effective in regulating and restraining the struggle for power on the international scene' and that the flawed method of positivism did not allow it to recognize this reality.[201]

However, in expressing his scepticism Morgenthau was not addressing the vast majority of rules that constitute international law. He was only concerned with international law rules that had 'a direct bearing upon the relative power of the nations concerned'.[202] In those instances he believed that 'considerations of power rather than of law determine compliance and enforcement'.[203] Morgenthau observed that in such cases from the 'iron law of international politics, that legal obligation must yield to national interest, no nation has been completely immune'.[204] But, little could be done to correct the situation as legal sanctions either did not

[198] Koskenniemi, *The Gentle Civilizer*, p. 459.
[199] See ibid.
[200] Morgenthau, 'Positivism, Functionalism', p. 265.
[201] See ibid.
[202] Morgenthau, *Politics among Nations*, p. 283.
[203] See ibid.
[204] Hans J. Morgenthau, *In Defense of the National Interest* (New York: Knopf, 1981), p. 144.

exist or could not be used against states.[205] Morgenthau reminded that there was no entity in the international legal system that had 'the monopoly of organized force'.[206] What was available to nations was merely the right of self-help.[207] Such a legal system is necessarily a weak system as the enforcement of the law is essentially left 'to the vicissitudes of the distribution of power between the violator of the law and the victim of violation'.[208] The two historic attempts to rectify the situation had failed i.e., in the Covenant of the League of Nations and the Charter of United Nations.[209] With respect to the latter he noted that in view of the reservations and qualifications attached to the collective security system the enforcement of international law remained almost entirely decentralized.[210] Morgenthau therefore described international law as 'a primitive type of law'.[211]

The decentralized nature of international society also had a serious effect on its legislative and judicial functions. Morgenthau noted that the provisions of treaties are 'vague and ambiguous' as they attempt to find a common basis on which divergent national interests can be reconciled and embodied, 'allowing all the signatories to read the recognition of their own national interests into the legal text agreed upon'.[212] Further, the reality of auto-interpretation in a decentralized society meant that states 'naturally interpret and apply the provisions of international law in the light of their particular and divergent conceptions of the national interest'.[213] The decentralized character of international law also impacted the judicial function. In the absence of mechanisms for peaceful change in international politics, 'imperialist' powers did not have patience with international law. In their eyes 'any system of existing law is of necessity an ally of the status quo, and the courts cannot fail to be its custodians'.[214] Nations desiring change knew that 'the court cannot grant their demands

---

[205] Morgenthau, *Politics among Nations*, pp. 220–221.

[206] See ibid., pp. 265–266.

[207] Morgenthau, *Politics among Nations*, p. 281.

[208] See ibid., p. 282.

[209] See ibid., p. 283.

[210] See ibid., and p. 298. Morgenthau writes: 'Wherever an attempt has been made to give international law the effectiveness of a centralized legal system, reservations, qualifications, and the general political conditions under which nations must act in the modern state system have nullified the legal obligations entered into for the purpose of establishing centralized functions'. See ibid., p. 298.

[211] See ibid., p. 265.

[212] See ibid., p. 269.

[213] See ibid., p. 270.

[214] See ibid., p. 411.

without destroying the very foundation on which its authority rests'.[215] It followed that 'imperialist' nations were unwilling to resort to the judicial settlement of disputes. According to Morgenthau, there can be 'no legal concepts to express that claim, let alone a legal remedy to satisfy it'.[216] This kind of dispute he designated as 'tensions' i.e., 'the unformulated conflicts of power'.[217] He concluded that 'the disputes which are most likely to lead to war cannot be settled by judicial methods ... No court, domestic or international, is equipped to settle the issue'.[218]

But, despite these weaknesses, Morgenthau warned against the underestimation of international law. First, states needed some agreed rules on the basis which to transact with each other.[219] Second, in a world without international law 'the weak would be at the mercy of the strong' and 'might would make right',[220] inviting the 'revolt' of those subjugated to power. Third, most of international law is observed most of the times.[221] The reason is that 'international law is overwhelmingly the result of objective social forces'[222] reflecting the 'identical or complementary interests of individual states'.[223] In the field of 'non-political international law', that is, rules that did not impinge on the relative power of nations, such as those relating to diplomatic privileges, territorial jurisdiction, extradition and so on, were generally observed.[224] It is only when there were no

---

[215] See ibid.
[216] See ibid., p. 412.
[217] See ibid.
[218] See ibid., p. 417.
[219] See ibid., p. 264.
[220] See ibid., p. 219.
[221] See ibid., p. 265.
[222] See ibid., p. 266; Morgenthau, 'Positivism, Functionalism', p. 284.
[223] See Morgenthau, *Politics among Nations*, p. 266.
[224] Morgenthau describes non-political rules thus:

> The main bulk of the concepts and principles of international law has been derived from municipal civil law. These concepts and principles have been developed within a legal system characterized by the extraordinary stability of the interests underlying it. Hence its application is, of necessity, restricted to legal systems based upon equally stable interests. In the international field such stable interests exist, for instance, with respect to diplomatic privileges, territorial jurisdiction, extradition, wide fields of maritime law, arbitral procedure, and so forth. This is the classical field of traditional international law as it has gradually developed in the practice of states since the sixteenth century. *We propose to call these rules non-political international law*, originating in the permanent interests of states to put their normal relations upon a stable basis by providing for predictable and enforceable conduct with respect to these relations.
>
> Morgenthau, 'Positivism, Functionalism', pp. 278–279; emphasis added

complementary interests, or in the instance of political international law when a situation of balance of power did not prevail, that international law was not complied with.[225] Fourth, judicial settlement of disputes is possible in a large number of cases as these can be decided on the basis of prevailing rules. Morgenthau distinguished between disputes relating to 'territorial concessions and legal adjustments within the framework of a recognized status quo' and those that 'pertain to the survival of the status quo itself'.[226] In his view, disputes of the first kind could be resolved through judicial settlement.

The realist understanding and critique of international law is not without merit. In this regard, it may also be borne in mind that when Morgenthau wrote his doctoral thesis and his first essays culminating in the 1940 article, critical approaches to international law were practically non-existent; the only other major critical approach, the Soviet approach to international law, was for ideological reasons not taken seriously in the West.[227] Therefore, the Morgenthau (and Carr) thesis on overestimating the role of international law and institutions came as a breath of fresh air. But, from an IMAIL standpoint, Morgenthau's critique of the deficiencies of international law was incomplete for three reasons. First, his critique of international law was rooted almost solely in the 'logic of territory' disregarding the 'logic of capital'. Morgenthau, therefore, did not take into account the relationship between universalizing capitalism (i.e., imperialism) and international law. As a consequence, he advanced a fractional critique of positivism that ruled out the emergence of truly interdisciplinary jurisprudence. As will be discussed in the next chapter, the occlusion of this possibility was precisely the complaint of the policy-oriented approach associated with Myres McDougal and Harold Lasswell.[228] Second, Morgenthau's critique was based on a limited understanding of

See generally Gerry Simpson, 'Dueling Agendas: International Relations and International Law (Again)', 1 (2004–2005) *Journal of International Relations & International Law,* pp. 61–75 at p. 67.
[225] Morgenthau observed that 'where there is neither community of interest nor balance of power, there is no international law'. Morgenthau, 'Positivism, Functionalism', p. 275. According to Morgenthau, even 'the balance of power operates as a decentralizing force only in the form of a general deterrence against violations of international law and in the exceptional cases when a violation of international law calls for a law enforcement action'. Morgenthau, *Politics among Nations,* p. 266.
[226] Morgenthau, *Politics among Nations,* p. 411.
[227] Of course there was E. H. Carr's *Twenty Years Crisis* (London: Macmillan & Co, 1940). For Morgenthau's view see Morgenthau, *Restoration,* pp. 36–43.
[228] See Chapter 3, p. 112–113.

the reasons why states obey international law. He was overly focused on the availability of sanctions and the prevalence of balance of power where political international law was concerned and the existence of complementary interests when it came to non-political international law. He did not appreciate the complex set of social and political reasons as to why states complied with international legal obligations. Third, Morgenthau did not seriously examine the phenomena of indeterminacy of rules which he traced merely to the manner in which rules of political international law were formulated and the fact of auto-interpretation. He did not explore the semantic and structural sources of indeterminacy which went to the heart of the matter. In sum, Morgenthau's critique of international law was deficient because he did not take into account the relationship of capitalism, imperialism and international law; could not recognize the range of reasons for which nations obey international law; and proposed a limited thesis on indeterminacy of international law rules. The result was that Morgenthau could not articulate a satisfactory basis for an anti-formalist jurisprudence. A brief discussion of each of the shortcomings that characterized Morgenthau's understanding of international law from an IMAIL perspective follows. It will help to delineate the distinctive realism of IMAIL, albeit as yet only in very bare and general terms.

A.   *The Logic of Capital and International Law*

On the face of it Morgenthau indicted positivist jurisprudence for embracing the fragmentation of social sciences. But, as already noted, his critique of positivism has to be read in the background of the assumption of the autonomy of the economic, political and legal spheres. It is only in the context of determining the effectiveness and validity of legal rules that he called for non-legal factors to be taken into account. The principal task of the lawyer remained to see if particular policies of a state were in conformity with existing rules of law.[229] In fact, political and legal formalism joined hands in the work of Morgenthau to avoid exploring the complex relationship between the sociological substratum of the international system and international law. Since political formalism was essentially concerned with the 'logic of territory' he did not pay attention to the 'logic of capital' and its influence on the evolution and development of international law. He could not see how universalizing capitalism had crucially shaped the doctrines and practices of international law. In the

---

[229] Morgenthau, *Politics among Nations*, p. 11.

event, Morgenthau did not speak of the deep and intricate relationship between the 'empire of rights', commerce and international law.[230] But, as historians of international law have shown, from Vitoria to Grotius to present times the 'logic of capital' has left its mark on the body of international law.[231] It was because Morgenthau did not delve into the 'logic of capital' that he was also unable to identify the variable interests of states. This failure led to a mistaken understanding of the place and role of law in a society. He conceived 'law' as a normative system which seeks to limit the struggle for power 'in the interest of *society as a whole* and *in the interest of its individual members*'.[232] From this perspective legal rules are '*not* the result of the mechanics of the struggle for power but are *superimposed* upon that struggle in the form of norms or rules of conduct by the will of the members of society themselves'.[233]

There is no doubt that a principal function of law is to limit the struggle for power in any society, but not always in the interests of the society as a whole. Very often the struggle for power is regulated by law in favour of groups or classes that hold political power. However, once the state is seen as standing above classes and representing the society as a whole, the rules it legislates are easily conceptualized as superimposed upon the power struggle taking place in society, rather than being a product of that struggle. The impression that law safeguards the interests of society as a whole and its individual members is sustained in modern societies through its generalized character, and the juridical concept of a person which proclaims the formal equality and freedom of all individuals in the domain of law. But, since society is not merely an aggregation of individuals but also the sum of the relationships in which these individuals stand to each other, the ideals of equality and freedom can easily turn into their opposites under conditions of capitalism.[234] While law does possess sufficient relative independence from dominant social groups and classes, and the idea of 'rule of law' has substance, it is not necessarily a neutral and non-partisan device.[235] Indeed, to oppose law to power is a fundamental

---

[230] See Martti Koksenniemi, 'Empire and International Law: The Real Spanish Contribution', 61 (2011) *University of Toronto Law Journal*, pp. 1–36; Antony Anghie, *Imperialism, Sovereignty and International Law* (Cambridge: Cambridge University Press, 2003).

[231] See in this connection Chapter 5, pp. 323–327.

[232] Morgenthau, *Politics among Nations*, p. 220; emphasis added.

[233] See ibid.; emphasis added.

[234] For a discussion from an IMAIL perspective of the intricate relationship between society and law, see Chapter 7, pp. 449–468.

[235] For the debate on the meaning of 'rule of law' being an unqualified good, see Chapter 7, pp. 457–458.

fallacy in the Morgenthau understanding of the role of law. On the face of it the conjunction of law and power is recognized, since the former has to be backed by sanctions. However, this recognition reflects only one dimension of the relationship between law and power. Morgenthau does not sufficiently appreciate that law itself takes sides in the struggle for power. As has been observed, 'for many years the emphasis that so-called realist political scientists placed on state power led to the stereotype that power was a force that worked in opposition to law. Today, very little political science research adopts the simple view of power; it looks, instead, at the ways that power interacts with other forces, including law, to shape outcomes'.[236]

What is true of internal law is also true of international law, especially non-political international law. But, Morgenthau did not interrogate in this regard the notion of 'complementary interests' that allegedly led to the observance of non-political international law. In giving examples of non-political law, Morgenthau referred to the most uncontroversial aspects of international law such as rules relating to the grant of diplomatic privileges. He did not explore, for instance, the rules of international economic law which are often one sided but are represented as embodying 'complementary interests'. But weak states are rarely in a position in such cases to obey the iron law of international politics that legal obligations yield to national interest. An important reason is that non-political international law is not always left to enforce itself. It is very often backed by a range of enforcement measures. Therefore, weak states have to obey rules of international law even when they do not benefit from them. But, since Morgenthau did not look at the role of sanctions in the context of non-political international law, he could not see that their use is not always a virtue.[237] The reason he did not so realize is that he was only concerned

---

[236] Hafner-Burton et al., 'Political Science Research', p. 51. They note that political and other social scientists distinguish between four distinct uses of power:

> The first is power in its most obvious, blunt form: the ability to coerce. The second is the ability to influence the decision-making agenda and process. The third is the ability to shape what people want and believe, such as through the spread of norms and the creation of interests and identities. The fourth face is discursive, which means that influence stems from the creation of systems of knowledge and social customs and from the ways that those phenomena shape laws and other systems of belief and practice.

See ibid., p. 52.

[237] As Harold Koh has observed, securing compliance is not 'always good per se. Indeed, securing compliance may even be undesirable if the treaties are themselves unfair or

with the survival and validity of the rules of international law;[238] only if legal sanctions follow violation is a rule a valid rule of international law.[239] He was not interested in the question of justice of rules.

If Morgenthau did not recognize the partisan dimension of international law, the same is true of the role of international institutions. He saw international economic institutions as belonging to the non-political sphere. Relying on the functionalist theory of David Mitrany, Morgenthau concluded that specialized agencies of the UN were non-political actors.[240] In reality, international economic institutions are as political as the political organs of the United Nations. But the neglect of the 'logic of capital' led him to an erroneous view of the nature and character of international institutions. International institutions, as Poulantzas has pointed out, 'express and crystallize class powers'.[241] They are not non-partisan institutions vis-à-vis subaltern groups and classes. Morgenthau, therefore, did not adequately appreciate the fact that international institutions are not only instruments of cooperation but also of domination.

B.   International Law as Primitive Law

Since Morgenthau was primarily concerned with the effectiveness and validity of rules he saw international law as an underdeveloped legal system that he described as 'primitive type of law'. He assumed in this respect that primitive societies and the international states system were comparable in a meaningful way.[242] The Morgenthau description elicited a variety of responses with Hersch Lauterpacht responding that 'civilized states are *not* primitive tribes'.[243] Likewise, Hoffman pointed out that states possess

---

enshrine disingenuous or coercive bargains'. Harold Hongju Koh, 'Why do Nations Obey International Law?', 106 (1996–97) *Yale Law Journal*, pp. 2599–2659 at p. 2641.

[238] Morgenthau, *Politics among Nations*, p. 271.

[239] See ibid., p. 221.

[240] See David Mitrany, *A Working Peace System*, 4th edn (London: National Peace Council, 1946).

[241] Nicos Poulantzas, *Classes in Contemporary Capitalism* (London: Verso, 1978), p. 70.

[242] In stating that international law was 'primitive law' Morgenthau spoke of it 'resembling the kind of law that prevails in certain preliterate societies, such as the Australian aborigines and the York of northern California'. Morgenthau, *Politics among Nations*, p. 265. Even if this were to be true, there is a degree of discomfort in terming the law of indigenous peoples as 'primitive law' rather than being simply different.

[243] Hersch Lauterpacht, *International Law: Collected Papers* (Cambridge: Cambridge University Press, 1975), vol. 2, 'The Law of Peace', Part I, p. 21; emphasis in original. For a critical assessment of the comparison, see A. Campbell, 'International Law and Primitive Law', 8 (1988) *Oxford Journal of Legal Studies*, pp. 169–196 at p. 178; Yoram

'highly institutionalized legal systems and differentiated political institutions' whereas 'primitive law is the law of a group whose components have
neither'.[244] In this view Morgenthau failed to see that there was no parallel
between the political structures of capitalist states and that of indigenous
peoples. However, what Lauterpacht and Hoffman did not point out was
that even if there were differences between laws of civilized states and
indigenous peoples it did not call for the characterization of the latter as
'primitive law'.

Be that as it may, it may be recalled in the context of this description that in assessing the effectiveness of non-political international law,
Morgenthau argues that given identical or complementary interests most
rules enforce themselves.[245] In his view, this fact explained why 'during the
four hundred years of its existence international law has in most instances
been scrupulously observed'.[246] But he added that 'when one of its rules
was violated, it was [...] not always enforced and, when action to enforce it
was actually taken, it was not always effective'.[247] It is worth reiterating that
this conclusion does not accurately reflect the state of international law
today as large segments of non-political international law are accompanied by relatively robust and effective enforcement mechanisms (e.g., WTO
law). In so far as political international law is concerned, Morgenthau was
of the firm belief that international law is ineffective 'in regulating and
restraining the struggle for power on the international scene'.[248] The only
real constraining factor in the struggle for power is the existence of balance of power. The problem in this instance is that Morgenthau assigned
different meanings to the notion of 'balance of power' considerably reducing its explanatory power.[249] Furthermore, since all states pursue the goal
of balance of power, the proposition that it contributes to the observance

Dinstein, 'International Law as a Primitive Legal System', 19 (1986–87) *New York Journal
of International Law and Politics,* pp. 1–32.

[244] Stanley Hoffman, 'International Law and the Control of Force' in Karl Deutsch and
Stanley Hoffman (eds.) *The Relevance of International Law* (New York: Anchor Books,
1971), pp. 34–66 at p. 38.

[245] See Morgenthau, *Politics among Nations,* p. 283.

[246] See ibid., p. 265.

[247] See ibid.

[248] See ibid.

[249] See ibid., p. 161 fn 1 where he assigns four different meanings to 'balance of power'. The
footnote reads as follows: 'The term "balance of power" is used in the text with four different meanings: (1) as a policy aimed at a certain state of affairs, (2) as an actual state
of affairs, (3) as an approximately equal distribution of power, (4) as any distribution of
power'.

of political international law is, as Inis Claude observed, 'a redundancy in his theory of international politics'.[250]

The reasons why states observe international law, both non-political and political, are far more varied and complex than Morgenthau provided for. These considerations have been explored by some of the best minds in the field over the last few decades. They have attempted to understand the rationale for states observing international law even when it lacks 'a coherent, recognized and comprehensive framework of sanctions'.[251] While this is not the occasion to undertake an extensive review of the literature, some reference may be made to approaches to compliance that show how it is a function of a range of factors.[252] In a well-known essay on the subject, Koh distinguishes between the 'managerial' approach of Abram Chayes and Antonia Chayes and the 'fairness' approach of Thomas Franck to the problem of compliance. Chayes and Chayes contend that 'the fundamental instrument for maintaining compliance with treaties at an acceptable level … is an *iterative process of discourse* among the parties, the treaty organization, and the wider public'.[253] Franck, on the other hand, argues 'that nations "obey powerless rules" because they are pulled toward compliance by considerations of legitimacy (or "right process") and distributive justice'.[254] He observes that 'if a decision has been reached by a discursive synthesis of legitimacy and justice … it is more likely to be implemented and less likely to be disobeyed'.[255] Koh himself advances a transnational legal process approach that goes beyond these approaches.

[250] Inis L. Claude Jr, *Power and International Relations* (New York: Random House, 1962), p. 37.

[251] Malcolm Shaw, *International Law* (Cambridge: Cambridge University Press, 2008), p. 5. What is more, Charter law has declared unlawful the idea of self-help or reprisals as a legitimate response to enforce legal obligations. See ibid., p. 1129. In fact to think that the existence of forceful sanctions is crucial to the validity of international law leads to 'the somewhat absurd result that the more force is controlled in international society, the less legal international law becomes'. See ibid., p. 5. It is, however, true that when force is unlawfully used by powerful states the international community is most often unable to enforce the law against these states. In these instances Morgenthau is perhaps right that international law is ineffective where relative power of nations is concerned.

[252] For an appraisal of the seminal literature on the subject see Koh, 'Why Nations obey'; and Oona Hathaway, 'Between Power and Principle: An Integrated Theory of International Law', 72 (2005) *The University of Chicago Law Review*, pp. 469–536.

[253] Abram Chayes and Antonia Handler Chayes, *The New Sovereignty: Compliance with International Regulatory Agreements* (Cambridge, MA: Harvard University Press, 1995), p. 25.

[254] Koh, 'Why Nations Obey', p. 2602.

[255] Thomas M. Franck, *Fairness in International Law and Institutions* (Oxford: Clarendon Press, 1995), p. 481.

He submits that 'both the managerial and the fairness accounts of the compliance story omit ... a thoroughgoing account of *transnational legal process:* the complex process of institutional *interaction* whereby global norms are not just debated and *interpreted,* but ultimately *internalized* by domestic legal systems'.[256]

Another leading scholar Oona Hathaway classifies the two principal approaches to compliance as 'interest based approach' and 'norm based approach' respectively, thereby taking on board the realist view of compliance. The 'interest based approach' argues 'that states create and comply with international law only when there is some clear objective reward for doing so; in other words, states follow consequentialist reasoning or what has been termed the "logic of consequences"'.[257] On the other hand, the 'norm-based approach' contends that 'governments create and comply with treaties not only because they expect a reward for doing so, but also because of their commitment (or the commitment of transnational actors that influence them) to the norms or ideas embodied in the treaties. In this view, states often follow what has been termed the "logic of appropriateness" rather than that of consequences'.[258] Hathaway then proceeds to advance an 'integrated theory of international law' that 'rejects the claim that where transnational legal enforcement is absent, international law cannot change state behavior',[259] but equally 'the claim that enforcement is irrelevant'.[260] Instead, she 'places such enforcement in a broader framework in which it plays an important, but not exclusive, role in generating compliance with international law'.[261] Hathaway, inter alia, speaks of legal enforcement by domestic actors 'using the domestic legal system and international bodies' and state members using 'means provided for in treaties' that have 'collateral consequences for state interests'.[262]

It is clear from even this cursory discussion that the international legal system encompasses not one but several processes, strategies and

---

[256] Koh, 'Why Nations Obey', p. 2602; emphasis in original.
[257] Hathaway, 'Between Power and Principle', p. 476.
[258] See ibid., p. 477.
[259] See ibid., p. 492.
[260] See ibid.
[261] See ibid.
[262] See ibid., p. 473. The latter 'arise when domestic and transnational actors premise their actions toward a state on the state's decision to accept or reject international legal rules. The reactions of these actors to the state's actions can affect, among other things, foreign investment, aid donations, international trade, domestic political support, and political contributions, and hence create powerful incentives for states to commit to and comply with treaties'. See ibid.

techniques for law enforcement. States have devised distinct arrangements in functional areas like disarmament, trade and finance, transport, human rights and disarmament to enforce agreed rules. These can
involve a host of means and measures that include inspection, surveillance, reporting, non-participation, condemnation, denial of resources
and punitive sanctions. Increasingly domestic actors and national institutions are playing a crucial role in enforcing international laws. There
are also reputational sanctions flowing from the 'logic of appropriateness',
that is, for violating an expected commitment to the idea of international
rule of law.[263] Therefore, to dismiss all but the critical moments in the
history of international law applications – which merely test the limits of
a particular form of enforcement, and is a phenomenon which characterizes the domestic legal order as well – as merely the doings of identical or complementary interests, is to fall prey to a deterministic logic. In
any case, the influence of international law on behaviour of states goes
beyond enforcement. It shapes their identity and interests in ways that
serve to induce compliance. Albeit admittedly it is often difficult to do
counterfactual analysis: 'if the law had not been in place, what would have
happened?'[264]

From an IMAIL perspective a principal weakness in the literature on
enforcement is that there is not sufficient recognition that the meaning
and implications of compliance depends on the theory of international
law that is used to assess their nature and consequences.[265] Realist theory
with its inability to conceptualize 'national interests', and working with a
constrained concept of 'power', tends to use an expansive concept of 'complementary interests' in the instance of non-political international law,
and narrowly conceived sanctions or an ill-defined concept of balance of
power in the case of political international law, to speak of the effective
enforcement of international law. While the liberal theories deployed by
Chayes and Chayes, Franck, Koh and Hathaway help broaden the concept of compliance and speaks of a variety of other factors that compel
compliance, these do not adequately take into account the role of power
asymmetry in the compliance process. For instance, it is interesting that

---

[263] Andrew T. Guzman, 'A Compliance-Based Theory of International Law', 90 (2002)
California Law Review, pp. 1826–1887.

[264] Hafner-Burton et al., 'Political Science Research', p. 90.

[265] Benedict Kingsbury, 'The Concept of Compliance as a Function of Competing
Conceptions of International Law', 19 (1998) *Michigan Journal of International Law*, pp.
345–372. See also Robert Howse and Ruti Teitl, 'Beyond Compliance: Rethinking Why
International Law Really Matters', 1 (2010) *Global Policy*, pp. 127–136.

while reviewing the seminal literature on the theme of compliance from the most ancient times to the present times Koh does not consider the writings of third world scholars who note how compliance is often the function of imperialism. Third world nations obey many a rule of international law not because of the legitimacy or justice of the rules but the lack of power or the inability to face the consequences brought upon them by global capital or the powerful nations that represent its interests. To put it differently, both the realist approach and its critics do not adequately appreciate that compliance with international rules is secured through interpenetrating modes of power viz., structural, institutional and productive modes of power. They do not, therefore, also recognize the importance of structural indeterminacy of doctrines and rules of international law in enabling powerful states to demonstrate compliance even when there is non-compliance.[266] While the structural indeterminacy critique advanced by the likes of David Kennedy and Martti Koskenniemi is totalizing, it does point to how the international law rules powerful nations obey is what they make of it in a decentralized society.

C.   Rules, Interpretation and World Politics

In this case, Morgenthau was ahead of his times. He was among the first to perceive the complex relationship between language, law and politics in a decentralized legal order. However, he did not go on to explore the different sources of indeterminacy of rules. A principal reason for this lapse was the assumption that only rules of political international law were visited by indeterminacy. Morgenthau saw indeterminacy as a function of the adoption of 'vague and ambiguous' provisions in the face of opposing national interests. The intrinsic element of indeterminacy in political international law was accentuated by the fact that the subjects of international law were the supreme authorities for interpreting rules. The problem could not be resolved through adjudication because of the use of inappropriate rules of interpretation borrowed from domestic law. Morgenthau pointed to the 'peculiar relationship' between social forces and rules of political international law that made the problem of interpretation show 'unique aspects' for which the traditional civil law techniques were 'utterly inadequate'. He contrasted in this regard an international treaty with contracts in municipal law. Morgenthau observed that 'when in the domestic field the meaning of a contract is ascertained by the usual

---

[266] See Chapter 5 for an extensive discussion of the work of Kennedy and Koskenniemi.

means of interpretation, the interpretive job is done. It is generally not too difficult to perform the same task with regard to an international treaty; but then the real problem of interpretation just begins'.[267] The problem starts because whereas a contract of civil law uses 'standardized language whose legal meaning is definite or at least can be ascertained according to objective, universally recognized standards', the 'real meaning' of international treaties was disguised with diplomatic language as 'national interests' are always subject to change.[268] In sum, Morgenthau identified the sources of indeterminacy as being political international law, auto-interpretation and the use of traditional rules of interpretation.

In so far as the problem of indeterminacy is traced to the nature of political international law, critics have argued that non-political international law is as indeterminate as political international law.[269] Morgenthau did not explore this possibility because he assumed that the existence of complementary interests caused the adoption of clearly formulated rules and shared interpretations. Such an understanding pre-empted him from examining the semantic and structural bases of indeterminacy of rules. However, these sources of indeterminacy received substantial attention from his contemporary Myres McDougal and later from Kennedy and Koskenniemi. It is, therefore, no longer possible to argue that non-political international law is any less indeterminate than political international law. It is another matter that the extent of indeterminacy of both political and non-political international law is exaggerated by McDougal, Kennedy and Koskenniemi. Both the subject-dependent indeterminacy view of classical realism and the radical indeterminacy position advanced by McDougal, Kennedy and Koskenniemi are rejected by IMAIL. The IMAIL critique of the radical indeterminacy position is dealt with in detail in later chapters.[270]

At this point, only a few observations may be made on the problem of auto-interpretation of political international law and the inadequacy in this regard of rules of interpretation borrowed from domestic law. The problem of auto-interpretation of international law cannot certainly be wished away. But it does not mean that any interpretation goes even in instances where a 'vague and ambiguous' rule is adopted. Broadly speaking, the interpretive process is constituted of a negative and a positive

---

[267] Morgenthau, 'Positivism, Functionalism', p. 282.
[268] See ibid., p. 279.
[269] Simpson, 'Dueling Agendas', p. 69.
[270] See Chapter 3, pp. 123–140, Chapter 4, pp. 188–192, and Chapter 7, pp. 524–534. In fact, it is recommended that these sections be read together.

moment wherein the former sets relatively strict limits to the possible interpretation that can be advanced. What is ruled out is reasonably clear, but is not to be confused with saying that it has a fixed meaning prior to the moment of interpretation.[271] The positive moment, which involves the determination of what is permissible, is more likely to be the arena of divergent interpretations.[272] But, if it is agreed that not all interpretations are equally persuasive, then opportunistic interpretations will be seen for what they are. But, unless interpretive relativism of a radical order is embraced, it is difficult to conclude that a provision of a political international treaty loses all restraining power when faced with pseudo interpretations. What is more, the international community proceeds to judgment with power and interest implications for the state that is advancing arbitrary interpretations. In a decentralized society auto-interpretation is matched by auto-judgment and in the case of the international states system with a difference: the relatively small number of actors. In other words, Morgenthau was not wrong in presuming that expedient interpretations would be advanced, but did not provide for the consequences that followed from the international community seeing it as such.

In so far as the unsuitability of common and Roman law principles of interpretation of political international law is concerned, there are a number of problems with the Morgenthau thesis.[273] He appears to set the interpreter a twofold task: to discover the 'real meaning' of the treaty which is concealed through the use of 'vague and ambiguous' provisions and to read it in the light of the political scenario prevailing at 'the time of

---

[271] See Francis Anthony Boyle, *World Politics and International Law* (Durham, NC: Duke University Press, 1985), pp. 70–72.

[272] See ibid.

[273] Oran Young, 'Compliance in the International System', in Richard Falk, Friedrich Kratochwil and Saul H. Mendlovitz (eds.) *International Law: A Contemporary Perspective* (Boulder CO: Westview Press, Inc., 1985), pp. 99–111, p. 104. A preliminary point that may be raised is that it is not perhaps correct to sharply contrast the international treaty with domestic contract. But presumably this response would be considered valid only in the case of non-political agreements, whereas Morgenthau's reference is to 'political agreements, especially treaties of alliance and their modern substitutes'. Morgenthau, 'Positivism, Functionalism', pp. 278–279. But the idea of 'strategic ambiguity' can inform non-political agreements as well, often the result of an inability to reach closure in the negotiations. For example, many of the clauses of WTO agreements reflect such 'strategic ambiguity'. B. S. Chimni, 'China, India and the WTO Dispute Settlement System: Towards an Interpretative Strategy' in M. Sornarajah and J. Wang (eds.) *China, India and the International Economic Order* (Cambridge: Cambridge University Press, 2010), pp. 217–250.

interpretation'. It is important to understand here that when Morgenthau speaks of modes of interpretation to discover the 'real meaning' of a political agreement he is not recommending a universal doctrine of interpretation, for it would not apply to contracts in the domestic sphere or to non-political agreements. He is proposing a regional theory of interpretation that will be able to come to terms with the peculiar subject matter of political international law. But it cannot be the task of the interpreter to determine the range of possible meanings that may be concealed in the provisions of a political agreement i.e., meaning that cannot be derived from the text. It is not for the interpreter of an agreement to say that in reality the parties never meant what they agreed upon. Turning to the application of the provisions of an agreement to constantly changing political scenarios, it is difficult to see how it calls for a unique method of interpretation. The interpreter cannot in the name of a changing political scenario assign meaning that has no basis in the text. It will be seen in the next chapter that in this regard the New Haven approach is one with Morgenthau, albeit in the case of the former the task of interpreter is tied to a particular understanding of law and the realization of certain world order values. At this point all that needs to be said is that international legal rules are adopted and given meaning in the backdrop of extant linguistic, social and political practices.[274] These practices constrain the kind of interpretation that is acceptable to the international community. While a state cannot be prevented from advancing a subjective interpretation, the international community can deprive the interpretation of legitimacy. It was noted earlier that Morgenthau recommends a policy of prudence in the world of power politics. There is no reason why it should not extend to the world of interpretation as well. But this suggestion raises issues regarding the relationship between international morality and international law that may now be considered.

V. International Morality, International Law and International Politics

Morgenthau viewed the role of international morality in international politics in three distinct ways.[275] First, he saw the role of international morality as part of a set of conditions that ensure the validity of international law rules. Morgenthau argued that 'the validity of any legal system

---

[274] See Chapter 3, pp. 123–140 and Chapter 7, pp. 524–534.
[275] Morgenthau, *Decline of Democratic Politics*, p. 59.

reposes upon a fundamental norm which itself cannot be of a legal nature, but belongs of necessity to the domain of ethics and *mores*.[276] It is only 'when ethics, *mores*, and law cooperate to realize a certain order of things, there is much greater likelihood that this order will be realized than when the law alone strives for the goal'.[277] In fact, Morgenthau lamented that the traditional science of international law did not even pose the question as to 'the empirical nature of the dual relationship between international law, on the one hand, and ethics and mores on the other'.[278] In making these observations he went beyond the realm of sanctions and balance of power to ground the effectiveness of legal rules in the domain and state of international morality. Second, Morgenthau saw morality attenuating the struggle for power in international relations in the same way it had done at the domestic level in Western civilizations.[279] In his view the actions of states could also be 'subject to universal moral principles'.[280] Morgenthau pointed out how statesmen and diplomats 'refuse to consider certain ends and to use certain means, either altogether or under certain conditions'.[281] Thus, an ethical impulse informed the 'moral condemnation of war',[282] as also the codification of international humanitarian laws with the aim of 'humanization of warfare' when war takes place.[283] Third, Morgenthau saw morality help stave off 'revolt against power' which, as he noted, was an aspiration that was 'as universal as the aspiration to power itself'.[284] In other words, morality plays an important role in lowering resistance to power by legitimizing its use in the eyes of those who are its subjects. However, Morgenthau did not clarify whether he was speaking here of the production of a certain social consensus in favour of power or the reduction of the possibility of resistance because of the prudent exercise of power. Since morality plays these different roles in limiting the struggle for power and rendering international law effective, he warned against underestimating its role in international politics.[285]

---

[276] Morgenthau, 'Positivism, Functionalism', p. 280.
[277] See ibid., p. 281.
[278] See ibid.
[279] Morgenthau, *Politics among Nations*, p. 223.
[280] Morgenthau, *Dilemmas of Politics*, p. 81.
[281] Morgenthau, *Politics among Nations*, p. 225.
[282] See ibid., p. 231.
[283] See ibid., p. 230. In delineating the role of international morality Morgenthau was entirely unconcerned with non-Western civilizations. If he were, he would have been pleasantly surprised to discover that non-Western civilizations gave life to similar ideas and practices long before Western civilizations came to embrace them.
[284] See ibid., p. 220.
[285] Morgenthau, *Politics among Nations*, p. 224.

But, Morgenthau also rightly cautioned against overrating the influence of ethics upon international politics. The reasons for his scepticism were twofold. First, in his view since 'moral rules operate within the consciences of individual men' the historical emergence of democratic rule within nation states transformed international morality 'from a reality into a mere figure of speech'.[286] The changeover from government by clearly identifiable men (the aristocratic rulers) to a polity in which responsibility is widely distributed among a great number of individuals answerable to collective institutions had undermined the role of morality in international politics. For the legal fiction of equating individuals and collective institutions is unacceptable in moral discourse. In short, 'the substitution of democratic for aristocratic responsibility in foreign affairs' diminished the role of morality in international affairs.[287] Second, Morgenthau pointed to the rise of the ideology of nationalism which was by its very nature 'particularistic and exclusive'.[288] Therefore, each nation considered its national ethics to be universal ethics, a tendency that easily led to foreign policy misadventures.[289] Furthermore, according to Morgenthau, the language of morality was often used by nations to disguise their real intent in international politics. The actual objectives were concealed behind moral rhetoric. In recent times the pro-democratic invasions of former Yugoslavia, Iraq and Afghanistan illustrate what Morgenthau had in mind. In view of these twin developments, i.e., the emergence of democratic responsibility and the ideology of nationalism Morgenthau was deeply sceptical about the role morality could play today in restraining the struggle for power at the international level. At the same time an amoral world was unacceptable to him as it would be a dehumanized world. Therefore, Morgenthau recommended a morality that could be practised in the modern world viz., a morality of prudence that carefully considers the consequences of political actions.[290] He pointed out that in the domain of power politics, the choice in modern times is not between morality and immorality but:

> between one type of political morality and another type of political morality, one taking as its standard universal moral principles abstractly formulated, the other weighing these principles against the moral requirements of concrete political action, their relative merits to be decided by a

[286] See ibid., pp. 241 and 240.
[287] See ibid., p. 235.
[288] See ibid.
[289] See ibid., pp. 235, 246.
[290] See ibid., p. 10.

prudent evaluation of the political consequences to which they are likely to lead.[291]

Morgenthau wanted states to follow 'an ethic of consequences' that places 'priority on ends rather than means' and 'on the goodness of the consequences rather than the abstract rightness of actions viewed in isolation'.[292]

It is evident that in discussing the reasons for not underestimating or overestimating the role of international morality in international politics, Morgenthau showed acute awareness of the complex ways in which the worlds of morality, law and politics intersect. But, he did not proceed to explore at any length both the positive and disquieting relationship between morality and law. To turn at first to the sanguine relationship, while Morgenthau looks at the role of international morality in enhancing the effectiveness of international law, as also in preventing and humanizing war, he did not delve into other aspects of the multidimensional relationship between law and morality in the modern era.[293] Some of these are worth indicating. First, the basic idea of 'international rule of law' which prevents the arbitrary exercise of power by states is at a fundamental level an ethical idea with a powerful draw among weak states even as there is recognition that law often aids power. Second, there are entire branches of international law such as international human rights law that are imbued with deep ethical values and go some way to humanize international law. Third, ethics plays a role in international adjudication when it comes to choosing between alternative interpretations of international law rules in issue.[294] Fourth, there are remedies in international law that are instilled with moral considerations (e.g., apology for historical wrongs). Fifth, many activities, decisions and resolutions of international organizations can be characterized as driven by an ethics of care, an instance being the provision of humanitarian assistance. Sixth, ethical

---

[291] Morgenthau, *Dilemmas of Politics*, p. 86. In the words of Frei, 'prudence presupposes practical wisdom and foresight, a power of imagination and combination, the ability to consider different things at the same time, sober detachment, and other qualities. In the final analysis, prudence represents sound judgment – *Urteilskraft* in German'. Frei, *Hans J. Morgenthau*, p. 225.

[292] Lea Brilmayer, 'Realism Revisited: The Moral Priority of Means and Ends in Anarchy' in Ian Shapiro and Lea Brilmayer (eds.) *Global Justice* (New York: New York University Press, 1999), pp. 192–215 at pp. 193, 197.

[293] Alexander Boldizar and Outi Korhonen, 'Ethics, Morals and International law', 10 (1999) *European Journal of International Law*, pp. 279–311 at p. 280.

[294] Rosalyn Higgins, 'Ethics and International Law', 23 (2010) *Leiden Journal of International Law*, pp. 277–289.

considerations allow attention to be drawn to negative outcomes that flow from compliance with substantive law (e.g., the troubling impact on the right to health by conforming to the WTO agreement on Trade Related Intellectual Property Rights). Finally, there is the principle of individual responsibility, including that of the individual international lawyer, for his or her own acts of omission and commission. These considerations show how the language of ethics helps make international law more humane and effective.

For the rest, in warning against overestimating the role of morality in international politics, Morgenthau offered a critique of moralism that is 'politically acute and salutary'.[295] The founders of historical materialism were as averse to moralism as Morgenthau. In their view too it denoted 'the vain intrusions of moral judgments in lieu of causal understanding' and lacked 'the exacting sense of material care and measure that is insep- arable from true moral awareness'.[296] Marx and Engels also believed that morality has no independent history and that its content evolves over time.[297] It is therefore crucial that the rules of morality are historicized and assessed in relation to their contribution to the expansion of human freedom in particular social formations or in relation to different phases of the history of international relations. The problem with the stand- point of Morgenthau is that in evaluating the changes in the nature and character of morality he confines himself to the political sphere, ignor- ing the 'logic of capital'. Therefore, he overlooks that on the international plane what principally constrains the role of morality in international politics is not modern democratic rule or nationalism but universal- izing capitalism which shapes the meaning of both in history. If it is

---

[295] Marshall Cohen, 'Moral Skepticism and International Relations', 13 (1984) *Philosophy and Public Affairs*, pp. 299–346 at p. 303.

[296] Perry Anderson, *Arguments with English Marxism* (London: Verso 1980), p. 86.

[297] Karl Marx and Frederick Engels, *Selected Works*, vol. 1 (Moscow: Progress Publishers, 1973), pp. 25, 42, 79. There is much literature on the relationship of Marxism and eth- ics. See Eugene Kamenka, *Marxism and Ethics* (New York: St. Martin's Press, 1969); Ziyad Husami, 'Marx on Distributive Justice', 8 (1978) *Philosophy & Public Affairs*, pp. 27–64; Allen Wood, 'Marx on Right and Justice: A Reply to Husami', 8 (1979) *Philosophy & Public Affairs*, pp. 267–295; Allen E. Buchanan, 'Marx, Morality, and History: An Assessment of Recent Analytical Work on Marx', 98 (1987) *Ethics*, pp. 104–136; Steven Lukes, *Marxism and Morality* (Oxford: Clarendon Press, 1985); Philip J. Kain, *Marx and Ethics* (Oxford: Clarendon Press, 1988); Kain Nielson, *Marxism and the Moral Point of View: Morality, Ideology, and Historical Materialism* (Boulder, CO: Westview Press, 1989); Cornel West, *The Ethical Dimensions of Marxist Thought* (New York: Monthly Review Press, 1991); Nicholas Churchich, *Marxism and Morality: A Critical Examination of Marxist Ethics* (Cambridge: James Clarke & Co, 1994).

correct to assume that intrinsic to the 'logic of capital' is the economics and politics of imperialism then the limits of the role of morality, including an 'ethic of consequences', becomes immediately apparent. In fact, as Morgenthau perceptively noted, morality is used by states to disguise real interests. This logic can be easily extended to international law which has historically served the interests of imperialism. The justification of colonialism in terms of a civilizing mission was one such effort to disguise real interests. However, Morgenthau did not recognize that a critical end of the rules of international morality and international law must be the creation of a non-imperialist world. He could not do so for at least three reasons. First, he posited the realization of 'national interest' as the single 'moral' standard in international politics. In this regard, Charles Beitz aptly observes that 'to say that the first principle of international morality is that states should promote their own interests denies the possibility that moral considerations might require a state to act otherwise'.[298] This is especially so when little consideration is given to identifying the variable 'national interests' through locating them in particular historical social formations. In speaking of an 'ethic of consequences', Morgenthau appeared to be merely suggesting that powerful Western capitalist states should not pursue imperialist policies without weighing its costs and benefits; subaltern nations and peoples were never of interest to him. He did not explore the limits the combination of 'logic of capital' and the 'logic of territory' placed on the practice of an ethic of consequences. It is the alliance between the two that gives rise to the politics of imperialism and imparts life to Morgenthau's iron law of international politics that international laws give way to national interests.

Second, Morgenthau mistakenly thought that the turn to modern democratic politics eliminated the role of morality in international affairs. It is not entirely correct to say that states cannot be the subject of moral conduct in the same way as aristocratic rulers were.[299] As Terry Nardin points out, 'morality consists of principles for individuals and, by extensions, for individuals acting in concert. While it is correct to say that

---

[298] Charles R. Beitz, *Political Theory and International Relations* (Princeton, NJ: Princeton University Press, 1979), p. 23. Brilmayer also notes that it is not clear as to 'how the consequences of actions are to be evaluated' and whether a 'statesperson is supposed to balance the interests of his or her own state against the interests of others'. Brilmayer, 'Realism Revisited', p. 214.

[299] Toni Erskine, 'Making Sense of "Responsibility" in International Relations: Key Questions and Concepts' in Toni Erskine (ed.), *Can Institutions Have Responsibilities? Collective Moral Agency and International Relations* (Basingstoke: Palgrave Macmillan, 2003), pp. 1–19 at p. 7.

moral concepts and principles apply largely and fundamentally to individual conduct, it does not follow that the conduct of states cannot be
judged in moral terms'.[300] Indeed, it is commonplace to pass moral judgment against the conduct of states. All that is perhaps necessary to see
is if states (and the institutions they create) 'possess a capacity for moral
deliberation' and are 'able to act on the basis of this deliberation'.[301] In this
regard, there is little doubt that the process of decision making in modern
states (and international institutions) involves a deliberative component.
Therefore, if international morality does not act as a constraint on power
politics or imperialism it is not because of the turn to democratic responsibility but the pursuit of parochial interests by powerful states with the
ideology of nationalism only accentuating the obsession with them.

Third, Morgenthau did not appreciate that the practice of prudence
depended far too much on the quality of political leadership of a nation.
It is easy for leaders to deceive themselves as to the common good that
will result from their actions. In any case, weak states cannot rely on wise
leadership alone to ensure that they do not become victims of imperialism. These states need legal guarantees as a shield against the politics
of imperialism. This perhaps explains why the political scientist Terry
Nardin believes that the best option for the international community is to
accept a rule-oriented ethic with the sole goal of promoting international
rule of law.[302]

In talking of a rule-oriented ethic, Nardin opposes it not only to the
'ethics of consequences' in the political sphere but also to an outcome-
oriented ethic in international law contending that 'though the consequences of observing a rule may be important in evaluating its desirability,
they cannot determine its validity'.[303] He may not be wrong to the extent

---

[300] Terry Nardin, *Law, Morality and the Relations of States* (Princeton, NJ: Princeton
University Press, 1983), p. 236.

[301] Nicholas Rengger, 'On "Good Governance", Institutional Design, and the Practices of
Moral Agency' in Toni Erskine (ed.), *Can Institutions Have Responsibilities?*, pp. 207–218
at p. 209.

[302] Terry Nardin, 'International Ethics and International Law', 18 (1992) *Review of
International Studies*, pp. 19–30 at p. 19.

[303] See ibid., p. 22. In other words, 'legality in international relations is a constraint, not an
outcome'. See ibid., p. 26. It is interesting to note in this context that in his own times
Grotius made natural law 'to approximate as far as possible to the condition of positive
law'. In fact, 'the ground on which the two idioms met most frequently was the law of
nations, the ius gentium'. The reason being that for the 'modern' natural-law theorists 'the
law of nations, although a human positive law, was that area where the teaching of the
law of nature could be translated into a body of enforceable precepts'. Anthony Pagden,
'Introduction' in Anthony Pagden (ed.), *The Languages of Political Theory in Early Modern*

that an outcome-oriented ethics can be used by powerful states to cause much harm to weak states. It may be recalled that the NATO action in former Yugoslavia was justified on the basis of the argument that it may have been illegal but was moral.[304] On the other hand, to suggest that the weak cannot seek to reform a valid rule through offering resistance is troubling as it squarely privileges the value of order over justice.[305] Alert to this fact, Nardin concedes that the international law tradition 'does not have an exclusive claim' to international morality.[306] In times of globalization, when the actions of states impact each other in myriad ways, especially the everyday life of individuals, an outcome-oriented ethic cannot be completely set aside. But its relevance has to be asserted along with an insistence that the basic or fundamental principles of international law as incorporated in the UN Charter or the Friendly Relations Declaration (1970) are observed. Thus, it is only a prudent mix of rule-oriented and outcome-oriented ethics that can safeguard the interests of the weak. The international legal community needs to support a mix that can promote a peaceful and just world order till a democratic world state comes into existence.

VI.   World Community, World State and International Law

In fact, Morgenthau believed that after the coming of the thermonuclear revolution, world peace cannot be achieved without a world state, foregrounding the ideational element in realism.[307] The arrival of nuclear weapons had in his view rendered the nation state obsolete and the idea of a world state no longer utopian.[308] According to Morgenthau, 'the

---

Europe (Cambridge: Cambridge University Press, 1987), pp. 5, 6. See also Richard Tuck, 'The Modern Theory of Natural Law' in Pagden (ed.), *Languages of Political Theory*, pp. 99–122.

[304] Antonio Cassesse, "Ex iniura ius oritur: Are We Moving Towards International Legitimation of Forcible Countermeasures in the World Community?", 10 (1999) *European Journal of International Law*, pp. 23–30; Thomas M. Franck, 'Break It, Don't Fake It', (July/August 1999) *Foreign Affairs*, pp. 116–118.

[305] Nardin, *Law, Morality*, pp. 12–13.

[306] See ibid., pp. 223 and 240.

[307] 'During the 1940s and 1950s, so-called "classical" Realists not only engaged extensively with proponents of radical global reform, but many of them advocated major alterations to the existing state system.' Scheuerman, 'Realism and the Left', p. 247.

[308] Morgenthau, *Truth and Power*, p. 260. The larger dilemma of total nuclear war, Morgenthau wrote, 'suggests the abolition of international relations itself through the merger of all national sovereignties into one world state which would have a monopoly of the most destructive instruments of violence. Both kinds of solutions are supported

availability of nuclear power as an instrument of foreign policy is the only revolution that has occurred in the structure of international relations since the beginning of history'.[309] For, the use of nuclear weapons could go to erase the critical distinction between victors and vanquished in a war. Morgenthau wrote that 'it is at this point that the realistic and utopian approaches to politics in general, and to international relations in particular, merge'.[310] A world state could create the conditions for preventing a nuclear war by ending the anarchical system[311] and obliterating the distinction between domestic law and international law.[312]

But while Morgenthau recognized the need for a world state he did not think that the conditions conducive to the creation of a world state were present. According to him, 'in no period of modern history were the moral, social, and political conditions of the world less favorable for the establishment of a world state'.[313] For a world state to be established a world community had to antedate it[314] but as yet there did not 'exist a supranational society that comprises all individual members of the nations' that was 'identical with humanity politically organized'.[315] Among other things, the ideology of nationalism stood in the way of a global demos coming into existence.[316] Morgenthau was spot on, as even decades after his pronouncement, there is continuing scepticism about the existence of an 'international community' which is largely deemed to be 'a juridical fiction'.[317] While the concepts of *erga omnes* and *jus cogens* may embody values that represent the legal building blocks of an 'international community', these are perceived as weak foundations on which

by the awareness of the unity of mankind underlying the inevitable fragmentation of international relations'. Cited in Campbell Craig, 'Hans Morgenthau and the World State Revisited' in Williams (ed.), *Realism Reconsidered*, pp. 195–215 at p. 206.

[309] See ibid.
[310] See ibid.
[311] Craig, 'Hans Morgenthau', p. 197.
[312] Oliver Jütersonke, 'Hans J. Morgenthau and the World State: Realism and the Legacy of Kelsenian Legal Formalism', paper prepared for British International Studies Association (BISA) Annual Conference, Manchester, April, 2011, p. 9.
[313] Morgenthau, *Politics among Nations*, p. 495.
[314] See ibid., p. 500.
[315] See ibid., p. 493.
[316] Lieber, 'Introduction', p. 15. Morgenthau did not consider the argument Alexander Wendt makes that 'far from suppressing nationalism, a world state will only be possible if it embraces it'. Alexander Wendt, 'Why a World State is Inevitable', 9 (2003) *European Journal of International Relations*, pp. 491–542 at p. 527.
[317] Gleider I. Hernandez, 'A Reluctant Guardian: The International Court of Justice and the Concept of "International Community"', 83 (2013)*British Yearbook of International Law*, pp. 13–60 at p. 59.

to claim that a genuine international community has been established. Indeed, contemporary scholars warn that an untimely search for 'international community' may lend itself to the legitimization of imperialist ambitions.[318] Morgenthau was also against any top down 'misguided and premature reform undertakings' which could lead to the creation of an undesirable world state.[319]

But, in thinking about the conditions for the emergence of a world community, Morgenthau focused once again on the political sphere neglecting the role of universalizing capitalism in creating a 'global social formation' and the conditions for the emergence of a world state.[320] He turned instead to the sphere of politics and to Mitrany's theory of functionalism for an answer.[321] Morgenthau believed that the work of specialized international institutions can 'overlay political divisions with a spreading web of international activities and agencies, in which and through which the interests and life of all nations would be gradually integrated'.[322] He even thought that these institutions 'could create by the very fact of their existence and performance a community of interests, valuations, and actions'.[323] In Morgenthau's view, they could help fashion 'common habits and interests',[324] overlooking the fact that even in his time the specialized agencies were 'sites of power, even of dominance'.[325] These institutions have from the beginning pursued an agenda prescribed by advanced capitalist states. Morgenthau does speak of 'economic imperialism' but did not think that international economic institutions were its vehicles. The reasons for Morgenthau's cognitive lapse were threefold: First, he assigned international economic institutions to the non-political domain. In his view only political organs of UN were the arena of power politics. Second, he never seriously concerned himself with the victims of 'economic imperialism' that is, the third world and its peoples.[326] His was a

---

[318] See ibid.

[319] Scheuerman, 'Realism and the Left', p. 247.

[320] On the meaning and emergence of a global social formation, see B. S. Chimni, 'Prolegomena to a Class Approach to International Law', 21 (2010) *European Journal of International Law*, pp. 57–82 at pp. 65–76.

[321] Morgenthau, *Politics among Nations*, p. 506. See also Scheuerman, 'Global Reform', p. 263.

[322] Morgenthau, *Politics among Nations*, p. 506.

[323] See ibid., p. 507.

[324] See ibid.

[325] Andrew Hurrell, 'Power, Institutions, and the Production of Inequality' in Barnett and Duvall, *Power in Global Governance*, pp. 33–59 at p. 56.

[326] Scheuerman observes that 'unlike Carr, Morgenthau in the postwar years consistently placed questions of cross-border economic distribution on the political back burner.

Eurocentric world. Third, in thinking of the world state his focus was on the European integration process for which a functionalist explanation appeared credible. But, in this instance, he failed to understand that it was European capital and not functional European agencies that were driving regional integration.[327]

In the event Morgenthau failed to see that a world state is emerging but not of the kind, nor driven by forces, that he envisaged. Today, in view of the accelerated globalization process that can be traced to the logic of late capitalism, a global social formation and a nascent world state is in the process of emerging under the guidance of a transnational capitalist class (TCC). A network of global economic laws that are creating a borderless global economic space have facilitated the emergence of this formation.[328] The policing of global economic laws have necessitated a greater role for international institutions to which sovereign functions of states have come to be ceded, turning them into building blocks of an embryonic world state.[329] The Mitrany vision is coming to be realized albeit in a perverse way. Even at the beginning of the globalization process Marxist scholars like Poulantzas were asking whether the extended reproduction of capital at the international level required the transformation of the functions of the nation state and the creation of super-state

---

Supranational society, it seemed, would somehow have to be built without economic redistribution between and among nation-state's'. Scheuerman, 'Global Reform', p. 264.

[327] Bastiaan van Appeldoorn, 'The Struggle over European Order: Transnational Class Agency in the Making of "Embedded Neo-Liberalism"' in Neil Brenner, Bob Jessop, Martin Jones and Gordon MacLeod (eds.), *State/Space: A Reader* (Oxford: Blackwell Publishing, 2003), pp. 147–165; Ian Manners, "Another Europe is Possible: Critical Perspectives on European Union Politics" in Knud Erik Jørgensen, Mark Pollack and Ben Rosamond (eds.), *Handbook of European Union Politics* (London: Sage, 2007), pp. 77–95; Nick Stevenson, 'Cosmopolitan Europe, Post-colonialism and the Politics of Imperialism' in C. Rumford (ed.), *Cosmopolitanism and Europe* (Liverpool: Liverpool University Press, 2007), pp. 51–72.

[328] Likewise, Chase Dunn and Inoue observe that 'the acceptance of the idea of a single global economy makes a single global political system easier to think of'. Christopher Chase-Dunn and Hiroko Inoue, 'Accelerating Democratic Global State Formation', 47 (2012) *Cooperation and Conflict*, pp. 157–175 at p. 163.

[329] B. S. Chimni, 'International Institutions Today: An Imperial Global State in the Making', 15 (2004) *European Journal of International Law*, pp. 1–39. Chase-Dunn and Inoue use the term 'global proto-state'. Chase-Dunn and Inoue, 'Accelerating Democratic', p. 162. According to Chase-Dunn and Inoue: 'the contemporary global proto-state is conceived as a constellation of institutions composed of the United Nations and its agencies, the International Financial Institutions (IFIs) such as the International Monetary Fund, the World Bank and the World Trade Organization, the Group of Eight and the Group of 20, as well as international regional security organizations, like NATO'. See ibid.

institutional forms.[330] What we are seeing today is the emergence of an incipient imperial world state constituted not by the disappearance of nation states but by international institutions. Instead of being an answer to the thermonuclear revolution, such a world state accentuates the threat flowing from nuclear weapons as for the present the emerging imperial world state will coexist with sovereign states. However, its constitution may be hastened in coming times. There are several neutral factors that may contribute to this process. According to Chase Dunn and Inloue, the factors include technological innovations, possible ecological, economic and political calamities, and networks and coalitions of social movements.[331] On the other hand, institutional innovations such as the creation of a Global Peoples' Assembly within the UN, along with other reforms such as making the UN Security Council more broad-based, may help to address to a degree some of its more disturbing consequences.[332]

There are of course those like the exponents of the network thesis, such as Anne-Marie Slaughter, who believe that a world government is both 'undesirable' and 'infeasible'.[333] Instead, what Slaughter supports is the idea of disaggregated sovereignty guided by Western liberal democratic states, especially the United States. The objective is to create an international community from below through greater interaction between the professional classes. In this respect, Slaughter points to the existence of a global network of legislators, judges, bank officials and police officials that are trying to address common global problems.[334] While Slaughter sees their functions as benign, others contend that the most important effect of global networks is 'the creation of a global bourgeoisie with a set of similar elite-class views' that advances the normative and enforcement agenda of global capital.[335] For the creation of a democratic world state that promotes peace, what is perhaps necessary is the creation of a genuine international community from below brought about by progressive global social movements. There is, however, a need for a thorough study of the conditions in

---

[330] Nicos Poulantzas, *Classes in Contemporary Capitalism* (London: Verso, 1978), p. 38.

[331] Chase-Dunn and Inoue, 'Accelerating Democratic', pp. 165 ff., p. 167.

[332] See in this regard Richard Falk and Andrew Strauss, *A Global Parliament: Essays and Articles* (Berlin: Committee for a Democratic U.N., 2011).

[333] Anne-Marie Slaughter and David Zaring, 'Networking Goes International: An Update', 2 (2006) *Annual Review of Law Society and Social Sciences*, pp. 211–229 at p. 225.

[334] Anne-Marie Slaughter, 'Sovereignty and Power in a Networked World Order', 40 (2004) *Stanford Journal of International Law*, pp. 283–327 at p. 288. See also Anne-Marie Slaughter, *A New World Order* (Princeton, NJ: Princeton University Press, 2004).

[335] Kenneth Anderson, 'Squaring the Circle? Reconciling Sovereignty and Global Governance through Global Government Networks', 118 (2005) *Harvard Law Review*, pp. 1255–1312 at p. 1272.

which a democratic world state can be created. It calls in this regard for the active collaboration between the disciplines of international relations (IR) and international law (IL). The proponents of the network thesis have already advanced what is called the IR-IL approach which contrasts with, and represents a departure from, the sceptical approach of Morgenthau. What needs consideration is the nature of collaboration suggested by the IR-IL approach and whether it can help achieve the desired goals of global peace and justice.

VII.   Classical Realism and the IR-IL Approach

Morgenthau's emphasis on the autonomy of the political and legal spheres and his scepticism about the role of international law in international politics diminished the possibility of any serious collaboration between the disciplines of IR and IL. Since realism was the dominant approach in the United States, the home of IR, in the Cold War era, it arguably caused a divorce between the disciplines of IR and IL.[336] It does not, therefore, come as a surprise that in the post–Cold War era 'IR and IL have rediscovered one another'.[337] Indeed it is significant that the first canonical text proposing collaboration between the disciplines of IR and IL was published by Kenneth Abbott in 1989,[338] followed by Slaughter's pioneering piece on the subject in 1993.[339]

---

[336] 'The dominance of the realist, and later, neorealist school of thought in international relations in the post-World War II era was perhaps the most significant reason for the divide between international law and international relations, as the realist school tended to promote the argument that law was largely derivative of international power politics'. Veronica Raffo, Chandra Lekha Sriram, Peter J. Spiro and Thomas Biersteker, 'Introduction: International Law and International Politics – Old Divides, New Developments' in Thomas J. Biersteker, Peter J. Spiro, Chandra Lekha Sriram and Veronica Raffo (eds.), *International Law and International Relations: Bridging Theory and Practice* (London: Routledge, 2006), pp. 1–23 at p. 4. They also contend that the divide was 'most visible in the United States'. See ibid., p. 5. Likewise, it has been argued that 'the reasons for the periodic divergence and reconvergence of the two fields have had more to do with the internalization of external events such as the Cold War and its end and the externalization of the internal dynamics of theory building and purported paradigm shifting'. Anne-Marie Slaughter, Andrew S. Tulumello and Stepan Wood, 'International Law and International Relations Theory: A New Generation of Interdisciplinary Scholarship, 92 (1998) *The American Journal of International Law*, pp. 367–397 at p. 393.

[337] Slaughter, Tulumello and Wood, 'International Law', p. 393.

[338] Kenneth W. Abbott, 'Modern International Relations Theory: A Prospectus for International Lawyers', 14 (1989) *Yale Journal of International Law*, pp. 335–411.

[339] Anne-Marie Slaughter Burley, 'International Law and International Relations Theory: A Dual Agenda', 87 (1993) *The American Journal of International Law*, pp. 205–239.

A principal reason for proposing collaboration is the growing signifi-cance of international law and institutions leading to the legalization of international relations.[340] The partnership had also became feasible as alternative approaches to IR such as rational institutionalism, liberalism and constructivism had gained ground in preceding years, offering also better tools to understand the increasing legalization and institutional-ization of world politics.[341] However, IR scholars felt that the discipline of IL was not yet ready for collaboration as it was overly focused on the internal logic, relations and dynamics of international law. International law scholarship was yet to take seriously the empirical analysis of key issues such as compliance or institutional design. International relations scholars believed that the discipline of IL, therefore, needed to borrow methodological tools from the discipline of IR. This suggestion raised the anxiety of IL scholars in the same way as the earlier critique of inter-national law by realist scholars like Morgenthau. The IR-IL approach appeared to demand that legal scholarship move away from its hermen-eutic orientation[342] and thereby raised visions of 'an imperialist invasion of the legal realm by political scientists armed with theories, epistemolo-gies, and conceptions of law that are fundamentally foreign to those of most legal scholars.'[343] Koskenniemi went further and accused the IR-IL school of seeing law as 'an irrelevant decoration'.[344] He observed that the IL-IR project:

> Is an American crusade ... the interdisciplinary agenda itself, together
> with the deformalized concept of law, and enthusiasm about the spread
> of 'liberalism', constitutes an academic project that cannot but buttress the
> justification of the American empire ... This is not because of bad faith or
> conspiracy on anybody's part. It is the logic of the argument ... that hopes
> to salvage the law by making it an instrument for the values (or better,
> 'decisions') of the powerful that compels the conclusion.[345]

---

[340] See special issue on 'Legalization and World Politics' 54 (2000) *International Organization* edited by Judith Goldstein, Miles Kahler, Robert O. Keohane and Anne-Marie Slaughter.

[341] 'Globalization, understood as multidimensional phenomenon, has put pressure on pol-ities everywhere, gradually circumscribing and delimiting political power. The operation of these transnational social forces has had a profound effect on both the functioning and the conceptualization of international law and international politics'. Raffo et al., 'Introduction', p. 1. For a brief account of the liberal institutionalists' and constructivists' different approach towards international law, see ibid., p. 5.

[342] See ibid., pp. 16–17.

[343] Dunoff and Pollack, 'International Law', p. 11.

[344] Martti Koskenniemi, 'Miserable Comforters: International Relations as New Natural Law', 15 (2009) *European Journal of International Relations*, pp. 395–422 at p. 410.

[345] Koskenniemi, *The Gentle Civilizer*, pp. 483–484.

In a response to this critique of the IR-IL school, Pollack argued that, in reaching his conclusion, Koskenniemi mistakenly assumed the continuing hegemony of realist theory within IR. In reality, 'while the legacy of realism remains important in teaching in particular, contemporary IR is not, nor for decades has been, dominated by realist theory'.[346] In the event 'Koskenniemi's critique of IR represents at best an anachronism, describing the early Cold War IR of our grandfathers rather than the contemporary field, and at worst a distortion of IR scholars' attitudes, aims, and influence on the legal profession'[347]. Pollack then went on to make the following other observations to counter the scepticism of Koskenniemi. First, 'Koskenniemi's image of IR as a policy science, devoted primarily or even largely to the making and justification of U.S. imperial policies, is no longer, if indeed it ever was, an accurate depiction of the field.'[348] Second, in contrast to Koskenniemi's assertion about the deformalization of the law 'much contemporary IR scholarship takes a naively *formalist* approach to international law, and that it engages in *too little* interdisciplinarity, relying too heavily on off-the-shelf concepts from IR theories and not enough on legal scholarship'.[349] Indeed, 'the rediscovery of international law over the past several decades has taken the form of an almost formalist approach to law-making, interpretation and compliance'.[350] Third, Pollack made the crucial point that irrespective of where one stands vis-à-vis scientific positivism:

> it seems clear ... that *the core social-scientific aim of understanding how international law is made, how it is interpreted and applied, and whether and when states comply with it, is not in itself incompatible with or hostile to legal scholars' normative, teleological aim of a world governed by law.* Indeed, to suggest that the goal of a world rules by law is somehow undermined by the social-scientific effort to *understand* how the law is made and how it works seems, frankly, bizarre.[351]

---

[346] See ibid., pp. 361, 364.

[347] Pollack, 'Is International Relations Corrosive?', p. 340. See also Jeffrey L. Dunoff, 'From Interdisciplinarity to Counterdisciplinarity: Is There Madness in Martti's Method?', 27 (2013) *Temple International & Comparative Law Quarterly*, pp. 309–338.

[348] See ibid., p. 364.

[349] See ibid., p. 365; emphasis in original.

[350] See ibid., p. 366.

[351] See ibid., p. 372; emphasis in original. From within the discipline of international law Schaffer and Ginsburg likewise argue that 'international lawyers should avoid prescription that are based solely on theoretical positions and that are also not grounded in empirical investigations'. Gregory Schaffer and Tom Ginsburg, 'The Empirical Turn in International Legal Scholarship', 106 (2012) *American Journal of International Law*, pp. 1–46 at p. 44.

Pollack concluded that 'the saddest feature of Koskenniemi's project is his effort to discourage interdisciplinary cooperation between IR and IL scholars, by presenting the former as an existential threat to the professional and moral integrity of the latter'.[352] Dunoff added that 'the fear of international law being colonized by international relations is exaggerated'.[353]

However, lately the IR-IL approach has reviewed its understanding of the basis of the proposed collaboration between the two disciplines. There are at least two reasons that account for the rethinking. The first is of course the sharp reaction of international lawyers to the proposed collaboration, especially the charge of denying 'law's normativity'.[354] While the IR-IL approach continues to reject the criticism that it is claiming that international law is "inconsequential and epiphenomenal"', especially given the 'move to law' and institutions in the era of globalization, the reaction of international lawyers compelled IR scholars to rethink the relationship.[355] The proponents of IR-IL approach have tried to reassure IL scholars that 'very few political scientists see law as unimportant force in world politics. Essentially all IR scholars find that international law, along with other international institutions, plays a substantial role in ordering relations between states'.[356] The second reason is the fact that, as Dunoff and Pollack point out, 'much of the early institutionalist, liberal, and constructivist literature understated the importance of state power as an explanatory variable in the making, interpretation, and enforcement of international law'.[357] In contrast, the discipline of IL had retained its focus on the state actor and with a 'turn to empiricism' was in a good position to contribute to the IR-IL approach. Dunoff and Pollack also noted with appreciation that international lawyers were increasingly addressing 'questions of institutional design, international judicial behavior, and enforcement and compliance, generating empirical findings and conceptual analysis that can be used to inform and enrich research in these areas'.[358]

---

[352] See ibid., p. 374.
[353] Dunoff, 'From Interdisciplinarity to Counterdisciplinarity', p. 332.
[354] Dunoff and Pollack, 'International Law', p. 19.
[355] See ibid., pp. 6, 9, 12.
[356] Hafner-Burton et al., 'Political Science Research', p. 97.
[357] See ibid.
[358] Dunoff and Pollack, 'International Law', p. 17. See in this regard Schaffer and Ginsburg, 'The Empirical Turn', pp. 1–46. Schaffer and Ginsburg document how 'a new generation of empirical studies is elaborating on how international law works in different contexts'. See ibid., p. 1.

The rethinking has led to the conclusion that IR-IL scholarship 'has been somewhat one-sided' and that there is a need to consider what 'IL can contribute to IR'.[359] In fact Pollack concedes that 'much IL/IR scholarship is not, in fact, truly interdisciplinary. Instead, it consists essentially of the application of IR as a *discipline* to the study of international law as a subject'.[360] According to Pollack, IR-IL scholarship is not fulfilling its potential 'in large part because of its failure to engage in fully interdisciplinary work that takes seriously the legal aspects of international norms, rules, and processes'.[361] In his view, 'externalism can become a vice if and insofar as IR scholars become interested only in the project of demonstrating extra-legal influences on the law, and thereby ignore the inner logic of the law, legal doctrine, and legal reasoning. The best defense against such a possibility, of course, is interdisciplinary scholarship that is sensitive to these legal issues'.[362] There is, thus, growing recognition that while quantitative methods in IR-IL scholarship have contributed 'substantial insights into international law' it has also in the process missed 'much that is fundamental about the international legal project, including formal legal doctrine and argumentation'.[363] Therefore, Dunoff and Pollack now speak of the need for a 'greater balance in intellectual terms of trade between the two disciplines' to tap into 'underutilized conceptual approaches and tools' of international legal theory and scholarship.[364]

Slaughter has also reassured that it is not the aim of IR-IL scholarship 'to erase the normative dimension of international law'.[365] She points out that 'it is precisely the contrast *between* IL and the empirical discipline of IR that brings out law's normative character. IR-IL scholars have to cross the empirical/normative boundary all the time, understanding how

[359] Kenneth W. Abbott and Duncan Snidal, 'Law, Legalization, and Politics: An Agenda for the Next Generation of IL/IR Scholars' in Dunoff and Pollack, *Interdisciplinary Perspectives*, pp. 33–56 at p. 33. Hafner-Burton, Victor and Lupu write that 'IR scholarship largely ignores or does not understand some matters of central importance to public international lawyers, such as the specific procedures for setting and interpreting the content of international treaties'. Hafner-Burton et al., 'Political Science Research', p. 48.
[360] Pollack, 'Is International Relations Corrosive?', p. 369.
[361] See ibid., p. 370.
[362] See ibid., p. 373.
[363] See ibid., pp. 373–374.
[364] Jeffrey L. Dunoff and Mark A. Pollack, 'Reviewing Two Decades of IL/IR Scholarship: What We've Learned, What's Next', in Dunoff and Pollack, *Interdisciplinary Perspectives*, pp. 626–661 at p. 627.
[365] Anne-Marie Slaughter, 'International Law and International Relations Theory: Twenty Years Later', in Dunoff and Pollack (eds.), *Interdisciplinary Perspectives*, pp. 613–625 at p. 624.

both theoretical and empirical scholarship in IR can inform law but never replace it'.[366] In fact, based on her experience in the Obama administration, Slaughter has gone on to observe that 'IR scholars need to know much more about how law is in fact made and what their international colleagues are doing not as IL-IR experts but as legal scholars'.[367] She now stresses the critical role international law was playing 'in shaping international reality', including its constitutive role.[368] In her view, IR-IL scholars need to generate 'new understandings of international law that draw from both traditions'.[369] Abbott and Snidal likewise emphasize the need to bring 'values/interests considerations and rationalist/normative approaches together' to 'understand how law (IL) and politics (IR) work together, in practice and in theory'.[370]

But, while there is increasing recognition of the implications of international laws' normative character, the reference point in so far as international law scholarship is concerned is mainstream scholarship or the New Haven approach that seek to further the Western liberal democratic project. There are few references in IR-IL literature to critical approaches to international law such as the third world, feminist or Marxist approaches to international law. The preference for certain approaches is no accident but a reflection of the goal of desired collaboration. On the other hand, the third world and left approaches have been at the forefront of questioning the Western hegemonic project and wish to conceptualize the IR-IL collaboration on the basis of an alternative sociology of international relations. Take the area of formulation of state interests. It is true that recognizing that 'interests (other than survival) are exogenous to realism', the IR-IL approach does lift the veil over the state to understand 'the formulation of state interests'.[371] But what is admitted is only a liberal understanding of the influence of domestic factors or non-state actors in the formulation of state interests. For instance, Andrew Moravcsik has shown how different interest groups 'compete with one another to

---

[366] See ibid.; emphasis in original.
[367] See ibid.
[368] See ibid.
[369] Dunoff and Pollack, *International Law*, p. 20.
[370] Abbot and Snidal, 'Law, Legalization', p. 34.
[371] Richard H. Steinberg, 'Wanted – Dead or Alive: Realism in International Law' in Jeffrey L. Dunoff and Mark A. Pollack (eds.) *Interdisciplinary Perspectives on International Law and International Relations* (Cambridge: Cambridge University Press, 2013), pp. 146–172 at p. 157.

define the national interest',[372] a view that in terms of its formulation is not very different from that of Morgenthau. This process of determination of national interests does not like the realist approach acknowledge the dominant influence of the 'logic of capital'. The liberal picture neglects the fact that in capitalist dispensations subaltern groups and classes are not able to shape national interests. The proposed collaboration between IR and IL then turns into a means for furthering and legitimizing the interests of the dominant classes in advanced capitalist countries. There are, therefore, justified apprehensions that in ideological terms the IR-IL is an imperial project. As US power declines, and the number of issues that have to be grappled with increase in a complex globalized world, it has to increasingly rely on international legal processes and institutions for sustaining its influence and realizing its 'national interests'.[373] It explains why, as one recent essay notes, 'there are large growing intersections between the fields' that 'are concerned with the design and impact of legal institutions'.[374] The interests of the United States are also being actualized through forging common interpretations and understandings of international laws through the collaboration of network of legal experts and judges. The IR-IL project hopes 'to craft solutions to policy problems in ways integrating legal and political analysis, and dealing with or working around the problematic role of the state'.[375] Slaughter, for instance, contends that a central feature of the new global order is that it replaces the concepts of 'power over' or 'power to' with 'power with'.[376] The concept of 'power with' is a reference to network of experts or non-state actors in a world of disaggregating sovereignty. In short, in the final analysis, the IR-IL initiative, like IR in general, is a US product that, in at least one view, 'cannot but buttress the justification of American hegemony in the world'.[377] It is, therefore, no accident that there is no prominent non-Western voice in the IR-IL project.

On the other hand, the problem with Koskenniemi's advocacy of IL rests on the fuzzy idea of 'culture of formalism'.[378] If the argument is

---

[372] See ibid.
[373] Raffo et al., 'Introduction', p. 16.
[374] Hafner-Burton et al., 'Political Science Research', p. 49.
[375] Raffo et al., 'Introduction', p. 20.
[376] Anne-Marie Slaughter, 'Filling Power Vacuums in the New Global Legal Order', (Symposium Issue) (2013) *Boston College International & Comparative Law Review*, pp. 920–936.
[377] Koskenniemi, *The Gentle Civilizer*, p. 20.
[378] For a detailed discussion of 'culture of formalism', see Chapter 5, pp. 333–344.

that interdisciplinary work per se leads to the marginalization of the language of law, then most of the critical approaches pursue that project without denying law's normativity; there is no particular reason why collaboration with IR alone will have that impact. Koskenniemi's 'culture of formalism' may, therefore, be seen as an attempt at differentiating and distancing itself from the third world, feminist and left approaches even as he seeks to appropriate their moral impulse. The result is that while he speaks of 'empire' Koskenniemi rarely speaks of capitalism other than in historical terms. Like Morgenthau he treats 'imperialism' as a political phenomenon or an ideological position. In contrast to both the mainstream IR-IL approach and Koskenniemi, the third world, feminist and left approaches share Morgenthau's scepticism about IL but *the sources of their scepticism go beyond* the power politics model of Morgenthau. The scepticism is not about the relevance of international law but about its biases which are inter alia a function of the 'logic of capital' and systems of patriarchy. International law has and continues to play a crucial role in the Western capitalist hegemonic project. The third world, feminist and left approaches do not deny that IR-IL or IL-IR scholarship can yield added insights for both the disciplines. The concern is that the IR-IL collaboration, essentially between US (or at best Western) IR and IL academia, may set an agenda that excludes the concerns of subaltern groups and classes in the Global South by, inter alia, leaving out key issues such as the role and influence of transnational capital in international politics.[379] So a central question is the theoretical frame from within which IR-IL collaboration is to take place viz., liberal, constructivist, feminist, third world, Marxist or post-structuralist. Each of these theories approaches IR-IL collaboration in a distinct way. In other words, there are different epistemological and ontological assumptions that inform attempts to advance an IR-IL approach. Some strands facilitate the Western hegemonic project and others seek to contest it. The critical IR-IL project seeks to address from the standpoint of subaltern groups and states the theme of capitalist globalization, imperialism and the increasing legalization and institutionalization of international relations.

---

[379] As has been noted in a recent essay, 'a particular blind spot, especially among political scientists, relates to firms. While transnational firms were central to much earlier work, the more recent literature tends to assume that the roles of firms in international cooperation are limited to a few tasks, such as performing functions that are delegated to them by governments'. Hafner-Burton, 'Political Science Research', p. 95.

VIII.   Conclusion

There are ebbs and flows in the lives of theories as in the lives of men and women. A theory that may be influential in one phase of history can come to be neglected in another but return to haunt those who have disregarded it. The biography of classical realism has followed this course. However, for a theory to be revived it has to be reinvented for new times.[380] It is, therefore, no accident that the rich intellectual lineage of Morgenthau, of which he himself left an account, is today receiving increasing attention. The intellectual sources are being revisited in a bid to give the very basic conceptual apparatus of Morgenthau greater depth. He was after all the ultimate purveyor of common sense realism encapsulated in accessible and aphoristic prose.[381] In order to lend greater credence to classical realism, researchers interested in its revival have turned to Freud, Nietzsche and Weber. But the effort runs the danger of redefining its essentials beyond recognition.[382] And if that risk is seen as unavoidable then there is no reason not to turn to Marx as Morgenthau himself noted the pioneering contribution of Marx to modern sociology.[383] Such an engagement would help lend depth to classical realism in at least two ways. First, it would assist in going beyond biological realism to seeing human nature also as 'an ensemble of social relations'. Second, it would allow greater attention to be paid to the 'logic of capital' and help map the complex linkages between the economic and political spheres and enable the articulation of a multidimensional conception of power and a substantive conception of 'national interest'; or to reverse the argument, if compatible insights from classical realism – flowing especially from the 'logic of territory' – are incorporated into IMAIL it would greatly enrich it.

[380] The intellectual roots of Morgenthau are also being explored in an attempt to address the lament that instead of attempting 'a period piece' like Carr, Morgenthau chose to propound a general theory valid for all times. E. H. Carr, *The Twenty Years Crisis, 1919–1939: An Introduction to the Study of International Relations* (London: Palgrave, 1981), p. viii. In the words of Hedley Bull, 'Carr's work was a polemic addressed to "the urgent task of the day" and disavowed all claims to universal and permanent validity. Morgenthau purported to present a comprehensive theory of all international politics derived from a distillation of its rational elements'. Hedley Bull, 'The Theory of International Politics 1919–1969' in Brian Potter (ed.) *The Aberystwith Papers: International Politics 1919–1969* (London: Oxford University Press, 1972), pp. 30–55 at p. 38.
[381] On 'common sense', see Antonio Gramsci, *Selections from the Prison Notebooks* (London: Wishart, 1971), pp. 323–333, 419–425.
[382] See Jeffrey W. Legro and Andrew Moravcsik, 'Is Anybody Still a Realist?', 25 (1999) *International Security*, pp. 5–55.
[383] Cozette, 'Reclaiming the Critical', p. 8; Morgenthau, 'Intellectual Autobiography', p. 66.

Meanwhile, it can be said that in view of the constraints flowing from his assumptions Morgenthau advanced an impoverished understanding of the history and dynamics of international law. First, since he did not ground his scepticism of the role of international law in the 'logic of capital', the relationship between capitalism, imperialism and the evolution and development of international law remained unexplored. Second, his thesis on indeterminacy of rules was unsustainably linked to the peculiar subject matter of international politics rather than to semantic and structural sources. Third, Morgenthau did not recognize the partisan dimension of international law and its consequences for weak states. This weakness can be traced to the fact that he only concerned himself with high politics leaving out of view the world of subaltern states. Fourth, he did not appropriately conceptualize his dualistic approach to international law. He was discerning enough to see that the role of international law cannot be underestimated, but grounded it in an unexplored and over-elaborated conception of complementary interests. He, therefore, also failed to appreciate the multifarious reasons that induce compliance with rules of international law. Finally, his assumption with regard to the autonomy of the political sphere prevented him from seeing that a universalizing capitalism was in the process of creating a global social formation and a nascent world state constituted by international institutions that could perpetrate violence on the weak and oppressed peoples and nations.

His critique of moralism like that of international law was valuable but again unsatisfying in the final analysis. First, he did not appreciate the intricate linkages between international ethics and international law. Second, his argument that it was the move to democratic responsibility that undermined international morality was unpersuasive as nations can be morally judged in the same way as individuals. What Morgenthau overlooked was that it is the 'logic of capital', of course, in alliance with the 'logic of territory', which presents the biggest hurdle to the conduct of moral international relations. Third, the principle of prudence Morgenthau recommended to evaluate the necessity of political actions depends far too much on the sensitivity and capability of particular leaders. It, therefore, provides little meaningful guidance in practice.[384] Finally, Morgenthau

---

[384] Hoffman, *Janus and Minerva*, p. 78. In the words of Ashley, many of the realist concepts, arguments and knowledge claims are 'too fuzzy, too slippery, too resistant to consistent operational formulation, and, in application, too dependent upon the artful sensitivity of the historically minded and context-sensitive scholar'. Richard K. Ashley, 'The Poverty of Neo-Realism', 38 (1984) *International Organisation*, pp. 225–286 at p. 231.

did not realize that the eventual goal of international morality should be to facilitate the creation of a world without imperialism.

The Morgenthau critique of legalism and moralism was at least one factor in the divorce between the disciplines of IR and IL in the period of the Cold War. With its end, and the acceleration of the globalization process, there are ongoing attempts to bring the disciplines of IR-IL together. There is little doubt that an equal exchange between the two disciplines can generate critical insights into the ways in which the world is changing, especially the implications of the growing role of international law and institutions. But there are genuine apprehensions that the IR-IL approach advanced by IR scholars may turn IL into an appendage of IR. These fears have been sought to be allayed by accepting the need for increased focus on the internal aspects of international law, that is, on its doctrines and distinct modes of argumentation. But what is still missing from the discussion is the question as to which approaches to IR and IL can combine to offer the best way forward. At present, liberal IR theory is seeking to collaborate with those IL approaches that help sustain the US hegemonic agenda. In other words, while there is a need for a debate on the benefits of collaboration between the two disciplines, it also needs to address the crucial question about the meaning and implications of particular approaches coming together. The integrated Marxist approach to international law believes that while the boundaries of IR and IL should be transgressed, it must be in the cause of emancipation of the marginal and oppressed groups and peoples in the world. To this end it would wish to collaborate with critical international relations theories articulated among others by neo-Gramscians, postcolonial theorists and feminists. But it is not known if critical IR theorists are interested in such collaboration. It is certainly time to think about it as each can lend the other insights and methodological tools that can advance the cause of weak groups, peoples and nations.

3

The Policy-Oriented or New Haven Approach to International Law: The Contributions of Myres McDougal and Harold Lasswell

I. Introduction

The policy-oriented approach or the New Haven approach to international law[1] deserves close study for many reasons: its incisive critique of political realism and positivism, its ability to raise vital questions and challenge established doctrines, its stress on the essential relationship between law and policy, its radical thesis on semantic and structural sources of indeterminacy, its articulation of interdisciplinary methods of inquiry for policy analysis, its meticulous investigation of diverse areas of international law,[2] its awareness of the growing interpenetration of international and municipal law, its commitment to the goal of human dignity and world public order, its emphasis on the edifying role of international lawyers,[3]

---

[1] The terms 'policy-oriented' and 'New Haven' approach are used interchangeably in the chapter. The latter was coined by Richard Falk. Richard Falk, *The Status of Law in International Society* (New Haven, CT: Yale University Press, 1970), p. 342. For a bibliography of writings on the policy-oriented approach, see Michael W. Reisman and Burns H. Weston (eds.), *Towards World Order and Human Dignity: Essays in Honour of Myres S. McDougal* (New York: The Free Press, 1976), pp. 587–591.

[2] It has been observed that the total impact of each of the [...] major books or treatise he [i.e., McDougal] co-authored 'was and continues to be magisterial'. Richard A. Falk, Rosalyn C. Higgins, W. Michael Reisman and Burns H. Weston, 'Myres Smith McDougal (1906–1998)', 92 (1998) *American Journal of International Law*, pp. 729–733 at p. 732. Falk has elsewhere observed that 'the jurisprudence's astonishing range of scholarly applications is likely to provide the most resounding vindication of the heroic efforts made by McDougal and Lasswell throughout their long, productive careers. On this secondary level of influence, writers on almost any topic of significance in international law can benefit from and are likely to keep consulting the McDougal treatment of broad subject-matter sectors'. Richard Falk, 'Casting the Spell: The New Haven School of International Law', 104 (1995) *Yale Law Journal*, pp. 1991–2008 at p. 1998.

[3] Hengameh Saberi, 'Descendants of Realism? Policy-Oriented International Lawyers as Guardians of Democracy' in Prabhakar Singh and Benoit Mayer (eds.) *Critical International Law: Postrealism, Postcolonialism, and Transnationalism* (Delhi: Oxford University Press, 2014), pp. 29–52.

and the fact that a host of illustrious names have confessed to being influenced by it.[4]

The policy-oriented approach was the outcome of close collaboration
between Yale professors Myres S. McDougal (1906–1998) and Harold
D. Lasswell (1902–1978), an association that was in the view of Michael
Reisman more productive than the team of Karl Marx and Friedrich
Engels.[5] Insofar as the world of international law is concerned, McDougal
was the principal figure, albeit he used a conceptual apparatus that was
entirely the work of Lasswell the political scientist. The New Haven
approach is today being carried forward principally by Reisman who has
always been seen as 'McDougal's semi-anointed successor'.[6] He is not only
viewed as 'an important contributor to the Lasswell-McDougal jurisprudence' but also 'its clearest articulator'.[7] Indeed, Reisman is said to have
given 'the New Haven School new insights and brought it into the twenty-
first century'.[8] According to Harold Koh, 'as great as McDougal was, it was
Michael [Reisman] who gave the New Haven School its modern relevance
and vitality'.[9] Indeed, there is little doubt that the New Haven approach is
'centered around him today'.[10] The present chapter, however, confines its
discussion to the work of McDougal and Lasswell, albeit including seminal writings of Reisman co-authored with them.

In recent years, there is said to have emerged a 'new' New Haven School
of International Law.[11] According to Koh, it persists with the five core
commitments of the policy-oriented approach even as it adapts them to
the contemporary era viz., 'commitments to theory and interdisciplinarity,

[4] Prominent names include Bill Burke, Lung Chu Chen, Richard Falk, Florento P. Feliciano,
     D. Johnston, Rosalyn Higgins, Morton Kaplan, Nicholas Katzenbach, John Norton Moore,
     B. S. Murty, Jordan Paust, and Burns Weston.
[5] Michael W. Reisman, 'Myres S. McDougal: Architect of a Jurisprudence for a Free Society',
     66 (1996) *Mississippi Law Journal*, pp. 15–26 at p. 17.
[6] Falk, 'Casting the Spell', p. 1998.
[7] Rosalyn Higgins, 'Closing Remarks at the Conference to Honor the Work of Professor
     Michael Reisman', 34 (2009) *Yale Journal of International Law*, pp. 605–613 at p. 613.
[8] Harold Hongju Koh, 'Michael Reisman, Dean of the New Haven School of International
     Law', 34 (2009) *Yale Journal of International Law*, pp. 501–504 at p. 502.
[9] See ibid.
[10] Siegfried Wiessner, 'Law as a Means to a Public Order of Human Dignity: The Jurisprudence
     of Michael Reisman', 34 (2009) *Yale Journal of International Law*, pp. 525–532 at p. 526. For
     a recent contribution of Reisman to the New Haven approach see Michael W. Reisman,
     *The Quest for World Order and Human Dignity in the Twenty-first Century: Constitutive
     Process and Individual Commitment: General Course on Public International Law* (The
     Hague: Hague Academy of International Law, 2012).
[11] Paul Schiff Berman, 'A Pluralist Approach to International Law', 32 (2007) *Yale Journal of
     International Law*, pp. 301–329 at p. 304.

transnationalism, process, normativity, and connecting law and policy through practice and public service'.[12] Laura Dickinson has also identified features that reflect continuity between the 'old' New Haven approach and those who draw on it today. First, as opposed to 'international law skeptics' the new scholarship also 'takes a normative stand' in favour of 'the rule of law, accountability, and human rights'.[13] Second, the new approach continues to take 'a flexible approach to the actors of international law' and 'adopts a practice-oriented study of the norms and processes of international law in action on the ground'.[14] Finally, 'new' New Haven scholars also 'adopt empirical and interdisciplinary approaches to the study of international law not only from political science but also other social science disciplines'.[15]

The 'new' New Haven approach has been associated with among others the work of Koh.[16] It has been observed that 'if there is a "new" New Haven School, then its roots spring in part from Harold Koh's melding of the original New Haven School with the legal pluralism of Robert Cover [another Yale icon]'.[17] He has attempted to refine New Haven School precepts through, inter alia, 'focusing on the ways that domestic legal systems diffusely incorporate, and ultimately come to obey, hard, international law'.[18] But since the Koh approach also goes by the name of the transnational legal process approach,[19] it may not be meaningful to speak of a 'new' New Haven approach.[20] In fact, as Saberi points out, the departures

---

[12] Harold Hongju Koh, 'Is there a "New" New Haven School of International Law', 32 (2007) *Yale Journal of International Law,* pp. 559–573 at p. 565.

[13] Laura A. Dickinson, 'Toward a "New" New Haven School of International Law', 32 (2007) *The Yale Journal of International Law,* pp. 547–552 at p. 549.

[14] See ibid., pp. 549–550.

[15] See ibid., p. 550.

[16] For other names see Dickinson, 'Toward a "new"', pp. 549–551.

[17] Berman, 'Pluralist Approach', p. 309.

[18] Janet Koven Levitt, 'Bottom-Up International Law Making: Reflections on the New Haven School of Law Making', 32 (2007) *Yale Journal of International Law,* pp. 393–420 at p. 416. See in this regard Chapter 2, p....

[19] See Harold Hongju Koh, 'Transnational Legal Process', 75 (1996) *Nebraska Law Review,* pp. 181–207. He however notes therein that 'process inquiries run through the work of Myres McDougal, Harold Lasswell and Michael Reisman at Yale Law School on the world constitutive process of authoritative decision'. See ibid., p. 186. See also Harold Hongju Koh, 'Jefferson Memorial Lecture: Transnational Legal Process After September 11th', 22 (2004) *Berkeley Journal of International Law,* pp. 337–354; Berman, ' Pluralist Approach', p. 304; and Mary Ellen O'Connell, 'New International Legal Process' in Steven R. Ratner and Anne-Marie Slaughter (eds.) *The Methods of International Law* (Washington, DC: American Society of International Law, 2004), pp. 79–109.

[20] Dickinson, 'Toward a "New"', pp. 551–552.

of the 'new approach' from the comprehensive original approach have been such that the 'new' approach 'barely resembles McDougal's policy science except in geographic name'.[21] If many of the so-called 'new' New Haven approaches do not attempt to closely follow the original approach, it is because it is considered, to use the words of Richard Falk, 'too idiosyncratic and demanding'.[22] It is difficult to disagree with this description as the 'old' New Haven approach remains 'enveloped in layers of mystification', a function among other things of the complex form in which it is framed.[23] The old approach was also a product of the Cold War that has

---

[21] Hengameh Saberi, 'Love It or Hate It, but for the Right Reasons: Pragmatism and the New Haven School's International Law of Human Dignity', 35 (2012) *Boston College International and Comparative Law Review*, pp. 59–144 at p. 65.

[22] Falk, 'Casting the Spell', p. 1997; see also Saberi, 'Love It or Hate It', p. 63.

[23] Saberi, 'Love It or Hate It', p. 59. Here perhaps a comment on McDougal's opaque form and style is in order. In evaluating any theory it is important that its content and form be considered together for you can often 'discern part of what a theory means by examining not only what it says but also how it says this'. Alvin W. Gouldner, *The Coming Crisis of Western Sociology* (New York: Basic Books, 1972), p. 199. In other words, style and substance possess a dialectical unity. Ignoring this element of interpenetration would be to miss out on a significant base of analysis. The form in which a framework or arguments are articulated, it may be added, can often go to determine the substance. For instance, where the content is encapsulated within an obscure form the critic could always be accused of misconstruing the content since the precise determination of what is actually said is perforce left to the author. Conversely, since it is imprecise and cumbersome, each scholar or policy maker could seek to interpret it as it best suits his purpose. Several perceptive scholars have noted these failings in McDougal's presentation. In fact, there are few reviews of his books or writings which do not refer to their often incomprehensible style. But there are others who have come to his defence. Falk, who is otherwise critical of the policy-oriented approach, has sought to defend it against the charge of obscurity of form. He points out that 'it is much more reassuring to reject a difficult author's book *ab initio* than to do so after a careful reading'. He submits that 'it is an insidious form of anti-intellectualism to insist that legal analysis can always be carried on in a fashion that allows its meaning to be evident to the uninitiated or hurried reader'. Moreover, he argues that the stylistic criticism is 'unfounded' since 'McDougal tries to achieve clear and precise expression. His sentences are almost always impossible to improve upon'. Richard Falk, *The Status of Law in International Society* (Princeton, NJ: Princeton University Press, 1970), p. 658. Falk's defence overlooks the fact that it is not the uninitiated reader alone who levies the charge. For instance, Sir Gerald Fitzmaurice in his well-known review *of Interpretation of Agreements and World Public Order,* observed that, 'it is written in a highly esoteric private language ... which renders large tracts of it virtually incomprehensible ... the reader, professional though he may be ... will be frequently be left with a feeling of honest doubt as to whether he has really – or fully – grasped the intended significance of what he has been reading'. He hastened to add that 'these strictures are not merely the carpings of a disgruntled reviewer forced for once to study and reflect, instead of only to skim and to scold', and proceeded to demonstrate it. He went on to conclude, perhaps harshly, that the 'linguistic esotericism' is 'in fact a deliberately employed technique'. Sir Gerald Fitzmaurice, 'Vae Victis or, Woe to the Negotiators! Your Treaty or our "Interpretation" of it?', 65 (1971)

long since ended.[24] In that era the primary objective of the New Haven approach was the defence of the actions of advanced Western capitalist

American Journal of International Law, pp. 358–373, pp. 360 and 361. However, even sympathetic reviewers of his works like Lissitzyn had pointed out that 'there is verbosity and needless repetition'. Oliver J. Lissitzyn, 'Book Review', 76 (1962–1963) Harvard Law Review, pp. 668–72 at p. 672. While it is true to say that it is insidious anti-intellectualism to always demand a product which is readily understandable it would not be wrong for the careful reader to expect the rewards to be commensurate with the labours expended. Here reading McDougal one is often reminded of the sentiments of Friedmann who speaking of the complex methodology and terminology of the school recalled 'the fable of the Sclaraffenland, where the visitor has to eat through a thick wall of rice before entering into the gourmet's paradise, where roast pigeons and other exquisite delicacies fly into his mouth'. Wolfgang Friedmann, 'Book Review', 64 (1944)Columbia Law Review, pp. 606–15 at p. 609. Finally, the fact that there are those who do not have the patience to give McDougal's cumbersome and voluminous works a careful reading is a double-edged sword. While it could mean ignorant criticism, it as well shields the author from adverse criticism of a large number of fellow travellers. Some of his contemporaries found his works fascinating precisely because they were unable to penetrate them, and yet overawed by the man and his standing within the international legal community were not too unwilling to glorify them. There were also other factors that gave McDougal his standing. Speaking of the pre-retirement, McDougal Eugene Rostow noted that there were not one but three McDougals: 'the first of these was [the only one which interests us here] Senator McDougal who was the spider at the center of a worldwide Old Boy network which was the marvel of the age. It dealt with the very stuff of power-appointments, promotions, honors, the makeup of key committees, assistance to a brother or sister in difficulty for the moment. A sabbatical, let us say, in Bangkok? The Deanship, hypothetically at Freiberg, or Florida, or Cornell? A grant and a visiting appointment to tide over a period of political turbulence at home? Appointment to the staff or even higher reaches of a federal government? Nothing was simpler.' Eugene V. Rostow, 'Afterword' in Reisman and Weston (eds.), Towards World Order, pp. 562–78 at p. 563. There is as well little doubt that his association with the Yale Law School contributed immensely to the acceptance and standing of his works. He had access to first rate students who were soon placed in important positions and able to win formal adherence to his approach. It is perhaps not without significance that it is largely those who had been his students (or their students in turn) who espoused the policy-oriented approach. Here Alvin Gouldner's observation on Talcott Parsons is quite appropriate: 'Because of its difficulty the work must be given an "interpretation". Its interpretation and understanding are, in part, dependent upon a personal acquaintance with the author, and knowledge of it often implies a special relation to him ... The very difficulty of interpreting the new doctrine heightens inter-communication among the first adherents, and this, along with its new, membership-symbolising vocabulary, draws them together into an intellectual community.' Gouldner, Coming Crisis, p. 202. Lastly, the fact that McDougal had always supported the foreign policy establishment policies won him its gratitude. However, it would be petty and churlish to assign these reasons alone for his eminence overlooking the immense contribution he made to the study of international law. It would also be absurd to discount their importance only because they are couched often in an opaque form and style. It is keeping this in view that a footnote has been chosen as the vehicle for making the foregoing comments.

[24] For a general discussion of the question as 'to what extent did the US geopolitical rivalry with communism (of various sorts) actually shape particular kinds of social-scientific

states against the socialist bloc countries and its third world allies. That context is no longer relevant today.

On the other hand, unlike the 'new' New Haven approaches, the original policy-oriented approach offers a comprehensive approach that is accompanied by matching ontological and epistemological premises. It potentially takes into account all the five logics that co-constitute world order even if in an unsatisfactory way viz., 'logic of capital', 'logic of territory', 'logic of Nature', 'logic of culture' and 'logic of law'. The fact that the 'old' New Haven approach is still considered valuable shows the continuing vitality of its method and vision.[25] The end of the Cold War offers the adherents of the policy-oriented approach the opportunity to articulate a jurisprudence that breaks away from the parochial understanding of 'human dignity' advanced by McDougal and Lasswell through focusing on the cause of subaltern groups, peoples and nations. After all, as Koh has reminded, the New Haven approach 'began life as a critical school'.[26] From this perspective, Falk, one of McDougal's outstanding students, and a critic of the extant liberal world order, can be seen as the true inheritor of the New Haven approach, with Reisman continuing to defend a bourgeois world order.[27] It will be argued that if the policy-oriented approach is to take a progressive turn its advocates will have to revisit its methods and commitments which were influenced by Cold War politics.[28] In this regard, the policy-oriented approach will need to take cognizance of alternative approaches to international law and world order articulated in recent times such as TWAIL, FtAIL and NAIL. Unless the policy-oriented approach spells out its response to the key issues raised by these three approaches, it cannot hope to reinvent itself for new times.[29]

activity during this period, as opposed to merely providing an *idiom* for work that might have taken place otherwise?', see Nils Gilman, 'The Cold War as Intellectual Force Field', (First View Article) (2015) *Modern Intellectual History*, pp. 1–17, at p. 7.

[25] The New Haven approach has also travelled east to Hong Kong where there is an annual event on the New Haven approach and its applications to a whole variety of contemporary problems. The Fifth International Conference on the New Haven approach jointly organized by the City University of Hong Kong's ('CityU') School of Law and Yale Law School was held at City University of Hong Kong on 17 and 18 September 2013. See www.hk-lawyer.org/en/article.asp?articleid=1516&c=136 (accessed 26 November 2015).

[26] Koh, 'Is There a "New"', p. 561.

[27] During the course of the Cold War McDougal was critical of Falk's work. See Myres S. McDougal, 'International Law and the Future', 50 (1979) *Mississippi Law Journal*, pp. 259–334 at pp. 263, 275.

[28] Eisuke Suzuki, 'The New Haven School of International Law: An Invitation to a Policy Oriented Jurisprudence', 1 (1974), *Yale Studies in World Public Order*, pp. 1–48 at p. 8.

[29] In this regard it also needs to heed the voice of the proponents of 'new legal realism' who believe that while the New Haven approach was 'an important precursor' for 'approaching

In this backdrop, the present chapter seeks to explore, analyse and critique from an IMAIL perspective, basic elements that go to constitute the policy-oriented approach. It especially focuses on the New Haven conception of law, its theses on indeterminacy of rules, and the theoretical and conceptual framework it advances to perform the intellectual tasks of jurisprudence and analyse the international process of decision making. The chapter proceeds as follows. In Section II an attempt is made to clarify and understand the policy-oriented conception of international law in the matrix of its critique of political realism and positivism and its borrowings and departures from American legal realism.

It is followed by a critical review in Section III of the position of policy-oriented approach on the semantic and structural sources of indeterminacy of rules that centrally informs its radical rule scepticism. It is argued that its theses on indeterminacy are difficult to sustain. Relying on the work of Ludwig Wittgenstein, J. L. Austin and others an attempt is made to demonstrate how the claim of semantic indeterminacy of rules is flawed. The section also goes on to look at the claim of structural indeterminacy and suggests that this charge is also exaggerated. The critique of policy-oriented approach lays the basis for the IMAIL understanding of interpretation of rules in Chapter 7.

Section IV outlines the intellectual tasks of jurisprudence that the policy-oriented approach prescribes viz., the clarification of goal values, the description of past trends in decision, the analysis of conditions affecting decision, the projection of future trends in decision, and the invention and evaluation of policy alternatives, and assesses the objectivity with which these are carried out. A thorough critique of the manner in which policy-oriented approach undertakes these tasks would require a separate tome as it calls for extensive engagement with social and political theory, especially the wide-ranging work of Lasswell. What is offered instead are broad observations pointing to some obvious weaknesses in the mode of analysis.[30] Broadly speaking, it is contended that the intellectual tasks that the policy-oriented approach recommends are carried out from an observational standpoint that neglects to review international law from class, gender and race perspectives. Further, while the policy-oriented

---

international law in an empirical and pragmatist vein', the 'New Legal Realism is distinct in its greater attention to and use of empirics'. Gregory Schaffer, 'The New Legal Realist Approach to International Law', 28 (2015) *Leiden Journal of International Law*, pp. 189–210 at p. 198.

[30] However, many of the themes considered are the subject of comment in other chapters. Readers may wish to consult the index in this regard.

approach is comprehensive enough to take cognizance of all five logics viz., 'logic of capital', 'logic of territory', 'logic of nature', 'logic of culture' and 'logic of law' that co-constitute world order, it is unable to success-fully explain and encompass the linkages between these logics. A prin-cipal reason is that the intellectual tasks were performed with a central focus on the Cold War which dictated complete opposition to Marxism. The policy-oriented approach therefore refused to accept the relative pri-macy of the 'logic of capital' and saw any attempt to do so as lapsing into 'economic determinism'.[31] Indeed, the policy-oriented approach wished to advance a theory which was as comprehensive as Marxism but with features that legitimized the Western liberal democratic framework.

Section V submits that given the inadequacies that inform the per-formance of the intellectual tasks, the detailed map and operation of the international decision-making process the policy-oriented approach offers – described in terms of participants, perspectives, situations, base values, strategies, outcomes and effects – is compromised. It ends up advancing a surfeit of concepts and categories that yield a vast amount of empirical materials that is not meaningful in the absence of any organizing principle(s). Its emphasis on the role of individuals, as against the reform of structures that constrain the realization of the goal of human dignity, does not allow the policy-oriented approach to advance a notion of power that offers serious guidance to participants on the choices to be made. In fact, the concept of power it deploys conceals the impact of dominant social, economic and political structures on the decision-making process.

Section VI discusses by way of illustration how the flaws in the policy-oriented approach lead to troubling views with regard to the most valued principle of contemporary international law viz., the principle of non-use of force in international relations.

Section VII contains some final remarks. These reflect on the principal weaknesses of the New Haven approach and the way forward in terms of articulating a progressive version of it.

II. Conception of Law and Function of Rules

In an effort to carve out a distinct identity for the policy-oriented approach McDougal advanced a critique of other approaches to international law,

---

[31] In the analysis to follow, the vocabulary of 'logics' is rarely used. But in reading the chap-ter readers could benefit by keeping these in mind. For a discussion of the 'five logics' see Chapter 1, pp. 30–35.

both past and present.[32] He was however most stridently opposed to the views of political realism and positivism that had dominated the field in the period after the Second World War.[33]

A.   Critique of Political Realism

McDougal disagreed in a fundamental way with the thinking of political realists like Hans Morgenthau who in his view essentially emphasized the pursuit of national interest through the use of naked power.[34] The McDougal critique of classical realism was at least six-fold. First, it worked with 'untested assumptions about the immutable nature of man'.[35] Second, classical realism was overly focused on the state actor to the neglect of other participants in international relations that included political parties, private corporations and international organizations. In McDougal's view these non-state actors were shaping in crucial ways the world social and legal process.[36] Third, the classical realist conception of power came 'perilously close to simple physical force'.[37] In its place McDougal suggested a 'more comprehensive notion of power' that included control over resources and wealth.[38] Fourth, classical realism neglected the growing 'interdependence' between peoples which made 'any conception of "national interest", apart from the interest of most of the peoples of the world, the sheerest of illusions'.[39] Fifth, the classical realist conception of law was confined to rules and its validity made dependent on the availability of the sanction of naked force.[40] In contrast, McDougal

---

[32] For a critique of theories about law, see Myres S. McDougal, Harold D. Lasswell and W. Michael Reisman, 'Theories about International Law: Prologue to a Configurative Jurisprudence', 8 (1968) *Virginia Journal of International Law*, pp. 188–299 at pp. 207ff. McDougal et al. divide theories about law into six groups: 'the non-law frame, the transempirical and metaphysical naturalistic frame, the historical frame, the analytical frame, the sociologistic frame, and the limited-factor frame'. See ibid.

[33] Berman, 'Pluralist Approach', p. 321.

[34] Levitt, 'Bottom-up', at p. 396.

[35] McDougal, Lasswell and Reisman, 'Theories about International Law', p. 212.

[36] Myres McDougal, 'Law and Power', 46 (1952) *The American Journal of International Law*, pp. 102–114 at p. 108.

[37] See ibid., p. 104. He observed that in view of the fact that in realism 'power processes are considered apart from the variables which affect the choices of various decision-makers and from the consequences of particular decisions upon other value processes, the understanding even of power is ... minimal'. Myres S. McDougal, 'The Realist Theory in Pyrrhic Victory', 49 (1955) *American journal of International Law*, pp. 376–378 at p. 378.

[38] McDougal, 'Law and Power', p. 107.

[39] McDougal, 'Law and Power', p. 109.

[40] See ibid., p. 110.

described the legal process in an inclusive manner assigning a secondary place to rules in the international legal order which could be enforced through a variety of means. Sixth, as compared to the classical realist view, McDougal assigned a greater role to international morality in the conduct of international relations.[41] The McDougal critique of political realism was extremely powerful.[42] However, in one respect the policy-oriented approach was no different from classical realism. McDougal like Morgenthau before him did not concern himself with the non-Western world; both were preoccupied with the high politics of the Cold War. Their lack of interest in the non-Western world goes to show the validity of the lament of postcolonial theory that social science theories can be formulated and advanced without any familiarity and engagement with the non-Western world.

B.   Critique of Positivism

McDougal was as critical of the positivist approach to international law as he was of classical realism. He was perturbed that positivism also unduly emphasized the place of rules in the international legal system. The rule scepticism of the policy-oriented approach had its roots in two different sources: first, it derived inspiration from the pragmatic stance of American legal realism that law should be seen as a means and not an end in itself. Second, it relied on theories of semantics, syntactic and commu-nication to contend that indeterminacy is a pervasive characteristic of a rule, and therefore, the conceptualization of law in terms of rules is not very meaningful. These dual sources of rule scepticism led McDougal to conclude that the intellectual task of jurisprudence should not be confined to merely determining the meaning and application of rules but to clarify and postulate policy goals accompanied by a realistic map of the inter-national decision-making process through which these can be realized. In fact as Reisman has observed, 'the Copernican Revolution in McDougal's jurisprudence was in unseating rules as the mechanism of decision.'[43]

---

[41] For instance, he spoke of the United Nations and associated projects as 'compelling evi-dence of moral perspectives that today transcend the boundaries of nation states'. See ibid., p. 112.

[42] It can today be extended to 'neo-conservative, nationalist critique of international law' advanced by among others Jack Goldsmith and Eric Posner. See Levitt, 'Bottom-up', p. 395; Jack L. Goldsmith and Eric A. Posner, *The Limits of International Law* (New York: Oxford University Press, 2005).

[43] W. Michael Riesman, 'Theory about Law: Jurisprudence for a Free Society', 108 (1999) *The Yale Law Journal*, pp. 935–939 at p. 937.

At this point, the policy-oriented approach went beyond American legal realism with whose confined understanding of the role of lawyers McDougal was not entirely satisfied. But, to begin with, American legal realism played an important role in alerting McDougal to the weaknesses of the positivist approach. A distinctive feature of the American legal realist movement was the functionalist stance it adopted. Its philosophical underpinnings were provided by pragmatism, summed up in the aphorism 'the life of law has not been logic but experience'.[44] It engendered a 'distrust of traditional legal rules and concepts' insofar as they purported to describe living law. To that view was counterposed a 'conception of law in flux, of moving law', with emphasis 'on evaluation of any part of law in terms of its effects, and an insistence on the worthwhileness of trying to find these effects'.[45] The resultant position that law is a means to an end provided a release from what was deemed a sterile debate about the definition of law. In other words, American legal realism offered to McDougal an escape from the narrow normative approach of traditional jurisprudence by allowing attention to be focused on the consequences of law for social behaviour.[46] It is the 'revolt against formalism' that inspired McDougal's harsh criticism of positivism.[47] According to him, 'the most fundamental obscurity in contemporary theory about international law secretes itself in over-emphasis, by most writers and many decision-makers, upon the potentialities of technical "legal" rules, unrelated to policies, as factors and instruments in the guiding and shaping of decisions'.[48] The critique was two-dimensional: of the function of jurists on the one hand and of the centrality of rules on the other. The pure theory of law of Hans Kelsen formed the perfect subject of this critique as it confined the function of legal scholars to the 'syntactic clarification' of

---

[44] The confluence of the realist movement and pragmatism is symbolized by Oliver Wendell Holmes whose association with C. S. Pierce and William James is well known. See generally Catherine P. Wells, 'Legal Innovation within the Wider Intellectual Tradition: The Pragmatism of Oliver Wendell Holmes, Jr', 82 (1988) *Northwestern University Law Review*, pp. 541–595; Jerome Frank, 'A Conflict with Oblivion: Some Observations on the Founders of Legal Pragmatism', (1954) Faculty Scholarship Series. Paper 4092. Accessed at http://digitalcommons.law.yale.edu/cgi/viewcontent.cgi?article=5109&context=fss_papers

[45] Karl Llewellyn, 'Some Realism about Realism', in *Jurisprudence: Realism in Theory and Practice* (Chicago, IL: The University of Chicago Press, 1962), pp. 42–76 at pp. 55–57.

[46] Alan Hunt, *The Sociological Movement in Law* (London: Macmillan, 1978), p. 48.

[47] W. Twining, 'The Significance of Realism', in Lord Lloyd of Hampstead and M. D. A. Freeman (eds.), *Lloyd's Introduction to Jurisprudence*, 5th edn (London: Stevens and Sons, 1985), p. 777.

[48] Myres S. McDougal, 'International Law, Power and Policy: A Contemporary Conception', 1 (1953) *Recueil des Cours*, pp. 137–258 at p. 143.

rules and their relationships. The jurist was 'regarded as neither author-ized nor qualified seriously to consider either the social context in which rules are generated or the socio-political consequences which rules, in turn, engendered in specific instances of application'.[49] According to the pure theory of law, the jurists' task was 'to apply the law as it is, after deter-mining if it is and what it is'.[50] This view of the role of legal scholars was, according to McDougal, 'at best irrelevant and at worst a guide to the magnification of the semi-relevant dimensions of law in the world com-munity'.[51] For McDougal, 'an interdisciplinary approach and an interdis-ciplinary jurisprudence offer[ed] the only effective means for delimiting and managing an area of inquiry which bristles with interdisciplinary problems.'[52] He, therefore, emphasized the essential relationship between law and policy and went on to observe that 'in the process of decision-making in the world arena, the technical rules that constitute the *lex lata* are continually being defined and redefined in the application of policy to ever-changing facts: in ever-changing contexts.'[53] In this formulation, the conception of law in flux found an expression that, as against the positiv-ist view, seriously discounts the operative role of rules in the international legal system. As Wiesner and Willard have noted positivism provided 'the counter-image' to policy-oriented school's 'empirical, dynamic concep-tion of law'.[54] From a policy-oriented perspective 'positivism remains fix-ated on the past, trying to reap from words laid down, irrespective of the context in which they were written, the solution to a problem that arises today or tomorrow in very different circumstances.'[55] The opposition to positivism has been articulated in an even sharper tone by Reisman who on one occasion observed as follows:

> The notion of law as a body of rules, existing independently of decision makers and unchanged by their actions, is a necessary *part of the intellec-tual and ideological equipment of the political inferior.* It makes no sense in a jurisprudence which conceives of law as a process in which human

[49] McDougal, Lasswell and Reisman, 'Theories about International Law', p. 243.
[50] See ibid.
[51] McDougal, Lasswell and Reisman, 'Theories about International Law', p. 260.
[52] Myres S. McDougal and W. Michael Reisman, 'The Changing Structure of International Law: Unchanging Theory for Inquiry', 65 (1965) *Columbia Law Review,* pp. 810–846 at pp. 810–811.
[53] McDougal, 'International Law, Power and Policy ', p. 156.
[54] Siegfried Wiessner and Andrew R. Willard, 'Policy-Oriented Jurisprudence and Human Rights Abuses in Internal Conflict: Toward a World Public Order of Human Dignity' in Ratner and Slaughter (eds.), *Methods of International Law,* pp. 47–79 at p. 52.
[55] See ibid.

beings try to influence the way social choices are made about the production and distribution of the things that they want, including considerations about the ways in which those decisions should be made.[56]

In the event, it is not very clear as to what role rules play in the policy-oriented approach. According to Rosalyn Higgins, rules do play a part but not an exclusive part in the policy-oriented approach.[57] But the Reisman position appears to see rules as an unnecessary constraint in the realization of common interests.

C.   Critique of American Legal Realism

That McDougal's views are more in accord with Reisman becomes clear when the reasons for his dissatisfaction with American legal realism are considered. McDougal observed that while legal realism performed a crucial role in contesting many of the key assumptions of analytical positivism, it failed to advance 'a positive systematic theory of its own'.[58] The McDougal critique of legal realism has been conveniently summarized by Reisman in terms of its 'six major mistakes'[59]:

> First, in their search for predicting how decisions would be made, they were still locked in the essential passivity of Positivism. They were predicting what someone else would do [i.e., courts]... Second, in their focus on courts or on the application of law, Realists were ignoring all the components of decisions-pre-law making, law-making, law-terminating, law appraisal-that preceded and followed courts and other institutions of application ... Third, in their focus on law, Realists were overlooking what political and legal struggles were about: life opportunities or 'values.' ... Fourth, in their focus on legal institutions, Realists were giving insufficient attention to the continuing impact of the rich dynamism of context and, in particular, to the role of power on decisions ... Fifth, in their focus on legal institutions, Realists did not grasp that the maintenance or adjustment of the institutions themselves was part of every decision and that

---

[56] W. Michael Reisman, 'The View from the New Haven School of International Law', 86 (1992) *American Society of International Law Proceedings*, pp. 118–125, at p. 121; emphasis added.

[57] Rosalyn Higgins, 'Integrations of Authority and Control: Trends in the Literature of International Law and International relations' in Reisman and Weston (eds.), *Towards World Order*, pp. 79–94 at p. 83.

[58] McDougal, Lasswell and Reisman, 'Theories about International Law', p. 261; Harold D. Lasswell and Myres S. McDougal, 'Criteria for a Theory about Law', 44 (1970–71) *Southern California Law Review*, pp. 362–394 at p. 373.

[59] W. Michael Reisman, 'Theory about Law: Jurisprudence about a Free Society', 108 (1999) *Yale Law Journal*, pp. 935–939 at p. 936.

the 'institutions and structures,' as political scientists called them, were products of an ongoing constitutive process ... Sixth, in their focus on the United States, Realists were ignoring the inevitable global dimension of influence and the impact of apparently local decisions.[60]

McDougal attempted to address these weaknesses by advancing a jurisprudence that was 'truly contextual, problem oriented, and multimethod'.[61] He made four principal moves to transcend the limits of legal realism in the world of international law, in particular its inability to move beyond the critique of positivism.

First, in order to address its acceptance of the 'passivity of positivism' and ensuing neglect of values that are at the basis of legal and political struggles, McDougal stressed the need for a conception of law and legal process that is explicitly concerned with the distribution of values in social systems. In the policy oriented view 'fundamentally, international law is a process by which the peoples of the world clarify and implement their common interests in the shaping and sharing of values'.[62] By 'common interests' McDougal meant interests 'whose fulfillment would benefit the entire community and which are held in common by most effective elites'.[63] In contrast, 'special interests' are 'demands made by only some effective elites, whose fulfillment will benefit only one segment of the community with a corresponding deprivation to the rest'.[64] The essential aim of pursuing 'common interests' is to promote the value of human dignity which anticipates 'a social process in which values are widely not narrowly shared, and in which private choice, rather than coercion, is emphasized as the predominant modality of power'.[65] The values at stake are identified as power, enlightenment, wealth, well-being, skill, affection, respect and rectitude. The realization of the goal of human dignity on the

[60] See ibid., pp. 936–937.
[61] Harold D. Lasswell, 'Introduction' in Reisman and Weston (eds.), *Towards World Order*, pp. xiii–xviii at p. xvi.
[62] Myres S. McDougal, Harold D. Lasswell and W. Michael Reisman, 'The World Constitutive Process of Authoritative Decision', 19 (1967) *Journal of Legal Education*, pp. 253–300 at p. 275.
[63] See ibid., p. 276. Further, as among the common interests, a distinction is made 'between those which are inclusive, in the sense that they may be enjoyed by all in the same modality (such as with respect to access to the oceans or the air-space over the oceans) and those which are exclusive in the sense that all may have comparable interests but not in precisely the same modality (such as with respect to the enjoyment of internal waters or of a territorial sea)'. McDougal and Reisman, 'Changing Structure', p. 814.
[64] See McDougal, Lasswell and Reisman, 'The World Constitutive Process'.
[65] Myres S. McDougal and Associates, *Studies in World Public Order* (New Haven, CT: Yale University Press, 1960) p. 16.

international plane required 'founding and maintaining minimum public order, in the sense of striving to eliminate the use of unauthorized coercion and violence; and in advancing toward an optimum public order, in terms of establishing and sustaining decision processes through which an ever-accumulating and wider enjoyment of values is realized'.[66]

Second, McDougal conceived of the legal process and law at a level of abstraction that was comprehensive enough to encompass its different phases, contexts and dimensions. He described law and the legal process as 'the making of authoritative and controlling decisions': 'Authority is the structure of expectation concerning who, with what qualification and mode of selection, is competent to make which decisions by what criteria and what procedures. By control we refer to an effective voice in decision, whether authorized or not. The conjunction of common expectations concerning authority with a high degree of corroboration in actual operation is what we understand by law'.[67]

The combination of elements of authority and control are necessary for 'when decisions are authoritative but not controlling, they are not law but pretense' and 'when decisions are controlling but not authoritative, they are not law but naked power'.[68] There is, of course, nothing particularly novel in arguing that decisions are authoritative when they possess legitimacy and controlling when they are effective. What was distinct in the McDougal approach was the conceptualization of 'authority' and 'control' in an inclusive manner, so as to encompass different 'components of decisions-pre-law making, law-making, law-terminating, law appraisal' and to move the concept of law beyond the world of rules so as to facilitate

---

[66] Wiessner and Willard, 'Policy-Oriented Jurisprudence', p. 61.

[67] McDougal and Associates, *Studies*, pp. 13–14. Elsewhere they write: 'Law will be regarded not merely as rules or as isolated decision, but as a continuous *process* of authoritative decision, including both the constitutive and public order decisions by which a community's policies are made and remade.' Lasswell and McDougal, 'Criteria for a Theory', p. 382.

[68] Lasswell and McDougal, 'Criteria for a Theory', p. 384. As Wiessner and Willard explain: 'For policy-oriented jurisprudence, only those decisions, i.e., communications with *policy* (or prescriptive) *content*, that are taken from communitywide perspectives of *authority* and backed up by *control* intent, are characterized as law. These are decisions that are made by the persons who are expected to make them, in accordance with criteria expected by community members, in established structures of authority, with sufficient bases in effective power to secure consequential control, and by authorized procedures. Compliance with the policy content of authoritative decision promises and/or generates significant benefits or indulgences in terms of any or all values; noncompliance is sanctioned by the threat and/or imposition of sever deprivations, again, in terms of any or all values.' Wiessner and Willard, 'Policy-Oriented Jurisprudence', p. 52; emphasis in original.

the determination that acts and omissions that help in the realization of 'common interests' are in accord with law.[69]

Third, McDougal stressed that law and policy cannot be separated not merely at the stage of law appraisal but at any stage (i.e., law making or law termination) of the legal process if goal values were to be realized. By policy McDougal meant 'the consequences of choice and decisions upon the values of individual human beings'.[70] He argued that 'the assessment of so-called extralegal considerations *is part of the legal process . . . There is no avoiding the essential relationship between law and politics*'.[71] In lieu of the intimate relationship between law and policy at all stages of the legal process, the policy- oriented approach worked 'toward a valid integration of "law and social sciences"' explaining the collaboration between McDougal and Lasswell.[72] It emphasized in this regard that the arrival of appropriate policies, including the identification of goals to be pursued, should be seen as an empirical and scientific enterprise.[73] Further, it endeavoured to locate authoritative decisions 'in the broader context of international relations',[74] allowing the New Haven approach to go beyond legal realism's

---

[69] In order to redress the failure of legal realists to appreciate that constituting, maintaining and adjusting legal institutions was part of the task of the legal process, McDougal identified two types of authoritative decisions termed 'constitutive' and 'public order' decisions: 'There are the decisions that establish [the] process of authoritative decision. These may be called *constitutive decisions*, decisions that say who the established decision-makers are and what the basic community policies are, decisions that create structures of authority, allocate bases of power, and specify the procedures that must be followed for a legal decision to emerge. The decisions that come out of this constitutive process may be described as *public order decisions*. They regulate every value process in the community, how wealth is shaped and shared, how health is protected, how education is fostered and shared, and so on through all the categories of values that a community may cherish.' Myres McDougal, 'Law and Minimum World Public Order: Armed Conflict in Larger Context', 3 (1984) *Pacific Basin Law Journal*, pp. 21–34 at p. 22. Ideally speaking, the aim of both constitutive and public order decisions is to advance 'common interests'. There are similar formulations with slight variations in his numerous writings. For instance, the process of authoritative decision is said to encompass 'constitutive decisions' 'which identify and characterize the different authoritative decision-makers, specify and clarify basic community policies, establish appropriate structures of authority, allocate bases of power for sanctioning purposes, authorize procedures for the different kinds of decisions, and determine the various modalities by which the law is made and applied'. McDougal, Lasswell and Reisman, 'Theories about International Law', p. 203.

[70] Myres S. McDougal and Michael W. Reisman, 'Harold Dwight Lasswell (1902–1978)', 73 (1979) *American Journal of International Law*, pp. 655–660 at p. 655.

[71] Higgins, 'Integrations of Authority', pp. 79–94 at p. 85.

[72] See ibid.

[73] See generally Anne Orford, 'Scientific Reason and the Discipline of International Law', 25 (2014) *European Journal of International Law*, pp. 369–385 at p. 379.

[74] McDougal and Reisman, 'Changing Structure', at p. 812

focus on the United States to stress the growing interdependence between peoples and nations. Indeed, McDougal can be seen as a pioneer of the international relations-international law (IR-IL) approach that has been advanced by Anne-Marie Slaughter, Kenneth Abbott and others.[75]

Fourth, in order to address legal realism's failure to take into account the 'continuing impact of the rich dynamism of context' and also the impact of 'role of power on decisions', McDougal distinguished between the role of the scholar and the decision maker. In the policy-oriented view, the scholar 'is thought to be preoccupied with aggregating the knowledge relevant to reaching the most informed decision, while the decision maker is conditioned by the dimension of power'.[76] In this light it prescribes two types of tasks for the scholar. The first is the performance of intellectual tasks that include the clarification of the goals of decision; description of the trends towards or away from the realization of these goals; analysis of the constellation of conditioning factors that appear to have affected past decision; projection of probable future developments, assuming no influence by the observer; and formulation of particular alternatives and strategies that contribute, at minimum net cost and risk, to the realization of preferred goals.[77] The second task involves the use of an 'analytic method for revealing the finer structure of any problem situation'.[78] Towards this end, the international decision-making process is to be examined through the analytic method by reference to the categories participants, perspectives, situations, base values, strategies and outcomes. Both these tasks are critically reviewed later in the chapter.

D.   Summing Up: Relationship of Law and Policy

In essence what the New Haven approach does is to offer a non-traditional conception of law and legal process and using the methods and materials of social sciences allows all relevant environmental factors to be taken into account and systematically analysed in the pursuit of 'common interest'. It is a separate question whether McDougal was successful in integrating law and social sciences. In the view of Oran Young, McDougal's contributions in this direction were '*not* particularly impressive' as he was not 'fully abreast of contemporary work in the social sciences' that

---

[75] For a discussion of the IR-IL approach see Chapter 2, pp. 93–101.
[76] Falk, 'Casting the Spell', p. 1992.
[77] McDougal, Lasswell and Reisman, 'Theories about International Law', p. 197.
[78] Wiessner and Willard, 'Policy-Oriented Jurisprudence', p. 58.

pertained to his work.[79] This view will be substantiated later in this chapter in the process of reviewing the manner in which McDougal performed the dual tasks he set international law scholars. What needs to be stressed here is that while correctly opposing the separation of law and policy McDougal all but obliterates the distinction between the two. In the New Haven approach it is not the rejection of the positivist or pure theory that is new, or the concern to take into account the sociological matrix within which international law evolves. What is new is the perception of the international legal process as an indistinguishable segment of the world social and political processes that unfold in particular (often special) arenas with specific conditions defining the nature of participation of actors with the goal of promoting human dignity. In other words, the legal process is not seen as a distinctive process which possesses its own internal structure, logic and dynamics. From within the New Haven framework an opposition between law and policy is meaningless inasmuch as the two are not distinguished. As Young observed:

> when law is defined in terms of the making of effective and authoritative decisions concerning the distribution of values in a society, the concept tends to lose discriminatory power for many purposes. That is, this conception encourages the inclusion of so much under the heading of law as a matter of definition that it often becomes difficult to identify law in a parsimonious fashion and then to analyze the connections between law and various other aspects of a social system without arriving at conclusions that are true by definition.[80]

To put it differently, McDougal's conception of law makes law an ever 'moving target', explaining the impatience with any conception of a legal system that assigns rules even a mildly important role.[81] As Wolfgang Friedmann noted:

> The basic ambiguity in the McDougal approach to the contemporary system of international law is uncertainty over the extent to which all international law is subject to requirements of policy. Obviously, if policy objectives are permitted to be the wholly controlling factor in the determination of the legitimacy or illegitimacy of a certain state action, international law as a minimum order binding upon all states ceases to have any meaning whatsoever, even as a system of 'positive morality' in the Austinian sense.[82]

---

[79] Oran R. Young, 'International Law and Social Science: The Contributions of Myres S. McDougal', 66 (1972) *American Journal of International Law*, pp. 60–76 at p. 63.
[80] See ibid., p. 64.
[81] See ibid., p. 65.
[82] Friedmann, 'Review', p. 610.

For those who see law as possessing a self-identity, an ego, and believe that the function of the international legal system is to effectively regulate international activity in the midst of diverse ideological dispositions that conceptualize 'common interest' in alternative ways the policy-oriented approach is debilitating. It ignores the elementary fact that 'without reference to a body of rules the idea of law is quite unintelligible'.[83]

This lapse explains why positivists have in turn been so sharply critical of the policy-oriented approach. As Bruno Simma and Andreas Paulus point out, 'the New Haven approach, by conflating law, political science, and politics plain and simple, fails to provide the very guidance that real-life decision makers expect from their lawyers'.[84] They go on to note that 'by not distinguishing clearly between norms and values, the New Haven approach ideologises international law, which is all too often based on a minimal consensus on means and not on ends'.[85] Of course Simma and Paulus concede that the New Haven approach 'may have considerable value for both the analysis of actual decision making and the formulation of policy proposals'.[86] But if rules are not assigned a significant place within the legal system, the result can only be free competition between different ideologies and corresponding interpretations and evaluations of particular rules, situations and events. In the words of Falk, 'McDougal sacrifices too many of the stabilizing benefits of a rule-oriented approach to international law by stressing policy flexibility'.[87] There is no gainsaying that it is important to uphold the crucial place of rules in the international legal system.[88] On the other hand, the problem with the positivist approach is that it treats the legal system as a self-enclosed

---

[83] Hedley Bull, *The Anarchical Society* (London: Macmillan, 19775), p. 128.

[84] Bruno Simma and Andreas L. Paulus, 'The Responsibility of Individuals for Human Rights Abuses in Internal Conflicts: A Positivist View' in Ratner and Slaughter (eds.), *Methods of International Law*, pp. 23–47 at pp. 27–28.

[85] See ibid., p. 28.

[86] See ibid.

[87] Richard Falk, *Legal Order in a Violent World* (Princeton, NJ: Princeton University Press, 1968), p. 89.

[88] The distinctive place of written rules is the function of a variety of factors that include: (1) that it is a written text; in writing language assumes a form which constrains interpretative freedom more than when it involves the interpretation of social action; (2) that it is a valid legal norm; the legal text can be distinguished from other written texts by the fact that it is validated by certain agreed procedures, and which operate to confer a particular status on it; (3) that its interpretation entails practical reasoning which excludes arguments over premises. This does not preclude debates concerning the substantial justification of the norm but merely points to the fact that it does not necessarily represent an internal moment.

system. The result is fetishism of the law. A balanced approach requires that these twin pitfalls be avoided. There is a need to recognize both the significance of rules in a legal system and the appraisal of the social consequences flowing from it. But the validity of rules cannot be internally linked to a particular conception of justice. To suggest that a particular justice standpoint be the basis for determining the validity of a rule is a recipe for imperialism. The weak in any legal system are wary of this stance because it is the powerful that will take advantage of tying the validity of rules to the idea of justice.

III.   Indeterminacy of Rules: Semantic and Structural Sources

It was noted that there are two sources of rule scepticism in the policy-oriented approach. The first source is the idea that confining the task of the international lawyer to interpretation of technical legal rules is not only to misconceive the relationship between law and policy but also to miss the opportunity of shaping the law to realize common interests. A second source of rule scepticism is the alleged semantic and structural indeterminacy of rules. The semantic basis of indeterminacy leads McDougal to contest the ordinary meaning rule codified in Article 31 of the Vienna Convention on the Law of Treaties, 1969 (VCLT) which inter alia states that 'a treaty shall be interpreted in good faith in accordance with the ordinary meaning to be given to the terms of the treaty in their context and in the light of its object and purpose'. The ordinary meaning rule is seen by positivist or mainstream international lawyers as being central to the interpretive exercise and to sustaining the idea of international rule of law. The structural basis of indeterminacy of rules has its foundation in both the New Haven concept of law that blurs the distinction between law and policy and the existence of a number of important and recurring concepts of international law are imprecise (e.g., state, independence, intervention and equality) or 'travel in opposites' (e.g., domestic jurisdiction and international concern, war and self-defence). The semantic and structural bases of indeterminacy led McDougal to conclude that indeterminacy is an 'all pervasive attribute of legal process'.[89] In what follows the semantic basis of rule scepticism is considered at first, followed by an analysis of the structural sources of rule scepticism. The overall argument is that the charge of indeterminacy of rules is exaggerated.

[89] Falk, *Legal Order*, p. 501.

A. Semantic Indeterminacy

Mainstream international lawyers subscribe to the ordinary meaning rule as in their view it helps determine both the intent and the rights and obligations of parties to an agreement and resolve disputes that may arise between them in an objective manner. But their views can differ on whether the application of the ordinary meaning rule should be viewed as the central aspect of the interpretative exercise or be seen as, in the words of Hersch Lauterpacht, 'no more than a starting point'.[90] According to Lauterpacht, 'no apparent amount of clarity is a sufficient justification for ruling out an independent investigation of intention (of the parties)'.[91] In his words, 'plain meaning may, at the highest, be treated as a rebuttable *presumptio juris* but not to be regarded as an irrefutable *preumptio juris et de jure*'.[92] But even if the 'starting point' thesis is accepted, differences may arise between writers and tribunals on the mode and implications of ascertaining the 'object or purpose' of an agreement. First, there may be disagreement over whether the process of determining the 'object or purpose' is to be confined to the text of the agreement or should a more comprehensive exercise be undertaken that does not neglect the text(s) but reviews all 'relevant materials' in order to discover the genuine shared expectations of parties. Second, differences may arise as to whether the act of interpretation should stop with the discovery of genuine shared expectations of parties to an agreement or it is the duty of the interpreter to advance interpretations that promote certain world order goals, especially in cases where an element of uncertainty prevails as regards the intention of parties.

McDougal answered both these questions in the affirmative. In his view, the genuine shared expectations of parties cannot be discovered from the text of the agreement alone as words do not possess 'ordinary meaning'. The principal reasons are that words possess multiple meanings and that reality is non-verbal. According to McDougal, modern studies in semantics, syntactics and communication indicate that only a comprehensive and systematic review of the relevant materials can help interpreters identify the genuine shared expectations of parties at the time of rule application. Where the text does not permit a clear determination of the genuine

---

[90] E. Lauterpacht (ed.), *International Law: Being the Collected Papers of Hersch Lauterpacht*, vol. 4 (Cambridge: Cambridge University Press, 1978), pp. 401–402.

[91] See ibid., p. 402.

[92] See ibid.

expectations of parties that interpretation should be adopted which furthers the goal of human dignity. Thus, the New Haven rejection of the 'ordinary meaning' rule rests on twin basis. The first ground for rejecting it is shared with Lauterpacht and others who believe that the ordinary meaning rule can only be the starting point of analysis to discover the intention of parties to an agreement. But McDougal is not as willing as Lauterpacht to concede that 'in so far as the process of interpretation must start from *somewhere*, it is not unreasonable – it is *essential* – that it should begin with what appears to be the natural, the common, the "plain" meaning of the terms used'.[93] That is to say, it is not clear whether McDougal agrees that the plain meaning rule is the *essential* starting point, albeit as shall be seen, at times he speaks of the act of interpretation in those terms. In any case the 'starting point' idea of Lauterpacht has to be located in McDougal's specific understanding of the process and purpose of interpretation. To McDougal only a comprehensive analysis of the context of communication allows the interpreter to find the genuine shared expectation of parties to an agreement at the time of application. This understanding makes the rule, including its object and purpose as found in the text, at best one element to be taken into account in the process of interpretation. In essence, McDougal challenged the extent to which the text of an agreement imposed serious constraints on an interpreter in arriving at the genuine shared expectations of parties. To understand his view of the process and purpose of interpretation it is best to begin with his critique of the VCLT formulation of the ordinary meaning rule.

B.   Critique of VCLT

McDougal advanced a critique of VCLT rules of interpretation even as the draft articles were being debated in the International Law Commission (ILC). He wrote that 'the great defect, and tragedy' in the ILC's final recommendations about the interpretation of treaties 'is in their insistent emphasis upon an impossible, conformity-imposing textuality'.[94] He summarized the ILC view as follows:

> In explicit rejection of a quest for the 'intentions of the parties as a subjective element distinct from the text', the Commission adopts a 'basic

---

[93] See ibid., p. 401; emphasis in original.

[94] Myres McDougal, 'The International Law Commission's Draft Articles upon Interpretation: Textuality Redivivus', 61 (1967) *American Journal of International Law*, pp. 992–1000 at p. 992.

approach' which demands merely the ascription of a meaning to a text. The only justification offered, and several times repeated as if in an effort to carry conviction, is that 'the text [of a treaty] must be presumed to be the authentic expression of the intentions of the parties' and hence that 'the starting point of interpretation is the elucidation of the meaning of the text, not an investigation *ab initio* into the intentions of the parties.' This arbitrary presumption is described as 'established law' because of approval by the Institute of International Law and pronouncements by the International Court of Justice. The Court, it is noted, 'has more than once stressed that it is not the function of interpretation to revise treaties or to read into them what they do not, expressly or by implication, contain'.[95]

In response to the ILC view, McDougal observed that by adopting the textual approach it was 'arrogating to one particular set of signs – the text of a document – the role of serving as the *exclusive index of the shared expectations* of the parties to an agreement' that reflected 'an *exercise in primitive and potentially destructive formalism*'.[96] He significantly pointed out that 'lest it be thought that the references to "context" and to "object and purpose" are intended to remedy the blindness and arbitrariness of "ordinary meaning," context is immediately defined as including mere text'.[97] He went on to emphasize that in the ILC view ' "object and purpose" do not refer to the actual subjectivities of the parties, rejected as the goal of interpretation, but rather to the mere words about "object and purpose" intrinsic to the text'.[98] McDougal therefore concluded:

> The truth is that in the absence of *a comprehensive, contextual examination of all the potentially significant features of the process of agreement*, undertaken without the blinders of advance restrictive hierarchies or weightings, no interpreter can be sure that his determinations bear any relation to the genuine shared expectations of the parties.[99]

He then went on to approvingly cite 'The Harvard Research in International Law' which had formulated the following rule of interpretation:

> A treaty is to be interpreted in the light of the general purpose which it is intended to serve. The historical background of the treaty, *travaux preparatoires*, the circumstances of the parties at the time the treaty was

---

[95] See ibid.
[96] See ibid., p. 997; emphasis added.
[97] See ibid., p. 993.
[98] See ibid., pp. 993–994.
[99] See ibid., p. 998; emphasis added.

entered into, the change in these circumstances sought to be effected, the subsequent conduct of the parties in applying the provisions of the treaty, and the conditions prevailing at the time interpretation is being made, are to be considered in connection with the general purpose which the treaty is intended to serve.[100]

But McDougal was not entirely satisfied even with this formulation. He went on to add:

> What the Harvard Research does not offer, in implementation of its insight about appropriate goal and necessary context, is *a comprehensive and systematic set of principles of content and procedure* designed effectively to assist interpreters in the economic examination of particular contexts in pursuit of their appropriate goal. Even the task of fashioning such a set of principles should not, however, be beyond the reach of contemporary scholars who enjoy the advantages both of a rich inheritance in tested principles and of access to *modern studies in semantics, syntactics, and other aspects of communication.*[101]

It is clear from these statements that the McDougal critique was not directed merely at the 'ordinary meaning' rule but at the broader idea of 'textuality'. He felt that to 'seek to construct a set of words that will automatically determine all future decisions and relieve human decision-makers of the anguish of choice and judgment' was a 'futile enterprise'.[102] According to McDougal the 'realist function' of rules is 'not mechanically to dictate specific decision but to guide the attention of decision-makers to significant variable factors in typical recurring contexts of decision, to serve as summary indices to relevant crystallised community expectations, and, hence, to permit creative and adaptive, instead of arbitrary and irrational, decisions'.[103] Stating that the primary aim of a process of interpretation by an authorized and controlling decision maker is to discover genuine shared expectations McDougal observed:

> The approach which seeks genuine shared expectations does not neglect the words of a purportedly final text, if any exists. It does, however, regard any initial version of their relation to shared expectations *as provisional*, and requires that the interpreter engage in a course of sustained testing and

---

[100] See ibid., pp. 999–1000.
[101] See ibid., p. 1000; emphasis added.
[102] Myres S. McDougal and Florentino P. Feliciano, *Law and Minimum World Public Order: The Legal Regulation of International Coercion* (New Haven, CT: Yale University Press, 1961), p. 151.
[103] See ibid., p. 57.

> revision of preliminary inferences about the pertinent subjectivities. And
> of course this calls for scrutiny of *the whole context of communication*.[104]

Thus, in the McDougal framework the text of rules is at best seen as 'special directives to contextual factors'. Legal rules are, to borrow the words of H. L. A. Hart, 'treated as displaceable presumptions or working hypothesis, to be modified or rejected if the predictable consequences of their application in a shifting social context proved unsatisfactory'.[105]

In sum, McDougal was extremely critical – 'in the light of modern developments in communication analysis' and 'modern techniques of linguistic analysis' – of the ordinary meaning principle of interpretation. In his view, the principle not only inflates the importance of a 'single contextual detail' but also encouraged an 'exaggerated assumption of clairvoyance on the part of the reader of a text, and de-emphasises an open-eyed quest for relevant information':[106]

> Although there is no reason to deny the usefulness of the common or public meanings of words as starting points in the process of interpretation, whenever a principle emphasising such meanings threatens to become transformed into a final, exclusive procedure, it must be rejected. No acceptable justification can be given for precluding an interpreter, whose goal is to determine the shared expectations of the authors of a document, from proceeding to examine all of the relevant features of the context prior to final decision.[107]

It is worth reiterating here that while McDougal speaks of plain meaning as a possible starting point of interpretation this move has to be understood in the light of the theory of semantics and syntactics that he deployed, the ambit of context he had in mind, and the idea that the genuine shared expectation may be subject to what McDougal termed the policing or integrative function.[108] Thus, the specific goals of interpretation were postulated by McDougal as follows:

General Statement: The goal is application of international agreements in terms of all community policies, including the policy of according the

---

[104] Myres S. McDougal, Harold D. Lasswell and James C. Miller, *The Interpretation of Agreements and World Public Order: Principles of Content and Procedure* (New Haven, CT: Yale University Press, 1967), p. xviii.

[105] H. L. A. Hart, *Essays in Jurisprudence and Philosophy* (Oxford: Clarendon Press, 1983), p. 131.

[106] McDougal, Lasswell and Miller, *Interpretation of Agreements*, pp. 95 and 97.

[107] See ibid., p. 97

[108] 'Contextuality', according to McDougal, 'implies that any interpreter of an outcome must be ready and able to explore the possible influence in concrete circumstances of the

highest possible deference, compatible with other constitutional policies, to the genuine shared expectations of the particular parties.

More specific statement:
Primary interpretation
Give deference to the genuine shared expectations of the particular
  parties to an agreement.

Supplementing interpretation
When expectations are ambiguous or vague, complete the argument in
  accordance with the goals of public order.

Policing and integrating interpretation

Negative
Do not give effect to the expectations of the parties when they conflict
  with the goals of the system of public order.

Affirmative
Encourage the conformity of future agreement making with the goals
  of public order.[109]

While the implications of this representation of the goals of interpretation are grave, these are considered later. At first it is the more fundamental thesis that the ILC principle of ordinary meaning is impossible of
application that is addressed.

C.   *Words Possess Ordinary Meaning: Function of a Sentence*

McDougal was certainly justified in his censure of Vattel's famous maxim
that 'it is not permissible to interpret what has no need of interpretation'
as rules do not come preinterpreted.[110] However, to say that a rule calls for
interpretation does not license a process that sees a rule or the agreement
of which it is a part as simply one variable in the process of arriving at the
genuine shared expectations of parties. It is not sufficient here to pay mere
obeisance to the words of the rule and the agreement as a whole but to
accept that together they place substantial limits on the scope of the interpretive exercise. But for this understanding to be accepted the principle

---

identity of communicators and audiences, of inclusive forums, of significant objectives, of
  base values and strategies'. McDougal, Lasswell and Miller, *Interpretation of Agreements*,
  p. xv. This dimension of the McDougal framework is considered infra pp. 157–171.
[109] See ibid., p. 44.
[110] McDougal, 'International Law', p. 996.

of 'ordinary meaning' must be capable of application. In other words, the shared expectations of parties cannot be found in the text when words do not possess 'ordinary meaning'. It brings the discussion to the crucial question as to what is the meaning of 'ordinary meaning'. Is it simply a reference to dictionary meanings or does it capture a more complex idea advanced by, among others, ordinary language philosophers like Ludwig Wittgenstein and J. L. Austin.[111]

To begin with, reference may be made to two propositions of Wittgenstein that are critical to clarifying the meaning of the words 'ordinary meaning' and the implications of words possessing 'ordinary meaning'. The first is that 'to understand a sentence means to understand a language' and the second that 'the meaning of a word is its use in the language'.[112] These two propositions help understand the significance attached by VCLT and the community of interpreters to the plain or ordinary meaning rule and to the broader idea of 'textuality'.

The significance of each of the two Wittgenstein propositions and their limitations may be considered in turn. The first proposition is that 'to understand a sentence is to understand a language'.[113] This formulation is crucial as there is a tendency to conclude that a word lacks 'ordinary meaning' without locating it in a sentence. This error in the instance of the New Haven approach can be traced back to the views of C. K. Ogden and I. A. Richards that were relied on by McDougal.[114] As Glanville Williams pointed out in his well-known essay on language and the law, Ogden and Richards 'direct their main attention to the meaning of individual words. They appear to regard syntactical meaning as a product or synthesis of the meaning of the separate words employed, when interpreted in the light of rules of grammar'.[115] In fact, Williams himself was 'concerned chiefly with

---

[111] It is perhaps important to clarify at the very outset that we do not entirely share Wittgenstein's view that (a) questions which have troubled philosophy originate in verbal confusion alone; and (b) that language is primarily constitutive of social life. It is, however, believed that Wittgenstein's use theory of meaning is a major contribution to comprehending social reality.

[112] Ludwig Wittgenstein, *Philosophical Investigations* (Oxford: Blackwell, 1958), rule 199 and rule 43 respectively.

[113] See ibid., rule 199.

[114] See discussion infra pp. 135–137.

[115] Glanville Williams, 'Language and the Law', 61–62 (1945–46) *The Law Quarterly Review*, pp. 71–86, 179–195, 293–303, 337–406 at p. 402. For this, Ogden and Richards are not to be singled out for blame because 'until recently, linguists have paid much more attention to lexical meaning (i.e., meaning of words) than they have to sentence-meaning'. John Lyons, *Language and Linguistics* (Cambridge: Cambridge University Press, 1981), p. 139.

the meaning of individual words'.[116] But the reality of alternate meanings of a word does not render the concept of 'ordinary meaning' redundant.[117] A rule is not to be seen as a mere 'collocation of letters' or a separate set of words for to do so is 'just as misleading as the claim that a painting is a *mere* concatenation of blobs of paint'.[118] Unfortunately, often linguists, and interpreters of legal rules, lay greater stress on the meaning of individual words than on their meaning in a sentence.[119] But 'properly speaking, what alone has meaning is *a sentence*'.[120] As J. L. Austin explains:

> of course, we can speak quite properly of, for example, 'looking up the meaning of a word' in a dictionary. Nevertheless, it appears that the sense in which a word or a phrase 'has a meaning' is derivative from the sense in which a sentence 'has a meaning': to say a word or a phrase 'has a meaning' is to say that there are sentences in which it occurs which 'have meanings': and to know the meaning which the word or phrase has, is to know the meanings of sentences in which it occurs. All the dictionary can do when we 'look up the meaning of a word' is to suggest aids to the understanding of sentences in which it occurs. Hence it appears correct to say that what 'has meaning' in the primary sense is the sentence.[121]

It is, therefore, wrong to direct attention primarily to the meaning of individual words and to regard syntactical meaning as a product of different words employed in a sentence. Such an approach tends to mystify a routine activity of assigning meaning to words – as Ogden and Richards do – by speaking of the role of dictionaries in maintaining 'fixity in references' of words.[122] But as Roy Harris pointed out in the context of the list of sixteen meanings of 'meaning' which Ogden and Richards drew up:

> by thus concentrating on how dictionaries are able to fulfil their definitional role, Ogden and Richards seem to miss the significance of what

[116] Williams, 'Language and the Law'.
[117] On surrogationalism, see Roy Harris, *The Language-Maker* (London: Duckworth, 1980), pp. 33–78, 84–89 and 91–96. Harris notes that 'the surrogationalism condemned by... Wittgenstein appears in two different basic forms throughout the Western tradition. What may be called "reocentric surrogationalism" supposes that the things words stand for are to be located "out there" in the world external to the individual language-user. On the other hand, what may be called "psychocentric surrogationalism" supposes that what words stand for is to be located internally, that is to say in the mind of the language-user.' See ibid., p. 44.
[118] G. P. Baker and P. M. S. Hacker, *Scepticism, Rules and Language* (Oxford: Basil Blackwell, 1984), p. 94, fn 41; emphasis in original.
[119] The reports of WTO panels and the Appellate Body are full of such examples.
[120] J. L. Austin, *Philosophical Papers*, 3rd edn (Oxford: Clarendon Press, 1979), p. 56; emphasis in original.
[121] See ibid.
[122] Cited by Harris, *Language-Makers*, p. 142.

> dictionaries treat meaning as. Relating words to other words is not just
> one among sixteen possibilities for the multiply ambiguous term *meaning*:
> it is one of only two types of procedure for identification of meanings.[123]

However, from the foregoing it would be wrong to conclude that an individual word has no meaning without being part of a sentence. All that is being asserted is that it is only with a sentence that we really say something – it is the 'minimal unit by which a move is made in the language-game'.[124] The dictionary meanings of a word being autonomous of any linguistic or empirical context provide no guidance other than indicating potential meanings. The dilemma of multiplicity of meanings is satisfactorily resolved only when the sentence is treated as of primary significance in the interpretive process. It immediately narrows down the context from the entire environment to that found in the sentence. In the words of Julius Stone:

> while the word, as the minimum expression of meaningful content, is the
> basic unit of communication by linguistic signs (or 'discourse'), discourse
> generally requires sentence, in which the syntactic relation of words to
> each other permits us to select among the multiplicity of meanings of each
> word so as to delimit somewhat what is communicated.[125]

In sum, it is only with a sentence that ordinary meaning of a word emerges. It resolves at the first level the meaning of a word. A possible objection may be considered here. It is that given its technical nature, 'legal language is not ordinary language; it is a language that must be learnt and a language to which special attention must be paid in the construction of legal documents and of statutory texts alike'.[126] The element of truth in this statement can be glimpsed from the fact that there are legal dictionaries besides 'ordinary' dictionaries. But this fact does not negate all that has been said about the ordinary meaning of words. First, of course, 'as compared with ordinary language, the incidence of ... strictly technical usage in judicial discourse is negligible'.[127] Second, what is meant by stating that 'legal language is not ordinary language' is that legal expressions possess an ordinary meaning within a 'language-game' (a term on which more is said presently). An expression could have an 'ordinary' as well as

---

[123] See ibid.
[124] Baker and Hacker, *Wittgenstein: Meaning*, p. 167.
[125] Stone, *Legal System*, p. 30.
[126] Peter Goodrich, *Reading the Law: A Critical Introduction to Legal Method and Techniques* (Oxford: Basil Blackwell, 1986), p. 107.
[127] Stone, *Legal System*, p. 35.

an 'ordinary legal' meaning. On the face of it McDougal appears to accept these understandings of ordinary meaning when he observes that:

> unless persuasive evidence is established to the contrary, assume that the terms of an agreement are intended to be understood as they are generally understood by the largest audience contemporary to the agreement to which both parties belong. The probabilities are that the more people who share a meaning, the more likely the particular parties are to have had that meaning.[128]

But he simultaneously relied on theories of semantics, syntactic and communications that confounded the issue and made him conclude that words possess no ordinary meaning. The reasons for rejecting the ordinary meaning rule went beyond determining the meaning of the text. In McDougal's view (1) the entire context of communication between parties cannot be captured by the text; (2) the search for genuine shared expectations must involve a comprehensive review of the materials at the time of rule adoption; and (3) the rule cannot determine its own application necessitating a survey of the relevant materials at the time of rule application. These concerns have only been partially addressed by showing that words possess 'ordinary meaning' when they become part of a sentence.

D. Words Possess Ordinary Meaning: Use Theory of Meaning

At this point it is important to recall the second proposition of Wittgenstein, that is, 'the meaning of a word is its use in the language'. The essential idea is that a word has ordinary meaning in a sentence because it captures a social practice(s) leading to 'agreement in judgments and in definitions'.[129] In this view, if the relationship between meaning and practice is snapped, a word can have any meaning. For it is not the black marks on a page that have meaning, but the social practice(s) that are signalled by them. It is another way of saying that language and social practices constitute each other. It cannot be otherwise. It can therefore be said that 'if there is no such thing as determinacy of sense, there is no such thing as absence of it. Since no expression could be determinate in sense, it makes no sense to ascribe to any expression the property of not having this "property".'[130]

---

[128] McDougal, Lasswell and Miller, *Interpretation of Agreements*, p. 59. See also p. 69.
[129] Ibid., p. 223.
[130] Baker and Hacker, *Scepticism*, p. 225.

The use theory of meaning may be clarified further by reference to the concepts of 'language game' and 'form of life' deployed by Wittgenstein. He used the notion of 'language game' 'to bring into prominence the fact that 'the *speaking* of language is part of an activity, or of a form of life'.[131] He therefore termed 'language and the actions into which it is woven, the "language-game".'[132] In so far as the notion of 'form of life' is concerned, Wittgenstein attempted to explain its meaning through the following observation: '"So you are saying that human agreement decides what is true and what is false?" It is what human beings *say* that is true and false; and they agree in the *language* they use. That is not agreement in opinions but in form of life.'[133] What Wittgenstein is doing here is to make more specific his generic use theory of meaning. He is suggesting that words have different meanings in different 'language games' or 'forms of life'. While philosophers debate whether there is a distinction between the ideas of a 'language game' and 'forms of life', the essential aim of both is the same viz., to link the meaning of words to a particular set of social practices which constitute the matrix in which the use theory of meaning assumes life.[134]

It can be said that *modern* international law is a distinct 'language game' that originated in the seventeenth century. It is constituted by practices of participants in the international legal process that have evolved over time. So when a word is used in the domain of international law it possesses ordinary meaning within the 'language game' of modern international law. Those who are participating in that 'form of life' understand each other. This understanding has family resemblance with Martti Koskenniemi's notion of a competent speaker who is steeped in the traditions of the discipline. (It is another matter that he mistakenly proceeds to argue the case for radical structural indeterminacy.)[135]

It may be further added in the context of written international agreements that since their drafting is an outcome of a lengthy process of negotiations competent speakers use words with care. These agreements go through several draft formulations which are debated threadbare

---

[131] Wittgenstein, *Philosophical Investigations*, rule 23; emphasis in original.
[132] See ibid., rule 7.
[133] See ibid., rule 241; emphasis in original. It is worth noting here that there are different ways of understanding what Wittgenstein meant by 'form of life'. See for instance J. F. M. Hunter, '"Forms of Life" in Wittgenstein's "Philosophical Investigations"', 5 (1968) *American Philosophical Quarterly*, pp. 233–243.
[134] See for instance Hunter, '"Forms of Life"', pp. 233–243.
[135] For Koskenniemi's views on indeterminacy and international law see Chapter 5, pp. 333ff.

by representatives of states not to mention that they are often carefully scrutinized by several government departments within each state.[136] Therefore, even when states resort to strategic ambiguity it is not difficult to discern this from the text itself.

In sum, words possess ordinary meaning as the problem of standard of correctness of the application of expressions is linked to social practices. Rules can be sufficiently transparent for 'whatever can be meant or intended must be capable of being expressed'.[137] It may be emphasized that the distinction between correct and incorrect uses only presumes 'the existence of tolerably definite practices of using expressions'.[138] In this respect, it is useful to draw attention to the following observations of J. L. Austin: (a) 'when we examine what we should say when, what words we should use in what situations, we are looking again not *merely* at words (or "meanings", whatever they may be) but also at the realities we use the words to talk about: we are using a sharpened awareness of words to sharpen our perception of, though not as the final arbiter of, the phenomena';[139] (b) that 'our common stock of words embodies all the distinctions that men have found worth drawing, and the connections they have found worth marking in the lifetimes of many generations';[140] and (c) 'words are not (except in their own little corner) facts or things: we need therefore to prise them off the world, to hold them apart from and against it, so that we can realize their inadequacies and arbitrariness, and can relook at the world without blinkers'.[141]

However, McDougal believed that 'one of the principal lessons which contemporary studies on semantics and linguistics offer is that every verbalisation, whether definitional or not, is an abstraction from the "unspeakable level of objective events"'.[142] The conclusion seemed to be derived from the works of C. K. Ogden and I. A. Richards, Alfred Korzybski and C. W. Morris.[143] Elsewhere McDougal wrote that 'it is

---

[136] Leo Gross, 'Treaty Interpretation: The Proper Role of an International Tribunal', (1969)*Proceedings of the American Society of International Law*, pp. 108–122 at p. 121.

[137] Baker and Hacker, *Scepticism*, p. 120. They explain this crucial point thus: 'A person may know more about what he means than he says, but not more than he can say or express ... Mental acts of meaning do not have the capacity by themselves to endow signs with meanings (intelligible uses)'.

[138] Williams, 'Language', p. 363.

[139] Austin, *Philosophical Papers*, p. 182.

[140] See ibid.; emphasis in original.

[141] Ibid.

[142] McDougal and Feliciano, *Law and Minimum World Public Order*, p. 154.

[143] Ibid., fn 90.

possible inadequacies in transmission – usually through *the inherent shortcomings in the capability of words and other signs to communicate shared subjectivities* – that place the communication analyst on guard that only a total contextual survey, systematically examining "who said what to whom through what channels and with what effects" will suffice in performing his difficult task of determining the genuine shared expectations of the parties".[144] With respect to these submissions Giddeon Gottlieb has noted that McDougal's observations on communication theory were 'unsatisfactory, referring loosely to a poorly identified body of scholarship".[145] But since the principal references were to authors of behaviourist theories of meaning,[146] it may be worthwhile to assess what this implies. In the behaviourist view of semantics and linguistics reality is unspeakable. A consequence is that all general concepts are in the final analysis meaningless, as abstractions are constituted through the 'omission of details".[147] From the behaviourist perspective reality is non-verbal: 'the objective level is not words, and cannot be reached by words alone".[148] Therefore, each ascending order of abstraction decreases its value for it represents 'only a shadow cast by the scientific object".[149] Thus, as Max Black noted of Korzybski, he 'thinks of the nervous system as a kind of coarse-grained sieve or filter; infinitely complex waves of physical energy distributions strike the filter, lose much of their individual detail in passing through it, and eventually produce the abstraction".[150] The result was a wholesale

[144] McDougal, Lasswell and Miller, *The Interpretation of Agreements*, p. 372. See also ibid., pp. 18–19; emphasis added.
[145] Giddeon Gottlieb, 'The Conceptual World of the Yale School of International Law', 21 (1968) *World Politics*, pp. 108–132 at p. 112.
[146] Those who are surprised at the inclusion of the work of Ogden and Richards under the label 'behavioral semantics' can refer to John Lyons, *Semantics*, vol.1 (Cambridge: Cambridge University Press, 1977), p. 98. Black observes of Ogden and Richards's *Meaning of Meaning* that 'while such terms as "thoughts", "feelings", "experiences", are freely used as interchangeable with locutions concerning "reactions to stimuli" and "adaptations of the organism"; and while the authors themselves claim that their doctrine is "neutral in regard to psycho-neutral parallelism, interaction, or double aspect hypothesis", there seems no doubt from the general progress of their argument that a *behaviouristic* theory is being presented'; (emphasis in original). Max Black, *Language and Philosophy: Studies in Method* (Ithaca, NY: Cornell University Press, 1949), p. 192, fn. 3.
[147] Black, *Language and Philosophy*, p. 236.
[148] Korzybski cited by Black, ibid., p. 239.
[149] According to Korzybski, the 'scientific object' is 'a mad dance of "electrons", which is different every instant, which never repeats itself, which is known to consist of extremely complex dynamic processes of very fine structure, acted upon by, and reacting upon the rest of the universe, inextricably connected with everything else and dependent on everything else'. Cited by Black, ibid., p. 235.
[150] See ibid., p. 243.

condemnation of abstractions. Speaking of Korzybski and Ogden and Richards, the philosopher John Passmore wrote that 'never have abstractions been assailed with such violence; whole areas of human thinking were dismissed with ignominy as congeries of empty abstractions'.[151] In the same vein, McDougal traced the semantic indeterminacy of a rule to the fact that while a rule is formulated in words reality is non-verbal. The problem of discovering the shared expectations of parties was accentuated by the fact that a constitutive feature of a word is a multiplicity of meanings. In the circumstances, McDougal found it difficult to see how any interpretation of a rule was possible without recourse to the entire context in which these words originated.

But if the use theory of meaning has validity a legal text can be separated from its ecology. The pre-understanding that it is the text of the rule and not the comprehensive context, both of the circumstances in which the rule was framed and in which it is applied, then needs to be respected. On the other hand, McDougal appears to suggest that before facts or events are to be evaluated with reference to a rule, the rule itself needs to be discovered through contextual interpretation. But this represents a perversion of the interpretive exercise for rules are what measure and not what are measured. In other words, the process of interpretation finds an inverted expression where instead of seeking to know whether certain facts or events are in accord with or in violation of a rule, the attempt is to discover the rule in the light of the contexts. But if each party is to discover the rule in this way there is little doubt that it would be formulated to suit subjective and expedient standpoints. To put it differently, the New Haven procedure of interpretation eventually leads to not merely different interpretations of a single rule, but rather, to singular interpretations of multiple rules arrived at on the basis of a comprehensive analysis of relevant materials. It is not an exercise in interpretation at all since new texts can emerge from the interpretive exercise. With the result that no judgment of facts or events is possible for while an act or an omission could be unlawful if one rule (ostensibly interpretation) is adopted, it could be perfectly legal if the other rule (ostensibly interpretation) is accepted. What separates them is the gulf of 'unshared' perceptions, often being completely divergent world views. The hermeneutic freedom that McDougal seeks for the interpreter in the name of discovering 'genuine shared expectations', and the pursuit of public order goals, is therefore subversive of international rule of law. McDougal disregards the fact that it is precisely the plurality of the 'unshared' perceptions which necessitates

---

[151] John Passmore, *A Hundred Years of Philosophy* (Middlesex: Penguin, 1972), p. 399.

agreement to be incorporated in a text. Ronald Dworkin has rightly noted in this context that:

> a social practice creates and assumes a crucial distinction between inter-preting the acts and thought of participants one by one, in that way, and interpreting the practice [in this case the rule] itself, that is, interpreting what they do collectively. It assumes that distinction because the claims and arguments participants make, licensed and encouraged by the prac-tice, are about what *it* means, not what *they* mean.[152]

In other words, the final text of a rule involves a process of self-alienation, and possesses an authenticity, which must be respected. In the words of Stone:

> the error of substituting *author's intention* for *meaning of language* is that it ignores the fact that a written work once created acquires a mean-ing which, though still dependent on men's usage, is still independent of its creator's motives; and interpretation is precisely a search for this meaning ... This is surely the deep basis of the judicial stress on the *ordin-ary* meaning of words when this does not lead to absurdity and the like.[153]

E.   Structural Indeterminacy

In response to the argument that words possess ordinary meaning, McDougal would be wont to point out that given the indeterminacy which characterizes international legal reasoning the matter does not end there. He laid particular emphasis on the fact that basic concepts/norms of international law came in complementary opposites making it difficult to provide definitive interpretive answers, the kind of argument later advanced by Martti Koskenniemi. Thus, for instance, the norm of non-use of force is accompanied by a norm that creates an exception in favour of self-defence.[154] While the existence of complementary concepts/

---

[152] Ronald Dworkin, *Law's Empire* (London: Fontana Press, 1986), p. 63; emphasis in ori-ginal. In this regard, Gottlieb has also noted that 'the *text* of the agreement must not itself be confused with the *process* of agreement that led up to it'. Gottlieb, 'Conceptual World', p. 114; emphasis in original.

[153] Julius Stone, *Legal System and Lawyer's Reasonings* (London: Stevens and Sons Ltd., 1964), pp. 32–33; emphasis in original.

[154] With respect to the law relating to the use of force McDougal writes:

> the rules of the law of war, like other legal rules, are commonly formulated in pairs of complementary opposites and are composed of a relatively few basic terms of highly variable reference. The complementarity in form and compre-hensiveness of reference of such rules are indispensable to the rational search for and application of policy to a world of acts and events which presents itself

norms cannot be denied, its significance is often overstated.[155] In fact, the international community delimits spheres of application fully aware that 'if complementary norms are equally plausible under most circumstances then no predictable impact upon behaviour derives from the adoption of a new prohibitive rule'.[156] Its perspective is translated into complementary concepts/norms with reasonably clear delineation of their spheres of application. To put it differently, the idea that a rule cannot determine its own application (to be differentiated from the proposition that a rule comes preinterpreted) is not as problematic as it appears. McDougal was right insofar as he assumed that a rule cannot be said to exist prior to an interpretation. But from this he mistakenly concluded that the text is of no great consequence. He did not adequately recognize that the rule and its consequence (acts which count as compliance with the rule) are internally related. That is to say, 'correctly viewed, the concept of a rule and the concept of what acts comply with it are not independent. We do not first grasp, understand, a rule, and then cast around to see whether we can understand what follows from it, or what counts as compliance with it'.[157] The very process of expressing a rule in words, it must be realized, involves its restatement in some other form of words clarifying as to what amounts to compliance with it. This becomes amply clear when you remember Wittgenstein's observation that to obey a rule is a custom and a practice. In other words, the picture of what counts as compliance with the rule is revealed by our social practices. That is precisely why Wittgenstein observed that 'interpretations by themselves do not determine meaning' for then everything could be made out to be in accord or conflict with the rule.[158] Norms have their roots in concrete social practices, that is, in particular historical experiences, and are assigned meaning only in their matrix. Thus, Article 2 (4) of the UN Charter was formulated in the

to the decision-maker, not in terms of neat symmetrical dichotomies or trichotomies, but in terms of innumerable gradations and alternations from one end of a continuum to the other; the spectrum makes available to a decision-maker not one inevitable doom but multiple alternative choices.

McDougal, *Law and Minimum World Public Order*, p. 57.

[155] Falk, *Status of Law*, p. 15. Falk further observed in this regard that 'to allege the pervasive complementarity of legal norms is to make a false allegation, as well as to blur the perception of quite another matter: namely, the idea that law can be manipulated to rationalise policy goals, even those of the most anarchic character'. See ibid.

[156] See ibid.

[157] G. P. Baker and P. M. S. Hacker, *Language, Sense and Nonsense: A Critical Investigation into Modern Theories of Language* (Oxford: Basil Blackwell, 1984), p. 265.

[158] Wittgenstein, *Philosophical Investigations*, rules 198 and 201.

backdrop of the history of the outlawry of war and the devastation caused by the Second World War. The principle of non-use of force can only be assigned meaning and applied in that context.

Yet, if scholars like McDougal did not find clearly etched areas of operation so far as Articles 2(4) and 51 are concerned, it was not because there were admittedly grey areas but because their analysis was ahistorical, non-system specific and self-serving.[159] It was also methodologically flawed inasmuch as he failed to discern the elements of unity and mutual interpenetration which characterize these opposites with implications for the interpretation of complementary norms, a matter illustrated at a later point.[160] It only needs to be added that the claim here is not that the spheres of application of the rule and the exception are fixed forever. But neither are they in constant flux. A new equilibrium can be reached between the norm and the exception, but this will be through the collective practices of states that are captured in a new rule or text.

IV.   The Intellectual Tasks of Jurisprudence

While McDougal's theses on indeterminacy of rules were flawed, his critique of legal formalism was incisive. His stress on the inextricable relationship between law and policy could not be faulted even as he went too far by obscuring the distinction between the two. It was seen that the inspiration for the attack on traditional jurisprudence came from American legal realism. But, as was noted, McDougal was equally dissatisfied with the negative orientation of the legal realists. As Lasswell put it, 'McDougal had a doubly negative orientation: he was dissatisfied with traditional jurisprudence; he was disenchanted with American legal realists. He at once perceived the possibilities of a comprehensive, affirmative and empirical method'.[161] As early as 1946, in a well-known article titled 'The Law School of the Future: From Legal Realism to Policy Science in the World Community', McDougal observed:

> The time has come for legal realism to yield predominant emphasis to policy science, in the world community and all its constituent communities. It

---

[159] Though theoretically McDougal admits that where ambiguities arise concerning the expectations of parties to a particular agreement 'it is enlightening to consider the practices that were current at the time the arrangement was made...', McDougal, Lasswell and Miller, *Interpretation of Agreement*, p. 60. However, the historical task itself is perceived in a manner which does not permit an objective assessment. See pp. 126–128.

[160] See infra pp. 171–174.

[161] Harold D. Lasswell, 'In Collaboration with McDougal', 1 (1971) *Denver Journal of International Law and Policy*, pp. 17–19 at p. 17.

is time for corrosive analysis and inspired destruction to be supplemented by purposeful, unremitting efforts to apply the best existing scientific knowledge to solving the policy problems of all our communities.[162]

Soon enough, Lasswell's configurative and policy-oriented approach was conjoined with a steadfast commitment to liberalism to produce a comprehensive and complex theoretical apparatus with which to do international law. It is here that the New Haven approach departed from critical legal studies (CLS) which also has its roots in American legal realism. McDougal addressed the difference between CLS and New Haven approach in the following way:

> We seek more emphasis upon deliberate creation and appreciation of policy than most prior framers of jurisprudence and we recognize the need for a comprehensive, integrated set of values to achieve this emphasis. It is here that we differ from the Critical Legal Studies people ... [W]e try to be constructive as well as destructive.[163]

For their part, as Saberi has noted, CLS 'would cringe' at 'New Haven's commitment to a scientific approach to decision-making'.[164]

The move towards a scientific policy-oriented approach required that appropriate intellectual tasks be performed, including developing a realistic understanding of the international decision-making process.[165] The intellectual tasks that McDougal and Lasswell identified included the clarification of goal values, the description of past trends in decision, the analysis of conditions affecting decision, the projection of future trends in decision, and the invention and evaluation of policy alternatives. It is emphasized that these tasks are to be performed 'systematically and configuratively in relation to specified problems in context',[166] by which McDougal meant 'choosing the phase at which a sequence of interactions [between participants in the world social, power and legal process] appears to culminate in choices enforced by sanctions and deprivation or indulgence'.[167] In sum, the policy-oriented

---

[162] Myres S. McDougal, 'The Law School of the Future: From Legal Realism to Policy Science in the World Community', 56 (1946–47) *Yale Law Journal,* pp. 1345–1355 at p. 1349.

[163] Cited in Saberi, 'Love It or Hate It', p. 63, fn 15.

[164] See ibid., p. 63.

[165] The order of analysis could also be reversed i.e., the map of the decision-making process could be analysed at first followed by the intellectual tasks that policy-oriented approach sets the scholar.

[166] McDougal, Lasswell and Reisman, 'Theories about International Law', p. 197.

[167] See ibid., p. 198. The 'intellectual tasks' have been termed 'principles of procedure' and the analysis of the process of decision making 'principles of content'. Wiessner and Willard, 'Policy-oriented Jurisprudence', pp. 58, 62.

approach calls for 'a contextual, problem-oriented, multimethod jurisprudence of international law'.[168]

A.   The Observational Standpoint

In performing the intellectual tasks, the policy-oriented approach lays
great stress on clarifying the observational standpoint of the scholar.[169]
It recommends an observational standpoint 'of citizens who are identified with the future of mankind as a whole rather than with the primacy
of any particular group'.[170] If the universal standpoint is to be faithfully
assumed, a scholar has to be aware of his or her class position, culture,
interest and personality.[171] In speaking of the observational standpoint,
the policy-oriented approach was in its times unique among contemporary approaches to international law. It was rare then to call for awareness of the factors shaping a scholar's thinking and interests. McDougal
also crucially distinguished the role of a scholar from that of the decision
maker of a particular community leading him to speak of 'theories *about*
law as contrasted with theories *of* law'.[172] In his view:

> when a jurisprudence fails to distinguish the theories required by a schol-
> arly observer for the performance of his intellectual tasks from the the-
> ories employed by the participants in the social process in making and
> justifying decisions (theories which are in fact a part of the events being
> observed), serious distortions in perception and reporting may occur.
> One of the gravest distortions that is attendant upon failure to determine
> and to maintain a consistent observational standpoint is the inability to

[168] See ibid., p. 196.
[169] Riesman, *View from the New Haven School*, p. 120. Reisman narrates that 'when a student in one of his [i.e. McDougal's] classes made some judgmental or appraisive statement, McDougal was likely to ask: "Who are you?"... Drawing on the philosophy of
science, McDougal understood that the momentarily dominant self in your bundle of
identities, at that point in time, or "history," if you prefer, will perceive and appraise
differently from other selves and that self-awareness and consistency in observation are
critical preconditions to the success of every other intellectual task'. Reisman, 'Theory
about Law', p. 938.
[170] Myres S. McDougal, Harold D. Lasswell and Lung-chu Chen, 'Human Rights and World
Public Order: A Framework for Policy-Oriented Inquiry', 63 (1969) *The American Journal
of International Law*, pp. 237–269 at p. 264.
[171] Therefore, McDougal made the 'strong recommendation that the scholar should be as
conscious as possible of the different communities with which he identifies, of which he is
a member, and upon which he has unavoidable impacts'. Lasswell and McDougal, 'Criteria
for a Theory', p. 380.
[172] McDougal and Reisman, 'Changing Structure', p. 813.

distinguish a comprehensive community perspective from that of particular participants.[173]

Yet McDougal himself rarely succeeded in assuming the observational standpoint of a global citizen who identified with the future of humankind. Indeed, as is discussed presently, McDougal proposed a provincial understanding of world order goals that saw him consistently endorse the standpoint of the US foreign policy establishment.[174] Of greater significance from a theoretical perspective is perhaps the fact that there is in McDougal's prodigious work 'no discussion of feminist, gay and lesbian, indigenous peoples', or black 'readings' of international law.[175] There is also little space devoted to 'the cartography of suffering and victimization that occurs within the sort of public order system, based on the principles of liberal democracy, of which they approve'.[176] In fact, as Falk observes, 'the absence of critical perspectives reflecting the interests of excluded constituencies (women, non-Westerners, the poor, indigenous peoples) is a fatal flaw' in the policy-oriented approach.[177] Falk is not alone in making this charge. Hilary Charlesworth has likewise written that while the policy-oriented approach school does attach significance to the clarification of the observer's standpoint it does not do so in practice. Speaking

---

[173] See ibid. Elsewhere they write:

> The primary concern of the scholar must be, as we have indicated, for *enlightenment* about the aggregate interrelationships of authoritative decision and other aspects of community process, while the authoritative decision-maker and others may be more interested in *power*, in the making of effective choices in conformity with demanded public order. If the scholarly observer does not adopt perspectives different from those either of the community member making claims or of the authoritative decision maker who responds to such claims, he can have no criteria for appraising the rationality in terms of community interest of either claims or decision. Hence, what the scholarly observer requires is a theory *about* law, designed to facilitate performance of the pertinent tasks in inquiry about decision, as distinguished from the theories *of* law which are employed by decision-makers and others for obtaining and justifying outcomes within the decision process and are, thus, among the variables about which the scholar seeks enlightenment.

Lasswell and McDougal, 'Criteria for a Theory', p. 376.
[174] See Leo Gross, 'Hans Kelsen', 67 (1973) *The American Journal of International Law*, pp. 491–501 at p. 493; Stanley Hoffmann, *Contemporary Theories of International Relations* (Englewood Cliffs, NJ: Prentice Hall, 1960), p. 10; Young, 'International Law', pp. 74–75; Saberi, 'Love It or Hate It', pp. 74–75.
[175] Falk, 'Casting the Spell', p. 2007.
[176] See ibid.
[177] See ibid., pp. 2007–2008.

from a feminist perspective, she observes that while the New Haven view was 'at first sight similar to the feminist concern with the politics of identity',[178] it was not the case in reality. In her words:

> from a feminist perspective, the New Haven School is interested in only a very narrow understanding of standpoint, failing to attribute any significance to the sex of the observer and the gendered world of international law. If law is a 'human artifact', is it not relevant that its makers are almost invariably men? The New Haven commitment to a world public order of human dignity also fails to consider the gendered dimensions of the notions of order and public dignity.[179]

Similarly, there is almost no attention paid to the standpoint of third world nations and peoples. In a well-known comment on the policy-oriented approach, Oran Young observed:

> Although he [i.e., McDougal] is concerned with the plight of the third world under the general rubric of achieving human dignity, he has not displayed a particularly high level of sensitivity to the extreme problems facing many of the developing nations in their efforts to 'catch up' within the framework of the existing international system.[180]

But more recently it has been claimed by Wiessner and Willard that there is a certain commonality between TWAIL and the policy-oriented approach:

> like Third World Approaches to International Law (TWAIL) ... policy oriented jurisprudence is concerned fundamentally with how power and other values are shaped and shared in the world community. Since law is a distinct element of power in every community, the ways in which law helps to establish and maintain particular distributions of power and other values is also a major issue policy-oriented jurisprudence shares with TWAIL. Moreover, we suspect that our conclusion that international law often works against efforts to achieve a public order of human dignity would be compatible with appraisals carried out by scholars associated with TWAIL.[181]

---

[178] Hilary Charlesworth, 'Feminist Methods in International Law' in Ratner and Slaughter (eds.), *Methods of International Law*, pp. 159–185 at p. 180.
[179] See ibid., pp. 180–181. This did not mean that McDougal did not address the issue of the rights of women. He certainly did so. See for instance Myres S. McDougal, Harold D. Lasswell, and Lung-chu Chen, 'Human Rights for Women and World Public Order: The Outlawing of Sex-Based Discrimination', 69 (2005) *The American Journal of International Law*, pp. 497–533. But he did not look at international law from a gender perspective.
[180] Young, 'International Law ', p. 74.
[181] Wiessner and Willard, 'Policy Oriented Jurisprudence', fn. 7.

Indeed they go on to add that 'from the perspective of policy-oriented jurisprudence, the common interest does not necessarily align with the demands and claims of dominant powers of past and present'.[182] This asser-tion brings to the fore the possibility of developing a critical New Haven approach. It also helps understand why in the past many third world scholars were not averse to embracing the New Haven approach.[183] But for a critical turn to become a reality the New Haven approach needs to internalize the different critiques of contemporary international law from race, class and gender standpoints. For as McDougal himself emphasized, 'the clarity and fidelity' with which the observational standpoint is main-tained 'affects every other feature of inquiry: how problems are defined, what goals are postulated, and what intellectual skills are employed'.[184]

The prospect of a critical New Haven approach of course raises the crucial question whether the New Haven approach is, as is sometimes claimed, an empty frame that can tolerate divergent value systems and following it different policy prescriptions. While its analytical frame-work is discussed in some detail presently, it may not be inappropriate to pose and consider the question in the context of the recommended observational standpoint. In the view of John Norton Moore 'the pol-icy plugged into the [New Haven] system is largely independent of the system. The analytic tools of the system will, like a computer, function equally well should someone postulate a public order of human indignity rather than the public order of human dignity espoused by McDougal and Lasswell'.[185] This view helps explain 'the inability of honest, intel-ligent, morally sensitive, and politically moderate individuals steeped in the New Haven approach to agree in the domain of policy applica-tion'.[186] Falk appears to concur with Moore when he observes that 'oppos-ing lines of interpretation by individuals of comparable intelligence and

---

[182] See ibid.

[183] In fact, Falk writes that 'the McDougal and Lasswell framework has had more influence in Third World countries than any other American jurisprudential perspective-a surprising result given the founders' penchant for applying their theory in justification of U.S. for-eign policy. This truth illustrates the power of the framework to structure decisions what-ever the observational stance of the user'. Falk, 'Casting the Spell', p. 1995. Albeit, one of the founder figures of TWAIL, a product of Yale Law School, R. P. Anand, never used the New Haven approach as he found it constraining to articulate the standpoint of third world states and peoples.

[184] John Norton Moore, *Law and the Indo-China War* (Princeton, NJ: Princeton University Press, 1972), p. 83.

[185] Ibid., p. 63. The Moore view can be traced to Lasswell who held a similar view, at least for some time. See Saberi, 'Descendants', p. 39.

[186] Falk, 'Casting the Spell', p. 2000.

virtue can reach utterly opposed policy conclusions on controversial matters even as they acknowledge their indebtedness to the McDougal and Lasswell jurisprudence'.[187] If Moore and Falk are right, a critical New Haven approach is a distinct possibility and Wiessner and Willard are right in suggesting that the TWAIL standpoint can be accommodated. However, the assumption that the policy-oriented approach is a neutral frame is open to question. Three points may be made here. First, it is a neutral frame only to the extent that like any theoretical approach it can tolerate different assessments of an empirical situation and following from it diverse policy recommendations. Second, it can be viewed as a neutral frame if the reference is to following a 'procedure' of conducting research in the mundane sense of the term, i.e., to having a checklist of tasks to be performed in pursuing scholarly work. But to so suggest is to reduce the policy-oriented approach to simply a mode of analysis rather than an approach based on a distinct epistemological and ontological framework accompanied by an appropriate methodology for conducting research. Third, to speak of a neutral frame beyond these possibilities is to neglect the critique that a framework of explanation cannot be accepted while rejecting its goal values.[188] For, as Charles Taylor explains, 'a conception of human needs [...] enters into a given ... theory, and cannot be considered something extraneous which we later add to the framework to yield a set of value judgments'.[189] And, if as is argued in the next section, the policy-oriented approach is committed to a certain schedule of values intimately associated with capitalism and liberalism it then makes it difficult to see how it is employing a neutral frame. While disagreements are permissible within any theoretical framework, it also sets the limits beyond which it cannot accommodate different policy prescriptions. Thus, for instance, the policy-oriented approach cannot certainly accept the prescription of abolition of private property. As a matter of fact, the policy-oriented approach was advanced during the Cold War in clear opposition to Marxism. This in turn means that the observational standpoint of a global citizen is assumed from within what is essentially a liberal framework. There is certainly potential from within the policy-oriented approach to pursue the goal of human dignity in an inclusive manner. But it can attend to class, gender, race and geographical divides only from within a liberal framework that does not call for structural

---

[187] See ibid., p. 2001.
[188] Charles Taylor, *Philosophy and the Human Sciences,* vol. II (Cambridge: Cambridge University Press, 1985), p. 75.
[189] See ibid. His critique of Lasswell is at pp. 77–81.

changes to be undertaken. In other words, the goal values to which the policy-oriented approach subscribes have a clearly liberal orientation. It is this theme that is now addressed.

B.   Clarification of Goal Values

An important contribution of American legal realism to understanding the process of adjudication was the view that judges should not surreptitiously introduce personal predilections while interpreting and applying the law, but instead should openly identify and debate them.[190] The policy-oriented approach likewise urges the explicit postulation of basic public order goals.[191] The overriding goal to which it commits itself is that of human dignity which, it is worth reiterating, anticipates 'a social process in which values are widely and not narrowly shared, and in which private choice, rather than coercion, is emphasized as the predominant modality of power'.[192] The postulation and clarification of a detailed map of goal values is not considered a 'mere exercise in faith' or 'derivation by exercise of logical (syntactic) skill' but an empirical exercise.[193] McDougal contends that the set of goal values he elaborates in relation to wealth, power, enlightenment and so on do not represent an 'idiosyncratic or arbitrary choice' but are those that 'are commonly characterized as the basic values of human dignity of a free society'.[194]

But it is not clear how McDougal ascertained the wishes of the peoples of the world. A perusal of his work reveals that he merely assumed the superiority of Western liberal values. McDougal for instance a priori ruled out any engagement with 'socialist values'. In the process, as Terry Nardin has pointed out, McDougal overlooked the 'circularity and arbitrariness' of his proposed value clarification:

> The clarification of values is supposed to be a purely empirical activity uninfluenced by preconceived moral principles, but at the same time certain values are excluded from the empirical canvas because they are

[190] Hart, 'Essays in Jurisprudence', p. 132.
[191] For among other things 'there can be no inquiry about international law, whether by scholarly observers or decision-makers, without consequences, in the enlightenment or obscurantism it produces, for global public order'. Myres S. McDougal and Michael W. Reisman, 'International Law in Policy Oriented Perspective', in R. St. J. Macdonald and D. M. Johnston (eds.), *The Structure and Process of International Law* (The Hague: Martinus Nijhoff, 1983), pp. 103–129 at p. 122.
[192] McDougal, *Studies*, p. 132.
[193] McDougal, Lasswell and Chen, *Human Rights*, p. 378. See also pp. 68–80.
[194] See ibid., p. 90.

morally offensive ... In the end, therefore, the value of human dignity is simply postulated.[195]

As Stone had earlier noted, while McDougal apotheosized individual human beings, he hedged against the need for empirical attention by observing that the complexity and range of the world process can 'dwarf, if not obliterate, the effectiveness of any one citizen'.[196] More significantly, in view of the fact that McDougal paid little attention to the perspectives of subaltern peoples and groups the values postulated by the elites in Western societies came to be represented as the common claims, aspirations and expectations of mankind.[197] As Rosalyn Higgins observed in the context of the third world nations, 'McDougal is concerned for human dignity in the new nations, as in all nations; but he does not see the developing countries as requiring the separate and urgent attention of the legal process'.[198] In fact, McDougal was rarely supportive of the claims of the peoples of underdeveloped nations.[199] His insensitivity to their concerns was symbolized by his support for US policies during the Vietnam War.[200]

The content of the value of human dignity is in fact derived from a bourgeois image of man. As Francis Boyle notes, 'it is evident that McDougal-Lasswell jurisprudence postulates capitalism to be the preferred economic system for the realization of its conception of fundamental human rights'.[201] In the debate on private property McDougal assumed a Lockean position.[202] In this view 'individuals have a natural right to property, a right prior to civil society and government, and not dependent on the

[195] Nardin, *Morality,* p. 204.

[196] Julius Stone, 'A Sociological Perspective on International Law' in Macdonald and Johnston (eds.), *Structure and Process,* pp. 263–303 at p. 274.

[197] Falk has also pointed out that 'McDougal tends to identify the representatives of governments with the well-being of the peoples of the world', an identification which 'runs contrary to fact with respect to any humanistic schedule of values'. Falk, 'International Legal Studies', p. 1012. See also Stone, 'Sociological Perspective', p. 277.

[198] Rosalyn Higgins, 'Policy and Impartiality: The Uneasy Relationship in International Law', 23 (1969), *International Organisation,* pp. 914–931 at p. 924. See also Falk, *Legal Order,* p. 83; and Young, 'International Law', p. 74.

[199] For a different view, see Alwyn Freeman, 'Professor McDougal's Law and Minimum World Public Order', 58 (1964) *American Journal of International Law,* pp. 711–716. See, however, Richard Falk's reply, 'International Legal Order: Alwyn V. Freeman vs. Myres S.McDougal', 59 (1965) *American Journal of International Law,* pp. 66–71.

[200] Richard Falk, *Status of Law,* pp. 577–579; and Young, 'International Law'.

[201] Francis A. Boyle, 'The Irrelevance of International Law: The Schism between International Law and International Politics', 10 (1980) *California Western International Law Journal,* pp. 193–219 at p. 213.

[202] See ibid., p. 212.

consent of others to it'.[203] There is no recognition that the capitalist path or the Western liberal democratic model is not the only viable alternative. In the words of Falk, McDougal 'presupposes a certain epistemological confidence which he never sustains with solid evidence'.[204] Yet scholars like Higgins defended him against Falk's reference to the competing model of Marxism and socialism. Higgins observed in response to Falk:

> If McDougal has failed to validate as opposed to postulate, the superiority of liberal democracy, Falk equally fails to deal with the question by mere reference to desirable objectives of Marxism which remain but a dream on paper. It surely behooves him to examine the competing political systems in operation and to ascertain whether the very nature of Marxism does not entail greater repressions of human dignity than does democratic capitalism with all its shortcomings.[205]

While it is certainly the case that at the time Higgins made this observation the Stalinist model of socialism led to extensive denial of human rights in the socialist world, it did not mean that the value of democracy and respect for human rights is necessarily incompatible with Marxism and socialism.[206] In fact the realistic possibility of democratic socialism explains why, despite the collapse of 'actually existing socialism', the attraction of a non-capitalist path has not diminished for subaltern groups and classes, in particular in the developing world.

The model of human dignity that McDougal offered suffers from another weakness. In McDougal's writings the treatment of human rights was pitched at such a general and abstract level that he did not address the problem of competing rights, that is, potential conflicts between preferred values. As Stone pointed out:

> with the list of 'values' which is so central a feature of Professor McDougal's policy-oriented legal science, national and international, the real difficulties begin after the values have been listed and named, either in general or for the particular conflict. It is after that, usually, that the crucial choices have to be made about which of them is to be sacrificed, and how far. For, except in the simplest cases, not all of them can be equally secured.[207]

Furthermore, McDougal did not sufficiently recognize that 'it is difficult to achieve a very high rank in terms of a stated value without having

---

[203] C. B. Macpherson, *Democratic Theory: essays in retrieval* (Oxford: Clarendon Press, 1973), p. 231.
[204] Falk, *Legal Order*, p. 89.
[205] Higgins, 'Policy and Impartiality', pp. 921–922; emphasis in original dropped.
[206] For a brief discussion of the Marxist conception of human rights, see Chapter 7, pp. 534–543.
[207] Stone, 'Notion of International Justice', p. 424.

substantial capabilities in terms of other values'.[208] In the absence of a serious analysis of the relationship between different values, the cause of a number of listed deprivations was often treated as a demand for a shared preferred value. For example, the 'lack of inadequate protection of the rights of property' is listed along with 'disparities in the distribution of wealth' among the deprivations. To put it differently, while theoretically 'any given value may be instrumental in the exercise of other values', the power and wealth values are significant determinants for the realization of other values. The means-end chain ensures that power-wealth is accumulated in states, classes and groups which already have an abundant share. In advancing this critique the plea is for a more open-minded clarification of values in the matrix of historical trends so as to effectively pursue and realize the goal of human dignity.

C.   Description of Past Trends

The description of past trends is an essential intellectual task that the policy oriented approach sets itself,[209] as 'we need to know whence we came, where we stand now, and in what direction we are moving, if we are to have any rational hope of transforming our aspirations of the present into the facts of the future'.[210] While in performing the historical task the policy-oriented approach avoids the classical problems of empiricism through an explicit statement of its goal values,[211] it embraces the other pitfall of thinking that since all history is interpretation the 'criterion of a right interpretation is its suitability to some present purpose'.[212] In this view, in the words of E. H. Carr, 'knowledge is knowledge for some

---

[208] Young, *Systems of Political Science*, pp. 67–68.

[209] The term 'trend' is used to specify 'the present distribution of goals sought, the degree of their contemporary realization, and the extent to which this realization has become greater or less through time'. McDougal, *Studies in World Public Order*, p. 19.

[210] McDougal, Lasswell and Chen, *Human Rights*, p. 423.

[211] As Suzuki rightly notes:

> objectivity cannot be achieved by simply collecting facts and presuming that they speak for themselves. Facts are not events; they are often the conclusions the observer has drawn from observing events. How the observer collects the facts necessary for his enquiry and how he establishes the causal relationship among them cannot be answered without some preconceptions as to the events he is observing and the goals he seeks.

> Suzuki, 'New Haven School of International Law', p. 15.

[212] E. H. Carr, *What is History* (Middlesex: Penguin, 1976), p. 27.

purpose. The validity of the knowledge depends on the validity of the purpose.'[213] And as Carr adds, 'even where no such theory has been professed the practice has often been no less disquieting'[214] as is the case with the policy-oriented approach. In other words, having assumed the preference for liberal democratic values embedded in Western capitalist societies, facts are selectively marshalled to confirm their validity and desirability.

While the choice of facts is a necessary process in any historical writing, it cannot be entirely arbitrary if it is to be sound history. There is a need to identify and distinguish 'real or significant facts' from secondary and accidental facts.[215] The historian must apply the 'right standard of significance' and place them within an acceptable interpretation of events.[216] A review of McDougal's statement of past trends in the field of human rights reveals that he does not meet this criterion. He opens with the remark that 'the changing trends and conditions relevant to human rights are evidently connected with the culture of cities'.[217] He then observes how the urban environment has developed over six thousand years altering the traditional role of kinship, but without recognizing in the beginning the 'human rights of the individual'.[218] While a complex division of labour evolved, it gave rise to great differences in wealth sanctioned by law. But according to McDougal, over time components of this urban environment have developed as a result of changing social relations resulting in 'the respect revolution'.[219] This trend has in his view gained ground in an increasingly 'interdependent urbanizing world'.[220]

In this simplistic portrayal of history McDougal glosses over the fact that over the last four centuries capitalism has generated a fictitious respect revolution that veils the serious constraints that continue to be imposed upon the freedom of choice and equality of opportunity of subaltern groups and classes. It is also disappointing that McDougal fails to examine the relationship between 'city' and 'country' at the global level for as Raymond Williams has observed 'one of the last models of "city

[213] See ibid.
[214] See ibid.
[215] See ibid., p. 120.
[216] See ibid., p. 123.
[217] McDougal, Lasswell and Chen, *Human Rights*, p. 424.
[218] See ibid.
[219] See ibid., p. 426.
[220] See ibid., pp. 427–428.

and country" is the system we now know as imperialism".[221] Instead, McDougal used the empty phrase 'interdependent urbanizing globe' without so much as a casual glance at the vast 'countryside' that it has spawned harbouring the wretched of the earth. The themes of gross violations of human rights and genocide in the colonial era hardly receive any attention. Neither does the continuing exploitation of third world peoples in the postcolonial era. In short, the McDougal description of past trends with respect to the realization of human rights leaves much to be desired, as he is silent on the most salient developments. A flawed understanding of the role of history also prevented him from acknowledging that the free societies he so valued were responsible for heinous crimes against humanity over the centuries.

D.   Identification of Conditioning Factors

At least one reason for the partial and subjective nature of McDougal's trend study of the realization of the goal of human dignity is because of an inadequate understanding of conditioning factors.[222] The policy-oriented approach describes the conditioning factors as being 'the interplay of the multiple factors affecting decision', an approach in which '*overwhelming importance will not be ascribed to any one factor or category of factors* (such as those relating to wealth)'.[223] It is evident that this understanding was counterposed to the alleged economic determinism of Marxism. In fact, in reviewing different approaches to human rights, McDougal made precisely that allegation. While he acknowledged Marxism's 'intense concern for human rights',[224] McDougal hastened to add that insofar as the conditioning factors necessary for realizing them was concerned it assigned 'exaggerated deference to the weight of the economic variable'.[225] He went to observe that 'it has become increasingly clumsy to divide all factors in psychological and social processes into "material" and the "non

---

[221] Raymond Williams, 'The New Metropolis' in Hamza Alavi and Teodor Shanin (eds.), *Introduction to the Sociology of Developing Societies* (London: Macmillan, 1982), pp. 363–365 at p. 363.
[222] As McDougal admitted, 'a trend study without reference to conditioning factors can be of little utility in determining how and in what degree goals have been achieved in the past and whether, given comparable conditions, the same strategies for goal realization will be useful in future projections'. McDougal and Reisman, 'International Law', p. 126. Therefore the task of identifying the most significant conditioning factors is crucial.
[223] McDougal, Lasswell and Chen, *Human Rights* , p. 92; emphasis added.
[224] See ibid., p. 77.
[225] See ibid., p. 79.

material".[226] He concluded his review of the Marxist approach by referring to the practices of 'actually existing socialism' that entirely negated individual human rights.[227]

It is interesting that the extensive footnotes to that section carry no reference to the writings of Karl Marx or those versions of Marxism that reject economic determinism.[228] More pertinently, the policy-oriented approach offers an understanding of conditioning factors that can best be described as economic indeterminism. The vulgar Marxist standpoint is replaced by its opposite, an incoherent policy-oriented approach that merely calls for taking cognizance of an endless array of variables that interact with each other to produce social effects. It advances an allegedly multicausal framework in which critical variables are treated as mere inputs for consideration and examination.[229] The outcome is the production of a vast amount of raw data which can be selectively used to support subjective determinations. In other words, in the absence of any kind of systems analysis that prioritizes causes, preferred conclusions can be arrived at with ease. Further, as Young noted of Lasswell, whose schema the policy-oriented approach adopts, that 'even his long-standing interest in such social phenomena as class developments and the nature of groups must be seen from the basic perspective of individuals. Though social aggregates occupy an important place in some of his work, such aggregates are ultimately composed of individuals pursuing interpersonal relations in various contexts'.[230] The multicausal approach that is espoused by McDougal must therefore be seen in the background of its inability to leave behind 'methodological individualism' and come to terms with the fact that the individual functions from within a set of given social relations, and not as he pleases.[231]

E.   Projection of Future Trends

The projection of future trends is another significant intellectual task to be attended to in the policy-oriented approach. In an effort to bridge the

---

[226] See ibid.
[227] See ibid., p. 77.
[228] On the concept of 'base-superstructure' model in Marx, see Chapter 7, pp. 449–461.
[229] As Young has noted, Lasswell's apparatus 'tends to hinder the development of theory severely by introducing excessive numbers of potentially relevant factors while the crucial problem in developing viable formal theories is to construct simple logical models by stripping away as many factors as possible without undermining the predictive accuracy of the resultant propositions'. Young, 'International Law', p. 69.
[230] Young, *Systems of Political Science*, p. 71.
[231] For a discussion of methodological individualism, see Chapter 5, pp. 276–279.

gap between the present and the desirable future, the latter is to be made 'conscious, explicit, comprehensive and realistic' as aid to the invention and evaluation of alternatives.[232] The desirable future of the international society is captured and projected by the policy-oriented approach with the phrase 'free people's commonwealth', a society characterized by 'shared participation in both production and enjoyment of all value processes'.[233] The forecast of future developments that could help realize this goal is not viewed as 'a simple-minded extrapolation of the past' leading to predictions in terms of 'inevitability'.[234] The procedure recommended is the formulation of developmental constructs 'that range through a broad spectrum or continuum of possibilities, *from the most optimistic to the most pessimistic*'.[235]

The pessimistic construct sees the world turned into 'a world of militarized, garrisoned communities, controlled from the centre and modeled on the prison'.[236] In such societies all values would be concentrated in few hands and subjected to the supreme value power. The role of military would grow in such societies and the potentialities of modern science and technology put to destructive use. The trends in favour of a pessimist construct were identified as growing military establishments, the increasing regimentation of society, concentration of wealth, erosion of individual liberties, the drying up of information, and so on. On the other hand, the factors in favour of the optimistic construct are listed as growing interdependence between peoples and nations, the acceleration of the tempo of change through science and technology, and the effort of world's intellectuals to clarify, affirm and implement the conception of human dignity.[237]

The question remains as to whether the trends in favour of the optimistic or pessimistic constructs are likely to prevail. This is where the flaws which afflict the process of investigation in the policy-oriented approach – clarification of goal values, description of past trends, analyses of conditioning factors – carry over into projection of alternative futures. In view of the absence of a serious history and sociology of international relations, and given the parochial conception of human dignity, it is difficult to imagine how any projection of future trends can have a sound basis.

---

[232] McDougal, Lasswell and Chen, *Human Rights*, p. 93.
[233] See ibid., p. 438.
[234] See ibid., pp. 437, 439. At another place McDougal uses the words 'a free and abundant peoples' commonwealth'. McDougal, 'International Law', p. 327.
[235] See ibid., p. 437; emphasis added.
[236] See ibid., p. 438.
[237] See ibid.

The fundamental idea seemed to have been to oppose the possibility of any world order other than that which is home to 'democratic capitalism'. In doing so the policy-oriented approach ignored the troubling consequences of universalizing capitalism and accompanying imperialism. It is, however, no surprise that the trends in favour of a pessimistic construct, that essentially signalled to McDougal a world in which 'actually existing socialism' became dominant, best captures today the state of a world dominated by 'actually existing capitalism'.

F.   The Invention and Evaluation of Alternatives

The final task of invention and evaluation of alternatives addresses the difficult question as to 'how strategies can be devised for spanning the distance between generalized goals and the more specific objectives suitable to a problematic situation'.[238] In performing this task the other intellectual tasks are to be synthesized and made relevant to the 'search for and promotion of integrative solutions characterized by maximum gains and minimum losses'.[239] A perusal of McDougal's writings shows that while he viewed changes in the environment or material conditioning factors relevant in bringing about a preferred world order, he essentially puts his faith in modifying the perspectives of peoples. According to him, the 'paramount task' for all who are genuinely committed to the goal values of a world public order of human dignity 'is that of creating in peoples of the world the perspectives necessary for accelerated movement toward such a public order'.[240] More specifically, he wrote, 'it is hardly a novel insight that the factors – culture, class, interest, personality, and crisis – which importantly condition peoples' perspectives can be modified to foster constructive rather than destructive perspectives'.[241]

In fact, McDougal appeared to have an illimitable faith in reason, so much so that he maintained that the predispositions of elites and decision makers – at the national and the global levels – can be transformed to support the cause of human dignity. He followed in the footsteps of John Stuart Mill (as also John Dewey and Alfred North Whitehead) who, treating the independent individual as the datum of social analysis, and asserting the primary role of ideas, argued that education can help

---

[238] See ibid., p. 440.
[239] See ibid., p. 93.
[240] See ibid., p. 443.
[241] See ibid.

overcome the fundamental contradictions in society.[242] In the process McDougal inflated the role of the free-choosing rational man and that of mental regeneration in transforming societies. On the other hand, he tended to ignore the serious constraints which social structures impose on the nature of reforms which can be introduced through education or modification of perspectives. In fact he observed that:

> the divisive effects of special *interests,* in different functional or territorial groups, may be minimized by candid exposure of narrow perceptions of interest and by according primacy to aggregate, long-term interests. The importance of developing multiple interests, especially through a wide range of pluralistic groups, may be stressed in positive programs to channel special interest in the direction of common interest.[243]

In this scheme of things McDougal assigned to the international lawyer the role of 'propagators of the idea of human dignity'. It was the responsibility of the international lawyer to perform an edifying role and in this light 'shape the future of the discipline'.[244] This task could not be carried out by those who had a constrained understanding of their vocation. More specifically, it could only be performed by those who saw the necessity of ensuring 'the future of liberal democracy'.[245]

The recommended strategy of transforming perspectives of individuals and groups to pursue common interests is clearly inadequate in the face of the power and influence of global capital over world social and power processes. In this regard, the heroic role McDougal assigns to the invisible college to transform the discipline, in order to realize a free people's commonwealth, places too heavy a burden on its shoulders. But it needs to be acknowledged that McDougal was among the first to envisage a crucial role for international lawyer in shaping the future of the world order. That he was ahead of his times can be seen from the fact that even today, in the era of accelerated globalization, when international law has acquired a critical role in human affairs, most international lawyers have a restrictive understanding of their role in influencing systems of global governance. They are seen as performing a narrow and technical rather than an edifying and critical function. In stressing the latter, Richard Falk and the founders of NAIL, David Kennedy and Marti Koskenniemi,

---

[242] Graeme Duncan, *Marx and Mill: Two Views of Social Conflict and Social Harmony* (Cambridge: Cambridge University Press, 1973), pp. 212–216.

[243] McDougal, Lasswell and Chen, *Human Rights,* p. 445; emphasis in original.

[244] Saberi, 'Descendants', pp. 44, 45.

[245] See ibid., p. 49.

have followed in the footsteps of McDougal. The problematic aspect of the McDougal vision was that he did not sufficiently appreciate the role of global social and political structures in engendering exploitation and oppression of individuals, groups and nations and limiting the role education can play in realizing 'common interests'.[246] To put it differently, a principal weakness of the policy-oriented approach is the absence of a serious theory of resistance that charts out ways of realizing the goal of 'human dignity'.

The restructuring of global social and political structures can of course be imagined in many ways. Thus, for instance, in conceptualizing alternatives to global capitalism, Michael Hardt and Antonio Negri proceed by rejecting what they see as false alternatives: it is to be 'neither private nor public, neither capitalist nor socialist' opening 'a new space for politics'.[247] Likewise, Boaventura de Sousa Santos argues that 'beyond the state and the market, a third social domain must be reinvented: a collective, but not state-centered, private but not profit-oriented, a social domain in which the right to a solidarity-oriented transformation of property rights will be socially and politically anchored'.[248] In short, a range of perspectives about alternative futures need to be explored, albeit with a degree of realism and a commitment to the goal of human dignity.[249]

V. The Process of Decision Making

In the policy-oriented approach, the effective performance of intellectual tasks has a critical bearing on international decision making. The inadequacies that characterize their execution directly impact the nature and outcomes of decision making. It is, therefore, not surprising that even the conceptualization and elaboration of the decision-making process leaves much to be desired. Before proceeding further it is important to recall that in the policy-oriented view law is not to be equated with mere rules but seen 'as a continuous *process* of authoritative decision, including both the constitutive and public order decisions by which a community's

---

[246] B. S. Chimni, 'Capitalism, Imperialism and International Law in the Twenty First Century', 14 (2012) *Oregon Review of International Law,* pp. 17–45.

[247] Michael Hardt and Antonio Negri, *Commonwealth* (Cambridge, MA: Harvard University Press, 2009), p. ix.

[248] Boaventura de Sousa Santos, 'Human Rights as an Emancipatory Script? Cultural and Political Conditions' in Boaventura de Sousa Santos (ed.), *Another World is Possible: Beyond Northern Epistemologies* (London: Verso, 2007), pp. 3–40 at p. 31.

[249] For the IMAIL vision, see Chapter 7, pp. 543–550.

policies are made and remade'.[250] In the circumstances, if the map and analysis of the international decision-making process does not approximate reality, it can distort the understanding of the nature, character and role of law in international affairs.

The policy-oriented approach offers an elaborate 'analytical framework' 'to bring into view the principal features of decision' that include 'the establishment of an authoritative decision process in the world community'.[251] It also allows a focus on decisions in particular arenas, especially in 'established authoritative arenas' to see if preferred values are advanced[252]. In this respect the policy-oriented approach offers a 'conceptual technique' involving what is termed a 'phase analysis' i.e., 'choosing the phase at which a sequence of interactions appears to culminate'.[253] It describes the process of authoritative and controlling decision (or legal process) in terms of participants, perspectives, situations, base values, strategies, outcomes and effects. This conceptual schema is to be applied to understanding the legal process 'as a whole or of each component context of interaction' in which '*Man* (actors, participants) acts to optimize *values* (preferred events) through *institutions* affecting *resources*'.[254] The categories of this conceptual schema are best understood in the shape of questions McDougal raises in understanding, explaining and evaluating decisions. The questions are:

1. Who acted or participated in roles of varying significance in the process which culminated in the decision (Participants)?
2. What were the significant perspectives of the participants? With whom were they identified? What value demand were they pursuing, with what expectations? (Perspectives).
3. Where and under what conditions were the participants interacting? (Situations).
4. What effective means for the achievement of their objectives were at the disposal of the different participants? (Base Values).
5. In what manner were these means or base values manipulated? (Strategies).

---

[250] McDougal, Lasswell and Chen, *Human Rights*, p. 382.
[251] Myres S. McDougal, Harold D. Lasswell and Michael W. Reisman, 'The World Constitutive Process of Authoritative Decision', in Richard A. Falk and C. G. Black (eds.), *The Future of the International Legal Order: Trends and Patterns* (Princeton, NJ: Princeton University Press, 1969), pp. 73–154 at pp. 79, 74.
[252] See ibid., pp. 78–79.
[253] See ibid., p. 80.
[254] See ibid., p. 79.

6. What was the immediate result – value allocation – of the process of interaction? (Outcomes).
7. What are the effects, of differing duration, of the process and outcomes? (Effects)[255]

The essential claim of the policy-oriented approach is that only a systematic mapping of the decision-making process allows a proper understanding of its dynamics and the evaluation of outcomes in terms of whether they promote the goal of human dignity. The comprehensive approach that it recommends helps the policy-oriented approach to move away from the narrow standpoints of political realism and positivism with their focus on either one or restricted set of participants, or a singular notion of power, or a limited understanding of the values that can be pursued through the legal process. In contrast, the policy-oriented view takes into account a range of participants that possess diverse perspectives, base values and strategies to pursue a variety of preferences that can be evaluated from the standpoint of the pursuit of common interests.

The problem with the policy-oriented approach to decision making is twofold. The first is its flawed conceptualization of power and the role it plays in the international decision-making process. Following Lasswell, McDougal defined 'power' as participating in 'making and influencing community decisions'.[256] This notion of power suffers from, as the Marxist political scientist Nicos Poulantzas has pointed out, two fundamental defects:

> it succumbs to a voluntarist conception of the decision-making process, through disregarding the effectiveness of the structures, and it is not able exactly to locate beneath the appearances the effective centres of decision inside which the distribution of power works; and (ii) it takes as a principle the 'integrationist' conception of society, from which the concept of 'participation' in decision-making is derived.[257]

In view of these dual weaknesses, the conception of power advanced by the policy-oriented approach is unable to accurately capture the role of structural power in international decision making and flowing from that of dominant groups in international societies. For instance, while it

See ibid., p. 80.
[256] Young, *Systems of Political Science*, p. 85. See also Harold Lasswell and Abraham Kaplan, *Power and Society* (New Haven, CT: Yale University Press, 1950), p. 75. 'Influence' was defined by Lasswell as 'the value position and potential of a person or group'. See ibid., p. 55.
[257] Nicos Poulantzas, *Political Power and Social Classes* (London: Verso, 1978), p. 104

is recognized that wealth is sometimes used to get political power, and political power is sometimes used to get economic power it does not 'treat these relations as central to the nature of political power'.[258] What is lost sight of is, inter alia, the fact that 'political power, being power over others, is used in any unequal society to extract benefit from the ruled for the rulers' or which is the same 'to maintain the extractive power of the class or classes which have extractive power'.[259] In other words, the policy-oriented approach advances a partial and reified concept of power. While McDougal was rightly critical of Morgenthau's narrow and unidimensional understanding of power, and instead offered a multidimensional conception of power, he was unable to identify the different ways in which political power worked in internal and international decision-making processes as he failed to locate it in social structures.[260] To put it differently, because of the inability to rigorously conceptualize the relationship between different conditioning factors in the internal social process the policy-oriented approach could not come to terms with the 'world power process'. As a result, it could not explain and understand on the international plane the exploitative relations between imperial and third world states and how this in turn manifested in the decision-making process.

Second, the map of the decision-making process is so complicated that a scholar or decision maker can get lost in a maze of details as each of the conceptual categories (e.g., participants, perspectives and outcomes) is further broken up into a number of elements.[261] Thus, for instance, the category 'outcomes' is disaggregated in terms of seven functions – intelligence, promotion, prescription, invocation, application, termination and appraisal.[262] The present section does not set itself the task of explaining each of the categories and the elements into which these are broken down for which the reader is best referred to McDougal himself. What follows are general observations on some of the questions or categories

---

[258] Macpherson, *Democratic Theory*, p. 46. And as he further observed, 'there could hardly be a clearer indication of the distance the empirical political theorists have put between themselves and the reality of power, than this assumption that political power *differs* from economic power in being power over others'. See ibid.; emphasis in original.

[259] See ibid., p. 47.

[260] For a discussion of different aspects of 'power' see Chapter 2, pp. 56–58.

[261] Saberi writes that McDougal's proposals 'reaches the outer limits of empirical possibility by requiring investigators to deal with eight value categories and seven phase categories with attendant sub-categories, an open-ended list of conditions of context, and five dispositional factors specifically related to scientific thinking (culture, class, interest, personality, and crisis)'. Saberi, 'Love It or Hate It', p. 109.

[262] McDougal, Lasswell and Chen, *Human Rights*, p. 248.

to argue that McDougal's map does not seriously contribute to a better understanding of the world constitutive process. The principal reason is that it is not integrally conjoined with an explanatory model which does not stop at simply describing various features of the decision-making process. It also does not, as noted before, assign appropriate weight to different conditioning factors and therefore cannot capture the central trends and contradictions in the world social and legal process (e.g., flowing from the relationship between the 'logic of capital' and the 'logic of law'). In the final analysis, McDougal merely presents a checklist of questions and categories that at best help arrange and systematize materials only to be (as in the instance of intellectual tasks) manipulated to serve a particular understanding of human dignity. More significantly, as Saberi points out, the value category 'colonizes the implications of all the other categories in its normative grasp'.[263]

A. Participants

A participant is designated as 'an individual or an entity' that 'can make claims or be subjected to claims'.[264] In adopting this understanding McDougal firmly rejected the traditional doctrinal position that states alone are participants or subjects of international law. He pointed out that 'historically, the greatest difficulty concerning participation in the world constitutive process has been this exaggeration of the role of the nation-state as the principal subject of international law'.[265] McDougal therefore proceeded to take cognizance of other transnational actors like international organizations, political parties, pressure groups, private associations and individuals.[266] He laid particular stress on the individual as a participant in the decision-making process for 'individuals participate as the ultimate actors for all the composite participants as well in their own right'.[267] In emphasizing the role of non-state actors in the international decision-making process he was ahead of his times: the law-making process in the era of globalization reveals the validity of his intuition. His

---

[263] She goes so far as to add that 'the reign of value judgment over all other variables of context and the fixity of value demarcation in the policy-oriented approach neither can nor does leave any hope for a genuinely contextual-oriented jurisprudence'. Saberi, 'Love It or Hate It', pp. 118, 128, 144.

[264] McDougal, Lasswell and Reisman, 'Constitutive Process', p. 81.

[265] McDougal, Lasswell and Chen, *Human Rights*, p. 178.

[266] McDougal, Lasswell and Reisman, 'Constitutive Process', p. 93.

[267] See ibid.

views can be contrasted with that of Jack Goldsmith and Eric Posner who even today continue to focus on the state actor and stress top down international law-making processes.[268] What is difficult to accept in the policy-oriented approach is the understanding that the nation state has today become a serious obstacle to ushering in a just world order. Four points may be made in this regard.

First, while it is true that given the growing interdependence between peoples and nations the nation state is under severe challenge,[269] the critical issue is the nature and consequences that flow from it. The process of modern interdependence between peoples and nations is not new. It can be traced back to the sixteenth century, that is, to the beginning of the capitalist era which created in its wake a world market.[270] But this interdependence, whether related to the power or the wealth process, manifested in the coexistence of metropolitan powers and colonies. It today tolerates a neocolonial relationship between the developed and developing countries. Instead of taking cognizance of this relationship, McDougal observed that 'the massive transformation of ex-colonies into independent states has typically failed to combine nationalism, democracy, and development into coherent and effective programs'.[271] He made no attempt to understand how far the nature of 'interdependence' was responsible for this state of affairs. The reasons for the failure of post-colonial states to deliver on welfare were viewed as entirely internal.[272] Therefore, while McDougal rightly observed that the demand for a new international economic order (NIEO) was 'in a profound sense a demand for human rights'[273] he never indicated the problems with the old order or the changes that have to be brought about to bring about a new order. Therefore, he did not also appreciate that developing countries invoke the principle of sovereignty to protect themselves from those features

---

[268] See Levitt, 'Bottom-up', pp. 409–410.

[269] One cannot but agree that 'the most striking fact about the global social process in which contemporary man pursues his basic values is in its comprehensive and ineradicable dependencies'. McDougal, Lasswell and Chen, *Human Rights*, p. 47.

[270] As Lasswell has noted, 'during the nineteenth century the spread of the capitalistic pattern brought ever widening tracts of the world into an inclusive activity area'. Harold D. Lasswell, *World Politics and Personal Insecurity* (New York: The Free Press, 1965), p. 9. For more detailed discussion of the history and evolution of the world economy and its structure see Chapter 7, pp. 477ff.

[271] McDougal, Lasswell and Chen, *Human Rights*, p. 99.

[272] See ibid., p. 229.

[273] See ibid.

of interdependence which seek to perpetuate colonialism without colonies.[274] In fact, McDougal was unhappy with the increasing democratization of the world power process through the adoption of the principle of sovereign equality of states as it was not based upon the existing distribution of base values.[275] He had thus no objection for instance to the weighted voting procedures in institutions like the IMF for whose democratization the developing nations have repeatedly demanded. In sum, as Stone had pointed out, McDougal did not acknowledge that the fact of growing physical and economic interdependence of nations 'did not in themselves give forth criteria for international justice, but left us with the really hard problems of choosing and articulating these'.[276]

Second, insofar as the growing significance of other transnational actors is concerned, there is insufficient recognition that it is often state action which establishes the primary normative framework within which these thrive and function. For instance, the interests and values pursued by multinational corporations – a major example of non-state actors participating in the world social and constitutive process –is facilitated by

---

[274] As Hedley Bull observed:

> it is no accident that … it is the countries of … the Third World that are most insistent on the preservation of state sovereignty … They regard the institution of sovereignty as one which provides safeguard against the attempts of more powerful states to wrest from them control of the economic resources they now enjoy. It has been by creating sovereign states in defiance of the colonial powers, and by defending these sovereign states against the intrusion and penetration of them by the so-called 'neo-colonial' powers, that the poorer and the weaker nations have been able to achieve for themselves some measure of international justice and, in some cases, of human justice for their inhabitants.

Bull, *Anarchical Society*, pp. 291–292.

[275] To quote McDougal:

> Since decisions are taken by numerical majority in many transnational arenas, effective power has shifted significantly to coalitions of the African-Asian states or of the Third World … This trend toward broader participation has not, however, always been accompanied by appropriate regard for the capabilities of new states to assume a responsible role in world constitutive process … The states of the world differ widely in size, population, resources, institutions, and projected public order systems. Hence, it is important to pierce the veil of the nominal "equality" of states for participating in a law of human dignity.

McDougal, Lasswell and Chen, *Human Rights*, p. 169.

[276] Julius Stone, 'Approaches to the Notion of International Justice' in Falk and Black (eds.), *Future of the International Legal Order*, pp. 372–462 at p. 450.

international investment regimes established through state action .[277] To put it differently, simply listing the multinational corporation as a participant in the world social and constitutive process that is marked by growing interdependence without disclosing its linkages to specific internal social structures mystifies their operation and role.[278] In other words, it is not the fact of different participants existing side by side, but their linkages and interrelationships which are of significance.[279] These observations are relevant even in the instance of international institutions which have become the principle vehicles of exercising hegemony over the poor world. While international institutions do possess relative independence in their functioning, their working is dictated by the interests of developed countries.[280]

Third, while there is little doubt that bottom-up law-making processes today are the outcome of 'a participatory, organic process that ensues in the trenches'[281] the non-state participants are most often from the Global North. Worse still, the underlying assumption that the state actor should not resist their normative weight has hegemonic connotations from the perspective of subaltern states in the international system. It is from this latter perspective that it maybe alleged that both the policy-oriented approach and their counterparts today have reached their conclusion on the eroding role of state actors based on a partial analysis of the features of the world constitutive and power processes.

---

[277] In the words of Falk, 'multinational corporations appear to depend on the state system even as they act as agents of its transformation'. Richard A. Falk, 'A New Paradigm for International Legal Studies: Prospects and Proposals', 84 (1974–75) *Yale Law Journal*, pp. 969–1021 at p. 1008.

[278] See generally James Petras and Ken Trachte, 'Liberal, Structural and Radical Approaches to Political Economy: An Assessment and an Alternative', 3 (1979) *Contemporary Crisis*, pp. 109–147 .

[279] On the other hand, McDougal concludes that:

> the whole controversy about the "subjects" of international law might be more explicitly recognized as a verbalistic quagmire … Whether an observer labels any one of these participants [individuals, private associations, international organizations, etc.] as a subject of international law or not is entirely a matter of preference in verbal aesthetics or a function of the argument he is trying to win.

Myres McDougal, 'Review of Hersch Lauterpacht's International Law and Human Rights (1950)', 60 (1951) *Yale Law Journal*, pp. 1051–1056 at p. 1055.

[280] B. S. Chimni, 'International Institutions Today: An Imperial Global State in the Making', 15 (2004) *European Journal of International Law*, pp. 1–39.

[281] McDougal, 'Review of Hersch', p. 1055. See also Berman, 'Pluralist Approach', p. 302.

Fourth, McDougal's emphasis on the individual as a subject of international law flows from methodological assumptions. It is a result of adopting Lasswell's conceptual frame in which the fundamental unit of analysis is the individual and therefore stress is laid on 'interpersonal relations, not abstract institutions or organisations'.[282] As a consequence no serious empirical assessment is undertaken of the role of the individual in the international legal process. On the empirical plane the conclusion can at best be that the individual is a subject of international law 'in particular contexts' (i.e., in her own right).[283] To so argue is not to deny the need for international law to concern itself with the promotion of individual or human rights. It is merely to situate the *international* movement of human rights in the crucible of history. For carried to its logical extreme 'the doctrine of human rights and duties under international law is subversive of the whole principle that mankind should be organised as a society of sovereign states'.[284] Some would not see any reason – as there is none in the abstract – to lament this trend, but despite the rhetoric about growing cosmopolitan consciousness it can hardly be denied, particularly insofar as developing countries are concerned, that not only are the Western states pursuing policies which often lead to, encourage and support the denial of human rights but also, when convenient, use the cause of human rights as a pretext to intervene in the internal affairs of weaker states.[285] The controversial doctrine of humanitarian intervention,

---

[282] Lasswell cited by Young, *Systems of Political Science*, p. 71. The underlying 'methodological individualism' is discussed in Chapter 5. It represents another feature that is common between new approaches to international law, as articulated by David Kennedy and Martti Koskenniemi, and the New Haven approach.

[283] Ian Brownlie, *Principles of Public International Law*, 4th edn (London: Clarendon Press, 1990), p. 67.

[284] Bull, *Anarchical Society*, p. 152. As Kelsen ruefully observed:

> Although there is nothing in the 'nature' of international law that precludes individuals from being the direct subjects of rights, obligations and responsibilities, individuals may be so only as an exception and not as a general rule. If and when the exception tends to become the general rule, the structure and technique characteristic of international law will be altered in such a way as to become indistinguishable from the structure and technique of municipal law … what has heretofore been a distinctive system of law would give way to a system of law the centralisation of which is but a synonym for the appearance of a world state.

Hans Kelsen, *Principles of International Law*, 2nd revised edn (New York: Holt, Rinehart and Wilson, 1967), p. 242.

[285] In the words of Falk, the 'contention that human rights, can easily serve as a cover for humanitarian imperialism is well taken, especially if advanced as a critique of the

and now responsibility to protect (R2P), owes its origin precisely to the doctrine of human rights and an important safeguard against its abuse is the shield of state sovereignty.[286]

B.   Perspectives

The perspectives that participants advance in the process of decision making have a significant bearing on the outcomes. An individual or a corporation or an international institution can be inclusive or exclusive in its orientation. The focus of McDougal, as has already been noted, is on the individual as 'individual human beings are claimants both in their own right and as representatives of groups'.[287] He recognized in this regard that 'in an epoch of exacerbated nationalism and accelerated nation build-ing' the 'dominant loyalties remain parochial and not universal'.[288] He also noted that 'exaggerated images of the difference between the "self" and "other" help to account for the continuing vogue of large scale depriv-ation'.[289] The result is that individuals and groups are unable to clarify 'common interests'[290] preventing the realization of an optimum world order with the maximum possible shaping and sharing of all values.[291]

In fact, the different perspectives (of self and other) culminate in 'con-tending systems of public order'.[292] While all systems commit themselves

pretensions of United States foreign policy since World War II'. He goes on to observe that the 'liberal internationalist' approach 'is unduly innocent about the imperial tendencies of big, dominant states, whatever their rhetoric and their domestic record of observance. Part of this innocence is expressed by the implicit assumption that humanitarian inter-vention is something that only happens to "others". The targets are always foreign soci-eties'. Falk, *Human Rights,* pp. 3–4.

[286] With respect to the doctrine of humanitarian intervention, one is left wondering with Falk as to 'whether this particular genie should be let out of the bottle, or more accur-ately, whether we should affix Angel's wings to the interventionary genie'. Richard Falk, 'Comment I' in John Norton Moore (ed.), *Law and Civil War in the Modern World* (Baltimore, MD: John Hopkins University Press, 1974), pp. 543–545 at p. 545. See also B. S. Chimni, 'For Epistemological and Prudent Internationalism', *Harvard Human Rights Journal* at http://harvardhrj.com/2012/11/for-epistemological-and-prudent-internationalism/; B. S. Chimni, 'Sovereignty, Rights and Armed Intervention' in Hilary Charlesworth and Jean- Marc Coicaud (eds.) *Faultlines of International Legitimacy* (Cambridge: Cambridge University Press, 2010), pp. 303–325.

[287] McDougal, Lasswell and Chen, *Human Rights,* p. 145.
[288] See ibid., p. 116.
[289] See ibid.
[290] See ibid., p. 117.
[291] See ibid., p. 401.
[292] See ibid., p. 119.

to the goal of human dignity, this is far from being the case in practice. In fact, as McDougal admits, 'special interests continue to assert themselves in effective sabotage of proclaimed objectives. There remains chronic tension among competing common interest, whose accommodation is always necessary'.[293] However, the policy-oriented approach has no serious theory of the factors that shape perspectives and make individuals claimants of special interests. This outcome is a result of adopting 'methodological individualism' and an inability to understand the impact of the ensemble of social relations that constitute a society. At times McDougal does note that 'organizational complexity in government, in the corporate world, and in other sectors of life is subjecting people to intense organizational pressures' affecting their autonomy and integrity.[294] But in advancing this proposition the essential focus was on totalitarian regimes in which 'society is practically swallowed up by government'.[295] There is, in the cases of non-totalitarian societies, no worthy explanation for why individuals make certain kinds of claims. While the observational standpoint is stressed in performing the intellectual tasks there is no clarity about the factors that shape individual perspectives.

C. Base Values – Strategies

It has been seen that McDougal criticized, validly it may be added, political realists (e.g., Morgenthau) for overemphasizing naked power and legal formalists (e.g., Kelsen) for laying too much emphasis on rules as 'summarising ambiguously ascribed perspectives' without taking into account 'operations' regarded as 'non-subjective events which constitute the behavior in the process of choice'.[296] In opposition to the narrow notions of power and operations McDougal advanced the categories of 'base values' and 'strategies'. 'Base values' are defined as 'any potential means of influencing decisions'.[297] These include the values of power, wealth, enlightenment, respect, well-being, loyalty, skill and rectitude. Each of the 'base values' is in turn 'composed of two components, one a pattern of symbols, the other a resource pattern'.[298] The former are ideological in

---

[293] See ibid.
[294] See ibid., pp. 123–124.
[295] See ibid., p. 125.
[296] Morison, 'Comparative Essay', p. 14.
[297] McDougal, Lasswell and Reisman, 'Constitutive Process', p. 108.
[298] See ibid.

their orientation and the latter are 'the physical magnitudes that figure in the operations'.[299] According to McDougal, 'the distribution of base values within the world social process obviously conditions the deprivation and fulfillment of values. The influence extends the distribution *among* and *within* states. As between states, the distribution is glaringly discrepant'.[300] Yet, McDougal did not examine the consequences of this disparity for weak nations in terms of pursuing policies for the welfare of their peoples. As has already been pointed out, the developing countries were never the focus of his attention.

It would have been noticed that in the policy-oriented approach values represent both 'ends in themselves' and 'also serve as instruments or means for achievement of other aspirations and goals'.[301] In the latter instance what is of concern is the 'operational' definition of values.[302] A key aspect of the 'operational' definition of base values, delineating its area of operation, relates to the jurisdictional apportionment between inclusive and exclusive spheres in international relations. According to McDougal, 'the chief trend is toward the attenuation of exclusive competence (domestic jurisdiction) and a broadening of exclusive authority'.[303] He went so far as to say that 'domestic jurisdiction means little more than a *concession* by the general community to particular states of a primary, but not necessarily wholly exclusive, competence over matters arising within the boundaries, and predominantly affecting the internal public order, of such states'.[304] Of course, he conceded that 'effective power continues to rest primarily in nation-state participants'.[305] He, however, felt that this situation should be rectified.

Such a view misreads past trends of community intervention into the internal affairs of states. The implication of the stress on 'international concern' as opposed to 'domestic jurisdiction' becomes clear when this dimension of base values is linked to 'strategies' defined as 'the modalities by which base values are manipulated in the decision-making process'; the strategies include diplomatic, ideological, economic and military strategies.[306] Such a linkage, keeping in mind the realities of international

---

[299] See ibid., pp. 108–109.
[300] McDougal, Lasswell and Chen, *Human Rights*, p. 131.
[301] Young, *Systems of Political Science*, p. 67.
[302] McDougal, Lasswell and Reisman, 'Constitutive Process', p. 109.
[303] See ibid., p. 110. See also McDougal, Lasswell and Chen, *Human Rights*, pp. 208ff.
[304] McDougal, Lasswell and Chen, *Human Rights*, p. 214; emphasis added.
[305] McDougal, Lasswell and Reisman, 'Constitutive Process', p. 112.
[306] See ibid., pp. 119–120.

power, often provides justification for intervention by the more powerful states in the internal affairs of the weaker nations. But McDougal
appeared to argue that this is desirable. He observed that 'the whole function of international law is to permit such intervention in affairs which
would otherwise be regarded as internal'.[307] He went on to recommend
that the United States should 'take the leadership in promoting such an
international law'.[308] When this standpoint is fused with the alleged superiority of the liberal democratic model of the implications are disturbing for third world states and peoples.[309] It establishes the basis for the
'pro-democratic' invasion proposition clearly unlawful under the Charter
of the United Nations and customary international law.[310] But given the
strong view of the New Haven approach on the matter it is no surprise
that Reisman continues to defend pro-democratic invasions or unilateral
armed humanitarian interventions.[311]

D.   Outcomes

The category of 'outcomes' of the constitutive process is in the policy-
oriented approach, as already noted, broken up into seven component
functions which comprise the various types of decision: intelligence,
promotion, prescription, invocation, application, termination and
appraisal.[312] These seven component functions represent 'functional distinctions' and are 'substitutes for the conventional view of legislative,

---

[307] Myres McDougal, 'Remarks on International Concern versus Domestic Jurisdiction',
(1954)*Proceedings of American Society of International Law*, p. 120.

[308] See ibid., p. 121.

[309] These connotations are articulated in Michael W. Reisman, 'Coercion and Self-
Determination: Construing Charter Article 2(4)', 78 (1984) *American Journal
of International Law*, pp. 642–645. See also Oscar Schachter's reply, 'The Legality
of Pro-Democratic Invasion', 78 (1984) *American Journal of International Law*,
pp. 645–650.

[310] The view neglects the ICJ decision in the *Nicaragua* case wherein the court stated
there were no general rights for states to intervene, directly or indirectly, with or without armed force, in support of an internal opposition in another state, whose cause
appeared particularly worthy by reason of the political and moral values with which
it was identified. Such a right was a fundamental violation of the principle of non-
intervention. *I. C. J. Reports* (1986), paras 206–9. See also Chimni, 'Sovereignty, Rights',
pp. 303–325.

[311] See, for example, W. Michael Reisman, 'Unilateral Action and the Transformations of
the World Constitutive Process: The Special Problem of Humanitarian Intervention', 11
(2000) *European Journal of International Law*, pp. 3–18 at p. 15.

[312] McDougal, Lasswell and Chen, *Human Rights*, p. 248.

executive, and judicial structures of the legal process'.[313] In view of the fact that the decentralized international arena does not possess a legislature, executive and judiciary of the kind within national legal orders it is perhaps useful to designate alternate, and more comprehensive, modes of making sense of outcomes. However, scholars like Wolfgang Friedmann rightly wondered whether it was 'necessary, or even helpful' to break down every outcome into the seven component functions.[314] The process simply complicated the tasks of the scholar and decision maker without yielding corresponding benefits. Furthermore, when these functions are located within a conception of law that displaces the role of rules, they only go to obfuscate analysis. That is to say, these component functions do little to enlighten if their subject is not law.

E.   Summing Up

It is time to sum up the discussion on the process of decision making. Young has written that 'the most serious intrinsic problems' of the Lasswell approach to politics and political processes that McDougal applied in the domain of international law 'stem from its extensiveness and almost overwhelming complexity'.[315] This complexity flows from the 'proliferation of concepts and conceptual boxes'.[316] The intricacy of the approach multiplies when it is realized that Lasswell developed 'complexes of concepts' that became 'fully meaningful when juxtaposed to the original structures in a fashion that produces multiples of the previous number of conceptual boxes'.[317] Thus, for instance, in any analysis of a decision-making process the category values makes its appearance both as ends and means. The result is a conceptual apparatus that 'becomes increasingly dysfunctional'.[318] The proliferation of concepts yields such a vast amount of empirical materials that it becomes impossible to make meaningful use of them. However, what it does make possible is their manipulation to support subjective perspectives. The commitment to realizing an optimum world public order easily translates into support for an imperial vision of world order. This outcome is also encouraged by the

[313] Morison, *Comparative Essay*, p. 31.
[314] Friedmann, *Changing Structure*, p. 609.
[315] Young, *Systems of Political Science*, p. 76.
[316] See ibid.
[317] See ibid., p. 77.
[318] See ibid.

fact that the policy-oriented approach focuses on ruling elites.[319] It is no accident that McDougal always stood by the foreign policy establishment of the United States.

VI.   Testing the Jurisprudence: Legal Regulation of International Coercion

Having considered the policy-oriented approach to international law (the function it assigns to rules, its theses on indeterminacy of rules, the intellectual tasks it sets the legal scholar, and the analysis of the process of decision making) and the criticisms which can be directed against it, a brief review of its perspective on the legal regulation of international coercion – peace being the central question in world politics – may be undertaken in order to pull the threads together and show how the inadequacies which characterize the methodological framework of policy-oriented approach lead to untenable positions in matters as grave as use of force. Indeed, the recommendations it makes in this regard effectively negate the goals of minimum world public order. These goals are according to McDougal the following: First, 'the prevention of alterations in the existing distribution of values among the nation-states by processes of unilateral and unauthorized coercion and the promotion of value changes and adjustments by processes of persuasion or by community-sanctioned coercion'; second, 'the reduction to the minimum, when the procedures of persuasion break down and violence is resorted to, of unnecessary destruction of values'; and third, 'the regulation of the conduct of coercion and violence in such a manner as to permit and facilitate the restoration of the processes of persuasion'.[320] However, these are goals which decision makers are advised to seek at a first level of 'abstraction and realism'.

At a second level of 'abstraction and realism' McDougal posits objectives which are in tension with the first set of goals and can only be implemented at times at their expense. He writes that 'on another level of abstraction and realism, reference may be made to such objectives as the maintenance or furtherance of varying contending systems or conceptions of world public order, compatible, in theory or in specific interpretation, in greater or lesser degree with *the values of free society*'.[321] This statement parallels and is to be read along with the policing and

---

[319] See ibid.
[320] McDougal and Feliciano, *Law and Minimum World Public Order,* pp. 41–43.
[321] See ibid., p. 43; emphasis added.

integrating function of interpretation which dictates that the interpreter does not give expression to the shared expectations of parties if they conflict with the goals of world public order. The formulation has grave implications when it comes to use of force as it tends to exonerate states for using force against societies which in their view are not committed to the values of a 'free society'. If such a standpoint is accepted, international law 'ceases to have any meaning' for its rules are by admission deemed slaves to a particular understanding of good society in a pluralistic world. It led Wolfgang Friedmann to query as 'to what extent does the McDougal school' 'require the universal observance of certain rules about the use of force?'.[322] According to Friedmann, once McDougal's premise is accepted it follows 'with dangerous ease, that different standards may have to be applied to those who incorporate "the values of a safe, free, and abundant society"', and those who, in the view of the writers, deny such values'.[323] Falk is even more forthcoming:

> It should be apparent that very practical consequences follow from McDougal's formulation if it is accepted as a serious jurisprudential appeal. Actors that accept McDougal's concept of human dignity are entitled to contaminate the atmosphere by nuclear testing, propose 'defensive' invasions ... and thereby *fulfill* the law. For the law turns out to be what helps a certain set of policies to prevail in the struggle for power. Identical claims to act by the enemies of McDougal's version of human dignity are, by the same reasoning, illegal, as their objectives deny the values of human dignity upon which law rests.[324]

Even Higgins, otherwise in sympathy with the perspective of the policy-oriented approach, is compelled to admit that:

> it is a very fine line between insisting that decision be taken in accordance with the policy objectives of a liberal, democratic world community and asserting that *any* action taken by a liberal democracy against a totalitarian nation is lawful. Falk correctly draws attention to this distinction, and I would share his concern that McDougal at times seems to step over the line.[325]

The alarming nature of the recommendations of policy-oriented approach becomes clear when its positions on the use of nuclear weapons are considered. McDougal candidly stated that 'a very strong case

---

[322] Friedmann, 'Book Review', p. 611.
[323] See ibid.
[324] Falk, *Legal Order,* pp. 88–89; emphasis in original.
[325] Higgins, 'Policy and Impartiality', p. 922; emphasis in original

would have to be made to establish that no possible uses of nuclear and thermonuclear weapons could conceivably be within the scope of military necessity *for objectives legitimate by standards making reference to human dignity*.[326] He considered a nuclear (pre-emptive) strike lawful as long as a state was 'intolerably threatened' and is pursuing the goal of human dignity. Such a rule, as Thomas Franck had noted, 'is so subjective as to be no rule at all'.[327] In fact, it is fraught with danger for the international community. In the final analysis, the introduction of a particular understanding of human dignity as a judgmental yardstick, ignoring the import of the use of nuclear weapons for the human situation, reveals a dogmatic attitude to what is the most serious problem of our age.[328] The international legal system is seen as existing to serve the interests of liberal democracies under the leadership of the United States.[329] In fact, McDougal's jurisprudence appears to give the impression of working itself backwards from this point, putting together elements which in combination can provide some form of intellectual rationalization and justification for every action that the United States undertakes.

In response to such criticisms McDougal argued that since 'totalitarian' states (a reference to the former Soviet Union and its allies) were committed to considering the use of law from their policy perspective it would be 'simple utopian idealism' for decision makers committed to non-totalitarian conceptions of world public order not to do likewise.[330] Here McDougal failed to distinguish his position from the more reasonable one that sees each state seeking to have its policy preferences incorporated in a legal rule, but once the latter is formulated and agreed to, there are limits placed to its manipulation to serve particular causes. McDougal, on the other hand, suggested that 'responsible decision-makers who share the values of a free society may appropriately give effect to such values

---

[326] McDougal and Feliciano, *Law and Minimum World Public Order*, p. 78; emphasis added.
[327] Thomas M. Franck, 'Who Killed Article 2(4)?', 64 (1970) *American Journal of International Law*, pp. 809–837 at p. 821.
[328] Sec Falk, *Legal Order*, pp. 92–94.
[329] Thus in the oft-quoted words of Anderson, 'the words of the law become mere wisps of sight or sound. Law is policy. Policy is human dignity. Human dignity is fostered in the long run by the success of American foreign policy. Therefore, law is the handmaiden of the national interest of the United States ... Law becomes merely an increment to power'. Stanley V. Anderson, 'A Critique of Professor Myres S. McDougal Doctrine of Interpretation by Major Purposes', 57 (1963) *American Journal of International Law*, pp. 378–383 at p. 382.
[330] Falk, *Legal Order*, p. 86; McDougal and Feliciano, *Law and Minimum World Public Order*, p. 66.

*not only in their formulation of principles but also in their specific inter-
pretations and applications'.*[331] This, however, is an erroneous proposition
and one which is subversive of international rule of law. Giving free reign
to auto-interpretation of law based upon self-serving notions of human
dignity is pure and simple negation of the international legal system. It
is not as if McDougal did not recognize the problems flowing from auto-
interpretation. At one place he explicitly stated that 'the special prerogative claimed by states to interpret their own obligation, and in a sense to
act as judges of their own cause, has long been regarded as a conspicuous Achilles' heel in international law'.[332] He also recognized that a single
state may not authoritatively impose its own interpretation upon other
states because 'by the principle of equality of states, each state has the
same licence'.[333] Yet overpowered by the belief in the absolute and eternal
validity of Western brand of liberal democracy he was unable to put this
view into practice.

VII.   Conclusion

The policy-oriented approach to international law is without doubt one of
the most ambitious attempts at disciplinary renewal. It articulates a comprehensive approach that seeks to integrate international law with social
sciences and offer detailed maps of the intellectual tasks of jurisprudence
and the process of decision making through which the goal of 'human
dignity' is to be realized. It thus attempts to address all five logics that go
to constitute world order viz., 'logic of capital', 'logic of territory', 'logic
of Nature', 'logic of culture' and the 'logic of law'. However, the effort to
present in the course of the Cold War a theoretical framework that was
the counter-image of Marxism and its alleged economic determinism, led
the policy-oriented approach to subscribe to an incomprehensible indeterminism in which the 'logic of capital' is a priori disregarded in analysing particular phases and events of the history of international relations
and international law. In the absence of any theory about the weights to
be assigned to a vast array of variables that are expected to be considered at multiple levels, or a procedure to determine the precedence of
causes within a framework of a multicausal analysis, the policy-oriented
approach merely generates an enormous amount of data that is amenable

---

[331] Falk, *Legal Order*, p. 96; emphasis added.
[332] McDougal, *Studies in World Public Order*, p. 188.
[333] See ibid., p. 189.

to sustaining subjective perspectives. It has, of course, been argued that the comprehensiveness is not a hurdle because the theory is 'capable of being made sufficiently precise'.[334] The problem is that it is not demonstrated as to how the move to the particular is dictated by the workings of the theoretical framework and not a predisposed mindset.

A second weakness of the policy-oriented approach is that it disregards the distinctiveness and the relative autonomy of the legal process – its specific form, internal structure, logic and dynamics. Its strength of course lies in the inclusive and interdisciplinary method that helps address the failings of positivism. It not only correctly draws attention to the inextricable relationship between law and policy but also rightly emphasizes that law is not an end in itself but a means to realize preferred goals. However, its process conception of law tends to blur the distinction between law and policy. The place and function of rules in the international system is further undermined by the flawed theses on the indeterminacy of rules. The ensuing rule scepticism was used in the period of the Cold War to generate an anxiety neurosis about the application of rules heightened with the reminder that the enemies of the free world are wont to manipulate it to secure oppressive visions of world order. What followed was a recommendation to the decision makers of the free world to be wary of the traps of rule-oriented thinking. It was accompanied by the suggestion that there is no alternative to the parallel manipulation of the legal process by the defenders of the free world to secure the goal of human dignity. This stark instrumentalist position would have much to commend it if it were true that indeterminacy is the pervasive characteristic of a rule. But this turns out to be a false allegation. Wittgenstein's teachings that 'to understand a sentence means to understand a language' and that 'the meaning of a word is its use in the language' provide the linguistic bases to demonstrate that the policy-oriented approach exaggerates the extent of indeterminacy. While an element of uncertainty will always prevail in the interpretation and application of rules, McDougal went too far in questioning the very possibility of arriving at the genuinely shared expectation of parties i.e., without a comprehensive review of all relevant materials and then subjecting the outcome to the policing or integrative function. The recommended procedure often led to bizarre interpretations of rules.[335] To

---

[334] McDougal and Reisman, 'Harold Dwight Lasswell', p. 655.
[335] For example, McDougal contended that interpreters of Article 51 mistakenly argued that the words 'if an armed attack occurs' means 'only if, an armed attack occurs'. Leo Gross, 'Problems of International Adjudication and Compliance with International Law: Some

put it differently, the problem with the policy-oriented approach is not merely the claim that the rules are not sufficiently determinate but the underlying assumption that only that meaning was valid which secured the ends of the free world. A social order of diverse ideological systems surely cannot produce rules whose explicit function is to achieve the goals of one of them.[336] In fact, it is the very plurality of visions that rules seek to safeguard. Unfortunately, the failure to appreciate this feature of the international legal process, and the fixation with 'actually existing social-ism', led McDougal to become an 'apologist for actions on the part of the United States'.[337]

Since the end of the Cold War the policy-oriented approach has been at crossroads. It has a choice of being relevant and progressive in changed times or fade away staying with an ideological orientation shaped by a politics that was obsessed with the contest between capitalist and socialist orders. Its central figure today, Michael Reisman, continues to tread the old path with the difference that the enemy today is any social force or nation that is opposed to the liberal international order. The element of continuity tends to suggest that the policy-oriented approach is not, as is sometimes suggested, an empty frame that can be filled with any content. It is a carrier of bourgeois ideology that supports and legitimizes a hege-monic global order. In the circumstances it is not surprising that all that the 'new' New Haven approach of Koh and others seeks to do is to refocus it on realizing the interests of advanced capitalist states in the era of glo-balization. Yet a progressive New Haven approach cannot entirely be ruled out given its future orientation and the accent on the realization of common interests of the international community. But if such a new New Haven approach has to evolve it has to take cognizance of the critique of New Haven school by TWAIL and FtAIL that show how it has ignored cri-tiques of international law from race and gender perspectives. However, as yet no serious attempt has been made to accommodate the feminist and third world critiques of international law. A progressive New Haven approach can only be arrived at with a different sociology of international relations combined with moderate rule scepticism, a more rigorous

---

Simple Solutions' in Leo Gross, *Essays on International Law and Organization* , vol. 1 (New York: Transnational Publishers, 1984), pp. 399–410 at pp. 404–405. Leo Gross aptly called this principle of interpretation the 'negative plain meaning'. See ibid., p. 405.

[336] McDougal criticized Falk for asserting otherwise observing that 'we may despair of his hope of the creation of an autonomous global law which can reconcile and accommodate incompatible value systems'. McDougal, 'International Law', p. 263.

[337] Young, 'International Law and Social Science', p. 74.

empirical method, and above all a willingness to listen to the voices of the weak in the international system. But at present the 'new' New Haven approach appears to shy away from questioning the constrained anthropology and politics that informs the work of McDougal. In this regard it can draw inspiration from the work of Richard Falk who arguably has for long advanced a new and progressive New Haven approach by subscribing to a view of international law that seeks to occupy the middle ground between McDougal's realism and Kelsen's formalism and a commitment to world order values that promote the interests of the weak in the international system. The critical stance of Falk is important for as Koh has observed what makes the New Haven attractive is that it does not see the role of international lawyers 'as "yes men" or scriveners'.[338]

The other possibility is that the policy-oriented approach advance a counter-hegemonic project through borrowing some of the deconstructive methods of new approaches to international law (NAIL) articulated by David Kennedy and Martti Koskenniemi, albeit without abandoning its reconstructive dimension. Arguably NAIL is a postmodern version of the policy-oriented approach, albeit it is averse to the suggestion that it is in any way similar to it or presents a 'new' New Haven approach. The comparison is not as farfetched as it may seem at first. There is a family resemblance between the two approaches inasmuch as both stress the relationship between law and politics, assert the pervasive indeterminacy of rules (albeit the NAIL emphasis is on structural roots of indeterminacy), embrace methodological individualism, pitch for an interdisciplinary understanding of the structure and process of international law, and focus on the ethical responsibility of international lawyers. Where NAIL departs from the New Haven approach is in abandoning its grand narrative and leaving behind any pretense to scientific and objective analysis of the values and strategies to be pursued through the formal decision-making process. It is another matter that in recent years NAIL has

---

[338] Koh observes:

> we should return to the post-World War II image of international law as a creative medium devoted to building a humane world public order. In an age of globalization, this means using transnational law to help organize the activities and relations of myriad transnational players, not simply nation-states, with the goal not of reflecting parochial state interests, but of advancing an enlightened global system dedicated to the promotion of human dignity. That was the basic endeavor of the original New Haven School and it should remain the enterprise of the "new" New Haven School as well.

Koh, 'Is There a "New"', p. 572.

assumed a position that sees value in the pursuit of common interests (the project of genuine universalism or distributive justice) through the process of law. But, as will be seen in Chapter 5, the NAIL counter-hegemonic project itself rests on shaky foundations. At first, however, there is a need to consider the counter- hegemonic approach articulated by Richard Falk for over five decades.

4

Richard Falk and the Grotian Quest:
Towards a Transdisciplinary Jurisprudence

I. Introduction

Among the most sensitive minds writing in the field of international law is that of Richard Falk. A student of Myres McDougal, whose influence he willingly acknowledges, Falk has articulated a distinctive 'intermediate' approach to international law that borrows the element of value relevance from the policy-oriented approach and combines it with the element of autonomy from the pure theory of Hans Kelsen.[1] He is thereby able to link law and policy without blurring the distinction between the two. Falk has used the 'intermediate approach' to address a whole range of subjects of international law including that of determinacy of rules. Along with McDougal, Falk is among the few international law scholars to deal in their work with all the five logics that co-constitute international law and world order viz., the 'logic of capital', the 'logic of territory', the 'logic of nature', the 'logic of culture' and the 'logic of law'. In his prolific writings Falk has examined key global problems like poverty, ecological decay, human rights violations, conflicts, and undemocratic international institutions, many of which did not receive adequate attention from the founding fathers of the New Haven approach.[2] Indeed, over a career spanning more than five decades, there are few issues of international law and world order that Falk has not addressed. The ambition that drives Falk's work is no less than the goal of humane global governance that assures every individual a life of dignity on planet Earth. He has actively pursued this project since the late sixties, including as one of the leading participants

---

[1] For his assessment of policy-oriented approach or New Haven jurisprudence, see Richard Falk, 'Casting the Spell: The New Haven School of International Law', 104 (1995) *Yale Law Journal*, pp. 1991–2008; Richard Falk, *The Status of Law in International Society* (Princeton, NJ: Princeton University Press, 1970), pp. vii–xii, 7–59, 342–379, 642–660; Richard Falk, *Legal Order in a Violent World* (Princeton, NJ: Princeton University Press, 1968), pp. 60–89.

[2] Richard Falk, 'A New Paradigm for International Legal Studies: Prospects and Proposals', 84 (1974–75) *Yale Law Journal*, pp. 969–1021 at p. 1012.

in the World Order Models Project (WOMP).[3] The demands made by it, coupled with the influence of the New Haven approach, have helped him transgress the conventional boundaries of international law. In fact Falk best exemplifies Edward Said's 'concept of secular criticism', that is, 'a criticism freed from the restrictions of intellectual specialisation'.[4] In his endeavour, Falk draws sustenance from a variety of intellectual traditions viz., 'libertarian socialism, philosophical anarchism, humanism, and militant non-violence'.[5]

His contributions to the study of international law and world order are many. An ardent advocate of world peace, Falk has resolutely campaigned for a nuclear free world, bringing to bear on the problem his considerable insight and skill in the technology of international law.[6] He has made significant contribution to clarifying the role of international human rights law in advancing the interests of exploited and oppressed groups. In fact Falk is among the few Western scholars to have shown sustained concern with the problems and struggles of third world peoples. He has also been among the first international law scholars to draw attention to the impending ecological crisis in his pioneering and path breaking work *This Endangered Planet* published a year before the Stockholm conference. Falk has also made notable contributions in clarifying and strengthening the role of the United Nations system. Falk has advanced novel proposals in this regard, including the creation of a global parliament. Above all, in pursuit of his project of humane global governance Falk has never hesitated to speak truth to power. He has always believed that a good patriotic citizen should not be 'a mindless supporter of nationalized truth'.[7] Indeed, he is a true symbol of courageous scholarship and therefore an inspirational figure for generations of scholars of international relations and

---

[3] For an autobiographical sketch of his intellectual journey, see Richard Falk, *The Promise of World Order: Essays in Normative International Relations* (Sussex: Wheatsheaf Books, 1987), pp. 13–24.

[4] Bill Ashcroft and Pal Ahluwalia, *Edward Said* (New York: Routledge, 1999), p. 15.

[5] Richard Falk, *The End of World Order: Essays on Normative International Relations* (New York: Holmes and Meir, 1983), p. 324.

[6] See Richard Falk, 'Shimoda Case: A Legal Appraisal for the Atomic Attacks on Hiroshima and Nagasaki', 59 (1965) *American Journal of International Law*, pp. 759–793; Richard Falk, Lee Meyrowitz and Jack Sanderson, 'Nuclear Weapons and International Law', 20 (1980) *Indian Journal of International Law*, pp. 541–595; and Richard Falk, 'Towards a Legal Regime for Nuclear Weapons' in Richard Falk, Friedrich Kratochwil, and Saul H. Mendlovitz. (eds.), *International Law: A Contemporary Perspective* (Boulder, CO: Westview, 1985), pp. 453–473.

[7] *The Writings of Richard Falk: Towards Humane Global Governance* (New Delhi: Orient BlackSwan, 2012), p. 481.

international law. Falk is from the days of the Vietnam War a critic of the imperial strain in US foreign policy.[8] In recent times he has forthrightly supported the rights of Palestinian peoples despite inviting considerable hostility, including from his own government and Israel.[9]

However, considerable as Falk's achievements are, the principal purpose of the present chapter is to focus on areas of disagreement. It is hoped that the analysis of these will help clarify the Integrated Marxist approach to International Law (IMAIL) perspective on several critical issues relating to international law and world order. The chapter proceeds as follows. Section II critically reviews the 'intermediate approach' to international law advanced by Falk. It contends that Falk does not sustain the intermediate approach with an appropriate sociology of international relations. More specifically, he does not recognize the centrality of the 'logic of capital' in shaping international law and therefore does not explore over time the critical relationship between capitalism, imperialism and international law. While Falk certainly devotes greater attention to the 'logic of capital' then the New Haven approach, it is not critical to his thinking on international law. In working out the intermediate approach, Falk has also not advanced a theory of interpretation that upholds the idea of relative autonomy of international law. While ably challenging the radical indeterminacy thesis put forward by the New Haven approach, Falk does not advance in this regard supportive theories of language and communication. In fact, it is argued that legal theory has never received the sustained attention of Falk, and certainly, international law literature is poorer for that.

---

[8] Richard A. Falk, 'International Law and the United States Role in the Vietnam War', 75 (1966) *Yale Law Journal*, pp. 1122–1160; Richard Falk, 'International Law and the United States Role in the Vietnam War: A Reply to Professor Moore', 76 (1967) *Yale Law Journal*, pp. 1095–1158; Richard Falk, 'What We Should Learn from Vietnam', 1 (1970–71) *Foreign Policy*, pp. 98–144. Also see the four volume series edited by Richard Falk, *The Vietnam War and International Law* (Princeton, NJ: Princeton University Press, 1968, 1969, 1972 and 1976). On Nicaragua, see Richard Falk, 'The World Court's Achievement', 81 (1987) *American Journal of International Law*, pp. 106–112. On the Gulf War, see Richard Falk, 'Reflections on Democracy and the Gulf War', 16 (1991) *Alternatives*, pp. 263–274; Richard Falk, 'UN Being Made a Tool of US Foreign Policy', *The Guardian Weekly*, 27 January 1991. See also fn 9.

[9] See in this regard Richard A. Falk and Burns H. Weston, 'The Relevance of International Law to Palestinian Rights in the West Bank and Gaza: In Legal Defense of the Intifida', 32 (Winter 1991), *Harvard International Law Journal*, pp. 129–157; Richard Falk, *Palestine: the Legitimacy of Hope* (Charlottesville, VA: Just World Books, 2014). See generally Richard Falk, *Human Rights and State Sovereignty* (New York: Holmes and Meir Publishers, Inc., 1981), pp. 9–32, 185–190, 218–223; fn 2.

Section III presents and analyses Falk's diagnosis of the ills of the contemporary global order. It is argued that his understanding of the global problematique is unsatisfactory. He essentially traces the problems of existing world order to the 'logic of territory', that is, to statism and the states system. The working and operations of global capitalism is merely treated as one variable that structures world order or what is termed 'global governance' today. Falk also does not explore and clarify with care certain basic concepts that are critical to his work such as 'state' or 'civil society' or 'global civil society'. While his pioneering analysis of the ecological crisis offers valuable insights, it is flawed inasmuch as he traces its roots to the arrival of industrial civilization and not to global capitalism. The notion of 'industrial civilization' lacks the analytical edge and purchase to adequately focus on the critical issues involved.

Section IV considers his proposed strategies of transition to a peaceful and just global order in different phases of his work. It identifies the three strategies that have informed his thinking over time: reform from above (1970–1985), reform from below (1985–1999), and reform through 'new internationalism' and 'legitimacy struggles' (1999–). These strategies are not mutually exclusive but reflect a change in emphasis over the years. It is contended that despite his reconsideration of strategies of transition these do not hold out a realistic possibility of realizing a humane world order as he does not address the question of reform of deep structures. There is, therefore, often a utopian air about his proposals.

Section V appraises the role he assigns to international law in the transition process in tandem with the different phases in his thinking on transition strategies. Beginning with a 1967 essay on 'new approaches to international law' he has continuously reflected on the role international law can play in the transition process. In recent years he has highlighted the significance of international law in strengthening 'legitimacy struggles'. Falk has emphasized in this regard the role of the global civil society in law making and law enforcement. He has also advanced novel proposals like a possible educative role for the International Court of Justice (ICJ). It is however not certain whether the new thinking or suggestions are likely to facilitate the realization of the posited goal of system transformation.

Section VI reviews Falk's writings on the theme of third world and international law. The purpose of the brief discussion is to consider how his views on the subject have evolved over the years. It is argued that overall his neglect of the 'logic of capital', and therefore imperialism, prevents him from looking at the deeper reasons for the inequality between developed and third world countries.

Section VII contains some concluding reflections.

II.   Legal Theory: The Intermediate View

Falk's approach to international law is most extensively explored in two companion volumes *Legal Order in a Violent World* and *The Status of Law in International Society* that comprise of essays published in the 1960s, albeit as he himself cautioned that even these can only be seen as offering no more than 'a prolegomena to a conception of international legal order'.[10] Falk defines in them his approach to international law more in the form of a critical response to principal theories of the times. It is primarily 'shaped by the intellectual dialectic that exists between the work of Hans Kelsen and Myres S. McDougal'.[11] According to Falk, 'Kelsen has gone too far to establish the autonomy of international law, whereas McDougal has gone too far to establish its relevance'.[12] What was required of legal analysis was 'to find a middle ground, conjoining law to politics without collapsing one into the other and attaining a realism that neither expects law to guarantee a peaceful world, nor concludes that law is irrelevant to international peace'.[13] He, therefore, proposed a constructive dialogue between the two distinct conceptions of international law, that is, of McDougal and Kelsen, one outcome of it being the 'intermediate view'.[14] But, as Rosalyn Higgins pointed out early on, it was the work of McDougal which was 'the catalyst for much of Falk's thinking on international law'.[15] In her view 'one cannot fully appreciate Falk's views and preoccupations without understanding what it is he shares with McDougal and where it is that they have parted company'.[16] Higgins herself traced their differences simply to 'different political dispositions' that found them holding 'opposing views'

---

[10] Falk, *Status of Law*, p. xii.
[11] See ibid., p. x.
[12] See ibid., p. xi.
[13] See ibid., p. 51.
[14] See ibid., pp. 41–60.
[15] Rosalyn Higgins, 'Policy and Impartiality: The Uneasy Relationship in International Law: Legal Order in a Violent World by Richard A. Falk', 23 (1969) *International Organization*, pp. 914–931 at p. 920. Falk himself unhesitatingly states that 'I regard McDougal as the most important international law theorist of our time'. Falk, *Status of Law*, p. 9.
[16] See ibid.

on the role of international law.[17] Falk believed that McDougal was overly 'preoccupied with cold-war confrontation to the neglect of the aspirations and needs of "the newer nations" and what is more was "partisan rather than objective and impartial"' when it came to assessing the legality of US actions in the period.[18] In his view, McDougal had transformed 'international law into a cold war ideology – almost the contradiction of Kelsen's image of an impartial restraint system'.[19] But at the same time Falk was critical of legal positivism for it did not help clarify the values that the international legal order should help realize. He rued the 'tendency to create an artificial distance between the "is" of international politics and the "ought" of international law'.[20] He noted how McDougal 'so ably demonstrated [that], one role of law is to help a social system move toward the attainment of its goals'.[21] The result was that Falk came to be dissatisfied with the conceptions of law offered by both Kelsen and McDougal. As he observed, 'the images of legal process and legal order embodied in the writings of both Kelsen and McDougal unduly impoverish the phenomenological reality of international law'.[22] The intermediate approach he advanced sought reconciliation between 'considerations of autonomy and relevance' deemed necessary if the international legal order was to exercise a positive influence in international affairs. Falk believed that through avoiding the pitfalls of policy-oriented reductionism and legal formalism international law could serve as a meaningful and purposive guide to action. He saw the intermediate approach as 'a means to express the simultaneous need for *minimum stability* in the relations among principal sovereign states and for *minimum social change* in the relations between the advantaged and disadvantaged sectors of international society'.[23] Falk concluded that 'the challenges set for law by the evolving needs of international life must be taken into account, but not at the expense of sacrificing the autonomy of the legal order'.[24]

Falk applied the intermediate approach to particular problems of international law. For instance, in his intervention on the debate on the legal

[17] Higgins, 'Reality and Impartiality', p. 921.
[18] See ibid.
[19] Falk, *Status of Law*, p. 44.
[20] Richard A. Falk, 'New Approaches to the Study of International Law', 61 (1967) *The American Journal of International Law*, pp. 477–495 at p. 488.
[21] See ibid.
[22] Falk, *Status of Law*, p. 52.
[23] See ibid., p. xii; emphasis in original.
[24] See ibid., p. 57.

status of resolutions of international organizations, in particular resolutions of UN General Assembly (UNGA), that so preoccupied the scholarly community in the 1960s and 1970s, Falk argued the case for 'attributing quasi-legislative force to resolutions of the General Assembly'.[25] This view occupied the intermediate space between what Mohammed Bedjaoui called 'legal paganism' which 'turns law into a new religion centred on itself'[26] and was therefore dismissive of UNGA resolutions based on the Charter provision describing them as mere 'recommendations', and the assertion that the most significant of them, such as the one on new international economic order, have a binding quality. In his own words, 'the idea of attributing quasi-legislative force to resolutions of the General Assembly expresses *a middle position* between a formally difficult affirmation of true legislative status and a formalistic denial of the law-creating role and impact'.[27]

Falk also reviewed much of the scholarly work in the period from the perspective of the intermediate approach.[28] Thus, in contrast to McDougal, he admired the work of Wolfgang Friedmann as he saw the latter extend the horizons of international law while respecting the autonomy of the law by carrying out the intellectual enterprise in a 'non-partisan spirit'[29] with a 'quest for objectivity'.[30] He endorsed the Friedmann critique that there should not be 'too easy an acceptance of George Scelle's conception of the *dedoublement fonctionnel*, the dual function of state authorities as organs of the perspective of the respective national communities and of the international community'.[31] But while Falk joined Friedmann in questioning McDougal's claim that national officials can take into account both national and common interests of the international community, insisting instead on the need to respect the autonomy of the legal sphere, he agreed with McDougal that social sciences needed to weigh in to determine the values to be pursued through international law. Falk felt that Friedmann

[25] Falk, *Status of Law*, pp. 174 and 177.
[26] Mohammed Bedjaoui, *Towards a new international economic order* (New York: Holmes and Meir, 1979), p. 100.
[27] Falk, *Status of Law*, p. 174.
[28] See his review of Morton A. Kaplan and Nicholas deBelleville Katzenbach, *The Political Foundations of International Law* (New York: Wiley, 1961) in Falk, *Status of Law*, pp. 486–495.
[29] See ibid., p. 470. The reference was primarily to Wolfgang Friedmann, *The Changing Structure of International Law* (New York: Columbia University Press, 1964).
[30] See ibid., p. 471.
[31] Cited by Falk; see ibid., p. 473.

wrote 'as if modern social science did not exist', contrasting it with the interdisciplinary work of McDougal.[32]

As is evident, the 'intermediate approach' essentially represents a negative view, rejecting the one-sidedness of the autonomy and relevance standpoints. It, therefore, merely represented a first step towards building a realistic jurisprudence. There remained the need to spell out the meaning of 'relevance' on the one side and the possibility and limits of 'autonomy' on the other. The former task involves exploring the intricate relationship between the international system and international law and the latter examining the limits of determinacy in the interpretation and application of the doctrines and rules of international law. It is worth noting here that most of the critical approaches to international law that include FtAIL, TWAIL and IMAIL broadly subscribe to the intermediate view. All of them accept that some mix of relevance and autonomy is required if the international law has to play a progressive role. But their analysis differs on both the sociological basis of international law and the question of indeterminacy of international legal rules. In other words, there can be and are a variety of intermediate approaches to international law. What calls for assessment is the validity of the particular intermediate view advanced. A few words are therefore necessary on the Falk understanding of the basis of international law and the issue of determinacy of rules.

A. On Basis of International Law

It is a truism to observe that law does not evolve in a vacuum and that its development is shaped by the sociological substratum of a system. The delineation of the substratum and its relationship with the legal sphere can engender different schools of jurisprudence. Falk attempts to capture the relationship between international law and the substratum with the notion of 'quasi-dependence' 'to express both the *subordination* of international law to the shape and character of the overall international environment and to identify areas of actual and potential *independence* wherein international law acts as a causative agent of its own'.[33] For Falk the sociological substratum is the decentralized international system that consists of sovereign states and other actors.[34] The notion of 'quasi-dependence'

---

[32] See ibid., p. 476.
[33] See ibid., p. 3; emphasis in original.
[34] See ibid., p. 9. It is because he saw McDougal as assessing this feature that he considered him as 'the most important international law theorist' of his times. See ibid., p. 9.

clearly has family resemblance to that of 'relative autonomy' used in the Marxist tradition.[35] The difference is that for Marxists the 'logic of capital' is as critical as the 'logic of territory' to the evolution and development of international law. Understanding the significance of the 'logic of capital' calls for looking at the internal constitution of states participating in the international system. It is not as if Falk does not recognize the significance of the domestic setting in shaping the international legal relations of states. In reviewing the work of Morton Kaplan and Nicholas Katzenbach on the political foundations of international law he pointed out that 'scant attention is given to the relevance of the internal distribution and orientation of power within participating national units'.[36] But Falk does not seriously travel beyond noting the need to take cognizance of the sources of power in domestic politics to seriously analysing different social formations and the ways in which these impact international law. The focus is on statism and the existing states system, a subject which is analysed in detail presently, and not on the nature and character of states that constitute the international system.[37] Therefore, Falk does not sufficiently recognize that the *modern* states system, and the external policies of key states within it, is a product of the evolution and development of capitalism and its universalizing thrust. If international law is to contribute to the process of transition to a just world order there must be clear understanding of the 'logic of capital' that involves exploring the linkages between capitalism, imperialism, the states system and modern international law. Such a perspective facilitates a realistic appraisal of the role which international law can play for it locates the notion of quasi-autonomy in the political economy of international relations. Since Falk does not do so he also fails to pay attention to the *form* modern international law assumes, the focus of Soviet jurist Evgeny Pashukanis's work while advancing a commodity form theory of international law.[38] While Falk refers to the inequality between states he does not see how the dynamic of it is framed by universalizing capitalism.[39] This is where his 'intermediate approach' to international law diverges from the 'relative autonomy' thesis of the Marxist approach which is discussed in detail in Chapter 7.

---

[35] For a detailed discussion of the Marxist idea of 'relative autonomy' of law see Chapter 7, pp. 458–461.

[36] See ibid., p. 493. The reference was to Morton A. Kaplan and Nicholas deBelleville Katzenbach, *The Political Foundations of International Law* (New York: Wiley, 1961).

[37] See discussion under sub-heading 'Problem of Statism and States System', infra, pp. 194–202.

[38] For a detailed discussion see Chapter 7, pp. 462–468.

[39] For a discussion of the work of Evgeny Pashukanis see Chapter 7, pp. 477–499, 506–517.

B.   On Indeterminacy of Rules

In identifying the distinctive characteristics of the international legal system, Falk lists its decentralized nature as the most significant one giving rise to the problem of auto-interpretation.[40] The problem of auto-interpretation is compounded by the claim that indeterminacy is the innate characteristic of international law. If the international legal order is to perform its function of guiding and controlling the acts of omission or commission of states, ways must be found to circumscribe their ability to rationalize any act through the process of interpretation. But in contesting the claims of indeterminacy it is necessary to enlist appropriate linguistic theories and procedures of interpretation with the aim of revealing the limits of hermeneutic freedom. In other words, in order to sustain his thesis on the autonomy of the law Falk had to address the issue of indeterminacy of rules flowing from particular theories of meaning and interpretation. Falk attempted to do so while reviewing the issue of indeterminacy of rules in the New Haven approach, but it cannot be said that his 'intermediate view' of interpretation is supported by an appropriate theory of meaning and interpretation.[41]

A principal reason is that as against the ordinary meaning rule adopted by the ILC in the Vienna Convention on Law of Treaties, 1969, Falk goes along with the New Haven theory of interpretation that contests it. Indeed, in considering the relative merits of the International Law Commission (ILC) and the New Haven approaches to interpretation, Falk opts for the latter in no uncertain terms. Falk notes that the policy-oriented approach contains 'the most persuasive account of treaty interpretation presently available'.[42] He goes on to observe that:

> The alleged self-evident clarity of textual language in isolation from its context entails a depleted understanding of language and communication; to rest interpretation on an essentially misleading view of language and communications, as does the ILC, rejects the role of reason and intelligence in the conduct of human affairs and seems to prefer implicitly the role of magic, myth, and authority.[43]

---

[40] According to Falk, international lawyers should 'place *due emphasis* on the decentralised character of international society'. Richard A. Falk, 'Comment I' in John Norton Moore (ed.), *Law and Civil War in the Modern World* (Baltimore, MD: The John Hopkins University Press, 1974), pp. 539–548 at p. 543; emphasis in original.

[41] This section is best read with that of the detailed discussion of the New Haven and ILC approaches to interpretation in Chapter 3, pp. 123–140.

[42] Falk, *Status of Law*, p. 348. For an elaborate critique of the New Haven approach to interpretation see Chapter 3, pp. 123–140.

[43] See ibid., p. 368.

Indeed, in Falk's view:

> It is misleading to suppose that a decision-maker can clearly interpret an international agreement by placing primary emphasis on textual language given controversy among the parties. Such a supposition exaggerates either the autonomy of language or the authority of interpreters, or both.[44]

This was to repeat verbatim the mistaken charges McDougal and his colleagues levied against the ILC view. As was suggested in the previous chapter, the theory of meaning adopted by the policy-oriented approach is flawed, and the ILC approach, despite suffering from inadequacies, offers a relatively more persuasive approach to interpretation of rules.[45]

While Falk did not contest the linguistic basis of the New Haven theory of interpretation, he was troubled by the policing function that McDougal espoused which led to a bias in favour of any interpretation that supported the foreign policy stance of United States. It may be recalled that McDougal calls for a policing or integrating function of interpretation which requires that the element of value relevance come into full play at the time of norm interpretation and application. Falk observed in this regard that McDougal's policy preference 'presupposes a certain kind of epistemological confidence which he never sustains with solid evidence'.[46] He was also troubled by the McDougal proposition that 'the law turns out to be what helps a certain set of policies to prevail in the struggle for power'.[47] Falk also did not accept the New Haven view that state officials, or for that matter scholars, are able to balance national interests and world community interests.[48] He found that scholars were also prone to accept the views of the government, as he discovered in relation to the Vietnam War. Even McDougal had contended that 'our moral – and legal – position in South Vietnam is sound'.[49] Falk wrote that 'this claim seems macabre and absurd in light of several million refugees and the untold devastation and destruction inflicted on Vietnam without even the prospect of successful military and political action'.[50] He attempted to find a way out of this conundrum by advancing an approach to interpretation that would accommodate the New Haven view on meaning but without

---

[44] See ibid.
[45] See Chapter 3, pp. 125–138.
[46] Falk, *Legal Order*, p. 89.
[47] See ibid., p. 88.
[48] Falk, *Status of Law*, p. 44.
[49] See ibid., p. 579.
[50] See ibid. See further Falk, 'International Law', pp. 1122–1160.

entirely undermining the autonomous role of rules in the international legal system:

> My own thinking on interpretation is heavily influenced by two kinds of factors that neither McDougal-Lasswell-Miller nor the ILC accord explicit attention: first, the *relevance of the decision-making locus,* whether national or international, whether judicial or executive, and whether governed by political officials or bureaucrats; and second, *the relevance of subject matter,* whether concerned with broad questions of national security in the war-peace sector or with more routine inter-actions.[51]

He went on to observe:

> I find both the ILC Draft Articles and the New Haven approach overgeneralized in their disagreement about the relative roles of text and context in the interpretative process. We need to develop more *functionally specific conceptions of interpretation* that give adequate weight to these factors through categorization of interpretative settings and through the suggestion of the *appropriate mix of text and context for each category.*[52]

This 'intermediate' or 'contextual' approach to interpretation is interesting for even as it is critical of the ILC approach there is implicit recognition of its merit, albeit accompanied by the suggestion that it be 'narrowly circumscribed to self-interpretation in the war–peace area'.[53] Falk thus calls for a 'more functionally specific conceptions of interpretation', which would give adequate weight to 'the relevance of subject matter'.[54] Accordingly, each instance of interpretation, depending on the locus of decision making and subject matter would require a different mix of text and context.

But the functional approach to interpretation advanced by Falk raises its own set of questions. Besides the fact that the very categorization of issues as being in the war or peace sector can become the arena of interpretive controversy, it is difficult to see how a 'misleading view of language and communications' adopted by the ILC can yield an appropriate or 'objective' interpretation when texts relating to grave issues are concerned and not do so where lesser issues are at stake. Or, to put it differently, how can subject matter, or for that matter the locus of decision making, control a theory of meaning. The Falk perspective can at best be seen as a spontaneous bid to achieve a satisfactory autonomy/relevance balance which

---

[51] Falk, *Status of Law,* p. 366; emphasis added.
[52] See ibid., pp. 366–367; emphasis added.
[53] See ibid., p. 366.
[54] See ibid., p. 367.

could restrain the opportunistic use of legal argument at least in the war–peace sector, having been witness to its blatant use in several contexts. But while the intention is noble, the strategy should have been to question the New Haven understanding of the meaning of meaning. A turn to the use theory of meaning advanced by Ludwig Wittgenstein (and J. L. Austin) would have greatly aided this process. As Wittgenstein noted, you do not first formulate a rule and then look around for its meaning. Rather a rule is formulated in the matrix of a shared social world and accompanying social practices that have already assigned it meaning. Such a perspective alone can sustain 'an intermediate position, one that maintains the distinctiveness of legal order while managing to be responsive to the extra-legal setting of politics, history and morality'.[55]

Falk, however, does address and contest more directly the New Haven thesis when it comes to the structural sources of indeterminacy of rules. He rightly notes that for the New Haven approach 'the pervasive reality of legal indeterminacy [...] is a consequence of the logical applicability of complementary structures of norms to any set of facts in contention';[56] the Koskenniemi view that the New Haven approach did not refer to structural basis of indeterminacy is therefore incorrect.[57] As Falk notes, in the McDougal view, 'legal rules co-exist in complementary pairs, permitting opposite arguments to develop in relation to each complementary norm'.[58] In the circumstances, it is better to indulge in explicit policy making than surreptitiously introducing value preferences in the course of the interpretation of particular rules.[59] However, Falk contested this view observing that 'the significance of complementary norms is exaggerated'.[60] He queries whether all arguments can be 'equally plausible'.[61] He also rightly concludes that McDougal 'sacrifices too many of the stabilizing benefits of the rule-oriented approach to international law by stressing policy flexibility'.[62] But once again he does not turn to relevant social and linguistic theories to make his argument. Instead Falk devotes himself to understanding the social and political reasons that prevented the international community of states from realizing a just world order.

---

[55] Richard Falk, 'The Interplay of Westphalia and Charter Conceptions of International Legal Order', in Falk et al., *International Law,* pp. 116–142 at p. 117.
[56] Falk, *Legal Order* , p. 84.
[57] For Koskenniemi's view, see Chapter 5, p. 316.
[58] Falk, *Status of Law,* p. 14.
[59] Falk, *Legal Order,* p. 84.
[60] Falk, *Status of Law,* p. 15.
[61] See ibid., p. 15.
[62] Falk, *Legal Order,* p. 89.

III.   Towards a Just World Order: Diagnosis

In the period 1968–1995 Falk was associated with the World Order Models Project (WOMP) as one of its leading figures. It marked a new phase in Falk's intellectual journey.[63] WOMP was an integral part of world order studies in general, albeit with a distinct identity which was sustained through a classification that saw it as a system-transforming approach in contrast to system-maintaining and system-reforming approaches.[64] It was driven by the realization of the following objectives: minimization of collective violence; maximization of economic well-being; maximization of social and political justice; and maximization of ecological quality.

WOMP has gone through two phases of transnational collaboration. In the first phase scholars from around the world were requested to con-tribute monographs on 'feasible utopias' that could be realized by the 1990s.[65] The resulting scholarship, published in the mid-1970s exhib-ited, according to Falk, 'the impatience and optimism of their authors' but with eventually little impact on the behaviour of states.[66] In the second phase WOMP attempted 'to produce an aggregate set of propos-als' that would have the consent of a diverse, albeit like-minded, set of scholars with a range of perspectives. But 'despite earnest efforts over a period of several years, the undertaking was abandoned as futile' as no consensus emerged.[67] However, one WOMP program called 'The Global Civilization: Challenges for Democracy, Sovereignty and Security Project (GCP)' led to a major publication.[68] More recently, Falk has asked whether

---

[63] For a brief history of WOMP, see Richard A. Falk, Samuel S. Kim and Saul H. Mendlovitz (eds.), *Towards a Just World Order* (Boulder, CO: Westview Press, 1982), pp. 1–9.

[64] Richard Falk, 'Contending Approaches to World Order' in Richard A. Falk, Samuel S. Kim and Saul H. Mendlovitz, (eds.) *Towards a Just World Order* (Boulder, CO: Westview Press, 1982), pp. 146–174.

[65] Richard Falk, *(Re)Imagining Humane Global Governance* (Abingdon, Oxon: Routledge, 2014), p. 183. The books included an 'overview' in Saul H. Mendolovitz (ed.) *On the Creation of a Just World Order: Preferred Worlds for the 1990s* (New York: Free Press, 1975); Rajni Kothari, *Footsteps to the Future: Diagnosis of the Present World and a Design for an Alternative* (New York: Free Press, 1974); Ali A. Mazrui, *A World Federation of Cultures: An African Perspective* (New York: Free Press, 1976); Richard Falk, *A Study of Future Worlds* (New Delhi: Orient Longman, 1975); Johann Galtung, *The True Worlds: A Transnational Perspective* (New York: Free Press, 1980); G. Logos and H. Godoy, *Revolution in Being: A Latin American View of the Future* (New York: Free Press, 1977).

[66] Falk, *(Re)Imagining Humane*, p. 183.

[67] See ibid.

[68] Richard Falk, *On Humane Governance: Toward a New Global Politics* (Philadelphia: Pennsylvania University Press, 1995).

it would be worthwhile to launch WOMP 2, a matter touched upon at the end of the chapter.

As an expert in international relations and law Falk made a major contribution to WOMP. From the beginning Falk argued the case for 'normative international relations' in opposition to realist thought. He of course understood the value of 'the antisentimental feature(s) of realist's thinking', including the idea that change cannot be brought about by appealing to the enlightened self-interest of ruling elites.[69] However, he felt that realist thought was insufficiently realist as it 'evade(d) critical questions' and showed 'an insufficient capacity to acknowledge emergencies' (flowing from presence of nuclear weapons and ecological crisis) and was therefore 'defective from a normative point of view'.[70] In the manner of the intermediate approach to international law Falk attempted to articulate a 'postrealist thought' that sought 'the creation of autonomous modes of discourse that are neither oblivious to the actualities of state power, nor so entrapped by these actualities as to be incapable of setting forth a non-statist array of planetary futures'.[71] Falk proposed the need for normative international relations whose ambitions were to be the 'diagnosis of the present, projection of the future, and discovery of creative space by which the predicted future can be brought into closer alignment with a preferred future'.[72] In what ensues, a critical examination of aspects of the diagnosis and the vision for the future is undertaken under the following heads:

1. Problems of statism and states system
2. Industrial civilization and the ecological crisis

It will be seen that Falk essentially traces the ills of present-day world order to the 'logic of territory'. In the instance of the ecological crisis the problems are additionally traced to an industrial civilization, to the relative neglect of the 'logic of capital'. That is to say, it is industrial civilization rather than capitalism that stands indicted for the ecological crisis. The critique of extant world order is accompanied by a strategy of transition for bringing about system transformation, principally through the agency of an emerging 'global civil society'. In the period of transition, international law is assigned an important role. In fact, WOMP has guided Falk's work in the field of international law. The strategy of transition in

---

[69] Falk, *End of World Order*, p. 11.
[70] See ibid., pp. 12–14. It may however be noted that among realists Morgenthau did change his views in response to the thermonuclear revolution. See Chapter 2, pp. 88–89.
[71] See ibid., p. 14.
[72] See ibid., p. 16.

bringing about system transformation, its different phases, and the role of 'global civil society' and international law proposed by Falk are dealt with in subsequent sections.

A.   Problem of Statism and States System

At the centre of Falk's diagnosis of the ills of contemporary world order is the 'dysfunctional territorial divisions of the planet and its peoples'; he contends that the states system is incapable of achieving set WOMP goals. Falk attributes the failure of the sovereign states system to deal with global problems to the fact that each state is in hot pursuit of its national interests, generating a system of international relations that is dominated by competition and conflict. According to Falk, such a system does not reveal any serious capacity for international cooperation as states are overwhelmingly guided by selfish interests.[73] Since the Westphalian system is captive to 'the dualistic thinking of "self" and "other"',[74] 'national governments formulate *planetary priorities* to reflect the ranking and character of *national priorities*'.[75] In the circumstances, 'the primary world order need is to find an alternative to statism'.[76]

Falk's own preference was initially for a 'central guidance system' at the international level implying 'a unified capacity for policy-formation – coordination and – implementation'.[77] But from the very beginning the declared obsolescence of the sovereign states system did not go unquestioned. For instance, Julius Stone noted that 'while state sovereignty should indeed be seen with all its faults, we must still remember that it *can* serve functions that are not *merely* a rationalisation of human greed, folly or madness'.[78] Hedley Bull emphasized that 'in the short run it is only national governments that have the information, the experience and the resources to act effectively in relation to these matters'.[79] In their view, there was no getting away from the fact that the state will be an important

---

[73] Richard Falk, *This Endangered Planet: Prospects and Proposals for Human Survival* (New York: Random House, 1971), p. 38.

[74] Falk, *(Re)Imagining Humane*, p. 5.

[75] Falk, *This Endangered Planet*, p. 40; emphasis in original.

[76] Falk, *End of World Order*, p. 291.

[77] Falk, *Study of Future Worlds*, p. 51. It may however be noted that the functional centralization was even then to be accompanied by a degree of political and economic decentralization.

[78] Julius Stone, *Visions of World Order; Between State Power and Human Justice* (Baltimore, MD: The John Hopkins University Press, 1984), p. 40; emphasis in original.

[79] Hedley Bull, *The Anarchical Society* (London: Macmillan, 1977), p. 294.

element of any projected solution to world order problems. But Falk believed that the states system can only sustain a 'meliorist vision of the future', which involves improving the managerial capacities of the existing system and therefore serves to perpetuate the status quo.[80] However, as will be discussed later, over the years Falk became increasingly conscious of the different facets of statism in the context of the North-South divide. In fact he has displayed a sensitive attitude to the developing nation affirmation of state sovereignty:

> for non-Western peoples, the acquisition of sovereignty has to be understood against a long history of dependence and domination. Statehood is a positive achievement, and the main task of the leadership is to consolidate this achievement, keeping the society truly independent in the face of a variety of pressures. Especially the Third World is suspicious at this time of 'globalist' schemes for world order, fearing some overarching framework designed to erode their sovereignty on behalf of Western economic and cultural interests.[81]

But this understanding did not mitigate the verbal assault on the states system. The reason is that Falk does not draw the appropriate lessons from the recognition that 'the role of the state has often been conceived in simplistic terms as the *bete noire* of world order'.[82] He also does not sufficiently appreciate that to trace most global problems to the 'logic of territory' to the exclusion of the 'logic of capital' is to ignore a primary cause for world order problems. To put it differently, instead of indicting the states system Falk should have examined the distinct character of states flowing from the universalizing 'logic of capital'. The characterization of different states has to be arrived at through an analysis of particular social formations over which these states preside. Such an exercise allows the identification of those social forces and states which are primarily responsible for the non-realization of WOMP values even if it were to be conceded that all states have made their individual contribution to sustaining an unjust world order and to bringing planet Earth to the brink of disaster.

A second reason why Falk does not distinguish between states that constitute the states system is the use of an anarchist theory of state that 'extend(s) the critique of the state ... to a critique of statism or the state system as a global framework for political organization'.[83] Falk observes

---

[80] See ibid.
[81] Falk, *Towards a Just World Order*, pp. 1–2.
[82] Falk, 'Contending Approaches', p. 169.
[83] Falk, *End of World Order*, p. 277.

that 'both liberal and Marxist theory underestimate the autonomous role of the state as an actor with its own set of interests distinct from those of the general population or from those of separate classes, ethnic identities, regions, or religions'.[84] In order to substantiate this proposition, Falk referred to the modern phenomenon of bureaucratism, the expanding role of the state, its complex relationship with technology, the encroachments on democratic processes made in view of the pressures of terrorism etc.[85] However, the core of his thesis is contained in the reference to 'the autonomous role of the state as an actor with its own set of interests'. It is partly with reference to its separate set of interests that he contends that world order risks are intrinsic to the operation of the states system. Falk did not explore the possibility of classification of states on the basis of their class (or gendered) character.[86]

The 'state for itself' thesis, according to which 'fundamental conflicts of interest might arise between the existing dominant class or set of groups on the one hand, and the state rulers on the other', has been persuasively contested by Marxist scholars.[87] As Ralph Miliband has pointed out, 'in relation to countries with a solid class structure and a well-entrenched dominant class, such a model does not seem appropriate'[88]:

> For it is surely very difficult to see, in such countries, what the interests of 'state rulers' would be which would also place these rulers in *fundamental* conflicts with *all* classes or groups in society … there are things which the state wants and does, and which are very irksome to the dominant class: but this is a very different matter from there being a fundamental conflict between them. Moreover, if such a conflict between them did occur, the state would in all likelihood be acting in ways that would favour some other class or classes. In other words, a new partnership would have been created; or the state would be acting, for whatever reason, in favour of a class or classes without any such partnership having been established. In neither case would the state be 'neutral', or acting solely 'for itself'.[89]

However, Miliband was willing to accept that since an 'economically dominant class' was often absent in the instance of developing countries

[84] See ibid., p. 63.
[85] See ibid.
[86] At times he speaks of key geopolitical actors representing 'the dominant class, gender, and race within their own territorial space'. Falk, *On Humane Governance*, p. 50. It may be worth noting that this volume is the outcome of a collaborative project.
[87] Ralph Miliband, 'State Power and Class Interests', 138 (1983) *New Left Review*, pp. 57–68 at p. 66.
[88] See ibid., pp. 66–67.
[89] See ibid., pp. 66–67; emphasis in original.

TOWARDS A JUST WORLD ORDER: DIAGNOSIS

the postcolonial state possessed 'a very high degree of autonomy' coming close to becoming a 'state for itself'.[90] The appearance of greater autonomy was, inter alia, a function of multi-structural societies in which the state functioned as an arbitrator amidst interacting modes of production (pre-feudal, feudal, capitalist) and corresponding classes (and their strata). Yet this did not prevent a combination of different classes (such as rich land-lords and the emerging capitalist class), along with transnational capital, from becoming the economically dominant class. In fact Miliband him-self qualified his remarks through reference to the existence of foreign interests.[91] Be that as it may, in the years since Miliband advanced his views the class structure in postcolonial societies has solidified as cap-italism has consolidated and become the dominant mode of produc-tion in their social formation, albeit it must be said that the relationship between dominant classes and the state continues to be the subject of much debate.[92]

An important reason Falk advocates 'the adoption of an anarchist perspective on global reform' is that it 'is alive to the twin dangers of socialism and capitalism if pursued within the structure of statism'.[93] In fact, he sees the immediate impact of anarchist thought as 'leavening the more deeply rooted political traditions of Marxism and liberalism' and 'providing a corrective for the bureaucratic and repressive tendencies of Marxist politics, and for the apologetics and rationalisations of liberal politics'.[94] Falk also believes that 'the basic anarchist impulse is towards something positive' and 'has something important to contribute to the emergent dialogue on the tactics and shape of global reform'.[95] In this respect, Falk recalls Bakunin's 'tentative advocacy of a universal confed-eration of peoples' and the conditions under which it could be created:

> It is absolutely necessary for any country wishing to join the free fed-
> eration of peoples to replace its centralized, bureaucratic, and mili-
> tary organizations by a federalist organization, based on the absolute

---

[90] Ralph Miliband, *Marxism and Politics* (Oxford: Oxford University Press, 1977), pp. 108 and 109. See also Nicos Poulantzas, *Political Power and Social Classes* (London: Verso, 1978), pp. 255 ff; and Bob Jessop, *State Theory: Putting the Capitalist State in Its Place* (Cambridge: Polity, 1990).

[91] See Miliband, *Marxism and Politics*, p. 109.

[92] Samir Kumar Das, 'Introduction: Surveying the Literature on State in Post-Independence India', in Samir Kumar Das (ed.) *Political Science: The Indian State*, vol. 1 (New Delhi: Oxford University Press, 2013), pp. 1–53, especially pp. 16–24.

[93] Falk, *End of World Order*, p. 294.

[94] See ibid., p. 283.

[95] See ibid., p. 279.

liberty and autonomy of regions, provinces, communes, associations, and individuals.[96]

In Falk's view such a vision is attractive and has much to contribute to creating just post-statal societies. It is also feasible because while the anarchist case for radical reform (i.e., for social revolution) 'was *chimerical within the confines of the state system*' the same is 'now being superseded'.[97] The globalization of social life 'allows … the anarchist vision (as epitomised in Bakunin's writings) of a fusion between a universal confederation and organic social forms of a communal character' to come into play.[98] Such a confederation 'represents the most acceptable normative sequel to the state system' including 'imperial consolidation, world state, regional federation, and intergovernmental functionalism'.[99]

The differences between Marxists and anarchists in this instance arises with respect to its viability and the role revolutionary forms of state can play in the long transition to a free confederation of peoples. However, at first, it is important to draw the attention of the reader to the deep roots of anti-statism in the thought of Marx, Engels and Lenin. Engel's pronouncement on the state withering away and finding its place in 'the museum of antiquities, by the side of the spinning-wheel and the bronze axe' is generally known.[100] What is less appreciated is that V.I. Lenin's views were as strongly anti-statist.[101] In his view, it is only when the state ceases to exist will complete democracy, democracy without exceptions, be possible and be realized.[102] Lenin stated categorically that 'so long as the state exists there is no freedom. When there is freedom, there will be no state'.[103] Thus, there is a family resemblance between anarchist and socialist thought in as much as both have the removal of state from the stage of history as their eventual goal. Where the two traditions differ is in the need for state power in the period of transition to a post-statal society, with the Marxist tradition favouring its use in the period of

---

[96] Cited by Falk, ibid, p. 280.
[97] See ibid., p. 288; emphasis in original.
[98] See ibid.
[99] See ibid., p. 291.
[100] Karl Marx and Frederick Engels, *Selected Works*, vol.3 (Moscow: Progress Publishers, 1973), p. 330. Also see pp. 34, 147 and 151.
[101] Ralph Miliband, 'Class Struggle from Above' in William Outhwaite and Michael Mulkay (eds.), *Social Theory and Social Criticism* (Oxford: Blackwell, 1987), pp. 175–184 at p. 180. According to Miliband, *The State and Revolution* is 'an anti-statist text if ever there was one'.
[102] V. I. Lenin, *Selected Works*, vol. 2 (Moscow: Progress Publishers, 1975), p. 303.
[103] See ibid., p. 308.

transition from capitalism to communism via socialism. In the case of anarchists the possibility of establishing a post-statal society also draws inspiration from the historical claim made by Kropotkin that 'anarchistic conceptions of organic institutions (of a cooperative character) were very successfully established over a wide geographical and cultural expanse [in European Middle Ages as also in non-West] until crushed by the emergent states of the fifteenth and sixteenth centuries'.[104] Thus, according to Falk, 'there is a kind of *prima facie* case for the plausibility of the anarchist model, although in a pre-state context'.[105] However, the accuracy of interpretations which Kropotkin made of these early societies has been contested, including their non-repressive nature.[106] It may also be questioned whether the obsolescence of the states system today is clearing the way for the anarchist vision of a post-statal society to be realized. Indeed, arguably a global imperial state constituted by a network of cities and international institutions is emerging in the era of neo-liberal globalization. This is perhaps the reason that at times Falk confesses that the anarchist prospect 'has slim chances for success'.[107]

In any case the confusion at the popular level between philosophical anarchism and the perception of anarchists as individuals who wish chaos to reign remains a serious hurdle to its acceptance. Therefore, more recently, Falk advocates what he terms 'anarchism without anarchism' or 'stealth anarchism' as it can help shake off the popular misunderstandings associated with the idea of 'anarchism'.[108] He calls for '*selectively* reviving the direction and underlying orientation of the tradition of philosophical anarchism'.[109] In his view, there are several encouraging developments in this respect. These include 'a primary reliance on non-state actors as the bearer of emancipator potential; seeking change on the basis of coercive nonviolence and soft power, including seeking control of the moral high ground in relation to social and political conflict; and reverence for nature and ancient wisdom'.[110] Falk is here speaking of undermining the states

---

[104] Falk, *End of World Order*, p. 287.
[105] See ibid.
[106] George Woodcock, *Anarchism* (Middlesex: Penguin, 1975), p. 22.
[107] Falk, *End of World Order*, p. 288.
[108] Falk, *(Re)Imagining Humane*, p. 149.
[109] See ibid., p. 151; emphasis in original.
[110] See ibid., p. 152. See generally Jonathan Purkis and James Bowen (ed.), *Changing Anarchism: Anarchist Theory and Practice in a Global Age* (Manchester: Manchester University Press, 2004).

system from below, making a distinction between the ideas of 'globalization from above' and 'globalization from below':

> the former being the de facto alliance of governments, banks, and cor-
> porations that were generating a particular menacing form of 'predatory'
> capitalism that had an unprecedented global wing spread, was intensifying
> inequalities, invalidating regulatory oversight, and operating without sig-
> nificant ideological opposition. In opposition, was an emergent collection
> of local, national, regional, and global social movements, initiatives, and
> visions, that is, 'globalization from below'.[111]

Falk believes that what makes the views of 'globalization from below' 'a vir-
tual species of anarchism in outlook, was the turn away from either situating
hopes in a reforming state, a revolutionary seizure of state power, or through
the global institutionalization of authority via the United Nations or the
establishment of world government'.[112] The social movements that constitute
'globalization from below' are informed by 'a global vision that allows its
overriding concern with freedom of the individual, autonomy of the group,
and harmony among groups to be responsive to the planetary imperatives
of a sustainable social life in the early twenty-first century'.[113] This vision can
be actualized 'by living locally and in accord with the mandates of voluntary
simplicity' drawing inspiration from the life world of indigenous peoples
and from the work and life of philosophical anarchists like Gandhi, Tolstoy,
Paul Goodman, Murray Bookchin and E. F. Schumacher among others.[114]

The Falk invocation of 'anarchism without anarchism' is certainly valuable. The state in the contemporary world is coming to have an all pervasive
presence. It uses diverse techniques of power to control and manipulate
individuals and communities aided by modern technologies. In fact, a
combination of networks of power and overt institutions presided over
by the state invades the life of an individual.[115] The state also overtly curbs

---

[111] See ibid. He has recently noted that 'this broad brush distinction is only a first
approximation ... The lines of actual conduct are shifting, complex, and far more con-
voluted and less dualistic'. Richard Falk, *Humanitarian Interventions and Legitimacy
Wars: Seeking Peace and Justice in the 21st Century* (London: Routledge, 2014), p. 181.

[112] See ibid.

[113] Falk, *(Re)Imaging Humane*, p. 148.

[114] See ibid., p. 157.

[115] See generally Nikolas Rose, Pat O'Malley and Mariana Valverde, 'Governmentality', (2006)
Annual Review of Law and Social Science, pp. 83–104. There are complex and insidious
ways in which micro and macro power manifest themselves in modern societies. The
Marxist scholar Bob Jessop therefore underlines the need to 'escape the dichotomy of
micro- and macro-power, the antinomy of an analytics of micro-powers and a theory of
sovereignty, and the problematic relation between micro-diversity and macro-necessity in

the power of citizens in the name of fighting a range of enemies including terrorism. In the event the ordinary citizen feels helpless before the leviathan. In the developing world the state can also inflict enormous violence and harm in the name of development.[116] In short, the 'dominant culture of the state' certainly needs to be challenged.[117] There is also good reason to be sceptical about the states system being in a position to address the critical issues that confront the world. In this respect too Falk is not entirely off the mark. A key lapse of Marxist theory is that it has tended to concern itself more with the state than the states system.[118] In this sense there is justification for the general observation of Michael Mann that 'theorists of *the* state abound, but they seem not to have noticed that *states* are plural'.[119] In other words, Marxist scholars have tended to neglect the fact that the 'logic of territory', that is the relationship between states constitutes, however partially, the structure and character of an individual state. The role and functions of a state cannot be understood outside the states system. However, it is equally problematic to assign primacy in the manner of Falk to the ontology of the states system. There is a need to theorize the different kinds of states that constitute the states system and the role particular categories of states play in interstate relations. To put

power relations'. Bob Jessop, 'From Micro-powers to Governmentality: Foucault's Work on Statehood, State Formation, Statecraft and State Power', 26 (2007) *Political Geography*, pp. 34–40 at p. 39. He points in this regard to the work of Michel Foucault. Bob Jessop notes that 'Foucault stressed three themes in his "nominalist" analytics of power: it is immanent in all social relations, articulated with discourses as well as institutions, and necessarily polyvalent because its impact and significance vary with how social relations, discourses and institutions are integrated into different strategies. He also focused on technologies of power, power-knowledge relations, and changing strategies for structuring and deploying power relations.' See ibid. In other words, Foucault contended that: 'One should study power where it is exercised over individuals rather than legitimated at the centre; explore the actual practices of subjugation rather than the intentions that guide attempts at domination; and recognize that power circulates through networks rather than being applied at particular points.' See ibid., p. 36.

[116] Ashis Nandy, *The Romance of the State: And the Fate of Dissent in the Tropics* (New Delhi: Oxford University Press, 2003), pp. 1–15.

[117] See ibid., p. 15.

[118] In this regard, see generally, Martin Shaw, 'War, Imperialism and the States System: A Critique of Orthodox Marxism for the 1980s' in Martin Shaw (ed.), *War, State and Society* (London: Macmillan, 1984), pp. 64–68.

[119] Michael Mann, *States, War and Capitalism: Studies in Political Sociology* (Oxford: Blackwell Publishers, 1988), p. viii. See also Andrew Linklater, 'Marxism and International Relations: Antithesis, Reconciliation and Transcendence' in Richard Higgott and J. L. Richardson (eds.), *International Relations: Global and Australian Perspectives on an Evolving Discipline* (Canberra: Australian National University, 1991), pp. 70–91.

it differently, it would not do to exaggerate the significance of either the 'logic of territory' or the 'logic if capital'.

B.   Industrial Civilization and the Ecological Crisis

The global environmental crisis has been from the 1970s a consistent theme in Falk's work.[120] As Falk describes at the beginning of *This Endangered Planet*, published in 1971, the process of questioning initiated by the Vietnam War led to the development of a 'counter-culture' and an 'explosion of concern among the young about the environment'.[121] A view gained ground that 'the rational consciousness of modern man has emptied nature of personality, and has deprived man of any sense of personal kinship with nature'.[122] It was thought that modern science taught dominance over nature accompanied by a misplaced confidence that 'science and technology can provide an answer to all the problems which are engendered'.[123] It discredited in the process all 'prescientific ways of thinking'.[124] In other words, the ongoing ecological crisis has its roots in an industrial civilization which misconceives the relationship between man and nature and portrays a picture of good life that ignores spiritual realities and is overly sanguine about coping with accumulating problems. The distinction here between capitalism and socialism is inapposite as was and is testified to by the record of 'actually existing socialism'. It was certainly worse than that of capitalism in so far as environmental protection is concerned.

Since the publication of *This Endangered Planet* Falk has continued to write about the impending ecological crisis and the response of the international community. He has identified two cycles of consciousness about 'ecological urgency'. The first cycle of ecological urgency began with the Stockholm Conference (1972) and ended with the Rio Earth Summit (1992) and was marked by the publication of the Brundtland Commission report.[125] This period saw many positives including growing public awareness, the increased role of civil society organizations, and the raising of justice issues by the Global South. But the period also witnessed

---

[120] The first clear statement on the subject was made in Falk, *This Endangered Planet*. See also Falk, *Study of Future Worlds*, pp. 46–48, 103–108.

[121] See Falk, *This Endangered Planet*, p. 17.

[122] See ibid., p. 39.

[123] See ibid., p. 34

[124] See ibid., p. 74.

[125] Falk, *Writings of Richard Falk*, pp. 179–184.

a backlash from vested interests, in particular the corporate world. Nevertheless the first cycle of ecological urgency generated 'a robust environmental movement' even if 'it lacked sufficient depth and perseverance' and therefore came 'to a grinding halt' without meeting its objectives.[126] The second cycle of ecological urgency which has its beginnings in the new century has seen diminished consciousness about the environmental challenge.[127] According to Falk, at least one significant reason is 'the hostility of neo-liberal ideology to regulation' and 'the regressive leadership of the United States'.[128] As the neo-liberal model came to be universalized it endangered planet Earth with sector after sector coming to be engulfed in crisis. Yet there is complete disregard today 'for sustainability of resources in the years and decades ahead, thereby reinforcing the tendencies that are producing environmental decay at an alarming rate and are especially damaging to the global commons (that is, seas, atmosphere, space – those domains of the earth's ecosystem lying beyond the territorial reach of states)'.[129] Falk also points out how modern warfare has caused severe environmental damage as in the instance of the Iraq war,[130] with the possibility of a nuclear war leading to 'the death of nature'.[131] But there continues to be 'deep denial' of ruling elites of the 'overall scale of the environmental challenge'.[132] The mood may have changed in the last few years with the problem of climate change coming to the fore in public discussions.[133] What have however not changed are two things: first, the view that the existing states system and the ideology of secular materialism can address the ongoing ecological crisis. Second, in speaking of global environmental governance there is still 'scant attention given to the bearing of fairness or justice on either the diagnosis of the environmental challenge or its cure'.[134] In fact 'the challenges of distributive justice relating to the environmental agenda are essentially ignored'.[135]

[126] See ibid., p. 184.
[127] See ibid., p. 185.
[128] See ibid.
[129] Falk, *On Humane Governance*, pp. 32–33.
[130] See ibid., p. 178.
[131] Richard Falk, *Explorations at the Edge of Time: The Prospects for World Order* (Philadelphia, PA: Temple University Press, 1992), p. 178.
[132] Falk, *Writings of Richard Falk*, p. 176.
[133] See ibid., pp. 185–186. For reflections on the challenge of climate change, see ibid., pp. 194–217.
[134] See ibid., p. 174.
[135] See ibid., p. 177.

In terms of how the ecological crisis is to be addressed, there are at least four broad responses that can be found in Falk's writings. First, there is the need to overcome 'the dualisms of the rational/scientific tradition, so dominant in the West' and creating 'a more unified sense of the inner/outer sensibilities'.[136] It calls for public education and lifestyle changes through learning from pre-industrial societies when men lived in harmony with nature through developing a sense of personal kinship with it. The stress should be on austerity, simplicity, self-reliance and communal living. In other words, the world economy would be reorganized so as to establish harmony between man and nature upset by the industrial revolution. Second, there has to be 'a concerted effort to establish an equilibrium between man and nature. The minimum requirement of such an equilibrium is some kind of ratio between technology and society enabling enough goods to be produced to satisfy the needs of everyone without resorting to a scale or modes of production that deteriorate the quality of the environment, including its resource base'.[137] The process of bringing about equilibrium will not involve the rejection of technology *per se* but object to the mindless marriage of technology to economic growth which encouraged high consumption lifestyles. Third, there should be efforts at demilitarization leading to a nuclear free world so that humankind does not self-destruct through causing an irreversible ecological crisis. Fourth, there must be greater cooperation between states to address the environmental crisis.[138] Falk proposes that the international community call 'a UN world conference devoted to the second cycle of environmental urgency, with attention to environmental justice as an imperative to environmental sustainability'.[139]

There is little doubt that central to the formulation of an ecological outlook is the perspective on man–nature relationship – structural considerations, the recorded past, the current impasse, and the beliefs and principles on which future societies should be organized. Falk comments on these issues in arriving at his particular ecological outlook 'whose essence is a political embodiment of man-in-nature, as the ideological underpinning for an adequate conception of world order'.[140] Both his analysis and recommendations to overcome the ecological crisis are not without merit. However, Falk does not address the principal issues

[136] Falk, 'Contending Approaches', p. 166.
[137] Falk, *This Endangered Planet*, p. 34.
[138] Falk, *Writings of Richard Falk*, pp. 207–208.
[139] Falk, *This Endangered Planet*, p. 189.
[140] See ibid., p. 21.

with the care and depth they deserve. It has been seen that it is rational-ist consciousness and industrial civilization in general along with statism and the states system which is placed in the dock. He does not indict the global capitalist system (as opposed to industrial civilization in general) that is arguably the principal cause of the global environmental crises. It is true that the historical record of 'socialist states' does not give room for optimism but it is important to understand that in the instance of Soviet Union there was the lack of understanding and in the case of China the problem is precisely its turn to capitalism and GNP consciousness.[141]

It is submitted that what is called for is a careful materialist analysis of the current ecological crisis. It is, therefore, not surprising that the last two decades have seen the emergence of a corpus of literature that explores the man–nature–society relationship from a materialist perspective.[142] This literature has, inter alia, mined the writings of Karl Marx and Friedrich

---

[141] See Zhihe Wang, Huili He and Meijun Fan, 'The Ecological Civilization Debate in China: The Role of Ecological Marxism and Constructive Postmodernism – Beyond the Predicament of Legislation', (November 2014) *Analytical Monthly Review*, pp. 35–56.

[142] J. O'Connor, 'Capitalism, Nature, Socialism: A Theoretical Introduction', 1 (1989) *Capitalism, Nature, Socialism*, pp. 11–38; James O'Connor, 'Political Economy and Ecology of Socialism and Capitalism', 3 (1989) *Capitalism, Nature, Socialism*, pp. 93–106; Neil Smith, *Uneven Development: Nature, Capital and the Production of Space* (Oxford: Blackwell, 1990); Reiner Grundmann, *Marxism and Ecology* (Oxford: Oxford University Press, 1991); Neil Smith, 'The Production of Nature' in G. Robertson et al. (eds.), *FutureNatural* (London: Routledge, 1996), pp. 35–54; Noel Castree, 'Marxism and the Production of Nature', 72 (2000) *Capital & Class*, pp. 5–36; Ted Benton, 'Marxism and Natural Limits: An Ecological Critique and Reconstruction', 178 (1989) *New Left Review*, pp. 51–86; Reiner Grundmann, 'The Ecological Challenge to Marxism', 187 (1991) *New Left Preview*, pp. 103–121; Ted Benton, 'Ecology, Socialism and the Mastery of Nature', 194 (1992) *New Left Review*, 55–72; P. Burkett, (1996) 'Some Common Misconceptions about Nature and Marx's Critique of Political Economy', 7 (1996) *Capitalism, Nature, Socialism*, pp. 57–80; P. Burkett, (1997) 'Nature in Marx Reconsidered', 10 (1997) *Organization and Environment*, pp. 164–183; John Bellamy Foster, *Marx's Ecology: Materialism and Nature* (New York: Monthly Review Press, 2000); Jason W. Moore, 'Environment Crisis and the Metabolic Rift in World-Historical Perspective', 13 (2000) *Organization & Environment*, pp. 123–157; John Bellamy Foster, 'Marx's Ecology in Historical Perspective', 96 (2002) *International Socialism*, available at www.marxists.org/history/etol/newspape/isj2/2002/isj2-096/foster.htm (accessed 17 September 2015); Brett Clark and John Bellamy Foster, 'Marx's Ecology in the 21st Century', 1 (2010) *World Review of Political Economy*, pp. 142–156; Michael Lowy, 'What is Ecosocialism', 16 (2005) *Capitalism, Nature and Socialism*, pp. 15–24; J. Kovel, *The End of Capitalism: The End of Capitalism or the End of the World?* 2nd edn (London: Zed Books, 2007); John Bellamy Foster, 'Ecology and the Transition from Capitalism to Socialism', 60 (2008) *Monthly Review*, available at http://monthlyreview.org/2008/11/01/ecology-and-the-transition-from-capitalism-to-socialism/ (accessed 17 September 2015); John Bellamy Foster, Brett Clark and Richard York, *The Ecological Rift: Capitalism's War on Earth* (New York: Monthly Review

Engels on the subject. However, as would be expected, these yield diverse interpretations of not only the thinking of Marx and Engels, but also the understanding of the contemporary ecological crisis and the ways of building an ecological civilization. But a common concern has been to overcome a dualist approach which at best 'instantiates the image of two "systems", one economic, the other ecological, which interact, albeit now in historically specific and relative ways'.[143] In the non-dualist understanding the 'production of nature is a continuous *process* in which nature and capital *co-constitute one another in temporally and geographically varied and contingent ways*'.[144] Such a view 'circumvents the absolutisms of *either* natural limits conservatism *or* social constructionist utopianism'.[145] The non-dualist approach helps reject mere managerial or technocratic solutions on the one hand and the romanticization of past on the other, as answers to the ecological crises. This view deserves brief elaboration.

In the non-dualist materialist view man is an integral part of nature and man-in-society is 'the everlasting Nature-imposed condition of human existence'.[146] It is this unitary matrix which is the subject of historical evolution, a process which man seeks to regulate, as thinking nature, to attain its own humanity, humanizing nature in the process. In the beginning there are elementary struggles between man and nature that is part of a necessary process imposed by nature itself. Soon the interaction of man with nature comes to be mediated by the labour of man which is, in the words of Marx,

> a process in which both man and Nature participate, and in which man of his own accord starts, regulates, and controls the material reactions between himself and Nature. He opposes himself to Nature as one of her own forces, setting in motion arms and legs, head and hands, the natural forces of his body, in order to appropriate Nature's productions in a form adapted to his own wants. By thus acting on the external world and changing it, he at the same time changes his own nature.[147]

The activities of man vis-à-vis nature assume different modes in different historical periods; in each economic epoch the relationship between

Press, 2010); Fred Magdoff and John Bellamy Foster, *What Every Environmentalist Needs to Know about Capitalism: A Citizen's Guide to Capitalism and the Environment* (New York: Monthly Review Press, 2011); John Bellamy Foster, 'The Epochal Crisis', 65 (2013) *Monthly Review,* pp. 1–12.
[143] Castree, 'Marxism', p. 23.
[144] See ibid., p. 28.
[145] See ibid., p. 28.
[146] Karl Marx, *Capital,* vol. I (Moscow: Progress Publishers, 1977).
[147] See ibid., p. 173.

man and nature is distinct.[148] In the past few centuries the relationship has come to be defined by the laws of motion of capitalism.[149] In studying the nature of capitalism Marx and Engels became aware of the negative implications of attempts to dominate and exploit nature. Attention may be drawn to a passage of Engels on the potential of capitalism to tame nature for the benefit of man:

> Let us not, however, flatter ourselves overmuch on account of our human victories over nature. For each such victory nature takes its revenge on us. Each victory, it is true, in the first place brings about the results we expected, but in the second and third places it has quite different, unforeseen effects which only too often cancel the first ... Thus at every step we are reminded that *we by no means rule over nature, like a conqueror over a foreign people*, like someone standing outside nature – but that we, with flesh, blood and brain, *belong to nature, and exist in its midst*, and that all our mastery of it consists in the fact that we have the advantage over all other creatures of being able to learn its laws and apply them correctly.[150]

This passage should help dispel the notion that Marxism advocates the subjugation of nature. Not only does it do no such thing – though some isolated passages in Marx may suggest this – but instead underlines man's unity with nature. It also cautions that a contrary conceptualization that pitches man against nature, as under capitalism, could lead to a serious ecological crisis. For example, writing of capitalist agriculture Marx observed that 'all progress in capitalistic agriculture is a progress in the art, not only of robbing the labourer, but of robbing the soil; all progress in increasing the fertility of the soil for a given time, is a progress towards ruining the lasting sources of that fertility'.[151] Likewise, he noted that 'the development of culture and of industry in general has ever evinced itself in such energetic destruction of forests that everything done by it conversely for their preservation and restoration appear infinitesimal'.[152] The examples of the concern of Marx and Engels about the impact of capitalism on environment can be multiplied, including their worries about the effects of capitalist urbanization on the environment and psyche of

---

[148] In the words of Marx, 'it is not the articles made, but how they are made, and by what instruments, that enables us to distinguish different economic epochs'. See ibid., p. 175.

[149] Narinder Singh, *Economics and the Crisis of Ecology* (New Delhi: Oxford University Press, 1976), p. 33.

[150] Frederick Engels, *Dialectics of Nature* (Moscow: Progress Publishers, 1974), p. 180; emphasis added.

[151] Marx, *Capital*, vol. I. pp. 474–475.

[152] Karl Marx, *Capital*, vol. II (Moscow: Progress Publishers, 1977), p. 248.

man.[153] But enough has been said to show that they were aware of the possible ecological disasters that capitalist exploitation of nature could engender. Indeed, anticipating the Brundtland Commission report Marx wrote that 'even a whole society, a nation, or even all simultaneously existing societies taken together, are not the owners of the globe. They are only its possessors, its usufructuaries, and, like *boni patres famil-ias*, they must hand it down to succeeding generations in an improved condition'.[154] But he grounded this concern in concrete historical analysis of the forces which dictated the domination of nature. To be sure, the practice of socialist states has not deviated significantly from the capitalist countries. Yet the theoretical critique of capitalism is of significance for in the words of Barry Commoner:

> we know that modern technology which is *privately* owned cannot long survive if it destroys the *social* good on which it depends – the ecosphere.

[153] Here is a passage from Engels describing London of his times:

> After roaming the streets of the capital a day or two, making headway with difficulty through the human turmoil and the endless line of vehicles, after visiting the slums of the metropolis, one realises for the first time that these Londoners have been forced to sacrifice the best qualities of their human nature, to bring to pass all the marvels of civilisation which crowd their city; that a hundred powers which slumbered within them have remained inactive, have been suppressed in order that a few might be developed more fully and multiply through union with those of others. The very turmoil of streets has something repulsive, something against which human nature rebels. The hundreds of thousands of all classes and ranks crowding past each other, are they not all human beings with the same qualities and powers, and with the same interest in being happy? And have they not, in the end, to seek happiness in the same way, by the same means? And still they crowd by one another as though they had nothing in common, nothing to do with one another, and their only agreement is the tacit one, that each keep to his own side of the pavement, so as not to delay the opposing streams of the crowd, while it occurs to no man to honour another with so much as a glance. The brutal indifference, the unfeeling isolation of each in his private interest becomes the more repellant and offensive, the more these individuals are crowded together, within a limited space. And, however, much one may be aware that this isolation of the individual, this narrow self-seeking is the fundamental principle of our society everywhere, it is nowhere so shamelessly barefaced, so self-conscious as just here in the crowding of the great city. The dissolution of mankind into monads, of which each one has a separate principle and a separate purpose, the world of atoms, is here carried out to its utmost extreme. Hence it comes, too, that the social war, the war of each against all, is here openly declared.

Frederick Engels, *The Condition of the Working Class in England* (Moscow: Progress Publishers, 1977), pp. 59–60.
[154] Karl Marx, *Capital*, vol. III (Moscow: Progress Publishers, 1977), p. 776.

Hence an economic system which is fundamentally based on private transactions rather than social ones is no longer appropriate and increasingly ineffective in managing this vital social good. The system is therefore in need of change.[155]

Marxists have not only subsequently elaborated on the relationship between capitalism and nature but also highlighted the phenomenon of 'ecological imperialism' that is an integral aspect of capitalism. John Bellamy Foster and Brett Clark have defined 'ecological imperialism' as follows:

Ecological imperialism [...] presents itself most obviously in the following ways: the pillage of the resources of some countries by others and the transformation of whole ecosystems upon which states and nations depend; massive movements of population and labour that are interconnected with the extraction and transfer of resources; the exploitation of ecological vulnerabilities of societies to promote imperialist control; the dumping of ecological wastes in ways that widen the chasm between centre and periphery; and overall, the creation of a global 'metabolic rift' that characterizes the relation of capitalism to the environment, and at the same time limits capitalist development.[156]

It may be recalled that while Falk does mention that the burden of environmental problems is shifted to the developing countries he does not trace this fact to the functioning of global capitalism but to power politics. Therefore, he does not see that the answer to the destruction of nature by capitalism and ecological imperialism does not lie in turning the historical clock back.

In the latter context it is important to remember that particular conceptions of man/nature relationship were held in ancient societies not because of their intrinsic merit but for the social functions they served. These societies were economically poor and technologically unable to come to grips with their natural environment. The ultimate dependence on the forces of nature led to the personification of natural phenomena.[157] In the words of Marx,

those ancient social organisms of production are, as compared with bourgeois society, extremely simple and transparent ... They can arise and exist

---

[155] Barry Commoner, *The Closing Circle: Nature, Man, Technology* (New York: Alfred A. Knopf Inc., 1971), p. 287; emphasis in original.

[156] John Bellamy Foster and Brett Clark, 'Ecological Imperialism: The Curse of Capitalism', (2004) *Socialist Register*, pp. 186–201 at p. 187.

[157] It played its part 'in the attempts of man to control his physical environment for his own economic and social ends'. Raymond Firth, *Human Types: An Introduction to Social Anthropology*, revised edn (New York: Mentor, 1958), p. 142.

only when the development of the productive power of labour has not risen beyond a low stage, and when, therefore, the social relations within the sphere of material life, between man and man, and between man and Nature, are correspondingly narrow. This narrowness is reflected in the ancient worship of Nature, and in the other elements of the popular religions. The religious reflex of the real world can, in any case, only then finally vanish, when the practical relations of everyday life offer to man none but perfectly intelligible and reasonable relations with regard to his fellowmen and to Nature.[158]

This passage arguably disregards the fact that certain attitudes towards nature have deep roots in cultural practices that cannot be traced merely to the primitive nature of the economic system. In any case there is admittedly something attractive about the respectful attitude of ancient societies towards nature. Levy-Strauss tells us of native communities unwilling to part with land even for ample compensation as it would be tantamount to exchanging their mother.[159] He writes of populations of wild-grain collectors (the Menomini of the Great Lakes region) perfectly aware of the agricultural techniques of their neighbours (the Iroquois), yet refusing to apply them to the production of their basic food (wild rice), although it is well suited to cultivation, for the reason that they are forbidden to 'wound their mother the earth'.[160] These attitudes can be encountered even today in one form or another in all civilizations. When juxtaposed to the narrow commercial outlook of capitalist civilization these sentiments seem so much more meaningful. It is for this reason that the economic and social features of ancient societies appear attractive in contrast to the industrialized world.[161] But moving forward the unity of outer and inner self, or respect for Nature, cannot be established without addressing the political economy of capitalism and imperialism. It may however be readily conceded that the ecological crisis 'requires us to put global histories of capital in conversation with the species history of humans'.[162] It calls for 'thinking simultaneously on both registers, to mix together the immiscible chronologies of capital and species history'[163] for 'the whole crisis cannot be reduced to a story of capitalism'.[164]

---

[158]   Karl Marx, *Capital*, vol. I, pp. 83–84.
[159]   Claude Levi-Strauss, *Structural Anthropology*, vol. 2 (Middlesex: Penguin, 1976), p. 321.
[160]   See ibid.
[161]   Karl Marx and Frederick Engels, *Collected Works*, vol. 28 (Moscow: Progress Publishers, 1986), pp. 411–412; emphasis in original.
[162]   Dipesh Chakrabarty, 'The Climate of History: Four Theses', 35 (2009) *Critical Inquiry*, pp. 197–222 at p. 212
[163]   See ibid., p. 220.
[164]   See ibid., p. 221.

IV.   Towards a Just World Order: Transition

Falk has from the beginning been conscious of the need to address the transition question. The realization was always there that if the vision of world order he was proposing was to be translated into reality then a strategy of transition had to accompany it.[165] However, his thinking on the transition question has gone through three phases: reform from above between 1970 and 1985, reform from below in the period 1985–1999 and the embrace of the ideas of 'new internationalism' and 'legitimacy struggles' since. There is a greater element of continuity in the latter two phases even as elements of all are to be found in the current phase.

A.   Reform from above: 1970–1985

Falk has always been conscious of the fact that ruling elites the world over will not voluntarily accept changes in the international system which do not help realize their parochial interests. It brought a negative reaction to the blueprint approach of Granville Clark and Louis Sohn which 'entrusted transition to the persuasive power of ideas directed at political elites'.[166] Falk was even at this stage against a heavy top-down model as it could bring about a world government 'so seriously flawed as to make us nostalgic for a world of states'.[167] Yet the strategy of transition that Falk set out in some detail in *A Study of Future Worlds* (1975) visualized a central guidance system.[168] Of course he clarified that a central guidance system was not the equivalent of establishing a world government but simply 'implied a unified capacity for policy-formulation, -coordination and –implementation, especially with regard to issues closely related to WOMP values'.[169] The recommended model anticipated 'a major build up of functional agencies at the regional and world level ... followed up by a shrinkage of state actors, especially the largest ones'.[170] In proposing this model of transition Falk borrowed from the insights of functionalism even as he was more aware of the limits of its logic then classical realists

---

[165] Falk, *Study of Future Worlds*, pp. 9, 277.
[166] Falk, *Towards a Just World Order*, p. 5. The Clark-Sohn approach is found in Grenville Clark and Louis B. Sohn, *World Peace through World Law*, 3rd edn (Cambridge, MA: Harvard University Press, 1966).
[167] Falk, *End of World Order*, p. 304.
[168] Falk, *Study of Future Worlds*, p. 158.
[169] See ibid., pp. 51, 229.
[170] See ibid., p. 226.

like Morgenthau.[171] He noted, for instance, that the UN system 'served mainly as extensions of the state system, not as alternatives to it' particularly in view of its financial dependence and the lack of capability to act independently. Indeed, his general conclusion was that the presence of international institutions was 'marginal to the state system, and often is so derivative from it that it has little or no independence'.[172] Falk therefore identified 'a sequence of changes that could bring about over time a dramatic and coherent set of results: first, value change via education; second, the growth of a world order reform movement via organisational activism; third, the institutional implementation of a new global consciousness via institutional innovation'.[173] He initially thought that this process could be completed in roughly three decades and proposed the following timetable: In the 1970s – political consciousness and the domestic imperative; in the 1980s – political mobilization and the transnational imperative; and in the 1990s – political transformation and the global imperative.[174]

Such a plan expectedly invited the charge of utopianism. Bull pointed out that while proponents of world order studies like Falk theoretically distanced themselves from the statement of mere blueprints and utopias they were unable to do so in practice.[175] He noted the naiveté about the plans for consciousness raising 'as if this had never been tried before'.[176] Stone challenged two of the underlying assumptions, namely, 'that state entities will not be aware of, or will be tolerant of, or will become so weak that they will submit to the truncation of their power in the transition to a planetary legal order' and 'that there will be such submission by sufficient number and range of state entities to allow the new planetary institutions to begin to function effectively'.[177] Stone also doubted whether people in the developed countries would be willing to sacrifice their own cultural and material interests for those geographically and culturally removed from them.[178] He was equally sceptical if the developing nations would be

---

[171] Falk, *End of World Order,* p. 300. He refers to the work of Ernest B. Haas, *Beyond the Nation-State* (Stanford, CA: Stanford University Press, 1964). For a brief summary of the functionalist position see Falk, *Study of Future Worlds,* pp. 194–195.

[172] See Falk, *End of World Order,* p. 302.

[173] See ibid., p. 220.

[174] Falk, *Study of Future Worlds,* p. 283.

[175] Hedley Bull, 'New Directions in the Theory of International Relations', 14 (1975) *International Studies* (New Delhi), pp. 277–286 at p. 282.

[176] Bull, *Anarchical Society,* p. 305.

[177] Stone, *Visions of World Order,* p. 36.

[178] See ibid.

willing to make sacrifices and exercise restraint with regard to issues like population growth and pollution.[179] Finally, Stone wondered if leaders of sovereign states would give preference to the long-term interests of the international community over their own short- and long-term interests.[180] Stanley Michalak, in a more detailed critique, also came to the conclusion that the proposal of consciousness raising, in particular in the time span indicated, was 'highly utopian'.[181] He pointed out that what Falk was recommending was revolution imposed 'from above' and such an exercise would involve more than 'a minimum of violence' than was envisaged.[182] In short, Falk did not seriously move beyond the Clark-Sohn strategy in as much as the emphasis remained on seeking change through the power of ideas on the basis of a blueprint of a preferred world polity. Falk admitted as much in his reply to Michalak. He confessed 'that *Future Worlds* overdoes the depiction of global structure. In this respect, its orientation is tied too closely to the political-legal heritage of world order studies'.[183] On reading the young Falk one is reminded of Engel's observation on the proposals of utopian socialists: 'the more completely they were worked out in detail, the more they could not avoid drifting off into pure phantasies.'[184] Engels had reminded the utopian socialists that the causes of social changes and political revolutions must in the final analysis be sought 'in the economics of each particular epoch'.[185] But, as has been argued, Falk neglects the central significance of the 'logic of capital'.[186] This eventually means a flawed diagnosis of world order, accompanied by an inadequate theory of state and a misconception of man–nature relationship. The circle was completed by a strategy of transition far removed from reality. Not surprisingly, it made little headway. In fact to his horror Falk found that

---

[179] See ibid.

[180] See ibid.

[181] Stanley J. Michalak, Jr., 'Richard Falk's Future World: A Critique of WOMP-USA', 42 (1980) *The Review of Politics*, pp. 3–17 at p. 11.

[182] See ibid., p. 7.

[183] Richard Falk, 'The Shaping of World Order Studies: A Response', 42 (1980) *The Review of Politics*, pp. 18–30 at p. 29.

[184] Marx and Engels, *Selected Works*, vol. 3, p. 119. See in this context Harry R. Targ, 'World Order and Future Studies Reconsidered', 5 (1979–80) *Alternatives*, pp. 371–383 at pp. 378–380.

[185] See ibid., p. 133; emphasis omitted.

[186] He had a chapter in *A Study of Future Worlds* on 'The World Economy as a World Order Dimension: Selected Aspects' that begins with the observation that previous world order studies from a non-Marxist perspective had neglected the 'character of the world economy' but himself did not go farther than noting some of its salient features. Falk, *Study of Future Worlds*, p. 350.

the language of world order came to be appropriated by the ruling elites to their own ends.[187]

B.   Reform from below: 1985–1999

By the mid-1980s Falk turned away from the top-down reform model. He now became 'solidly aligned with those social forces committed to grassroots globalism' and concluded that 'the positive prospect rests on further emergence of what is called "global civil society"'.[188] The new strategy of 'reform from below' had several elements. First, it involved the rejection of 'conventional party politics' or 'normal politics' as it had lost its potential to deliver on the promise of enhancing people centred security.[189] It was, however, conceded that governments too may contribute to the process of enhancing human welfare,[190] albeit the caveat followed that too much may be expected from state power leading to disappointments when it comes to enhancing human security.[191] Second, it placed reliance on new social movements concerned with promoting new politics related to democracy, human rights, feminism, ecology and peace.[192] Third, it rejected 'violent forms of revolutionary politics' as it was not likely to enhance the realization of world order values.[193] Fourth, there was grudging recognition that 'in general, nationalism (as a counter to colonial memories and interventionary policies) is a more positive ideology for social movements in the South – especially if it upholds the political, economic and cultural autonomy of a country – than it is in the North, where it is associated with imperial projection, the arms race, and war-making'.[194] Finally, Falk proposed 'an agenda for the 1990s' even as he recognized that 'it is pretentious, and even arrogant, for intellectuals to prescribe from the safety and isolation of their ivory tower'.[195] The agenda was 'five-dimensional': denuclearization, demilitarization, depolarization, sustainable development and democratization.[196]

---

[187] Falk, 'Contending Approaches', p. 148.
[188] Falk, *Explorations at the Edge of Time*, p. 2.
[189] See ibid., pp. 125–126.
[190] See ibid., p. 131.
[191] See ibid., p. 127.
[192] See ibid, pp. 125–126.
[193] See ibid.
[194] See ibid., p. 126
[195] See ibid., p. 133.
[196] See ibid., pp. 134–135.

The central and innovative feature of this strategy of transition was the reliance on 'global civil society' and new social movements for transformation politics. Yet nowhere did Falk seriously delve into the complexities of the idea and workings of 'global civil society' or deal with the organizational structure and dynamics of non-governmental organizations (NGOs) and social movements, or with their possible role in different political contexts.[197] He did not in particular pay adequate attention to the fact that the concept and role of 'civil society' is contested.[198] For instance, critics have argued that liberal notions of 'civil society' are not entirely applicable to non-Western societies.[199] Partha Chatterjee speaks of a 'political society' instead, a space outside 'civil society' that does not speak in the language of rights in the absence of legitimate legal claims.[200] In as much as 'civil society' plays a role it has been varyingly evaluated, as in the instance of India.[201] Likewise, there are a whole set of issues related to the concept, priorities and role of 'global civil society'. The achievements of an emerging 'global civil society' are of course well known in terms of initiatives to adopt international treaties, organize protests and hold sovereign states to certain ethical and legal standards vis-à-vis how they treat their citizens.[202] Global civil society organizations also provide information and analysis to less equipped developing countries in international forums. They have helped introduce transparency into international

---

[197] Falk 'defines' global civil society in general terms. He writes: 'Just as civil society is a construct without spatial dimensions, global civil society is a construct of the mind and imagination, a device for recording initiatives of transnational scope and global implication and for acknowledging normative aspirations to build the inevitable globalism of the future on democratic foundations, thereby resisting and regulating the globalism from above that arises out of the technocratic elitism of modernism.' See Falk, *Explorations at the Edge of Time*, p. 50.

[198] For an initial exploration see Helmut. K. Anheier, Marlies Glasius and Mary Kaldor, 'Introducing Global Civil Society' in Helmut. K. Anheier, Marlies Glasius, and Mary Kaldor (eds.) *Global Civil Society* (Oxford: Oxford University Press, 2001), pp. 3–22; Laura Pedraza-Farina, 'Conceptions of Civil Society in International Lawmaking and Implementation: A Theoretical Framework', 34 (2013) *Michigan Journal of International Law*, pp. 606–673.

[199] Partha Chatterjee, 'Introduction: The Wages of Freedom: Fifty Years of Indian Nation-State' in Partha Chatterjee (ed.), *Wages of Freedom: Fifty Years of Indian Nation-State* (New Delhi: Oxford University Press, 1998), pp. 1–20 at p. 10.

[200] Partha Chatterjee, *The Politics of the Governed: Reflections on Popular Politics in Most of the World* (Delhi: Permanent Black, 2004), pp. 40–41.

[201] See for instance Neera Chandhoke, ' "Seeing" the State in India', 40 (2005) *Economic and Political Weekly*, pp. 1033–1039.

[202] See generally Marlies Glasius, *The International Criminal Court: A Global Civil Society Achievement*. (London: Routledge, 2005).

negotiations and at least partially addressed the issue of democratic deficit of international institutions.[203] Through these measures 'global civil
society' initiatives have helped embed elements of 'deliberative democracy' in the international process of decision making. But there are
troubling questions as well. There are issues relating to 'representative-
ness and accountability' of civil society organizations and 'the norms that
are privileged by global civil society actors'.[204] In the latter context, Neera
Chandhoke points out that 'the idea that all groups across the world who
are struggling against the inequities of globalization, either have access
to global civil society or equal voice in this space, is both unrealistic and
misleading'.[205] In her view it is a 'chimera'.[206] The problem of representation raises its own set of concerns. According to Ernesto Laclau, 'no pure
relation of representation is obtainable because it is of the essence of the
process of representation that the representative has to contribute to the
identity of what is represented'.[207] In other words, the question is 'are citizens of countries of the South and their needs *represented* in global civil
society, or are citizens as well as their needs *constructed* by practices of
representation?'[208] Without undermining the substantial achievements of
'global civil society', Chandhoke expresses the hope that global civil society 'does not replicate the hegemony of the West in yet another sphere of
the world system'.[209] To take one instance, the work of powerful Western
international non-governmental organizations (INGOs) can facilitate,
propel, and legitimize unilateral armed humanitarian intervention into
third world nations. Finally, the internal structure of civil society organizations is a matter of concern.[210] In the absence of democratic internal

---

[203] See generally Marlies Glasius, 'Does the Involvement of Global Civil Society Make
International Decision-Making More Democratic? The Case of the International Criminal
Court' at www.orfaleacenter.ucsb.edu/sites/secure.lsit.ucsb.edu.gisp. d7_orfalea-2/files/
sitefiles/publications/Glasius_OBii.pdf (accessed 17 September 2015).

[204] Neera Chandhoke, 'How Global is Global Civil Society?' 11 (2005) *Journal of World-Systems
Research*, pp. 355–371 at p. 359. See also Kenneth Anderson, 'The Ottawa Convention
Banning Landmines, the Role of International Non-Governmental Organizations and the
Idea of International Civil Society', 11 (2000) *European Journal of International Law*, pp.
91–120.

[205] Chandhoke, 'How Global', p. 360.

[206] See ibid.

[207] Ernesto Laclau, *Emancipation(s)* (London: Verso. 1996), p. 85.

[208] Chandhoke, 'How Global', p. 362.

[209] See ibid., p. 370.

[210] History also suggests that what appears attractive on paper is not easy to implement in
practice. For example, Bakunin, that great champion of individualism, defied his own
beliefs when it came to organizational practice. To quote E. H. Carr, 'for the revolutionary
party, he desired "absolute effacement of individuals, of wills, in collective organisation and

structures, the priorities and activities of civil society organizations are capable of being manipulated by powerful actors.[211]

C. New Internationalism and Legitimacy Struggles (1999–2015)

In the past two decades there has been a shift in the vocabulary with which Falk speaks of the process of transition. However, both continuity and change mark the new strategy of transition. There is continuity in as much as Falk subscribes to the idea that there is no 'zero-sum rivalry' between reform from above and reform from below.[212] He has therefore continued to support the reform of UN as it would 'be wrong to regard the UN as either only a geopolitical instrument or as exclusively a bastion of law, justice, and peace. For better or worse it is both'.[213] What Falk finds problematic is the fact that the UN 'has not accommodated the rise of global civil society by giving non-state actors a more robust role within the Organization'.[214] Therefore, at times Falk speaks of 'the *impossibility* of UN reform' from within the Westphalian imaginary and system[215] undermining its legitimacy claims.[216] Falk contends that 'the commitment to UN reform by civil society actors is the worthwhile path, although the realization of its vision cannot even be imagined at this point'.[217] Such a possibility requires 'giving civil society actors serious modes of participation in the United Nations' but is yet to happen.[218]

But he has simultaneously suggested possible reform in UN including the need for independent financing of UN and the creation of new mechanisms such as a volunteer peace force, an economic security council and a global peoples' assembly.[219] Among these the last proposal has received much attention. Falk repeatedly notes that 'to date, the institutions of world order, including the UN, have given lip service to the relevance

action"; and in practice, though not in theory, he readily enough conferred on himself the dictatorship of the revolutionary party'. E. H. Carr, *Michael Bakunin* (New York: Vintage Books, 1961), p. 455.

[211] Even in lesser instances 'internal deliberation' has not always been encouraged as in the case of the coalition of NGOs intervening in the negotiations that led to the adoption of the Rome Statute. Glasius, *The International Criminal Court*, p. 13.

[212] Falk, *Humanitarian Interventions*, p. 191.

[213] Falk, *(Re)Imagining Humane*, p. 57.

[214] See ibid., p. 71.

[215] Falk, *Writings of Richard Falk*, p. 91.

[216] See ibid., p. 78.

[217] See ibid., p. 95.

[218] See ibid., p. 79.

[219] See ibid., pp. 161–165.

of global civil society, but have not been willing to alter the membership and participation rules and procedures to accommodate the spectacular quantitative and qualitative development of this CS [civil society] dimension of world order'.[220] Falk is of course against the idea of a world government as 'such a utopian project is dystopian, and should be rejected'.[221] But a top-down post-Westphalian conceptions of world order[222] is different from attempts to deepen global democracy through creating appropriate institutional structures. Therefore, since the late 1990s, in collaboration with Andrew Strauss, Falk has been suggesting the creation of a Global Peoples Assembly to democratize global governance.[223] For at least one way to address the democratic deficit in global governance system is the creation of a 'popularly elected global body'.[224] Falk and Strauss do not believe this to be a fanciful proposal, as in their view the creation of the European Parliament has helped rectify 'a regional democratic deficit'.[225] Even a simple advisory role for a Global Peoples Assembly would allow 'some democratic oversight of international organizations such as the IMF, the WTO, and the World Bank'.[226] Falk and Strauss also think that a citizen elected Global Parliamentary Assembly 'would offer disaffected citizens a constructive alternative to terrorism and other forms of political violence'.[227] Their thinking on the pragmatics of the creation of such an assembly has evolved from an 'early endorsement of a parliament or assembly created by civil society to ... an interstate treaty created parliament'.[228] Even there not all states in the world need to sign up from the beginning. The experiment can begin with twenty to thirty states with the expectation that there will be pressure on others to join later.[229] The global

---

[220] Falk, *Humanitarian Interventions*, p. 161.
[221] See ibid., p. 163. It is seen as being dystopian on several grounds: 'a tendency to freeze the existing structures of inequity and to create a rigid hierarchy of power, privilege, status; an ensured dynamic of resistance on the part of those sovereign entities and popular forces that fear the authoritarianism; and the likelihood that a globally central government structure would overcome opposition by relying on oppressive means, which would undoubtedly include high levels of surveillance and reliance on drones to patrol the world'. See ibid.
[222] See ibid.
[223] For a collection of these articles, see Richard Falk and Andrew Strauss, *A Global Parliament: Essays and Articles* (Berlin: Committee for a Democratic U.N., 2011).
[224] See ibid., p. 21.
[225] See ibid., p. 25.
[226] See ibid., p. 24.
[227] See ibid., p. 132.
[228] See ibid., p. 16.
[229] See ibid., p. 27.

parliament along with the UN General Assembly can 'eventually become part of a bicameral global legislative system'.[230]

But critics like Joseph Nye have suggested that it is an impractical proposal because of the absence of a 'strong sense of community' at the global level which alone can induce a minority to subject itself to a majority.[231] Falk and Strauss respond that not only does this argument assume 'a model of Athenian democracy' that prevails nowhere it also does not recognize that 'political communities are often formed by institutions rather than preceding them'.[232] They are also unconvinced by the Nye contention that what they are suggesting is a nightmare scenario whereby 'citizens of around 200 states would be willingly to be continually outvoted by more than a billion Chinese and a billion Indians'.[233] According to Falk and Strauss, the delegates from these nations are unlikely to adopt a unified position, as they will reflect diversity of interests that prevail within them.[234] But they recognize that formidable obstacles remain. For instance, civil society organizations may not wish to establish such a body that lay claim to 'the mantle of voice of the global citizenry' being a 'popularly elected body'.[235] Even more fundamental issues have been raised. Thus, for example, David Kennedy has expressed concern that 'the image of politics embedded in the proposal for a global parliament seems outmoded, even part of the problem'.[236] For it is based on the dubious assumption that 'our domestic political order is up to the challenges of contemporary life, and that its parliamentary form is reason why'.[237] According to Kennedy, such a view is problematic because 'the decisions which affect the distribution of things are not made in a parliament – they are made in the capillaries of economic and social life, by experts, officials, private actors, and public officials'.[238] Therefore, the answer perhaps lies in paying more attention to 'the work of professionals and experts working in the institutions that operate in the background of public and private life'.[239] What Kennedy

---

[230] See ibid., p. 160.
[231] See ibid., p. 164. See Joseph S. Nye, 'Globalization's Democratic Deficit: How to Make International Institutions More Accountable', 80 (2001) *Foreign Affairs*, pp. 2–6.
[232] Falk and Strauss, *Global Parliament*, p. 165.
[233] See ibid.
[234] See ibid.
[235] See ibid., p. 17; emphasis deleted.
[236] David Kennedy, 'Speech: Assessing the Proposal for a Global Parliament: A Skeptics View', XIII (2007) *Widener Law Review*, pp. 395–399 at p. 395.
[237] See ibid.
[238] See ibid., pp. 395–396.
[239] See ibid., p. 396.

is implicitly suggesting here is the need 'to multiply the sites' of resistance rather than 'condensing them in a center'.[240] The Kennedy critique is
insightful even as his alternative approach to bring about change is rooted
in a problematic methodological individualism that is examined in the
next chapter. In any case the two choices may not be viewed, despite the
different visions that inform them, in either/or mode but be conceived as
a pincer attack on the problem of democratic deficit in the global system.
But most certainly Falk and Strauss need to pay attention to those features
and complexities of global governance that might make their proposal
acceptable to social forces such as an emerging transnational capitalist
class (TCC) that may see in the Global Peoples Assembly an opportunity
to legislate for itself. Yet the proposal is not without its merits as it does
seek to empower ordinary citizens and progressive elements of 'global
civil society' vis-à-vis hegemonic global social forces and institutions. It
could also complement the idea of global administrative law (GAL) with
which Falk and Strauss surprisingly do not engage at all. The endeavour
of injecting the values of participation, transparency and accountability in
international bodies is with all its limitations an important effort at democratizing their functioning.[241]

In the new strategy of transition Falk has most crucially spoken of 'new
internationalism' and 'legitimacy struggles'. The 'new internationalism'
(another phrase for reform from below) has seen 'transnational social
forces promote the adoption of legal standards in coalition with like-
minded governments'.[242] These have inter alia given birth to the Convention
on the Prohibition of the Use, Stockpiling, Production and Transfer of
Anti-Personnel Mines and on their Destruction, 1997 (the Landmines
Treaty) and Rome Statute of the International Criminal Court, 1998. But
perhaps the more significant idea that Falk has advanced in recent times is
that of 'legitimacy struggles' to bring about historical change. The essence
of 'legitimacy struggle' is, according to Falk, 'its reliance on soft-power
initiatives that draw on the capacity of people to serve as the principal
agents of historical change'.[243] What 'legitimacy struggle' does is 'to shift

---

[240] See ibid., p. 397. For a critical discussion of the role of experts see Chapter 5, pp. 272–294.
[241] Among their numerous writings, see Benedict Kingsbury, Nico Krisch and Richard B.
Stewart, 'The Emergence of Global Administrative Law', 68 (2005) *Law and Contemporary
Problems*, pp. 15–63. For a critique see B. S. Chimni, 'Cooption and Resistance: Two faces
of Global Administrative Law', 37 (2005) *New York University Journal of Law and Politics*,
pp. 799–827.
[242] *Writings of Richard Falk*, p. 25.
[243] Falk, *Palestine*, p. 19.

the emphasis from *governments* and *governing elites* to *people* and *civil society* as the principal agents of historical change, and, at the same time, subordinate hard-power forms of resistance to soft-power tactics'.[244] It envisages 'taking control of the commanding heights international law and morality, as well as international human rights standards'.[245] As Falk emphasizes, 'it is when the people become centrally engaged in a struggle that the political potency of soft-power instrument is exhibited'.[246] In his view, 'legitimacy struggles' that rely on militant non-violent and spiritual politics can be an effective weapon against hegemonic states and social forces. Falk believes that 'the potentialities of constructing a world order on the basis of soft power principles is gaining support, shifting non-violent geopolitics from the domain of utopianism to an emerging status of plausible political project'.[247] Of course, the practice of non-violent politics requires visionary leaders like Mohandas Karamchand Gandhi and Martin Luther King who had 'a spiritual orientation toward the meaning of life'.[248] The move to non-violent politics is based on the important lesson 'that political violence is not the answer. It brings neither security nor liberation'.[249] He could not be more right.

Falk is optimistic that history is on the side of those who may be weak but speak the language of justice. As he perceptively observes, 'most of the outcomes of the political struggles of the last seventy-five years have been won by the side with inferior military capabilities'.[250] He goes on to note that 'this generalization includes the outcomes of the anticolonial struggles of the 1960s and 1970s, the indigenous resistance against the huge high-tech American military intervention in Vietnam, the 1980s movements challenging Soviet rule in Eastern Europe, and the global campaign against apartheid in South Africa'.[251] In recent times this has included 'the election of an African-American as president of the United States, and the Arab Spring'.[252] This history is testimony to the fact that when weak people struggle to bring about historical change using soft power and the weapon of non-violence they are mostly successful. This is what Gandhi had demonstrated in the Indian freedom movement. The non-violent

---

[244] See ibid., p. 206; emphasis in original.
[245] See ibid., p. 19.
[246] See ibid., p. 207.
[247] Falk, *(Re)Imagining Humane*, p. 37.
[248] Falk, *Palestine*, p. 225.
[249] See ibid., p. 184.
[250] See ibid., p. 20.
[251] See ibid.
[252] See ibid., p. 45.

struggle of the weak will also more readily receive the support of a 'global solidarity movement' dedicated to peace and justice.[253]

V.   The Transition Process and International Law

It has been natural for Falk to consider the place and role of international law in the process of transition to a just world order. The 'intermediate view', formulated largely before the WOMP phase, was developed in that direction. There was an effort to consider the role of international law in terms of the needs of a rapidly evolving international system that faced widespread threats ranging from nuclear war to a deteriorating environment. As early as 1967, Falk wrote about the need for 'new approaches to the study of international law'[254] (a generic title used later by David Kennedy to describe the work of a new generation of critical scholars). Falk examined therein three broad trends and five different approaches in the United States to the role of international law. The trends were the rejection of positivism in order to bring the study of international law into closer association with social sciences,[255] a move away from commitment to national interest to allegiance to a common law of mankind;[256] and the search for ways to take into account the role of non-state actors.[257] The five new approaches to international law that he considered were policy science, functionalism, quantitative empiricism, systems theory and the phenomenological perspective.[258] He found that each of these approaches had something to offer as against legal positivism that contrived a distinction between the 'is' and 'ought' of international law.[259] He was, therefore, willing to draw on their insights in order to move away from the rationalization role of the international lawyer to a more 'scientific' and constructive role in realizing certain world order values.

In 1974, around the time that he was writing *Future Worlds* with its focus on the central guidance system, Falk delivered the Sherrill lectures at Yale University, in which he recommended 'a new paradigm for

[253] See ibid., p. 231.
[254] Falk, *Status of Law*, pp. 447–469. Originally published as Richard A. Falk, 'New Approaches to the Study of International Law', 21 (1967) *American Journal of International Law*, pp. 477–495.
[255] See ibid., p. 449.
[256] See ibid., p. 454.
[257] See ibid., p. 455.
[258] See ibid., p. 459.
[259] See ibid., p. 459.

international legal studies'.[260] He asked a series of questions to clarify the role of an international lawyer in the period of transition:

> What can we learn from [...] prior transition process, which culminated in the birth of the state system? What roles were played by international law and lawyers? To what extent is this historical experience transferable to the present transition context? How can international law and international lawyers help ensure the emergence of a new post-state system of world order that is relatively more peaceful and just? To what extent does the participation of international lawyers reflect specific national, ideological, cultural, socioeconomic concerns? Is it possible to formulate a position on the means and ends of transition that could serve as the basis for a transnational or global consensus? Could such a global consensus provide for the normative grounding for a political movement dedicated to global reform?[261]

Recalling the contribution of Grotius to the articulation of the Westphalian paradigm in a period of transition, Falk imaginatively invoked the image of 'timeless-ness of the Grotian quest for openings to the future through shadow land exploration'.[262] According to Falk, the Grotian quest was of significance 'because it is normatively grounded and future oriented, synthesises old and new, and cherishes continuities while welcoming discontinuities'.[263] It was his lament that international law scholars remained unmindful of both the need for system change and for new approaches that advanced the process of transition in a progressive direction.[264] On his part he noted five elements that could together constitute a new paradigm of international legal studies:

> (a) a framework of inquiry that is global, explicitly normative, futurist, and systematic; (b) an orientation towards inquiry that is shaped by an appreciation of the transitional character of the international system; (c) a recognition that the outcome of transition will be the emergence of a system of non-territorial central guidance; (d) an understanding that the actual shape of the emergent non-territorial central guidance system will be conditioned by the interplay of statist, business, and populist social forces; and (e) a consensus that the most beneficial of the central guidance options will reflect the priority of populist claims for peace, economic equity, social and political dignity, and ecological balance.[265]

---

[260] Richard A. Falk, 'A New Paradigm for International Legal Studies: Prospects and Proposals', 84 (1975) *The Yale Law Journal*, pp. 969–1021.
[261] See ibid., pp. 972–973.
[262] Richard Falk, 'The Grotian Quest' in Falk et al. (eds.) *International Law*, pp. 36–42 at p. 39.
[263] See ibid., p. 41.
[264] Falk, 'New Paradigm', p. 1071
[265] See ibid.

In the 1980s, Falk pursued the Grotian quest by supporting all initiatives which promoted international cooperation that were based on global
sentiments that created organizational capabilities to uphold the common
good. The United Nations Convention on Law of the Sea, 1982 was one
such initiative.[266]

A.   Reimagining the World Court

But he also advanced imaginative proposals flowing from the need for
reorienting existing international legal institutions towards world order
goals. Thus, for instance, in an essay written in 1984 Falk called for 'a
value-oriented and educative jurisprudence' through greater use of the
World Court's advisory opinion capability.[267]. According to Falk:

> the most important aspect of a new jurisprudence for the Court would
> entail a commitment to an educative mission in which the primary audi-
> ence of the Court, in addition to the parties to a dispute, would become a
> non-professional constituency of concerned *planetary* citizens.[268]

It would involve evolving progressive jurisprudence of global orientation to embrace an agenda 'associated with a visionary world order for
all peoples and stages of development'.[269] The new 'judicial culture' would
require the Court to willingly deal 'with the equities of the past and present, especially as these are evident in North-South relations' and also
concern itself with longer-term issues of world order, including 'questions
touching on war and peace, mass poverty, oppression of various types
and ecological decay'.[270] What Falk was suggesting is that the primary role
of ICJ should be to educate and guide state elites and civil society movements, an agenda subversive of its traditional function that primarily
entails resolving disputes between sovereign states.

Two decades later, reflecting on the ICJ advisory opinion rendered in the
Wall case, Falk reiterated that 'reliance on a narrow reading of the "advisory" language no longer serves the best interests of international society,
if it ever did, and that the term should at least be construed in the future to
conform more with the authoritativeness of the Court's pronouncements

---

[266] Falk et al., *International Law*, pp. 522–523.
[267] Richard A. Falk, 'The Role of the International Court of Justice', 37 (1984) *Journal of
International Affairs*, pp. 253–268 at p. 267.
[268] See ibid., pp. 265–266; emphasis in original.
[269] See ibid; emphasis in original.
[270] See ibid., p. 267.

on international law'.[271] Falk argued that 'the ICJ has made its more recent important contributions to the development of international law in the exercise of its advisory jurisdiction, dispensing legal guidance on issues of fundamental importance to the peoples and governments of the world (including on matters of decolonization, self-determination, the status of nuclear weapons, and the duty to pursue nuclear disarmament negotiations)'.[272] He also felt that 'the advisory route is the only way... to bring nonstate actors into the formal workings of the World Court'.[273]

Falk has, however, not provided altogether convincing reasons for enhancing the advisory function of ICJ. When Falk had first advanced the proposal, Leo Gross had aptly asked as to 'why replace the Court, with all its accomplishments and shortcomings, with an academy?'[274] This is certainly not an argument against a forward looking and progressive court but against it primarily wearing the 'educative' mantle, for in doing so it would discount the seriousness of its principal function, that is, to provide a forum for settling disputes which do not require it to pronounce on the present and future course of world history.[275] In fact, the legal system can effectively contribute to world order goals, including advancing views on critical issues before humankind, only if it is seen as doing what it is meant to do and not if it is collapsed into other forms of communication. In this instance, Falk's proposal appears to run against the 'intermediate view' that called for maintaining the autonomy of law, stressing the 'is' as against the 'ought', and thereby lending stability to the international system.

In any case, there is no guarantee that in providing advisory opinions the ICJ can rise above the political realities of the time. Thus, for instance, the advisory opinion of the Court in the *Nuclear Weapons* case stopped short of delegitimizing nuclear weapons because the nuclear weapon powers were averse to such an outcome. In the event the Court by a majority decided that 'in view of the current state of international law, and of the

---

[271] Richard A. Falk, 'The ICJ Ruling on Israel's Security Wall', 99 (2005) *The American Journal of International Law*, pp. 42–52 at p. 46. For the text of the opinion, see 'Legal Consequences of the Construction of a Wall in the Occupied Palestinian Territory', Advisory Opinion I.C.J, 9 July 2004, available at www.icj-cij.org/docket/files/131/1671 .pdf (accessed 6 September 2015).

[272] See ibid., p. 49.

[273] See ibid.

[274] Leo Gross, 'Review of Reviving the World Court', 82 (1988) *American Journal of International Law*, pp. 166–175 at p. 175.

[275] And as Gross has rightly pointed out, it does even perform an educative function at present. See ibid.

elements of fact at its disposal, the Court cannot conclude definitively whether the threat or use of nuclear weapons would be lawful or unlawful in an extreme circumstance of self-defence, in which the very survival of a State would be at stake'.[276] To put it differently, in rendering its opinion the Court was not guided by desired world order goals but by a positivist understanding of international law and more significantly a view of the limits of its role in system transformation. The majority did not follow the exhortation of Judge Christopher Weeramantry in his dissenting opinion to overcome the 'Western jurisprudential bias against nonpositivist styles of analysis' or the politics of the day.[277]

What Falk does not recognize is that the role of international courts is system maintenance and not system transformation. While individual judges may give separate or dissenting opinions that underline the need for system transformation it would be mistaken to think that the ICJ can play the role of a radical agency that will offer the necessary ideological and legal guidance in bringing about historical change. To be sure, social forces and states seeking system transformation in favour of the weak, and to address the ecological crisis, must seek to use all available legal institutions to advance that cause. From this perspective Falk is right to stress that the 'civil society should make maximum use of international law and global legal institutions to wage a legitimacy war against the possession and normalization of legal weaponry'.[278] This is what the civil society had done by getting Marshall Island to file a case against UK and other nations in the ICJ.[279] In short, the ICJ can certainly play a part in the 'legitimacy struggle' that Falk has recently come to emphasize. But there has to be a realism that informs that effort. After all in the context of nuclear weapons Falk himself lamented that it is unfortunate that 'even the unanimous view of the International Court of Justice that the nuclear weapon states had a legal obligation under Article VI of the NPT to pursue nuclear disarmament in good faith had no effect whatsoever on the policy process'.[280]

---

[276] Legality of the Threat or Use of Nuclear Weapons, Advisory Opinion, *I.C.J. Reports* 1996, pp. 226–267 at p. 266 available at www.icj-cij.org/docket/files/95/7495.pdf (accessed 6 July 2015).

[277] Richard Falk and David Krieger, *The Path to Zero: Dialogues on Nuclear Dangers* (Boulder, CO: Paradigm Publishers, 2012), p. 139.

[278] See ibid., p. 134.

[279] For the majority judgment of the Court declining jurisdiction, see for instance, *Obligations Concerning Negotiations Relating to the Cessation of the Nuclear Arms Race and to Nuclear Disarmament (Marshall Islands vs. U.K.): Preliminary Objections,* available at www.icj-cij .org/docket/files/160/19198.pdf (accessed 6 November 2016).

[280] Falk and Krieger, *Path to Zero,* p. 122.

It is not as if Falk imagines that the Court can play a principal role in system transformation. But by giving the impression that judges of the ICJ, or the ICJ as an institution, can contribute to the effort, he portrays an establishment body, essentially committed to the status quo, as an agent of historical change. At best institutions like ICJ can, keeping in view the stability of the existing system, protect the interests of the weak from predatory states. Even there, given the consent-based nature of its jurisdiction, it will rarely have the opportunity to play a role in a 'legitimacy struggle' as it did in the *Nicaragua* case. The ICJ may even contribute to conflict in the international system. For example, in the recent advisory opinion on *Unilateral Declaration of Independence by Kosovo* case the Court failed to understand the implications of its own opinion and thereby possibly contributed to future conflicts rather than peace. While the ICJ clarified in this case that it was not concerned with 'remedial secession' it provided implicit legitimacy to the idea by recognizing that the unilateral 'declaration of independence' by the Provisional Institutions of Self-Government of Kosovo 'did not violate international law'.[281] In his address to the Russian parliament in 2015, President Vladimir Putin mentioned the case to justify the annexation of Crimea.[282]

B.   Role of Global Civil Society

In keeping with his emphasis on the role of 'global civil society' in bringing about system transformation Falk has also stressed the need for

---

[281] Accordance with International Law of the Unilateral Declaration of Independence in Respect of Kosovo, Advisory Opinion, *I.C.J. Reports 2010*, pp. 403–453 at p. 453. www.icj-cij.org/docket/files/141/15987.pdf (accessed 27 May 2015).

[282] President Vladimir Putin noted in his address that:

> the Crimean authorities referred to the well-known Kosovo precedent – a precedent our western colleagues created with their own hands in a very similar situation, when they agreed that the unilateral separation of Kosovo from Serbia, exactly what Crimea is doing now, was legitimate and did not require any permission from the country's central authorities. Pursuant to Article 2, Chapter 1 of the United Nations Charter, the UN International Court agreed with this approach and made the following comment in its ruling of July 22, 2010, and I quote: 'No general prohibition may be inferred from the practice of the Security Council with regard to declarations of independence,' and 'General international law contains no prohibition on declarations of independence.' Crystal clear, as they say.
>
> 'Address by President of the Russian Federation' on
> 18 March 2014 at http://en.kremlin.ru/events/
> president/news/20603 (accessed 27 May 2015).

grassroots or non-governmental efforts at framing 'legal' documents and/ or making 'legal' pronouncements. An early example of such an effort was the 1976 Algiers Declaration on the Rights of Peoples.[283] In recent decades, as already noted, 'global civil society' initiatives have led to the adoption of the Land Mine Treaty and the Rome Statute.[284] Mention may also be made of the work of MSF which led to the adoption of the 2001 Doha Declaration on TRIPS and Right to Health. It may also be recalled that the global civil society has played a key role in getting the UN General Assembly to seek an advisory opinion from the ICJ on the question of legality of nuclear weapons.[285] In the latter regard Falk and associates have advanced other proposals such as 'a new international treaty, a nuclear weapons convention for the phased, verifiable, irreversible, and transparent elimination of nuclear weapons'.[286] Falk has alongside also called for 'a focused campaign to advocate a No First Use Policy as a sign of political life in the antinuclear global civil society movement'.[287]

A second way in which the 'global civil society' can be expected 'to increase the ethical and political relevance of international law' is 'by illuminating the geopolitical manipulation of law and by forming its own parallel institutions that focus on the criminality of the strong and the victimization of the weak'.[288] According to Falk, 'until international law has the capacity to treat equals equally, the corrective checks of progressive civil society are a vital ingredient of a jurisprudence of conscience despite their lack of governmental legitimacy'.[289] He thus highlights the role of global civil society tribunals such as the Bertrand Russell International Criminal Tribunal on the American role in the Vietnam War (1966–1967), the Istanbul World Tribunal on Iraq (2005), the Russell Tribunal on Palestine (2011), and Kuala Lumpur War Crimes Tribunal (2011) on

---

[283] The text of the Algiers Declaration is available at www.algerie-tpp. org/tpp/en/ declaration_algiers.htm (accessed on 16 September 2015). It is also available in Falk, *Towards a Just World Order*, pp. 432–434.

[284] See generally, Barbara K. Woodward, *Global Civil Society in International Law Making and Global Governance: Theory and Practice* (Leiden: Brill, 2010).

[285] See Richard Falk, 'The Nuclear Weapons Advisory Opinion and the New Jurisprudence of Global Civil Society', 7 (1997) *Transnational Law & Contemporary Problems*, pp. 333–352; Richard Falk, 'Nuclear Weapons, International Law and the World Court: A Historic Encounter', 91 (1997) *The American Journal of International Law*, pp. 64–75. See generally, Steve Charnowitz, 'Nongovernmental Organizations and International Law', 100 (2006) *American Journal of International Law*, pp. 348–372.

[286] Falk and Krieger, *Path to Zero*, pp. xv–xvi.

[287] See ibid., p. 198.

[288] Falk, *Humanitarian Interventions*, p. 46.

[289] See ibid.

Iraq.[290] Global civil society can also play a role in strengthening internal rule of law.[291]

In short, there is no doubt that global civil society activism can promote global democracy and justice through the progressive development and enforcement of international law.[292] But, as noted before, there is a troubling side to the work of 'global civil society' which is not free of weaknesses. For instance, the West-dominated 'global civil society' has been silent on prosecuting Western leaders responsible for war crimes and crimes against humanity. Even Falk concedes that 'the NGO community has, by and large, been opportunistic, supporting efforts to hold officials accountable for their implementation, seeming to reason that a glass half full is preferable to an empty glass'.[293] If that is so, efforts have to be undertaken to make 'global civil society' organizations accountable, an accountability that should go beyond 'mutual intertwining' and convenient conferring of legitimacy between international organizations and NGOs.[294]

C.   *International Law and Legitimacy Struggles*

In recent years Falk has assigned a critical role to the language of international law as part of the strategy of 'legitimacy struggles'. Since international law serves 'as a universal language for the communication of claims and grievances'[295] weaker states can effectively use it to protect their interests.[296] Falk is therefore critical of 'new approach' of Martti Koskenniemi, for 'the apology/utopia dualism is too simplistic in a number of respects, including overlooking the significance of law as relevant for gaining control over the often crucial high moral ground in a conflict situation, in all manner of "new wars", especially in those conflicts highlighting the role of social movements and non-state actors'.[297] Falk argues

---

[290] See ibid., pp. 45–46.
[291] Maria Dakolias, 'Legal and Judicial Development: The Role of Civil Society in the Reform Process', 24 (2000) *Fordham International Law Journal*, pp. S26–S55.
[292] Falk, *Humanitarian Interventions*, p. 81.
[293] See ibid., p. 38.
[294] See generally Kenneth Anderson, ' "Accountability" as "Legitimacy": Global Governance, Global Civil Society and the United Nations', 36 (2011) *Brooklyn Journal of International Law*, pp. 841–890.
[295] Falk, *(Re)Imagining Humane*, p. 53. See also Richard Falk, *Law in an Emerging Global Village: A Post-Westphalian Perspective* (Ardsley, NY: Transnational, 1998).
[296] See Falk, *(Re)Imagining Humane*, p. 53.
[297] See ibid., p. 54. Falk is more sympathetic to the Koskenniemi idea of 'culture of formalism'. See ibid., p. 64 fn.6.

that international law 'supplies markers of the impermissible' and can be deployed by those struggling for global justice.[298] In fact, violent resistance is increasingly being replaced by soft power instruments such as the force of law.[299]

The greater accent on the role of international law in Falk's recent writings can inter alia be traced to the current shift in Palestinian strategy to 'legitimacy struggle' that involves 'taking control of the commanding heights of international law and morality'.[300] While Falk is realistic enough to recognize that 'legitimacy struggle' is a complicated and complex process he believes that it helps in 'influencing the climate of global public opinion relevant to diplomacy and perceptions of relative justice of the two sides' positions'.[301] He is of the view that the egregious violation of international law by a state delegitimizes it in the eyes of the international community. This explains why while defying international law Israel 'still cashes in its most expensive diplomatic chips to avoid censure whenever possible'.[302] According to Falk, Israel also recognizes that being seen to flagrantly violate international law can deny it easy access to its language:

> when Israel subjects the whole of Gaza to a punitive blockade ... imprisons thousands of Palestinians in conditions below international legal standards, and refuses to implement the World Court's near-unanimous advisory opinion on the unlawfulness of its annexation wall, it has lost all credibility to rely on international law on those few occasions when it works to Israel's disadvantage.[303]

Therefore, Falk exhorts weaker sides, in this case the Palestinian people, who have international law on their side, to use it to good effect:

> *It seems clear* that international law supports Palestinian claims on major issues in contention: borders, refugees, Jerusalem, settlements, resources water, land, statehood, and human rights. Then why not insist on resolving the conflict by reference to international law with such modifications as seem mutually beneficial?[304]

---

[298] See ibid., p. 63.
[299] See ibid.
[300] Falk, *Palestine*, p. 19.
[301] See ibid., p. 140.
[302] See ibid., p. 148.
[303] See ibid., p. 156.
[304] See ibid., p. 186; emphasis added. On the factual situation in relation to Palestinians and Israelis Falk writes that 'truth and accuracy are my litmus tests of objectivity, and as such, they knowingly defy that sinister god who encourages the substitution of balance for truth'. See ibid., p. 167.

The significance that Falk attaches to reliance on the language of international law by oppressed and exploited groups and peoples today has, however, not compelled Falk to revisit his theory of interpretation or issues related to semantic and structural sources of indeterminacy. More so in the light of the fact that in recent years the founding figures of New Approaches viz., David Kennedy and Martti Koskenniemi lay so much emphasis on the structural indeterminacy of rules on grounds similar to that of policy-oriented approach. They follow the New Haven approach in stressing the unavoidability of choice. Falk could have pursued this course as well. But he has rightly chosen not to stress in recent times the indeterminacy of rules. Instead, he has suggested that rules possess a core meaning that can legitimize the cause of the weak.

Falk's sustained engagement with the struggle of the Palestinian peoples has made Falk realize more than ever before the dual essence of the role of international law in the contemporary world. His understanding that international law is part of the problem and solution is shared by third world scholars and states. Like many TWAIL scholars Falk speaks of 'a creative tension of international law as an instrument for Orientalist domination and exploitation of the non-Western peoples of the world, on the one hand, and international law as a fragile, yet indispensable, humanist enclave embedded in realist and imperialist geopolitical behaviour, which has provided the normative foundations for resistance against and emancipation from contemporary forms of imperialism, on the other'.[305] Falk knows that international law cannot entirely restrain hegemonic states from pursuing their 'national interests'. In fact, from the beginning he was struck by how powerful actors violated their professed ideals on the international stage.[306] In the late 1960s, as the Vietnam war progressed, he wrote that 'a special irony attaches to the efforts by the United States to champion the rule of law in world affairs at this time; it requires only a little objectivity to perceive that the United States has become the most flagrant violator of legal rules and procedures governing the use of violence'.[307] He writes today with similar anguish about Israel's violation of international law. But yet he has never been dismissive of the role of international law. Falk recognizes that it has a protective function

[305] Falk, *Writings of Richard Falk*, p. 54. On the TWAIL view, see for instance B. S. Chimni, 'International Law Scholarship in Post Colonial India: Coping with Dualism', 23 (2010) *Leiden Journal of International Law*, pp. 23–51.
[306] He wrote that 'the United States government is doing one set of things and saying another'. See Falk, *Status of Law*, p. 595.
[307] See ibid.

that takes the shape of providing legitimacy to the causes and struggles of the weak. He also emphasizes the positive role of international law in pursuing goals such as observance of human rights, removal of poverty and achieving ecological justice. In his view 'international law is a project of global civil society, as well as an instrument useful to state actors that project their power beyond their borders'.[308]

A key issue, however, is whether a strategy of transition that relies on 'global civil society' and the constructive role of international law and international institutions such as the UN and ICJ help realize the goal of system transformation. Any realistic assessment would suggest otherwise. The real struggles for change take place at the local and national levels through the organized struggles of old and new social movements, including those led by left parties, and supported on the international plane by a coalition of weak states. The demand of these movements and coalitions today is the retrieval of national sovereign economic space ceded to international institutions. To put it differently, the answer to system transformation in the era of neo-liberal globalization paradoxically lies in strengthening the nation state and not in the erosion of sovereignty.[309]

VI.   The Third World and International Law

It may be useful at this point to review the views of Falk on the subject of third world and international law as it helps highlight once again the strengths and weaknesses of the WOMP approach to international law. It also provides the occasion to see how his views on the subject have evolved over the years. But what can be said without hesitation is that Falk has nearly always, temporary aberrations like on the use of force by NATO against Afghanistan apart, advocated the cause of the developing world. Indeed, it was his principal grievance with the New Haven approach that it did not.[310] However, it is argued subsequently that given his diagnosis of the problems that afflict the global order his writings on the third world have suffered from certain weaknesses. These include: the problem of political determinism that flows from attributing primary significance to the 'logic of territory'; a critique of hegemonic politics and law not rooted in a

[308] See ibid., p. 57.
[309] B. S. Chimni, 'Anti Imperialism: Then and Now' in Vasuki Nesiah, Michael Fakhri and Luis Eslava (eds.) *Bandung and Beyond* (Cambridge: Cambridge University Press, forthcoming).
[310] See supra, p. 179.

deeper understanding of the relationship between capitalism and imperialism; the absence of serious engagement with the history of international law, especially the evolution, development and implications of colonial international law; and the neglect of non-Western scholarship, especially in the early years.

A.   Early Years

Falk was among the few US international law scholars to address the concerns of 'new states' in the immediate years after decolonization. In fact he chose to give his 1965 Hague Lectures, delivered at the age of thirty-five, on the theme *The New States and International Legal Order*.[311] This move may be contrasted with critical scholars who came afterwards (such as David Kennedy and Martti Koskenniemi) who in their early years never engaged with the problems of the third world.[312] Falk not only considered the condition of third world peoples but did so in a spirit of solidarity. He was of the view that the viability and legitimacy of international law depended on how far it met the interests of the poorer states.[313] Falk was also critical of writers of the time who saw the participation of 'new states' as a setback to the integrity of the international legal order.[314] Falk perceptively noted that while 'new states' advanced an ideological critique of colonial international law it was accompanied by an interest-based assessment of present possibilities.[315] He went on to occupy the middle ground between F. S. C. Northrop who argued that there was a distinctive cultural approach and Wolfgang Friedmann who contended that the third world nations worked with a purely interest-based approach to international law. Falk was of the view that while 'new states' were responding to international law essentially in terms of how it was serving their interests it was 'premature to deny influence to factors associated with cultural background'.[316]

---

[311]   Richard A. Falk, 'The New States and International Legal Order', II (1966) *Recueil Des Cours* (Leyden: A. W. Sijthoff, 1968), pp. 1–102.

[312]   See in this respect Chapter 5, pp. 257–258, 321–322.

[313]   Falk, *New States*, p. 35. He concurred here with the views of B. V. A. Roling expressed in *International Law in an Expanded World* (Amsterdam: Djambatan, 1960). Falk observed that 'the international legal order to remain viable must accommodate the interests of the new states'. Falk, *New States*, p. 31.

[314]   Falk, *New States*, pp. 32–33.

[315]   See ibid., p. 17.

[316]   See ibid., p. 40.

However, despite his empathetic view of the standpoint of 'new states', Falk did not sufficiently appreciate the deep impact of colonialism on their prospects. In fact he pointed out that 'colonial rule is blamed, *perhaps unfairly in many cases*, for retarding the rate of economic development'.[317] In his work of the 1960s there is no mention of dependency theory (Samir Amin, Andre Gunder Frank and the rest) or the world systems theory of Immanuel Wallerstein. His focus was even at this stage on the dysfunctional nature of the states system, that is, as against the 'logic of capital'. The fact that Falk did not take into account the meaning and implications of imperialism in the postcolonial era meant that while he did recognize the factor and consequences of inequality between states he did not have a theoretical explanation for it beyond the 'logic of territory'. It can then only be surmised that Falk accepted the realist explanation for 'the power of a nation vis-à-vis other nations' viz., geography, natural resources, military preparedness, national character, national morale, quality of government and so on.[318]

Falk also charged 'new states' of 'adopt(ing) a double standard on issues of force and non-intervention'.[319] He was critical of the fact that 'the commitment to end colonialism and to eliminate racial discrimination' had taken 'precedence for the new states over their allegiance to the Charter prohibitions concerned with the regulation of force in world affairs'.[320] Therefore, for instance, despite showing a degree of understanding of India's act of liberating Goa in 1961 he did not find persuasive the formulation that the violation of the UN Charter was acceptable if it clashed with the goal of decolonization. He found problematic the willingness of new states to 'pick and choose among rules of international law'.[321] His rap for 'new states' was however accompanied by the forthright critique of 'the official American position ... to allow ... international law to be used by the colonial powers to resist the pressures for decolonization'.[322]

In examining the 'new states' approach to international law in these early years, Falk neglected the available writings of third world scholars like R. P. Anand, S. P. Sinha or J. G. Syatauw, and even the path-breaking essays

---

[317] See ibid., pp. 20–21; emphasis added.
[318] Hans Morgenthau, *Politics among Nations: The Struggle for Power and Peace* (New York: Alfred A. Knopf, 1967), pp. 106–144.
[319] Falk, *New States*, p. 51.
[320] See ibid.
[321] See ibid., pp. 54, 55.
[322] See ibid., p. 56.

of C. H. Alexandrowicz published in the *British Yearbook of International Law* and *Indian Yearbook of World Affairs*, contesting the Western telling of the history of international law.[323] In the voluminous *The Status of Law in International Society*, a leading scholar like R. P. Anand, also a student of McDougal, is mentioned in a footnote and C. H. Alexandrowicz not at all. It was still a phase of international law scholarship when Western scholars did not pay attention to the writings of third world scholars or explore the meaning of the new narrative of the history of international law. Postcolonial theory had yet to emerge and underline the theoretical need to listen to voices from the Global South.[324]

B.   Later Years

But in recent years Falk has become much more sensitive to the need for third world scholars to represent their understanding of international law and the standpoint of third world peoples and nations. In an essay on the theme of 'Orientalism and international law' he acknowledges that 'while insisting on a progressive undertaking, I still cannot pretend to adopt a subaltern voice but rely on others for an enactment of subalternity'.[325]

---

[323] But he correctly noted the paradox that Afro-Asian diplomats 'reveal an exaggerated deference to traditional and conservative interpretations of the requirements of international law'. See ibid., p. 24.

[324] It is at least one reason he failed to appreciate the realism of R. P. Anand when he opined that the role of UN General Assembly resolutions as an instrument for legal change was a limited one. Falk was critical of R. P. Anand who wrote that 'although these resolutions are not formally binding and no more than "recommendations", their effects on the course of international law must not be underestimated'. Cited in ibid., p. 42. Falk responded: 'Mr. Anand's conclusion, however correct in its deference to traditional thinking, is a misleading way to affirm the dynamic quality of international legal order. It is essential to confirm that under conditions of requisite formality and consensus these resolutions set forth authoritative claims to control behaviour and constitute, at the very least, "legislative facts" by which the appropriate decision-makers in national and international arenas can infer a new calculus of legal duty expressive of the will of the international community'. See ibid., pp. 42–43. The reason for these observations was perhaps that Falk wished to place UN General Assembly resolutions on a firmer legal basis. But, as history testifies, Anand reflected greater realism than Falk in his assessment of the legal status of General Assembly resolutions. Be that as it may, as time went on, especially as the Vietnam War unfolded, Falk became more and more inclined towards the views of third world scholars and states.

[325] Falk, *Writings of Richard Falk*, p. 58. He has elsewhere noted examples of early third world thinking such as Judge Radhabinod Pals' dissent as an Indian member of Tokyo War Crimes Tribunal that have been ignored. Falk writes that 'Pal's dissent is an exemplary instance of anticolonial jurisprudence, and not only does the Western academic literature

This shift in understanding is in particular reflected in his writings on the struggle of Palestinian peoples where he pointedly notes that it is:

> important to understand, especially for non-Palestinians, that it is the Palestinians who should retain control over the discourse on their struggle, vision, and strategy. It is up to the rest of us, those who side with the Palestinians in the struggle to uphold their rights, that we not encroach on this political space and appreciate that our role is secondary: to aid and abet, to accept a responsibility to act *in solidarity*.[326]

In the context of the discourse of international law, he observes that 'any proper investigation of the Orientalist traditions embedded in international law would include ... a close reading of the work of non-Western jurists, both critical and apologetic'.[327] However, while Falk is more alert today to how international law has been shaped by Orientalism it has not compelled him to delve into the profound and complex ways in which it did so in the past and has strong resonance in the present. In fact, the history of international law has never seriously engaged the attention of Falk. There are almost no reflections in his prodigious writings on the recent turn to history in international law to which TWAIL scholarship has made an important contribution.[328] Yet it is not difficult to agree with his general conclusion 'that despite the pervasive Orientalism of the main traditions of international law scholarship and doctrine, it is from international law that we derive the most geopolitically relevant framing of humanist resistance to the criminalization of world politics over the course of recent decades'.[329] This is precisely the dualist strategy that third world scholars subscribed to from the very beginning of the postcolonial era.[330]

But since Falk does not assign sufficient significance to the 'logic of capital' he still does not see the phenomenon of imperialism as a crucial explanation for the inequality of states in modern international relations. It is true that in recent years Falk does speak at times of 'the strong tendency of capitalism to operate in particular cruel ways ... reinforcing structures of inequity, misappropriation of resources, and neglect

---

ignore it, but it is not published in a text that is readily available in most libraries'. Falk and Krieger, *Path to Zero*, p. 140.

[326] Falk, *Palestine*, p. 206. See also pp. 131–133.

[327] Falk, *Writings of Richard Falk*, p. 58.

[328] See for instance Antony Anghie, *Imperialism, Sovereignty and International Law* (Cambridge: Cambridge University Press, 2003).

[329] See ibid., p. 54.

[330] See B. S. Chimni, 'International Law Scholarship', pp. 23–51.

of those most impoverished'.[331] He also writes that 'the current phase of capitalism is especially polarizing with respect to both class relations and center/periphery patterns'.[332] Falk even goes on to use the metaphor 'global apartheid' to describe the racist structure of geopolitics.[333] But flowing from the neglect of history of colonial international law and the internal relationship between capitalism and imperialism he still does not attach fundamental importance to the 'logic of capital'.

C.   On Sovereignty and Equality of States

However, while his explanation for the inequality of states in the international system can be faulted, he has to his credit constantly drawn attention to its manifestation in a number of areas of international relations. These are worth noting to highlight his progressive politics. First, Falk is a critic of neo-liberal globalization or what he terms predatory globalization that continues to sustain a North-South divide.

Second, he has aptly pointed out that the nuclear non-proliferation regime is an 'oligarchy among nuclear weapon states' that are unwilling to comply with the disarmament provisions of Article VI of the Nuclear Non-Proliferation Treaty.[334] He rightly observes that 'the overall preoccupation with the nonproliferation regime misleadingly implies that the principal danger arises from the countries that do *not* possess nuclear weapons rather than from those that do'.[335] It distracts attention from the need for nuclear-weapon states 'to engage in serious disarmament negotiations' rather than simply seek 'the efficient and safe management of existing nuclear arsenals'.[336] Falk laments that states have paid little heed to the 'carefully reasoned assessment' of the ICJ in the *Nuclear Weapons* case that states must enter into nuclear disarmament negotiations under NPT.[337] Instead, 'international law is appropriated to make effective a legal regime that reflects an approach to nuclear weapons that rejects the fundamental legal principle of treating equals equally'.[338]

---

[331] Falk, *On Humane Governance*, p. 47. It may be noted that this volume is an outcome of a 'collaborative effort' and saw his role more as a 'rapporteur'. See ibid., p. xv.
[332] See ibid., p. 48.
[333] See ibid., pp. 50–52. More recently he has noted that 'in the early twenty-first century confidence in capitalism has further retreated, especially in the aftermath of a global recession that started in 2008...'. Falk, *(Re)Imagining Humane*, p. 21.
[334] Falk, *Humanitarian Intervention*, p. 158.
[335] Falk, *(Re)Imagining Humane*, p. 10. Emphasis in original.
[336] See ibid., p. 11.
[337] See ibid., p. 73.
[338] See ibid., p. 74.

Third, Falk writes against 'one-sided warfare' waged by Western countries against third world countries.[339] He has been critical in this respect of the United States wars against Vietnam and Iraq, and the NATO intervention in Kosovo.[340] In his considered view, Israel's approach to occupied Palestine is the most glaring example of 'one-sided warfare'.[341]. He concludes that 'the historical record demonstrates that one-sided warfare has been consistently and frequently waged for centuries, especially against the "darker" peoples of the Third World, as well as against indigenous peoples everywhere'.[342]

Fourth, Falk notes that 'the implementation of international criminal law is undertaken only against individuals on the losing side who are indeed responsible for substantive wrongdoing, while exempting individuals on the winning side'.[343] He notes in this respect the cases of Slobodan Milosevic, Saddam Hussein and Muammar Qaddafi.[344] In contrast, the US government has never even expressed remorse for the use of nuclear weapons on Hiroshima and Nagasaki.[345] Indeed, there is the irony that 'Hiroshima was bombed on August 6, 1945, the Nuremberg Charter was signed on August 8, 1945, and Nagasaki was bombed on August 9, 1945'.[346] In other words, 'Allied war crimes took place immediately before and after the Allies agreed to hold Axis leaders accountable for their crimes'.[347] In recent years 'crimes against peace have basically been marginalized as an international crime'.[348] The attempts to claim universal jurisdiction by regarding states 'as agents of the international legal order' has had to be more or less abandoned by European states under Washington's pressure.[349] Falk therefore calls for a 'jurisprudence of conscience' in implementing international criminal law.[350]

Fifth, Falk has explored 'the tension between rights and power' in the discourse and practice of human rights.[351] He has forthrightly noted that

[339] Falk, *Writings of Richard Falk*, pp. 227–242.
[340] See ibid., p. 229.
[341] See ibid.
[342] See ibid., p. 238.
[343] Falk, *Humanitarian Interventions*, p. 36.
[344] See ibid., p. 42.
[345] See ibid., p. 37.
[346] Falk and Krieger, *Path to Zero*, p. 125.
[347] See ibid.
[348] See ibid., p. 40.
[349] See ibid., pp. 44–45.
[350] Falk, *Humanitarian Interventions*, pp. 35–47.
[351] Falk, *Writings of Richard Falk*, p. 351.

'rights of power prevail over the power of rights almost always when strategic interests of major state actors are stake'.[352] The Palestinian question is perhaps the most conspicuous example of the exercise of the 'rights of power':

> If the underlying conflict between Israel and Palestine were to be assigned to an independent third-party mechanism to assess the claims of the two sides from the perspective of law and morality, there is little doubt that the outcome would favor the Palestinians on every key disputed issue: that is, ending the occupation by requiring an immediate Israeli withdrawal from Palestinian territory; by resolving territorial claims and reestablishing borders that existed before the 1967 War; by determining the legal status of Israeli settlements in accordance with the Fourth Geneva Convention; by carrying out the mandate of the World Court in its Advisory Opinion relating to the legality of Israel's security force constructed on occupied Palestinian territory; by restoring the demographics and boundaries of Jerusalem, and by invalidating the assignment of sovereign rights over the city to Israel; by upholding the legal entitlements of Palestinian refugees claiming a right of return; and by determining the use rights of access to ground water aquifers located beneath Palestinian territory.[353]

But Falk believes that this fact does not diminish the 'power of rights'. It encourages an engagement that seeks justice for the exploited, oppressed and marginalized peoples.

Finally, Falk notes the tendency of the North in relation to the ecological crisis 'to shift as much of the burden of blame and adjustment in relation to environmental policy as possible to the South'.[354] It is most recently manifested in the Climate Change Accord of December 2015.

In view of inequities between states that have been sustained over time Falk has on occasions been receptive to the third world position on state sovereignty. In his book *On Humane Governance* (1995), perhaps because it was an 'outcome of collaborative effort', Falk takes a more nuanced approach to 'sovereignty', statism and states system.[355] He observes that 'sovereignty and statehood remain a normative horizon for most peoples of the word, especially for those victimized'.[356] He also notes 'the *defensive* roles of sovereignty'[357] and that 'all is context and interpretation'.[358]

---

[352] See ibid.
[353] See ibid., p. 355.
[354] Falk, *On Humane Governance*, p. 74.
[355] See ibid., p. xv.
[356] See ibid., p. 80.
[357] See ibid., p. 81; emphasis in original.
[358] See ibid., p. 85.

He, therefore, stresses the need 'to distinguish among various invocations of sovereignty as positive, anachronistic, and regressive'.[359] According to Falk, there is 'no way to escape the ambiguity of sovereignty as concept and organizing principle in this period of transition. It represents both an expression of self-determination and human rights and an instrument of geopolitics'.[360] Falk reiterates that 'abandoning sovereignty prior to overcoming the regressive sides of geopolitics would remove, especially in certain settings, one of the few means of protection available to weak and vulnerable states'.[361] He, therefore, understands why the Palestinian peoples, for example, would want their own state.[362] Falk writes that the intent is not to either 'demonize or romanticize the idea of sovereignty or the role of the state', but to call for revaluation in the light of 'changing global and human circumstances'.[363] This includes the danger of 'the emergence of some new oppressive political order that might be historically described as "global fascism", a political fix without historical precedent'.[364] This is possible as the United States today 'is a global state in addition to being a territorial entity due to its force projection on a global scale (its network of hundreds of foreign bases; navies in every ocean; military dominance of space; CIA penetration and surveillance; special forces operations in foreign countries; globalization of capital and finance)'.[365]

Yet his constant refrain in other writings remains that the Westphalian system cannot prevent 'the consequences of nuclear winter, of global warming and ozone depletion, of rainforest destruction, of air and ocean pollution'.[366] On these occasions Falk does not historicize the problem of sovereignty. The sovereignty as anachronism thesis has its roots in thinking in terms of binaries and fixed essences. In the real world opposites come to be linked as a part of a dynamic process of internal development,

---

[359] See ibid., p. 90.
[360] See ibid., pp. 91–92.
[361] See ibid., p. 92.
[362] See ibid., p. 90.
[363] See ibid., p. 100.
[364] See ibid., p. 24.
[365] Falk, *Humanitarian Interventions*, p. 160. He stresses the fact 'it seems more useful to abandon the notion of "state" and signal the conceptual rupture by considering it be the first instance of a "global state"'. Falk, *(Re)Imagining Humane*, p. 13. He also notes that 'the advocates of the new imperialism emphasize its benevolent potentialities, with reference to the spread of constitutional democracy and human rights, and the geopolitical availability of peacekeeping capabilities that could act far more effectively than what could be achieved by reliance on the United Nations'. See ibid., p. 23.
[366] Falk, *Explorations at the Edge of Time*, p. 199.

in this case universalizing global capitalism. In other words, a proper appreciation of the dual role of the principle of sovereignty calls for dialectical thinking.[367] The problem with formal logic is that it does not deal seriously with the concept of time. It 'is predominantly concerned with the scaffolding of a *static* world. Propositions we are usually told are either true or false, but both true *and* false. All this is true enough, granting that the world does not change. Where it does their truth-value can vary with time.'[368] Historical change involves motion and development of which contradiction is the motivating force. The opposites in this case – sovereignty and globalization – cannot be transcended without transforming the nature and character of contemporary global capitalism. The tensions between sovereignty and globalization are manifested in all spheres of international life expressing the innermost contradiction of our age: a global system of production and a national system of governance and accountability. To put it differently, the principle of sovereignty can be seen as helping overcome or transcending its own essence. Once it helps establish a firm linkage between globalization and justice it would have rendered the principle redundant.

Such a view would also enable a better understanding of a range of global events and development. Take the case of self-determination of Palestinian peoples. In the period 2008–2014 Falk was the Special Rapporteur on Occupied Palestine for the UN Human Rights Council.[369] Before and in this period Falk showed great moral and legal clarity and indomitable courage that is necessary for anyone criticizing Israel. He has supported the Palestinian cause 'in the face of a determined campaign of defamation and dirty tricks, which unfortunately comes with the territory'.[370] He has not hesitated to speak truth to power. In fact Falk has forthrightly observed that 'truth and imbalance are my litmus tests of objectivity, and as such, they knowingly defy that sinister god who encourages the substitution of balance for truth'.[371] The question however is what explains the United States' sustained support for Israel? Why is it that 'despite Israel's relative affluence, American taxpayers foot the bill for

---

[367] As Frederick Jameson puts it, 'if at every moment in which we represent something to ourselves in a unified way, we try to undo that and see the contradictions and multiplicities behind that particular experience, then we are thinking dialectically'. Michael Hardt and Kethi Weeks (eds.), *The Jameson Reader* (Oxford: Blackwell, 2000), p. 160.

[368] Georg Henrik Von Wright, *Philosophical Logic* (Oxford: Basil Blackwell, 1983), p. 92.

[369] Falk, *Palestine*, p. 17.

[370] See ibid., p. 17. For details see pp. 187–191.

[371] See ibid., p. 167.

more than three billion dollars per year, more than is given to the whole of Africa and Latin America'?[372] Is the tragedy of the Palestinian peoples simply an outcome of the workings of the states system? Or was the holocaust and tragedy of the Jewish peoples an outcome of the states system alone? It is here that Falk's analysis is left wanting in terms of diagnosis of the extant world order. To be sure, there is no singular reason that can explain historical situations and events. The forces of global capitalism and imperialism are not the only explanations. It would be crass determinism to so suggest. But is it enough to say by way of analysis that it is due to 'the entanglement of geopolitics' and 'the moral, legal and political inadequacy of the contemporary world order' that prevents such an outcome?[373] The question is what undergirds the contemporary world order to produce the colonization of Palestinian peoples? Falk's diagnosis of the contemporary world order fails to provide a persuasive answer.

VII.   Conclusion

It is time to assess the contribution of Falk to international law and world order studies, as well as the bridge he has endeavoured to build between them. It can be said without hesitation that Falk has made pioneering and significant contributions to both. But his work is also characterized by certain conceptual and theoretical gaps. By way of conclusion it is worth schematically listing his achievements and the weaknesses that characterize his work.

The intermediate approach to international law that Falk advances as an alternative to legal formalism and policy-oriented reductionism represents an important step forward in developing a realistic jurisprudence that while accepting the inextricable link between law and policy does not erase the distinction between the two. The strength of the intermediate approach is that it does not sacrifice the stabilizing and progressive role of rules in the international legal system. Falk's current stress on the role international law plays in 'legitimacy struggles' succinctly captures the possibilities that the language of international law holds in resisting structures of domination. The view that international law is not merely a vehicle for domination but also that of resistance helps avoid an overly pessimistic view of the role of law in international affairs. Falk aptly stresses the need to reform and recast it for realizing a peaceful and just

[372] See ibid., p. 135.
[373] See ibid., p. 29.

world order. The weakness of the intermediate approach to international law is that it does not offer a systematic theory of international law. First, while the intermediate view does conceptualize the relationship between the sociological substratum and international law through the notion of 'quasi-dependence', it essentially confines the former to the 'logic of territory'. It thereby disregards the primary role of the 'logic of capital'. As a consequence Falk has never come to appreciate the internal and historical links between imperialism and international law. Second, the fact that the ills of current world order are traced to statism and the states system means that the categories 'class' 'race' and 'gender' are neglected in analysing the nature and character of international law.[374] The use of these categories offers rich insights into the workings and differential impact of international law on different groups and nations. Third, the intermediate approach does not methodically address the question of indeterminacy of rules in order to sustain the idea of relative autonomy of law in the international system. Falk's support for a 'functionally specific conceptions of interpretation' with a focus on the subject and locus of decision making is not convincing, as it is not grounded in matching theories of language and communication. Fourth, while Falk has consistently addressed the concerns of developing countries, and in recent years written sensitively on the theme of 'Orientalism and international law', the intermediate approach only weakly imbibes third world scholarship.

Insofar as world order studies are concerned Falk was greatly influenced by the far-reaching ambitions and method of the New Haven approach. He therefore realized early on that the realm of law, dominated as it was by formalism and positivism, was not the site from which the struggle for transformational changes in world order could be imagined, mapped or launched. It prompted Falk to make world order studies, with its wider canvas and scope, his intellectual home. He has in the past decades offered penetrating analysis of a whole range of world order issues including the implications of the states system, the problems associated with neo-liberal globalization, the causes and impact of the ecological crisis and the role of global civil society is realizing a just world order. Few can disagree with his specification of values that should inform a just world order viz., minimization of collective violence, maximization

---

[374] As Engels observed of Bakunin, the latter did not 'regard capital i.e., the class antagonism between capitalists and wage workers which has arisen through social development, but the *state* as the main evil to be abolished'. Frederick Engels, 'Letter to Theodor Cuno' in Karl Marx and Friedrich Engels, *The Individual and Society* (Moscow: Progress Publishers, 1984), p. 262.

of economic well-being, maximization of social and political justice and maximization of ecological quality. In realizing it, his reflections on the contemporary relevance of philosophical anarchism are invaluable at a time when the state is coming to have an overwhelming presence in the lives of ordinary citizens, especially in the developing world. But his writings on world order are marked by certain conceptual and theoretical gaps. First, even as Falk speaks of predatory role of industrialized states in international economic relations, he does not consider the critical or foundational role of the 'logic of capital' in shaping modern world order, that is, as against the 'logic of territory'. Second, despite his emphasis on the 'logic of territory', Falk expends little effort at clarifying the theory of 'state' he works with beyond an odd essay on anarchism. Therefore, the occasional recognition of the different faces of statism (for example, the value of the principle of sovereignty for weak states) is not theoretically integrated into his understanding of the states system. Third, his diagnosis of the ecological crisis is wanting in as much he lays the blame at the door of industrial civilization in general, leaving unexplored the extent to which it is an outcome of the working of global capitalism. Fourth, in speaking of agents of change Falk does not explore the meaning and role of 'civil society' or 'global civil society' in any depth, especially in the context of the non-Western world. Finally, while his analysis of international institutions is insightful and balanced, it is again weakly theorized. He, therefore, makes no attempt to identify for instance the social forces that influence the working and operations of contemporary international institutions, in particular international economic institutions. These theoretical gaps result in a deficient diagnosis of the ills of world order and in turn impacts the strategy of transition proposed.

In the beginning, Falk's legal orientation resulted in a top-down model of reform with emphasis on a 'central guidance system' that involved the restructuring of the UN system. In subsequent decades this vision has been replaced by stress on reform from below, emphasising the role of an emerging global civil society in bringing about change. But to his credit even in this phase he does not neglect the role of UN in bringing about reform in the international system. He aptly recognizes that it has played a key role in standard setting, in educating world public opinion through organizing global conferences on threats or problems confronting humankind, in mitigating conflict through peacekeeping efforts and providing urgent humanitarian assistance to those in need. His proposal for democratizing and enhancing the role of UN through the creation of global people's assembly or global parliament is novel and welcome. The combination of reforms from above and below, along with the recognition of the significance of international law in 'legitimacy struggles', has lent a greater degree of realism to his strategy of transition. However, in the final analysis systemic change can only come about through restructuring global capitalism by the combined resistance of all democratic and left social forces at the local and national levels, supported on the global plane by a coalition of progressive states, international institutions, and 'global civil society' organizations. The 'global civil society' or international institutions such as UN can only complement these efforts. It is hoped that Falk's intense engagement with the struggles of the Palestinian peoples will make him rethink questions of agenda and agents of social transformation.

Falk hints as such a possibility in speaking about the need to revive WOMP to explore anew the horizons of desire and its realization in the twenty-first century.[375] The revived WOMP 2 would need to address with greater care the complex theoretical issues involved in the diagnosis of global problematique as well as the strategy of transition to a just world order, including the role of international law in it. It would above all have to, as Falk admits, 'incorporate non-Western perspectives into the very sinews of the undertaking'.[376] Besides, WOMP 2 can also make a fresh effort in theorizing questions of international law and the contribution it can make in bringing about reforms in the international system. It can provide in this regard an effective counterpoint to the liberal IR-IL initiatives of Anne-Marie Slaughter and others.[377] It is the great strength of Falk that he has always shown a willingness to engage with and learn from his critics. It is, therefore, hoped that Falk will undertake the creation of WOMP 2.

Any assessment of Falk's work would be incomplete without mentioning his courage to speak truth to power. His most illuminating writings are those where he is analysing particular situations of oppression and injustice. From Vietnam War to the rights of the Palestinian peoples he offers acute analysis of the issues at hand. The invisible college of international lawyers needs to learn from Falk and be committed to ethical and ecological imperatives for a just world order to be realized. In fact it can draw much inspiration from the words and deeds of this extraordinary scholar.

---

[375] Falk, *(Re)Imagining Humane*, p. 183ff. He has also wondered if WOMP 2 should 'put more stress on what is attainable, or should it accept its role as cartographer of the highly unlikely, yet desirable and necessary, in the domain of "future worlds"'? See ibid., p. 186.

[376] See ibid., p. 191.

[377] See in this regard Chapter 2, pp. 93–101.

New Approaches to International Law:
The Critical Scholarship of David Kennedy and
Martti Koskenniemi

I. Introduction

David Kennedy and Martti Koskenniemi are without doubt two of the most gifted international law scholars on the contemporary scene. They are the 'founding fathers' of New Approaches to International Law (NAIL)[1] which is articulated by 'a group of legal academics' wishing to 'experiment with new methods and ideas'.[2] The creation of NAIL owes much to the imagination and energy of Kennedy but Koskenniemi has been a crucial partner in the project.[3] The initial intellectual impulse for

[1] Anne Orford, 'The Destiny of International Law', 17 (2004) *Leiden Journal of International Law*, pp. 441, 474. For a NAIL bibliography, see Thomas Skouteris, 'New Approaches to International Law', Oxford Bibliographies at www.oxfordbibliographies.com/obo/page/international-law (accessed 5 February 2015); David Kennedy and Christopher Tennant, 'New Approaches to International Law: A Bibliography', 35 (1994) *Harvard International Law Journal*, p. 417.

[2] David Kennedy, 'When Renewal Repeats: Thinking Against the Box', 32 (2000) *New York Journal of International Law and Politics*, pp. 335, 489.

[3] For an alternative account of the origin of NAIL, see Akbar Rasulov, 'New Approaches to International Law: Images of a Genealogy' in Jose Maria Beneyto and David Kennedy (eds.), *New Approaches to International Law: The European and the American Experiences* (The Hague: T. M. C. Asser Press, 2013), pp. 151–191 at p. 160. Rasulov writes:

> the first formative experiences that prepared the stage for NAIL's emergence almost certainly took place on the opposite side of the Atlantic and the basic ideological framing they evolved in quite unmistakably derived from a completely different intellectual context than the US CLS. A good decade before anyone even began using the NAIL label, three of its four founding figures – Philip Allott, Martti Koskenniemi and Anthony Carty – had already started their first explorations in critical international legal theory. All three of them proceeded in their endeavours by drawing on a decidedly European tradition of critical-theoretic inquiry. All three, furthermore, lived and worked in Europe and openly identified themselves as cultural Europeans. None of them, in the final analysis, had managed to find the magic solution that would bring NAIL into existence, and so it was only when the fourth founding figure, David Kennedy, brought all their different breakthroughs together – while adding

NAIL came from Critical Legal Studies (CLS) which was influential at the time Kennedy entered law school.[4] Critical Legal Studies scholars had 'developed a range of doctrinal, historical, and theoretical accounts' that revealed 'the general limitations of liberalism in law'.[5] It is as part of the CLS community that Kennedy honed his skills that he was to later bring to bear on the world of international law.[6] While critical legal studies left a deep impact on his work, its experience and fate also taught him that 'if criticism cannot be expressed in ... the field's known spectrums of disagreement, it often just cannot be heard'.[7] Since his project was never 'to discover a better answer to the field's enduring questions', such as whether international law was law at all, Kennedy knew that he would come to be 'placed outside the field'.[8] This understanding was reinforced in the early phase by 'lots of rejections from all the major law journals' which had less to do with the quality of his work and more with the alien nature of his project viz., the deconstruction of the internal structure of international law[9]. In a short introduction that Kennedy has written to the work of the radical feminist legal scholar Catherine MacKinnon he notes how her two most influential writings were published not in leading law journals but in *Signs* – a journal on 'women, culture and society' as 'the voice and style

also a tremendous amount of his own original work – that the pieces finally started to fall into place.

But even Rasulov admits that 'it would be pointless to deny that in both of its practical hypostases the "idea" of NAIL took off for the first time at Harvard and that all throughout their early years both the NAIL movement and the NAIL tradition remained closely affiliated with the US branch of the CLS enterprise'. See ibid.

[4] Kennedy, 'When Renewal Repeats', p. 481. Duncan Kennedy, a mentor, had just published his seminal piece 'Form and Substance in Private Law Adjudication', 88 (1976) *Harvard Law Review*, p. 1685. The first CLS conference was held in 1977. There is vast literature on CLS. For one bibliography on the subject see Duncan Kennedy and Karl Klare, 'A Bibliography of Critical Legal Studies', 94 (1984) *Yale Law Journal*, pp. 461–490. See generally Roberto Mangabeira Unger, 'The Critical Legal Studies Movement', 96 (1983) *Harvard Law Review*, p. 561; Mark Kelman, *A Guide to Critical Legal Studies* (Cambridge, MA: Harvard University Press, 1977); and Roberto Unger, *The Critical Legal Studies Movement* (Cambridge, MA: Harvard University Press, 1986).
[5] David Kennedy and William W. Fisher III (eds.), *The Canon of American Legal Thought* (Princeton, NJ: Princeton University Press, 2006), p. 832.
[6] Kennedy, 'When Renewal Repeats', p. 489. However, in later years as the CLS movement 'accumulated a lot of baggage' he carved out his own path. Kennedy notes that 'for many young scholars and students, "critical legal studies" seemed at once passé, dangerous, too politicized, too much associated with a "line" of some sort'. See ibid.
[7] See ibid., p. 459.
[8] See ibid., p. 460.
[9] See ibid., p. 483.

of these articles precluded their publication in law journals at the time'.[10] He then goes on to observe that yet 'MacKinnon's articles changed not only what one could write about but how one could write legal scholarship'.[11] The same was in a sense true of his writings as most of his important articles were initially published not in 'leading' law journals. Even his influential book *International Legal Structures* (ILS) was brought out by a German publisher unknown in the English-speaking world.[12] It is interesting that his fellow traveller Koskenniemi's seminal work *From Apology to Utopia* (FATU) was also at first brought out by a Finnish publisher rather than by an established publishing house in the field of international law.[13] What was for Kennedy a necessity in the beginning soon became a style. It is notable that even today Kennedy has not published in premier mainstream journals of international law like the *American Journal of International Law* or *European Journal of International Law*.[14] It would appear that Kennedy believed that he could publish in lesser-known law journals and yet be a leading light of the discipline on the strength of his argument. His more recent books have, however, been published by prestigious university presses reflecting a changed view of the culture and politics of publication. It is also symbolic of a semblance of acceptance of his work by a segment of mainstream scholars who view his current cogitations on the fluidity of international law as in accord with their own intuitions. Yet by and large he still remains an outsider in the discipline.

The early rejections seemed to have also taught Kennedy the lesson that innovators in the discipline had to actively recruit adherents and build an audience if their work had to become influential.[15] Only if a critical mass of scholars came to be associated with any new scholarship could it acquire credence necessary to challenge mainstream scholarship. He therefore set about creating a NAIL community using the resources and prestige of Harvard Law School (HLS), a fact that he does not conceal. He writes that 'the whole experience would have been quite different had I not been fortunate early on in my career' i.e., of being a tenured faculty

---

[10] Kennedy and Fisher III, *Canon of American Legal Thought*, pp. 831, 839.

[11] See ibid.

[12] David Kennedy, *International Legal Structures* (Baden-Baden: Nomos Verlagsgesellschaft, 1987).

[13] Martti Koskenniemi, *From Apology to Utopia* (Helsinki: Lakimiesleton Kustannus, 1989).

[14] For a Harvard law professor that is unusual. Or perhaps because he is a Harvard professor, and the prestige and influence that come from being one, he can afford to neglect standard ways of signalling the stature of a scholar.

[15] See Kennedy, 'When Renewal Repeats', pp. 466ff, 495.

at HLS.[16] He succeeded in what he set out to do through organizing conferences and workshops that helped create a NAIL community that appreciated 'new thinking' and eventually helped establish a relative 'balance of
power' with mainstream thinking.[17] Kennedy also thereby demonstrated
to the mainstream that he could conjure a parallel world of international
law scholarship in which insiders were outsiders. He was, however, realistic enough to appreciate that in this endeavour he required at least the
quiet support of a few established figures. This is the role that some senior
scholars like Louis Sohn and Thomas Franck appeared to have played in
the NAIL movement.[18]

There was from the beginning the realization that in order to create a
strong critical community, the NAIL project had to be 'diffuse'.[19] It had
to accept serious differences within the group. Kennedy therefore projected NAIL as 'an eclectic project, a project of difficult alliances and
unfinished dialogs'.[20] However, over the years, groups that were initially
sought to be subsumed under NAIL, such as for instance TWAIL II,
began to mark out and reclaim their separate identity. The NAIL movement formally 'ended' in the spring of 1997 with a conference named 'Fin
de NAIL: A Celebration'.[21] In a sense it had to cease as its institutionalization would have made it seem like other critical approaches (such as
CLS) that keep going till they fade away; being different was in some ways
a defining element of NAIL. What is more, for Kennedy 'new thinking'
was principally a 'performance'. He writes that 'whenever I think of the
NAIL, I think of it as a performance artwork'.[22] Its ending was also part
of this theatre. NAIL was viewed as 'a lived experience' that had to end
like life does with death.[23] The 'Fin De NAIL' celebration was also meant
to demonstrate that 'illumination cannot become a possession' and that
Kennedy was willing to 'decenter his own sovereign position'.[24] While

---

[16] See ibid., p. 484.
[17] See ibid., p. 467ff.
[18] See ibid., p. 483. 'Of course, people in the established field have been terribly important, as
    friends, as mentors, offering encouragement, training, criticism.' See ibid., p. 467.
[19] See ibid., pp. 491ff.
[20] See ibid., p. 497. Kennedy writes that 'The NAIL was not a movement of ideas or the work-
    ing out of a general disciplinary problem, but a specific effort by a group of legal academics
    in particular institutions to encourage one another's work, hold conferences, write more
    and differently, get to know people they would not otherwise have met, experiment with
    new methods and ideas.' See ibid., p. 489.
[21] See ibid., p. 490.
[22] See ibid., pp. 497–498.
[23] See ibid., p. 499.
[24] Orford, 'Destiny of International Law', p. 475

there may have been more mundane reasons that may have prompted the announcement of its 'death' – such as the need to continuously mobilize resources to stage NAIL– it left an impression.

But there is life after death for NAIL. However, those who currently do 'new approaches' apparently share more common ground. Kennedy has identified the key features of NAIL today.[25] First, of course, in common with other critical approaches NAIL scholars recognize 'the depth of the injustice' in the world today 'and the urgency of change'.[26] Second, among NAIL scholars there is 'an impulse to step back from contemporary common sense about the nature of global order and the available paths for reform, as well as a recognition that despite decades of careful study, we still lack a good picture of how we are, in fact, governed at the global level'.[27] Third, NAIL scholars believe that 'the most well-intentioned efforts to strengthen global governance and reinforce international law may, in fact, be as much a part of the problem as of the solution'.[28] In fact, much of Kennedy's work in recent times (e.g., on human rights and humanitarian laws) goes to demonstrate this thesis and partially explains the reluctance of NAIL to 'have a persuasive program of action'.[29] But arguably this view has been somewhat revised in the past few years. The current Kennedy take is that there can be no just global governance 'until the political economy of the world has been rebuilt'.[30] That is to say 'the relationship between the institutional frameworks for economic life and the channels for politics will need to be remade, a project demanding institutional innovation and experimentation'.[31] The possibility of reform is thus not ruled out, but the proposals for reform turn on working out the 'mysteries of global governance'. It can, however, be said that as a result of coming to terms with the critique of NAIL scholarship, recent years have seen a hint of change in its oeuvre. Kennedy's recent book *A World of Struggle* (2016) captures some subtle changes in his thinking. Meanwhile, since the beginning of the new century, especially since the publication of the *Gentle Civilizer of Nations* (GCN), Koskenniemi's work has also

[25] David Kennedy, 'Preface' in Jose Maria Beneyto and David Kennedy (eds.), *New Approaches to International Law: The European and the American Experiences* (The Hague: T. M. C. Asser Press, 2013), pp. v–xv. For another version, see Rasulov, 'New Approaches', pp. 164ff.
[26] See ibid., p. ix; emphasis added.
[27] See ibid., p. vii.
[28] See ibid.
[29] See ibid.
[30] See ibid., p. x.
[31] See ibid.

reflected new thinking. He has articulated a neo-formalist approach (termed 'culture of formalism') now expressed in the 'field's known spectrums of disagreement'. Both have also turned to doing political economy in recent years, with Koskenniemi concerned more with its historical aspects and Kennedy with its contemporary shaping of international law. In a sense, both Kennedy and Koskenniemi have returned to doing more mainstream critical scholarship.

The aim of this chapter is *not* to offer a comprehensive survey of the work of Kennedy and Koskenniemi but merely to review some key themes in their scholarship. The chapter follows the following scheme. Section II attempts to identify the principal features that united the work of Kennedy and Koskenniemi in the initial years. In this period Koskenniemi was very much the student and to his credit has always acknowledged his intellectual debt to Kennedy. Some of these elements continue to inform their work even as each has modified them and moved ahead in different ways.

Section III offers a critical assessment of select aspects of the Kennedy scholarship from an IMAIL perspective. It will be seen that much of Kennedy's work is written in the deconstructive mode with the aim of identifying internal contradictions in international legal discourse that go to reveal a divided self. The section considers in turn his internal critique of the structure of international law, of histories of the discipline of international law and institutions, and the role of experts and expertise, and thereafter sequentially his views on law and political economy, the complex role of law in war, the problem with the human rights movement and governance humanitarianism. Thereafter, after schematically listing out some of his seminal contributions, an attempt is made to briefly compare and contrast his approach with some mainstream and critical approaches to international law. It is worth reiterating here that the chapter does not discuss his contributions in many areas of international law such as international comparative law. It is left to someone attempting a full-length study of Kennedy's work to offer a more detailed survey and assessment of the same.

Section IV discusses Koskenniemi's key writings especially his basic theses on international law, his work on the history of international law, and his concept of 'culture of formalism'. The theme of indeterminacy of international law with which his name is closely associated is only cursorily dealt with it as it has been explored in the chapters on the New Haven approach to international law and IMAIL.[32] Where his views on

---

[32] See Chapter 3, pp. 123–140 and Chapter 7, pp. 524–534.

international relations and international law scholarship are concerned these have been considered in the chapter on classical realism.[33] The section concludes with a comparative assessment of his work vis-à-vis other critical approaches to international law.

II. Beginnings: Commonalities

Before looking separately at the scholarship of Kennedy and Koskenniemi it is useful to identify the features that initially united their work, and in an important measure continue to do so, explaining why the two are often spoken of together.[34] The common method and vision that informed their early writings is confirmed by Kennedy and Koskenniemi. Thus, for instance, in his reflections on reissued FATU, Kennedy writes that both ILS (1987) and FATU (1989) 'pursued similar themes' with FATU 'developing an analytic framework parallel to my own'.[35] The reason for this convergence was that they 'shared the feeling that the intellectual tradition sustaining the field of international law had come to an end – the field was, in some sense, over'.[36] Therefore, both wished 'to rewrite the entire history and all the doctrines of international law in a new way, in a single unified intellectual framework'.[37] In order to do so both were 'reading and borrowing from all the then fashionable currents of European social theory'.[38] In fact, both have pioneered the import of postmodern and post-Marxist social theories into the field of international law.[39] The result was that their 'basic arguments were quite similar'.[40] It may help the reader to schematically list out the common ideas and themes that informed the early work of Kennedy and Koskenniemi. Insofar as these features go, it is worth reiterating that Kennedy is very much the master and Koskenniemi the pupil, albeit the sameness was expressed in their work in different sensibilities imbibed in dissimilar legal cultures.

---

[33] See Chapter 2, pp. 93–101.

[34] About their association Kennedy writes that 'In the early 1980s, I met Martti Koskenniemi at a conference in Geneva – he was the first international lawyer I met who seemed interested in the project I was trying to pursue.' Kennedy, 'When Renewal Repeats', p. 482.

[35] David Kennedy, 'The Last Treatise: Project and Person (Reflections on Martti Koskenniemi's *Apology to Utopia*)', 7 (2006) *German Law Journal*, pp. 982–983 at p. 982. FATU was reissued in 2005 by Cambridge University Press with a new Epilogue.

[36] See ibid., p. 983.

[37] See ibid., p. 984.

[38] See ibid.

[39] See ibid.

[40] See ibid., p. 985

First, both Kennedy and Koskenniemi turned their attention to the internal structure of international law. Kennedy sought to deconstruct 'public international law from the *inside*',[41] in order to demonstrate the contradictions in the conceptual and doctrinal framework of international law.[42] In a similar vein, Koskenniemi proceeded to show that 'law's indeterminacy was a property *internal to the law itself*, not introduced to it by "politics" from the outside'.[43] As a consequence, 'the legal argument inexorably, and quite predictably, allowed the defense of whatever position while simultaneously being constrained by a rigorously formal language'.[44]

Second, both Kennedy and Koskenniemi argued that international law had no particular relationship with external reality. Kennedy wrote that 'rather than a stable domain which *relates* in some complicated way *to* society or political economy or class structure, law is simply the practice and argument about the relationship between something posited as law and something posited as society'.[45] Koskenniemi followed suit,[46] albeit his view is best captured in a later observation stating that 'different legal language-games do not possess greater or smaller distance from something that could be called an independent "reality". The methods create their own "realities" '.[47]

Third, both viewed international law as a process of argumentation informed by a distinctive style.[48] Koskenniemi described, 'the choice

---

[41] David Kennedy, 'A New Stream of International Law Scholarship', 7 (1988) *Wisconsin International Law Journal*, pp. 1–49 at p. 11; emphasis in original.

[42] In so suggesting Kennedy followed in the footsteps of his mentor Duncan Kennedy as also Roberto Unger. Duncan Kennedy noted that 'we need to understand far more than we now do about the content and internal structure of legal thought before we can hope to link it in any convincing way to other aspects of social, political or economic life'. Duncan Kennedy, 'The Structure of Blackstone's Commentaries', 28 (1979) *Buffalo Law Review*, pp. 209–382 at p. 221. David Kennedy was to repeat this verbatim later. See infra pp. 256–265. Unger wrote that his critique 'treats liberal doctrine as a set of interlocking conceptions whose relationship to society is disregarded. The study of the internal structure of the theory has been pursued at the cost of awareness of theory's social significance'. Unger, 'Critical Legal Studies', p. 602.

[43] Martti Koskenniemi, 'Letter to the Editors of the Symposium' in Steven R. Ratner and Anne-Marie Slaughter (eds.), *The Methods of International Law* (Washington, DC: The American Society of International Law, 2004), pp. 109–126 at p. 114; emphasis added.

[44] See ibid.

[45] Kennedy, 'New Stream', p. 8; emphasis in original. Kennedy repeats the same words later in David Kennedy, 'The Disciplines of International Law and Policy', 1 (1999) *Leiden Journal of International Law*, pp. 9–133 at p. 83.

[46] Koskenniemi, *From Apology to Utopia*, pp. 468–469, 473–474.

[47] Koskenniemi, 'Letter', p. 123.

[48] David Kennedy, 'Book Review: How Nations Behave (2d ed.) by Louis Henkin New York: Columbia University Press 1979', 21 (1980) *Harvard International Law Journal*, pp. 301–320 at pp. 301, 304.

lawyers are faced with as being not one of method (in the sense of external, determinate guidelines about legal certainty) but of language or, perhaps better, of style'.[49] In this view, there are no alternative methods of doing international law but merely alternative styles: 'legal styles are styles of argument, of linguistic expression'.[50] The style 'unifies and identifies a group of people as a community (of diplomats, practitioners, academics)'.[51] For Kennedy as well, it is the style, including sensibilities and mission of different groups of scholars, which differentiated them from one another.[52]

Fourth, both Kennedy and Koskenniemi were critical of the view that international law is 'an ideological neutral framework for intercourse' that is achieved by the 'separation of law and politics'.[53] They also agreed that those who seek to occupy the middle ground by referring to 'how nations behave' do not sufficiently appreciate that the position translated into 'unmediable opposition' in practice.[54] In fact, Kennedy indicated at an early stage the swing of international legal argument from 'apology to utopia'.[55] The intimacy between law and politics and the reality of indeterminacy rendered international law, as Koskenniemi famously put it, 'singularly useless as a means for justifying or criticising international behaviour'.[56]

---

[49] Koskenniemi, 'Letter', p. 117.
[50] See ibid., p. 122.
[51] See ibid., p. 123. In Koskenniemi's understanding 'the distinctive contribution of alternative styles lies in their ability to shed light on mainstream law's hidden priorities'. See ibid., p. 120. But Koskenniemi is self-conscious of the problem of relativism. Since 'any style of legal argument may work as a mechanism of blindness', 'to describe legal method as a style is to bracket the question of law's referential reality. As such, it may be assumed to lead into "anything goes" cynical scepticism, the giving up of political struggle and the adoption of an attitude of blasé relativism'. See ibid., pp. 120 and 124. He recognizes the 'danger of being transformed into a means of status quo arguments'. See ibid., p. 124. But how do styles then come to 'articulate experiences of injustice'? Koskenniemi suggests that perhaps the literary route offers possibilities: a novel or a letter. But to so suggest is to concede that 'experiences of injustice' cannot be articulated and opposed in the language and world of international law. Koskenniemi soon realized the weakness in this argument. His turn to formalism (or his understanding of it) and Kennedy's turn to political economy is to an extent explained by the latent nihilism in their position. Both these 'turns' are discussed later in the chapter.
[52] Kennedy 'New Stream', p. 8, pp. 47ff; David Kennedy, 'The International Style in Postwar Law and Policy', 7 (1994) *Utah Law Review*, pp. 7–103.
[53] Kennedy, 'Book Review: How Nations', pp. 301, 304.
[54] See ibid., p. 308.
[55] See ibid., pp. 309–311.
[56] Koskenniemi, *From Apology to Utopia*, p. 48.

Fifth, both Kennedy and Koskenniemi suggested that international law creates the illusion of progress through an 'obsessive repetition of a rather simple narrative structure': 'as movements from imagined *origins* through an expansive process towards a desired substantive goal'.[57] Both ILS and FATU attempted to demonstrate that the internal contradictions that characterized the discourse of international law trapped and consumed all attempts at the progressive transformation of international law. Kennedy therefore spoke of an 'uncanny continuity' in reform efforts and their criticism.[58]

Sixth, both Kennedy and Koskenniemi subscribed to some guiding scepticisms. There was scepticism in particular towards the so-called larger forces of history to be captured in grand theory.[59] In their view, there was 'no general problem, and no general solution', though one may become involved in particular redistributional struggles.[60]

While these features united Kennedy and Koskenniemi, there were even at the early stage differences between them. For instance, Kennedy noted with respect to Koskenniemi that 'at times his agnosticism annoys'.[61] More recently, Kennedy has written that 'for some reason, I have never quite shared Martti's yearning for a "culture of formalism" which could redeem the promises of the liberal cosmopolitan vision he associates with the best in the European international law tradition'.[62] The differences remain. But perhaps what is of greater significance is that both have simultaneously moved away from some of their earlier held positions. For example, while

---

[57] Kennedy, 'New Stream', p. 2; emphasis in original; Kennedy, 'Disciplines of International Law', p. 92.

[58] David Kennedy, 'A New World Order: Yesterday, Today, and Tomorrow', 4 (1994) *Transnational Law & Contemporary Problems,* pp. 330–375 at p. 358. See also David Kennedy, 'Move to Institutions', 8 (1987) *Cardozo Law Review,* pp. 841–988..

[59] This was a reflection of 'a Lyotardian-style loss of faith in all traditional meta-narratives that swept through the intellectually progressive circles in the US academia in the early to mid-1970s'. Akbar Rasulov, 'CLS and Marxism: A History of an Affair', 5 (2014) *Transnational Legal Theory,* pp. 622–639 at p. 625. The problem was 'coupled with the general ideological exigencies of the Cold War [which] made it highly unlikely... that any [...] new enterprises could organize themselves as an extension of the traditional Marxist theoretical project ... as a matter of practical academic reality Marxism remained the ultimate slur word'. See ibid., p. 626. In the circumstances it was entirely understandable that 'a very considerable part of what CLS scholars have had to say about the Marxist legal tradition (MLT) seems essentially useless from the point of view of a Marxist legal scholar'. See ibid., p. 631.

[60] See generally Kennedy, 'A New World Order' pp. 374–375.

[61] David Kennedy, 'Book Review', 31 (1990) *Harvard International Law Journal,* pp. 385–391 at p. 387.

[62] Kennedy, 'Last Treatise', p. 989.

both Kennedy and Koskenniemi had rejected the idea that political economy and law are related, even in 'any complicated way', they have now
turned to doing political economy, albeit in different ways. Koskenniemi
is looking at the relationship of law and political economy in historical
terms while Kennedy is attempting to understand contemporary aspects
of the political economy of global governance. One reason for this departure is arguably the emergence of other critical approaches such as TWAIL,
MAIL and some strands of FtAIL that have (re)stressed the salience of
political economy to the understanding of international law. Meanwhile,
in the intervening decades, Kennedy and Koskenniemi addressed different themes of international law to produce a corpus of significant work. It
is time to consider their individual contributions.

III.   Seeing Like Kennedy: The Internal View

Among the very first pieces Kennedy wrote,[63] he declared the discipline
of international law in crisis.[64] He contended that 'no one seemed to think
that international law was intellectually rich' or 'that international legal
theory could offer a more than an easy patois of lazy justification and
arrogance for a discipline which had lost its way and kept its jobs'.[65] This
was a necessary move for someone who wished to rewrite the history and
doctrines of international law; a radically new approach could be justified
only if the discipline was in a state of decay. He was not altogether wrong
about the state of the discipline, but he certainly exaggerated the claim,
even in the context of the United States. It was perhaps true that by and
large mainstream international law scholars had failed to see that the discipline was mired in contradictions and lacked the intellectual resources
to identify and address the most pressing issues of the time. However,
he neglected several ongoing efforts, with beginnings in the 1960s, to
attend to the poverty of the discipline of international law. The initiatives
included the policy-oriented approach of Myres McDougal and Harold
Lasswell with its theses on rule scepticism and indeterminacy and reliance on interdisciplinary materials in pursuit of the goal of human dignity, and the 'intermediate approach' of Richard Falk who was not only
exploring fresh ways of thinking about international law but also about a

---

[63] A complete list of publications of David Kennedy can be found at www.law.harvard.edu/
faculty/dkennedy/publications/
[64] David Kennedy, 'Theses about International Law Discourse', (1980) *German Yearbook of
International Law*, pp. 353–391 at pp. 356, 390.
[65] Kennedy, 'New Stream', p. 6.

range of world order issues.[66] It was also a time when scholars like Thomas Franck had identified a cutting edge international law agenda (for the 1980s) that included 'seven major items: Palestine, South Africa, the new international economic order; arms control; human rights; disaster prevention and relief; and revamping the multilateral lawmaking and problem solving machinery'.[67] But Kennedy did not take too much notice of the diverse theoretical developments, or engage with the new agenda, as he had something distinct in mind when it came to disciplinary renewal.[68] He wanted to look at international law from the inside.

This move also prevented Kennedy from looking towards the Global South to see if there was new thinking among postcolonial scholars that could invigorate the discipline. If he had he would have found that a third world approach to international law was being articulated that offered a sharp critique of mainstream international law scholarship (MILS) from the standpoint of the decolonized world. An entire generation of third world scholars was challenging received history and doctrines of international law and also calling for the transformation of traditional international law rules. R. P. Anand had written his well-known book *New States and International Law* in 1972 and Mohammed Bedjaoui published his important work *Towards a new international economic order* only a year before Kennedy pronounced the entire discipline in crisis. In the process, Kennedy overlooked the sense of excitement among third world scholars that was traceable to several developments in the field of international law: a review of the foundational principles of international law culminating in the 1970 Friendly Relations Declaration, the ongoing negotiations of a new law of the sea convention with the active participation of third world countries, the call for a new international economic order to restructure the rules that regulated the world economy, the emergence of new coalitions such as G-77 to take the postcolonial economic agenda forward, and the creation of new international institutions like UNCTAD to lend weight to the voices of third world peoples and countries. In fact

---

[66] Indeed, one of the essays of Richard Falk was titled 'New Approaches to the Study of International Law', 61 (1967) *The American Journal of International Law*, pp. 177–195. For a discussion of the work of Richard Falk see Chapter 4.

[67] Cited later by Kennedy himself in David Kennedy, 'Tom Franck and the Manhattan School', 35 (2003) *NYU Journal of International Law and Politics*, pp. 397–437 at p. 422.

[68] It explains why till the present author applied to Harvard Law School for affiliation in 1995 (as a requirement for the grant of a Fulbright fellowship) he had never read David Kennedy. Indian international law scholars keenly followed the writings of US scholars like Richard Falk who engaged with third world concerns.

not until his now well-known TWAIL students arrived in the 1990s at Harvard Law School (Antony Anghie, James Gathii, Celestine Nyamu, Vasuki Nesiah, Balakrishnan Rajagopal, Hani Syed and Amr Shalakny among others) did Kennedy give serious thought to how third world scholars, peoples and states were attempting to recast the discipline.

In the early years Kennedy was entirely preoccupied with his project of deconstructing international law and offering an original account of the structure of international law. As one observer put it, he had arrived 'on the international legal scene with a manifesto in his hand and revolution in his heart'.[69] The intellectual sources of the manifesto were 'critical legal scholarship', 'linguistic and literary theory', 'structuralism and post-structuralism' and 'literatures of psychiatry and feminism'.[70] The revolution he sought to bring about was in the way of looking at international law. Kennedy scrupulously eschewed an external critique of the 'relationship between international legal materials and their political and interpretive milieu'.[71] He was at this stage 'not concerned about the context within which arguments are made and doctrines developed'.[72] Kennedy believed that the discipline could overcome its crisis only by interrogating and understanding the internal structure of international law that necessitated a distinct style of doing international law. Therefore, in ILS he set out to find the 'rhetorical structures and maneuvers' that could help 'clarify and relate a number of otherwise somewhat perplexing and disparate texts'.[73]

Kennedy was of course self-conscious about 'the difficulties and eccentricities' of his approach, but appears to have believed that 'by thinking about the field from the inside' a more 'heterodox discipline' could be developed.[74] He did generate genuine insights that he later used to present brilliant alternative accounts of different spheres of international law. His work on the dark side of human rights movement and international humanitarian law are examples of the rich fare the internal view has to offer. But his internal critique was so disconnected from the mainstream, or other critical ways of doing international law which were principally

---

[69] Nicholas Onuf, *International Legal Theory: Essays and Engagements, 1996–2006* (London: Routledge-Cavendish, 2008), p. 275.
[70] Kennedy, 'New Stream', pp. 7–9.
[71] See ibid., pp. 10, 11; emphasis in original.
[72] See ibid., p. 10. See fn 40 in this regard.
[73] Kennedy, *International Legal Structures*, p. 9.
[74] See ibid, p. 8. Kennedy was also driven like most others by 'the register of disciplinary desire'.

concerned with material outcomes, that in the early years it was largely ignored. The mainstream could not sufficiently appreciate that it is not as if Kennedy was not concerned with distributional issues. He merely felt that in the final analysis only the effective deconstruction of international law could bring a proper focus on them. Arguably, he also wanted to distance himself from the traditional left view that traced the growing North-South divide to the workings of global capitalism. Here too he wished to carve out his own distinctive path. He adopted methodological individualism as his creed and concluded that international governance, law and institutions did not reflect the rule of capital or any such thing but that of experts who should learn to assume responsibility for their actions. Only recently has he begun to look in a relatively more conventional way at material outcomes by turning to political economy and advance the beginnings of an external critique of international law. In all these regards, it may help to proceed systematically to analyse his work. In what follows, critical reflections are offered of his internal view, his narration of the history of international law from this standpoint, his early thinking on the role of experts and expertise in global governance, the turn to political economy and law, his current thinking on the role of experts and expertise, and finally his insights on particular areas of international law.

A. The Idea of Internal Critique

The distinction between 'internal' and 'external' critique has been succinctly captured by Andreas Paulus: 'An "internal" critique unveils the internal inconsistency of "mainstream" international law, an "external" critique points towards the ideological and political bias of supposedly "neutral" legal rules'.[75] The former avers that 'the indeterminacy of rules and the arbitrariness of the application of principles and values preclude a definite outcome of legal analysis' and the latter critique is about 'preservation of male or imperialist meta-structures'.[76] Kennedy pursued his internal critique through the 'unorthodox' treatment of 'familiar materials'. He focused on 'the relationships among doctrines and arguments and upon their recurring rhetorical structure'.[77] Kennedy contended that

---

[75] Andreas L. Paulus, 'International Law after Postmodernism: Towards Renewal or Decline of International Law?', 14 (2001) *Leiden Journal of International Law*, pp. 727–755 at p. 731.
[76] See ibid., pp. 731–732.
[77] Kennedy, *International Legal Structures*, p. 7.

the structure along with the accompanying manoeuvres 'always shrewdly locates the moment of authority and the application in practice else-where',[78] that is, depending on where these are first located, among the dis-cursive areas of sources, process and substance of international law.[79] In order to understand the ensuing thesis that the doctrines of international law do not stand on firm ground, it may help to touch on Kennedy's treat-ment of the doctrine of sources of international law.[80] In his analysis, Kennedy makes the crucial point that the discourse on sources continu-ally oscillates between consent and community without reaching closure. Thus, in his view, 'it is difficult to categorize the sources of Article 38 as either soft or hard'[81] because while 'a "hard" argument' 'seek(s) to ground compliance in the "consent" of the state to be bound', it relies for its effect-iveness on a 'soft' argument, that is, 'upon some extraconsensual notion of the good or the just',[82] explaining why in 'the Vienna Convention on the Law of Treaties consent vies with justice for supremacy as a source of obligation to abide by treaty law'.[83] In fact, because each of the sources has a 'double nature' the 'argument about the sources of international law' assumes the form of 'an endless project of differentiation and recombin-ation'.[84] Thus both the elements of consent and justice must '*temper* the other in important ways and the discourse as a whole must seem to move forward from autonomy to community'.[85] In other words, 'contemporary sources discourse is uncomfortable with both hard and soft rhetoric in their extreme forms',[86] as at the end of the day the sources doctrine is

---

[78] See ibid., p. 293. See also Kennedy, 'New Stream', pp. 36–39.
[79] 'Sources doctrine is concerned with the origin and authority of international law-a con-cern it resolves by referring the reader to authorities constituted elsewhere. Process doc-trine – the bulk of modern international public law – considers the participants and the jurisdictional framework for international law independent of both the process by which international law is generated and the substance of its normative order. Substance doctrine seems to address issues of sovereign co-operation and conflict more directly. Like sources doctrine, it does so largely by referring to the boundaries and authorities established in other doctrinal fields'. Kennedy, *International Legal Structures*, p. 8.
[80] For a more detailed discussion see Anthony Carty, 'Critical International Law: Recent Trends in the Theory of International Law', 2 (1991) *European Journal of International Law*, pp. 1–26 at pp. 6–11.
[81] David Kennedy 'The Sources of International Law' (1987) 2 *The American Journal of International Law and Policy*, pp. 1–96 at p. 24.
[82] See ibid., p. 20.
[83] See ibid., p. 42.
[84] See ibid., p. 28.
[85] See ibid., p. 89; emphasis in original.
[86] See ibid.

about 'normative authority in a system of autonomous sovereigns',[87] which already presumes the legal order.[88] But, by assuming the existence of an international legal order, the sources doctrine simply defers the moment in which its absence (or weak presence) returns to haunt it 'opening up an endlessly proliferating field of legal argumentation'.[89] International law thus often seeks to establish order through a doctrinal edifice built on bad faith. What Kennedy is doing through undertaking this exercise of decon-struction is 'addressing patterns of illusion ... The system works, but in an apparently self-deceptive way'.[90] In view of the structural indeterminacy that characterizes international legal argument, the international lawyer is 'without a law at her disposal', but bad faith allows her to become 'a political arbiter without any further legitimacy than her own individual preferences'.[91]

This conclusion partly explains Kennedy's lack of interest at this stage in the traditional left mode of doing international law with its emphasis on an external critique, as also his later focus on the role of experts and expertise for realizing preferred values. Indeed, Kennedy acknowledges that 'better international law arguments, doctrines, and institutions' were never his 'first concern' even though this could have helped left-liberal causes.[92] In his writings, he repeatedly makes the point that the inter-national law academia was 'more in need of in-reach than outreach'.[93] In fact, what Kennedy had found most frustrating is 'navigating the disci-plinary demand for usefulness', that is, for proposals that lead 'to concrete reforms'.[94] He was of course acutely aware that he was ' "side stepping" the real world'.[95] He knew that he was likely to be asked as to 'what about

[87] See ibid., p. 92.

[88] See ibid., p. 95.

[89] See ibid., pp. 87, 96. In this regard Kennedy also perceptively pointed out that the sources doctrine proceeds 'independently of the norm's particular content or application'. See ibid. It is sociologically neutral.

[90] Carty, 'Critical International Law', p. 8. See also Edward M. Morgan, 'International Law in a Post-Modern Hall of Mirrors: International Legal Structures by David Kennedy', 26 (1988) Osgoode Hall Law Journal, pp. 207–233 at pp. 214–218.

[91] Paulus, 'International Law', p. 743. Paulus aptly notes the resemblance of the contention with the New Haven approach insofar as the posited role of international lawyer is con-cerned: 'the political expectations towards the lawyer remain the same', that is, minus the scientific methodology of New Haven to arrive at solutions. See ibid., p. 737. The resem-blance is reflected in the idea that 'the person of the lawyer, and not the law, is in the central position'. See ibid., p. 739.

[92] Kennedy, 'When Renewal Repeats', p. 478.

[93] See ibid.

[94] See ibid., p. 461.

[95] See ibid., p. 400.

reality, real problems, real solutions, real conditions, real statecraft, real politics, and real suffering?'[96] After all, as he put it, even a genius must know that the connection 'to usefulness is crucial'.[97] The point Kennedy was making is that it is not as if he does not engage with the real world, it is merely in a different way. In his view no particular way of dealing with the real world should be privileged over other ways of doing so. But researchers imagined that they were engaging with the real world if only they were doing it in one way (the external way) rather than another way (the internal way). In this regard, he perceptively observes that 'international lawyers often feel that rejecting the critic for the reformer would *itself* be progress'.[98] One consequence of this view has been that the US mainstream was 'rather quick to reject socialism, anarchism, Marxism, and even anti-colonialism in its most innovative phase' and also 'been very hesitant in absorbing the waves of intellectual innovation' that swept the American legal academy in the last century.[99]

But the real problem with his internal critique is not that he chooses one way of dealing with the real world over another, it is that his internal critique is neither particularly novel nor of great value. First, the rhetorical moves he identifies as informing an interminable legal argument on doctrines of international law given the 'continual oscillation' between autonomy and community is the state of being of the 'international' in an anarchic system. The internal structure of international law is simply an expression of the absence of a world state that can help the argument reach closure. In other words, the contradictions in the internal structure of international law are not the outcome of some flawed logic but a mere reflection of the nature of international society. The discovery of certain recurring rhetorical structures in international legal discourse is in that sense not especially interesting. Of course, Kennedy does contribute to understanding the ways in which international legal discourse (for instance, on sources doctrine) ties itself in knots. He also ably demonstrates how the rhetorical moves between sources, process and substance sustain the illusion of international law. But the lack of internal coherence

---

[96] See ibid., p. 464.
[97] See ibid., p. 400. Therefore, 'however violently an innovative scholar might rearrange the terms with which the discipline responds to problems, even the genius does not rethink the problem set itself, neither the discipline's mission of more law among states, nor the definition of what counts as practical. Doing so would place the effort outside the scope of evaluation and adoption by practitioner-beings'. See ibid.
[98] See ibid., p. 464; emphasis in original.
[99] See ibid., p. 467.

or the inability of doctrinal discourse to reach closure has been evident from the beginning. Indeed, the centuries-old debate on the problem of compliance in a decentralized international society is an expression of attempts to come to terms with the contradictions that inform the idea of international law.[100] In an essay on 'international law and nineteenth century', Kennedy himself brilliantly recounts the historical vacillation between naturalism, positivism and pragmatism as possible but unsustainable responses to overcoming the structural defects flowing from the 'logic of territory'.[101] But what he does not adequately recognize is that the genius of international lawyers over the ages has been to acknowledge that the social construction of an imagined community can make a real difference. The real problem in fact is that this community was and is imagined in particular ('Eurocentric') ways by Western international lawyers that cannot be addressed by merely looking at the internal structure of international law.

Second, his internal critique of international law is profoundly ahistorical and apolitical. Anthony Carty has aptly observed that Kennedy 'stops short of questioning the context of the discourse which he deconstructs. He does not treat it basically as an historical conditioned discipline. Nor does he question the uses to which it is put'.[102] He instead 'appears to treat international legal discourse as an aesthetic achievement. Its very aimlessness is the mark of its perfection: international law for the sake of international law, a beautiful exercise in perpetual and "successful" evasion'.[103] In other words, Kennedy does not explore how the internal tensions in the body of international law have played out, and with what consequences for weak groups, peoples and nations in different phases of history. How did for instance the opposing concepts of 'autonomy' and 'community' or 'consent' and 'justice' evolve in the colonial era? What were the rhetorical moves that helped evade the internal contradictions to allow international law to facilitate the colonial project? For example, the entire idea of a political entity being assigned sovereignty so that it could be signed

---

[100] See in this regard Chapter 2, pp. 73–78.

[101] David Kennedy, 'International Law and the Nineteenth Century: The History of an Illusion', 17 (1997) QLR, pp. 99–136.

[102] Carty, 'Critical International Law', p. 4. It is perhaps worth noting here that in an attempt to explain the absence of 'context', Kennedy has later asserted that he 'focuses on the background rather than context' by which he means 'impersonal forces' like 'global capital' or 'interests of the ruling class' and the like explaining its absence even at the early stage. David Kennedy, 'Challenging Expert Rule: The Politics of Global Governance', 27 (2005) Sydney Journal of International Law, pp. 1–24 at p. 5. This matter is discussed presently.

[103] Carty, 'Critical International Law', p. 4.

away shows how closure was reached on questions of autonomy and community through the exercise of power.[104] The expedient relationship between autonomy and community in the colonial era continues to manifest itself even today, albeit assuming new forms. The relationship reflects an *internal* link between imperialism and international legal structures (i.e. the sources, substance and process of international law) that Kennedy does not explore. Instead, in attempting to advance a purely internal critique, he posits a static understanding of the basic concepts and categories of international law.[105] Such a critique is fractional unless it proceeds in conjunction with a historical critique of the universalizing logic of capital. To be sure, there are two separate 'insides' to be deconstructed here, that of law and capital respectively, with each sphere having its own internal logic. But in history the two separate logics also interpenetrate.[106] The reality and ideology of universalizing capital configures and circumscribes the ideas of autonomy and community in different ways in different eras. The hypothesized oscillation between autonomy and community is therefore not to be investigated in the abstract but in terms of their particular relationship in different periods of history. In overlooking this, Kennedy ends up offering a partial and therefore flawed critique as he looks at the internal structure of international law after delinking it from the logic of imperialism.[107]

It is because Kennedy did not make the connections between the internal structures of law and capital, or of law and society, that critics found ILS 'eerily empty and ultimately uninteresting'.[108] The internal view was seen as 'another grand theory unfortunately unconnected with the real world of international politics'.[109] The particular critic went on to

---

[104] In the colonial period 'the only occasion when native "sovereignty" or "personality" is bestowed or recognized is in a context where the personality enables the native to transfer title, to grant rights – whether trading, to territory, or to sovereignty itself'. Antony Anghie, *Imperialism, Sovereignty and the Making of International Law* (Cambridge: Cambridge University Press , 2003), p. 105.

[105] See generally, Akbar Rasulov, 'International Law and the Poststructuralist Challenge', 19 (2006) *Leiden Journal of International Law*, pp. 799–827 at pp. 800–801.

[106] As Rasulov neatly puts it: 'No entity can ever keep at bay that analytical antithesis on whose ontological isolation its identity depends. Or, to put it slightly less abstractly, every Self carries within it an ineradicable trace of its external Other, which is to say that the Other is never really external, and moreover, never really an Other.' See ibid., p. 801.

[107] Paulus, 'International Law', p. 737.

[108] Phillip R. Trimble, 'International Law, World Order, and Critical Legal Studies', 42 (1990) *Stanford Law Review*, pp. 811–845 at p. 823.

[109] See ibid.

conclude that 'I do not understand the point of his elaborate exercise.'[110] To be sure, such critics disregard the fact that Kennedy demonstrates with great acumen the logical impossibility of equilibrium between sources, substance and process of international law. But it has also to be conceded that it would have been more meaningful to have gone further and linked the hopelessness of reaching equilibrium in international law with the impossibility of reaching equilibrium under global capitalism, that is, demonstrate the internal contradictions in law and material structures flowing from both the 'logic of territory' and 'logic of capital'. It would have lent the internal critique of international law greater depth and relevance. Kennedy would have been able to capture multivalent dimensions of international law.

B. Towards Internal History

In this respect, it is puzzling that while Kennedy's understanding of international legal structures is ahistorical, he was from the beginning interested in the history of international law. Starting around the same time as he wrote ILS, Kennedy published several historical pieces in the next two decades. But the puzzle resolves itself the moment the historical essays are approached. He clarifies therein that their objective is less to do history and more to deconstruct particular phases of the evolution of the discipline of international law that he classified as primitive, traditional and modern. In his 1986 essay on 'primitive legal scholarship'[111] Kennedy notes at the very outset that it is 'neither a history of the development of legal doctrines nor a social history' but an attempt 'to explain the work of the primitives as extensively and as sympathetically as possible within the four corners of their own lexicon'.[112] His project was the deconstruction of the 'inside' of international law scholarship in particular phases of history. In this particular instance it was about how the primitive texts of Vitoria, Suarez, Gentili and Grotius are misconstrued, the way they should be read, what lent internal coherence to them, how sources of authority were invoked, why these sources were often cited unreflectively, what differentiates one primitive text from another, whether the primitives imagined

---

[110] See ibid., p. 832.
[111] David Kennedy, 'Primitive Legal Scholarship', 27 (1986) *Harvard International Law Journal*, pp. 1–98.
[112] See ibid., p. 13.

a distinction between the spheres of morality and law or that between municipal and international law and so on.

There is of course no reason why the 'internal structure' of primitive texts cannot be analysed to inter alia show that contemporary scholars misread these, often seeing continuity or discontinuity where there is none.[113] This is what Kennedy demonstrates and with skill and insight. On the other hand, once again he does not appreciate that material developments infiltrate texts, including their internal composition and constructs. It would surely be reductionist to draw a simple relationship between internal structure of texts and external realities; the former has its own distinctive history. But it would be equally mistaken to overlook the historical context in which these texts originated. Or, as significantly, the texts to which these texts were a particular response. The Cambridge school of history has long since alerted us to the errors that can result from ignoring these multiple realities.[114] Thus, for example, it is difficult to understand John Selden's *Mare Clausum* (1636) without keeping in sight Hugo Grotius' *Mare Liberum* (1609). Because the different historical contexts and texts to which the primitive texts were a response are ignored, it does not come as a surprise that Kennedy concludes his reflections on the primitives (turning now cursorily to the material context) with the observation that 'it is difficult to speculate about the causes of the shift from primitivism'.[115] Albeit he does go on to observe that it may be because 'the general scheme of Suarej, Vitoria, Gentili and Grotius had become unsatisfactory for various reasons'.[116] In this respect, he mentions nationalism and 'developing trends towards international political decentralization',[117] but there is no word on capitalism or colonialism. The 'logic of capital' is completely left out of the picture.

Kennedy's particular focus explains why he was not attentive to the fact that primitive legal scholarship was among other things driven by the necessities of the colonial project. He was primarily concerned at this time with unravelling disciplinary texts in order to show continuities where others found discontinuity or breaks where continuity was perceived. Kennedy was not interested in exploring primitive scholarship in relationship to developments in the material world which saw the emergence

---

[113] See ibid., p. 37.
[114] See generally Quentin Skinner, *Visions of Politics*, vol. I: *Regarding Method* (Cambridge: Cambridge University Press, 2002).
[115] Kennedy, 'Primitive Legal Scholarship', p. 97.
[116] See ibid.
[117] See ibid.

of an 'empire of rights'.[118] He would otherwise have certainly taken cognizance of the well-known fact (to continue with the earlier example) that Grotius was often defending in his writings the imperial interests of Holland.[119] In other words, what is absent in the essay on 'primitive legal scholarship' is a sensibility that takes notice of the colonization of non-western nations.[120] Kennedy's deconstructive obsession with 'internal structures' made him miss obvious linkages. Like many CLS scholars he appears to have been concerned that he should not be seen as doing some kind of reductionist Marxist history. In the process, he was unwittingly incarcerated in a Eurocentric discourse of international law. While he was offering fresh ways of approaching and reading primitive legal texts, his understanding in the final analysis represented more continuity then discontinuity with mainstream international law scholarship (MILS) reading of 'primitives' insofar as the missing colonial project was concerned.

How else does one explain the nature of Kennedy's engagement with the work of Vitoria, especially the 'law governing relations with American Indians and the law of war'?[121] It is fascinating that he goes over the same ground as Antony Anghie two decades later but with different results. Thus, for instance, he writes that 'Vitoria imagines that legitimate title might be obtained either by Indian consent or as a result of some Indian violation of some Spanish "right" which entitled the Spanish to "right" the "wrong" to enforce the precepts of divine law'.[122] He then goes on to note that according to Vitoria 'the wrongs by which Indian authorities might deprive themselves of their authority are numerous, relating to generally to obstructing the Spanish freedom to trade and proselytize. These freedoms are grounded in natural law'.[123] But he does not draw the relationship

---

[118] As will be seen later in the chapter, Martti Koskenniemi is attempting to fill this lack in his recent scholarship.

[119] Mathew Craven citing Richard Tuck observes, 'it is no longer possible to read Grotius without attending to the fact that much of his work seemed to be written as an "apology for the whole Dutch commercial expansion into the Indies"'. Mathew Craven, 'Colonialism and Domination' in Bardo Fassbender and Anne Peters (eds.), *The Oxford Handbook of the History of International Law* (Oxford: Oxford University Press, 2012), pp. 862–890 at p. 862. See also R. P. Anand, 'Maritime Practice in South-East Asia until 1600 A.D. and the Modern Law of the Sea', 30 (1981) *International and Comparative Law Quarterly*, pp. 440–454; R. P. Anand, *The Origin and Development of Law of the Sea* (The Hague: Martinus Nijhoff, 1983).

[120] On the other hand, arguably Anghie does not sufficiently acknowledge how his thinking was shaped by earlier third world scholarship allowing him to make the connections that Kennedy did not.

[121] Kennedy, 'Primitive Legal Scholarship', pp. 23ff.

[122] See ibid., p. 27.

[123] See ibid., p. 28.

Anghie draws between the writings of Vitoria and the colonial project.[124] The reason is that Kennedy is focused on internal logic of the text than on historical realities that prompted Vitoria to cogitate on the subject of Indians. He entirely misses out on the significance of the evolution of the development of the 'empire of private rights' in the period. The result is that he fails to link the primitive texts to the 'logic of capital'.

A year after his take on 'primitive legal scholarship', Kennedy turned his attention to the history of modern international institutions, a history that is usually traced to the creation of the League of Nations.[125] He now proceeded to explore the 'internal structure' of the 'discipline of international institutions' which distinguished itself from public international law that usually traces its modern origins to the Treaty of Westphalia, 1648.[126] Once again Kennedy explicitly disavowed the objective of narrating a history of international institutions.[127] His concern was with 'a set of ideas about institutionalization illustrated by some narratives told by the discipline of international institutions about its origin and practice'.[128] In other words, his reflections were on how the discipline of international institutions constructed the history of institutions in a particular way, beginning with ascribing its origins to the League of Nations. He pointed to the insightful fact that the discipline of international institutions was seen as being less about words (or texts) and more about deeds and therefore had its own distinctive self-image.[129] The birth of international institutions was thus seen to signal a move from 'chaos to order'.[130] Kennedy perceptively noted how the history of international institutions was told by the discipline as a narrative of progress with successive institutions overcoming gaps and weaknesses in earlier incarnations. In fact, he offers a dense history of the rhetoric that is mobilized to sustain a progress narrative. His intricate analysis helps sustain a healthy scepticism towards the idea of relying on international institutions to build a just world order. He points out how international institutions have had to constantly negotiate between ideals and reality, principles and practices, and sovereignty and ethics to achieve a desired order.

---

[124] Anghie, *Sovereignty, Imperialism,* chapter 2.
[125] David Kennedy, 'The Move to Institutions' , 8 (1987) *Cardozo Law Review*, pp. 841–988.
[126] See ibid., p. 842.
[127] See ibid., p. 849.
[128] See ibid.
[129] See ibid., p. 843.
[130] See ibid., p. 855.

But Kennedy said little about the realities, practices and sovereignties that prevented the realization of a progressive world order. Once again what is surprising is that in an essay that deals at length with the League of Nations there is little engagement with the central issues of the times viz., colonialism and inter-imperialist rivalries that led to two wars and provided the impulse for the creation of international institutions. Indeed the fate of colonies hardly gets any attention.[131] Instead, what assumes precedence is the internal structure of arguments of different contending paradigms in the creation of League of Nations. Kennedy of course skilfully reveals the contradictions in each approach. Thus, for instance, he demonstrates how those who wished to keep law and politics apart had to allow politics in and those who do not think too much of law relied on it to frame politics.[132] The same ambivalence characterized the relationship between diplomacy and the organization, at once keeping the other away and then drawing it back in.[133] This is very much the kind of internal tensions that Kennedy brilliantly captured in explaining the moves from autonomy to community while discussing the sources of international law. In the instance of the League there is likewise 'a movement from reality to utopia and from utopia to reality'.[134] Kennedy deconstructs in this regard every aspect of the text of the Covenant of the League of Nations: from the articles dealing with the institutional structure to those concerned with procedural dimensions that include the working of the plenary or the structure of voting. But in all this the external reality of capitalism, colonialism and imperialism once again does not make an appearance. It is interesting to contrast the Kennedy piece with the work of Anghie on the Mandate System of the League of Nations a quarter of a century later. Anghie's argument is entirely different and distinctive. In his words:

> My argument is that colonialism profoundly shaped the character of international institutions at their formative stage, and that by examining the history of how this occurred we might illuminate the operations and character of contemporary international institutions.[135]

Admittedly, the Kennedy goal is confined to revealing the internal contradictions that mark the disciplinary discourse on international institutions

---

[131] Colonial territories get mentioned but only incidentally. See ibid., pp. 914, 926–928.
[132] See ibid., pp. 868–869.
[133] See ibid., p. 861.
[134] See ibid., p. 873.
[135] Anghie, *Sovereignty, Imperialism*, p. 117. It could however be said that Anghie does not sufficiently acknowledge his debt to Kennedy for bringing him to the point where he simply had to add the reality of colonialism to articulate his particular thesis on international law.

and is not intended to look at the external realities in the matrix of which their creation is undertaken. But in so limiting his objective Kennedy misses the opportunity to demonstrate that these tensions often arise out of trying to come to terms with troubling historical realities.

A decade after his essay on 'primitive legal scholarship' Kennedy returned to the history of legal scholarship in an essay on 'International Law and the Nineteenth Century: The History of an Illusion'. This time however he begins by observing that he had 'been working for some time on a general history of international law, focusing, like most histories of the discipline, on the modern period and on the early writers of the seventeenth and eighteenth centuries'.[136] He then notes that in writing this history he found himself 'returning again and again to the nineteenth century, and to the break which opened the modern period at the beginning of this century [i.e., twentieth century]'.[137] Kennedy then goes on 'to stress a few counterpoints' to the conventional narrative that sees the nineteenth century way of doing international law as a thing of the past.[138] In contrast to the experiencing of the 'modern international lawyer' of disciplinary developments in the twentieth century 'as a maturation', he argues that 'sovereignty, formalism, positivism, and a rule of coexistence rather than cooperation, all remain with us, not only as echoes and remnants to be excised root and branch, but as dreams, projects, and goals for our work'.[139] This continuity in twentieth-century disciplinary argument makes him 'skeptical of the claim that a shift away from formalism or sovereignty can ensure, or even mark an argument as progressive, or internationalist, or modern'.[140] He is 'drawn to the hypothesis' that a certain understanding of the classical synthesis has been 'generated by very twentieth century argumentative habits'.[141] Thus, the theme of continuity and discontinuity in his writings continues, seen as constructs of the community of international lawyers. In this way of seeing things the moderns are compelled to represent the past in particular ways to present themselves as moving forward with the times. They like to see the disciplinary developments in the twentieth century 'as a progressive story of modernization, internationalization, and of the left'.[142] But the imagined narrative of theoretical and

---

[136] Kennedy, 'International Law and the Nineteenth Century', p. 99.
[137] See ibid.
[138] See ibid., p. 102.
[139] See ibid., pp. 101, 102–103.
[140] See ibid., p. 103.
[141] See ibid., p. 103.
[142] See ibid., p. 102.

methodological progress runs up against the hard rock of the very realities that the discipline grappled with in the nineteenth century. To put it
differently, there have been no momentous ruptures that mark the discipline. Old ideas and concepts seem to go away only to return under new
conditions serving new masters assuming new forms. Such is for example
the concept of sovereignty. Too much before the First World War, less in
the inter-war period and immediate post-war period, more after decolonization, less after globalization and so on. Kennedy helps us see these
twists and turns. But once more in all this the 'logic of capital' or the phenomenon of imperialism does not figure in a central way. However, this
time around, since the essay is written in the period in which his TWAIL
student Anghie had already published his work centrally focused on colonialism, it finds a presence.[143] The continuities between the nineteenth
and the twentieth century are now also linked to the imperial project, i.e.,
to external realities. Kennedy observes for instance how 'the problem of
engaging and governing the culturally different has preoccupied the field
across a wide range of historical periods, scientific methods and doctrinal
conventions'.[144] While the theme of colonialism and international law find
an echo throughout the essay the centrality of imperialism to the story of
international law is still not the subject of reflection.[145] The impact of the
Soviet Union and its East European allies on the doctrines and workings
of international law are also left uncommented. Kennedy appears to be
held back by the emphasis he had placed in his earlier essays on looking at
the inside of international law. What you, therefore, still get is essentially
an internal history of the discipline that matches the concern with exploring the tensions in the internal structure of international law. The analysis,
therefore, continues to suffer from the same frailties. Despite the wealth of
insights Kennedy runs the risk of his work being neglected or castigated
for not addressing central issues. If it can ever be said of any historical
writing that it is ahistorical by design then Kennedy's writings epitomize
the proposition. However, the deeper flaw remains the inability to grasp
the impact of external realities on the internal structure or inside of the
history of international law. The external or material realities and internal
structures do not operate in parallel universes. These more often than not
partake of each other.

---

[143] The very first page of the essay makes a reference to an essay by Anghie and his then
unpublished thesis. See ibid., p. 99, fn 1.
[144] See ibid., p. 103.
[145] See ibid., p. 103.

C.   Rule of Experts: First Take

At least one important reason Kennedy tends to leave out the real world in his writings is perhaps his view that it is not easy to know how material structures cohere and work. Implicit in this way of thinking is a critique of Marxism with its claim of having discovered the laws of motion of capitalism and its relationship to the sphere of law. It may be recalled that Kennedy had early on made the argument that there is no stable relationship between political economy and law. He, therefore, chose to concentrate on deconstructing and exposing the tensions that characterize the discourse on international legal structures or the history of the discipline. To put it differently, the critique of a functional or reductionist reading of the relationship between the 'logic of capital' and international law led Kennedy to doing a kind of history and theory that assumed that both the constitution of the material world and its relationship to international law were difficult to map with any confidence.

This standpoint explains why Kennedy is wont to speak of 'the mystery of global governance'.[146] The constant refrain is 'how little we in fact know about how we are governed ... about the structure of global society'.[147] There are simply too many variables, processes, and structures to be identified and understood. In the circumstances 'it is not at all obvious how power is put together on the global stage, let alone how its exercise might be rendered just or effective'.[148] Kennedy raises a number of questions that in his view are not paid sufficient attention.[149] In advancing them he is suggesting that that there are no easy answers to how and in what ways material structures are constituted or cause particular outcomes and the role of law in all this. First, there are questions related to 'how does the world remain so unequal; how are hierarchy and domination reproduced?'[150] Second, 'what does law have to do with the organization of politics and economics?'[151] Third, how do we assess the implications of 'the sheer density of rules and institutions in the global space'; there is 'law

---

[146] David Kennedy, 'The Mystery of Global Governance in Jeffrey L. Dunoff and Joel P. Trachtman (eds.), *Ruling the World? Constitutionalism, International Law, and Global Governance* (Cambridge: Cambridge University Press, 2009), pp. 37–68.

[147] See ibid., at p. 38.

[148] See ibid., p. 56.

[149] See ibid., p. 57.

[150] See ibid., p. 55.

[151] See ibid., p. 55.

and regulation at every turn'.[152] Fourth, what is one to make of 'the dis-
orderliness, the pluralism, the uncertainty, the chaos, of all of those rules
and principles and institutions'.[153] The reference here is to 'the informal
and the clandestine – to customary norms, background patterns of private and public expectation, black markets, and illegal flows'.[154] Finally,
there are questions 'about who will win and lose' and who 'one expects' to
bring about just global governance.[155]

It is not difficult to agree with Kennedy that the international system
comprises multiple and complex structures, agencies, and processes
whose workings and effects cannot be fully mapped and grasped. But to
move from acknowledging a certain inadequacy of methods and knowledge to speaking of 'the *mystery* of global governance' is to ignore what
we do know. There is for instance enough credible theoretical, historical
and empirical literature available to demonstrate that there are structures,
laws, institutions and practices that facilitate and legitimize the exploitation and oppression of subaltern groups, peoples and nations.[156] In talking about the unknown and unknowable dimensions of global governance,
Kennedy once again appears to be attempting to displace traditional left
categories such as capitalism and imperialism or centre or periphery used
to analyse its nature and character. Instead of these categories that inter
alia refer to structural and historical constraints on the development of
weak peoples and states, he seeks to stress the critical role of experts in
global governance and speak of the fluidity of the international system
in which the identity of the exploited and the exploited or the oppressor
and oppressed is not always clear. In the paragraphs to follow the role
of experts in the Kennedy scheme of things is considered followed by
his views on the fluidity of the international system. Subsequently, his
changed views on the role of experts and expertise in his more recent
work are discussed. These implicitly acknowledge the weaknesses in his
earlier formulations.

Kennedy is for at least the past two decades focused 'on the work of
experts and the significance of expert knowledge in governing our

---

[152] See ibid., p. 55.
[153] See ibid.
[154] See ibid., p. 56.
[155] See ibid., p. 57.
[156] Indeed, Kennedy himself worries that 'everywhere global capacity is not only too anemic
or irregular to confront the stakes of global poverty, conflict, injustice; it is also the instrument of that poverty, those conflicts, and that injustice'. See ibid., p. 60.

world'.[157] His ambition is to propose 'a general model of expertise and the work of experts in global governance'.[158] Therefore, in speaking of the problems of global governance, Kennedy eschews the vocabulary of structures or interests of state and non-state actors. He insists that 'we are increasingly governed by experts. Not by the American empire, not by 'global capital' – but by experts'.[159] In the event to speak of 'impersonal forces' such as 'the means of production' or 'the interests of the ruling class' is to take attention away from where the real work is done: 'power lies in the capillaries of social and economic life'.[160] From this perspective, the experts do much of the work and produce 'that actual global governance regime'.[161] Indeed, the myriads of decisions taken by experts can be said to have 'colonized' structures of global governance.[162] Kennedy therefore laments that 'we downplay the work of experts' tending to focus on big categories like empire, state, capital and labour. Of course, the experts themselves 'are generally loathe to think of their work in political terms'.[163] They feel that they 'advise, they interpret, but they do not rule'.[164] It is this belief that they do not govern which allows experts to take flight from the experience of 'freedom and responsibility'.[165] In contrast, Kennedy urges us 'to see the expert as free – rather than as determined by interest or ideology'.[166] The expert must therefore assume responsibility for his decisions and actions. This is especially so in the domain of international law as it is characterized by structural indeterminacy allowing expert preferences to play a critical role in the interpretation and application of rules.

In fact, the idea that experts do much of the work in global governance even leads Kennedy to suggest that rather than describe international law as 'the law governing interstate relations', 'it is more accurate to think

---

[157] See ibid., p. 53.
[158] Kennedy, 'Mystery of Global Governance', p. 53. Kennedy is convinced that if only we 'were to understand the mutually constitutive relationship between professional practice and knowledge, we would have displaced the agent-versus-structure debate that has so paralyzed much of the social sciences with respect to international affairs. Rather than agents in structures, we might come to see people with projects, projects of affiliation and disaffiliation, commitment and aversion, and with wills to power and to submission'. Kennedy, 'Mystery of Global Governance', p. 54.
[159] Kennedy, 'Challenging Expert Rule', p. 2.
[160] See ibid., pp. 4, 3.
[161] See ibid., p. 6.
[162] See ibid, p. 12.
[163] See ibid., p. 11.
[164] See ibid.
[165] See ibid., p. 24.
[166] See ibid., p. 23.

of international law as a practice of argument among a rather narrow range of people scattered about in the world, often about the relationship between something that they posit as "international law" and something they refer to as "international society".[167] This group of people share 'professional tools and expertise, as well as a sensibility, viewpoint, and mission ... Their disciplinary consciousness or lexicon is composed of typical problems, a stock of understood solutions, a vocabulary for evaluating new ideas, a sense about their own history and a way of looking at the world'.[168] The group comprises of individuals with projects: 'In my image of the discipline individuals have projects – personal, professional, political – which they pursue in, around and through the argumentative, doctrinal, and institutional materials the discipline offers'.[169] The individual projects are usually identified amidst the 'national' ecology of the discipline (the 'field of origin') and therefore often aligned with national projects. It results in the diversity of professional sensibilities.[170] These projects are 'different in different places'[171] and as a consequence 'international law is applied differently in different places'.[172] But 'the pluralism of professional perspective' is very little understood adding to the mystery of global governance.[173]

The attempt to describe international law in terms of the role of experts, and viewing them as 'individual with projects', is seeing like Kennedy again.[174] Kennedy advances this view essentially to critique the self-understanding of experts that their role in the international legal process is essentially a limited one. The tendency is to attribute outcomes to decisions of actors such as states and international institutions. But in reality it is their decisions that often go to make international law 'very much part

---

[167] Kennedy, 'Disciplines of International Law', p. 84.
[168] David Kennedy, 'My Talk at the ASIL: What is New Thinking in International Law', ASIL Proceedings of the 94th Annual Meeting, April 5–8, 2000, pp. 104–125 at p. 104.
[169] Kennedy, 'Challenging Expert Rule', p. 14.
[170] David Kennedy, 'One, Two, Three, Many Legal Orders: Legal Pluralism and the Cosmopolitan Dream', 31 (2006–07) N.Y.U. Review of Law & Social Change, pp. 641–659 at p. 648.
[171] See ibid, p. 642; Kennedy, 'Disciplines of International Law', p. 17.
[172] Kennedy, 'One, Two, Three', p. 642. As Kennedy observes: 'International lawyers in New Delhi and Washington or Beijing and Paris have different jobs, different professional sensibilities, different relationship to statecraft, and different interpretations of a common professional vocabulary.' See ibid, p. 648. A lack of understanding of legal pluralism has meant the absence of 'strong' science of comparative international law. See ibid., p. 649.
[173] See ibid., p. 642.
[174] Kennedy, 'Disciplines of International Law', p. 14.

of the problem'.[175] Kennedy thus helps to foreground the work of experts and expertise in the production and reproduction of global governance.[176] But to move from reminding the individual expert of his responsibility to suggest that categories such as 'global capital' and 'ruling class' are without purchase is not only unnecessary but also questionable. The 'methodological individualism' that underlies the Kennedy argument, whose sources range from the sociology of Max Weber to the post-structuralist deconstructive work of Michel Foucault, has been for long the subject of debate in social sciences. A few words on the subject are in order to identify its weaknesses and to clarify the IMAIL perspective on the subject. In *Economy and Society*, Max Weber wrote that in doing sociological work scholars often talk about various 'social collectivities, such as states, associations, business corporations, foundations, as if they were individual persons'.[177] But in his view 'these collectivities must be treated as solely the resultants and modes of organization of the particular acts of individual persons, since these alone can be treated as agents in a course of subjectively understandable action'.[178] In general this view is used for 'discrediting historical materialism' with its alleged focus on structures and neglect of individual agents.[179] Be that as it may, in recent times analytical Marxists like Jon Elster (and G. A. Cohen) have come to accept the value of 'methodological individualism', that is, 'the doctrine that all social phenomena (their structure and their change) are in principle explicable only in terms of individuals – their properties, goals, and beliefs'.[180] But, as Elster goes

---

[175] Kennedy, 'One, Two, Three', p. 647.
[176] Thus, for instance, this view helps in showing that 'the political values of experts' within criminal tribunals 'shape the outcome of the process. These experts manage the background norms that permeate the value structure of the tribunals'. Sujith Xavier, 'Theorizing Global Governance Inside Out: A Response to Professor Ladeur', 3 (2012) *Transnational Legal Theory*, pp. 268–284 at p. 281.
[177] Max Weber, *Economy and Society*, Guenther Roth and Claus Wittich, (eds.) (Berkeley: University of California Press, 1968), p. 13.
[178] See ibid.
[179] 'Methodological Individualism' *Stanford Encyclopedia of Philosophy* http://plato.stanford .edu/entries/methodological-individualism/ (accessed on 28 June 2013).
[180] Jon Elster, 'Marxism, Functionalism and Game Theory: The Case for Methodological Individualism', 11 (1982) *Theory and Society*, pp. 453–482 at p. 453. Levine, Sober and Wright define methodological individualism thus: 'Methodological individualism is a claim about *explanation*. It is the view that all social phenomena are best explained by the properties of the individuals who comprise the phenomena; or, equivalently, that any explanation involving macro-level, social concepts should in principle be reduced to micro-level explanations involving only individuals and their properties.' Andrew Levine, Elliot Sober and Erik Olin Wright, 'Marxism and Methodological Individualism', 162 (1987) *New Left Review*, pp. 67–84 at p. 69.

on to add, 'many properties of individuals ... are inherently relational, so that an accurate description of one individual may involve reference to others'.[181] He is not alone in adding this qualification. In fact, scholars subscribing to methodological individualism qualify it in varied ways giving rise to different versions of it.[182] These range from 'versions requiring that social phenomena be fully explained in terms of individuals, to versions requiring only that they be partly explained in terms of individuals'.[183] In exploring the role of experts and expertise Kennedy does not indicate the version of methodological individualism he subscribes to.[184] On the face of it, he embraces, at least at this stage, its strong version, albeit this is not always clear. All that can be concluded is that Kennedy shoots down what is called 'radical holism'. It has been described in the following way:

> Radical Holism stands in sharp contrast to methodological individualism. For radical holists, particular relations among individuals are essentially epiphenomenal with respect to social explanations ... Macro-social categories – capitalism, the state, class relations – are not merely irreducible to micro-level processes. They are unaffected by these processes.[185]

---

[181] Jon Elster, *Making Sense of Marx* (Cambridge: Cambridge University Press, 1985), p. 6.

[182] As one prominent commentator on the subject observes: 'The participants in the debate appear frequently to misunderstand one another and argue at cross-purposes ... One reason for this, no doubt, is that methodological individualism exists in a number of different versions, which must be distinguished for rational debate to be at all possible. It is necessary to know if we have to do with an ontological thesis about social reality, an epistemological thesis about possible knowledge, or a strictly methodological principle about the road to knowledge. It is also necessary to know if methodological individualism is to be understood as a principle concerning concepts, explanations, or laws. It is, above all, necessary to distinguish between strong and weak versions of methodological individualism before discussing its pros and cons and to take a stand in the debate about it.' Lars Udehn, 'The Changing Face of Methodological Individualism', 28 (2002) *Annual Review of Sociology*, pp. 479–507 at p. 480. Udehn goes on to observe that 'to know that a particular social scientist, or philosopher, is a methodological individualist is not very enlightening until you know what kind of methodological individualist he or she is'. See ibid., p. 502.

[183] See ibid., p. 498.

[184] Thus, for instance, it is not clear whether Kennedy subscribes to 'methodological individualism' or 'institutional individualism': 'there is clearly an important difference between the original principle of methodological individualism and institutional individualism. The difference is this: In the original version of methodological individualism, social institutions are something to be explained in terms of individuals. They appear only in the explanandum or, better, the consequent of an explanation, but never in the explanans, or antecedent. In institutional individualism, on the other hand, social institutions explain and, therefore, also appear in the explanans, or antecedent of an explanation'. See ibid., p. 489. This is a critical distinction as in the real world individuals are constrained by social institutions. Kennedy appears to neglect this fact.

[185] Levine, Sober and Wright, 'Marxism', p. 73.

However, critical social science approaches rarely subscribe to the idea of radical holism, albeit some lazy formulations of Marxists, perhaps the target of the Kennedy critique, tend to suggest it. In reality Marxism 'attaches great importance to the "microfoundations" of macroexplanations'.[186] Indeed, few Marxists would disagree with Elster when he observes that 'as a practical matter, the specification of micro-mechanisms is often indispensable for establishing the credibility of macro-level explanations'.[187] But 'microfoundations' can itself mean different things:

> There are four possible explanatory connections between social phenomena and individuals' properties: first, individuals' properties can explain social phenomena; second, social phenomena can explain individuals' properties; third, individuals' properties can explain individuals' properties; and fourth, social phenomena can explain social phenomena. The critique of radical holism implies that the fourth of these explanatory connections is legitimate only when the causal chain in the explanation involves combinations of the first two. That is, social phenomena explain social phenomena only insofar as there are linkages – causal mechanisms – that work through the micro-individual level. Social structures explain social structures via the ways they determine the properties and actions of individuals which in turn determine social structural outcomes. The investigation of such micro-pathways through which macro-structures have their effects is the study of microfoundations.[188]

In other words, the study of microfoundations is complicated by the fact that the different connections between social phenomena and individual properties can be explained in distinct ways.[189] This is, however, not the occasion to rehearse any further the debate on methodological individualism. It may only be observed that some form of methodological individualism is theoretically indispensable in as much as acts of social collectives, and the use of abstract categories to capture them, do not make sense without bringing the individual back in. But in correcting one mistaken perception (that of radical holism) Kennedy appears to contribute another (radical individualism). While it is true that at the end of the day there are only individual experts that take decisions, the intentions of individuals do not exist 'only as psychological states in the heads of

---

186 See ibid., p. 79.
187 See ibid.
188 See ibid., p. 79.
189 It can for instance be explained by 'the Marxist theory of ideology, understood as a theory of the process of forming social subjects'. See ibid., p. 83.

individuals'.[190] These can also be said to lie 'directly embedded in irreducible social practices' and therefore 'the identification of any intention
is impossible without examining the social context within which agents
think and act'.[191] It will be seen later that Koskenniemi commits the same
error in describing the role international lawyers should play, even as
Kennedy attempts to provide a corrective in his latest work on experts
and expertise titled *A World of Struggle*.

It is being argued that the radical individualism of Kennedy at this stage
makes the expert and expertise responsible for much and social forces
and structures for little. He does not sufficiently recognize that experts are
not free to make any choice. A distinction has to be made between the fact
that it is the individual who acts in the final analysis and the suggestion
that he acts under no constraints, whether internal or external. In fact it
is surprising that for someone who refers to the literature on psychiatry
as an intellectual source he does not speak of internal constraints. These
constraints are a creation of both biology and 'an ensemble of social relations'.[192] But to stay with external constraints Kennedy's proposition leads
to exaggerating the actual freedom experts possess while doing their job.
In reality there are serious constraints on individuals that are the function of social structures constituted by what Marxists call the 'mode of
production' and 'relations of production'. These inter alia comprise a set of
institutions, social practices, and modes of thought that tend to divide a
society into different groups that have a great bearing on the choices that
an individual makes. There are, therefore, good reasons for using collective categories such as class, gender, race and caste to understand societies as their membership impacts the choices of individual experts. For
instance, a male expert acts in a particular way because of the workings
and influence of the institutions of patriarchy and accompanying practices. To disconnect the structural constraints from the decision of the
individual expert is to ignore the complex social processes that influence
the decisions of experts. In other words, the existence of macrostructures
that condition the decisions of experts cannot be neglected.[193] Needless
to add, all this does not take away from the significance of the Kennedy

---

[190] Rajeev Bhargava, *What Is Political Theory and Why Do We Need It?* (New Delhi: Oxford University Press 2010), pp. 315–326 at p. 315.
[191] See ibid., pp. 315–316. See also Rajeev Bhargava *Individualism in Social Science* (Oxford: Clarendon Press, 1992).
[192] See the discussion in Chapter 2, pp. 50–53.
[193] Kennedy himself speaks of the 'national ecology' that shapes the orientation of experts.

reminder to the invisible college for 'the exercise of responsible human freedom'.[194]

Indeed, the legal profession needs to face the dark sides of its own work.[195] It too often likes to see itself as speaking truth to power even as it shares power. But that does not make individual decisions responsible for everything and social structures for nothing. Thus, for example, it may be true that expert advice and individual decisions mattered in the invasion of Iraq. But to suggest that the experts alone are responsible for the choices that were posed and not oil or geopolitics is to displace other important reasons and accuse a few individuals of not exercising their freedom well. To be sure it can be argued that it is experts who define economic and geopolitical interests in the first place. But the point is that they do not do it as they please but in the matrix of preceding decisions and continuing interests. If one individual resists taking an unpleasant decision another will be found. The decision to resist must of course be applauded. But one must not forget that the need for resistance arose because of the existence of certain social relations and structures that dictated particular decisions.[196]

However, since Kennedy believes that it is the rule of experts and not of capital or any such thing he is also unable to explain the continuity of

---

[194] Kennedy, 'One, Two, Three', p. 645. He explains: 'The experts who rule our world affect the wealth, status, and power of other people in thousands of small steps, interpreting and enforcing their background norms and institutions that structure activity in the market, in the state, in the family. Their routine work establishes and refurbishes this complex, transboundary legal and institutional milieu, while giving them the experience at every moment that someone else, somewhere else, had the responsibility. We are ruled by experts who structure their world to deny themselves the experience of discretion and responsibility and the rest of us the opportunity to challenge their action'. See ibid., p. 647.

[195] See ibid., p. 646.

[196] There are, of course, choices that experts make that in turn lead to being confronted with difficult choices. Thus, an expert need not join a corporation or an international institution with a track record of human rights violation. But once inside these corporations and institutions – for instance, the two international financial institutions – these individuals are not only socialized into a new culture, but are constrained by the fact of their employment to reach particular interpretations of situations or rules or to take certain decisions. In so far as taking responsibility for particular interpretations and decisions is concerned the causal chain between the expert decision and harm caused is not always easy to establish. These interpretations and decisions are also often taken collectively leading to a reduced sense of individual responsibility. To be sure, Kennedy is right in suggesting that there is always a certain degree of flexibility in every situation and external constraints may often be hyped to avoid responsibility. On the other hand, it is difficult to imagine that the top management of International Monetary Fund would permit experts exercise particular choices that went against institutional policies.

ideas among experts, especially of Western experts.[197] It is ironic in this respect that Kennedy constantly reminds his 'colleagues' in the field that what they think is 'new' is really 'old' and that it is time to ponder over this discursive reality. This charge, of course, discomforts the invisible college as no individual, or a community of scholars, likes to be reminded that what is advanced as a new idea is in reality a pale imitation of a product marketed decades ago in the bazaar of ideas.[198] But the more crucial point is that methodological individualism does not allow Kennedy to seriously explore the reasons for why moments of renewal are déjà vu moments. He does not consider the possibility that acts of renewal are constrained by deep structures that limit the space for fresh or innovative thinking. There is arguably a link between capitalism, imperialism and particular legal projects that cannot be snapped, even as they may assume distinct forms in different historical phases giving a sense of break and renewal. It is therefore not entirely an accident that 'rarely [Western] international lawyers argue for particular projects in terms of the specific distributional or strategic consequences for particular groups'.[199] The answer lies in talking about global structures that have been in place since the sixteenth century. These are the structures of global capitalism that shape international legal structures. This is not to invoke some kind of old Marxist base-superstructure model, or deny the role of experts, but simply to remind that the answer to the nature and character of law and legal process cannot be found in the decisions of individual experts alone, other than in the mundane sense that individuals alone act in the final analysis.[200] An internal critique of the law and the critical role of experts only go so far to explain the state of the law and discipline and no further. The realization of the limits of internal critique and the role assigned to experts is perhaps one factor that explains Kennedy's turn to political

[197] As he points out 'the conventional tale of international legal history is a progress narrative, a fable about how the discipline grew and who its enemies are – above all, this history teaches, turn your back on politics and ideology, and then also on philosophy, theory, and form'. Kennedy, 'Disciplines of International Law', p. 92.

[198] 'Kennedy suggests that while successive generations of international lawyers seem committed to understanding their professional role as one of engaging in renewal, reform or 'new thinking', in fact 'international lawyers return repeatedly to two basic axes of philosophical disputation, each with its own well-developed vocabulary: the relationship law should seek to strike between an international community and sovereign autonomy and the most effective balance between a more or less formal law'. Orford, 'Destiny of International Law', p. 468.

[199] Kennedy, 'When Renewal Repeats', pp. 372–373.

[200] For a detailed discussion on the metaphor of base and superstructure see Chapter 7, pp. 449–461.

economy and more recently to a slightly less extravagant understanding of the role of experts and expertise.[201]

D.   On Law and Political Economy

It has been the burden of argument of the previous section that individuals and social structures co-constitute each other in complex ways. In his recent writings Kennedy admits that just global governance is not possible 'until the political economy of the world has been rebuilt'.[202] He attributes the conclusion to the fact that 'government everywhere is buffeted by economic forces, captured by economic interests, engaged in economic pursuits'.[203] In this respect, he also lays stress on the constitutive nature of law which is not mere epiphenomenon but 'a language in which governance is written and performed'.[204] According to Kennedy:

> It is now clear that the elements of economic life – capital, labor, credit, money, liquidity – are creatures of law. The same can be said for the elements of political life – power and right. Law not only *regulates* these things, it creates them. The history of political and economic life is therefore also a history of institutions and laws. Law constitutes the actors, places them in structures, and helps set the terms for their interaction. It often provides the language – and the stakes – for economic and political struggle. As a result, legal arrangements offer a privileged window onto political economic dynamics.[205]

In view of the critical role law plays in shaping global economic structures and processes, he suggests that 'scholars should not shy away from *developing macro-scale pictures of global political economy*, if only because thinking about more technical matters often rests on broad convictions about the nature of the world which no longer hold'.[206] They should among other things address the crucial question of 'the dynamic relationship

---

[201] It is difficult to believe that as astute a thinker as Kennedy would not have realized before long the limitations of 'methodological individualism'.

[202] Kennedy, 'Preface', p. x.

[203] See ibid., p. ix.

[204] See ibid., p. xi.

[205] David Kennedy, 'Law and the Political Economy of the World', 26 (2013) *Leiden Journal of International Law*, pp. 7–48 at p. 8. He notes that his insights are drawn from 'heterogeneous, institutionalist, realist, critical, sociological, postmodernist, post-Marxist, progressive' intellectual traditions. But he essentially follows Karl Klare, Duncan Kennedy and others of the 'old CLS' in laying stress on the significant role law plays in creating and shaping economic actors and institutions.

[206] See ibid., p. 9; emphasis added.

between centres and peripheries'.[207] He also exhorts international lawyers to pay attention to the distributional impact of international laws and institutions. Kennedy argues that if this is not on the agenda of international law experts it is because they are keeping economics, politics and law apart through 'simply doing their job', that is, by interpreting their role in a manner that leaves others to do economics and politics.[208] Instead, he calls on international lawyers 'to break free of the technical agendas which orient the work of the professions'.[209]

This invitation to international law experts to shed formalism and embrace political economy is most welcome. However, two departures from Kennedy's earlier positions need to be flagged. First, the turn to political economy represents a move away from the view of young Kennedy that there is no stable domain that relates political economy to law. In the new understanding they co-constitute each other in a manner that 'legal arrangements offer a privileged window onto political economic dynamics'. But as he enters the field Kennedy contends that 'surprisingly little scholarship in the international legal field aims to illuminate the global distribution of political authority and economic growth'.[210] This move parallels the one he made in his early writings in which he declared the discipline in crisis, neglecting efforts to address it. In this instance, both TWAIL and MAIL have been for long analysing 'the global distribution of public authority and economic growth'.[211] In fact, TWAIL contends that an approach to international law that ignores the power of Western states in shaping international law and institutions and the economic divide between and within the Global North and the Global South is ignoring the central questions of international law today. Be that as it may, Kennedy has now recognized the limits of the focus on the internal structure of international law. Second, his views on 'law and political economy' depart from the earlier reluctance to speak about 'structures' or 'global capital'. He now invites scholars to develop 'macro-scale pictures of global political economy'. He speaks about law placing actors in 'structures' and shapes their 'interaction'. He uses categories like 'capital' and 'labor'. He of course still speaks of the role of experts and expertise. But he now appears to subscribe to a weak version of methodological individualism.

---

[207] See ibid., p. 12.
[208] See ibid., pp. 15, 26.
[209] See ibid., p. 20.
[210] See ibid., p. 9.
[211] A single reference to Antony Anghie is all there is in a lengthy article on the subject. There are no references to the work of other TWAIL scholars.

This version is entirely compatible with different versions of Marxism that do not subscribe to, as most do not, radical holism. But on his part, to make his version of methodological individualism internally coherent, Kennedy needed to revisit his thesis on the role of experts i.e., expert counts for everything and structures for nothing. As we shall see presently, he has done so in his most recent work.

It is time to analyse some of his contestable propositions on global political economy focusing particularly on his thesis on fluidity of international law. A good example of which is his statement that 'the difference between the First and Third Worlds has eroded because all nations now face political, social, and economic challenges once typical of the Third World'.[212] He writes that 'centre–periphery is not a strong model of *power* or *domination* focused on the identification of agency, causation, and effect. It is a model of relative *positions* in a field and the dynamics which develop between them over time. The point is not that the centre does this or that *to* the periphery'.[213] He explains:

> To claim that *this* is peripheral to *that* requires a suspension of awareness of life's complexity, irrationality, and unpredictability. Even then, it can be difficult to tell just who is the centre and who is the periphery. There are centres in the periphery, peripheries in the centre. More importantly, perhaps, centres can *feel* peripheral, style themselves marginal, bemoan their distance from power. And in every family we can identify the peripheral drama queens around whose instability and weakness the entire family rotates. In the end, centre–periphery analytics *are both interpretations* – this is how things are – and, when the interpretation holds, persuades, reconfigures the situation, interventions. To call out the perpetual drama queen victim on his centrality is to name and to shame, whether the ostensible victim is an adolescent or a nation.[214]

Even conceding 'life's complexity, irrationality and predictability' many of the formulations on centre-periphery in this passage is puzzling. Take for instance the view that 'it can be difficult to tell just who is the centre and who is the periphery'.[215] This is certainly true in some ways. For

[212] Kennedy, 'Law and the Political Economy', p. 10.
[213] See ibid., p. 25.
[214] See ibid., p. 29; emphasis added.
[215] This understanding was earlier advanced by Hardt and Negri who wrote that concepts such as centre and periphery are now all but useless, because 'it is no longer possible to demarcate large geographical zones as center and periphery, North and South'. According to Hardt and Negri, there are today '"no differences of nature" between the United States and Brazil, Britain and India, "only differences of degree"'. Michael Hardt and Antonio Negri, *Empire* (Cambridge ,MA: Harvard University Press, 2000), p. 335.

example, the operation of international finance capital has undermined the sovereignty of both first and third world states. Neither world can effectively regulate its boundless mobility, complex operations and fantasy products. It may also be readily conceded that there is a periphery in the centre as there is a centre in the periphery. It can equally be admitted that there are emerging powers today that can be classified as centres vis-à-vis the rest of the periphery. But Kennedy goes much further when he claims that centre–periphery analytics are *merely interpretations* that have little to do with reality. In effect what Kennedy is seeking to do here is to undermine the material reality of imperialism. It makes him overlook, at least at the methodological level, the sufferings of millions of people in the periphery because of the 'imperial' doings of the centre *to* the periphery. A vast majority of nations in the periphery do not simply *feel* peripheral but *are* peripheral. The periphery still remains the principal site of exploitation with its growing reserve army of labour. The periphery is also the geographical space in which force is used to secure commercial advantages.[216] The fluidity of relations between the centre and periphery are not such that positions of states in the Global South can be exchanged with nations of the Global North. For the rest TWAIL and MAIL have advanced the argument that the nature of imperialism is changing. It has inter alia been argued that the transnational fractions of the capitalist classes in the emerging powers have a coincidence of interests with their counterparts in the first world leading to the emergence of a transnational capitalist class (TCC).[217] But Kennedy is not speaking of fluidity in global class forces or of a global class divide replacing or being superimposed on the geographical divide. He is speaking within the frame of a sovereign state system. In the event, to deny that power and domination of the first world continues to be a palpable reality is to embrace the position of the mainstream. Further, even if it were to be accepted that the first and third world face the same 'challenges' it needs to be acknowledged that these are met in situations and circumstances mostly defined by the centre. The relative positions of centre and periphery, or the fluidity of position, are constituted in the matrix of their historical relationship. It cannot be overlooked that the shape and content of international laws and institutions have been determined by Western imperialist states since the

---

[216] James Thuo Gathii, *War, Commerce, and International Law* (New York: Oxford University Press, 2010).

[217] B. S. Chimni, 'Capitalism, Imperialism and International Law in the Twenty First Century', 14 (2012) *Oregon Review of International Law*, pp. 17–45.

sixteenth century. That advantage has not suddenly withered away. In other words, the centre does do 'this or that *to* the periphery'. If Kennedy does not see it this way it is because of the kind of history and social science he does in which capitalism, colonialism and imperialism rarely figure. It is, therefore, not surprising that his (early) writings on the aspects of the history of international law and institutions simply do not address the theme of imperialism and international law.

The missing category of 'imperialism' in the Kennedy writings leads him in the final analysis to go along with the liberal view of changing global order. It is important to note that the category is missing not only because of the way he does his history but also the manner in which he approaches the subject of political economy (or perhaps it is the other way around). He entirely rejects 'the idea that questions of political economy can best be answered *either* by large scale narratives of historical necessity – the nature of capitalism, and so forth –*or* by ethnographies and micro-sociological study of the impact of "globalization" on very particular communities and transactions'.[218] Once Kennedy discards arguments related to the 'nature of capitalism' he is also able to dispense with the phenomenon of imperialism. He is, so to speak, able to rid of explanations of imperialism linked to the universalizing nature of capitalism offered by the likes of a Rosa Luxemburg or a David Harvey. His 'macro scale picture of global economy' is instead focused 'on the middle range':

> The idea is to use the background world of law and legal expertise as a window for *interpreting the foreground of world political economy*. The hypothesis is that law offers an index of tools and stakes for interaction between centres and peripheries in the world political economic system.[219]

But even if the 'best' way of doing political economy is to perform 'middle range' law jobs there is no reason that it cannot be accomplished while studying the nature of capitalism or micro-sociological studies of the impact of globalization. Indeed, it can be argued that addressing the 'middle range' without keeping the nature of capitalism and the impact of globalization on quotidian life firmly in view can lead to serious distortions of understanding of the political economy of global governance. In any case there is no reason to choose between the different possible ways of doing political economy even as a researcher may decide to dedicate oneself to one or other level of analysis. Thus, TWAIL and MAIL have not only looked at the nature of capitalism and imperialism, but

---

[218]   Kennedy, 'Law and the Political Economy', p. 26.
[219]   See ibid.; emphasis added.

also done extensive work in 'the middle range' to show how third world countries lose critical policy space through the workings of international laws and institutions.[220] On the other hand, to suggest that 'the middle range' has nothing to do with the 'nature of capitalism', or to disregard it, is to accept the mainstream narrative of the workings of the liberal international order.

An important reason that Kennedy focuses on the middle range is that it is more in consonance with his position on the central role of experts and expertise in global governance. The insistence on 'interpreting the foreground of world political economy' is explained by the concern that while moving away from radical methodological individualism he does not wish to stray too far as it would compromise his earlier position. Kennedy wishes to occupy the middle ground between large scale narratives and micro-sociological studies in a way that allows him to retain his previous and continuing emphasis on the role of experts. For instance, in an essay on the different phases of the evolution of law and development thinking since the Second World War, he begins by observing that he will 'say very little about how thinking in these phases was linked to broader social and political events'.[221] Instead he seeks to 'track the changing relationship between economic and legal ideas in development expertise' to unravel 'the mystery of their possible political associations'.[222] Kennedy

[220] See B. S. Chimni, 'WTO, Democracy and Development: A View from the South', 40 (2006) *Journal of World Trade*, pp. 5–36; B. S. Chimni, 'International Institutions Today: An Imperial Global State in the Making', 15 (2004) *European Journal of International Law*, pp. 1–39; B. S. Chimni, 'The Political Economy of the Uruguay Round of Negotiations: A Perspective', 29 (1992) *International Studies*, pp. 135–158; James Thuo Gathii, 'How Necessity May Preclude State Responsibility for Compulsory Licensing Under the TRIPS Agreement', 31 (2006) *North Carolina Journal of International Law and Regulation*, pp. 943–970; James Thuo Gathii, 'Construing Intellectual Property Rights and Competition Policy Consistently With Facilitating Access to Affordable Aids Drugs to Low- End Consumers', 53 (2001) *Florida Law Review*, pp. 728–788; Obiora C. Okafor, 'Between Elite Interests and Pro-Poor Resistance: The Nigerian Courts and Labour-led Anti-Fuel Price Hike Struggles (1999–2007)', 54 (2010) *The Journal of African Law*, pp. 95–118; Obiora C. Okafor, 'Irrigating the Famished Fields: The Impact of Labour-led Struggles on Policy and Action in Nigeria (1999–2007)', 27 (2009) *Journal of Contemporary African Studies*, pp. 159–175; Obiora C. Okafor, 'Remarkable Returns: On the Influence of a Labour-led Movement on Legislative Reasoning, Process and Action in Nigeria', 47 (2009) *Journal of Modern African Studies*, pp. 241–266.
[221] David Kennedy, 'The "Rule of Law," Political Choices, and Development Common Sense in David M. Trubek and Alvaro Santos (eds.), *The New Law and Economic Development: A Critical Appraisal* (New York: Cambridge University Press, 2006), pp. 95–173 at pp. 95–96.
[222] See ibid., p. 98.

appears to suggest that it is simply the way that the relationship between law and development is conceived or political economy imagined by experts that determines whether nations fail or succeed. In different eras there are different models that capture the imagination of experts and drive the law and development agenda. It has nothing to do with large scale narratives and imperatives of capitalism or imperialism.

A second reason that accounts for the stress on the middle range is that it allows Kennedy to reinforce the idea of fluidity of the relationship between the centre and the periphery. It is in the middle range that fluidity is most easily evidenced. Thus examples can be given of the periphery organizing itself to wrench some concessions from the centre in particular legal regimes. There is also the phenomenon of emerging powers becoming part of G 20 and allegedly having a voice in the shaping of global governance. In the circumstances, to speak of large scale narratives of imperialism is beside the point.

In the final analysis, what Kennedy hopes to do is to reclaim the critical edge of NAIL from other critical schools such as TWAIL and MAIL. He is trying to carve out a distinct approach while caricaturing those who talk about the 'nature of capitalism' or 'international law from below'. In the process he is forgetful that you cannot look at the 'middle range' as a completely autonomous phenomenon suspended as if it were in mid-air. In actuality it is merely a particular manifestation of macrostructures constituted by global capitalism that impact everyday life. Second, he hopes to advance a critique of the political economy of global governance that is more acceptable to mainstream international law scholars. By speaking to the 'middle range' he is not only engaging with the world that most interests the mainstream but is also able to avoid using traditional left vocabulary that troubles the former. Indeed, he is able to suggest that the centre does not do anything to the periphery. It would however be a tragedy of sorts if he were now to join, admittedly through a 'complex, irrational and unpredictable' process, the mainstream that he has been so rightly critical of.

E.   Rule of Experts: Take Two

While that has not yet been the case, his views are evolving in a conventional direction. In his latest work Kennedy makes two moves that deserve attention. First, as will be seen, he explicitly gestures towards the constraints within which experts and expertise play a role. Earlier he had merely used phrases such as 'national ecology' to indicate the matrix

in which expertise evolves. This of course does not mean that his penchant for the inside view has diminished. He still speaks of developing
'an approach to conflict in global affairs from the inside out' and in this
respect offers 'a cartographic model of expert struggle from the perspective of those who engage in it'.[223] Yet the accent on external constraints is
discernible. Second, he adopts a more mainstream critical stance towards
the role of international law in producing inequality and injustice. He
earlier avoided doing so and in any case chose to emphasize the need to
look at international law from the inside. He is less hesitant today. It is
worth reviewing these subtle shifts in his views.

Insofar as the role of experts and expertise is concerned, Kennedy
continues to argue that both play a critical role in the international legal
process. Since 'expert rule mobilizes knowledge as power'[224] he wishes to
'bring knowledge practices and power practices into the same frame'.[225]
He sees them 'as the crossroads where they intersect'.[226] But now Kennedy
frames his focus on experts and expertise more to point to 'the limits of
system analytics'.[227] He accepts the value of the 'conventional approach',
but wishes to 'compensate for some classical limitations of the actor/
structure/system framework'.[228] He wishes to reveal 'the tendency to reify
the actors and structures one sees, a bias towards order, and the potential to overlook the knowledge work of experts with the result that their
shared logic is treated as the logic of the system itself'.[229] He is merely concerned that effects or outcomes are traced to social forces or abstractions
like capital or corporations or international institutions suggesting that
'no actual person did anything' or that individual as experts are not 'ruling or distributing: they are advising, interpreting, informing'.[230] He therefore continues to stress the need to explore 'the way experts forget their
struggles and their role in distribution' or refuse to know 'its power and
limit'.[231] He stresses once again how 'we excuse experts – as experts excuse
themselves – from responsibility for the outcomes of their work'.[232] This is

[223] David Kennedy, *A World of Struggle: How Power, Law, and Expertise Shape Global Political
Economy* (Princeton, NJ: Princeton University Press, 2016), p. 55.
[224] See ibid., p. 7.
[225] See ibid., p. 4.
[226] See ibid.
[227] See ibid., p. 75.
[228] See ibid.
[229] See ibid.
[230] See ibid., pp. 28, 3.
[231] See ibid., p. 5.
[232] See ibid., p. 277.

because it is believed that the experts are not central to global governance and it is others who decide.[233] But when the two set of observations are read together it can be said that Kennedy is veering towards a mild methodological individualism position. He now notes the constraints placed on decision making by the 'context' which 'include the "drivers" that the decision makers are ready to ignore at their own peril: technological, historical, social, economic or political "realities"'.[234] Kennedy goes on to observe:

> This is what social scientists speak of as 'structure': the arrangements that shape and constrain the decisions of agents. Here we find the impersonal forces of the material world and the social system as well as the immutable beliefs of ideology or religion. The context is not a black box of subjective preference, nor the brute force of objective necessity. It is the settled outcome of background work. Interests and facts relevant for decision are socially constructed. The place where that happens – and could happen differently – is the 'background'[235].

According to Kennedy, 'the *background* is the space where people argue about and make real the claim that something or someone is foreground or context'.[236] While Kennedy goes some way to accept constraints and mitigate methodological individualism by adopting its weak version, he continues to treat the 'material world' as 'socially constructed'. He is able to do so by limiting himself once again to the intermediate decision-making processes. He speaks again of 'midlevel observations and hypotheses' or of exploring the area 'between big systems and ethnographic study' where his thesis works more than in other spaces where these decisions assume more predictability.[237] Later he speaks of 'the midlevel processes by which individual actions aggregate into systemic actions' but stresses that these 'remain obscure'.[238]

All in all there is little doubt that there is a delicate shift away from his earlier positions. Expert rule now takes place amongst structures and processes that may have been put in place by experts and their expertise but yet limit the alternatives that can be explored in making the world a better place to live in. It is no longer about relatively free experts and expertise shaping the world but experts embedded in a world even if it

---

[233] See ibid., p. 278.
[234] See ibid., p. 112.
[235] See ibid.
[236] See ibid., p. 114; emphasis in original.
[237] See ibid., pp. 2–4.
[238] See ibid., p. 77. See also p. 81.

is of their own making. Kennedy now seeks to combine the insights of Max Weber and Michel Foucault with that of Pierre Bourdieu[239] who is concerned with 'the domain within which expertise simultaneously arises and is practiced'.[240] He then goes on to observe that the well-known category 'habitus' used by Bourdieu 'expresses the difficulty of articulating what people think and do together in a reciprocal relationship with the context in which they do it rather than a solution'.[241] But he does not tell us how far the influence of Bourdieu extends and how he combines his insights with that of Weber and Foucault. In fact Kennedy never makes his theory explicit leaving it to readers to arrive at it from his analysis. Be that as it may, he appears to be moving towards the idea that men do not make history as they please but in a given world of social relations, with the difference that in the case of Kennedy the world of ideas is seen as constitutive in ways that inverts Marx's famous *Preface to the Contribution to Political Economy*. Both see them as co-constitutive but the one assigns primacy to the material world and the other to ideas as it works through experts and expertise. However, it may be added that he describes the work of experts in so many different ways that it is often difficult to tell which position he is aligned to. On the one hand, he now uses categories like 'ruling classes' or 'the global managerial class'[242] and on the other he believes that the experts can together change the world.[243] It is not as if the two propositions are irreconcilable, but an effort has to be made in that direction.

The value of his approach to experts and expertise are many. He has a point when he says that particular institutional arrangements 'are not absolute requirements'.[244] That would be to be captive to a functional logic that is debilitating for any critical analysis that also believes in reforms. He is in this regard also right to suggest the 'plasticity' of institutional forms or of law[245] and the malleability of expertise.[246] He aptly asks you to bear in mind that it is 'common to overestimate the rigor of expert analytics'[247] or the internal coherence of ideologies.[248] His model is useful

[239] On the influence of Bourdieu, see ibid., p. 282 fn. 7.
[240] See ibid.
[241] See ibid.
[242] See ibid., pp. 41, 44.
[243] See ibid., p. 279.
[244] See ibid., p. 42.
[245] See ibid., pp. 64, 84.
[246] See ibid., p. 136.
[247] See ibid., p. 3.
[248] See ibid., pp. 138–139.

in understanding how changes can take place within a particular 'context' (or 'system') and presumably slowly, step by step, work towards transform-ing it. Kennedy provides an important corrective to the lazy or determin-ist Marxist views that deduce outcomes from general propositions. He is also correct in suggesting that 'it is all too common to picture the impact of ideas as a straightforward capture: the actor becomes the agent of the idea, belief, or ideology'.[249] In those scenarios you always know in advance the conclusion of ongoing negotiations or disputes or any other legal process. But Kennedy overcompensates for the determinist view. What should have been proposed as an important corrective to the reductionist Marxist critique which uses reified categories like 'state' 'global capitalism' and 'corporation' is presented as a full-blown theory that replaces them. It is at this point that his understanding ceases to be helpful. He makes a theory of 'midlevel processes' a theory of all processes. It seeks to colonize all theories of non-midlevel processes. In attempting to do so he snaps the link of ideas with developments in the material world that he other-wise accepts co-constitute each other. To put it differently, his views are insightful and productive till he confines himself to midlevel processes in which experts and expertise produce the system.[250] It helps highlight the role of individuals and therefore their ethical responsibility in mak-ing some kinds of arguments and avoiding others. The problem arises when he turns his midlevel theory to a grand theory. Kennedy is also not alert to the fact that his views can be co-opted by the mainstream and deployed to sustain a 'narrative of progress'. Otherwise it would have been expected that Kennedy would explore the limits of transformation that can be brought about through the work of experts and expertise. In other words, how plastic are institutional forms or law? Is a just world order constrained only by the language and work of of experts and expertise? Are actors in no way agents of ideas, beliefs or ideologies? Not everything is fluid or in flux. But Kennedy does not attempt to demonstrate this.

But in keeping with his reference to 'constraints' he is now more willing to, as if it were, look at international law from the outside. He does not any longer insist that the internal view deserves priority. In fact, Kennedy repeatedly observes that 'when people reflect on the role of law in global affairs, they rarely focus on law as an instrument of distribution or cause of inequality'.[251] Usually they think of it 'benignly as a sign of the potential of

[249] See ibid., p. 77.
[250] See ibid., p. 84.
[251] See ibid., p. 218. For the same sentiment, see also pp. 171, 177, 217 and 219.

order and justice in global affairs'.[252] It is surprising however that he does not mention in this context the contribution of TWAIL, FtAIL and MAIL. If he were speaking only of the United States, he may have mentioned Richard Falk's WOMP and others. The target of his critique is perhaps the mainstream to which his observations certainly apply. But he could have noted that the other critical schools do think of international law as impacting distribution and producing inequality and justice. Be that as it may, Kennedy now sees international law as 'an ever more powerful struggle tool for people struggling for advantage on the global scale'.[253] He writes that 'legal arrangements everywhere affect the balance of power between groups, changing the bargaining power of individuals and firms in ways they are not able to change or negotiate away on their own'.[254] Further that 'global inequalities rest not only on the legal outcomes of individual and group struggles settling the status of forces among them but on arrangements that affect the dynamic interactions among those who lead and those who lag'.[255] In his view, 'legal arrangements structure patterns of interaction between rich and poor in a variety of ways that encourage the compounding of gains'.[256] Therefore, law 'enables the capture of gains, distributes power and resources between groups, and structures relations between leading and lagging regions, firms, and nations'.[257] He then goes on to correctly note that 'people who readily understand allocations among firms, industries, or nations as the outcome of struggle nevertheless interpret patterns of social inequality as in some way natural'.[258]

That is as external (or instrumental) a picture of international law as it can get. It may not be difficult to pull out observations from Kennedy's earlier work to this effect, but these were not as stark and systemic as now and also unaccompanied by the emphasis on looking at international law from the inside. The external view now firmly coexists with the internal view. In this instance, the concern is that Kennedy is unable to effectively bridge the internal and external divide. He works with binaries, treating the inside and outside as separate spaces, and therefore misses the intimate and dialectical relationship between the two. But on the positive

[252] See ibid.
[253] See ibid.
[254] See ibid., p. 196.
[255] See ibid., p. 199.
[256] See ibid., p. 200.
[257] See ibid., p. 217.
[258] See ibid., p. 197.

side Kennedy sets the balance right between the inside and the outside. He has perhaps realized that the engagement with external dimension of international law cannot be avoided in view of the growing legalization of international affairs. Kennedy writes that 'the expansion of law's reach in global affairs and the breadth of practical innovation since the nineteenth century are difficult to overstate'.[259] Therefore, 'the legalization of global political and economic life has made legal expertise a predominant language of engagement in transnational struggle'.[260] This is a phenomenon that TWAIL and MAIL have been long emphasizing. In fact, it may not be wrong to surmise that in the face of powerful external critiques advanced by TWAIL, FtAIL and MAIL the internal counterpart did not look as interesting as it earlier did when it was certainly refreshing. Kennedy was therefore compelled to look at material dimensions of the growth of international law. The problem, however, is the lack of an integrated view of international law that combines the internal and external understanding so as to explain the form and content of international law as two aspects of the same phenomenon.

F.   On Law and War

In the last decade or so, prior to turning to political economy and to explicating his 'new' views on experts and expertise, Kennedy turned his gaze to other dimensions of international law, in particular the institution of war. He came up with searing insights. Rather than accept the widely held view that international law is opposed to war, and disciplines its conduct when it takes place, he views it in great measure as part of the problem. Kennedy here relies on the insight of CLS scholars who have noted that whatever the social phenomenon 'law is always "in" from the start'.[261] In the same mode Kennedy argues that it is difficult to separate the realm of law from the institution of war as 'there is law at every turn'.[262] In fact, 'law and force flow into one another'.[263]

---

[259] See ibid., p. 221.
[260] See ibid., p. 171.
[261] Karl Klare (2008) 'Critical Legal Studies in a Nutshell'. Paper distributed at the British Critical Legal Studies Conference, Glasgow, September 2008, p. 1 (on file with the author).
[262] David Kennedy, *Of War and Law* (Princeton, NJ: Princeton University Press, 2006), p. 25.
[263] See ibid., pp. 165. Kennedy goes on to write of 'the delicate partnership of war and law' and the fact that 'law no longer stands outside violence, silent or prohibitive. Law also permits injury, as it privileges, channels, structures, legitimates, and facilitates acts of war'. See ibid., p. 167.

It is, of course, widely recognized that the institution of war is constituted in complex ways by international law. The international legal process defines, among other things, what 'force' means, when the use of force is permissible, and the limits on the use of force. But what Kennedy underscores is that there is nothing 'natural' about any of the rules relating to *jus ad bellum* and *jus ad bello*; these can be differently imagined, constituted, interpreted and applied. In fact the relevant rules are derived from distinctive human experiences and ways of doing international law. The latter methods range from formalism to pragmatism to pluralism. But the persistent theme has been to present as 'natural' particular rules, interpretations and applications of the law relating to the use of force in terms of geography, ends and disciplines.

The underlying idea that international law tends to facilitate and legitimize war is not new. Traditional international law legitimized unspeakable violence against colonial peoples in the name of bringing civilization to them; the laws of war were never made applicable to them.[264] What is perhaps new in the Kennedy argument is that in the contemporary world states harness 'law as a weapon, law as a tactical ally, law as a strategic asset, and instrument of war'.[265] States are able to use law in these different ways for a number of reasons. First, there is a proliferation of 'sites at which official rules of war are given meaning'; these sites are both national and international. The international sites range from 'peacekeeping' to international criminal tribunals; the context of each site makes it possible to advance different considerations creating space for interpretations of rules of war that assist warfare.[266] Second, there are the 'ambiguities, gaps and contradictions' that mark legal categories (such as 'force' or 'self defense') that are the basis of distinguishing between situations of war and non-war.[267] These legal categories have become 'far too spongy', that is to say, 'legal materials are elastic enough to permit diverse interpretation'.[268] In the instance of international humanitarian laws (IHL) this can impact even basic distinctions like that between combatants and civilians. Third, the military decision making apparatus is able to use the indeterminacies

---

[264] Frederick Megret, 'From "savages" to "unlawful combatants": A Postcolonial Look at International Humanitarian Law's "other"' in Anne Orford (ed.), *International Law and its Others* (Cambridge: Cambridge University Press, 2006), pp. 265–317.

[265] David Kennedy, 'Lawfare and Warfare' in James Crawford and Martti Koskenniemi (eds.), *The Cambridge Companion to International Law* (Cambridge: Cambridge University Press, 2012), pp. 158–184 at p. 160.

[266] See ibid., pp. 163, 165.

[267] See ibid., p. 161.

[268] See ibid., pp. 165, 167.

in modern law of war and the sharing of responsibility in decision making to avoid assuming ethical responsibility for death and suffering caused in the course of war.[269]

A significant reason that law has come to be deployed as a weapon is because 'law-legal categorization' has today become 'a communication tool'.[270] It is mobilized by either a state or the military or private security companies to explain the use of violence in the name of justice. It has meant that 'those who exercise power as truth' are increasingly 'pulled toward ever more hyperbolic invocations of justice and law'.[271] In this process, states and their experts are able to exploit even the efforts of those who use the language of the law to speak truth to power. In fact, Kennedy contends that by making the move the truth speakers enter into 'a strategic alliance with those whose power becomes truth' and in the process 'find themselves drawn into the collaborative exercise of violence'.[272] More precisely, by engaging the Other in the name of realism and pragmatism, and indeed on the very ground of law and justice, the critics concede ground to power. Those who wield power take that opportunity to more loudly proclaim their commitment to law, humanity and justice.

However, the question arises if the critics are eternally trapped by the language of international law into playing into the hands of the 'enemy'? To be sure, Kennedy's emphasis on the manipulation of law and legal categories is well taken. So is his stress on assuming personal responsibility for causing harm. But Kennedy's understanding of the legal process is totalizing as it suggests that law and legal arguments can be endlessly manipulated. Therefore, these can never be used to speak truth to power. Such a view leaves no space for articulating critical opposition in the language of law as it inevitably becomes complicit with power. In his understanding there can be no effective distinction made in the terrain of law between good and bad arguments. While there is an element of truth in this proposition it assumes an extreme form in not leaving room for the creative use of law to oppose power. But Kennedy always seems happy to look at the intricacies of a subject without suggesting ways and vocabularies in which to do what should be done, in this instance to oppose war and mindless violence.

Kennedy also does not sufficiently recognize that the opposition to the institution of war is not merely in the domain of arguments (i.e., the

---

[269] Kennedy, *Of War and Law*, pp. 168–169.
[270] Kennedy, 'Lawfare and Warfare', p. 166.
[271] See ibid., p. 178.
[272] See ibid., p 178.

discourse of experts) but also at the level of social movements against war and violations of laws of war. The opposing legal arguments are given meaning and power through resistance. Or maybe he does recognize this and is suggesting that that is where energy should be concentrated rather than indulge in pragmatic engagement in the terrain of law. Power may still prevail in the final analysis, but the engagement will not at least provide legitimacy to the institution of war. But the lingering feeling remains that Kennedy does not sufficiently appreciate that legal arguments also de-legitimize power and that international rule of law matters. It is true that legal categories can be manipulated but they cannot be endlessly so. Their abuse can be exposed through counter-hegemonic narratives.

G. On Human Rights

Kennedy has also brought his deconstructive method to bear on international human rights law. He has argued that 'on balance' the human rights movement today is 'more part of the problem ... than part of the solution'.[273] Kennedy readily admits that 'human rights movement has done a great deal of good, freeing individuals from great deal of harm, and raising the standards by which governments are judged'.[274] But, it is precisely this positive contribution that has made the language of human rights 'a universal ideology, an international standard of legitimacy for sovereign power, a common vernacular of justice for a global civil society'.[275] It has resulted in the human rights movement 'bit(ing) off more than it could chew'[276] and taken attention away from alternative vocabularies of justice. Indeed, human rights movement has become 'a status quo project for a stable time'.[277] It has even become 'a vocabulary of the centre against the periphery'.[278] The pervasive presence of human rights movement has meant that it is not simply opposing power but is also imbued with power. It today gets to share power with ruling elites. In

---

[273] David Kennedy, 'The International Human Rights Movement: Part of the Problem?', 14 (2002) *Harvard Human Rights Journal*, pp. 101–126 at p. 101.

[274] David Kennedy, 'The International Human Rights Regime: Still Part of the Problem' in Rob Dickinson, Elena Katselli, Colin Murray and Ole W. Pedersen (eds.), *Examining Critical Perspectives on Human Rights* (Cambridge: Cambridge University Press, 2013), pp. 19–34 at p. 19.

[275] See ibid., p. 20.

[276] See ibid., p. 21.

[277] See ibid., p. 34.

[278] See ibid., pp. 25–26.

many a case it is the human rights movement that decides when the ruling elites of powerful states should exercise power, most often in the periphery. The movement can thus legitimize the use of force in the name of human rights.[279] When it does so, the costs do not matter for after all it is the movement that has taken the decision. It is thus both judge and jury. But for these very reasons time may be running out for the human rights movement as it has failed to deliver on its promises. In fact, Kennedy concludes that 'human rights was a late twentieth century project' that is now 'in some sense, over'.[280] He does, however, suggest a way forward. The movement should stop treating human rights as 'an object of devotion' and instead approach it in a pragmatic way,[281] encouraging 'open engagement about differing pragmatic assessments'.[282] There must be dispassionate evaluation of the benefit and costs of particular human rights initiatives.[283] This evaluation must be 'in comparative terms', that is, how they impact other emancipatory projects to realize the rights of individuals and groups.[284]

How does one assess the Kennedy theses on human rights and human rights movement? In a brief response to Kennedy, the feminist scholar Hilary Charlesworth has raised some pertinent points. She begins by noting the pedagogic value of Kennedy's work: it is 'an excellent teaching resource'.[285] The criticisms directed against Kennedy are threefold. First, he needs 'to be clearer about his own views and commitments'.[286] According to Charlesworth, Kennedy does not disclose which dimensions of international human rights movement are worth supporting. Second, Kennedy does not offer 'specific examples' to illustrate his criticisms with the result that he generalizes across national spaces and movements.[287] For instance, speaking of Australia Charlesworth contends that human rights talk is still valuable and not simply 'a dominant and fashionable vocabulary for thinking about emancipation'.[288] Third, Kennedy does not explain who the addressees of his plea for a 'more pragmatic attitude are'.

---

[279] See ibid., p. 22.
[280] Kennedy, 'Preface', p. viii.
[281] Kennedy, 'The International Human Rights', p. 101.
[282] See ibid., p. 103.
[283] See ibid., p. 102.
[284] See ibid., p. 104.
[285] Hilary Charlesworth, 'Author! Author!: A Response to David Kennedy', 15 (2002) *Harvard Human Rights Journal*, pp. 127–131 at p. 127.
[286] See ibid.
[287] See ibid.
[288] See ibid.

Neither is it entirely clear what a pragmatic approach to international human rights movement is[289] These are valid criticisms. Kennedy has a tendency to make broad generalizations without supporting evidence. In fact, it is somewhat paradoxical that while he is against the idea of grand theory he never explores diverse local histories at any length before drawing conclusions. The result is the neglect of the enormous diversity in the impact of the human rights movements in different contexts and in different spaces.

Yet Kennedy is right in recognizing that the real problem with the human rights movement today is its imperial aspirations undermining in the process alternative vocabularies of justice. It has become in a profound sense 'the last utopia'.[290] But, while Kennedy does speak of 'alternative vocabularies of justice or real justice', he does not go beyond vague formulations about what these are. His refusal to engage in a critique of the structures of global capitalism and imperialism means that his indictment of human rights movements does not go deep enough. It is not as if all human rights violations have in the final analysis to be traced to structures of global capitalism. That would be plain reductionism. There are a whole host of local social and political factors that account for human rights violations. The answer to these violations are also local or national struggles that seek redress and justice. But Kennedy does not seriously address the diverse causes of human rights violations, what the approach of human rights movements should be to them, or dispassionately assess the outcomes of struggles for human rights.[291] For the rest it is worth recalling that the argument about the limits of human rights discourse was made by Marx more than a century and half ago.[292]

---

[289] See ibid., pp. 129–130.
[290] Samuel Moyn, *The Last Utopia: Human Rights in History* (Boston, MA: Harvard University Press, 2010).
[291] Susan Marks, 'Human Rights and Root Causes', 74 (2011) *The Modern Law Review*, pp. 57–78 at p. 77.
[292] Karl Marx, 'On the Jewish Question'; Karl Marx, 'Critique of the Gotha Programme' in Karl Marx and Frederick Engels *Selected Works*, vol. 3 (Moscow: Progress Publishers, 1977), pp. 9–30. In the world of international law Susan Marks captures the left critique in her work. She points out how human rights have become 'a language of exoneration and justification'. Susan Marks, 'Human Rights in Disastrous Times', *The Cambridge Companion*, pp. 309–327 at p. 320. She makes the following points among others: First, 'what is not in is out'. Second, there are 'in-built exceptions and qualifications'. Third, human rights can be 'made to speak in the service of particular people and particular purposes'. That is to say, the resources of human rights are available to all including the global ruling classes. See ibid., p. 320. If this situation has to change then the critique of

H.   On Governance Humanitarianism

Kennedy also explores the broader theme of humanitarianism in his writings. The conclusion is the same viz., humanitarian projects are 'as much part of the problem as of the solution'.[293] But in this case, in order to pre-empt the critique of indulging in broad generalizations that are globally applicable, he hastens to add that his focus is on the humanitarian work of well-meaning people in the United States.[294]

Kennedy's concern is once again less with the better implementation of humanitarian efforts and more with the dark side of '*best* efforts themselves'.[295] He is concerned with what is called governance humanitarianism. According to Kennedy, the humanitarians have a hard time focusing on the costs of humanitarianism because they do not think of themselves 'as rulers'. In their view '*other* people govern, and it is our job to hold *them* responsible'.[296] In this discourse, the practice of humanitarianism is framed in a manner that 'it is easy to think of the activist as *outside* and the official as *inside* the exercise of power'.[297] In fact, humanitarians like to believe that they speak truth to power whereas they are complicit with power. As Kennedy points out, international humanitarians are in reality 'rulers in flight from rulership' and use their pragmatic expertise to avoid responsibility for their actions.[298] In fact, the more pragmatic and virtuous international humanitarians are, the more blind they are to the dark side of their activities. Kennedy exhorts these humanitarians to assume responsibility for their actions, albeit he realizes that they are trapped in the circle of virtue that power spins. Power also reinforces the self-image of humanitarians being pragmatic experts. Kennedy is therefore sceptical that the humanitarian impulse can be made truly humanitarian,[299] for the dark sides of humanitarianism are 'the dark side(s) of pragmatic renewal itself'.[300]

---

structures of global capitalism and its relationship to imperialism cannot be avoided. This is where the Kennedy way of doing political economy is unhelpful.

[293] David Kennedy, *The Dark Sides of Virtue: Reassessing Humanitarianism* (Princeton, NJ: Princeton University Press, 2004), p. xiii.
[294] See ibid, p. xv.
[295] See ibid., p. xviii; emphasis in original.
[296] See ibid., p. xix; emphasis in original.
[297] See ibid., p. 344; emphasis in original.
[298] See ibid., pp. xxiv–xxv.
[299] See ibid., p. 342.
[300] See ibid.

But Kennedy is wary of being accused of humanitarian nihilism. He therefore expresses the hope that 'good-hearted people will continue to try and make the world a better place, more just, more humane'.[301] This time around he even offers 'a series of suggestions for those who seek to move beyond pragmatic renewal in their search to understand and manage the dark sides of international humanitarianism'.[302] These assume the form of 'maxims or heuristics' that inter alia suggest that humanitarians should no longer avert their eyes from rulership;[303] 'embrace "the full range" of effects of humanitarianism on the world';[304] unearth 'the sites and terms experts use' to 'heighten the dark side and contest them politically';[305] focus on outcomes to 'bring to the table the dark consequences we are more comfortable leaving in the shadows';[306] view humanitarianism as 'an interest among others, as a culture among others' and not as 'neutral engagement in far away places';[307] realize that speaking for 'the under-represented, the powerless, the voiceless, the public interest, the unborn', does not immunize them 'entirely from responsibility for both truth and power';[308] abandon progress narratives and instead 'imagine constructing programs, making proposals, without the metaphors of primitive and mature';[309] imagine a humanitarianism 'whose *end* was criticism, whose *knowledge* was critique … imagine international humanitarianism – or a human rights movement – as an antiestablishment establishment'.[310] The eventual hope being to 'build a new humanitarian community. Forged in disenchantment. Embracing the dark sides. Deciding – at once uncertain and responsible'.[311] If these suggestions are accepted, it would certainly help Western humanitarians avoid the human costs of humanitarian projects. The insights and suggestions may not be new but are nevertheless welcome.

It is, however, doubtful if the Kennedy advice will be taken. It may be recalled that humanitarianism is the ideology of imperialism since the sixteenth century. The colonial project was viewed by humanitarians

[301] See ibid., p. 347.
[302] See ibid., p. xxv.
[303] See ibid., p. 348.
[304] See ibid., p. 349.
[305] See ibid.
[306] See ibid., p. 350.
[307] See ibid., p. 351.
[308] See ibid.
[309] See ibid., p. 353.
[310] See ibid.; emphasis in original.
[311] See ibid., p. 357.

of the times as a humanitarian project.[312] Indeed, the community did
some good work even as it supported and legitimized imperialism.
Humanitarianism in the era of globalization is no different.[313] It is
merely wearing new garbs. Therefore, Kennedy does well to remind the
current humanitarians that they may often be active participants in the
project of domination. His 'maxims and heuristics' can certainly help
humanitarians avoid complicity with power and to think of alternative ways that the humanitarian project can be advanced. But, in the
absence of any serious reflection and reform of deep structures that contribute to the creation of humanitarian crisis, the Kennedy suggestions
will not go far in transforming the contemporary humanitarian regime.
Unfortunately, even at this stage, the Kennedy obsession with the
inside – of how humanitarians view or approach their task –continues,
in this case with the internal tensions in the vision, discourse and practice of humanitarianism.

I.   Contribution to International Law Scholarship

It was noted in the introduction to the chapter that its critical focus does
not allow justice to be done to the rich body of work of Kennedy. In an
attempt to set the balance right, and before touching on the response of
other approaches to Kennedy's work, it is worth listing schematically his
many contributions to international law scholarship, some of which have
been mentioned or alluded to in the discussion.

First, Kennedy has been able to reveal the untenable propensity of
mainstream to treat the language and grammar of international law as
internally consistent even as it is mired in contradictions. Through focusing on the internal relations of international law he has shown how the
feature of indeterminacy characterizes all international legal discourse.
Indeed, under his gaze much that is solid melts into air.

Second, Kennedy has been able to effectively debunk the mainstream
narrative of progress by showing how old ideas are recycled as new by the
international community. He has been able to reveal the continuities that
mark past and present scholarship and thereby create space for a more

---

[312] Uday Singh Mehta, *Liberalism and Empire: A Study in Nineteenth-Century British Liberal
Thought* (Chicago, IL: Chicago University Press, 1999).
[313] See B. S. Chimni, 'Globalization, Humanitarianism and the Erosion of Refugee Protection',
13 (2000) *Journal of Refugee Studies*, pp. 243–264.

profound critique of mainstream that thrives on the self-image of constant forward movement based on learning from past experiences.

Third, Kennedy ably shows how global governance is crucially shaped by the mutual interaction of law and economic phenomena. He goes on to reveal the multifarious ways in which law constitutes 'economic structures' and impacts distributive outcomes. Further, in his more recent work, he persuasively contends that problematic distributive outcomes cannot be corrected without suitably restructuring the critical intersections of the relationship.

Fourth, the Kennedy critique of international institutions is most salutary. He is able to expose the opposing impulses that inform their creation and working, causing an easy movement between idealism and realism or law and politics in ways that eventually allows power to have its day. In fact, his scepticism about the international institutions as a way of addressing global problems is refreshing in the face of the general belief that they promote international cooperation.

Fifth, Kennedy's insight that international lawyers are partaking in power while imagining themselves as powerless is both powerful and original. Kennedy demonstrates the subtle yet deep linkages between knowledge and power in the course of global governance. He also shows how the complicity with power is presented by the mainstream as a moment of opposition and resistance.

Sixth, the Kennedy understanding that power can be resisted anywhere and everywhere and not merely in privileged spaces through particular agents is compelling. He is, therefore, able to make the significant point that international lawyers can further the goal of human dignity in all professional locations. Kennedy has himself chosen to promote critical international law scholarship through organizing conferences/workshops, providing support to individual scholars, and encouraging new generations of international law scholars to pursue critique in their separate ways.

Last, but not the least, there is the pedagogic value of Kennedy's work. In fact, he has helped liberate generations of international law scholars from the confines of arid positivism by revealing inconsistencies in the heart of the liberal project. The application of his theoretical insights in different fields of international law brilliantly reveals how power infiltrates and circulates in progressive discourses. He thereby helps reject sentimental views of how international laws can be used to advance the cause of the weak.

J.   Kennedy and Others

But Kennedy's work has not always received the appreciation it deserves. As has been argued, at least one crucial reason is the failure to connect with material realities or engage with current concerns of the international community and advance policy prescriptions. The mainstream has never seen great value in the project of deconstruction of international law. It has also been troubled by the fact that Kennedy caricatured their work and projects.[314] It has found especially disturbing the proposition that international law and the international legal profession are most often part of the problem.[315] The mainstream is also upset by the claim that the community of international lawyers is looking for answers in the wrong places and that international lawyers are often pursuing personal projects while imagining they are pursuing the global common good. The mainstream laments that instead of using his considerable talents in the service of international law Kennedy is mocking those with faith in its capacity to transform the world.[316] He has unfortunately made a virtue of looking at the dark side of things and questioning attempts at 'renewal' or 'reform' of international law and institutions, representing such efforts as nothing other than more of the same. It is therefore not at all surprising that there has been a relative lack of engagement with his work.

To the extent his work is commented upon by the mainstream, it is the subject of searching questions. Has not much of what Kennedy has to say been said before by the New Haven approach?[317] Why is his work full of

[314] Anthony D'Amato, 'Old Approaches to International Law', 36 (1995) *Harvard International Law Journal*, pp. 509–512 at p. 509.
[315] In Kennedy's words, 'in some ways the international legal profession has often made the very thing it claims to care most about less likely, [and] that the professional discipline is part of the problem'. Kennedy, 'When Renewal Repeats', p. 456. According to Kennedy the reason international lawyers in the United States find his view disturbing is because 'at least in the United States, the field has been associated with pacifism, with the critique of the American empire, with the progressive movement, with the left, with law as an instrument of social change, as well as with an insistently pluralist and cosmopolitan attitude towards the national political and legal culture. The mainstream players in the field announce themselves as "the left" in the national political culture, suggesting that if you are critical of their vocabulary, you must be pretty wacky indeed'. See ibid., p. 469.
[316] Kennedy, 'When Renewal Repeats', p. 470.
[317] As Rosalyn Higgins points out comparing CLS and New Haven approach: 'For both schools, the legal theory is applicable to law in general and not just international law ... Both take as the starting-point the contention that law is deeply rooted in social theory. Both locate legal process in social context and make the place of values quite explicit. Both reject law as rules and exceptions'. Rosalyn Higgins, *Problems and Process: International Law and How*

generalizations that are unsupported by hard empirical evidence?[318] Has not his corrosive cynicism led to the 'soulless deconstruction' of international law?[319] Why does he not have a reconstructive agenda?[320] For the rest the response of the mainstream is that despite a wealth of critiques international law is not 'helpless or superfluous' but useful and necessary.[321] What is more 'despair ultimately supports power',[322] especially when unaccompanied by 'a contemporary theory of reconstruction'.[323]

But in more recent times some sections of the mainstream are coming to recognize the 'new realism' in Kennedy's later writings. According to Crawford, at least on the face of it, 'a reversal of sorts appears to have occurred in Kennedy's later work'.[324] There is now some willingness to recognize the value of international law and in proposing, as in his work on humanitarianism, a reconstructive agenda. It shows that his obsession with the 'dark side' of things flows from an impulse to improve things. Some among the mainstream have come to appreciate his idea of fluidity of international politics as it does not hold hegemonic powers solely responsible for the problems of the world.[325] However, the mainstream remains sceptical about Kennedy's thinking as in its view he continues to argue the need for 'law to abandon the search for binding rules and principles, and to content itself with simply critiquing policy, the shaping of which is for others'.[326]

Kennedy's work shares a complex relationship with other critical approaches. In many ways his approach overlaps with those advanced by

---

We Use It (Oxford: Clarendon Press, 1994), p. 9. Third world critics have also noted the 'many commonalities' with the schools such as policy science that Kennedy sets out to critique. J. Oloka-Onyango and Sylvia Tamale, '"The Personal is Political", or Why Women's Rights are Indeed Human Rights: An African Perspective on International Feminism', 17 (1995) *Human Rights Quarterly*, pp. 691–731 at p. 722. See also Chapter 3, pp. 177–178.

[318] Charlesworth, 'Author, Author', p. 127. More generally, Schaffer laments that critical legal scholars 'do not engage with the empirical study of law for pragmatic decision-making'. Gregory Schaffer, 'The New Legal Realist Approach to International Law', 28 (2015) *Leiden Journal of International Law*, pp. 189–210 at p. 196.

[319] See ibid., p. 128.

[320] James Crawford, *Chance, Order, Change: The Course of International Law. General Course on Public International Law* (Brill, 2014)(On file with author), p. 123

[321] Paulus, 'International Law' p. 729. See also Schaffer, 'New Legal Realist', pp. 189–210.

[322] See ibid., p. 735.

[323] See ibid., p. 739.

[324] Crawford, *Chance, Order, Change*, p. 123.

[325] See Robert Howse and Ruti Teitl, 'Does Humanity-Law Require (or Imply) a Progressive Theory of History? (and Other Questions for Martti Koskenniemi)', 27 (2013) *Temple International & Comparative Law Journal*, pp. 377–398 at p. 396.

[326] Crawford, *Chance, Order, Change*, p. 123.

TWAIL, MAIL and FtAIL in as much as these agree that international law is very often part of the problem. What is different about Kennedy is that he thinks it is part of the problem not because of structures of global capitalism or patriarchy but principally because of indeterminate doctrines and rules and the fact that experts do not exercise their freedom in a responsible manner. His commitment to methodological individualism, and to an abstract conceptualization of the relationship between knowledge and power, prevents him from offering a serious critique of the material constraints on the choices that an expert makes. He therefore rarely relies on the categories of class, gender, and race to indict contemporary international law.

In so far as TWAIL is concerned, Kennedy's work in recent years has arguably been influenced by its scholarship. In fact, one way of looking at the different phases of Kennedy's work is to see it as pre- and post-TWAIL II phases (beginning circa 1995). In the pre-TWAIL II phase he relentlessly pursued the project of advancing an internal critique of international law. In this period his work was in the realm of impassive abstractions. There was little engagement at this stage with the non-Western world or with third world scholarship. In this respect he was no different from CLS of which it was observed that their work begins and ends 'within the western context – an analysis divorced from the essential role and function of the dimension of imperialism in the evolution of that law'.[327] Despite being interested in the history of international law, Kennedy never gave serious consideration to the role of colonialism and imperialism in the evolution and development of international law. As was pointed out, this absence is striking as by the time Kennedy arrived on the scene of international law the first generation of third world scholars (i.e. TWAIL I) had been for some time contesting the Eurocentric history of international law. Yet in an early essay on 'a new stream of international law scholarship' when Kennedy noted the names of others pursuing critical projects in the field of international law he included only one name from the third world viz., Surakiart Sathirathai.[328] He did not acknowledge key figures like R. P. Anand, Georges Abi-Saab, Mohammed Bedjaoui, T. E. Elias and others. It is not until his third world students produced work on the relationship between imperialism and international law that the theme found its way into his writings; as has been mentioned before, from the early 1990s he was the supervisor of many of the key figures of TWAIL II. However, it is not entirely clear whether Kennedy recognizes the influence

[327] Oloka-Onyango and Tamale, ' "The Personal is Political" ', p. 722.
[328] Kennedy, 'New Stream', p. 2.

of TWAIL II on his work as he views it as 'in one way or another, grown out of the peculiar tradition of international law in the United States, even if they are largely a reaction against it, and even if a large majority of their practitioners have not, in fact, been citizens of the United States'.[329] The Kennedy observation is meant to diminish the distinctive contribution of TWAIL II to the theory and practice of international law.[330] The argument appears to be that the personal projects of core figures of TWAIL II have been defined by their academic exposure in the United States or suggested or influenced by mentors there and not by their prior experiences and learning. While his TWAIL students have always acknowledged their debt to Kennedy, it is not very clear how much of it is for the sustained support they received to pursue their work and how much for intellectual borrowings.[331] On occasions, however, Kennedy does acknowledge TWAIL as an independent effort and 'one of the most interesting and sustained grand projects of reimagination'.[332] This recognition appears to be in line with his current engagement with international law from the outside.

When it comes to MAIL the differences are substantial. Kennedy is extremely wary of being labelled an unsophisticated Marxist scholar who is unable to recognize the complexities, contingencies and irrationalities that inform international politics. His reasons for rejecting the 'traditional left', in so far as these can be inferred from his writings, are on the lines of mentor Duncan Kennedy's objections. Karl Klare ably summarizes the unflattering objections which are essentially twofold. First, 'many traditional leftists believe that they actually possess a complete and coherent, descriptive and prescriptive analysis of social life'.[333] Second, leftists believe 'that critique is easy and fun whereas reconstruction is much more

---

[329] Kennedy, 'Discipline of International Law', p. 15.
[330] He even lists the present author in the TWAILERS he mentions which include Antony Anghie, Robert Chu, James Gathii and Celestine Nyamu, Balakrishnan Rajagopal and Amr Shalakany. Kennedy, 'Discipline of International Law', fn. 15). This author had already produced the first edition of this very book before arriving as a Fulbright scholar at Harvard in 1995. Antony Anghie had worked on the *Nauru* case with Judge Christopher Weeramantry which had considerably influenced his thinking, especially about the history of colonial international law. See in this regard Antony Anghie, 'The Heart of My Home: Colonialism, Environmental Damage and the Nauru Case', 34 (1993) *Harvard International Law Journal*, pp. 445–506.
[331] This is a conclusion derived from conversations with many of his TWAIL students. It is however not to be to be attributed to them in any way. In fact it is quite possible that many of them hold an entirely different view.
[332] Kennedy, 'Mystery of Global Governance', p. 50.
[333] Karl E. Klare, 'The Politics of Duncan Kennedy's Critique', 22 (2001) *Cardozo Law Review*, pp. 1073–1103 at pp. 1095–1096. It may be noted that the entire debate is in the context of the role of the traditional left in the United States.

difficult and less glamorous, bit what serious "leftists" do'.[334] In short, traditional leftists 'are self-righteous, self-certain, sanctimonious, desperately
seeking to be loved, and boring' who 'will foist their incipient totalitarianism on the rest of us'.[335] Klare goes on to ably defend the traditional
left against the caricatured views attributed to them. He aptly argues that
their understanding is much more sophisticated than Duncan Kennedy
makes them out to be. The traditional left has not only imbibed the lessons of the past but also come to accept many of the flaws in traditional
left thinking.[336] Indeed, while it borrows core tenets from Marxism, the
same is combined with a range of other intellectual sources. Be that as
it may, Klare was defending the traditional left against the criticism of a
Duncan Kennedy who pursues 'particular reconstructive projects' and is
also one with the left when it aims 'at transformation of existing social
structures on the basis of a critique of their injustice, and specifically...
the injustices of racist, capitalist patriarchy'.[337] In fact, according to Klare,
Duncan Kennedy 'is militant in the cause of class, racial, gender, and
sexual justice, and an enthusiastic advocate of redistribution of wealth
and power'.[338] While David Kennedy may accept these justice goals, he
moves in a different direction in terms of both diagnosing the reasons
for persisiting inequalities and ways of addressing them. His rejection of
the study of 'impersonal forces' such as 'means of production' or 'interests of the ruling class' or 'global capital' makes his repudiation of traditional left thinking more complete than that of Duncan Kennedy who
continues to draw on Marxism to build alternative understandings of law
and the legal sphere.[339] To the extent the critique of structures of capitalism (and imperialism) is fundamental to the left standpoint, it is not clear

[334] See ibid., p. 1098.
[335] See ibid., pp. 1095–1096. Duncan Kennedy opposes the traditional left with his version of
modernism/postmodernism:

> [The mpm version of leftism] chooses the ethos of post-ness, doubleness,
> yearning irony and the aesthetic, the element of self-conscious formal manipu-
> lation in the name of unknowable primal underforces and dangerous supple-
> ments, cut by the critiques of the subject and of representation. It chooses them
> over the traditional course of leftist righteousness (whether in the mode of
> post-Marxist 'systemacity' or of identity politics) and, with equal intensity, over
> the compromises of left liberalism.

Cited by Klare; see ibid., p. 1074.
[336] See ibid., p. 1101.
[337] See ibid., p. 1088.
[338] See ibid.
[339] See ibid.

where David Kennedy currently stands, as it has been seen his most recent writings have in some ways advanced a more conventional external critique of international law. Turning to ways of realizing different justice projects David Kennedy would readily accept the distinction that Duncan Kennedy makes 'between particular reconstructive projects' which he thinks are okay 'and a project of reconstruction in the name of a totalizing, alternative model, with its own ethical foundations and institutional assumptions (not okay)'.[340] But his understanding of 'particular reconstructive projects' is more profoundly linked to the role of individual experts and expertise than it is in the case of Duncan Kennedy who is not openly committed to methodological individualism. Therefore, David Kennedy's theoretical basis for rejecting the traditional left goes deeper.

Finally, where FtAIL is concerned, liberal feminists like Charlesworth have been critical of his approach more on the lines of the mainstream; her critique of the Kennedy take on human rights is an example.[341] In fact, he has much in common with critics of governance feminism like Janet Halley that liberal feminists are so sceptical of.[342] If IMAIL opts for socialist feminism Kennedy turns to critical legal feminism or more precisely postmodern feminism for its insights as these are more in line with his thinking.

K.   Conclusion

Kennedy is undoubtedly among the most perceptive contemporary scholars of international law. He has ably advanced an internal critique of the doctrines and discourses of international law, of particular narratives of the history of the discipline and the role of experts and expertise. He has used the ensuing insights to examine particular fields or regimes of international law. In the process he has produced work that is remarkably fresh and novel at both the methodological and empirical levels. The newness of his thinking lies in revealing unexpected continuities and discontinuities in the telling of the history of the discipline. It lies in revealing indeterminacy as a structural feature of international law. It lies in delineating the critical role of experts in the making and working of international

---

[340] See ibid., p. 1098.
[341] Kennedy had met Hilary Charlesworth as a fellow student who was 'also interested in launching a broad feminist reexamination of the field'. Kennedy, 'When Renewal Repeats', p. 482.
[342] For a detailed discussion see Chapter 6, pp. 380–386.

law. It lies in his insight that those who see themselves speak truth to power often partake in power. It lies in demonstrating that law and violence share a deep intimacy. In a profound sense Kennedy's strength as a scholar lies in offering counter-intuitive understandings of international law. If you think international law is about rules he will show you how it is about personal projects. If you think your proposal is a new one, he will demonstrate that it is another recycled idea. If you think moral responsibility can be evaded through invoking corporate decision-making he will show you how the individual is deeply implicated. If you celebrate international human rights law he will help you see its dark side. If you think international humanitarian law helps make war less brutal he will show you how it facilitates war. In short if you think international law is part of the solution he will show you how it is part of the problem. These inverted understandings make Kennedy's work of enormous pedagogic value. These help destabilize standard understandings of international law and open up space for critical and creative thinking. Kennedy has gone further and expended great effort at creating networks of researchers with critical projects. He convenes for this purpose regular workshops and conferences of promising international law scholars. This mission has great potential as it helps draw the attention of new generations of international law scholars to the narrow world of mainstream and opens up new horizons in the process. It also helps sensitize them to the need for taking an ethical view of international law.

But in advancing his internal critique of international law Kennedy tends to leave the 'real world' entirely out of the frame. It is mostly written without mentioning material developments, or to state it differently, without reference to the realities of capitalism, colonialism and imperialism that crucially influenced the evolution and development of modern international law. His critique of the structure of international law or the history of the discipline is therefore profoundly ahistorical. The obsession with looking at international law from the inside has also meant that he often fails to make obvious connections between the internal and the external as can be seen in his reflections on Vitoria where he does not link the views of the Spanish thinker to the colonial project. Likewise, he fails to connect his critique of the disciplinary narrative on League of Nations with inter-imperialist competition of the times. His initial work on the role of experts and expertise suffers from not being located in impersonal structures traceable to the embrace of a relatively strong version of methodological individualism. The focus on the internal also blinds him to the fact that many of the incongruities in the structure of international legal argument merely manifest the anarchic international system. In short, Kennedy works with the binary concepts of internal and external or inside and outside that result in a fractional and often sterile critique of international law. His is more an aesthetic critique.

Kennedy's recent reflections on international law have however seen a subtle shift in emphasis. The beginnings of an external critique can be discerned in his cogitations on the relationship between political economy and law and his consideration of structural constraints that bear on the role of experts and expertise. These moves provide a corrective to his earlier obsession with the internal view. It can only be surmised as to how far the shift has been a response to the emergence of other critical approaches such as TWAIL II, FtAIL and MAIL that combine an internal and external critique by concurrently examining the form and content of international law. The problem with the external view Kennedy advances is once again that it is not embedded in either structures of global capitalism or patriarchy or in the geographical divide between the Global North and the Global South or anything else. He does not attempt to investigate the deep structures that bear upon international law and international institutions. The reason is that the external critique is overly focused on 'midlevel' legal and institutional processes. Such a move is necessitated by the need to sustain his views on the crucial role of experts and expertise. For it is here that they do much of their work: it is easier to demonstrate their vital role in 'midlevel' processes. In the event Kennedy makes too much of the 'mystery of global governance' and the element of fluidity in the international system that subverts categories such as centre and periphery. Indeed, he comes close to concluding that imperialism is a thing of the past. With the result that his critical reflections on the role of international law in the differential distribution of gains between groups, firms and nations appears to be no different from that of the mainstream.

It also deserves mention that since Kennedy advances his internal and external critiques in different phases of his academic journey these do not always cohere. The one comes after the other and often proceeds on separate lines. In this regard he has either to convincingly demonstrate that what appears to be an external critique is in reality an internal critique or revisit his earlier work to offer an integral or holistic view of international law. From a theoretical standpoint he has to explain how the different intellectual resources he uses, one set being Foucault, Weber and Bourdieu, to advance the internal and external critiques yield a coherent system of explanation and understanding. While eclecticism informs much contemporary theorization, including IMAIL, there is a burden on those deploying eclectic theory to show how it comes together. Kennedy does not effectively discharge that burden. This lapse threatens to undermine the integrity of his work.

It is difficult to know what the current political orientation of Kennedy is.[343] But the distinct nature of his work has meant that it remains contentious. In his comment on the work of MacKinnon, Kennedy observes how 'MacKinnon remains an extremely controversial figure' a description that as yet fits him.[344] Like MacKinnon, Kennedy is best seen as a resource for rethinking the field. Each individual can dip into his work and take away from it that which fits his or her orientation or project.

IV.   Writing like Koskenniemi: Flair and Imagination

Martti Koskenniemi is among the most erudite and versatile of contemporary critical scholars of international law. He is at home in several European languages and his writings draw on, as in the case of Kennedy, a range of sources from humanities, social sciences and the literature on philosophy.[345] He has had a rich and diverse work experience in the world of international law having served the Finnish Foreign Ministry and been a member of the International Law Commission.[346] He has also been elected to the *Institut de Droit International*. He has through deep study and wide-ranging work experience acquired a strong command over traditional international law materials. This has made his critical work much more acceptable and influential than that of Kennedy. As Kennedy himself has noted, Koskenniemi's strength is that 'his criticism is rooted in the materials of the discipline itself – its cases, its histories, its arguments, and its professional contexts'.[347] In fact, he 'integrates doctrinal,

---

[343] At one place he writes that 'my own position often seems to fade quite easily into neo-conservatism'. Kennedy, 'New Stream', p. 8.

[344] Kennedy, *Canon of American Legal Thought*, p. 839.

[345] His landmark work *From Apology to Utopia* begins with the following sentences: 'This is not only a book in international law. It is also an exercise in social theory and political philosophy'. Martti Koskenniemi, *From Apology to Utopia*, p. xiii. The book was reissued in 2005 by Cambridge University Press with an 'Epilogue'. With the exception of references to the 'Epilogue' all other references to FATU are to the original edition. In the former case the year of publication of reissued FATU is added.

[346] On his life and education see Emmanuelle Jouannet, 'Koskenniemi: A Critical Introduction' in Martti Koskenniemi, *The Politics of International Law* (Oxford: Hart Publishing, 2011), pp. 1–32 at pp. 1–4.

[347] Kennedy, 'Book Review', p. 386. Further Kennedy writes, 'while he produces "a criticism that is internal" based on diverse social science theories it is "ultimately, situated in the best traditions of the discipline"'. See ibid.

historical, and theoretical materials into a single image of the discipline.[348] He is, therefore, more effectively able to demonstrate the internal tensions and contradictions that mark the body and discourse of international law. In the process, Koskenniemi has liberated many an international law scholar from methods that have little room for new thinking and experimentation.

Koskenniemi is also a prolific writer with a body of work that ensures his place among the greats of the discipline. He is highly regarded by even those who are openly in disagreement with him. For there is no area of international law that he turns to that he does not offer new insights. In fact Koskenniemi has made original and striking contributions to the study of international law. He has been aptly described as 'a dazzlingly original' scholar.[349] But it may be said that many of his contributions have assumed the form of adding depth or distinctive dimensions to new themes that have originated in the work of others in the field.[350] Much of his early work on the structural indeterminacy of international law draws on the writings of Kennedy even as he clarifies, elaborates and takes it forward. Koskenniemi generously acknowledges the same in his foreword to FATU. He writes that 'whatever merit this book may have is due to my having been able to acquaint myself with him [i.e. Kennedy] and his work.'[351] His later historical writings, which represent a move from 'structure to history', are certainly more creative and written with great flair and imagination. But these essentially add a facet to the story of imperialism and international law narrated by Antony Anghie and others in recent years. Once again Koskenniemi admits in the preface to *The Gentle Civilizer of Nations* (GCN) observing that he 'draws on the work of Professors Antony Anghie and Nathaniel Berman, and from discussions I have had with them over the years'.[352] However, few writers have such a deep understanding of the history of European international law and of

[348] See ibid., p. 391.
[349] See Jeffrey L. Dunoff, 'Engaging the Writings of Martti Koskenniemi: Introduction to the Symposium', 27 (2013) *Temple International & Comparative Law Journal*, pp. 207–214 at p. 207. The journal carries a symposium on his work with the title 'Engaging the Writings of Martti Koskenniemi'.
[350] Koskenniemi himself makes no claims to the originality of his work. But it is a part of the onerous task of assessing any individual scholars' work to evaluate such judgments by placing it in relationship to ongoing trends in the field. It is merely in that spirit that the subject is touched upon.
[351] Koskenniemi, *From Apology to Utopia*, p. VI.
[352] Martti Koskenniemi, *The Gentle Civilizer of Nations: the Rise and Fall of International Law 1870–1960* (Cambridge: Cambridge University Press, 2004) p. xi.

the key figures that shaped its course, especially in the nineteenth century; the history is written with great empathy.[353] Koskenniemi's more recent history of international law between the sixteenth and eighteenth centuries is without doubt groundbreaking. The attempt to use the emergence of the 'empire of rights' to explain and understand the role of modern international law represents a crucial move in understanding the history of modern international law. But even this history is somewhat on the lines of customary materialist history on the evolution of law under capitalism. At this point it is worth noting that his historical writings came after he had advanced a structural critique of international law raising the question whether the structure and history of international law—or as in the case of Kennedy the internal and external aspects of international law—can be separately explored without impoverishing the understanding of both. Some of the drawbacks in the notion of 'culture of formalism' that he has advanced can be traced back to this procedure. However, overall he remains among the most influential figures in the international law academia. Even a reference from him to your work can lend it weight beyond its merits. His silences are therefore meaningful. His reluctance to directly engage with other critical approaches such as FtAIL and TWAIL that share the dualist thinking which informs the idea of 'culture of formalism' is a case in point.

In the discussion to follow there is no attempt to offer a comprehensive review of Koskenniemi's work. In fact it is impossible in the space of half a chapter to even touch on the innumerable themes and subjects that he has addressed.[354] The ensuing analysis merely attempts to understand aspects of his central theses on the working and history of international law and offer a critique from an IMAIL perspective. The chapter opens with Koskenniemi's essential theses on the structure of international law. It then goes on to discuss his move from structure to history, mentioning some concerns with the history he narrates, and finally attempts to grapple in some detail with the idea of 'culture of formalism' he has advanced.[355] In his recent work he appears to have already moved beyond the theme of 'culture of formalism.'

353 It perhaps explains his relatively greater popularity among European international law scholars.
354 Some aspects of his work are dealt with in other chapters. See for his views on the relationship of IR-IL and critique thereof Chapter 2, pp. 93–101.
355 It is not possible in the space of this chapter to discuss at any depth his elaborate and insightful work on the history of international law and the international legal profession. It will have to be left to a future essay to analyse his historical writings at greater length, including his 'history of international law histories'. See in latter regard, Martti Koskenniemi, 'A History of International Law Histories' in Fassbender and Peters (eds.),

But it is important to consider the idea as whatever new formulations on international law that he may offer in the future the idea of 'culture of formalism' will remain a turning point in his thinking.

A.   The Essentials: Theses on International Law

Koskenniemi advances four *overlapping* theses on international law. His first thesis is that the relationship between international law and politics 'is not one of two entities colliding against each other but one of identity'.[356] That is to say, the relationship is not that between 'international law *and* politics' as international law is intrinsically political.[357] At the same time, he is against any attempt to erase or abolish the identity of formal international law.[358] In his epilogue to reissued FATU he writes that he was 'disappointed by "political" treatments according to which international law was best seen as an instrument for more or less shared "values" or "interests" or its significance lay in whether it made nations "behave" towards some postulated end-state'.[359] In his view, there is a need to 'resist' both 'the pull of excessive "formalism" or excessive policy-oriented "realism" '.[360] The idea of 'culture of formalism' which attempts to conceptualize and capture a possible middle ground receives detailed treatment later in the chapter. For the present it may only be noted that the attempt to find a via media between excessive formalism and excessive realism is a task that many others have pursued in the past. Thus, for instance, Richard Falk also advanced the 'intermediate view' seeking to find the middle ground

---

Oxford Handbook, pp. 943–972. What is on offer is a broad critique of the general thrust, significance and methodology of his work.

[356] Koskenniemi, *Politics of International Law*, p. v.

[357] See ibid.; emphasis added.

[358] As Jouannet points out, it would 'be an error to conclude that Koskenniemi rehabilitates politics in order to dissolve the formal specificity of law. Indeed, it is for precisely this dissolution of law in politics that he criticizes realist and instrumentalist approaches'. Jouannet, 'Koskenniemi', p. 21.

[359] Martti Koskenniemi, *From Apology to Utopia: The Structure of International Legal Argument* (Cambridge: Cambridge University Press, 2005), p. 564. Hereafter *From Apology to Utopia* (2005).

[360] See ibid. In his epilogue to the reissued FATU Koskenniemi writes that the sentiment that gripped him while writing it was 'the simultaneous sense of rigorous formalism and substantive or political open-endedness of argument about international law '. See ibid., p. 562. He was therefore 'frustrated by attempts to fix the meaning of individual rules, principles or institutions in some abstract and permanent way, irrespective of the changing situations in which legal interpretations were produced'. See ibid., p. 564.

between the excessive formalism of Kelsen's pure theory of law and the excessive realism of the policy-oriented approach.[361]

Koskenniemi's second thesis is that international law suffers from structural indeterminacy. He traces this feature to the 'contradictory premises' on which the doctrines and discourses of international law are founded. In other words, these are 'not an externally induced distortion' but 'a structural property of the international legal language itself'.[362] According to Koskenniemi, international law is '*in constant movement from emphasizing concreteness to emphasizing normativity and vice versa* without being able to establish itself permanently in either position'.[363] Therefore, international law 'remains both over- and underlegitmizing: it is overlegitimizing as it can be ultimately invoked to justify any behavior (apologism), it is underlegitmizing because [it is] incapable of providing a convincing argument on the legitimacy of any practices (utopianism)'.[364] Koskenniemi has been at pains to distinguish his thesis on structural indeterminacy of international law from that of semantic indeterminacy. He laments that his view on indeterminacy has sometimes 'been misunderstood as a point about the semantic open-endedness or ambiguity of international legal texts'.[365] In fact his claim of indeterminacy is '*not at all* that international legal words are semantically ambivalent'.[366] It is rather a 'much stronger (and in the philosophical sense more "fundamental")' claim that 'even where there is no semantic ambivalence whatsoever, international law remains indeterminate because it is based on *contradictory premises* and seeks to regulate a future in regard to which even single actors' preferences remain unsettled'.[367] In distinguishing between

---

[361] See Chapter 4, pp. 183–186.
[362] Koskenniemi, *From Apology to Utopia*, p. 44.
[363] See ibid., p. 46; emphasis in original.
[364] See ibid., p. 48.
[365] Koskenniemi, *From Apology to Utopia* (2005), p. 590.
[366] See ibid.; emphasis added. Jouannet sums up Koskenniemi's view on indeterminacy thus: 'Put simply, legal norms might be absolutely clear, but they would nonetheless remain – always and inevitably – imprisoned within the structure created by the play of legal argumentation; a structure that renders them interdependent, and within which each is defined not in isolation but in relation to the others'. Jouannet, 'Koskenniemi', p. 11. In other words, 'the solutions adopted and decisions taken no longer find their ultimate justification in the formal language of the law; rather, they belong to the actual world of politics – which is that of determination and commitment, just as it is that of manipulation and exploitation'. See ibid., p. 12.
[367] Koskenniemi, *From Apology to Utopia* (2005), p. 590; emphasis added. It follows that 'it is possible to defend *any* course of action – including deviation from a clear rule – by professionally impeccable arguments that look from rules to their underlying reasons, make

semantic and structural sources of indeterminacy Koskenniemi is seeking to distance his view of indeterminacy from that of others like Myres McDougal who are seen to have relied on the pervasiveness of semantic indeterminacy to sustain their thesis on rule scepticism. But it was seen in Chapter 3 that this is not entirely true. For even as McDougal placed emphasis on semantic indeterminacy to maintain his views on rule scepticism he also identified structural sources of indeterminacy.[368] Be that as it may, Koskenniemi's thesis on structural indeterminacy is flawed in as much as he assumes that the oscillation between concreteness and normativity is independent of how the operation of these spheres has been historically delimited by states in practice. As was argued in chapter 3, in the real world, states and scholars have reduced the possibility of the move 'from apology to utopia' through sustained critique of certain kinds of arguments and practices.[369] To put it differently, an interpenetration of opposites takes place over time, considerably limiting the opportunity to advance certain kinds of arguments to justify problematic practices. As was also seen in chapter 3, the work of Wittgenstein has much to offer in this regard.[370] It would not help to go over the same ground again.

Third, Koskenniemi argues that since the feature of indeterminacy represents the state of being of international law it should be seen less as a problem and more as an opportunity. In the face of structural indeterminacy he seeks to re-establish 'the identity of the ... international lawyer as a social agent'.[371] The international lawyer 'must take seriously the moral-political choices they are faced' and 'should be responsible for them'.[372] It will allow him to 'live a conscious and meaningful life as a lawyer in the midst of the actuality of social and political conflict'.[373] The international lawyer must relate to international law in a way 'which makes it possible to live in the present without losing the sense of beyond'.[374] As Jason Beckett explains, 'perhaps the most common mistake made by FATU's

choices between several rules as well as rules and exceptions, and interpret rules in the context of evaluative standards ... indeterminacy is an absolutely central aspect of international law's acceptability. It does not emerge out of the carelessness or bad faith of legal actors (States, diplomats, lawyers) but from their deliberate and justified wish to ensure that legal rules will fulfill the purposes for which they were adopted'. See ibid., p. 591.

[368] See Chapter 3, pp. 138–140.
[369] Ibid.
[370] See Chapter 3, pp. 133–138. See also Chapter 7, pp. 524–534.
[371] Koskenniemi, *From Apology to Utopia*, p. 490.
[372] See ibid., p. 479.
[373] See ibid., p. 495.
[374] See ibid., p. 490.

readers is to *assume* that the demonstration of radical indeterminacy was a critique, that Koskenniemi had brought indeterminacy to light, that we might eradicate it, and "save" the international legal project'.[375] Instead, as he points out, 'Koskenniemi perceives the radical indeterminacy of international law as a *good thing*'; as 'an absolutely central aspect of international law's acceptability'.[376] It is the feature of indeterminacy that allows the possibility of pursuing a politics of emancipation through the language of international law. Indeed, Koskenniemi's ambition is 'to provide resources for the use of international law's professional vocabulary for critical or emancipatory causes'.[377] The view that structural indeterminacy is a 'good thing' is not shared by mainstream scholars who accuse him of 'trashing the system' and 'of eliminating international law', thereby doing more harm than good.[378] They are concerned that it is difficult to sustain the idea of international rule of law in the face of the strong structural indeterminacy thesis.[379] Further, in Koskenniemi's scheme of things the burden to realize common good appears to fall on individual members of the invisible college who are expected to make the right choices. The methodological individualism that this view is based on, as in the case of Kennedy, has always been present in Koskenniemi's work. According to Outi Korhonen, the aim of the final chapter of FATU titled 'Beyond Objectivism', was 'to restore the meaning and relevance of international law by theorizing a new positive identity for the international lawyer'.[380]

---

[375] Jason A. Beckett, 'Rebel Without a Cause? Martti Koskenniemi and the Critical Legal Project', 7 (2006) *German Law Journal*, pp. 1045–1088 at p. 1059; emphasis in original.

[376] See ibid., p. 1060. Beckett further explains that there is thus "an intimate connection between Koskenniemi's critical and constructive (or ethical) projects. From this perspective, the critical project both identifies the conceptual space, and secures the political space, within which the ethical project takes place; and thus the ethical project drives the critical". See ibid., p. 1046.

[377] Koskenniemi, *From Apology to Utopia* (2005), p. 589.

[378] Outi Korhonen, 'New International Law: Silence, Defence or Deliverance?', 7 (1996) *European Journal of International Law*, pp. 1–28 at pp. 13, 3. Koskenniemi anticipated the charge of nihilism but observed that: 'to renounce critical reflexion simply as one feels that it will lead into nihilism is not in itself a rational counter-argument. It simply betrays another, and possible aggravated, version of nihilism as it argues, in effect, that it is better to continue living in an illusion, whatever the consequences, rather than to analyze what part of the illusion might be worth preserving and what simply obstructs constructive effort'. Koskenniemi, *From Apology to Utopia*, p. 478.

[379] Koskenniemi anticipates this criticism as well but does not say much about it in FATU. Koskenniemi, *From Apology to Utopia*, p. 479. See also Beckett, 'Rebel Without A Cause', p. 1065.

[380] Korhonen, 'New International Law', p. 24. Koskenniemi writes: 'one is not committed to irrationality or to an "anything goes" morality even if one rejects the view that law

As we have seen, Koskenniemi himself speaks about how 'one can *live* in and through it' in order to 'live a conscious and meaningful life as a lawyer'.[381] Thus, 'Koskenniemi proposes the adoption of a personal perspective. From this perspective the international lawyer or scholar could observe or act without having to insist on any other foundation'.[382] Or as Koskenniemi puts it, he seeks to re-establish the international lawyer as a social agent.[383] He must exercise his freedom in the face of choices that are ever-present. It is partly this understanding that informs the notion of 'culture of formalism' that Koskenniemi has advanced and is examined presently.

The fourth thesis is a critique of the narrative of progress that informs much writing about international law. Initially, following Kennedy, as the latter himself pointed out in his 1990 review of FATU, Koskenniemi 'challenge(d) the enlightenment story of intellectual and institutional progress' and presented 'a comprehensive criticism of modern public international legal doctrine and argument'.[384] However, in the epilogue to reissued FATU Koskenniemi nuances his position and writes: 'it does not seem possible to believe that international law is *automatically or necessarily* an instrument of progress. It *provides resources for defending good and bad causes*, enlightened and regressive policies'.[385] In other words, while a narrative of progress is problematic 'good causes' can be pursued through international law. But Koskenniemi hastens to add that 'the positive aspect of the critical programme is considerably more difficult to outline'.[386] Therefore, the critical programme is primarily assigned a procedural meaning. Thus Koskenniemi conceives politics as 'a human practice of continuous criticism of and conversation about the present conditions of society and the ways to make them more acceptable'.[387] He

---

contains an external, privileged vision of society. It simply gives effect to the intuition that the lawyers' expectations of certainty should be downgraded and that they – as well and States and statesmen – must take seriously the moral-political choices they are faced with even when arguing "within the law" and accept the consequence that in some relevant sense the choices are theirs and that they therefore should be responsible for them'. Koskenniemi, *From Apology to Utopia*, p. 479.

[381] Koskenniemi, *From Apology to Utopia*, pp. 490, 495.

[382] Korhonen, 'New International Law', p. 24.

[383] Koskenniemi, *From Apology to Utopia*, p. 490.

[384] Kennedy, 'Book Review' p. 385. On the narrative of progress, see generally Thomas Skouteris, *The Notion of Progress in International Law Discourse* (The Hague: T. M. C. Asser Press, 2010).

[385] Koskenniemi, *From Apology to Utopia* (2005), p. 613; emphasis added.

[386] Koskenniemi, *From Apology to Utopia*, p. 484.

[387] See ibid., p. 480.

notes that two conditions must be satisfied in arriving at a 'solution', partial or otherwise:

> first, the solution must be arrived at through an open (uncoerced) discussion of the alternative material justifications; two, the critical process must continue and put that rival justification – as it will now have become part of the dominant consciousness – to future criticism. The legitimacy of critical solutions does not lie in the intrinsic character of the solution but in the openness of the process of conversation and evaluation through which it has been chosen and in the way it accepts the possibility or revision – in the authenticity of the participants' will to agree.[388]

In other words, there must be a culture of conversation accompanied by 'the ideal of *authentic commitment*' that encapsulates an 'ethic of responsibility'.[389] But a dialogic conception of international law does not rule out commitment of any kind in which to anchor the conversations. In so far as Koskenniemi is concerned, 'it positively *excludes imperialism and totalitarianism*. Beyond that, however, it makes no pretension to offer principles of the good life which would be valid in a global way'.[390]

These theses and reflections are reconfigured and later integrated in the notion of 'culture of formalism'. Before turning to its exegesis and critique, it is important to review Koskenniemi's move from structure to the history of international law, and the particular stories he tells, as it coincides with and informs both the move to neo-formalism and a hint of moving beyond.

B.   The Turn to History

The challenge Koskenniemi posed to the mainstream understanding of international law in FATU was limited to deconstructing the structure and doctrines of international law relying on linguistic and post-structural theories. Later, he came to appreciate the importance of the history of international law in understanding the nature and character of international law.[391] Koskenniemi realized that a critical theory

---

[388] See ibid., p. 487.

[389] See ibid., p. 488; emphasis in original.

[390] See ibid., p. 497; emphasis in original.

[391] It can be conjectured that the work of the work of TWAIL scholars like Anghie played a role in this regard. Antony Anghie, `Heart of My Home', pp. 445–506; Antony Anghie, 'Francisco de Vitoria and the Colonial Origins of International Law', 5 (1996) *Social Legal Studies*, pp. 321–336; Antony Anghie, 'Finding the Peripheries: Sovereignty and Colonialism in Nineteenth Century International Law', 40 (1999) *Harvard International*

of international law cannot be advanced without taking the history of international law seriously, especially the centrality of the colonial project. It was the beginning of a historical turn in Koskenniemi's work. One phase of this work was completed with the publication of GCN which represented, in his words, a 'move from structure to history'.[392] In it he essentially traced the history of international legal profession in Europe between 1870 and 1960. Since GCN, Koskenniemi has written much on the history of international law that include essays on the contribution of Spanish scholastics of sixteenth century to the emerging 'empire of private rights' and on Grotius and the emergence of mercantile capitalism in the seventeenth century. The recent history is written in the materialist mode and suggests a somewhat different understanding of international law from that contained in FATU and GCN. Koskenniemi has been later tempted to read his historical work back into FATU. But as Balakrishnan Rajagopal observed in his reflections on reissued FATU: 'It is hard to see how FATU, when originally published, could be seen to express a critique of the way international law helped to sustain an unequal relationship between a powerful North and a weak South. Koskenniemi's work between FATU's first and second editions (between 1989 and 2005) has in fact focused significantly on the central intuition that he attributes to the first edition, viz., that international law is structurally biased against the South.'[393]

In what follows, four submissions are made with respect to Koskenniemi's historical writings and its implications. First, it is argued that the Koskenniemi assumption that his historical work leaves his

Law Journal, pp. 1–80; Antony Anghie, 'Colonialism and the Birth of International Institutions: Sovereignty, Economy and the Mandate System of the League of Nations', 34 (2002) New York University Journal of International Law and Politics, p. 513; Anghie, Imperialism. In his book The Gentle Civilizer of Nations he notes the writings of Anghie but in a footnote in the first chapter (fn 6 and one more time), but clubs his work along with 'David Bederman, Nathaniel Berman, Anthony Carty, David Kennedy, Karen Knop, Outi Korhonen, Carl Landeur, and Annelise Riles'. While the others have certainly contributed to the history of international law, many of these writings are not in a central way about the colonial project and the evolution of international law. It may be noted that his footnote is to the statement that 'much of the new work has concentrated in describing international law as part of the colonialist project'. Koskenniemi, Gentle Civilizer, p. 9. It is left to readers to decide as to how many of them have actually directly, or some cases even indirectly, talked about 'international law as part of the colonialist project'. It is also worth noting that there is no mention of TWAIL I scholars like R. P. Anand and Nagendra Singh, or T. E. Elias and Mohammed Bedjaoui.

[392] Koskenniemi, Gentle Civilizer, p. 5.
[393] Balakrishnan Rajagopal, 'Martti Koskenniemi's From Apology to Utopia: A Reflection', 7 (2006) German Law Journal, pp. 1089–1094 at p. 1093.

contentions about the structure of international law intact is deeply problematic. Second, it is suggested that his recent historical work, written in
the materialist mode, runs against his general thesis about the absence
of determinate 'causes' of legal developments. Indeed, there is even out
there the hint of a 'grand narrative'. Third, it is contended that his history
of European international law is flawed as it is written in the monologic
mode, that is, without taking into account histories written by non-
Western scholars. Fourth, it is submitted that he makes a misplaced point
about the absence of 'autochthonous' histories of international law among
those who seek to 'provincialize Europe'. It leads to the false idea that a
Eurocentric history of international law can, even after critique has had its
day, may legitimately be portrayed as a universal history of international
law. Each of these submissions is examined in turn.

C.   *From Structure to History*

Because of the crucial omission of the relationship between colonialism
and international law in FATU, Koskenniemi had failed to see that despite
the infirmities that characterized the structure of international law it was
uniquely productive in facilitating and legitimizing imperialism. The neglect of the relationship between colonialism and international law meant
that the structure of international law that he described and analysed in
FATU was deeply flawed, at least in capturing historical realities. The relationship between the abstract and the concrete was snapped in his analysis of international law. International law in the colonial period was not
'substantively open ended' as far as the colonized were concerned. Nor
did politics or law assume a dialogic form. The colonized were preventing
from speaking any language, whether of politics or law, unless allowing
them to speak was the first step in silencing them.[394] In fact the colonized
were banished from the kingdom of international law and international
politics.

   However, the move from structure to history did not compel
Koskenniemi to revisit his thesis on the internal structure of international
law. He did not appreciate that you cannot post facto add history to
structure to arrive at a realistic portrayal of international law. There is an
intimate and dialectical relationship between the history and structure of
international law that cannot be captured through an arithmetic procedure but only, as if it were, in a single motion. It could perhaps be argued

[394] Anghie, *Imperialism*, p. 105.

that Koskenniemi later amended his earlier understanding of the workings of international law. Thus, for instance, he diluted his claim on structural indeterminacy as can be deduced from his lament that one sentence
from FATU on the irrelevance of international law was insistently cited to
make him say more than he wished to.[395]

His idea of 'culture of formalism' can also be viewed from this perspective. He took his earlier reflections on 'beyond objectivism' and gave them
new meaning through his thesis on neo-formalism. As will be seen later
he did this in two ways. First, he attributed the role of international law
in the colonial period to what he terms its 'instrumental use' which did
not undermine the fact that international law was a carrier of values of
universality. Second, he argued that while most European international
lawyers of the period supported the colonial project they were nevertheless committed to liberal internationalism. This move was necessary not
only to mitigate the complicity of European international lawyers but also
to assign international lawyers a heroic role as he does in the frame of
'culture of formalism'. But as will be argued presently, he thereby delinked
the story of international law from the story of universalizing capitalism.
He also appears to confine the idea of resistance to individual lawyers,
thereby neglecting among other things the epic struggles of the formerly
colonized peoples, along with the subaltern classes in the Metropolitan
nations, over the centuries.[396]

D.   Towards a Grand Narrative?

In recent years, working backwards, Koskenniemi has turned to the study
of the contribution of Spanish scholastics Vitoria and Suarez. In an essay
on the subject he argues that the legal basis of colonialism was the 'empire
of private rights' articulated by among others Vitoria and Suarez in the
sixteenth century. His claim is that 'the principal legacy of the Salamanca
scholars lay in their development of a vocabulary of private rights (of
dominium) that enabled the universal ordering of international relations
by recourse to private property, contract, and exchange. This vocabulary
provided an efficient articulation for Europe's "informal empire" over
the rest of the world and is still operative as the legal foundation of global relations of power'.[397] Thus, in his view, the more important way of

---

[395] Koskenniemi, *From Apology to Utopia* (2005), p. 600.
[396] For an explanation of this tendency see infra pp. 342–343.
[397] Martti Koskenniemi, 'Empire and International Law: the Real Spanish Contribution', 61
(2011) *University of Toronto Law Journal*, pp. 1–36 at p. 1.

thinking about 'imperial relations' is 'through the universal functioning of such private-law rules as those concerning property and contract'.[398] In Koskenniemi's view, scholars like Antony Anghie, China Miéville and Robert Williams omitted this dimension in their work and focused instead on 'the relations that pertained between princes and sovereigns'[399] or 'subjugating non-European cultures under a rhetoric and trustee-ship'.[400] Koskenniemi has of course no quarrel with a critique of the work of Vitoria and Suarez from the latter perspective, albeit, he does not fail to mention 'the liberal retort' 'on the good intentions of the Spaniards and their personal courage'.[401] But the crucial point Koskenniemi makes is that 'by ignoring those aspects of their work that deal with the universal operation of property and contract, we receive a truncated and one-sided image not only of what they were doing but of the nature of the legal system that has persisted much more powerfully as part of global history than did any formal empire'.[402] Vitoria and others were addressing, among other things, 'the emergence of a global economic system based on pri-vate ownership and the search for profit'.[403] It is in that context that they spoke of 'the beneficial nature of private property and the transactions connected with it'.[404] This understanding helps explain why 'the univer-salization of private dominium rights by *ius gentium* was accompanied by rules on their enforcement under the theory of just war'.[405] According to Koskenniemi, in the final analysis Vitoria, Suarez and others were lay-ing the foundations of 'a structure of human relationships that we have been accustomed to label "capitalism" '.[406] He therefore concludes that 'far more important than their writings on the Indies are the texts discussing dominium as the (subjective) right of property that is valid universally under the *ius gentium* and that can be together with the derivative rights of travel and trade, enforced by just war'.[407] In short, as Koskenniemi puts it 'the world was an empire, but an "empire of private rights" '.[408] It has to be said that his critique of Anghie and others is in order as it is the rise of capitalism and its universalizing thrust, which has gone through different

---

[398]   See ibid., p. 2.
[399]   See ibid., p. 31.
[400]   See ibid., pp. 1, 10.
[401]   See ibid., p. 10.
[402]   See ibid., p. 3.
[403]   See ibid., p. 12.
[404]   See, ibid., p. 18.
[405]   See ibid., p. 28.
[406]   See ibid., p. 32.
[407]   See ibid.
[408]   See ibid., p. 28.

phases, that accounts for the phenomenon of imperialism since the six-teenth century.[409]

Koskenniemi's subsequent essay on 'international law and the emer-gence of mercantile capitalism' shows how 'Grotius followed the 16th century Spanish scholastics who had already made a firm link between private rights, commutative justice, property and sovereignty'.[410] He writes in the context of the rise of Dutch power that 'the Dutch policy did not differ significantly from that of other European powers in the 17th century. All of them advocated free trade and free passage as long as they were ascending; once established, their political interest was in monop-oly'.[411] Koskenniemi observes that the links between economic progress, private traders, free trade and the imperial state are clear:

> For the Dutch as well as those other powers, economic progress was inex-tricable from State-building and it would be hard (and perhaps pointless) to identify one part of the project as conceptually or ideologically prior to the other. Trade served statehood, and statehood served the interests of private traders. This was the very engine on which Europe's ascent to world dominance at this time was based.[412]

In the case of the Dutch in particular Koskenniemi emphasizes the 'close connection between the merchant elite and the State'.[413] Turning to the emergence of a capitalist legal system Koskenniemi notes the continu-ities and observes that 'the basic legal elements of property and contract that we usually link with "capitalism" were already present in the Spanish scholastics. Grotius and his followers detached them from what was left of the Aristotelian framework and reinstated them in the language of the legal form'.[414] He concludes that the 'changes in patterns of eco-nomic activity is sufficient for understanding the need of legal innovation during early modernity'.[415] It necessitated 'a well operating legal system that would guarantee the security of private property and the speedy and reliable handling of commercial disputes'.[416] This narrative is once again

---

[409] For a synoptic history of international law along these lines, see Chapter 7, pp. 477–499.

[410] Marti Koskenniemi, 'International Law and the Emergence of Mercantile Capitalism', p. 9, at www.helsinki.fi/eci/Publications/Koskenniemi/MKMercantileCapitalism.pdf (accessed 21 January 2014).

[411] See ibid., pp. 21–22.

[412] See ibid., p. 22.

[413] See ibid., p. 23.

[414] See ibid., p. 22.

[415] See ibid.

[416] See ibid., p. 25. Koskenniemi also notes two other features about the thinking of Grotius that deserve attention in the context of materialist history of the period. First, that 'although Grotius accepted something like "state sovereignty", most of the long discussion

sound, albeit akin to a 'grand narrative' about the relationship between
the empire of private rights, imperialism and international law. Indeed,
this is good materialist history that involves the determination of 'legal
innovation' by 'changes in pattern of economic activity' a proposition far
removed from his earlier position that saw any such linkage as part of the
old economic determinism argument.[417]

What Koskenniemi is attempting here is to reveal in historical terms
the relationship between law and political economy in the same ways as
Kennedy is seeking to do with reference to contemporary international
law. But like Kennedy he does not explain his departure from, or so it
seems on the face of it, the view that advancing 'any grand history' or 'any
particular theory about causal determination of ideas or by ideas of something else' would involve 'implied philosophical, methodological, and
political assumptions' that are 'hard to sustain'.[418] However, to his credit,
Koskenniemi draws attention to the significance of the 'empire of private
rights' to the story of international law. It was a central development in
the period of transition from feudalism to capitalism in Europe. In fact,
as Michael Tigar and Madeline Levy write in their book *Law and Rise of
Capitalism*: 'by 1600 the main principles of bourgeois private law, that law
regarding interpersonal dealings in contract, property, and so on, had in
theory though not everywhere in practice replaced personal feudal relationships'.[419] The principles of bourgeois private law were carried to other
parts of the world by roving capitalism. These principles gave a certain
shape to the evolution and development of international law. As already
pointed out, TWAIL scholars like R. P. Anand have demonstrated how
legal thinking in this era was often driven by imperial interests, as in the

---

of the matter in *De jure belli ac pacis* attacked the view that the "people" itself might in any
way be thought of as the "proper" holder of sovereignty'. See ibid., p. 24. Second, Grotius
rejected the right of resistance: 'Resistance was legitimate only in case of "extreme and
inevitable", that is to say mortal, danger. Otherwise subjects should either obey or emi-
grate'. See ibid. The idea was 'the restoration of order, a prerequisite of economic resur-
gence'. Immanuel Wallerstein cited in ibid., p. 24.

[417] In a later essay Koskenniemi notes 'the close relationship that has always existed between
sovereignty and property, public and private law in external government and empire'. He
goes on to say that it is this understanding that he has tried to capture in his recent work.
Martti Koskenniemi, 'Histories of International Law: Significance and Problems for a
Critical View', 27 (2013) *Temple International & Comparative Law Journal*, pp. 215–241 at
p. 235.

[418] Koskenniemi, *Gentle Civilizer*, pp. 2, 6. He later attempts to explain this by stating that he
was doing different kinds of history. See 'Histories of International Law'.

[419] Michael E. Tigar (with the assistance of Madeleine R. Levy), *Law and the Rise of Capitalism*
(New York: Monthly Review Press, 1977), p. 183.

case of Grotius advancing the doctrine of freedom of the seas to defend Dutch maritime interests.[420] Be that as it may, what Koskenniemi has to say on the subject of the relationship between the 'empire of private rights', imperialism and international law is welcome. It is another matter that he does not carry this analysis and understanding to the present.

E. European International Lawyers, Colonialism and Cosmopolitan Vision

His current take on the history of international law is also refreshing because in the history he narrates in GCN of the role of European international lawyers in late nineteenth century there is not much on the relationship between patterns of economic activity and legal developments both in domestic and international law. GCN was written before he had made the connections between universalizing capitalism, imperialism and the evolution of international law. It may of course be argued that the essays in GCN had a different purpose. These represented, in his own words, 'a kind of experimentation in the writing about the disciplinary past in which the constraints of any "rigorous" method have been set aside in an effort to create intuitively plausible and politically engaged narratives about the emergence and gradual transformation of a profession that plays with the reader's empathy'.[421] The focus was apparently on 'how the profession ended up being what it is today'.[422]

The history of the profession that he narrates is unique in the sense that he seems to care about European international law scholars in a way that no one has in recent times, empathetically describing their individual and political projects. Of course, Koskenniemi does not hesitate to show how European international lawyers fell prey to 'nationalism',[423] justified the colonial project,[424] displayed little respect for other religions[425] and despised 'socialism'.[426] But he also goes on to point out how European international lawyers 'integrated their nationalism in a larger, humanist vision of European

---

[420] See chapter 4 titled 'Mare Liberum vs Mare Clausum' in R. P. Anand, *Origin and Development of Law of the Sea: History of International Law Revisited* (The Hague: Martinus Nijhoff Publishers, 1983).

[421] Koskenniemi, *Gentle Civilizer*, pp. 9–10.

[422] See ibid., p. 7.

[423] See ibid., p. 64.

[424] See ibid., p. 75.

[425] See ibid., p. 66.

[426] See ibid., p. 69.

civilization'.[427] The general idea is to suggest that these 'white men' were not reactionary and heartless but merely the product of their times. That is to say, while they were certainly vulnerable to the prejudices of the colonial era, they also offered a vision of international law that was cosmopolitan and universal. Indeed, Koskenniemi argues that despite being complicit in the colonial project European international lawyers never forsake liberal internationalism. He buttresses his point by gesturing towards the nature of world order after decolonization:

> The story of international law and formal empire in 1870–1914 may be a story of arrogance, misplaced ambition, and sheer cruelty. But it is indissociable from the wider narrative of a liberal internationalism that thinks of itself as the 'legal *conscience* of the civilized world' and whose humanitarian aspirations cannot be dismissed as a set of bad-faith justifications for Western domination ... That most international lawyers enthusiastically welcomed decolonization was completely conditioned by their interpretation that this meant the final universalization of Western forms of government.[428]

Thus Koskenniemi, while being critical of European international lawyers of the nineteenth century, portrays them as far-sighted people who accurately perceived the drift of history.[429] This is an interesting move for that reading can be extended to the era of neo-colonialism and global imperialism as well. But if the history of the profession is to offer any guidance to present and succeeding generations it is important not to present international lawyers complicit in the colonial project as 'progressive' minds. But this is precisely the hazard of writing a monologic history of European international law. For the Other does not participate in the writing of this history.

Indeed, a fundamental problem with the history Koskenniemi tells of nineteenth-century international lawyers is the belief that the history of European international law can be told without taking into account history written by Others. More precisely, he does not believe in a 'participatory

---

[427] See ibid., p. 63.

[428] See ibid., p. 176; emphasis in original.

[429] 'Koskenniemi's nuanced account of debates over colonialism presents a picture of international lawyers who were sincerely concerned with the well-being of native populations, but who more often than not supported the imperial policies of their own states'. Jeffrey L. Dunoff, 'From Interdisciplinarity to Counterdisciplinarity: Is There Madness in Martti's Method?', 27 (2013) *Temple International & Comparative Law Journal*, pp. 309–339 at p. 317. See also Andrew Lang and Susan Marks, 'People with Projects: Writing the Lives of International Lawyers', 27 (2013) *Temple International & Comparative Law Journal*, pp. 437–453 at pp. 445–446.

search for truth' that comes through engaging with the history told from the perspective of those who had been colonized.[430] This is particularly troubling as Other histories of international law had been written before Koskenniemi wrote his history of European international law and the legal profession, even if these are different kinds of histories.[431] But he writes his history as if there are no Other histories of the period. He also ignores the fact that there are no unique histories after the emergence of capitalism, as we saw he argues later, when considering the contribution of Vitoria and Suarez. In fact there are only intersecting histories: therefore there cannot be 'an understanding of Europe that springs out of itself as a fully autonomous phenomenon'.[432] Koskenniemi cannot justify the neglect of Other histories by stating that he is simply writing the history of European international law or lawyers. As Andrew Davison et al. point out, 'but this is *the point*'.[433] Europe cannot narrate its story without dialogue with Others as 'all understanding takes place within relationships of otherness'.[434] In a radical rendering of Hans Gadamer, Davison et al. make him cross colonial borders for reaching understanding.[435] In this view narrating the history of European international relations cannot but be a dialogic process. It is not a choice for there is no other way a history that aspires to 'truth' can be told. To be sure, the history of the self and other do not merge but there is a 'fusion of horizons'.[436] In other words, 'the point is not that the Other always has it "right", only that the Other, like the self, always has a shared part to play in illuminating the self to the self by provoking the self to understand the Other's experience of the self'.[437]

---

[430] Andrew Davison, Himadeep Muppidi, Freya Irani and Dror Ladin, 'Europe and Its Boundaries: Toward a Global Hermeneutic Political Theory' in Andrew Davison and Himadeep Muppidi (eds.), *Europe and Its Boundaries: Words and Worlds, Within and Beyond* (Lanham, MD: Lexington Books, 2009), pp. 83–111 at p. 84.

[431] It reveals how the European international lawyer believes that she does not have to engage with the view of the Other about this history. For another recent example of such neglect see Emmanuelle Jouannet, *The Liberal-Welfarist Law of Nations* (Cambridge: Cambridge University Press, 2012).

[432] Davison et al., 'Europe and Its Boundaries', p. 85.

[433] See ibid., p. 91; emphasis in original.

[434] See ibid., p. 92.

[435] See ibid., p. 99.

[436] The term 'fusion of horizons', as Dallmayr explains, 'should not be taken in the sense of a complete merger or a Hegelian synthesis, but in that of an engaged dialogical encounter'. Fred Dallmayr, 'Self and Other: Gadamer and the Hermeneutics of Difference', 5 (1993) *Yale Journal of Law and the Humanities*, pp. 507–529 at p. 516.

[437] Davison et al., 'Europe and Its Boundaries', p. 101. Davison et al. therefore speak of 'the anticolonial potential of Gadamerian hermeneutics'. See ibid., p. 102.

The co-narration is a relational account that is meaningful for both the self and the Other.[438] It is the only way that the 'truth' emerges. It is surprising that for someone who lays emphasis on dialogue in the course of interpretation and application of international law Koskenniemi does not see its import in doing history, be it of international law or the profession.

F.   Search for Autochthonous Histories

Writing some years later, Koskenniemi appears to accept the fact that 'the view that there is a single, universal international law with a homogeneous history and an institutional-political project emerges from a profoundly Eurocentric view of the world'.[439] He also notes that 'the point of view the "Other" is being researched in studies on East Asian, Chinese, Japanese, Latin American, Ottoman and Islamic systems of international relations and law'.[440] But instead of speaking of a dialogue with these researches he goes on to observe that these studies:

> tend to receive their perspective, concepts and standards from European historiography, not least because of most of the respective scholars have been trained in and usually continue to work with European or (perhaps more often) US academic institutions. This may be impossible to avoid, and in any case, the more important problem may be that much of this work is constrained within the conceptual confines of 'Empire' and 'colonization'– European notions and experiences of European rule. *The question remains how to identify and compare autochthonous forms of thinking about inter-community relations that would not necessarily be subsumable under European legal categories but would stand on their own and thus also provide a wider comparative perspective under which European categories could be examined as equally 'provincial' as others.*[441]

It would be noticed that the 'comparative' dimension is conceptualized as each nation or region having its own history and not about intersecting histories or a history written in conversation with the Other. The demand is for 'autochthonous' histories that 'would stand on their own' to expose European categories as 'provincial'. This confuses issues once again. After the beginning of the colonial era the

---

[438] See ibid., p. 107.
[439] Martti Koskenniemi, 'The Case for Comparative International Law', 20 (2009) *Finnish Yearbook of International Law*, pp. 1–8 at p. 4.
[440] See ibid. For some reason he leaves out India and South Asia unless he is subsuming them under East Asia.
[441] See ibid., pp. 4–5; emphasis added.

trap of essentialism awaits those who attempt 'autochthonous' histories. These do not exist so far as *modern* international law is concerned.
There could be multiple interpretations of the relationship between
Europe and the Other. But these would be different global histories –
the debate will be about *that* history and not about unique histories of
regions. Undoubtedly there will yet be a surplus history that is indigenous, both pre-colonial and colonial. In the former instance that history
is not that of modern international law, albeit important from the point
of view of recording the contribution of the non-West to the evolution
and development of international law. In the case of the colonial period,
the surplus history will be about practices that existed in Asia and Africa
that allowed the European traders and local rulers to speak the same
language as in the case of India.[442] But when Koskenniemi demands an
'autochthonous' history of international law in the Global South and
points out that the leaders of the freedom movement used European
ideas, he neglects the universalizing logic of capital and the constraints
it imposed upon them.[443] To 'provincialize Europe' does not mean that a
pure indigenous history has to be counterposed to the historical narrative of European international law. A global history of international law
comprises three different strands. First, there is the history of relations
between political entities in the pre-colonial period that produced basic
rules of inter-state conduct. In some instances these rules and practices
contributed to the evolution and development of international law. This
is not a claim (as Koskenniemi insensitively suggests) that 'we were also
Europeans'.[444] It is simply drawing attention to the idea that the rules of
international law are a product of unavoidable social realities and not of
the unique genius of particular peoples. But since Koskenniemi thinks
and writes in the monologic mode it is also difficult for him to appreciate the additional claim that there may be something to learn from
the history of pre-colonial international law.[445] The term 'Eurocentrism'
and 'Eurocentric history' is used for the denial of precisely such claims.
Second, there is the history of modern European international law that

---

[442] See R. P. Anand, *Development of Modern International Law and India* (New Delhi: Indian
Society of International law, 2006), pp. 24–25. See Chapter 7. pp....

[443] Vivek Chibber, *Postcolonial Theory and the Specter of Capital* (New Delhi: Navayana
Publishing Pvt. Ltd., 2013).

[444] Koskenniemi, 'Histories of International Law', p. 223. He has repeated this charge recently.
See Koskenniemi, *Politics of International Law* p. 963.

[445] B. S. Chimni, 'Legitimating International Rule of Law' in Crawford and Koskenniemi,
Cambridge Companion, pp. 290–309 at pp. 305–306.

cannot be told separately from the story of colonial international law. As Anghie demonstrates, in this period the destiny of European international law was internally linked with the colonial project.[446] Third, certain tenets of European international law, earlier made inapplicable to the colonial world, were universalized through the struggles of third world peoples against colonialism and neocolonialism; the democratization of international law came about through these struggles but still subject to the universalizing logic of capital leading to many European legal categories and principles being adopted by postcolonial states.[447] If the claim is that Europe contributed to these ideas it is not off the mark. But these ideas were part of the repertoire of other ideas that justified colonialism and continue to justify imperialism. If pride has to be taken in some ideas it has to be accompanied by the remorse that genocide, exploitation and violence against other peoples were an intrinsic part of that world of ideas.[448] Indeed, the two sets of ideas cannot be easily separated.[449] Finally, as one observer notes in the context of India:

> In recent years the history of India from the sixteenth century has become a field of astonishingly fertile contestation, with strikingly revisionist suggestions on both historical and conceptual questions. Historians working on vernacular textual sources have suggested an autochthonous process of 'early modernity' which was partly accelerated and partly negated by the arrival of colonialism which introduced institutional forms from modern Europe.[450]

This nascent revisionist history has to be read in the light of the fact that postcolonial theory highlights viz., 'the more modernity expands and spreads to different parts of the world the more it becomes differentiated

---

[446] Anghie, *Imperialism*.

[447] See generally the sketch of history in Chapter 7, pp. 477–499.

[448] In a more recent essay Koskenniemi reiterates that 'the history of international legal ideas is intensely Eurocentric'. Martti Koskenniemi, 'International Law in the World of Ideas' in Crawford and Koskenniemi (eds.). *Cambridge Companion*, pp. 47–63 at p. 54. He tells the story about international law as part of 'the history of European ideas'. See ibid., p. 50. There is not even the usual reference to the ideas of international law in the history of the non-Western world. There is much here that he could have learnt from the many writings on the subject challenging the idea that international law is a product of European Christian civilization (e.g., the work of C. H. Alexandrowicz, R. P. Anand, and Christopher Weeramantry).

[449] See Mehta, *Liberalism*.

[450] Sudipta Kaviraj, 'On the Enchantment of the State: Indian Thought on the Role of the State in the Narrative of Modernity', 46 (2005) *European Journal of Sociology*, pp. 263–296 at p. 272.

and plural'.[451] Western social sciences have yet to come to terms with the idea of myriad trajectories of modernity that arise not only from different ways in which separate elements of modernity come together or are historically sequenced, but also from 'initial conditions' in which elements of modernity are embedded.[452] These have a great bearing on the nature of modernity and modern international law that now have no centre. It is hard however for Koskenniemi to let go of the centrality of Europe in global history.

G.   The Turn to Culture of Formalism

It is no accident that in the years that Koskenniemi produced his historical work that he also began to argue the case for a 'culture of formalism'. He wanted to salvage from the history of colonial international law the liberal cosmopolitan vision of European international lawyers.[453] He proceeded to hive off the vision from colonial realities and in combination with his thesis on structural indeterminacy advanced the notion of 'culture of formalism'. He formulated it in the following manner in the epilogue to reissued FATU:

> Recently, I have argued in favor of a 'culture of formalism' as *a progressive choice*. This assumes that although *international law remains substantively open-ended*, the choice to refer to 'law' in the administration of international matters – instead of, for example, 'morality' or 'rational choice' – is not politically innocent. Whatever historical baggage, including bad faith, such culture entails, *its ideals include those of accountability, equality, reciprocity and transparency* and it comes to us with an embedded vocabulary of (formal) rights.[454]

[451] Sudipta Kaviraj, 'An Outline of a Revisionist Theory of Modernity', 46 (2005)*European Journal of Sociology*, pp. 497–526 at p. 504.

[452] 'When we are talking about modernity, we are talking about a number of processes of social change which can be studied or analyzed independently of each other – such as, capitalist industrialization, the increasing centrality of the state in the social order (Foucault's "governmentality"), urbanization, sociological individuation, secularization in politics and ethics, the creation of a new order of knowledge, vast changes in the organization of family and intimacy, and changes in the fields of artistic and literary culture'. See ibid., p. 508.

[453] Others have tried to find a degree of continuity with FATU and noted that the last chapter 'Beyond Objectivism' offers an early rendering of it. Florian Hoffman, 'An Epilogue on an Epilogue', 7 (2006) *German Law Journal*, pp. 1095–1102 at p. 1096. But it is being argued that the sources of that early statement were different and therefore it could not have been given the form it has been given now. Koskenniemi's use of the word 'recently' must be seen in that light.

[454] Koskenniemi, *From Apology to Utopia*, p. 616; emphasis added.

The meaning and implications of idea of 'culture of formalism' is best understood through identifying its principle features as found in Koskenniemi's different pronouncements on the subject. In order to faithfully represent his views reliance is placed on his own formulations even as questions are raised with respect to them. The following six overlapping features of the 'culture of formalism' can be culled from his writings.

First, he continues to assume that 'international law remains substantially open-ended'.[455] Koskenniemi does not revise his celebrated thesis on the structural indeterminacy of international law despite the fact that in the colonial era international law was not open-ended but severely constrained from the standpoint of the Other. Even today domination and oppression does not result from international law being substantively open-ended. International law is often oppressive in a straightforward and uncomplicated way. It simply codifies the interests of powerful social forces and actors.

Second, Koskenniemi contrasts the culture of formalism with the culture of instrumentalism arguing that 'the instrumental perspective is typically that of an active and powerful actor in possession of alternative choices; *formalism is often the perspective of the weak actor relying on law for protection*'.[456] In civilizational terms Koskenniemi describes 'European instrumentalism' in the following way:

> *Instrumentalism* is the view that sees international law as *our* possession, part of *our* civilized identity that it seeks to bear upon what it sees as power, chaos, and anarchy outside itself. Law as civilization against the barbarism of politics. This view bridges the gap between the particular and the universal by a historical fable – Kant's view of Europe as the pinnacle of progress … What is taken as given here is that, as we are civilized, we are also in advance of history while the lives of others are only provisional. Hence the mission; hence arrogance and racism. Nothing is at stake for us; everything is at stake for them.[457]

---

[455] The structural indeterminacy that characterizes the language of international law, with every principle having a counter-principle, leaves no escape from rule scepticism: 'Each general principle seems capable of being opposed with an equally valid counter-principle'. Koskenniemi, *From Apology to Utopia*, p. XV; emphasis added. This understanding appears to assume a strong version of structural indeterminacy thesis whereas in his epilogue to FATU Koskenniemi distances himself from his famous sentence of international law being useless in justifying any position. Koskenniemi, *From Apology to Utopia* (2005), p. 600.

[456] Koskenniemi cited in Beckett, 'Rebel without Cause', p. 1079; emphasis added.

[457] Martti Koskenniemi, 'International Law in Europe: Between Tradition and Renewal', 16 (2005) *European Journal of International Law*, pp. 113–124 at p. 123.

He goes on to add that 'we Europeans share this intuition: the international world will be how we are'.[458] Koskenniemi therefore speaks of 'the constant danger of *false universalism*, the universalism of Empire'.[459] He emphasizes the need to be alert to international law serving as a hegemonic technique. Koskenniemi describes the logic of hegemony in the following way: 'the attempt by *me* to represent *my* interests and *my* values as universal, *my* rule as community'.[460] He writes that 'colonialism illustrates the functioning of the logic of hegemony behind an argument about the international community'.[461]

Third, while Koskenniemi distinguishes between 'false and genuine universalism' he rejects relativism. He observes that 'from the fact that there is no authentically universal position, it does not follow that all positions are the same'.[462] Koskenniemi however recognizes that 'the real difficulty lies in being able to make that distinction'.[463] On what basis does one distinguish between hegemonic politics and 'a politics of universal law'? The answer he offers is professional competence and 'sensitivity' of the practitioner (including the academic) and their enlightened understanding of the deep grammar of international law.[464] But as Outi Korhonen observes, the end result is that 'the whole subjectivism versus objectivism debate

---

[458] See ibid., p. 117.

[459] See ibid., p. 116.

[460] Martti Koskenniemi, 'Comments on Chapters 1 and 2' in Michael Byers and Georg Nolte (eds.), *United States Hegemony and the Foundations of International Law* (Cambridge: Cambridge University Press, 2003), pp. 91–100 at p. 95; emphasis in original.

[461] See ibid., p. 94

[462] Koskenniemi, 'International Law in', p. 119.

[463] See ibid. Yet he goes on to write: 'The fact that international law is a European language does not even slightly stand in the way of its being capable of expressing something universal. For the universal has no voice, no authentic representative of its own. It can only appear through something particular; only a particular can make the universal known. A danger and a hope are involved. The danger is that of mistaking one's preferences and interests for one's tradition – and then thinking of *these* as universal, a mistake we Europeans have often made. Therefore, I will suggest that *we should take much more seriously those critiques of international law that point to its role as a hegemonic technique.* Once that critique has been internalized, however, I want to point to its limits. If the universal has no representative of its own, then particularity itself is no scandal. The question would then be: Under what conditions might a particular be able to transcend itself? What particular politics might we have good reason to imagine as a politics of universal law?' See ibid., p. 115; emphasis added.

[464] Koskenniemi, *From Apology to Utopia* (2005), p. 617. To Koskenniemi professional competence inter alia means a grip over 'a complex argumentative practice in which rules are connected with other rules at different levels of abstraction and communicated from one person or group of persons to another so as to carry out the law jobs in which international lawyers are engaged'. See ibid., p. 566.

dichotomy is instigated all over again' with no real escape from 'relativist pragmatism'.[465] Koskenniemi further complicates matters by pointing to the limits of the critique of the hegemonic technique. He writes that:

> If the universal has no representative of its own, then particularity itself is no scandal. The question would then be: Under what conditions might a particular be able to transcend itself? What particular politics might we have good reason to imagine as a politics of universal law?[466]

The real difficulty underlying this formulation is his unwillingness to indicate the 'conditions' that would promote 'the politics of universal law'. He does not reveal his hand. Thus, for instance, it is difficult to know whether he endorses or opposes the extant liberal international order. It is also not clear with what methods he judges the difference between false and genuine universalism on specific questions. International lawyers seem to have an especially heavy burden to carry in the face of agnosticism with respect to material structures that underlie questions of false and genuine universalism.

Fourth, 'a culture of formalism cannot tolerate – the transformation of the formal into a façade for the material in a way that *denies the value of the formal as such*'.[467] From this perspective he distinguishes the idea of formalism from that of Rule of Law:

> The Rule of Law hopes to fix the universal in particular, positive space (a law, a moral or procedural principle, an institution). A culture of formalism resists such fixation. For any such connection will make the formal appear merely a surface for something substantive or procedural, and thus destroys it. In this sense *universality (and universal community) is written into the culture of formalism as an idea (or horizon), unattainable but still necessary*.[468]

In his view, the culture of formalism 'represents the possibility of the universal (as Kant well knew) but it does this by remaining "empty", a negative instead of positive datum, and thus avoids the danger of imperialism'.[469] The negative translates into the question 'what is it that we lack? *The ability to articulate this lack, and to do this in universal terms, is what the culture of formalism provides*'.[470] Therefore, the culture of formalism

---

[465] Korhonen, 'New International Law', p. 24.
[466] Koskenniemi, 'International Law', p. 115; emphasis added.
[467] Koskenniemi, *Gentle Civilizer*, p. 501; emphasis in original.
[468] See ibid., p. 507; emphasis added.
[469] See ibid., p. 504; emphasis added.
[470] See ibid., p. 506; emphasis in original.

'has no essence, and its techniques are constantly redefined in the context of political struggle: what the particular lacks cannot be decided once and for all'.[471] It is presumably an endless process of claims and counterclaims that will move the particular towards the universal and make the world more humane and just. He anticipates that he may be accused of 'a rather worn-out form of legalism' and 'a systematic conservatism'.[472] He denies this. He explains that 'there is room for a culture of formalism even after the critique of rules has done its work. It is precisely because the critique is correct that formalism cannot be permanently associated with any of the substantive outcomes it may have co-existed with ...To assess the culture of formalism by reference to its substantive alignments is, as Kelsen well knew, to mix up categories that should be held distinct'.[473] A 'culture of formalism' simply 'gives voice to those who have been excluded from decision-making'; it '*provides a platform* on which claims about violence, injustice, and social deprivation may be made even against the dominant elements'.[474] But it is not clear whether this platform is the values embedded in law or constituted by law or whether any platform does law work as long as it allows claims of justice to be advanced. In any case, as noted earlier, how is one to know 'what is that we lack?' Who is to arbitrate between different versions of the lack in a world in which power and resources are unequally distributed?

Fifth, in Koskenniemi's view of the cultural of formalism is an antidote to the 'recasting problems of politics as problems of expert knowledge'.[475] The reason international law is 'a progressive choice' is not because 'of the sophistication of its rules or institutions' or 'their moral value' but because

> the tradition of international law has often acted as *a carrier of what is perhaps best described as the regulative idea of universal community*, independent of particular interests or desires. This is Kant's cosmopolitan project rightly understood: not an end-state or party programme but *a project of critical reason* that measures today's state of affairs from the perspective of an ideal of universality that *cannot be reformulated into an institution, a technique of rule, without destroying it*. The fate of international law is not a matter of re-employing a limited number of professionals for more cost-effective tasks but of re-establishing hope for the human species.[476]

[471] See ibid., p. 507.
[472] See ibid., p. 503.
[473] See ibid.
[474] Koskenniemi, *Politics of International Law*, pp. 265–266; emphasis added.
[475] Martti Koskenniemi 'The Fate of Public International Law: Between Technique and Politics', 70 (2007) *The Modern Law Review*, pp. 1–30, at p. 9.
[476] See ibid., p. 30; emphasis added.

In this instance he again speaks of 'an ideal of universality'. But how is this ideal to be realized? What is the project of 'critical reason'? Are there not different kinds of 'critical reason'? Which 'critical reason' is to be privileged? Is the dark past of international law or the dark sides of international laws merely due to the absence of 'critical reason'? Were colonial policies simply a manifestation of lack of 'critical reason'? Or was there more to it? Do the categories capitalism and imperialism help understand the reasons for the absence of critical reason? Or is hope for the human species to be simply re-established through a process of communicative action? Is this another form of Jurgen Habermas's theory communicative action? Koskenniemi speaks of 'a commitment to listening to others' claims and seeking to take them into account' and includes 'in political contestation the question about *who* are entitled to make claims and *what kinds* of claims pass the test of validity'.[477] But is it possible to have communicative action outside the domain of power and what is to be 'the test of validity' of outcomes?

Sixth, in Koskenniemi's view of the culture of formalism the site of resistance can be anywhere where the language of international law is used. He explains (in his Epilogue) that when in FATU he

> refrained from proposing new institutional structures, instead calling upon the imagination of new institutional practices, this gave voice to the insight that progressive legal work was available in a number of different professional environments ... Progress towards just distribution might be much more efficiently reached through work in a national administration, a transnational economic organization or even a multinational company. This, however, few colleagues were ready to hear.[478]

This theory of resistance, as in the case of Kennedy, has its basis in methodological individualism. It explains why there is rarely any discussion in Koskenniemi about collective agents of change or of social movements of any kind.

It may be helpful at this stage to schematically identify the features and critique of the idea of 'culture of formalism'. The various facets of the idea of 'culture of formalism' may be summarized in the following points. First, a culture of formalism assumes that there is 'no zone of non-law' in the tradition of international law. Second, it is based on the belief that despite its dark past the tradition of international law is 'progressive'

---

[477] Martti Koskenniemi, ' "The Lady Doth Protest Too Much" Kosovo, and the Turn to Ethics in International Law', 65 (2002) *The Modern Law Review,* pp. 159–175 at p. 174.
[478] Koskenniemi, *From Apology to Utopia* (2005), p. 605.

because it is a carrier of the ideal of universality holding out the promise of justice. Third, it is defined in opposition to instrumentalism by which is meant the use of international law to achieve particular civilizational goals or interests that has historically led to colonialism or what is termed 'false universalism'. Fourth, a culture of formalism does not mean that 'all positions are the same'. It distinguishes between false and genuine universalism, between 'honesty and cheating'. It is, however, noted that there lies the 'real difficulty', that is, the basis for distinguishing between the two. In this regard, faith is put in professional competence which encompasses the sensibility to understand the deep grammar of international law and its ideals of universality. Fifth, a culture of formalism means that the 'weak' are 'heard and protected'. International law 'provides the platform on which claims about violence, injustice, and social deprivation may be made against dominant elements'. It is committed to the ideals of 'accountability, equality, reciprocity, and transparency' that are part of an 'embedded vocabulary of (formal) rights'. Sixth, the idea of 'culture of formalism' is not to be equated with the idea of 'rule of law' as the latter 'hopes to fix the universal in particular, positive space (a law, a moral, or procedural principle, an institution)'. In fact 'the culture of formalism resists such fixation'.[479] Seventh, a culture of formalism 'has no essence' and its 'techniques' are being constantly refined to oppose 'hegemonic techniques' in political struggle. Eighth, it is clarified that the reference to 'formal rights' does not mean reference to the basic principles of international law such as the principle of sovereign equality of states.[480] For the 'culture of formalism' discards 'the assumption that there is a set of substantive rules or principles of "international law" that would be worthy of the kind of total commitment or rejection'.[481] Ninth, a culture of formalism assumes that progress towards genuine universalism can be achieved 'in different professional environments', not necessarily through privileging some spaces and practices over other. Tenth,

---

[479] Koskenniemi, *Gentle Civilizer*, p. 507. Thus, the 'culture of formalism' is not to be equated with some form of 'positivism'. As Jouannet explains, Koskenniemi is not seeking here 'to defend a formalism whose goal is neutrality, masking political choices and conflicts; he is not proposing a positivistic formalism, but rather a committed, political and cultural formalism'. Jouannet, 'Koskenniemi', p. 21.

[480] However, at one point Koskenniemi writes that whereas 'lawyers from the United States [are] suspicious of institutional formality and claims of sovereign equality and reconceiving international law – including the UN – from the perspective of its instrument usefulness', European lawyers take 'an extremely formal view of international law and especially of the UN Charter'. Koskenniemi, *From Apology to Utopia* (2005), p. 612.

[481] Koskenniemi, 'Fate of Public International Law', p. 2.

since the universal has no voice under some conditions the particular can transcend itself and become the universal. But the conditions in which this can happen have to be determined. Finally, given the structural indeterminacy of international law the international lawyer, and others speakers of its language, cannot escape moral and ethical responsibility for choices made and preferences expressed. The idea of 'culture of formalism' thus signifies an ethical position.[482] In sum, Koskenniemi believes that international law is a field of professional practice, that is, of interpretation in which contestation takes place between different preferences in the matrix of values that promotes the interests of the weak. Indeed, the empire of law is internally constituted by values such as equality, accountability, reciprocity and transparency that are imbibed in the process of acquiring professional competence to speak the language of international law. Having understood its deep grammar, competent professional speakers can contest attempts to present particular interests as universal interests and push the discourse towards 'genuine universalism' to realize the goal of justice.

How helpful is the idea of 'culture of formalism' in realizing the ideals of universality and justice? Undoubtedly there is a certain value to opposing it to the 'deformalization' of law resulting from realist critiques advanced by Hans Morgenthau and others who privilege the political over the legal approach.[483] But serious questions remain to be answered. How can a language that has been shaped by false universalism now serve as a vehicle for realizing genuine universalism?[484] How are the weak to explain the dark present? Why is it that barring honourable exceptions competent speakers of hegemonic states do not interpret the values and rights which are internal to the kingdom of law to protect the weak from the strong? Since the basic principles of international law do not have a 'fixed' content how can a hegemonic technique be condemned in the face of structural indeterminacy that characterizes all legal interpretation?[485] Koskenniemi himself justified the unilateral armed intervention in Kosovo in the name

---

[482] Jan Klabbers, 'Towards a Culture of Formalism? Martti Koskenniemi and the Virtues', 27 (2013) *Temple International & Comparative Law Journal*, pp. 417–436 at p. 420.

[483] Dunoff, 'From Interdisciplinarity', p. 321.

[484] See in this respect, James Tully, *Strange Multiplicity: Constitutionalism in the Age of Diversity* (Cambridge: Cambridge University Press, 1995).

[485] As one critic observes, 'we must recognize that the abstract, supposedly empty frame of international law is already itself complicit in the perpetuation of the current status quo'. Paavo Kotiaho, 'A Return to Koskenniemi, or the Disconcerting Co-optation of Rupture', 13 (2013) *German Law Journal*, pp. 483–496 at p. 494.

of humanity even as most of the third world opposed it. Was it not a case of professional competence being used to support 'false universalism'? The sharply different views on Kosovo again raises the crucial question as to how competent professionals distinguish between different false and genuine universalism.[486] Koskenniemi's invocation of the 'tradition of international law', and his reference to Kelsen, seems to suggest that the extra-vernacular is kept out of this process. It makes Orford observe that for Koskenniemi 'being an effective user of legal language, whether within the world of practice or the world of academy, involves accepting the constraints of a discipline that is anti-theory and anti-philosophy'.[487] But this idea, as she goes on to point out, is 'profoundly conservative' as it means that 'all appeals to reason and method that stand outside the received conventions and wisdom are superfluous'.[488] It implies the neglect of the material structures and processes that have crucially influenced the evolution and development of the tradition. This omission is also in tension with the history of international law Koskenniemi narrates of the period between sixteenth and eighteenth centuries that speak of the relationship between economic activity, private rights and empire. It may be recalled that the notion of 'culture of formalism' that lays critical stress on the moral agency and ethical responsibility of international lawyers was articulated at a time he was doing a particular kind of 'experimental' history with a focus on the sensibilities of individual international law professionals. Since then he has done a different kind of history, but has not revised his idea of 'culture of formalism'. The more materialist history has not made him rethink the exclusive stress on individual responsibility. His explanation of course is that he is doing different kinds of histories with dissimilar aims but this is not convincing beyond a point. Even as Koskenniemi's historical project has led him to speak of capitalism and empire he does not tell us where he stands vis-à-vis capitalism today (in any of its forms). While he condemns colonialism and imperialism, he often treats them as ideological phenomena and critiques them in those terms. He also does not disaggregate the idea of 'weak': for instance, the categories class and gender play little role in his understanding of the tradition of international law.

---

[486] In this respect, it may be recalled Kennedy had perceptively observed at an earlier stage that 'at times his agnosticism annoys'. Kennedy, 'Book Review', p. 387.

[487] Anne Orford, 'A Journal of the Voyage from Apology to Utopia', 7 (2005) *German Law Journal*, pp. 994–1010 at p. 998.

[488] See ibid., p. 999.

At the end of the day all Koskenniemi seems to be saying is that the tradition of international law is valuable despite its dark past as it is a carrier of certain values and provides a vocabulary in which different particular interests can be contested in the face of the structural indeterminacy of international law to work out outcomes that move the international community towards genuine universalism. He exhorts the international law professional to use his competence to move us in that direction. In this respect, Andrew Lang and Susan Marks in an important intervention, referring to an earlier debate between E. P. Thompson and Perry Anderson, helpfully distinguish after Anderson between three kinds of personal projects which may be described as purely personal, projects undertaken in association with others 'directed at public goals, whether pursued individually or collectively', and projects 'which aim at the transformation of existing social relations. These may take the form of political movements, grassroots organizing, or – an historical rarity – revolutionary campaigns'.[489] Lang and Marks note that 'the essential characteristic of this third kind of project is that it seeks to subject to democratic control the fundamental framework within which social life unfolds'.[490] They go on to observe that 'a call for moral responsibility on its own may do little to bring forth projects that challenge the taken-for-granted context of our social relationships'.[491] To those professionals interested in the third kind of project the historical question to be asked is how international legal professionals have contributed to them? Where do individual professionals stand vis-à-vis them today?[492] Koskenniemi does not pose the question at all. Lang and Marks finally go on to stress 'the reality that effective human agency depends not just on a sensibility or set of mental attitudes, beliefs, and images, but also on a cognitive infrastructure that is capable of providing insight into the historical conditions within which any collective project will fall to be realized'.[493] A suitable cognitive apparatus is needed inter alia to identify the critical factors that shape particular social formations without the understanding of which collective projects will remain unrealized.[494]

---

[489] Lang and Marks, 'People with Projects', p. 450.
[490] See ibid., p. 451.
[491] See ibid.
[492] See ibid.
[493] See ibid, p. 452.
[494] See ibid.

It has also to be accompanied by a theory of collective resistance that goes beyond the role of the individual legal professional. But presumably because Koskenniemi is not interested in the third kind of project he does not have a serious theory of resistance, i.e., beyond stating with Kennedy that it can be practised by the individual professional at all sites.[495] He does not address the idea that the weak can be protected and international law used for the common good primarily through the struggles of oppressed and marginalized groups and peoples and not merely through the moral agency of competent professionals working the 'culture of formalism' . It is not surprising then that he tells the story of European international law and lawyers without mentioning the sustained resistance of third world peoples to achieve independence from colonial rule and subsequently against the practices of neocolonialism and global imperialism to make international law the carrier of values that he so commends. He also disregards the fact that the history of the profession does not give confidence that given that different versions of 'genuine universalism' can be articulated in the frame of 'the tradition of international law' it will back that which furthers the goal of emancipation of man. On the cognitive plane it is also not always clear what he means by 'sensibility';[496] it is perhaps a certain approach towards the concerns of the weak. It is then presumed that good argument will prevail, at least in the long run, to realize genuine universalism. It is not as if it never does. In the battle of arguments the weak have often vanquished the strong. The idea of law certainly needs to be valued insofar as it allows good arguments to be advanced. But its autonomy is undermined by Koskenniemi by the claim of structural indeterminacy of rules which leads to, much in the New Haven mode, the collapse of 'law' into politics.[497] On the other hand, Koskenniemi does not wish to speak of the material structures that give life to 'false universalism' or speak of collective resistance of groups and states to realize 'genuine universalism' as it would make him sound like the traditional left. All in all the idea of 'culture of formalism' is a fuzzy idea that does not hold

---

[495] In his neglect of resistance, there is a similarity with Grotius, albeit in the latter case there was a more active rejection of the right of resistance.
[496] Lang and Marks note that 'Martti's use of the term "sensibility" is not always easy to pin down'. Lang and Marks, 'People with Projects', p. 448.
[497] As Jouannet notes, 'if law comes down to the individual policies of different actors, is there not a risk of an inevitable dilution of law in politics, thus turning international law into the law of the most powerful?' Jouannet, 'Koskenniemi', p. 29.

much attraction for the weak or legal professionals who really wish to advance the cause of the weak.

H.   Comparing and Contrasting

At least one reason that arguably prompted Koskenniemi to advance the idea of 'culture of formalism' (as also his history of 'empire of private rights') was the persuasiveness of the critique and proposed reconstruction of international law elaborated by TWAIL, MAIL and FtAIL scholars in the period after FATU was published. These approaches demonstrated that the central issue was not the structural indeterminacy of international law but the structures of imperialism and patriarchy. Koskenniemi may also have found attractive the idea that despite the incisive critiques these approaches advanced they did not (with the exception of an odd scholar) assume a nihilist attitude towards international law. But it could well be that it was the appeal of 'enlightened positivism' that caused him to reformulate his earlier views. In any event it can be said that the idea of 'culture of formalism' seeks to capture, albeit in a distinctive way, the dualism of TWAIL, MAIL, and FtAIL. However, Koskenniemi's version of critique and faith is not as persuasive as it is delinked from the material substratum that shapes international law. His deconstructive method does not help a realistic assessment of the constraints and opportunities that exist in the international legal system. In this regard it may be useful to compare and contrast, albeit in telegraphic language, the idea of 'culture of formalism' with the views of TWAIL, MAIL, FtAIL and MILS.

I.   TWAIL and 'Culture of Formalism'

In his post-FATU writings, Koskenniemi often uses the concepts of colonialism and imperialism to describe and understand modern international law. However, these terms rarely occurred in FATU, nor were these mentioned in Kennedy's review of FATU in 1990, or to be found in the index of the book. The reason was that the relationship between colonialism, imperialism and international law eluded Koskenniemi in the FATU phase. As noted earlier, this is surprising in the case of both Kennedy and Koskenniemi because by the time ILS and FATU came to be written the first generation of third world scholars (TWAIL I) had not only launched a scathing critique of the Eurocentric history of international law, but also demonstrated how the doctrines and rules of international law had facilitated and legitimized the colonial project. But, while the work of key figures of TWAIL I such as Georges Abi-Saab, R. P. Anand, Mohammed Bedjaoui, T. E. Elias among others is listed in the bibliography of FATU, their critique of colonial international law is not to be found in its pages. Of these scholars only Bedjaoui finds a mention in the text.[498] But even his work had not compelled Koskenniemi to look back at the history of imperialism and its intimate connectedness to the development of international law, including 'the structure of international legal argument'.[499] After the publication of FATU, TWAIL II scholars like Anghie underscored *the centrality of the colonial project* to the history and development of international law. It arguably made Koskenniemi turn to exploring the theme of colonialism and international law.

Yet Koskenniemi rarely engages with the contribution of TWAIL II to the understanding of the history, nature and character of international law. Indeed, TWAIL as an approach is rarely mentioned in his work, albeit there are occasional references to individual TWAIL scholars. In one essay, since it was required by the format of the symposium to which it was a contribution, there is a critical reference to TWAIL for which too he used a footnote as the vehicle.[500] Koskenniemi contends therein that while TWAIL II authors claim to speak for 'the lived experience of Third World peoples' they do not reveal in this regard their theory of representation.[501] It is therefore worth clarifying here that the TWAIL claim is not that it is the authentic voice of third world peoples. Any theory of political representation has it is said 'a robust non-normative descriptive sense' that 'results from an audience's judgment that some individual, rather than some other, is a representative of a particular group'.[502] It is in this non-normative descriptive sense that TWAIL scholars are widely seen as 'representing' third world peoples. Such representation is not necessarily legitimate or deserving of approval as it is after all a case of self-authorized representation.[503] The ultimate test of legitimacy is whether a particular

---

[498] Koskenniemi, *From Apology to Utopia*, pp. 183–184.

[499] The focus was on the deconstruction of international law. It is perhaps worth observing here that it is often difficult for third world international lawyers to understand the impact of Koskenniemi's work on colleagues in Europe because they have always known that political choices were being made in the language of international law, albeit not merely in the process of interpretation and application but also in the negotiation and adoption of international legal rules. The third world international lawyer has always been speaking of ethical choices in the context of oppressed subaltern nations and peoples.

[500] Koskenniemi, 'Letter'.

[501] See ibid., p. 117 fn. 8.

[502] Andrew Rehfield, 'Towards a General Theory of Political Representation', 68 (2006) *Journal of Politics*, pp. 1–21 at p. 2.

[503] See ibid., p. 4.

act(s) of representation advances the cause of democracy (and justice).[504] In the case of TWAIL scholars, as in all other cases, the assessment has necessarily to be left to others. For the rest it is too late in the day to deny that in democratic politics of any kind self-authorized representation is not an acceptable act.[505] But it should usually involve the recognition of others who make a similar claim even if it be as critique. But such acknowledgment is not forthcoming from Koskenniemi. In so far as Koskenniemi often speaks for the weak Pierre-Marie Dupuy has observed that:

> Koskenniemi in fact takes up a discourse that has been around for a long time. This theme was introduced mainly by the proponents (whether jurists or diplomats) of the critical thought emanating from developing countries on the threshold of independence, more than 40 years ago.[506]

It makes him conclude that 'Koskenniemi's critique, for all its skilful exposition, is neither new nor particularly original'.[507] It is difficult to protest that judgment.

But there are also key differences between TWAIL II and the 'culture of formalism'. At least two deserve to be mentioned. First, generally speaking, TWAIL II accepts the idea of rule of law and also does not subscribe to the strong indeterminacy thesis. To illustrate the differences between TWAIL II and Koskenniemi reference may be made to his views on the NATO action in Kosovo. Koskenniemi had forthrightly noted that the action was 'formally illegal' but 'morally necessary'[508]:

> Lawyers who held the bombing illegal base this on the formal breach of Article 2(4) of the UN Charter that was involved. *As is well-known*, the article admits of only two principal exceptions: authorization by the Security Council and self-defence under Article 51. Neither was present. Ergo, *the bombing was illegal.* Although *there is little doubt of the professional*

---

[504] As has been observed, 'the challenges for democratic theory are to understand the nature of these representative claims and to assess which of them count as contributions to democracy and in what ways'. Nadia Urbinati and Mark E. Warren, 'The Concept of Representation in Contemporary Political Theory', 11 (2008) *Annual Review of Political Science*, pp. 387–412 at p. 404.

[505] See ibid.

[506] Pierre-Marie Dupuy, 'Some Reflections on Contemporary International Law and the Appeal to Universal Values: A Response to Martti Koskenniemi', 16 (2005) *European Journal of International Law*, pp. 131–137 at p. 132. See also Ignacio de la Rasilla del Moral, 'Martti Koskenniemi and the Spirit of the Beehive in International Law', 10 (2010) *Global Jurist*, pp. 1–53 at p. 13.

[507] Dupuy, 'Some Reflections', p. 132.

[508] Koskenniemi, ' "The Lady Doth" ', p. 162.

correctness of this conclusion, it still seems arrogantly insensitive to the humanitarian dilemmas involved.[509]

The fact that Koskenniemi had no hesitation in stating that the NATO action in Kosovo was illegal sustains the TWAIL view that international law constrains; it is not as open-ended as it is made out to be by Koskenniemi. In the circumstances to reject the idea of 'rule of law' allows strong states to disregard basic or fundamental principles of international law in the name of universal values.[510] It brings to the fore the question of the basis on which to arbitrate between false and genuine universalism. As is well known, the Kosovo intervention was opposed by third world states.[511] These countries saw Western commentators as being insensitive to their concerns in the name of pursuing humanitarian values. It is precisely this attempt to present particular ethics as universal ethics that classical realists had also warned against. The TWAIL view is that 'rule of law' should be valued even as third world nations and peoples contest, resist and reform particular legal regimes. Any other view facilitates the rule of the strong over the weak.

Second, in contrast to Koskenniemi, TWAIL II lays stress on deep structures to explain the historic bias of international law. Koskenniemi does not do so, albeit he does observe at one place that 'irrespective of indeterminacy, *the system still de facto prefers some outcomes of or distributive choices to other outcomes and choices*'.[512] But he does not answer the question as to why and how do particular distributive choices come to prevail? In the TWAIL view the intimate relationship between imperialism and international law is only in a secondary sense facilitated by the indeterminacy that characterizes the structure of international legal argument.[513] Koskenniemi appears to accept this in his recent narration of the

---

[509] See ibid., p. 163; emphasis added.

[510] The assessment cannot but be a historical assessment of the character of international law. The idea of 'international rule of law' is relevant today as its fundamental principles provide a shield to the weak against the strong. See generally, B. S. Chimni, 'Sovereignty, Rights, and Armed Intervention: A Dialectical Perspective' in Hilary Charlesworth and Jean-Marc Coicaud (eds.), *Fault Lines of International Legitimacy* (Cambridge: Cambridge University Press, 2010), pp. 303–326.

[511] See 'Ministerial Declaration of the Twenty-Third Annual Meeting of the Ministers for Foreign Affairs of the Group of 77' (24 September 1999) Para 69 available at www.g77.org/doc/Decl1999.html; and B. S. Chimni, 'Sovereignty, Rights', pp. 303–325.

[512] Koskenniemi, *From Apology to Utopia*, p. 606; emphasis in original.

[513] For instance, the WTO Agreement on Trade Related Intrellectual Property Rights (TRIPS) is patently against the interests of third world peoples even as the element of

history of international law from Vitoria to Grotius. But he is yet to revise his views on 'culture of formalism' in this light.

J.   MAIL and 'Culture of Formalism'

How does Koskenniemi's notion of 'culture of formalism' compare with MAIL? There is arguably a family resemblance to the Marxist relative autonomy thesis which can for the present purposes be roughly summarized as follows.[514] International law codifies the interests of dominant social forces and states at a particular historical conjuncture that are portrayed as universal interests. These interests are also served by manipulating the structural and semantic indeterminacies that characterize international concepts and rules. But in order to sustain the legitimacy of the international legal system the strong states accommodate from time to time the interests of the weak and also uphold the idea of international rule of law. In short, the Marxist view involves the 'simultaneous rejection of both an instrumentalist or reductionist approach, which denies that the legal order possesses any autonomy from the demands imposed on it by actors of the capitalist society in which it is embedded, and a formalist approach, which asserts an absolute, unqualified autonomy of the legal order from this society'.[515]

The idea of 'culture of formalism' is somewhat on the lines of the Marxist concept of relative autonomy as the 'hegemonic technique' argument is simply a restatement of the view that ruling classes present their particular interests as universal interests. Likewise, on the lines of the Marxist approach Koskenniemi notes that 'a culture of formalism cannot tolerate – the transformation of the formal into a façade for the material in a way that *denies the value of the formal as such*'.[516] However, as has been seen, for Koskenniemi the 'formal' does not include the idea of 'rule of law'. But the real difference between MAIL and the neo-formalism of Koskenniemi is the absence in the latter's work of a historical sociology

---

indeterminacy is also used (both semantic and structural indeterminacy) by powerful actors to inject it with a particular content.

[514] For a discussion on the concept of 'relative autonomy', see Chapter 7, pp. 458–462.

[515] Isaac D. Balbus, 'Commodity Form and Legal Form: An Essay on the "Relative Autonomy" of the Law', 11 (1977) *Law & Society Review*, pp. 571–588 at p. 571. However, the Marxist view 'cannot be understood as a compromise between the instrumentalist and formalist positions; rather it purports to transcend the opposition between these positions by rejecting the common conceptual terrain on which they are based and elaborating a wholly different theoretical terrain'. See ibid., p. 573.

[516] Koskenniemi, *Gentle Civilizer*, p. 501; emphasis in original.

of international relations that explains the exclusion of the weak from the benefits of international law. More specifically, there is the absence of a social and political theory that can explain the relationship between capitalism, imperialism and the 'weak' in history. The idea of 'culture of formalism' also does not incorporate a theory of resistance. There is hardly any discussion in Koskenniemi of the (multiple) historical agents and modes of resistance that inform what he terms 'political struggle' in the arena of international law.

K.   FtAIL and 'Culture of Formalism'

Insofar as FtAIL is concerned its proponents have accused Koskenniemi of completely neglecting the marginality of gender in the discourse of contemporary international law. Hilary Charlesworth minced no words when she wrote of FATU that:

> Koskenniemi's impressive familiarity with a great range of philosophical, political and sociological literature does not appear to extend to standard feminist works, although feminism has been one of the most lively and productive fields of intellectual enquiry for more than two decades.[517]

She went on to note that while Koskenniemi and others argued that 'critical-normative' practice is possible, 'they are *frustratingly vague on what this actually entails*'.[518] Indeed, as she elaborated, Koskenniemi

> does not provide any criterion to distinguish between competing understandings of the appropriate resolution in any particular dispute. The audience Koskenniemi is addressing often seems a very narrow one: his message appears to be directed more at Western male international legal advisers to states than at international lawyers working for nongovernmental organizations, minorities, Third World nations, groups without formal international legal personality and women.[519]

She therefore concluded that 'it is clear that Koskenniemi's project and those of feminists are very different indeed' as 'he does not observe the deeply gendered nature of the current international law game'.[520] In her view, it was 'unlikely that Koskenniemi's reimaginings of the game will be

---

[517] Hilary Charlesworth, 'Subversive Trends in the Jurisprudence of International Law', (1992) *ASIL Proceedings*, pp. 125–131 at p. 29 fn. 12.

[518] See ibid., p. 127; emphasis added.

[519] See ibid.

[520] See ibid., p. 129.

any different in this respect: *gender is simply not anywhere on his agenda*.[521]
More than a decade later she writes of his 'culture of formalism':

> Koskenniemi seems to be advocating acceptance of the framework of inter-
> national law because, flawed as it is, it is some protection from untram-
> meled subjectivity and politics. My argument … is that international law
> does not provide even a 'partial, consensual, formal distance' from subject-
> ivity. It is intertwined with a gendered subjectivity and reinforces a system
> of male symbols.[522]

It is of course possible for Koskenniemi to argue that the idea of 'false universalism' is capacious enough to cover the gender (or class) perspective. But
the fact that despite the feminist critique he appears to have made no effort
to allay concerns at both epistemological and ontological planes shows that
he is somewhat indifferent to the destiny of different subaltern groups.

L.   The Missing Indigenous Peoples

It is significant in this regard that Koskenniemi entirely overlooks the
concerns of 'indigenous peoples' who in several Western liberal nations
are the living symbols of false universalism.[523] In this respect it has been
pointed out that 'the critical assumption that we all speak the same professional language skirts the issues of those who speak this language but
remain unheard or ultimately reject its fundamental, statist grammar'.[524]
In those instances, the principles and doctrines of international law need
to be recast to make them more inclusive. Indeed, there is an urgent need
for a 'gesture toward the myriad Indigenous legal traditions that would
fruitfully inform alternative and critical histories of international law
for the purposes of accuracy, decolonization, and justice'.[525] It deserves
emphasis that it is not merely a question of redressing the past but also
responding to the 'ongoing colonial encounter in North America';[526] the

---

[521] See ibid.; emphasis added.
[522] Hilary Charlesworth, 'Feminist Methods in International Law' in Ratner and Slaughter (eds.), *Methods of International Law*, pp. 159–184 at p. 182.
[523] It is perhaps inane to charge a scholar with not dealing with everything. After all there are a myriad matters that an individual researcher may not have addressed. The point here is that the concerns excluded should have been central to the theoretical position of the researcher and therefore it is not misplaced to refer to their absence.
[524] Amar Bhatia, 'The South of the North: Building on Critical Approaches to International Law with Lessons from the Fourth World', 14 (2012) *Oregon Review of International Law*, pp. 131–176 at p. 139.
[525] See ibid., p. 145. See also pp. 141–142.
[526] See ibid., p. 149.

vote of Australia, Canada, New Zealand and the United States against the 2007 UN Declaration on the Rights of Indigenous Peoples is a manifestation of that encounter.[527].

It may not be out of place to note here that the neglect of indigenous peoples is also in evidence in postcolonial states. In that instance too the oppression of indigenous peoples goes a long way back. For instance, in postcolonial Latin America it can be traced back to Creole consciousness – 'Creoles' being American-born elite of Spanish descent. Creole legal consciousness has been described as 'certain ideas about the law held by the Creole literati in the post-independence era' whose essence was '*completing civilization* in Latin America'.[528] The Argentinian jurist Carlos Calvo, who belonged to the Creole elite, justified 'the conquest and management of native populations in the region' in the name of a civilizing mission.[529] In other words, as Obregon writes, 'Creoles had a critique of sovereignty, as abused by Europeans, but supported internal imperial attitudes of conquest and colonization. That is, they proposed to reject European and US interventions in their territories, but at the same time supported the national appropriation of indigenous lands in their own countries'.[530] While in postcolonial Asia there was no Creole consciousness to be contended with, the approach to indigenous or tribal peoples has not been very different. For instance, despite constitutional protections for indigenous peoples in India, the land and cultures of tribal peoples has been the subject of a 'development mission'; their land has been appropriated and cultures invaded. Such has been the violence heaped upon tribal peoples that in *Nandini Sunder vs. State of Chhattisgarh and others* the Supreme Court of India quoted Joseph Conrad's *Heart of Darkness* to indict the Indian state for its predatory policies in tribal areas.[531] In short, critical approaches 'cannot ignore the experiences of Indigenous peoples within international law' as Koskenniemi (and many of us) does.[532]

---

[527] See UNGA/10612, 'General Assembly Adopts Declaration on Rights of Indigenous Peoples', www.un.org/News/Press/docs/2007/ga10612.doc.htm

[528] Liliana Obregon, 'Completing Civilization: Creole Consciousness and International Law in Nineteenth Century Latin America' in Anne Orford (ed.), *International Law and Its Others* (Cambridge: Cambridge University Press, 2006), pp. 247–265 at pp. 249, 253.

[529] See ibid., p. 257.

[530] See ibid., p. 263.

[531] *Nandini Sunder vs. State of Chhattisgarh and others* AIR 2011 SC 2839.

[532] Bhatia, 'The South of the North', p. 171.

M.   MILS and 'Culture of Formalism'

It is time to look at the views of MILS on the idea of 'culture of formalism'.[533] Despite the turn to formalism, which should have made Koskenniemi's work more acceptable to mainstream scholars, it has remained suspect in their eyes. Emmanuelle Jouannet makes the following observations in this regard. First, she charges Koskenniemi with deliberately caricaturing mainstream understanding of the working of the international legal system. In her view, he often presents their views 'in absolutist terms in order to make the task of critiquing them easier'.[534] Second, Jouannet contends that in as much as Koskenniemi speaks of 'European instrumentalism' or 'false universalism' he does not adequately recognize that in at least so far as contemporary international law is concerned there is an 'intersubjective agreement' on 'ethical principles, including those of law, and in particular of human rights'.[535] Third, Koskenniemi does not explain why for him 'conflict is the fundamental reality of the social world and political decision the only available means of defusing it'.[536] Or why he does not 'believe in the possibility of a political praxis capable of generating a common good through the mutual respect – spontaneous or imposed – of those involved in the discussion'.[537] Fourth, Jouannet points out that in Koskenniemi there are 'only two alternatives: either we can liberate ourselves sufficiently from the structure of language and make a choice, or we are conditioned and do not thus make a genuine choice. Yet Koskenniemi seems caught between the two: he presents us with the disconcerting idea not only of the necessity of making a choice, but of a choice that remains conditioned'.[538] Indeed, Jouannet finds this position 'extremely complex and difficult to understand'.[539] In a sense she is right for as has been noted, in contrast to other critical approaches Koskenniemi 'fully accepts the

---

[533] Koskenniemi has noted three kinds of criticism against FATU: 'one of them focuses on the semantics of the linguistic analysis ... another on its pragmatics ... A third criticism is a more fundamental attack on the normative pretensions of the book'. Koskenniemi, *From Apology to Utopia* (2005), p. 590.

[534] Jouannet, 'Koskenniemi', p. 22. The act of interpretation and application of international law is presumably one area in which Koskenniemi can be said to have adopted such a strategy.

[535] See ibid., p. 23.

[536] See ibid., pp. 25–26.

[537] See ibid.

[538] See ibid., p. 28.

[539] See ibid.

tradition of international law and its institutional forms', severely constraining the possibility of the pursuit of 'genuine universalism'.[540]

In a more elaborate intervention, Rob Howse and Ruti Teitl have challenged 'Koskenniemi's arguments that humanity-law [i.e., contemporary
international law] is associated with a dogmatically progressive theory
of history, that it is oriented toward a world government, that it relies
on a version of historical determinism, that it posits a false universalism,
and that legal indeterminacy undermines its claims'.[541] In short, they contest all of Koskenniemi's reading of 'how contemporary international law
works'.[542] In contrast to Koskenniemi, Howse and Teitl stress that 'the post-
Cold War human rights or humanity-law trend encompasses demands of
economic justice against the state and the revival of social and economic
rights (human security)'.[543] In their view the state today 'is internationally accountable for how and to what extent it realizes responsibilities
for social and economic justice among others'.[544] Of course, Howse and
Teitl recognize that humanity law may 'relapse into brutal, inhumane violence, and political oppression'.[545] But contra Koskenniemi they believe
that 'humanity-law knows its own normative logic, and requires humanity in means as well as ends'.[546] In other words, humanity-oriented legal
internationalism is conscious of the risk that the value and goal of universalism can be misused. Therefore, 'humanity-law considerably narrows
the window for humanitarian intervention by insisting that its agents and
its beneficiaries comport themselves in accord with humanity-law obligations'?[547] In any case, Koskenniemi himself supported for instance the
bombing of Serbia stating that it was 'illegal but necessary'.[548] All in all in
this view humanity law is playing a positive role in international affairs.
Howse and Teitl therefore go on to accuse Koskenniemi of 'a form of neocolonial condescension'.[549] They point to the fact that third world states
use international law effectively without 'worrying about re-colonizing

---

[540] Orford, 'Journal of the Voyage', p. 996.
[541] Howse and Teitl, 'Does Humanity-Law Require?', p. 396.
[542] See ibid., p. 397.
[543] See ibid., p. 383.
[544] See ibid.
[545] See ibid., p. 378.
[546] See ibid., p. 386.
[547] See ibid., p. 388.
[548] See ibid.
[549] See ibid., p. 385.

themselves'.[550] Most significantly, Howse and Teitl write that unlike Kennedy, Koskenniemi does not recognize the dialectics of history:

> Often David Kennedy's and Koskenniemi's critical perspectives on inter-national law are viewed as similar or identical. Yet, Kennedy grasps the fluidity and interchangeability of roles and identities; indeed for Kennedy the activist who denies that she is also a functionary suffers from a lack of self-conscious knowledge, one that is dangerous.[551]

Howse and Teitl suggest that they share with Kennedy the notion that 'we free ourselves to grasp the humanity-law moment as a new conjunc-tion of forces, a situation of fluidity that demands clarity about both the risks and opportunities through the endlessly dynamic relation of law to social reality as appreciated already by Grotius and Montesquieu (and perhaps even Aristotle)'.[552]

It would appear that the principal objection of Howse and Teitl is to Koskenniemi's pessimistic views about the role of 'humanity law' which often sounds to their ears like TWAIL and MAIL critiques. Their emphasis is instead on the possibility of realizing genuine universalism through humanity law. However, a dispassionate assessment of the state of human-ity law today would tend to side with the judgment of Koskenniemi; the sheer amount of violence against subaltern states and peoples is sufficient evidence for arriving at that verdict. Secondly, while there is a certain amount of fluidity in relations between states, and interchangeability of roles and identities reflected among other things in the arrival of emer-ging powers, it does not *necessarily* reduce the threat of false universal-ism. It has only spawned a different material and ideological matrix in which hegemonic techniques are used by a new actor i.e., an emerging transnational capitalist class (TCC).[553] In other words, a sharpened global class divide today accompanies the old North-South divide reducing the possibility of subaltern states fulfilling their responsibilities of ensuring social and economic justice to their people. But both Howse and Teitl and Koskenniemi do not look at the character of third world states or the impact of humanity law on different groups within them. Both do not explore the substratum of contemporary humanity law or the con-sequences of the pursuit of neo-liberal globalization policies today. It is

---

[550] See ibid.
[551] See ibid., p. 395.
[552] See ibid., p. 396.
[553] For a discussion on the role of TCC see Chapter 7, pp. 507–509.

therefore difficult for them to see that the danger of false universalism arises today as a result of the vision, influence and practices of a TCC that presents its particular interests as universal interests. The source of policies of false universalism is not merely liberal Western states but also third world states that pursue the interests of particular classes. To put it differently, the differences between Howse and Teitl and Koskenniemi are not serious. It is simply about whether the glass of humanity law is half full or half empty. Overall, it is the fuzziness of the idea of 'culture of formalism' that accounts for the fact that Koskenniemi is accused by the mainstream of being overly pessimistic about the possibilities of advancing humanity law and his left critics of being overly optimistic about using the tradition of international law in furthering genuine universalism. It often seems that the mainstream is staging a skirmish with Koskenniemi to get him not to yield evaluative ground to TWAIL and left critics. They want him to openly declare that he is a liberal.[554]

V. Conclusion

There is little doubt that in terms of sheer range and depth Koskenniemi is among the most exceptional international law scholars on the contemporary scene. His major works FATU and GCN have come to lend gravitas to international law scholarship. Relying on sophisticated social and linguistic theories he has deconstructed international law in a manner that has revealed internal contradictions that go to the very core of its being. He has shown how the discrepancies offer an opportunity to international lawyers to help realize 'genuine universalism' and reminded them of their ethical responsibility in this regard. He has also produced quality historical scholarship to demonstrate how the tradition of international law was implicated in the pursuit of 'false universalism', especially in the colonial era. He has made an original and path breaking contribution to

---

[554] In as much as the thinking of Koskenniemi centres on a self- determining individual, the liberal project has always been there. In this regard, Sahib Singh aptly points out that 'at the precise historical juncture that Koskenniemi's text seeks to challenge the main tenets of liberalism, his text offers a subject who sees her emancipation on the same foundations as that of the liberal subject'. For as he notes: 'Liberalism has established, sustained and rejuvenated itself by constantly furnishing us with an image of the individual who is always self-determining and always capable of making any choice she wishes to. Not only is freedom equated with choice, but this choice is an ever-present possibility and always absolute. The liberal subject is seduced (and often, ironically shamed) into believing that she is the alpha and omega in her relations with the world.' Sahib Singh, *The Critical Subject* (Cambridge: Cambridge University Press, forthcoming). On file with the author.

understanding the world of European international law, especially the impulse that informed the vision and work of scholars in the nineteenth century. We cannot but also admire his masterful assemblage of diverse philosophical, linguistic and legal materials to make imaginative interventions on different themes of international law. In short, his writings have played an important role in advancing the understanding of the history, structure, process and substance of international law.

Yet for all his achievements it is not easy to assess the true significance of Koskenniemi's contributions to the discipline of international law. The claims he has advanced in his writings have not always withstood scrutiny. His allegation with respect to the structural indeterminacy of international law was certainly exaggerated in FATU, and later admitted as such. A principal reason for the overstatement was that he deconstructed the structure of international law before he studied the history of international law. It prevented him from seeing that in so far as the weak are concerned international law has been rather determinate over the centuries. Yet when Koskenniemi turned to writing the history of European international lawyers and law, he wrote in a monologic form. Koskenniemi did not appreciate the need for undertaking the exercise in dialogue with the Other. In the absence of such an effort it is not surprising that the idea of a 'culture of formalism' that he advances is deeply flawed. His affirmation of the tradition of international law in a manner that excludes reasons and methods that are placed outside it also takes away the critical edge from his work. Furthermore, the notions of professional competence and sensibility are made to carry too heavy a burden in the pursuit of genuine universalism. This is especially so when the bases for distinguishing between false and genuine universalism are not made clear.

Koskenniemi, very much like Kennedy, does not see that it international law is shaped in a fundamental way by the deep structures of capitalism, imperialism and patriarchy. He rarely deploys the categories class, gender, race or indigenous peoples to understand the nature and character of international law. Koskenniemi also does not have a serious theory of resistance constrained as he is by methodological individualism. He hardly ever speaks about the historical struggles of colonial peoples in the past and different oppressed groups today against neo-liberal globalization. His politics is also difficult to pin down. The debate with his liberal critics seems to be more about whether the glass of 'humanity law' is half full or half empty. It can be said that today he stands at crossroads. His current work on the history of international law (examining the work of Spanish theologians Vitoria and Suarez and the Dutch thinker Grotius) using materialist methods and insights can make him advance a left radical critique of international law. This would involve a revision of his particular understanding of the 'culture of formalism'. It is equally possible that this history is used to announce his arrival in the liberal camp that believes that despite the flaws in capitalism that is the only game in town. That move would also help save his idea of 'culture of formalism' as it is currently formulated.

To sum up, it can be said that if critical reason is to promote genuine universalism it must at least have the following features: First, it must contest local and global structures of oppression, be it the global capitalist system or microstructures of oppression. Second, it must believe in what Boaventura de Souusa Santos calls cognitive reciprocity and justice between different knowledge systems including Western and non-Western knowledge frameworks and between different civilizations without essentializing any civilization or system of knowledge.[555] Third, it must engage with and address different fractures in society, be it along class, race or gender lines. Fourth, critical reason must take resistance movements seriously as they express knowledge from below or vernacular knowledge. This does not mean endorsing all such knowledge but the neglect of resistance movements is problematic. Fifth, critical reason must be self-reflective so as to be able to see the grounds of its own genesis and the historical limits of its relevance. Sixth, critical reason must state its normative preferences about alternative futures. Koskenniemi is found wanting on all these counts. Be that as it may, there are few scholars who write with greater style than Koskenniemi.

---

[555] Boaventura de Sousa Santos, *Epistemologies of the South: Justice against Epistemicide* (Boulder, CO: Paradigm Publishers, 2014).

6

Feminist Approaches to International Law: The Work of Hilary Charlesworth and Christine Chinkin

I. Introduction

A seminal contribution to rethinking and recasting the role of international law has been made by feminist approaches to international law. While the history of women's movement and its struggle for women's rights goes back many centuries,[1] the beginnings of feminist engagement with international law can be traced to the International Congress of Women which met in The Hague in 1915 and called for the peaceful settlement of disputes.[2] Women activism came into to its own in international institutions with the League of Nations; its history is however yet to be written.[3] In the post–Second World War period, feminist approaches to human rights came to be elaborated, both within and outside the United Nations.[4] The period of the 1970s saw the flowering of feminist theories of law.[5] These developments contributed to the adoption of the 1979 Convention on the

---

[1] Arvonne S. Fraser, 'Becoming Human: The Origins and Development of Women's Human Rights', 21 1999 *Human Rights Quarterly*, pp. 853–906.

[2] Freya Baetens, 'The Forgotten Peace Conference: The 1915 International Congress for Women', *Max Planck Encyclopedia of Public International Law* (Oxford: Oxford University Press, 2010) available at http://opil.ouplaw.com/home/epil (accessed on 29 June 2015). For text of resolutions, see 'Resolutions Adopted', International Congress of Women, The Hague, 28 April-1 May 1915, available at www.ub.gu.se/kvinndata/portaler/fred/samarbete/pdf/resolutions_1915.pdf (accessed on 4 June 2015). See also B. S. Chimni, 'Peace through Law: Lessons of 1914', 3 (2015) *London Review of International Law*, pp. 245–265.

[3] 'The history of feminist activism in the League of Nations is only beginning to be written, but such activism was significant'. Gulay Caglar, Elisabeth Prugl and Sussane Zwingel, 'Introducing Feminist Strategies in International Governance' in Gulay Caglar, Elisabeth Prugl and Sussane Zwingel (eds.) *Feminist Strategies in International Governance* (London: Routledge, 2013), pp. 1–18 at p. 7.

[4] Karen Engle, 'International Human Rights and Feminisms: When Discourses Keep Meeting' in Doris Buss and Ambreena Manji (eds.) *International Law: Modern Feminist Approaches* (Oxford: Hart Publishing, 2005), pp. 47–66 at pp. 47, 49.

[5] See generally Martha Chammalas, *Introduction to Feminist Legal Theory* (New York: Wolters Kluwer Law & Business, 2013); Joanne Conaghan (ed.) *Feminist Legal Studies: Critical Concepts in Law* vols. I-IV (London: Routledge, 2009); Nancy Levitt and Robert R. M. Verchick, *Feminist Legal Theory: A Primer* (New York: New York University Press, 2006);

Elimination of Discrimination against Women (CEDAW) which in turn gave an impetus to feminist engagement with international law. But the first articulation of a feminist approach to international law (FtAIL) had to await the end of the Cold War, usually traced to an essay of that title written by Hilary Charlesworth, Christine Chinkin and Shelley Wright in 1991.[6] Subsequently, Charlesworth and Chinkin elaborated FtAIL in their path breaking book *The boundaries of international law: A feminist analysis*.[7] In the period since the publication of their pioneering essay, the feminist approach to international law has come to be advanced from varying theoretical standpoints by a number of scholars that include Karen Engle, Janet Halley, Ratna Kapur, Karen Knop, Prabha Kotiswaran, Vasuki Nesiah, Celestine Nyamu, L. A. Obiora, Anne Orford, Dianne Otto and Kerry Rittich.[8]

The focus of this chapter is however on the work of Charlesworth and Chinkin. The reasons for this are at least twofold. First, Charlesworth and Chinkin have between them engaged with different trends in feminist thinking on law, including a critique of the work of key figures like Catherine MacKinnon and Janet Halley.[9] Second, their book remains the single most important text on FtAIL. It deals with some of the central topics of international law like sources and subjects of international law, state responsibility, human rights, use of force and humanitarian laws, all from a distinctive feminist perspective. Further, since the publication of their book Charlesworth and Chinkin have continued to write from a feminist standpoint on various themes of, and developments in, international law.

This chapter sets itself two objectives. First, it attempts to articulate a critique of the feminist approach advanced by Charlesworth and Chinkin. It is argued that their approach to international law is best described as

Katherine Bartlett and Rosanne Kennedy (ed.) *Feminist Legal Theory: Readings in Law and Gender* (Boulder, CO: Westview Press, 1991).

[6] Hilary Charlesworth, Christine Chinkin and Shelley Wright, 'Feminist Approach to International Law', 85 (1991) *American Journal of International Law*, pp. 613–645.

[7] Hilary Charlesworth and Christine Chinkin, *The boundaries of international law: a feminist analysis* (Manchester: Manchester University Press, 2000).

[8] Dianne Otto, 'Feminist Approaches' in Tony Carty (ed.) *Oxford Bibliographies Online: International Law* (New York: Oxford University Press, 2012), available at www.oxfordbibliographies.com/obo/page/international-law (accessed 5 November 2015). There is a vast scholarship on the theme of gender and human rights. However, it is not the direct subject of analysis in this chapter. For a representative collection see Dianne Otto (ed.) *Gender Issues and Human Rights* Volumes 1–3 (Cheltenham: Edward Elgar Publishing Limited, 2013).

[9] While the views of Charlesworth and Chinkin may slightly differ from each other in their writings beyond the book these are sufficiently identical to allow common treatment.

mainstream feminist international law scholarship (MFILS) because like mainstream scholars they do not explore the critical relationship between the deep structures of capitalism and imperialism and international law. Indeed, in their writings Charlesworth and Chinkin barely touch on the 'logic of capital'. This weakens their analysis of international law because to develop a critique without examining the relationship between patriarchy and capitalism or the phenomenon of imperialism is to omit discussing the structures that have critically shaped its evolution over the last four centuries. The absence of any discussion of international economic law or international economic institutions in their work is a reflection of this lapse.

Second, the chapter seeks to make a case for a socialist feminist approach to international law that incorporates the insights of postcolonial theory. The pitch for what can be called a postcolonial socialist feminist approach to international law proceeds on the assumption that the ideology, institutions and practices of patriarchy have in the modern era been shaped in a crucial way by the 'logic of capital', albeit with differential impact on varied social formations resulting in their specific and distinctive articulations in metropolitan, colonial and postcolonial spaces. While the realities of global capitalism and imperialism do not exhaust the institutions and practices of patriarchy it is believed that a critique of both is imperative if the emancipation of women is to be promoted, both in the Global South and the Global North. What is needed is 'an anti-imperialist, anticapitalist, and contextualized feminist project to expose and make visible the various, overlapping forms of subjugation of women's lives'.[10] It is contended that socialist feminism is in a position to effectively undertake the critique of structures of patriarchy, capitalism and imperialism through deploying the central tenets of Marxism. It also enables socialist feminism to undertake intersectional and dialectical analysis of the relationship between gender, class and race to talk of, both on the national and international planes, the emancipation of all marginal and oppressed groups. This is in contrast to MFILS that skims over deep structures and is, therefore, both unable to come to grips with

---

[10] Chandra Talpade Mohanty, ' "Under Western Eyes" Revisited: Feminist Solidarity through Anticapitalist Struggles', 28 (2003) *Signs*, pp. 495–535 at p. 515; emphasis added. It may be said that Mohanty subscribes to postcolonial feminism but that would be to ignore the fact that in many instances there can be a significant overlap between postcolonial and socialist feminisms. It explains why her work has been included in a recent reader on socialist feminism. See Nancy Holmstrom (ed.) *The Socialist Feminist Project: A Contemporary Reader in Theory and Politics* (New Delhi: Aakar Books, 2011).

the complex constitution and workings of patriarchy in the third world or the need for concerning itself with the fate of all subaltern groups and classes. But socialist feminism suffers from at least two weaknesses. First, while it has the theoretical potential its proponents do not always pay sufficient attention to the particular views and concerns of women in the third world. In this respect it needs to assimilate the concerns flagged by postcolonial and third world feminisms. Second, while it is concerned with the legal status of women under capitalist patriarchy socialist feminism does not advance a general theory of law. It is contended that the insights of socialist feminism can be productively situated within a Marxist theory of law. Thereafter, once the concerns of postcolonial theory are absorbed, it can be the basis for articulating an Integrated Marxist approach to International Law (IMAIL).[11]

The chapter proceeds as follows. Section II reflects on the reasons why FtAIL emerged in the post-Cold War period and why its dominant form has assumed the shape of FMILS.

Section III offers thumbnail sketches of four approaches to feminism viz., radical feminism, critical or 'governance feminism', third world feminism and socialist feminism. It is contended that from the perspective of developing IMAIL the engagement with radical feminism of Catherine MacKinnon is particularly helpful, for by opposing feminism to Marxism in her early work she helps clarify the basis on which a relationship between the two can be re-established. In recent times MacKinnon herself facilitates this by accepting the need for intersectional analysis, albeit from within the constrained framework of radical feminism. On the other hand, by advancing the concept of 'governance feminism' and advising a 'break from feminism' at a time when it is being co-opted by hegemonic forces, Janet Halley assists in understanding the limits of both radical and liberal feminism and the reasons why the two feminisms are often

---

[11] Broadly speaking, socialist feminists are more concerned with the institution of capitalist patriarchy than with capitalism per se whose critique is central to articulating a Marxist theory of law and international law. Socialist feminists essentially provide, like postcolonial theory, a standpoint critique of legal institutions and practices. Its particular critique needs to be located in Marxism to offer a more general critique of society and law. The 'integration' of socialist feminism and Marxism can assume a variety of formulations. Apart from the fact that not all socialist feminists are Marxists and not all Marxists subscribe to socialist feminism their synthesis can be captured in a variety of ways. The views offered here is just one possible way of taking cognizance of the concerns of socialist feminism. It may also be noted that the term 'socialist' is used here for indicating post capitalist futures that promise justice to marginal and oppressed groups located both in the third and first worlds. See in this regard Chapter 7, pp. 543–550.

fellow travellers.[12] The section proceeds to argue that socialist feminism can not only accommodate the central concerns of these approaches, but also explore and critique deep structures that prevent the emancipation of women and other exploited and oppressed groups across different geographical spaces and histories.[13] It is submitted that in contrast the eclectic method that Charlesworth and Chinkin use, incorporating the insights of 'a variety of analytic strategies', does not seriously moving beyond the liberal idea of equality of sexes.[14]

Section IV discusses the views of Charlesworth and Chinkin on different aspects of international law. The objective is to offer a brief exposition and critique of their views on crucial topics and themes of international law. It is often accompanied by a bare observation or two on how socialist feminists would approach these. It is worth noting that the analysis does not seek to provide a comprehensive review of the individual work of Charlesworth and Chinkin on international law.[15] It only reviews writings that directly pertain to the elaboration of FtAIL. In the process the responses of other theoretical approaches to FtAIL are also touched upon. Generally speaking, while mainstream international law scholarship (MILS) has welcomed FtAIL, it is concerned that by challenging the neutrality and objectivity of international law FtAIL is undermining the very language that could be used to promote equality between sexes.[16] The worry of MILS is that the divisive orientation of FtAIL may only go to

[12] According to Ferdinand Teson, Charlesworth uses both 'liberal' and 'radical' feminist analysis. Hilary Charlesworth, 'Feminist Critiques of International Law and Their Critics', 13 (1995) *Third World Legal Studies-1994*, pp. 1–16 at p. 6 accessed at http://scholar.valpo.edu/twls/vol13/iss1/1. Her response was that 'the labels "liberal" feminist or "radical" feminist are not particularly meaningful in the international context'. See ibid. She also argued that 'liberal feminism does not go far enough in responding to the subordination of women'. See ibid., p. 7. But she never seriously travels beyond the frames of radical and liberal feminism.

[13] The chapter does not separately discuss 'critical race' and 'postcolonial' feminisms, albeit it refers to some of its scholarship.

[14] Charlesworth and Chinkin, *Boundaries of international law*, p. 50.

[15] It does not therefore review their other writings. See, for instance, Alan Boyle and Christine Chinkin, *The Making of International Law* (Oxford: Oxford University Press, 2014); Hilary Charlesworth, *Democracy and International Law* (Leiden: Martinus Nijhoff Publishers, 2015); Hilary Charlesworth and Emma Larking (eds.), *Human Rights and the Universal Periodic Review: Rituals and Ritualism* (Cambridge: Cambridge University Press, 2014); M. Freeman, C. Chinkin and B. Rudolf (eds.), *The UN Convention on the Elimination of All Forms of Discrimination against Women: A Commentary* (Oxford: Oxford University Press, 2012).

[16] Anthony D'Amato, 'Book Review: Rebecca J. Cook ed., Human Rights of Women: National and International Perspectives', 89 (1995) *American Journal of International Law*,

destabilize and delegitimize the universal character of contemporary international law. On the other hand, the concern of critical legal scholarship is that the liberal feminist approach of Charlesworth and Chinkin does not seriously depart from MILS in many regards.[17] In fact, like MILS it tends to ignore the central themes and concerns of Third World Approaches to International Law (TWAIL), New Approaches to International Law (NAIL), and Marxist Approaches to International Law (MAIL). To be sure, Charlesworth and Chinkin have attempted to accommodate the concerns of third world feminism through accepting its distinctive voice. But they have largely ignored the internal critique of international law offered by NAIL and the historical critique of deep structures advanced by TWAIL and MAIL, as also some third world feminists. At the same time, it has to be conceded that there has been no sustained engagement of non-feminist approaches with FtAIL or the work of Charlesworth and Chinkin. The state of affairs is best captured and expressed by the phrase 'talking to ourselves' used by Charlesworth to lament the lack of effort by either the mainstream or other critical approaches to enter into a dialogue with FtAIL.[18]

Section V contains some concluding reflections on FtAIL.

---

pp. 840–844 at p. 843. It is interesting that he does not see Charlesworth as a fellow liberal but as someone holding a' radical view of international law'. See ibid., p. 842.

[17] The liberal feminists, according to Charlesworth and Chinkin, are those who cast their arguments 'in terms of individual rights' and 'their primary goal is to achieve equality of treatment between women and men in public areas such as political participation and representation, and equal access to and equality within paid employment, market services and education'. Charlesworth and Chinkin, *Boundaries of international law*, pp. 38–39. Another description of liberal feminism is that provided by Janet Haley who describes it thus: 'Liberal feminism is characterized by a view that women and men are, for all legitimate purposes, the same; equality is its central social and legal goal. For liberal feminists, the hard part is deciding what constitutes a legitimate purpose. In recurrent ambivalence on this question, liberal feminism has veered from equal treatment to special treatment; from formal equality to substantive equality; from empty theories of gender to particularized ones'. Janet Halley, *Split Decisions: How and Why to Take a Break from Feminism* (Princeton, NJ: Princeton University Press, 2006), p. 79. The ambivalences Halley refers to are reflected in the work of Charlesworth and Chinkin and are the impulse for adopting the 'eclectic method' that borrows from other feminisms.

[18] Hilary Charlesworth, 'Talking to Ourselves?: Feminist Scholarship in International Law' in Sari Kouvo and Zoe Pearson (eds.) *Between Resistance and Compliance? Feminist Perspectives on International Law in Era of Anxiety and Terror* (Oxford: Hart, 2011), pp. 17–32. Elsewhere she writes: 'Looking at the major writings in international law and theory over the past decade, it is very hard to detect any real attempt to engage with feminist theories of international law, or indeed with any outsider perspectives. Feminist theories seem to remain in a scholarly ghetto, at most a brief footnote, in international legal scholarship'. Hilary Charlesworth, 'Feminist Ambivalence about International Law,'

II. Delayed Beginnings: Impact of Cold War

In each discipline a certain approach to its study comes to be advanced at a particular historical juncture. Its origins and substance often becomes a subject of deep reflection.[19] The reason is that the timing of the emergence of a particular theoretical approach has something to tell about the proposed approach, the discipline itself, and the times in which it is advanced. It is therefore of interest to understand the reasons why the feminist approach in the field of international law originated only after the end of the Cold War.[20] This reality becomes intriguing when account is taken of the fact that the same is true in the cognate discipline of international relations. In the same year as Charlesworth, Chinkin and Wright published their celebrated essay on a feminist approach, Ann Tickner was writing her pioneering work *Gender in International Relations*.[21] In the introduction to her book Tickner notes that the first conferences she attended on the subject were in June 1988.[22] It can therefore be surmised that as the threat of socialism and Marxism began to recede it created the space for critical approaches to international law and international relations to emerge in the West. This understanding is supported by the

11 (2005) *International Legal Theory*, pp. 1–8, at p. 2. See also Dianne Otto, 'The Exile of Inclusion: Reflections on Gender Issues in International Law over the Last Decade,' 10 (2009) *Melbourne Journal of International Law*, pp. 11–26.

[19] Thus, for instance, there is much deliberation on the emergence of the positivist method and its meaning in the literature on international law. For one view, see Antony Anghie, *Sovereignty, Imperialism and International Law* (Cambridge: Cambridge University Press, 2003), pp. 32–65.

[20] Chinkin traces 'the first feminist intervention into international law within the academy' to a conference in Canberra held in 1990. Christine Chinkin, 'Feminist Interventions into International Law,' 19 (1997) *Adelaide Law Review*, pp. 13–24 at p. 13. It is possible to tell the story of 'arrival' in alternative ways depending on how doing international law is defined. In the period of the Cold War there was feminist engagement with international human rights law and what may be termed international development law. But this literature did not represent a systematic feminist approach to international law or methodically address core doctrinal issues as Charlesworth and Chinkin did. It is therefore usual to associate the beginnings of the feminist approach to international law with their work. But as is mentioned presently the time of arrival is also dictated by a Eurocentric telling of the history of feminist approach to international law.

[21] J. Ann Tickner, *Gender in International Relations: Feminist Perspectives on Achieving Global Security* (Columbia, NY: Columbia University Press, 1992).

[22] See ibid., p. 2. It led to the publication of her well known essay viz., J. Ann Tickner, 'Hans Morgenthau's Principles of Realism: A Feminist Reformulation,' 17 (1988) *Millennium*, pp. 429–440.

fact that even the New Approaches to International Law (NAIL) originated in the same period.[23]

It is not as if Western international law scholarship in the period of the
Cold War was not marked by serious internal differences. It was often
characterized by sharp differences as can be seen for instance by comparing the classical realist approach with the New Haven approach to
international law. However, these differences did not involve the foundational questioning of the history, structure and process of international
law.[24] Thus, for instance, both the classical realist and the policy-oriented
approaches did not address the theme of colonialism and international
law or speak of class, gender and race perspectives to international law as
these could have been read as supportive of the Soviet view of international
law.[25] Even Richard Falk with an avowed interest in system transforming
approaches did not throw a fundamental challenge to Cold War thinking
on international law; his critique was essentially confined to workings of
the states system. It is also of interest that in the period of the Cold War
Western approaches and scholars tended to neglect TWAIL in so far as it
was raising fundamental questions in relation to the origin, evolution and
development of international law. In other words, the Cold War environment was simply not conducive for critical approaches such as FtAIL to
emerge. Indeed, the environment had not been favourable for feminist
legal thinking ever since the October Revolution. Even at the domestic
level there was a tendency in the West, especially in the United States, to
neglect the issue of gender differences. Karen Offen writes that 'following
the Russian Revolution of 1917 and the development of a strong anti-
communist reaction in the United States during the 1920s, feminist intellectuals veered sharply in the direction of downplaying sex differences'.[26]
It was also the case that 'U.S. women's organizations were continually

---

[23] The end of the Cold War is certainly not the only factor in explaining the arrival of NAIL
but it was certainly an important factor. For discussion of NAIL see Chapter 5.
[24] For an exposition of different mainstream approaches in the international law in the
United States, see David Kennedy, 'The Disciplines of International Law and Policy', 12
(1999) *Leiden Journal of International Law*, pp. 9–135.
[25] This did not mean that some of the approaches of the time were not concerned with the
rights of women. See, for instance, Myres S. McDougal, Harold D. Lasswell and Lung-chu
Chen, 'Human Rights for Women and World Public Order: The Outlawing of Sex-Based
Discrimination', 69 (2005) *The American Journal of International Law*, pp. 497–533.
[26] Karen Offen, 'Defining Feminism: A Comparative Historical Approach', 14 (1988) *Signs*,
pp. 119–157, at p. 143

obliged to negotiate national (state) interests in their international work.[27] In fact, as has been recently argued, feminist scholarship in the US academy in the period of the Cold War tended to mirror its hegemonic interests.[28] In the circumstances, even when the radical feminist approach to law eventually came to be articulated in the early 1980s it was in the form of a critique of Marxism.[29] At a time when strong anti-Marxist sentiments prevailed gender differences could only be brought centre stage by counterposing feminism to Marxism, a trend admittedly encouraged also by the feminist disenchantment with the left. It is therefore difficult to accept the 'stock narrative' that academic feminism was 'inherently oppositional to the Cold War geopolitics'.[30] There is also good reason for scepticism with respect to the claim that feminism received its impulse from new social movements of the times; as has been observed such a narrative is 'inherently incomplete'.[31] In reality, 'notable portions of the academic feminist knowledge project were rooted in the geopolitics of the Cold War era'.[32] In fact, the consequent limited engagement with the 'socialist model of development' was 'part of the discursive context within which feminist scholarship's central concepts, theories, and epistemologies [...] emerged, and thus they necessarily haunt many presumptions, debates, and trajectories within feminist scholarship'.[33] The idea of socialist feminism was thus marginalized within academic feminism in the United States, and given its influence in such matters, in the Western academia. In other words, the critique of patriarchy by academic feminism was advanced from within the confines of a liberal discourse on capitalism. The study of

---

[27] Celia Donert, 'Women's Rights in Cold War Europe: Disentangling Feminist Histories', 8 (2013) *Past and Present*, pp. 178–202 at p. 182. See also Helen Laville, *Cold War Women: The International Activities of American Women's Organizations* (Manchester: Manchester University Press, 2002).

[28] Kelly Coogan-Gehr, *The Geopolitics of the Cold War and Narratives of Inclusion: Excavating a Feminist Archive* (New York: Palgrave Macmillan, 2011), p. 2. The study uses 'the history of *Signs: Journal of Women in Culture and Society* during its first ten years of publication (1975–1985) as a case study'. See ibid. The journal looked for funding from philanthropic institutions and United States Agency for International Development (USAID) which indirectly shaped its agenda. There is no conspiracy theory being proposed here or any attempt to underplay the contribution of *Signs,* but a simple narration of how the publication came to reflect the geopolitical interests of the United States.

[29] Kate Sutherland, 'Marx and MacKinnon: The Promise and Perils of Marxism for Feminist Legal Theory', 69 (2005) *Science and Society*, pp. 113–132 at p. 114. Albeit, it is interesting that radical feminists often used Marxist tropes.

[30] Coogan-Gehr, *The Geopolitics of the Cold War*, pp. 34–35.

[31] See ibid.

[32] See ibid., p. 51.

[33] See ibid., pp. 84–85.

third world women was also undertaken to consider the role they could play 'as agents possessing the capacity to spread democratic and capitalist ideologies' in the beginning of the neo-liberal era.[34] It may be recalled here that in the period of the Cold War anti-communist governments in the third world were opposed to transnational feminism because they saw it as aligned to communism.[35]

In these circumstances, it is somewhat understandable that in the paranoid world of Western international law there was no space for feminist or other critical approaches until after the end of the Cold War. What was, however, entirely acceptable and even encouraged was a feminist approach to human rights as it brought focus on the poor human rights record of Soviet bloc countries.[36] These writings did contribute to the adoption of CEDAW. The end of the Cold War saw FtAIL being not only articulated but receive some attention, even if often accompanied by scepticism with regard to its usefulness, in the Western international law academia. The reasons for the relatively positive reception of FtAIL in the post Cold Ware era deserve to be noted. First, of course, a facilitative environment had been created by feminist scholarship in human rights along with the UN conferences on women in the matrix of a growing transnational women's movement.[37] Second, the fact that scholars like Charlesworth and Chinkin were merely suggesting that contemporary international law needed to promote the equality of sexes and protect women from sexual violence made it more acceptable than the more radical critiques of international law being advanced by NAIL and TWAIL. In other words, the reason why MFILS received recognition, that is to the extent it did, was because it did not contest the Western neo-imperial project, as also because of the unintended consequence of fracturing critical theories on gender lines. Third, by drawing attention to the deeper inequalities and the greater oppression of women in the third world it helped legitimize

---

[34] See ibid., p. 116.

[35] Jacqueline Castledine, ' "In a Solid Bond of Unity": Anticolonial Feminism in the Cold War Era', 20 (2008) *Journal of Women's History*, pp. 57–81.

[36] Rittich writes that 'although feminist analyses of human rights norms began to appear with some degree of regularity by the 1980s, analysis of mainstream international law was sporadic at best'. Kerry Rittich, 'Book Review', 14 (2001) *Leiden Journal of International Law*, pp. 935–939 at p. 935.

[37] Mohanty observes: 'Feminist theory and feminist movements across national borders have matured substantially since the early 1980s, and there is now a greater visibility of transnational women's struggles and movements, brought on in part by the United Nations world conferences on women held over the last two decades'. Mohanty, ' "Under Western Eyes" Revisited', p. 508.

the Western international security agenda. This was not possible in the period of the Cold War because, as Carol Harrington points out, 'women's politics in the UN system formed a terrain of superpower struggle'.[38] To the dismay of the West, the Soviet argument that 'the problem of "women's oppression" should be located within a broader analysis of international political economy attracted many women's organizations active in the UN'.[39] This changed with the collapse of the Soviet Union. In other words, 'the sudden unity forged in the post-Cold War UN field of women's politics owe[d] less to the intrinsic properties of the violence against women issue than to a sudden absence of superpower conflict'.[40] The end of the Soviet Union also 'transformed discourse on both "women" and "human rights" as problems for international government' as the United States 'pose[d] as leader of the democratic world and defender of women and children against brutal men who instigate "new wars" characterized by mass rape'.[41] The stage had thus been set for a feminist approach that was written from within the received framework of radical and liberal feminism that did not interrogate the implications of globalizing capitalism. As the idea of 'governance feminism' has signalled, radical and liberal feminisms, and the two combine in the work of Charlesworth and Chinkin, can be deployed to help legitimize the US hegemonic project.[42] Finally, as has been suggested by Nancy Fraser, the liberal discourse on feminism came to be co-opted by the ongoing neo-liberal globalization

---

[38] Carol Harrington, 'Resolution 1325 and Post-Cold War Feminist Politics', 13 (2011) *International Feminist Journal of Politics*, pp. 557–575 at p. 558. See also Helen McCarthy, 'The Diplomatic History of Global Women's Rights: The British Foreign Office and International Women's Year, 1975', 50 (2015) *Journal of Contemporary History*, pp. 833–853. McCarthy writes that the British foreign office 'reading of IWY [International Women's Year] was refracted through the prism of Cold War politics and postcolonial struggles. Gender politics was conceptualized by diplomats – including, significantly, the small number of female diplomats in post – as essentially a proxy for these larger ideological battles. This was an approach with origins in the [...] anti-communist propaganda campaigns after the Second World War, which had identified women as an important target group for pro-western publicity'. See ibid., pp. 836–837.

[39] Harrington, 'Resolution 1325', p. 558.

[40] See ibid.

[41] See ibid. She further observes that 'according to security experts, the "new wars" of the post-Cold War era require new forms of peacekeeping that include attention to women's rights, particularly violence against women. Ironically, these new forms of peacekeeping create environments in which sexual violence, abuse and exploitation flourish'. See ibid.

[42] MFILS did not assign sufficient significance to the fact that in the colonial era too there was a focus on the reform of the position of third world women, an accent that offered special justification for the colonial project.

process.[43] The focus on identity and difference, and flowing from it on issues such as violence and reproduction, coupled with the absence of a critique of capitalism and imperialism allowed liberal feminism to enter into a 'dangerous liaison' with neo-liberal globalization.[44] For instance, the emphasis on equality translated into greater participation of women in the workforce facilitating the implementation of the neo-liberal mantra of labour flexibility.[45] The answer, of course, does not lie in the absence of participation in the workforce but a critique of structures of global capitalism that exploit the new situation. To be sure, and this point needs to be emphasized, the impulses that informed the articulation of MFILS were not driven by a neo-imperial agenda. In fact, Charlesworth and Chinkin have not only opposed 'imperial feminism' but have also played a signal role in sensitizing the community of international lawyers to the gender question, including to the concerns of third world feminism. But their theoretical position is open to interpretations that militate against their individual concerns, especially where the neo-liberal agenda is concerned. By not addressing deep structures, MFILS made it possible for its project to be used, often over the protests of the pioneers of the approach, to legitimize neo-imperial ends.

In this regard, MFILS also did not sufficiently appreciate that 'a feminist analysis of international law that focuses on gender alone, without analyzing the exploitation of women in the economic "South", would operate to reinforce the depoliticized notion of "difference" that founds the privileged position of the imperial feminist'.[46] There was insufficient realization that by not critically examining key branches of international law such as international economic law (on which more later) MFILS was taking a step backwards from the feminist discourse on human rights and development. It is worth emphasizing here that by the time MFILS came to be articulated the essence of the third world and socialist feminist approach had come to be embodied in the preamble to CEDAW that inter alia states:

> Concerned that in situations of poverty women have the least access to food, health, education, training and opportunities for employment and other needs,

---

[43] Nancy Fraser, 'Feminism, Capitalism and the Cunning of History', 56 (2009) *New Left Review*, pp. 97–117.

[44] See ibid., pp. 108–109.

[45] See ibid., p. 110.

[46] Anne Orford, 'Feminism, Imperialism and the Mission of International Law, 71 (2002) *Nordic Journal of International Law*, pp. 275–296 at p. 285. MFILS also neglects the ways in which globalization 'produces a gendered international division of labor'. See ibid., p. 286.

> Convinced that the establishment of the new international economic order based on equity and justice will contribute significantly towards the promotion of equality between men and women,
>
> Emphasizing that the eradication of apartheid, all forms of racism, racial discrimination, colonialism, neo-colonialism, aggression, foreign occupation and domination and interference in the internal affairs of States is essential to the full enjoyment of the rights of men and women.

These preambular paragraphs show how third world feminism and socialist feminism had already shaped the thinking on women's rights.[47] The link of violation of women's rights with poverty, an unequal international economic order and imperialism was after all at the centre of third world and socialist feminist thinking.[48] It may be recalled that CEDAW was adopted only a few years after the landmark resolutions on the 1974 Programme and Declaration of action on a New International Economic Order (NIEO) and the Charter of Economic Rights and Duties of States (CERDS) both of which underlined the relationship between the international economic order and the welfare of third world peoples, including women. The contribution of third world feminism (including postcolonial feminism) and TWAIL to the text of CEDAW has however rarely been acknowledged by Western scholars of international law. Instead, as in the case of international law in general, the origin and development of feminist approach to international law is solely attributed to Western feminist scholars, movements and practices. With that narrative the claim that international law is the product of European civilization continues. It is a useful reminder of the complex relationship between knowledge and power in tracing the genealogy of a discipline.

III.   Different Approaches to Feminism

In this backdrop some of the feminist theories that have a presence in the legal field may be considered. There is no attempt to offer either a general or detailed survey of the different feminist theories but to briefly discuss

---

[47] Throughout the 1960s 'the socialist bloc joined forces with the non-aligned countries in lobbying for a separate Declaration for the Elimination of all Forms of Discrimination against Women, a forerunner to the binding convention of the same name that would enter into force in 1979'. Donert, 'Women's Rights', p. 199.

[48] See ibid. See also Raluca Popa, 'Translating Equality between Women and Men Across Cold War Divides: Women Activists from Hungary and Romania and the Creation of International Women's Year' in Shana Penn and Jill Massino (eds.) *Gender Politics and Everyday Life in State Socialist Eastern and Central Europe* (London: Palgrave Macmillan, 2009), pp. 59–74.

those that facilitate the explication of the work of Charlesworth and Chinkin and help make the case for socialist feminism.[49] In discussing different approaches, it is useful to distinguish between two broad stances in feminist scholarship that can help frame debates on the subject. These ideal types may be termed 'autonomous' and 'integrative' theories.[50] What unites them in the field of law is the general aim of 'freeing women as well as legal scholarship'.[51] Broadly speaking, 'autonomous' theories hold the view that the category 'gender' is central to understanding not only the status of women but society as a whole. While autonomous theories can certainly be extended towards intersectional analysis, and can take cognizance of historical and cultural differences, the extensions and inclusions are not allowed to displace the centrality of the category 'gender'. In contrast the integrative theories are not only more willing to work 'across different feminist approaches',[52] but also ready to accommodate other social theories that allow a focus on all subaltern groups and classes. It is believed that integrative theories can stop the marginalization of feminist approaches by framing them as inclusive theories of social transformation. The mixing of feminist and other social theories does not necessarily mean that the former loses its edge for the latter are profoundly transformed in the process. However, not all integrative stances may be equally persuasive from the perspective of both feminist and social theories as also in terms of explaining and understanding international legal structures. It will be seen that the 'eclectic method' that Charlesworth and Chinkin use essentially combines the insights of radical feminism with liberal social and political theory to offer an approach that does not analyse deep structures or even the internal contradictions that mark the international legal system. It has led to a peculiar outcome: on the one hand, Charlesworth and Chinkin assume positions more radical than radical feminists like MacKinnon by rejecting the sanguine assessment of the advances that have been made in international law to address the concerns of women and, on the other hand, they appear to endorse a

---

[49] In the event it is the nature of different feminisms rather than their perspective on the role of law that is in focus.

[50] These ideal types are adopted from Amy G. Mazur, 'A Feminist Empirical and Integrative Approach in Political Science: Breaking Down the Glass Wall?' in Harold Kincaid (ed.) *The Oxford Handbook of Philosophy of Social Science* (New York: Oxford University Press, 2012), pp. 533–558, at p. 536.

[51] Catherine MacKinnon, 'Foreword' in Beverley Baines, Daphne Barak-Erez and Tsvi Kahana (eds.) *Feminist Constitutionalism: Global Perspectives* (Cambridge : Cambridge University Press, 2012) pp. ix–xii at p. xii.

[52] Mazur, 'A Feminist', p. 536.

narrative of progress where other areas of contemporary international law are concerned.[53] They are thus radicals in one direction and conservative in other respects. It is argued later that an integrative theory that combines the insights of socialist and postcolonial feminism with Marxism offers the most productive basis for articulating a theory of international law which can simultaneously promote equality between sexes and the goal of emancipation of all subaltern groups and classes.

A.   Radical Feminism

The radical or structural feminist approach to law is best approached through the writings of Catherine MacKinnon.[54] In an early and famous essay MacKinnon describes the essence of radical feminism by comparing it to Marxism:

> Sexuality is to feminism what work is to marxism: that which is most one's own, yet most taken away … the molding, direction, and expression of sexuality organizes society into two sexes – women and men – which division underlies the totality of social relations … the organized expropriation of the sexuality of some for the use of others defines the sex, woman.[55]

MacKinnon extended the sexual subordination thesis advanced here to the oppression of women in general. As Mariana Valverde observes:

> MacKinnon took gender structuralism to the extreme and claimed that sexual objectification is not just one amongst many patriarchal evils – as liberal and socialist feminists generally believed – but is in fact the foundation of patriarchy as such, lying at the root of all the other oppressions suffered by all women, regardless of economic class, geography, or culture.[56]

MacKinnon does accept that social and cultural factors come into play in how sexual subordination manifests itself in different societies. She also concedes that gender structuralism plays out differently in different periods of history. In her words, 'feminists do not argue that it means

---

[53] D'Amato, 'Book Review'; José E. Alvarej, 'Book Review', 95 (2001) *The American Journal of International Law*, pp. 459–464.
[54] Radical feminism, according to Charlesworth and Chinkin, 'explains women's inequality as the product of domination of women by men'. Charlesworth and Chinkin, *Boundaries of International law*, p. 42.
[55] Catharine A. MacKinnon, 'Feminism, Marxism, Method, and the State: An Agenda for Theory', 7 (1982) *Signs*, pp. 515–544 at pp. 515–516.
[56] Mariana Valverde, 'The Rescaling of Feminist Analyses of Law and State Power: From (Domestic) Subjectivity to (Transnational) Governance Networks', 14 (2014) *UC Irvine Law Review*, pp. 325–352 at p. 336.

the same to women to be on the bottom in a feudal regime, a capitalist regime, and a socialist regime; the commonality argued is that, despite real changes, bottom is bottom'.[57] But MacKinnon does not attempt to identify the social forces in pre-capitalist or socialist societies that ensure that 'bottom is bottom' or the forms in which it manifests itself.[58]

Having advanced the subordination feminism thesis MacKinnon turns to understanding the nature of the capitalist state and law. She argues that a capitalist society 'institutionalizes male power' in significant ways through law.[59] But, unlike Marxists who talk about the transformation of capitalist social relations and capitalist law through the working class capturing state power, MacKinnon does not speak of transforming the legal regime through deposing the patriarchal state and the rule of men. Instead, she posits the aim of feminist politics as 'consciousness raising' which means 'the collective critical reconstitution of the meaning of women's social experience, as women live through it'.[60] According to MacKinnon, 'conscious raising is the major technique of analysis, structure of organization, method of practice, and theory of social change of the women's movement'.[61] It is only through consciousness raising that 'women grasp the collective reality of women's condition from within the perspective of that experience, not from outside it'.[62] Women learn that 'they have learned that men are everything, women their negation, but that the sexes are equal'.[63] The goal of 'consciousness raising' inexorably leads her to accept in the final analysis the liberal feminist position of fighting for equality between sexes within the existing order of things.[64]

---

[57] MacKinnon, 'Feminism, Marxism', p. 523.

[58] As Valverde observes: 'MacKinnon does not provide any discussion, however tentative, of either a prepatriarchal past or a postpatriarchal future. Her frame therefore lacks any feminist equivalent of what Marxists used to call the motor forces of history. Therefore, the subjectivity that is theorized in MacKinnon's work of the 1980s is even more structured, so to speak, and less "agentic," than that of the hardest of hard-line structuralist Marxists.' Valverde, 'Rescaling ', p. 337.

[59] Catharine A. MacKinnon, 'Feminism, Marxism, Method, and the State: Toward Feminist Jurisprudence', 8 (1983) *Signs*, pp. 635–658 at pp. 644 and 645.

[60] MacKinnon, 'Agenda for Theory', p. 543.

[61] See ibid., p. 519.

[62] See ibid., p. 536.

[63] See ibid., p. 542.

[64] Sutherland, 'Marx and MacKinnon', pp. 114, 128. According to Sutherland, the relationship between being and consciousness is theorized in ways that have her 'mired in an impossible quandary': 'Women need to be extricated to provoke social change, yet women cannot be extricated without social change. No one is outside the system, but no one can provoke change from within it.' See ibid., p. 128.

The underlying assumption, of course, is that eventually the struggle for equality would lead to the general transformation of society. She is not alone in making this assumption. It has been observed that 'the dominant assumption in twentieth-century feminist theory is that consciousness-raising is itself a form of praxis that is revolutionary'.[65] In the consciousness raising process MacKinnon accords 'the legal arena a central place in feminist struggles'.[66] But doubts have been expressed as to whether in the 'closed system' of radical feminism law can serve as a liberatory tool for women.[67]

On the other hand, since MacKinnon understates the significance of Marxism's 'transformative potential for feminist legal theory',[68] and is also, as shall be seen, critical of postmodernism, she cannot offer a radical critique of law. She is of course not entirely wrong in complaining that 'Marxist theory *has* traditionally attempted to comprehend all meaningful social variance in class terms ... Marxists typically extend class to cover women, a division and submersion ... inadequate to women's divergent and common experience'.[69] She may also be right in suggesting that even female Marxists did not think otherwise: 'Women as women, across class distinctions and apart from nature, were simply unthinkable to Luxemburg, as to most Marxists.'[70] But she is equally critical of 'socialist feminism' for not recognizing 'the depth of the antagonism or the separate integrity of each theory'.[71] In her view at best 'an uneven combination is accomplished' by socialist feminism with the result that the 'woman question' 'is always reduced to some other question, instead of being seen as the question, calling for analysis on its own terms'.[72] On her part MacKinnon subsumes class inequality under sex inequality. She sees 'women as even more inextricably oppressed within patriarchy than are workers within capitalism'.[73] To put it differently, MacKinnon does not accept the idea that the eventual aim of the Marxist project is social transformation for all, including the emancipation of women. She also rejects the Marxist understanding that the problem of subordination of women

[65] Josephine Donovan, *Feminist Theory: The Intellectual Traditions Fourth Edition, Revised and Expanded* (New York: Continuum, 2012), p. 84.
[66] Sutherland, 'Marx and MacKinnon', p. 130.
[67] See ibid., p. 129.
[68] See ibid., p. 131.
[69] MacKinnon, 'Agenda for Theory', p. 520; emphasis in original.
[70] See ibid., p. 521.
[71] See ibid., p. 524.
[72] See ibid., pp. 526–527.
[73] Sutherland, 'Marx and MacKinnon', p. 130.

cannot be seriously addressed within a capitalist system. In the process, MacKinnon 'jettisons or overlooks some of the most liberatory aspects of Marxism'.[74] It comes as no surprise then that she rejects the view of social-ist feminists that 'a re-engagement with Marxist theory offers alternate possibilities for feminist praxis in the legal arena'.[75] The offer is spurned not only because of the poor record of 'actually existing socialism', but also because she does not see the need for thinking of the women's question along with the destiny of other subaltern groups.[76]

However, in recent times, perhaps realizing the circularity and limits of radical feminism, MacKinnon explores the idea of intersectionality even though sex inequality remains for her the primary contradiction that characterizes all human society. She makes two moves in this regard. First, MacKinnon rejects the charge of essentialism and reductionism by not-ing that she had never claimed that 'gender is all there is' which 'explains everything' or that 'everything reduces to gender, that it is the only regu-larity or the only explanation for things, the single cause of everything, or the only thing there'.[77] Second, MacKinnon notes the benefits of reject-ing a 'monocular vision' and adopting an intersectional framework.[78] According to her, 'intersectionality both notices and contends with the realities of multiple inequalities as it thinks about ' "the interaction of" those inequalities in a way that captures the distinctive dynamics at their multidimensional interface'.[79] Using the work of Kimberlé Crenshaw, MacKinnon describes 'intersectionality' as a method that 'does not sim-ply add variables' but offers 'a distinctive stance' embodying 'a particular

---

[74] See ibid.

[75] See ibid., p. 114.

[76] In so far as the record of 'actually existing socialism' is concerned it is worth noting that Soviet initiative in the very early years 'was nothing short of dramatic. The Bolshevik gov-ernment rewrote family law on assumptions of equality between woman and man, reject-ing the law as it existed in the West'. John Quigley, *Soviet Legal Innovation and the Law of the Western World* (Cambridge: Cambridge University Press, 2007), p. 20. V. I. Lenin is said to have observed that 'in the course of two years of Soviet power in one of the most backward countries of Europe, more has been done to emancipate woman, to make her the equal of the "strong" sex, than has been done during the past 130 years by all the advanced, enlightened, "democratic" republics of the world taken together'. Cited by Quigley, see ibid., p. 26.

[77] Catharine MacKinnon, 'Points Against PostModernism', 75 (2000) *Chicago-Kent Law Review,* pp. 687–712 at p. 695. MacKinnon cites Tracy Higgins on the meaning of essen-tialism: 'the rejection … of the idea that particular characteristics can be identified with over time and across cultures'. See ibid., p. 697.

[78] Catharine MacKinnon, 'Intersectionality as Method: A Note', 38 (2013) *Signs,* pp. 1019–1030 at p. 1020.

[79] See ibid., p. 1019.

dynamic approach to the underlying laws of motion of the reality it traces and traps while remaining grounded in the experience of classes of people within hierarchical relations "where systems of race, gender, and class domination converge" criticizing a rigidly top-down social and political order from the perspective of the bottom up'.[80] She approves of Crenshaw drawing on 'the combined effects of practices which discriminate on the basis of race, and on the basis of sex'.[81] In other words, in MacKinnon's view, intersectionality 'is animated by a method in the sense of an operative approach to law, society, and their symbiotic relation, by a distinctive way into reality that captures not just the static outcomes of the problem it brings into view but its dynamic and lines of force as well. It is this that makes it transformative'.[82] She thus accepts the Crenshaw understanding that the different bases of oppression and subordination are greater than the sum of its parts. Finally, MacKinnon notes that 'capturing the synergistic relation between inequalities as grounded in the lived experience of hierarchy is changing not only what people think about inequality but the way they think'.[83] But, despite the engagement with the idea of intersectionality, its implications are not entirely clear as she has not revised the centrality of the sexual subordination thesis. Arguably, the move to intersectionality allows, by broadening the base of critique of third world societies, to more effectively justify her current support for military interventions in the name of feminism. For the rest, the concept of intersectionality can only do limited work within the confines of the m/f binary. It is only a socialist feminist framework that allows the idea of intersectionality to be 'integrated coherently and systematically' in a comprehensive theory of social transformation.[84]

---

[80] See ibid., p. 1020. For an early writing of Crenshaw on intersectionality see Kimberlé Crenshaw, 'Demarginalizing the Intersection of Race and Sex: A Black Feminist Critique of Antidiscrimination Doctrine, Feminist Theory and Antiracist Politics', (1989) *University of Chicago Legal Forum*, pp. 139–167.

[81] MacKinnon, 'Intersectionality as Method: A Note', p. 1020.

[82] See ibid., pp. 1023–1024.

[83] See ibid., p. 1028.

[84] Nancy Holmstrom, 'Introduction' in Nancy Holmstrom (ed.) *The Socialist Feminist Project: A Contemporary Reader in Theory and Politics* (Delhi: Aakar, 2011), p. 8. See also Johanna Brenner, 'Intersections, Locations, and Capitalist Class Relations: Intersectionality from a Marxist Perspective' in Nancy Holmstrom (ed.) *The Socialist Feminist Project: A Contemporary Reader in Theory and Politics* (Delhi: Aakar, 2011), pp. 336–348; Maxine Molyneux, 'Conceptualizing Women's Interests' in Nancy Holmstrom (ed.) *The Socialist Feminist Project: A Contemporary Reader in Theory and Politics* (Delhi: Aakar, 2011), pp. 250–257.

Yet from the standpoint of socialist feminism the move to intersection-ality acquires salience in the backdrop of her critique of postmodernism, that is, despite the fact that MacKinnon's turn to intersectionality is ani-mated by her justification of imperial feminism. This is because her cri-tique of postmodernism for ignoring empirical realities makes a case for feminism that not only takes cognizance of multiple bases of oppression in society but is also rooted in the real world of oppression.[85] Her cri-tique of postmodernism is based on the perfectly valid assumption that 'practical confrontation with the specific realities of sexual and physical violation' is what 'created feminist theory'.[86] The gendered nature of these realities were 'not assumed, posited, invented, or imagined'.[87] Women 'could know it was real' because their bodies 'collectively, lived through it'.[88] On the other hand, postmodernism's 'main target is, precisely, real-ity'.[89] According to MacKinnon, postmodernism 'derealizes social reality by ignoring it, by refusing to be accountable to it ... by openly repudiating any connection with an "it" by claiming "it" is not there'.[90] In her view, 'the fact that reality is a social construction does not mean that it is not there; it means that it is there, in society, where we live'.[91] The postmodern critique is thus in her view 'an abstract critique of abstract subjects'.[92] In any case 'if everything is interpretation, you can never be wrong'.[93] Radical feminism on the other hand 'does not assume that anyone's culture, including their own, is valid'.[94] In contrast what postmodernism offers 'is a multicultural defense for male violence – a defense for it whatever it is, which in effect is a pretty universal defense'.[95] The politics of postmodernism is thus a 'politics of abdication and passivism'.[96] According to MacKinnon, 'if the postmodernists took responsibility for changing even one real thing, they would learn more about theory than everything they have written to date

---

[85] For an early Marxist critique of postmodern academic feminism see Carol A. Sabile, 'Feminism and the Ends of Postmodernism' in Rosemary Hennessy and Chrysn Ingraham (eds.) *Materialist Feminism: A Reader in Class, Difference, and Women's Lives* (Routledge: London, 1997), pp. 395–408.

[86] MacKinnon, 'Points', p. 688.

[87] See ibid.

[88] See ibid., p. 689.

[89] See ibid., p. 693.

[90] See ibid.

[91] See ibid., p. 703.

[92] See ibid., p. 710.

[93] See ibid., p. 704.

[94] See ibid., p. 699.

[95] See ibid., p. 700.

[96] See ibid., p. 710.

put together'.[97] The implication of her critique of postmodernism for the idea of intersectionality is that it is validated by empirical reality and is 'not assumed, posited, invented, or imagined'.

Having touched upon MacKinnon's views on Marxism, socialist feminism and postmodernism it is time to briefly consider her pronouncements on the world of international law.[98] It is interesting in this instance to contrast the views of MacKinnon with Charlesworth. Whereas MacKinnon is sanguine about the role international law can play in promoting equality between sexes, Charlesworth believes that MacKinnon has 'a rather romantic view of the international legal arena where women's rights remain hotly contested'.[99] Before turning to Charlesworth's critique it would only be appropriate to recount the reasons MacKinnon offers for her view that women have 'been effective at using the international arena against masculine dominance'. First, she notes that 'sex equality, although subject to varying interpretations, is nearly universally embraced as an international norm'.[100] Second, the international locale helps women emerge as a transnational group (perhaps on the lines of 'workers of the world unite') and therefore 'the international is the authentic locale for the fight of women's rights'.[101] Third, new initiatives like the Optional Protocol to CEDAW offers 'the possibility of reinvigorating the international human rights framework and hope for equality of women'.[102] But while MacKinnon places her faith in international law she is also not sparing in her critique. However, her critique draws on an essentialist standpoint that invites the charge of complicity with hegemonic forces. For example, she asks as to why violence against women does not 'receive a response in the structure and practice of international law anything approximate to the level and focus of determination inspired by September 11th attacks?'.[103] Or why is the fate of Afghan women 'imprisoned in their clothes and homes for years ... not rank with terrorism' and invite military action?[104]

---

[97] See ibid., p. 711.

[98] Catharine MacKinnon, *Are Women Human? And Other International Dialogues* (Cambridge, MA: Harvard University Press, 2006).

[99] Hilary Charlesworth, 'Book Review: Catherine A MacKinnon, Are Women Human? And Other International Dialogues' , 107 (2013) *American Journal of International Law,* pp. 719–214.

[100] MacKinnon, *Are Women Human?*, pp. 9–10.

[101] See ibid., p. 120.

[102] See ibid., p. 67.

[103] See ibid., p. 269.

[104] See ibid., p. 270.

The Charlesworth critique is as follows. First, MacKinnon overestimates the contribution of international law which while it 'carries a certain glamour and allure' has been 'a disappointing mechanism for redress
of women's rights'.[105] Thus, for instance, the Optional Protocol to CEDAW
has achieved little as it has led to few cases.[106] Second, 'MacKinnon's elevation of the international system as the most accommodating for wom-
en's rights understates the critical role of national and local systems for
women'.[107] Charlesworth argues in this respect that women turn most
to local and national systems to carry forward their struggles. In any
case, international norms have to be incorporated and transformed into
national norms to be effective.[108] Third, Charlesworth finds MacKinnon's
suggestion of military action 'troubling' for 'it effectively endorses armed
intervention as a method of achieving change, despite all the evidence
that such intervention is counter-productive, tending to install even more
repressive political orders inimical to women's rights'.[109] Indeed, in her
view, MacKinnon's remedy 'fails to recognize male power operates in
complex ways and cannot be snuffed out by the use of force. It also buys
into a deeply gendered understanding of dispute resolution and short-
circuits a more sustained discussion about the ways to achieve equality'.[110]

The question that is left open by Charlesworth is whether her critique
of MacKinnon implies the rejection of essentialism or implies its affirmation by suggesting that international law cannot seriously undermine
male power. It is perhaps more the case that the Charlesworth critique
simply reflects a different assessment of the progress made in international law in promoting the rights of women. She is also apprehensive
that the MacKinnon view could be placed in the service of hegemonic
forces.[111] But, as will become clear later, her critique of MacKinnon does

---

[105] Charlesworth, 'Book Review', p. 722.
[106] See ibid.
[107] See ibid.
[108] See ibid.
[109] See ibid.
[110] See ibid. While Charlesworth writes that MacKinnon is 'stung by criticism when it comes
from feminist and progressive scholars' it is also perhaps the case that she does not receive
fair commentary. Thus, for example, she writes of MacKinnon's critique of postmodernism that it 'verges on parody'. See ibid., p. 723.
[111] It is interesting that Chinkin appears to take a different position. She writes that 'the
invisibility of women in any legal justification for the use of force is striking. When assessing the impact of possible responses to aggression the concerns and needs of women
are simply not raised by governments or even by other groups'. Christine Chinkin, 'A
Gendered Perspective to the International Use of Force', 11 (1991) *Australian Yearbook
of International Law*, pp. 279–293 at p. 291. Indeed, Chinkin observes that: 'It must be

not necessarily mean a rejection of essentialism or a move beyond the liberal feminist project.[112]

B. *Critical Legal Feminism*

In recent years the term 'governance feminism' (GF) has come into vogue. The critical legal feminist scholar Janet Halley has coined this phrase to refer to:

> the incremental but by now quite noticeable installation of feminists and feminist ideas in actual legal-institutional power … Feminists by no means have won everything they want – far from it – but neither are they helpless outsiders…. international legal order is increasingly receiving feminists into its power elites and that feminist law reform is emerging as a formidable new source of legal ideas.[113]

Like MacKinnon Halley believes that 'many of the most breathtaking advances have been made in the rapidly evolving world of international law'.[114] The field of international humanitarian law (IHL) is seen as a good example with GF winning significant victories in the Rome Statute.[115] Feminism is also seen as playing an important role, if not 'running things', in 'the European Union, the human rights establishment, even the World Bank'.[116] Halley is not alone among critical feminist scholars in making claims about the successes of feminism and its growing presence in global

acknowledged that inclusion of gender issues in determining norms of international law and in assessing what behavior is contrary to those norms will pose a major challenge to the prevailing legal notions of authority and sovereignty located in nation States'. See ibid., p. 293.

[112] Thus, for instance, Charlesworth would not accept the view of Pierre Bourdieu who points out that ' the relation of complicity that the victims of symbolic domination grant to the dominant can only be broken through a radical transformation of the social conditions of production of the dispositions that lead the dominated to take on the point of view of the dominant on the dominant and on themselves'. Pierre Bourdieu, *Masculine Domination* (Cambridge: Polity Press, 2001), pp. 41–42. Symbolic violence is defined as 'the *violence which is exercised upon a social agent with his or her complicity*'. Pierre Bourdieu and Loïc Wacquant, *An Invitation to Reflexive Sociology* (Cambridge: Polity Press, 1992), p. 167; emphasis in original.

[113] Janet Halley, Prabha Kotiswaran and Hila Shamir, 'From the International to the Local in Feminist Legal Responses to Rape, Prostitution/Sex Work, and Sex Trafficking: Four Studies in Contemporary Governance Feminism', 29 (2006) *Harvard Journal of Law & Gender*, pp. 335–423 at pp. 340 and 419.

[114] See ibid., p. 340.

[115] See ibid., pp. 342 ff.

[116] Janet Halley, *Split Decisions*, p. 20.

governance. There are others who endorse the idea of GF.[117] For instance, Chantal Thomas writes that feminism has 'against very steep odds of governmental indifference and patriarchal hostility' succeeded 'in achieving recognition of and response to social justice claims on behalf of women everywhere. The feminist movement has proven truly international, and as such stands as an exemplar of the potential for 'global governance'.[118] In her view the situation today is very different from three decades ago when 'it was possible to state with certainty that the international human rights framework did not recognize that "women's rights are human rights"'.[119]

But Halley is sceptical whether GF represents real advance for feminism. Indeed, despite her 'positive' assessments of the role of international law in advancing the cause of women's rights Halley advises 'a break from feminism'.[120] She recommends that feminism rethink two overlapping issues. First, whether feminism has in all cases to begin and end with the concerns of women. Halley speaks of divergentist forms of feminism to indicate a feminism which 'is prepared to see political splits and split decisions within its feminism'.[121] In this view, 'feminism need not be the normative or political measure of the goodness of the results' or 'be the ultimate form of the product' or 'be the constituency on whose behalf it works'.[122] From this perspective, the idea of taking a break from feminism does not necessarily require moving away from the feminist tradition but merely to go beyond radical or subordinate feminism. However, while this

---

[117] See for instance Cyra Akila Chowdhury, 'Governance Feminism's Imperial Misadventure: Progress, International Law, and the Security of Afghan Women', FIU Legal Studies Research Paper No.14-04, February 2014, can be accessed at http://ssrn.com/abstract=2320004. At the domestic level too GF is said to have had its day. Thus Sutherland writing on radical feminism states that: 'even as MacKinnon's influence has waned among feminists, it has increased among legislators and judges. For example, in recent years she has had an enormous impact on the crafting of U.S. sexual harassment laws and of Canadian obscenity laws. While such legal developments may have produced victories for individual women, they have done little to counter systemic inequality. Indeed, they have often exacerbated systemic inequality, particularly when gender inequality intertwines with discrimination based on class, race, sexual orientation, or disability'. This has led to "liberal co-optation" of the work of radical feminists. Sutherland, 'Marx and MacKinnon', p. 114.

[118] Halley et al., 'From the International', p. 347. According to Chantal Thomas, GF is 'feminism that seeks not only to analyze and critique the problem, but to *devise, pursue and achieve reform to address the problem in the real world*'. See ibid., p. 348; emphasis in original.

[119] See ibid., p. 352.

[120] Halley, *Split Decision*.

[121] See ibid., p. 26. See also p. 30.

[122] See ibid.

critique opens the space for integrative feminisms, Halley is pessimistic about the role of socialist feminism, at least in so far as the United States is concerned where it is 'like a patient etherized upon a table'.[123] Despite the geographical caveat, the underlying suggestion is that if socialist feminism does not have a presence in the United States it cannot have life elsewhere. But the significant point perhaps is that she recognizes that a positive feature of socialist feminism (as also of postcolonial and critical race feminisms) is that it may require that radical feminism be left behind.[124]

A second issue on which Halley calls for critical reflection is 'the institutionalization of feminist ideas in law and other sites of formal power'. While Halley concedes that 'governance feminism has been, in manifold ways, a good thing',[125] she believes that 'it has a dark side'.[126] In other words, GF has both intended and unintended consequences. As Hila Shamir explains, the term GF 'is normatively empty: it signifies a certain form of power – which in itself is not *necessarily* bad, but the fact that it is feminist does not make it *necessarily* good either'.[127] Like Halley she finds it unsettling that 'the current form of GF tends to deny its own power, and consequently *systematically* overlooks the shifts in bargaining power, distributive consequences, and production of winners and losers yielded by feminist legislative reforms'.[128] A real concern is that feminism may be co-opted by hegemonic social forces and states at the international level. Taking the example of the trafficking regime Thomas writes of its 'contribution ... to the border control agendas of states – particularly rich states – at the expense of delivering actual aid to victims of trafficking' harming the very people that are to be helped.[129] Prabha Kotiswaran has

[123] See ibid., p. 81.
[124] See ibid., p. 20.
[125] See ibid., p. 32.
[126] See ibid. There is a parallel between the Kennedy emphasis on experts and the need to exercise responsibility and the Janet Halley notion of GF. According to Kennedy, 'we have a hard time focusing on costs in part because we do not think of ourselves as rulers. *Other* people govern, and it is our job to hold *them* responsible'. David Kennedy, *The Dark Sides of Virtue: Reassessing Humanitarianism* (Princeton, NJ: Princeton University Press, 2004), p. xix; emphasis in original. He terms the phenomena 'governance cosmopolitanism'. David Kennedy, 'One, Two, Three, Many Legal Orders: Legal Pluralism and the Cosmopolitan Dream', 31 (2006–07) *N.Y.U. Review of Law & Social Change*, pp. 641–659 at p. 646.
[127] Halley et al., 'From the International', p. 360.
[128] See ibid., p. 361.
[129] See ibid., p. 388. 'Thomas and Halley both note that GF reforms sometimes end up ratifying national(ist) arrangements without paying much attention to the possible downsides

shown how the national and international GF interface to facilitate the mobilization of international law by hegemonic forces. In her view, while the international does not determine the national it can become complicit in shaping national agendas to institute hegemonic discourses.[130] It is therefore possible to speak of the collaboration between national and international GF in the same way as Marxists speak of the collaboration between capitalist classes across national borders. Yet GF 'refuses to own its will to power' and does not reflect on the distributive effects it has in the world.[131] It 'pretends it is always the underdog'.[132] Therefore, care must be taken by feminists to avoid complicity with power. In this regard Halley calls for the study of 'the much larger technologies of power into which GF inserts itself'.[133] In fact, in her view, unless feminism takes a break from itself 'it can't see injury to men by women. It can't see other interests, other forms of power, other justice projects'.[134]

In assessing the idea of GF advanced by critical legal feminists three distinct points need to be separated. The first point is whether there have

of doing so: feminist indifference to the repatriation of trafficked women to their "proper" location on the globe and the collaboration of feminists with ever-intensifying border-control politics is not a pretty sight; nor is feminist indifference to possible ethnic-nationalist deployments of their rules on rape'. See ibid., pp. 420–421. On the trafficking regime Engle also notes that: 'The restrictions on trafficking raise questions about the representations of women with regard to trafficking, whether women should be able to sell their sexuality both here and abroad, and the extent to which anti-trafficking efforts function to restrict migration and avert attention from the socioeconomic pressures that make women and children vulnerable to trafficking'. Karen Engle, 'Liberal Internationalism, Feminism, and the Suppression of Critique: Contemporary Approaches to Global Order in the United States', 46 (2005) *Harvard International Law Journal*, pp. 427–439 at p. 439.

[130] Halley et al., 'From the International', p. 376. For a demonstration of this argument see Vasuki Nesiah, 'Uncomfortable Alliances: Women, Peace, and Security in Sri Lanka' in Ania Loomba and Ritty A. Lukose (eds.) *South Asian Feminisms* (New Delhi: Zubaan, 2012), pp. 139–161.

[131] Halley, 'From the International', p. 420. According to Otto, Halley and her colleagues 'describe Governance Feminism as providing a "dock" for particular strands of feminist thinking associated with the "radical" or "sexual-subordination" feminism of MacKinnon which, because of its preoccupation with (hetero)sexuality as an arena of danger for women, has much in common with religious and social conservatives. As they observe, feminist ideas that emphasise women's vulnerability and powerlessness are particularly susceptible to serving hegemonic power in international law and ... sexual panics mobilise irrational fears about sexuality and can catch feminists in a "conservative impulse" that drastically narrows the terms of feminist discourse'. Dianne Otto, 'Power and Danger: Feminist Engagement with International through the UN Security Council', 32 (2010) *The Australian Feminist Law Journal*, pp. 97–121 at p. 119.

[132] Halley, *Split Decisions*, p. 33.

[133] Halley et al., 'From the International', p. 422; emphasis added.

[134] Halley, *Split Decisions*, p. 33.

been major advances made in the field of international law so far as rights and status of women are concerned. Second, whether feminism can see injury to men, especially in the domain of sexuality.[135] The third is the larger point whether feminism can set aside the radical or subordination model to see other projects of justice. Instead of focusing on the critical third issue Halley essentially engages with matters of 'sexuality' i.e., with the 'erotic' and 'sexual orientation'. These are the concerns that she has in mind when she states in her book *Split Decisions* that 'it's about sex'.[136]

On her part Charlesworth merely contests the idea of GF, that is, the Halley claim that 'feminism has now achieved considerable clout in many areas – governance, society and culture – and refusal to acknowledge this is a form of bad faith'.[137] As in the case of MacKinnon (who in many ways symbolizes governance feminists), Charlesworth counters Halley by noting that her claims are 'exaggerated in light of the evidence'.[138] She argues that while some international institutions may have accepted feminist urgings 'they have reduced feminist ideas to ritualized incantations. Despite all talk of women, gender and gender mainstreaming, women's lives remain on the periphery of international institutions'.[139] In her view, Halley seems to have been dazzled by the inclusive language, but *she has not looked beneath the surface*'.[140] Charlesworth goes on to observe that 'Halley's critique of feminism is focused on its manifestation in law, but *feminist goals and methods extend far beyond the law*'.[141] For, among other things, 'while increasing women's participation in institutions is important, it does not itself change institutional agendas'.[142] She therefore

[135] Halley characterizes 'MacKinnon's work in the 1990s and 2000 as dogmatic, totalizing and so focused on male power that it is unable to recognize the power of women and feminism'. Halley, *Split Decisions*, p. 21.
[136] See ibid., p. 23.
[137] Charlesworth, 'Talking to Ourselves', p. 21.
[138] Charlesworth, 'Talking to Ourselves', p. 23; emphasis added. Franks writes that 'the evidence Halley provides for the charge that feminism is both powerful and in denial about its power lacks concrete or historical support'. Mary Anne Franks, 'Book Review', 30 (2007) *Harvard Journal of Law & Gender*, pp. 257–267 at p. 258. She goes on to observe: 'Is it the case that all Halley is really after in *Taking a Break from Feminism* is the reinstatement of patriarchy? Not quite. In some ways, it is much worse than that'. See ibid., p. 261. Franks also criticizes Halley for not providing evidence of denial by feminists of some success: 'Of course it is true that feminists have impacted international law and therefore obtained some kind of power; Halley asserts that all feminists would strenuously deny this, but fails to offer a single quotation or reference to support this claim'. See ibid., p. 260.
[139] Charlesworth, 'Talking to Ourselves', p. 23.
[140] See ibid; emphasis added.
[141] See ibid., p. 31; emphasis added.
[142] See ibid., p. 30.

does not accept the Halley critique of GF. Dianne Otto agrees with this assessment of Charlesworth when she writes that 'the feminist project in international law is losing ground, even as many are celebrating its victories'.[143] She does not accept the Halley critique of GF, that is, 'its failure to be critically self-reflective, its reliance on state-centred forms of power, its promotion of the "sexual subordination" feminism of Catharine MacKinnon, and its persistent self-representation as the "political underdog"'.[144] Instead, Otto calls for an empirical analysis that can distinguish moments of genuine advance from setbacks.[145]

Returning to Charlesworth, she does not sufficiently appreciate that the assessment of the achievements of feminism, and its complicity with power, is only one dimension of the problem that leads Halley to call for a break from feminism. The reason is that in her writings Charlesworth herself does not look 'beneath the surface' or move 'beyond the law' as she confines the scope of 'beneath' and the 'beyond' to the status of women and their agendas to the legal domain. The debate seems to be once again about whether the glass is half full or half empty. While her assessment of what has been accomplished in the past decades to ensure equality between sexes may not be inaccurate, she is unable to satisfactorily explain why there is such halting progress at the global level; the monocausal explanation of radical or subordination feminism is plain reductionism. Of course, Halley fares no better on this and other counts.

---

[143] Dianne Otto, 'Power and Danger: Feminist Engagement with International Law through the UN Security Council', 32 (2010) *The Australian Feminist Law Journal*, pp. 97–121 at pp. 97–98.

[144] See ibid., p. 97.

[145] For instance, Otto looks at the UNSC resolutions on Women, Peace and Security and concludes: 'Clearly R1820 fits into this mould, with its panicked proposal to evacuate women and girls facing an imminent threat of sexual violence and its silences about sexual violence directed at men and boys. However, the other three resolutions draw from a broader range of feminist ideas, and there is a hint of "sexual positivity" in R1889's call for the recognition of women's "sexual" as well as "reproductive" health needs. Even R1888, despite its focus on sexual violence, addresses the issue in the broader context of women's (and perhaps men's) empowerment instead of their inherent vulnerability. When taken together, these resolutions have not harboured the ideas of "sexual-subordination" feminists, as feminist advances in international criminal law and antitrafficking measures appear to have done. While those ideas have a presence in the Council's resolutions, they have not had the effect of occupying the field and shutting out the influence of other feminist ideas.' See ibid., p. 119. The relevant UN Security Council Resolutions are SC Res 1325 UN SCOR 4213th mtg, UN Doc S/RES/1325 (31 October 2000) (R1325); SC Res 1820 UN SCOR, 5916th mtg UN Doc S/RES/1820 (19 June 2008) (R1820); SC Res 1888 UN SCOR 6195th mtg UN Doc S/RES/1888 (30 September 2009) (R1888); and SC Res 1889 UN SCOR, 6196th mtg UN Doc S/RES/1889 (5 October 2009) (R1889).

First, since the reasons for FtAIL gaining prominence in the post-Cold War period are not explored, she does not realize that GF was always on the agenda. Secondly, she does not offer the tools to understand the process of co-option of feminist agendas by power or the ways in which 'other interests, other forms of power, other justice projects' are to be pursued. On her part, Charlesworth does not seriously engage with deep structures or propose the need for intersectional analysis to look beyond the law or beneath the surface to endorse other justice projects. This is the essence of the critique advanced by third world feminism.[146]

C.   *Postcolonial and Third World Feminism*

It is, therefore, unsurprising that from the early stages Charlesworth and Chinkin have had to confront the critique that 'the dominant mode of international feminism reflects the dominant character and color of international relations, Bourgeois/white, often predatory, and paternalistic'.[147] Oloka-Onyango and Tamale also drew attention to the fact that 'the political economy of international law and relations' was coming to crucially shape 'the internal domestic structure' of third world nations and only 'a truncated feminism' could ignore its impact on the lives of women.[148] In response to such critiques Chinkin conceded that 'a gendered perspective of international law must include the experiences of non-Western women'.[149] She recognized that third world feminists coming from a 'tradition of struggle against colonialism and foreign domination are drawing

---

[146] See generally Gayatri Chakravarti Spivak, 'Three Women's Texts and a Critique of Imperialism', 12 (1985) *Critical Inquiry*, pp. 243–261; Kumari Jayawardena, *Feminism and Nationalism in the Third World* (London: Zed, 1986); Gayatri Chakravarti Spivak, 'Can the Subaltern Speak?' in C. Nelson and L. Grossberg (eds.) *Marxism and the Interpretation of Culture* (Basingstoke: Macmillan education, 1988), pp. 271–313; Sara Suleri, 'Woman Skin Deep: Feminism and the Postcolonial Condition', 18 (1992) *Critical Inquiry*, pp. 756–769; Ania Loomba, *Colonialism/Postcolonialism* (London: Routledge, 1998).

[147] J. Oloka-Onyango and Sylvia Tamale, ' "The Personal is Political", or Why Women's Rights are Indeed Human Rights: An African Perspective on International Feminism', 17 (1995) *Human Rights Quarterly*, pp. 691–731 at p. 698. For one of the early critiques of feminism along these lines see Valerie Amos and Pratibha Kumar, 'Challenging Imperial Feminism', 17 (1984) *Feminist Review*, pp. 3–19.

[148] See ibid., pp. 697 and 703. It may be worth noting here that Onyango and Tamale were advocating 'a united front' based on the universality of women's concerns.

[149] Chinkin, 'Gendered Perspective', p. 284. Elsewhere Chinkin writes that 'Western feminism too often … assumes an essentialist female identity and agenda that ignores factors of race, class, history, economic well-being, religion, nationality, ethnic origin, and culture which all identify and construct a person as well as gender'. See Christine Chinkin, 'Gender Inequality and International Human Rights Law' in Andrew Hurrell and Ngaire

the political connections between what occurs at home and international structures; the same forces that operate to maintain marginalization and oppression of women at home operate internationally in actions by stronger States against weaker States'.[150] Later, Charlesworth joined Chinkin in noting that 'third world feminist have argued that feminism must have a broader agenda than the eradication of oppression based on sex and gender. It must pay attention to the complex interaction of gender, race, class, colonialism and global capitalism'.[151] But the sentiments did not contribute to reconstituting their method or moving them beyond liberal feminism. As Engle has observed,

> this compromise fails to attend to the most radical potential of third world feminist critiques, which is their refusal to separate the cultural from the economic. Taken seriously, such critiques require attention to the gendered and cultural dimensions of the global distribution of wealth and to the economic dimensions of politics and policies about gender and culture.[152]

However, in her view, such an integrated approach is not possible because 'culturally sensitive universalism' is as far as liberal feminism can go.[153]

Woods (eds.) *Inequality, Globalization, and World Politics* (Oxford: Oxford University Press, 1999), pp. 95–121 at p. 116. In this context reference may be made to Otto who compares TWAIL and Feminism and notes that they have 'much in common': 'Both are bodies of theory about power, and how it works systematically to privilege the interests of some groups over the majority of disadvantaged "others". Both bodies of work are aiming to better understand how hierarchical systems of power reproduce themselves, and thus to find ways to contest and transform them. In the field of international law, both feminists and TWAILers are deeply committed to understanding more about how law serves elite interests, in the hope that we will come to a more effective understanding of laws' emancipatory potential and how we might assists its realization. These commonalities enable feminists and TWAILers to work together when our theories and goals converge'. Dianne Otto, 'The Gastronomics of TWAIL's Feminist Flavorings: Some Lunch-Time Offerings', 9 (2007) *International Community Law Review*, pp. 345–352 at pp. 347–348. But she feels that 'there are also many limits to what is shared'. She gives the example of 'sexual autonomy and freedom of expression' which 'is often considered out of step with a Third World Perspective'. See ibid., pp. 348, 349. According to her, 'the heterosexual presumption tends to become a site of division rather than a source of strength'. See ibid., p. 350. At some point feminism may have to take a break from TWAIL and vice versa depending on the prioritization of the agenda for change.

[150] Chinkin, 'Gendered Perspective', p. 284. Chinkin notes that 'the newly independent State has too often replicated the patriarchal power structures of the colonizing State with women again consigned to the private, non public domain, possibly even losing the societal positions they may have held in pre-colonial times'. See ibid., p. 285.

[151] Charlesworth and Chinkin, *Boundaries of international law*, pp. 47–48.

[152] Engle, 'International Human Rights', p. 50.

[153] See ibid.

It explains why when Charlesworth turned to the idea of 'feminist internationalism', that is, 'the elaboration of transnational principles and standards to advance the position of women', it still did not travel beyond 'culturally sensitive universalism'.[154] To be sure, she does refer to Martha Nussbaum's capability approach which 'transcends the traditional division of civil and political rights on the one hand and economic and social rights on the other'.[155] But her focus on civil and political rights does not change. Of course, she is not entirely wrong in cautioning with Nussbaum that 'in the name of antiessentialism, some scholars, otherwise committed to the advancement of women, have espoused reactionary, oppressive, and sexist positions'.[156] In this context, she also rightly mentions the resistance from states to international norms with respect to women. These norms are viewed as 'illegitimate because they may challenge national culture, traditions, policies, and laws'.[157] Indeed, it is at least one reason that 'the norm of nondiscrimination on the basis of sex has in practice a much reduced status in international law ... Claims of culture and religion readily trump women's rights'.[158] It is, therefore, not surprising that CEDAW 'is subject to an extraordinary number of formal reservations ... in the name of preserving a state's religious or cultural traditions'.[159] In contrast 'few reservations have been made to the substance of the obligation of nondiscrimination on the basis of race'.[160]

But even as Charlesworth advances her critique of certain forms of antiessentialism she admits that 'the search for "universal" women's predicaments can obscure differences among women and homogenize women's experiences'.[161] But her plea for what is termed strategic essentialism leads to the very result and worse.[162] It helps create space for the depiction of a 'subordinate victim'. Ratna Kapur for instance accuses radical and liberal

[154] Hilary Charlesworth, 'Martha Nussbaum's Feminist Internationalism', 111 (2000) *Ethics*, pp. 64–78 at p. 64.
[155] See ibid., p. 74.
[156] See ibid., p. 74.
[157] See ibid., p. 64.
[158] See ibid., p. 66.
[159] See ibid., pp. 67–68.
[160] See ibid., p. 68.
[161] See ibid., p. 73.
[162] The term "strategic essentialism" is used in the common sense parlance than in the way Gayatri Chakravarti Spivak has used. For this see Joanne Conaghan, 'Reassessing the Feminist Theoretical Project in Law' in Costas Douzinas and Colin Perrin (eds.) *Critical Legal Theory: Critical Concepts in Law* vol. III (London: Routledge, 2012), pp. 108–142 at p. 117.

feminism of representing the third world woman as the 'authentic victim subject'[163] through inter alia 'its focus on violence against women (VAW)'.[164] Kapur's contention is that 'the focus on the victim subject in the VAW campaign reinforces gender and cultural essentialism in the international women's human rights arena'.[165] She, therefore, decries 'the fiction of a universal sisterhood, bonded in its experience of victimization and violence' as 'there is no space in this construction for difference or for the articulation of a subject that is empowered'.[166] She is concerned that the stereotyped images of 'women as weak, vulnerable, and helpless' feed 'into conservative, right-wing agendas for women, which are protectionist rather than liberating'.[167] In Kapur's view the challenge of feminists has been 'to express their politics without subjugating other subjectivities through claims to the idea of a "true self" or a singular truth about all women'.[168] Instead, there is a need to bring to the feminist project 'the possibility of imagining a more transformative and inclusive politics'.[169]

The 'culturally sensitive universalism' position of Charlesworth may also be contrasted with that of Mohanty who proposes that 'cross-cultural feminist work must be attentive to the micropolitics of context, subjectivity, and struggle, as well as to the macropolitics of global economic

[163] 'The victim subject is a transnational phenomenon. It occurs, at least within legal discourse, in both the "West" and the Third World. However, the Third World victim subject has come to represent the more victimized subject; that is, the real or authentic victim subject. Feminist politics in the international human rights arena, as well as in parts of the Third World, have promoted this image of the authentic victim subject while advocating for women's human rights'. Ratna Kapur, 'The Tragedy of Victimization Rhetoric: Resurrecting the "Native" Subject in International/Post-Colonial Feminist Legal Politics', 15 (2002) *Harvard Human Rights Journal*, pp. 1–37 at p. 2.

[164] See ibid.

[165] See ibid. 'The significant impetus provided by the NGOs has come from largely Western organizations. In contrast, the majority of topics under consideration has focused on slavery-like practices in the Third World.' Kathryn Zoglin, 'United Nations Action against Slavery: A Critical Evaluation', 8 (1986) *Human Rights Quarterly*, pp. 306–339 at p. 315.

[166] Kapur, 'Tragedy of Victimization', p. 36.

[167] See ibid., p. 36.

[168] See ibid., p. 37.

[169] See ibid. In a similar vein Engle writes: 'In the decade preceding September 11, Third World feminists, including many in the United States, had been engaged in a critique, both of international law and of Western feminist critiques of international law, largely challenging First World feminist understanding and use of culture to call for changes in women's lives in the third world. For these critics, First World feminists often essentialized culture and defined Third World women by that essentialized culture. In doing so, First World feminists were seen to deny Third World women's agency within or in opposition to their "culture."', Engle, 'Liberal Internationalism', p. 433.

and political systems and processes'.[170] For this she invokes 'the use of historical materialism as a basic framework and a definition of material reality in both its local and micro-, as well as global, systemic dimensions'.[171] Mohanty sees 'the politics and economics of capitalism as a far more urgent locus of struggle today' for 'global economic and political processes have become more brutal, exacerbating economic, racial, and gender inequalities, and thus they need to be demystified, reexamined, and theorized'.[172] In this respect, she laments that the antiglobalization movement 'has not been a major organizing locus for women's movements nationally in the West/North'.[173] As against this absence it has 'always been a locus of struggle for women of the Third World/South because of their location' and that 'this contextual specificity should constitute the larger vision'.[174] She recalls that 'women of the Two-Thirds World have always organized against the devastations of globalized capital, just as they have always historically organized anticolonial and antiracist movements. In this sense they have always spoken for humanity as a whole'.[175] In other words, what is deeply problematic about radical, liberal and postmodern feminisms, that of MacKinnon, Charlesworth or Chinkin, and Halley, respectively, is that these do not speak about the structures of global capitalism and imperialism that is at the basis of exploitation and oppression of third world women or their struggles against them.[176] In contrast, African women activists for instance have long 'understood that their liberation as women was as connected to issues of imperialism and racism as to sexism. In fact, these oppressions *could not be* disaggregated'.[177] Therefore, both in the period of colonialism and today there is 'a reluctance to embrace a solely feminist identity, even in the process of waging struggle against

---

[170]   Mohanty, ' "Under Western Eyes" Revisited', p. 501.

[171]   See ibid; emphasis added.

[172]   See ibid., p. 509.

[173]   See ibid., p. 516; emphasis added.

[174]   See ibid.

[175]   See ibid.

[176]   Jacquette has observed that 'contemporary western feminist theory is offering little concrete support and failing to address the most critical issues for women of the Global South, including the need for a renewed commitment to redistributional politics and a recognition of the need to reform, as well as transform, politics'. Jane S. Jacquette, 'Feminism and the Challenges of the "Post-Cold War" World', 5 (2003) *International Feminist Journal of Politics*, pp. 331–354 at p. 332.

[177]   Cheryl Johnson-Odim, "For their freedoms": The anti-imperialist and international feminist activity of Funmilayo Ransome-Kuti of Nigeria', 32 (2009) *Women's Studies International Forum*, pp. 51–59 at p. 52; emphasis in original.

indigenous patriarchy, and certainly not when waging struggle against international patriarchy and oppression'.[178] The point Mohanty and others are making is that it is not sufficient to recognize difference and address cultural issues but also to acknowledge the global mechanics of exploitation and oppression of third world women if 'feminist internationalism' is to mean anything.[179] This view is also endorsed by others such as Vrushali Patil who reject feminist methodological nationalism because 'the potential and actual interrelationships of historically and geographically specific patriarchies to [...] transterritorial and transnational processes' such as European imperialism and colonialism and neoliberal globalization is neglected.[180] Patil speaks of transnational intersectionality as opposed to domestic intersectionality and thus rejects the 'ongoing Eurocentricity in intersectional productions of knowledge'.[181]

However, in order to address fractures within postcolonial societies, third world feminism is not averse to use of domestic intersectionality. For instance, postcolonial feminists in India have rightly been called upon to address the lament of Dalit feminists that upper caste and upper class feminisms have neglected their concerns and produced a 'dalit women free feminism'.[182] But, as Sharmila Rege has written in response, the Dalit feminist view 'cannot flourish if isolated from the experiences and ideas of other [marginalized] groups'.[183] The same advice of an integrationist approach may go to Western feminist scholars. In short, Mohanty, Patil

---

[178] See ibid.

[179] Mohanty further observes: 'I wish to better see the processes of corporate globalization and how and why they recolonize women's bodies and labor. We need to know the real and concrete effects of global restructuring on raced, classed, national, sexual bodies of women in the academy, in workplaces, streets, households, cyberspaces, neighborhoods, prisons, and social movements'. Mohanty, ' "Under Western Eyes" Revisited', p. 516.

[180] Vrushali Patil, 'From Patriarchy to Intersectionality: A Transnational Feminist Assessment of How Far We've Really Come', 38 (2013) *Signs*, pp. 847–867 at p. 848.

[181] See ibid., p. 853. Incidentally, Patil is not sparing of anti-colonial spokesmen of the Global South as well. She notes 'the largely male anticolonialist speakers in the General Assembly [who] advanced the argument for decolonization in another way – on the gendered terrain of nature, violation, and masculinity'. According to Patil, 'these anticolonial men attempted to reclaim that subjectivity by reclaiming adulthood and masculinity'. See ibid., pp. 859–860.

[182] Indira Jalli, 'Dalit Feminism and Indian Academics', (2003) *Indian Association for Women Studies Newsletter*, p. 31; Sharmila Rege, *Writing Caste, Writing Gender: Reading Dalit Women's Testimonies* (New Delhi: Zubaan, 2006).

[183] Sharmila Rege 'Dalit Women Talk Differently: A Critique of "Difference" and towards a Dalit Feminist Standpoint Position', 33 (1998) *Economic and Political Weekly, Women Studies*, pp. 39–46 at p. 45.

and Rege are pleading for an integrative feminism and a strategy of inclusive resistance and politics that begins with 'difference' but proceeds to embrace the struggles of all exploited and oppressed groups.

D.   Liberal (Eclectic) Feminism of Charlesworth and Chinkin

It is time to consider liberal feminism, especially as found in the work of Charlesworth and Chinkin, who seek to combine it with insights from other feminist perspectives. According to Charlesworth and Chinkin, liberal feminists are those who cast their arguments 'in terms of individual rights' and 'their primary goal is to achieve equality of treatment between women and men in public areas such as political participation and representation, and equal access to and equality within paid employment, market services and education'.[184] Along the same lines Janet Haley describes liberal feminism as 'a view that women and men are, for all legitimate purposes, the same; equality is its central social and legal goal'.[185] According to her the difficult part for liberal feminists is 'deciding what constitutes a legitimate purpose'.[186] As she goes on to note, 'in recurrent ambivalence on this question, liberal feminism has veered from equal treatment to special treatment; from formal equality to substantive equality; from empty theories of gender to particularized ones'.[187] These ambivalences are reflected in the work of Charlesworth and Chinkin and are the impulse for their adopting the 'eclectic method'. They claim that they do not embrace any particular feminist approach to examine the international legal system.[188] In their view, since 'no single theory is adequate in the context of international law',[189] it is best to approach it 'with a variety of feminist perspectives and techniques to indicate the gendered and sexed nature of its structures, processes and substance'.[190] These include liberal feminism, cultural feminism, radical feminism, postmodern feminism and third world feminisms.[191] It leads Charlesworth and Chinkin to adopt 'the method described by Margaret Radin as "situated judgment" – using a variety of analytic strategies rather than a single

---

[184] Charlesworth and Chinkin, *Boundaries of international law*, pp. 38–39.
[185] Halley, *Split Decisions*, p. 79.
[186] See ibid.
[187] See ibid.
[188] Charlesworth and Chinkin, *Boundaries of international law*, p. 18.
[189] See ibid., p. 23.
[190] See ibid., p. 18.
[191] See ibid., pp. 38–48.

feminist theory'.[192] However, as they themselves recognize, the 'eclectic method may also attract charges of theoretical incoherence'.[193] While the burden is certainly on them to show how the different approaches can be sensibly combined, the anticipated criticism is off the mark. The influence of the feminist standpoints other than radical feminism is largely peripheral to the liberal perspective they adopt, as is clear from the critique advanced by third world feminism of their work.

The impact of radical feminism on the other hand becomes evident when despite the critique of MacKinnon at the level of practical gains, Charlesworth and Chinkin observe while discussing the problem of 'essentialism' that 'feminist analyses rest on the commitment to challenge male dominance of women'.[194] It also informs their conclusion that 'the international legal system fails all groups of women'.[195] The question is how relevant is the radical feminist standpoint from the perspective of advancing the woman cause. It may be readily admitted that some form of 'woman-centredness' is necessary to take the feminist project forward. But, as Tanesini observes, '.to recognize that gender, race, class, or sexual orientation are not neatly separable does not entail that nothing can be said about gender without mentioning all the other aspects. It means, however, that this is possible only in limited and carefully chosen contexts'.[196] As Conaghan also notes, the real issue is not the category 'woman' but 'to the uses to which it is put'.[197] She goes on to point out that:

> Anti-essentialism is, in no sense, a prescription for abandoning a concern
> with women's disadvantage; it does, however, direct us to an understanding

[192] See ibid., p. 50. Charlesworth and Chinkin explain: 'In some contexts, we rely on "liberal" feminist techniques to point out that modern international law has failed to deliver on its promises of neutrality and equality and to challenge its illusory universality. Women have been almost completely excluded from international law-making arenas and it is important to document this and then to argue for the need for proper representation and participation of women. Simply "adding women and mixing" is by itself inadequate because *the legal system is itself gendered*. Its rules have developed as a response to the experiences of a male elite. Feminist analysis must thus explore the unspoken commitments of apparently neutral principles of international law and *the ways that male perspectives are institutionalized in it*. This involves some of the techniques and concepts suggested by "cultural", "radical", "post-modern" and "third world" feminisms. *All these approaches are useful in examining the sex and gender of the building blocks of the international legal order...*'. See ibid., p. 50; emphasis added.

[193] See ibid.

[194] See ibid., pp. 22 and 49.

[195] See ibid., p. 2.

[196] Alessandra Tanesini, *An Introduction to Feminist Epistemologies* (Oxford: Blackwell, 1999), p. 146.

[197] Conaghan, 'Reassessing', p. 119.

of disadvantage as multiple, intersecting, and complex and requires us to consider the implications of such an understanding for feminist theory and strategy.[198]

At the same time, Conaghan rightly cautions against both overstating the case of anti-essentialism as that is to 'engage in a form of essentialism'.[199] The short point is that Charlesworth and Chinkin have not seriously considered occupying a nuanced but structured middle ground in order to move beyond the essentialism/anti-essentialism binary. Thus, for instance, while they do take cognizance of cultural and economic differences that characterize the lives of women in different geographical spaces, Charlesworth and Chinkin do not criticize the liberal international economic order that is central to the reproduction of economic differences between women in the Global North and the Global South.[200] They also do not consider undertaking a transnational intersectional analysis that would help go beyond a debilitating essentialism even as the woman question is given its due. In the circumstances, the Charlesworth-Chinkin contention that an 'eclectic approach' is being followed is difficult to sustain other than in the ordinary sense of some reference to other approaches in their work. The reality is that radical and liberal feminisms are fellow travellers at the international level. Halley explains the reasons for 'why, given the vast differences between them, has liberal feminism been so willing to go to bed with dominance feminism?'[201] In her view, this is because

> Though they may disagree about whether to promote minimalist or maximalist definitions of coercion, and about whether to use criminal law or "softer" legal tools to address the problems of domination, liberal and dominance feminisms have fallen in together on making [...] accommodation to liberal legalism.[202]

Therefore, despite the objection to MacKinnon's muscular prescriptions at the policy level, the influence of radical feminism is evident in the work of Charlesworth and Chinkin.

The problems and limits of combining radical and liberal feminism may be further considered by reflecting on the 'recurring female subjectivities'

---

[198] See ibid., p. 120.

[199] See ibid.

[200] There are occasional references in their writings that suggest the beginnings of a critique but this is not elaborated. See, for instance, Chinkin, 'Gender Inequality', pp. 97, 119, 121.

[201] Janet Halley, *Governance Feminism: An Introduction* (October 2014) p. 25 (On file with the author).

[202] See ibid.

in international legal instruments. As Otto has noted, 'the privileged subject always bears the masculine characteristics of the gendered duality. In fact his dominance *depends* on his dissimilarity with the discourse's feminine "others"'.[203] It compels her to raise the critical question as to 'whether a focus on women's specificities, in the framework of universality, will ever achieve women's full inclusion in universal representations of humanity, because it is those very specificities against which the privileged figure of the masculine universal is defined'.[204] The problem is that on the one hand, 'to ignore women's specificities ... is to misrepresent the reality of women's gendered disadvantage'.[205] But on the other hand 'the cost of women's "inclusion" may be their continuous marginalization; that the project of disrupting gender hierarchies through human rights may be impossible'.[206] Her pessimism exposes the limits of a liberal feminist approach embedded in radical feminism and draws attention to the need to move beyond 'women's specificities'. To do so does not mean to give up the separate struggle for equality between sexes. It only means looking for deeper roots of women's oppression, often also the cause of oppression of other marginal groups in society.

Of course Charlesworth and Chinkin believe that the benefits that would arise from addressing the women's issue 'would not be limited to women'.[207] They do express the hope that while they offer an explicitly feminist account of international law, 'its methods will be of value to other groups outside the boundaries of international law'.[208] The underlying belief is that the liberal feminist approach has the most potential to address the concerns of all marginalized and oppressed groups. Among 'other groups' they mention 'indigenous peoples, disabled persons, ethnic minorities and other non-state groupings'.[209] But the radical feminist underpinning of their approach limits the possibilities of dealing with the concerns of other groups. Charlesworth and Chinkin make the mistake of thinking that not speaking directly to the concerns of women is not to be concerned with their fate at all. They are surely right in contending that none of the other methods of international law display 'sustained concern

---

[203] Dianne Otto, 'Lost in Translation: Re-scripting the Sexed Subjects of International Human Rights Law' in Anne Orford (ed.) *International Law and Its Others* (Cambridge: Cambridge University Press, 2006), pp. 318–356 at pp. 320–321.

[204] See ibid., p. 351.

[205] See ibid.

[206] See ibid.

[207] Charlesworth and Chinkin, *Boundaries of international law*, p. 61; emphasis added.

[208] See ibid., p. 19.

[209] See ibid.

with gender or, indeed, with the position of women as an international law issue'.[210] But it is one thing to argue that the problems of women are not *separately* addressed and another that it is *not* addressed at all? Is not a critique of imperialism advanced by TWAIL and MAIL addressing issues of concern to women? Are women not the principal victims of imperialism? Whether it is the invasion and occupation of societies by imperialist states or the pursuit of neo-liberal policies at the behest of international economic institutions the principal victims are women. It may therefore be legitimately asked if the absence of the critique of global capitalism and imperialism, or their manifestation in the world of international law and institutions, is not complicity with male-centric MILS. Indeed, it could be argued that a feminist analysis that does not critique imperialism is less feminist than an approach that does so. For the modern institution of patriarchy is integrally related to structures of capitalism and imperialism. The argument is not about the absence of need for separately addressing the women's question. That is what feminism is about. The issue is how the Otto concerns can be overcome.

What is at stake in not taking intersectional analysis seriously or adopting an integrationist approach is nothing less than the fate of feminist legal scholarship. Its status is telling in this regard. While its aim has been both 'freeing women as well as legal scholarship' it has yet to be fully accepted in the legal academy. As MacKinnon observes, 'feminist analysis is not yet considered an expertise; it remains regarded as autobiographical and ideological ... unbecoming and unscholarly' to pursue 'as the backbone or compass of an intellectual agenda'.[211] Therefore, 'tokenism is the practical organizing principle of this ghettoizing reduction. One is a feminist legal scholar, not a legal scholar with particular information and focus and perspectives to offer'.[212] But instead of reflecting on the reasons for this state of affairs, especially in the context of the constraints radical feminism imposes, MacKinnon simply sees it as 'another way of maintaining male dominance'.[213] It has already been seen

[210] Hilary Charlesworth, 'Feminist Methods in International Law' in Steven R. Ratner and Anne-Marie Slaughter (eds.) *The Methods of International Law* (Washington, DC: The American Society of International Law, 2004), pp. 159–185 at p. 180.
[211] MacKinnon, 'Foreword', p. xii.
[212] See ibid. These understandings may not sit well with her own view of the success that feminism has had in the field of international law. However, her argument perhaps is that despite the successes feminism does not have the presence in the legal academia that it should have had.
[213] See ibid. Mohanty also notes how her work is (mis)appropriated 'through a citational politics (use of Mohanty as "a totemic symbol"), a rhetorical gesture disconnected from the

that the MacKinnon move to intersectional analysis is undertaken without reframing radical feminism.

It comes as no surprise that the state of feminist scholarship in the third world is no different. In the case of India it has been observed that 'the feminist scholar is left largely in dialogue with other feminists'.[214] For instance, speaking of feminist historiography Janaki Nair mentions that a typical response is 'a politically correct gesturing towards the formidable body of feminist scholarship without engaging with it in any way'.[215] It has been pointed out for instance that 'it is a striking feature of the first six volumes of Subaltern Studies that, with the exception of a solitary piece by Tanika Sarkar, the work of no women practitioners of Indian history was on display'.[216] Nair rightly wonders 'why there has been a very public engagement with Subaltern studies, which in turn has generated a cottage industry of its own, while the equally large, empirically rich, and infinitely more representative Indian feminist work, produced over a longer period of time, has not sustained similar engagement'.[217]

It is therefore worth asking if the neglect can be traced to the influence of radical feminism on all feminisms. To put it differently, the question is whether there can be a feminist approach that is not focused on women alone.[218] Or to reiterate a point made earlier, 'is gender the appropriate category of analysis in all instances where women are present?'[219] According to Vasuki Nesiah:

> if feminism was going to be about a politically relevant and engaged analytics, it may not always begin with gender as the starting point of analysis; critical feminist analysis will be precisely that which can eschew such pieties in understanding and challenge the enabling conditions and distributive implications of international law in ways that are intellectually versatile and politically relevant.[220]

---

systematic and materialist analysis of power'. Chandra Talpade Mohanty, 'Transnational Feminist Crossings: On Neoliberalism and Radical Critique', 38 (2013) *Signs*, no. 4, pp. 967–991 at p. 981.

[214] Janaki Nair, 'Indian Historiography and its "Resolution" of Feminists' Questions' in Anjan Ghosh, Tapati Guha-Thakurtha and Janaki Nair (eds.) *Theorizing the Present: Essays for Partha Chatterjee* (New Delhi: Oxford University Press, 2011), pp. 35–65 at p. 41.

[215] See ibid., p. 44.

[216] Vinay Lal, *The History of History* (New Delhi: Oxford University Press, 2003), p. 189.

[217] Nair, 'Indian Historiography', p. 45.

[218] See ibid., p. 47.

[219] See ibid.

[220] Vasuki Nesiah, 'Priorities of Feminist Legal Research: A sketch, a draft agenda, a hint of an outline...', 1 (2011) feminists@law, p. 3. She explains why the structural explanation

This point is significant as it recognizes the need for analysing social relations beyond gender relations. In terms of international law it calls for analysis of particular regimes (trade, environment or sea) that equally focuses on their outcomes for other categories of exploited and oppressed groups.[221] But, despite attempts by radical and liberal strands of feminist scholarship to travel beyond the fate of women, they remain the addressees, and not humankind. This fact often keeps others away from serious engagement with their work. The critics, especially left critics, believe that the emancipation of women cannot come about without general social transformation that also promises emancipation of other exploited and oppressed groups. Therefore, feminist scholarship must build appropriate theoretical and methodological tools that help address the emancipation of humankind in general. In fact intersectional studies have 'exposed how single-axis thinking undermines legal thinking, disciplinary knowledge production, and struggles for social justice'.[222] In the instance of Charlesworth and Chinkin this point can be clarified by comparing their work with MILS. If you are a liberal international lawyer MILS is more attractive than MFILS. For in contrast to MFILS, MILS believes that it can through the liberal international order not only address the concerns of women but also that of other groups. In contrast MFILS appears a partial and segmented approach to international law.

It may be argued that in an important sense all critical approaches are structured around particular categories, e.g., the Marxist approach around the category class. Even if this is conceded, the liberal feminist approach is seen as more limiting than the others. To take the Marxist approach, while the use of a singular category 'class' is true, the consequences are less serious because it is an inclusive category, albeit in practice its use often tends

and understanding was where beginnings had to be made: 'Two decades back feminist scholarship addressing international law still occupied outsider status in many arenas. Early interventions in the field outlined the priorities of feminist research in international law as the mainstreaming and consolidation of feminist insights in other terrains into international legal analysis, inclusion of feminist perspectives within mainstream legal practice, and the expansion of feminist analysis of public/private onto the international law stage.' See ibid., p. 1.

221 'For instance, if we are looking at the distributive dynamics of international trade, we cannot begin with an a priori assumption that gender is the starting point to challenging the legal architecture of the international trade regime.' See ibid.

222 Sumi Cho, Kimberlé Williams Crenshaw and Leslie McCall, 'Toward a Field of Intersectionality Studies: Theory, Applications, and Praxis', 38 (2013) *Signs*, pp. 785–810 at p. 787. 'Intersectionality was introduced in the late 1980s as a heuristic term to focus attention on the vexed dynamics of difference and the solidarities of sameness in the context of antidiscrimination and social movement politics'. See ibid.

to exclude the concerns of women. But as Amartya Sen explains, 'no other source of inequality is fully independent of class' and therefore 'the basic issue is complementarity and interrelation rather than the independent functioning of different disparities that work in seclusion (like ships passing at night)'.[223] In other words, class is critical to understanding inequalities based on race, gender and caste discrimination. But it does not either subsume them or exhaust their analytical and political potential.[224] To sum up, all that is being said is that it is not patriarchy per se but capitalist patriarchy at work in shaping international law. As Mohanty writes, 'capital as it functions now depends on and exacerbates racist, patriarchal, and heterosexist relations of rule'.[225] For the rest, intersectional analysis does not signify a closed system. According to Cho et al., 'since the beginning' intersectional studies have been 'posed more as a nodal point than as a closed system – a gathering place for open-ended investigations of the overlapping and conflicting dynamics of race, gender, class, sexuality, nation, and other inequalities'.[226] It is 'best framed as an analytic sensibility': 'what makes an analysis intersectional – whatever term it deploys, whatever its iteration, whatever its field or discipline – is its adoption of *an intersectional way of thinking about the problem of sameness and difference and its relation to power*'.[227] In the final analysis intersectional studies is about all forms of 'political and structural inequalities'.[228]

The benefit of analytic sensibility of intersectional analysis can also be illustrated through the concept of 'hegemonic masculinity' that helps to come to grips with the fact that men are not a homogeneous group but with 'different identities and power positions' and therefore with different relationship to women with 'different identities and power positions';[229]

---

[223] Amartya Sen, *The Argumentative Indian* (London: Penguin Books, 2005), pp. 207, 208; see also Rosemary Hennessy and Chrysn Ingraham (eds.) *Materialist Feminism: A Reader in Class, Difference, and Women's Lives* (Routledge: London, 1997), pp. 2–3.

[224] The precedence of class does not necessarily make women only a 'secondary contradiction' or 'a niche question' as even Mies suggests. Maria Mies, *Patriarchy and Accumulation on a World Scale: Women in the International Division of Labour* (London: Zed Books, 1998), pp. viii and xii. What is called for is contextual analysis to reveal social and economic situations in which one or the other fracture is dominant.

[225] Mohanty, '"Under Western Eyes" Revisited', p. 510; emphasis added.

[226] Cho, Crenshaw and McCall, 'Toward a Field', p. 788.

[227] See ibid., p. 795; emphasis added.

[228] See ibid., p. 797. See also Leslie McCall, 'The Complexity of Intersectionality', 30 (2005) *Signs: Journal of Women in Culture and Society*, pp. 1772–1799.

[229] Gillian Youngs, 'Feminist International Relations: A Contradiction in Terms? Or; Why Women and Gender Are Essential to the World We Live In', 80 (2004) *International Affairs*, pp. 75–87 at p. 85.

'masculinity is not more monolithic than femininity'.[230] The absence of homogeneity can be addressed through intersectional analysis as the categories class and race get factored in. The analysis can also be done at the global level by rejecting methodological nationalism and adopting a transnational intersectional analysis. This is where MFILS in particular falls short. Even when Charlesworth and Chinkin accept the need to move beyond gender, intersectional analysis is not taken seriously and also confined to the nation state. A systematic transnational intersectional analysis is more productively undertaken by socialist feminism as it appreciates the intimate relations between patriarchy, capitalism, and imperialism.

E.   Towards Socialist Feminism

There exists considerable literature on socialist feminism.[231] However, the effort in what follows is merely to identify key features of the idea of socialist feminism and to show how it goes beyond radical and liberal

[230] See ibid., p. 86.
[231] There is considerable literature on the subject. It includes Sheila Rowbotham, Lynne Segal and Hilary Wainwright, *Beyond the Fragments: Feminism and the Making of Socialism* (Boston, MA: Alyson Publications, 1981); Holmstorm, *The socialist feminist project*; Nancy C. M. Hartsock, 'The Feminist Standpoint: Developing the Ground for a Specifically Feminist Historical Materialism' in Sandra Harding and Merrill B. Hintikka (eds.) *Discovering Reality: Feminist Perspectives on Epistemology, Metaphysics, Methodology, and Philosophy of Science* (Dordrecht: Kluwer Academic Publishers, 1983), pp. 283–310; Hennessy and Ingraham, *Materialist Feminism*; Linda Briskin, 'Socialist Feminism: From the Standpoint of Practice', 30 (1989) *Studies in Political Economy*, pp. 87–114; Colin Farrelly, 'Patriarchy and Historical Materialism', 26 (1) (2011)*Hypatia*, pp. 1–21. For a synopsis of Marx's views on gender see Donovan, *Feminist Theory*, pp. 63–72; Martha E. Gimenez, 'Capitalism and Oppression of Women: Marx Revisited', 69 (2005)*Science & Society*, pp. 11–32; Heather Brown, 'Marx on Gender and the Family', (June 2014)*Analytical Monthly Review* , pp. 45–53. It is worth noting that the 'socialist feminist' tradition has often grappled with a distinct set of questions: 'A central concern of contemporary socialist feminism has [...] been to determine the role of the household in capitalist society: The most extensive analysis has revolved around the question of domestic labour and its contribution to capitalism. A second area of discussion on the "woman question" concerns the direct relationship women may have with the modes of production as wage-earners. Third is the connection between women and class. Fourth, theory has developed around the question of the home or family's role in ideological socialization. A final direction in contemporary feminist theory that derives from Marxist categories is that which focuses on the idea of praxis and on questions about ideology and the nature of consciousness.' Donovan, *Feminist Theory*, p. 74. These questions, other than the relationship between gender and class, are also not being addressed here. These are detailed debates that do not have a direct bearing on the broad methodological point that is being made about the meaning and relevance of socialist feminism.

feminism.[232] But it is further argued that socialist feminism in turn needs to incorporate the insights of postcolonial theory to lend it greater relevance and depth.

The bare fundamentals of socialist feminism may at first be elaborated by reference to two essays published in the 'second wave' of feminism. The first article is that of Herbert Marcuse. It is admittedly an odd place to start an exposition of socialist feminism, but useful in the present instance because like the present author Marcuse advances his reflections on feminism looking in as if it were from the outside, that is, from a male and Marxist standpoint. However, his cogitations on the subject captured important dimensions of the idea of socialist feminism. Marcuse made the following observations. First, while 'women are not a class in the Marxian sense' there are 'good reasons' to use the general categories 'woman' and 'man' for patriarchal civilization has historically subjected women to specific forms of repression.[233] Second, despite biological differences between men and women 'the feminine characteristics are socially conditioned' or in current parlance socially constructed.[234] Third, while a separate women's movement is a necessity, its goals call for 'changes of such enormity in the material and intellectual culture, that they can be attained only by a change in the entire social system'.[235] The very logic of women's movement demands 'freedom for men and women',[236] as freedom for women is in a profound sense linked to the transformation of the world of men. Fourth, while social, cultural and economic equality may be achievable under capitalism it will not be a society in which 'the established dichotomy between masculine and feminine is overcome in the social and individual relationship between human beings'.[237] As Marcuse succinctly puts it 'equality is not yet freedom'.[238] Fifth, the constitutive relationship between

---

[232] It may be noted that 'the names for the knowledges that have emerged out of the intersection of Marxism and feminism' is 'sometimes designated as marxist feminism, socialist feminism, or materialist feminism. These signatures represent differences in emphasis and even in concepts, but all signal feminist critical engagement with historical materialism'. Rosemary Hennessy and Chrys Ingraham, 'Introduction: Reclaiming Anticaptialist Feminism' in Rosemary Hennessy and Chrysn Ingraham (eds.) *Materialist Feminism: A Reader in Class, Difference, and Women's Lives* (Routledge: London, 1997), pp. 1–14 at p. 4.

[233] Herbert Marcuse, 'Marxism and feminism', 2 (1974) *Women's Studies*, pp. 279–288 at p. 280.

[234] See ibid.

[235] See ibid., p. 281.

[236] See ibid., p. 285.

[237] See ibid., p. 281.

[238] See ibid., p. 285.

capitalism and patriarchy means that even in advanced capitalist societies
male domination is a reality. In contrast, 'socialism, as a qualitatively different society, must embody the antithesis, the definite negation of the
aggressive and repressive needs and values of capitalism as a form of male
dominated culture'.[239] Sixth, feminism can develop a distinct morality
that goes beyond bourgeois morality and can thereby approach issues of
sexuality in an open and democratic manner.[240] Marcuse concluded that
'feminism is a revolt against decaying capitalism, against the historical
obsolescence of the capitalist mode of production'.[241] He certainly recognized that 'actually existing socialism' did not achieve the goal of emancipation of women. In his view, it represented continuity with capitalism by
remaining focused on productive forces rather than on the realm of freedom by 'making life an end in itself'.[242] However, Marcuse did not raise
questions of 'sexual autonomy and freedom of expression' that are central
issues for many feminists.[243] This is where socialist feminism may wish to
take a break from Marxism.[244]

A year or two after Marcuse's intervention, Barbara Ehrenreich in a well-
known essay articulated in a more direct way the merits of adopting a socialist feminist approach to social relations and of course to the emancipation of
women.[245] She felt that it had great advantage over radical feminism. In her
view the problem with radical feminism was that:

> it doesn't go any farther. It remains transfixed with the universality of male
> supremacy – things have never really changed; all social systems are patri-
> archies; imperialism, militarism, and capitalism are simply expressions of
> innate male aggressiveness. And so on.[246]

---

[239] See ibid., p. 282.

[240] See ibid.

[241] See ibid., p. 288.

[242] See ibid., p. 286.

[243] See Otto, 'The Gastronomics', p. 349.

[244] But Amos and Parmar have explained the relatively less concern with 'sexuality' issues
in the potcolonial world in the following way: 'The struggle for independence and self
determination and against imperialism has meant that for Black and Third World women
... sexuality as an issue has often taken a secondary role and at times not been considered
at all'. Valerie Amos and Pratibha Parmar, 'Challenging Imperial Feminism', 17 (1984)
Feminist Review, pp. 3–19 at p. 12.

[245] Barbara Ehrenreich, 'What is Socialist Feminism?', (2005) *Monthly Review,* available at
http://monthlyreview.org/2005/07/01/what-is-socialist-feminism (accessed on 21 July
2013). (Originally published in WIN Magazine on 3 June 1976, p. 2.) Reproduced in
Hennessy and Ingraham, *Materialist Feminism,* pp. 65–70.

[246] See ibid., p. 4.

According to Ehrenreich, radical feminism neglected the fact that if we are 'to understand our experiences of women today, we must move to a consideration of capitalism as a system'.[247] For this it was helpful to turn to Marxism. She reminded readers that 'Marxism and feminism have an important thing in common: they are critical ways of looking at the world'.[248] While 'Marxism rips away myths about "democracy" and its "pluralism" to reveal a system of class rule that rests on forcible exploitation', 'feminism cuts through myths about "instinct" and romantic love to expose male rule as a rule of force'.[249] But Ehrenreich went on to note that to combine both in a coherent manner you need a 'socialist feminist kind of feminism and a socialist feminist kind of socialism'.[250] She therefore urged 'mechanical Marxists' to understand 'capitalism as a social and cultural totality'.[251] While in the final analysis the 'woman question' is not a separate issue but is 'at the very heart of their class',[252] there is a need for 'synthesis in our understanding of sex and class, capitalism and male domination'.[253]

Two decades later Maria Mies advanced her important understanding of socialist feminism in the book *Patriarchy and Accumulation on a World Scale*.[254] She argued even more forcefully against a socialist feminist approach that simply adds feminism to Marxism. Instead, she called for 'a new theory of society altogether'.[255] In her view, what was needed was 'a new historical and theoretical analysis of the interrelation between women's exploitation and oppression, and that of other categories of people and of nature'.[256] From this perspective she critiqued feminist theories in which 'the structural roots' of the woman question, that is 'its connection with capital accumulation remain invisible'.[257] She especially took Western feminists to task for not talking of capitalism.[258] While the women's question was not for her, as for some old socialists, a 'secondary contradiction' or belonging 'to the sphere of ideology, the superstructure or culture', she

[247] See ibid., p. 5.
[248] See ibid., p. 2.
[249] See ibid., p. 3.
[250] See ibid., p. 4.
[251] See ibid.
[252] See ibid., p. 6.
[253] See ibid., p. 7.
[254] Mies, *Patriarchy and Accumulation*, p. 12.
[255] See ibid.
[256] See ibid., p. 13.
[257] See ibid.
[258] See ibid., p. 22.

was also persuaded that 'the feminist movement cannot ignore the issues of class, or the exploitative international division of labor, and imperialism'.[259] The woman question must be understood 'in the context of all social relations that constitute our reality today, that means in the context of a global division of labor under the dictates of capital accumulation'.[260] She aptly observed that 'if we do not want to fall into the trap of moralism and individualism, it is necessary to look below the surface and to come to a materialist understanding of the *interplay* of the sexual, the social and international division of labor'.[261] Mies was also critical of the growth model of development and argued that 'as women have nothing to gain in their humanity from the continuation of the growth model, they are able to develop a perspective of a society which is not based on exploitation of nature, women and other peoples'.[262] She thus combined the theme of the exploitation and oppression of all subaltern groups and peoples with that of 'logic of capital' and the 'logic of nature' and thereby laid the basis for a comprehensive approach to the question of emancipation of women.

The socialist feminist approach has, in contrast to the view expressed by Halley, continued to find adherents. Nancy Holmstorm has recently noted that socialist feminism 'is alive and well today', albeit it is known by a variety of names including materialist feminism or feminist materialism.[263] Using 'socialist feminism' as a generic term Holmstorm defines a socialist feminist as 'anyone trying to understand women's subordination in a coherent and systematic way that integrates class and sex, as well as other aspects of identity such as race/ethnicity or sexual orientation, with the aim of using this analysis to help liberate women'.[264] She argues that 'feminist theory that is lost in theoretical abstractions or that depreciates economic realities will be useless for this purpose. Feminism that speaks of women's oppression and its injustice but fails to address capitalism will be of little help in ending women's oppression'.[265] In her view 'all socialist feminists see class as central to women's lives, yet at the same time none would reduce sex or race oppression to economic exploitation...class is always gendered and raced'.[266] On the other hand, 'the brutal economic

---

[259] See ibid., p. 1.
[260] See ibid., p. 2.
[261] See ibid., p. 11.
[262] See ibid.
[263] Holmstrom, 'Introduction', p. 1.
[264] See ibid.
[265] See ibid., p. 2.
[266] See ibid.

realities of globalization make it impossible to ignore class, and feminists are now asking on a global level the kinds of big questions they asked on a societal level in the 1970s'.[267]

In recent years the socialist feminist tradition is carried forward in the important work of Nancy Fraser. She has sought to help revitalize socialist-feminism theorizing through attempting to 'integrate the best of recent feminist theorizing with the best of recent critical theorizing about capitalism'.[268] Fraser attempts to bring together 'three analytically distinct dimensions of gender injustice: economic, cultural and political'.[269] She also endorses the ' "intersectionist" alternative that is in her view widely accepted today'.[270] According to her, despite differences 'most second-wave feminists – with the notable exception of liberal-feminists – concurred that overcoming women's subordination required radical transformation of the deep structures of the social totality'.[271] To second wave feminists 'feminism appeared as part of a broader emancipatory project, in which struggles against gender injustices were necessarily linked to struggles against racism, imperialism, homophobia and class domination, all of which required transformation of the deep structures of capitalist society'.[272]

But 'that project remained stillborn' with the rise of neo-liberalism. It saw second wave feminism 'overextend the critique of culture, while downplaying the critique of political economy'.[273] According to Fraser, 'what had begun as a needed corrective to economism devolved in time into an equally one-sided culturalism' that suited the neoliberal project.[274] Feminism became simply identity politics.[275] In other words, second-wave feminism had inadvertently provided a new ingredient to 'the new spirit of neoliberalism'.[276] She concludes that 'we should reconnect feminist critique to the critique of capitalism – and thereby re-position feminism squarely on the left'.[277] The Fraser point is supported by the fact that

---

[267] See ibid., p. 8.
[268] Fraser, 'Feminism, Capitalism', p. 98. She has, however, also been classified as a post-Marxist. See Hennessy and Ingraham, 'Introduction', pp. 5–6.
[269] See ibid., p. 99.
[270] See ibid., p. 103.
[271] See ibid., p. 104.
[272] See ibid., p. 107.
[273] See ibid., p. 108.
[274] See ibid.
[275] See ibid.
[276] See ibid., p. 110.
[277] See ibid., p. 116.

in the period of accelerated globalization or neo-liberalism, 'the living conditions of many women deteriorated' worldwide.[278] It has worsened still after the global financial and economic crisis. But as Brigitte Young writes, global financial sector policies 'have inscribed in them a series of biases that have gender as well as class- and race-based outcomes'.[279] Therefore, an integrationist approach is most appropriate for undertaking a critique of neo-liberalism. It leads Young to the view that 'increasing female representation in decision-making bodies is a necessary but not sufficient precondition to safeguard specific female interests'.[280] According to her, 'female representation only makes a difference if it comes with an alternative concept of financial order'.[281]

Among those who prefer to use the term 'materialism feminism' in place of 'socialist feminism' is Kotiswaran.[282] She believes that 'materialist feminism' is a better term because 'socialist feminism in its bid to reinvent itself is now no longer concerned only with gender and class, but also with race, ethnicity, and sexual orientation'.[283] Secondly, she does not wish to 'sharply delineate and fetishize the distinctions between the material and the social or cultural' for it 'fails to recognize the mutually constituted nature of these realms, besides the political histories they embody'.[284] It would appear from these ruminations that Kotiswaran is merely uncomfortable with the category 'socialist feminist' for most of her objections have for long been accepted interpretations of, or amendments to, the Marxist approach; only the most dogmatic Marxists would assert otherwise. In fact, her views

[278] Caglar, Prugl and Zwingel, 'Introducing Feminist Strategies', p. 9.
[279] Brigitte Young, 'Structural Power and the Gender Biases of Technocratic Network Governance in Finance' in Gulay Caglar, Elisabeth Prugl and Sussane Zwingel(eds.) *Feminist Strategies in International Governance* (London: Routledge, 2013), pp. 267–282 at p. 267. She goes on to observe that: 'the crisis has turned a spotlight on the low or even nonexistent female representation in top positions of financial institutions and the decision making bodies in key regulatory institutions, central banks, formal and informal financial networks. The same applies to today's efforts at global regulatory reform that excludes those who are affected most by the financial crisis: workers, minorities, women and representatives from the civil society, and less developed countries'. See ibid., p. 268.
[280] See ibid., p. 269.
[281] See ibid.
[282] However, to begin with she notes in the context of India that 'far from being an alien language, socialist feminism resonates well, both within the Indian feminist and sex worker communities'. Prabha Kotiswaran, *Dangerous Sex, Invisible Labor: Sex Work and the Law in India* (New Delhi: Oxford University Press, 2012), p. 50. The term 'materialist feminism' appeared on the scene only in the late 1970s.
[283] See ibid., p. 51.
[284] See ibid.

are well within the tradition of socialist feminism of which she rightly observes there are multiple renditions. Her version maybe called post-colonial materialist feminist theory that attaches significance to the cultural turn within it as it can be productively used to underscore and attend to the concerns of third world women.[285] In fact, in as much as postcolonial feminism brings to the fore the distinctive voices of third world women, its contribution greatly enriches the socialist feminist approach.

In sum, socialist feminism is very much alive today and remains the most persuasive of feminist theories as it simultaneously critiques economic, social and cultural dimensions of the exploitation and oppression of women in all geographic spaces. Its proponents stress the need to systematically evolve a socialist feminist theory that does not simply add feminism to Marxism or anticipate a merger. The essential point may be summarized with reference to an earlier debate on what was termed 'dual systems' theory. According to the dual systems theory, 'women's oppression arises from two distinct and relatively autonomous systems' viz., patriarchy and capitalism.[286] It was argued that 'patriarchy should be understood as a system of domination distinct from capitalism, with its own "laws of motion"'.[287] The theoretical problem that the 'dual systems' approach posed was whether socialist feminists could 'synthesize Marxian theory and radical feminist theory into a viable theory of social reality in general or and of women's oppression in particular'.[288] There was a need for synthesis because of the intrinsic weakness of 'dual systems' theory. On the one hand, 'it allows Marxism to retain in basically unchanged form its theory of economic and social relations, onto which it merely grafts a theory of gender relations'.[289] On the other hand, as Iris Marion Young pointed out, some versions of 'dual systems' theory see patriarchy as a system that has prevailed over time and appear to make the absurd suggestion 'that women as women stand outside history'.[290] The 'practical

---

[285] However, as has been observed of many 'materialist feminists', Kotiswaran tends to privilege cultural dimensions of the oppression of women over class analysis. Hennessy and Ingraham, 'Introduction', p. 9.

[286] Iris Marion Young, 'Socialist Feminism and the Limits of Dual Systems Theory' in Rosemary Hennessy and Chrysn Ingraham (eds.) *Materialist Feminism: A Reader in Class, Difference, and Women's Lives* (Routledge: London, 1997), pp. 95–106 at p. 95. There have been different versions of 'dual systems' theory that have been advanced that need not be gone into here. See ibid., pp. 97–98.

[287] See ibid., p. 100.

[288] See ibid., p. 96.

[289] See ibid., p. 98.

[290] See ibid., p. 99.

dangers' of this version of 'dual systems' approach is that 'it tends to create a false optimism regarding the possibility of a common consciousness
among women. This can lead to serious cultural, ethnic, racial, and class
biases in the account of the allegedly common structures of patriarchy'.[291]
Young rejected 'dual system' theory to argue that:

> We need not merely a synthesis of feminism with traditional Marxism, but
> also a thoroughly feminist historical materialism, which regards the social
> relations of a particular historical social formation as one system in which
> gender differentiation is a core attribute.[292]

A significant point that Young makes from the perspective of the
women's movement is that 'feminist consciousness should be so incorporated that one could justifiably understand oneself as engaging in feminist work on issues not immediately concerning women's situation'.[293] In
other words, what Young proposes is that 'a feminist historical materialism must be a total social theory, not merely a theory of situation and
oppression of women', albeit gender differentiation will always be its starting point.[294] The monist approach uses intersectional analyses to stress the
need for an integrationist framework accompanied by a strategy of social
transformation that links the emancipation of women with the emancipation of all exploited and oppressed groups. Such a framework does not
require one category of oppressed to be a priori privileged over the other,
but calls for a flexible contextual approach that responds to the problem
or situation to be addressed. In order to avoid a Eurocentric orientation,
monist socialist feminism also needs to integrate the insights of postcolonial theory. It must not disregard historical and cultural differences
across nations and treat the Western as the universal.[295] On the other
hand, the problem with postcolonial theory is that it is primarily confined
to the domain of culture neglecting material structures that underlie gender and other forms of oppression.[296] It is here that Marxism fills a crucial
gap by inter alia stressing the significance of universalizing capitalism in
shaping non-Western societies. It only remains to be reiterated that the
insights of socialist feminism, Marxism and postcolonial theory can be
integrated because these theories, or rather particular interpretations of

---

[291] See ibid.
[292] See ibid., p. 102; italics in original dropped.
[293] See ibid., p. 104.
[294] See ibid.
[295] See generally in this regard Chapter 1, pp. 22–30.
[296] Young, 'Socialist Feminism', p. 104.

them, are entirely compatible.[297] This is the assumption on which IMAIL proceeds. It is believed that it offers conceptual and theoretical tools that help explain and understand the contemporary nature and character of international law through linking it to the workings of global capitalism and its differential impact on groups and societies with varying histories and cultures. In what follows, the insights of a monist socialist feminism are deployed to appraise the views of Charlesworth and Chinkin on diverse aspects of international law.

IV. Liberal (Eclectic) Feminism and International Law

The burden of the argument in this section is that despite its far-reaching ambition what distinguishes the liberal feminist outlook of Charlesworth and Chinkin from MILS, even in its eclectic incarnation, is in the final analysis its focus on the 'woman question'. In fact, it is because the liberal feminist approach to international law is otherwise indistinguishable from the mainstream approach (i.e. other than by its focus on the need for equality of sexes) that it 'initially produced shock and even ire' among mainstream scholars.[298] Antony D'Amato even advised Charlesworth to learn rather than critique the language of international law in order to advance women's rights.[299] In fact, much before MacKinnon and Halley, he argued that international law is more receptive to women's rights then domestic law.[300] D'Amato is not alone in making this point. One researcher goes so far as to claim that 'international law is gendered neither conceptually nor procedurally, and that most of its substance exhibits no gender bias'.[301] In this view, 'while Charlesworth and her colleagues offer several interesting insights into the suffering and underrepresentation of women internationally, their criticism really applies to the overwhelming economic, political, and social gender inequality within states, not in the international legal system'.[302]

---

[297] For a more detailed analysis see Chapter 1, pp. 18–30.
[298] Alvarej, 'Book Review', p. 459. Most mainstream international law scholars tended to ignore feminist interventions. In an early assessment of the impact of feminist approaches, Chinkin lamented that fact that eminent scholars such as Thomas Franck neglected them in their work on fairness in international law. See Chinkin, 'Feminist Interventions', p. 22.
[299] D'Amato, 'Book Review', p. 843.
[300] See ibid., p. 844.
[301] Aaron Xavier Fellmeth, 'Feminism and International Law: Theory, Methodology, and Substantive Reform', 22 (2000) *Human Rights Quarterly*, pp. 658–733 at p. 661.
[302] See ibid., p. 662.

The view that the liberal feminist approach and MILS possess family resemblance does in a sense grave injustice to the former. The feminist critique of international law is foundational in as much as it problematizes the history, principles, concepts and categories of international law. It is not simply about realizing women's rights within the present frame of international law but of using gender lens to rethink and recast the structure and process of international law. But the reluctance of liberal feminism to critique deep structures that account for the exploitation and oppression of women and other subaltern groups pre-empts the ambition from being realized. The failure to address the problems associated with universalizing capitalism, or imperialism, both in its historical and present phase, makes the liberal feminist approach appear similar to MILS. In the final analysis it merely relies on the structural element of radical feminism to distinguish itself from MILS. But liberal feminism then finds itself in the odd position of assuming a more critical position than radical feminism. Thus, it was seen that Charlesworth takes MacKinnon to task for suggesting that substantial progress in the world of international law has been made on the woman question. The critique is, of course, driven by the apprehension that a sanguine assessment would lend credence to the thesis on 'governance feminism'. But the glass half full view is difficult to reconcile with the liberal stance of Charlesworth as most certainly some progress has been made in realizing women's rights. Yet in the light of her disagreement with MacKinnon Charlesworth is unwilling to revisit and rethink the limits of the structural and liberal standpoints. The eclectic elements of their approach are not used to transgress the boundaries of liberal feminism. It is submitted that a monist socialist feminism offers one way out of the conundrum. It can help differentiate FtAIL from MILS by locating the critique of international law in structures of global capitalism and the different ways in which it has historically impacted postcolonial societies. In order to sustain this contention it is best to begin at the beginning by noting the structural critique of international law by Charlesworth and Chinkin.

A.   The Structural Critique

On the very first page of their book *Boundaries of International Law: A feminist analysis* Charlesworth and Chinkin state their main thesis:

> Its central argument is that the absence of women in the development of international law has produced a narrow and inadequate jurisprudence

that has, among other things, legitimated the unequal position of women around the world rather than challenged it.[303]

They go on to note that:

> women are on the margins of the international legal system. Their participation in the development of international legal principles is minimal and the international legal order appears impervious to the realities of women's lives ... whenever women come into focus at all in international law, they are viewed in a very limited way.[304]

Charlesworth and Chinkin conclude:

> At a deeper level, the very nature of international law has made dealing with the structural disadvantages of sex and gender difficult. The realities of women's lives do not fit easily into the concepts and categories of international law...international law is constructed upon particular male assumptions and experiences of life where "man" is taken to represent the "human".[305]

The structural critique of international law using the male/female (m/f) binary is not unique to Charlesworth and Chinkin. Thus, for example, Rosa Brooks writes that 'international law seems to have very little to say to women'.[306]

The charge of essentialism that the structural critique of international law invites from fellow feminists is rejected by stating that it 'is an easy and in some contexts meaningless critique deployed by feminists against each other. The political force of feminism rests precisely on identifying common experiences'.[307] But as Otto rightly points out, while the

---

[303] Charlesworth and Chinkin, *Boundaries of international law*, p. 1. It may be noted that Charlesworth had earlier too expressed a radical feminist critique: 'Since the very basis of feminist theory is the experience of women, there will be an inevitable tension between universal theories and local experience in any feminist account of international law. But patriarchy and the devaluing of women, although manifested differently within different societies, is almost universal.' Charlesworth, 'Subversive Trends', p. 128.

[304] See ibid., p. 48.

[305] See ibid., p. 17. It is of significance that Charlesworth and Chinkin begin with an empirical review of the status of women in the world so as to 'provide a context for an analysis of international law that takes women seriously'. See ibid., pp. 4–14 at p. 5. Their theory is embedded in the real lives of real women. It is on the basis of data that they reach the conclusion that 'the world over, women's quality of life is less then men's'. See ibid., p. 14. This informs their historical evaluation of the role of international law. They note that 'to date, the longstanding efforts of women's organizations in the international arena have had little effect on the substance and process of international law'. See ibid., p. 16.

[306] Rosa Ehrenreich Brooks, 'Feminism and International Law: An Opportunity for Transformation', 14 (2002) *Yale Journal of Law & Feminism*, pp. 345–361 at p. 346.

[307] Charlesworth, 'Book Review', p. 723.

structural critique has led to 'the institutionalization of feminist ideas, in international law and politics', the underlying essentialism 'has divested them of their radical potential'.[308] She goes on to caution that 'a relentlessly dualistic understanding of gender is [...]easily recolonized by naturalized accounts of biological sex'.[309] The consolidation of 'protective' responses in international human rights law and practices through assuming the vulnerability and dependency of women is then only a step away.[310] In the process, male subjectivities are projected 'as fully human, which includes the expectation that they provide protection for women'.[311] The result is 'the continued naturalization of gender identities that normalize women's secondary status and men's power and authority'.[312] What is worse, the feminist cause is co-opted to serve hegemonic powers, including the justification of the use of force to address the oppression of women.[313] While Charlesworth and Chinkin may oppose protective responses or the use of force at the level of policy, they do not entirely appreciate that the MacKinnon view on use of force for preventing the oppression of women is a natural extension of radical feminism that they do not sufficiently question. In that sense, MacKinnon is consistent in her position as she always recognized the intimate relationship between radical and liberal feminism.[314] Otto is therefore right in speaking of the need for 'rethinking gender dualism and asymmetry from within feminism'.[315] She appropriately stresses the need for 'reframing sex/gender as multiple and shifting'[316] so as to take cognizance of 'abuses suffered by men and others, whose gender expressions and identities fall outside the gender binary (m/f) system, such as intersex and transgendered people, gender transients, multi–gendered people, androgynes, butch lesbians, transvestites and others who may identify as an "in–between" or third sex'.[317] However,

---

[308] Dianne Otto, 'Prospects for International Gender Norms', 31 (2011) *Pace Law Review*, pp. 873–881 at p. 875.
[309] Dianne Otto, 'International Human Rights Law: Towards Rethinking Sex/Gender Dualism' in Margaret Davies and Vanessa E. Munro (eds.) *A Research Companion to Feminist Legal Theory* (London: Routledge, 2013), pp. 197–215 at p. 199.
[310] See ibid.
[311] See ibid.
[312] See ibid., p. 197.
[313] Otto, 'Prospects', pp. 876–877.
[314] Sutherland, as earlier noted, writes that when pursuing change through law radical feminists 'are highly vulnerable to liberal co-optation'. Sutherland, 'Marx and MacKinnon', p. 115.
[315] Otto, 'International Human', p. 198.
[316] See ibid.
[317] See ibid.

the Otto attempt to overcome 'gender dualism' essentially touches on issues of 'sexuality'. The lack of engagement with the world beyond 'sexuality' takes away the edge from her questioning of gender dualism. While it is theoretically possible to do so, the contestation does not travel in a fundamental away from the frame of radical feminism as articulated by MacKinnon. Although Otto speaks of 'intersectional forms of discrimination against women' she does not link it to the need to use the category of 'gender' alongside the categories of class and race to analyse contemporary international law. She also does not situate intersectional forms of gender discrimination in international political economy; the overall sense that you get is that discrimination is a cultural phenomenon.[318] At least two moves need to be made here to overcome gender dualism. The first is not only to speak of sexuality and sexual subordination but all kinds of subordination. The second is to look at deep structures that result in the oppression of women and other subaltern groups and classes. This is where socialist feminism can lend the critique of contemporary international law epistemological and ontological depth and help evolve a suitable non-dualist approach.[319] The insights of socialist feminism are not merely helpful in macro analysis of international law but also, through intersectional analysis, in promoting the rights of women and other subaltern groups in particular contexts.

B.   On State

Since the state remains the principal subject of international law, Charlesworth and Chinkin begin by addressing its gendered character. They rightly point out that international lawyers treat the state 'as being without a sexed identity, a neuter, and thus without consequences for sex or gender'.[320] In reality the patriarchal character of the state 'makes it difficult to represent women's interests in international legal discourse'.[321] It also explains why discrimination on the basis of sex is not treated as seriously as racism. As a result sex discrimination 'has never been proposed

---

[318] See ibid., p. 207. However, she does worry that 'there is no frame for imagining what comes after the enterprise of addressing sexual violence'. Otto, 'Prospects', p. 875.

[319] On philosophy and gender see generally Cressida J. Heyes (ed.), *Philosophy and Gender: Critical Concepts in Philosophy* vol. 1 (London: Routledge, 2012); Miranda Fricker and Jennifer Hornsby (eds.) *The Cambridge Companion to Feminism in Philosophy* (Cambridge: Cambridge University Press, 2000).

[320] Charlesworth and Chinkin, *Boundaries of international law*, p. 125.

[321] See ibid.

as a barrier to the creation of a state, even where there is an effective system of apartheid based on sex'.[322] Charlesworth and Chinkin are not entirely wrong here, but in the absence of an historical and integrative approach there is a lack of recognition of the intersections between discrimination based on sex and race. In the process of contrasting how the international community approaches discrimination based on sex and race, Charlesworth and Chinkin neglect the fact that racism has been associated with extreme forms of violence such as genocide, slave trade, colonialism and neocolonialism that have had grave consequences for the well- being of women. The cognitive lapse here is not unusual among feminist scholars. As Mies points out:

> Following the general ahistorical trend in social science research, racial discrimination is put on the same level as sexual discrimination. Both appear to be bound up with biological givens: sex and skin color. But whereas many feminists reject biological reductionism with regard to sex-relations and insist on the social and historical roots of women's exploitation and oppression, with regard to race relations, the past and ongoing history of colonialism and of capitalist plunder and exploitation of the black world by white man is almost forgotten.[323]

This critique does not mean that sex discrimination is not deeply abhorrent and harmful. The essential point is that sex discrimination must not be seen in isolation from other forms of discrimination and oppression in determining the nature and character of a state.[324] Therefore, while agreeing that states are not 'neuter', socialist feminists would add that only an inclusive analysis of the bases of discrimination and oppression within society at a particular historical conjuncture can yield an appropriate characterization of a state. They would argue that the simple assertion of the 'sexed identity of the state' prevents a more accurate understanding of the character of particular states for all other modes of exclusion and oppression are assigned a secondary significance leading to what may be termed 'gender determinism'. An important consequence is the lack of realization that you cannot change the destiny of one exploited

---

[322] See ibid., p. 136.

[323] Mies, *Patriarchy and Accumulation*, p. 11.

[324] Fellmeth 'argue(s) that feminists "overstate" the role of sovereign states in international law and that, to the extent that states do play an important role in international law, historical power dynamics and not gender bias explain their existence'. Fellmeth, 'Feminism and International', p. 660. Further, he contends 'that neither the concept of states nor their practical consequences themselves reflect a "male voice" or inherently ignore women's interests'. See ibid., p. 660.

and oppressed group without changing that of others. There are in other words limits to what single issue social movements can achieve within nation states and in the international arena. The point once again is not that there should not be a separate women's movement or that its focus on discrimination based on sex is inappropriate, but merely that a fundamental change in the relationship between sexes cannot come about without general social transformation. In other words, the problem in the case of much feminist scholarship is its fixation with the category 'sex' in the same way as Marxists are often fixated with 'class'.

The tendency to speak of a gendered state also makes it difficult for Charlesworth and Chinkin to come to terms with the phenomenon of imperialism. What is more, in the absence of engagement with the consequences of universalizing capitalism, and based merely on the record of attending to discrimination based on sex, the imperialist state can be characterized as a relatively progressive state. It is because of the exploitation and oppression of third world women by imperialism that socialist and postcolonial feminists support anti-imperialist sentiments of third world states even as they simultaneously recognize that these states are often the embodiment of patriarchal oppression. If imperial oppression had been borne in mind Charlesworth and Chinkin would have been less critical of newly independent states (or TWAIL) for not mentioning the gendered nature of international law.[325] For, their emphasis on 'international law's Western origins and biases' is simultaneously a reference to the relationship between imperialism and the oppression of third world women.[326] Likewise, while it is troubling that many third world states are insensitive to gender considerations and inter alia have used cultural considerations to make extensive reservations to CEDAW, their general collective contestation of neutrality and objectivity of international law complements the feminist approach. But Charlesworth and Chinkin make no attempt to take into account the working and impact of global capitalism. It is as if male agency per se and not a certain combination of capitalism and patriarchy that achieves the subordination of women. The problem of essentialism thus crops up again and again in the analysis. It deserves repetition that the issue goes beyond the need for affirming strategic essentialism at times. The m/f binary invades their entire analysis of international law.

The focus on women continues in the discussion on the principle of self-determination. Charlesworth and Chinkin are of course entirely

---

[325] Charlesworth and Chinkin, *Boundaries of international law*, pp. 17–18.
[326] See ibid.

correct in their claim that there is no 'single relevant "self"'.[327] They aptly point out that 'the fact that half of the group comprising the "people" are accorded unequal status and are allowed little input into its decisions is not considered relevant at international law'.[328] But, by the same reasoning, a class critique of the principle of self-determination is equally persuasive. In other words, socialist feminists could argue that the principle of self determination not only masks the fact that the 'self' is defined by men but also by men belonging to a particular class. The only way out of the selective attitude is to adopt an integrative feminist approach.

Turning to the subject of state responsibility, Charlesworth and Chinkin write that in keeping with the public/private distinction 'the law of state responsibility distinguishes "public" actions for which the state is accountable from those "private" ones for which it does not have to answer internationally'.[329] For instance, violence in the private sphere 'is typically not regarded as an international legal issue'.[330] According to Charlesworth and Chinkin, 'the failure of the legislative, executive and judicial branches of the state to ensure the prevention, investigation and punishment of violence against women should incur international legal responsibility'.[331] They also rightly go on to add that while 'the notion of individual state responsibility' would represent a progressive move, 'the notion is inadequate in capturing the global nature of domination of women, and the way that international society reinforces this'.[332] But their refusal to critique the liberal international order that results in this domination makes this sentiment an empty gesture. In contrast, socialist feminism would critique deep structures that result in the global domination of women.

C.   *On International Law-Making*

An authoritative statement of the sources of international law is contained in Article 38(1) of the Statute of the International Court of Justice.[333]

---

[327] See ibid., p. 162.
[328] See ibid.
[329] See ibid., p. 148.
[330] See ibid.
[331] See ibid., p. 149.
[332] See ibid., p. 151.
[333] Article 38 (1) of the Statute if ICJ states:

> The Court whose function is to decide in accordance with international law such disputes as are submitted to it, shall apply: (a) international conventions, whether general or particular, establishing rules expressly recognized by the contesting States; (b) international custom, as evidence of a general practice

Charlesworth and Chinkin argue that 'the accepted sources of inter-national law sustain a gendered regime'.[334] They make two salient points in this regard. First, texts dealing with women's rights are very often adopted by the international community of states as non-binding soft law (e.g., the UNGA declaration on the elimination of violence against women).[335] Charlesworth and Chinkin trace the reason for resistance to the trans-lation of the interests of women into binding law to inter alia the fact that 'international law operates in the public, male world' with private issues 'left to national, rather than international, regulation'.[336] Second, Charlesworth and Chinkin argue that the claims of customary status of norms relating to the welfare of women tend to be rejected.[337]

It is interesting to note here the commonality of views between FtAIL and TWAIL on the constraints imposed by the authoritative sources of international law to bring about change in the international system. The arguments of TWAIL with respect to salient principles and norms incor-porated in the Program and Declaration on New International Economic Order (NIEO) and Charter of Economic Rights and Duties of States (CERDS) being classified as 'soft law' norms were no different.[338] TWAIL scholars had argued that despite their repeated affirmation in a range of texts these were not given the status of customary international law.[339] TWAIL would therefore readily accept the view that dominant sections of the 'invisible college of international scholars' who assess develop-ments in international law are 'fettered' by 'prejudices of racism, sexism and colonialism'.[340] Yet, despite the coincidence of views, there is almost no reference by Charlesworth and Chinkin to the contentions of TWAIL. The reason perhaps is that the TWAIL standpoint was not advanced

as accepted as law; (c) the general principles of law recognized by civilized nations; (d) judicial decisions and the teachings of highly qualified publicists of the various nations, as subsidiary means for the determination of rules of law.

[334] Charlesworth and Chinkin, *Boundaries of International law*, p. 62.
[335] See ibid., p. 77.
[336] See ibid., p. 56.
[337] 'It is difficult to assert the existence of custom in the face of consistent opposition from powerful and influential states. Even if an international prohibition of violence against women became widely accepted, it is possible that opposing states could claim to be "per-sistent objectors" to the norm'. See ibid., p. 77.
[338] Mohammed Bedjaoui, *Towards a new international economic order* (Paris: Holmes and Meir, 1979).
[339] See B. S. Chimni, *International Commodity Agreements: A Legal Study* (London: Croom Helm, 1987), chapter 12.
[340] Charlesworth and Chinkin, *Boundaries of International law*, p. 92.

with respect to women's rights but in relation to the international economic order. However, writing a decade later, Charlesworth conceded that the TWAIL perspective 'has considerable resonance with feminist approaches to international law',[341] but with the renewed complaint that it does not 'connect the power of international law to its gendered character, nor indeed the use of gendered images of the Third World'.[342] The critique reveals once again the unfortunate influence of radical feminism. Even a far-reaching critique of the liberal international economic order is seen as non-feminist for it does not directly address gender concerns. While, as has been noted earlier, TWAIL certainly needs to explicitly address the world of gender, it arguably has a feminist orientation even in its absence as it critiques deep structures that cause the oppression of women; a monist socialist feminist standpoint would support such an understanding. It is altogether another matter that TWAIL has by way of third world feminisms directly engaged with the rights of women; the writings of Nesiah and Nyamu are examples.

Be that as it may, in discussing the fact that the sources of international law sustain a gendered regime, Charlesworth and Chinkin surprisingly ignore the issue of indeterminacy of rules, especially because the lack of neutrality and objectivity is at the heart of their critique of international law.[343] The reason advanced for this neglect is that unlike critical legal studies (CLS) or New Approaches to International Law (NAIL) the feminist approach 'is not consumed with avoiding objectivism and flies an unequivocal flag for the fundamental value of women's equality with men'.[344] Socialist feminists would share this viewpoint, but would at the same time argue that the problem of lack of objectivity and neutrality does not disappear once international law affirms the equality of men and women. To put it differently, socialist feminists would take the problem of indeterminacy seriously for the problems of absence of neutrality and objectivity do not come to an end with the adoption of hard law or the acceptance of the existence of customary norms of international law on the rights of women. Albeit, they would disagree with the strong indeterminacy thesis advanced by the New Haven approach and NAIL as these tend to overlook the fact that international law in most instances facilitates in a direct way the oppression of women.[345]

[341] Charlesworth, 'Feminist Methods', p. 181.
[342] See ibid.
[343] See ibid., p. 180.
[344] Charlesworth, 'Subversive Trends', p. 128.
[345] For a materialist theory of interpretation, see Chapter 7, pp. 524–534.

D.   On Women's Rights

Charlesworth and Chinkin identify from a feminist perspective a range of problems with existing human rights instruments and institutions, including those directly dealing with women's rights. It is worth listing these schematically. First, general human rights instruments do not adequately address the rights and world of women.[346] Second, ' "mainstream" human rights institutions have tended to ignore the application of human rights norms to women'.[347] Third, 'ineffective implementation of existing provisions relating to women's rights to equality have reduced the force of international legal regulation'.[348] Fourth, reservations made to CEDAW tend to reduce the significance of women's rights.[349] Fifth, 'the existing law identifies sexual equality with equal treatment'[350] ignoring 'the underlying structures and power relations that contribute to the oppression of women'.[351] Sixth, the attention human rights instruments 'pay to the idea of family' 'discourages intervention and proper scrutiny of whether the rights to life, liberty, freedom from slavery and security of the person are realized in particular family contexts'.[352] Seventh, 'powerful entities in the private arena, such as religious and commercial institutions, benefit from the lack of international human rights scrutiny' making it difficult to realize women's rights.[353] Eighth, 'the international legal definition of the right to development' reflects 'the privileging of a male perspective and a failure to accommodate the realities of women's lives'.[354] Ninth, the attempt at gender mainstreaming in the general human rights instruments and in IOs 'has had a mixed fate'. There is a ritualistic character to it with the absence of, among other things 'the systematic questioning of states'.[355] Finally, Charlesworth and Chinkin note the challenges to the rights regime being posed by 'the forces of religious extremism and of economic globalization'.[356] The weaknesses in the existing rights regime make

[346] Charlesworth and Chinkin, *Boundaries of International Law*, pp. 214–216.
[347] See ibid., p. 218.
[348] See ibid., p. 220.
[349] See ibid. Chinkin writes that 'reservations to the Women's Convention have had a paralyzing effect'. Chinkin, 'Gender Inequality', p. 110.
[350] See ibid., p. 229.
[351] See ibid., p. 231.
[352] See ibid., p. 232.
[353] See ibid., p. 233.
[354] See ibid., p. 241.
[355] See ibid., p. 247.
[356] See ibid., p. 249.

Charlesworth and Chinkin ask the fundamental question as to whether the human rights canon can respond at all to the concerns of women? In their considered view it 'can play a useful, strategic role in advancing women's equality, particularly when used in conjunction with other political and social strategies, but that the limited nature of rights must be acknowledged'.[357] That is to say, 'while the acquisition and assertion of rights is by no means the only solution for the domination of women by men, it is an important tactic in the international arena'.[358] However, they conclude that all in all 'the significance of rights discourse outweighs its disadvantages'.[359]

This conclusion cannot really be faulted. But the views of Charlesworth and Chinkin are susceptible to two kinds of criticisms. First, they do not have a theory of rights that locates the possibility of realizing women's rights in particular social formations. Second, the term 'gender' is used 'as a synonym for "women", which undermines the idea that it is a social and relational category and threatens to reduce women again to biology'.[360] Otto suggests that it is perhaps these lapses of liberal feminism that made Halley call for taking a break from feminism.[361] However, even when Otto and Halley speak for instance of men suffering harm the primary reference is to sexual violence based in many instances on their racial or ethnic identities.[362] What is surprising is whether it is Charlesworth and Chinkin or Otto and Halley they do not view the question of gender relations in the context of the political economy of human relations. While Charlesworth and Chinkin do speak of 'the underlying structures and power relations that contribute to the oppression of women' the reference is essentially to the institution of patriarchy.[363] They do not articulate a theory of rights that explains the distinctive features of the institution of patriarchy with

---

[357] See ibid., p. 210.

[358] See ibid.

[359] Others have commented on the value of 'the promotional character of human rights law'. See Caglar et al., *Feminist Strategies*, p. 11 and fn. 36. Brooks writes that while international law 'does oppress and injure women' international human rights law 'has a transformative potential that we ignore at our peril'. Brooks, 'Feminism and International Law', p. 347.

[360] Otto, 'International Human', p. 205. Otto is disappointed that treaty bodies like the Human Rights Committee or the Committee on Elimination of Racial Discrimination 'use "gender" as a synonym for women'. See ibid., p. 207. But she believes that many human rights bodies are moving in the right direction i.e., 'the inclusion of gendered harms experienced by men'. See ibid., pp. 206ff.

[361] See ibid.,

[362] See ibid., p. 207.

[363] Charlesworth and Chinkin, *Boundaries of international law*, p. 231.

reference to particular social formations. On their part, Otto and Halley merely seek to extend the scope of analyses by taking the category 'gender' seriously, highlighting once more the need for a socialist feminist perspective that uses intersectional analysis but combines it with cultural and economic critiques.

The recognition that gender is 'a social and relational category' has many implications. One of which is the idea that in the final analysis the 'social relations of production' is of critical significance in understanding the oppression of women. A particular social formation manifests institutions of patriarchy in specific ways, a phenomenon that cannot be captured by structural or radical feminism. As postcolonial feminists note, what third world women and men are struggling against is a particular combination of capitalism, imperialism and patriarchy with differential impact on 'gender'. Therefore, unless global capitalism undergoes serious reform, and the phenomenon of imperialism addressed, it is not possible to adequately realize women's rights or address the concerns of men.

E.   On Use of Force

Turning to the subject of use of force, Charlesworth and Chinkin note that 'women are rarely involved in decisions about the use of armed conflict and in its processes'.[364] They believe that the exclusion of the voices of women is 'a great strategic mistake'.[365] Of course, Charlesworth and Chinkin admit that it is not entirely clear what the participation of women in decision making on the use of force would mean.[366] But in their view

---

[364] See ibid., p. 257.

[365] Hilary Charlesworth and Christine Chinkin (2002), 'Editorial Comment: Sex, Gender and September 11', 96 (2002) *American Journal of International Law*, pp. 600–605 at p. 604. Charlesworth and Chinkin argue that 'sex has been a crucial aspect of the events of September 11 and the response to them. Men have been the major players in all contexts and women have been cast as victims without real agency to affect the future. The public and political debate has largely ignored the considerable initiatives and activity of Afghan women aimed at contributing to the design of their future. The exclusion of over half the world's population from the formal decisions of great international significance is more than a question of justice and human rights; it is also a great strategic mistake'. See ibid., p. 604. More recently, in the context of 'new Wars' Chinkin and Kaldor have written that 'much greater participation of women is needed in all international roles, in peacekeeping, law enforcement, and at all levels of peace negotiations'. Christine Chinkin and Mary Kaldor, 'Gender and New Wars', 67 (2013) *Journal of International Affairs*, Fall/Winter pp. 167–187 at p. 182.

[366] 'Gender as "the socially and culturally constructed categories of masculinity and femininity" does not refer to the characteristics of particular men and women. Indeed, it

'it would at least allow for a greater diversity of considerations to be taken into account'.[367] According to them:

> The problem with all types of gendered discourse is that it makes some courses of action impossible to contemplate. Thinking in dichotomous terms limits the ways we can analyze the situation; it confines our perspective to simple either-or propositions; it makes certain actions seem inevitable or nonnegotiable.[368]

In other words, gendered ways of thinking 'do not allow us to understand the complexity of the situation, or to devise long-term solutions'.[369] On the other hand, a feminist perspective enables 'broader and more durable solutions' to problems.[370] Thus, for instance, post-September 11 the United States could have responded 'not just (or not at all) through military action', but by programs that acknowledged the fact that it is 'the economic and political desperation felt by so many of the world's disenfranchised' that 'helps fuel misdirected acts of terrorist violence'.[371] Feminist policy makers would also have 'looked harder for ways to target Al Qaeda without so much devastation to Afghan civilians'.[372] They may also have insisted 'that regimes and cultures which systematically exclude or oppress women must change if they are to be our allies'.[373]

In advancing a feminist perspective on the use of force what Charlesworth and Chinkin do not explore once again is the link between imperialism and violence against peoples of weak nations. Such a move would have helped explain why women in power in the imperial world are equally trapped within mainstream security discourse.[374] Women policy makers cannot easily brush aside the dominant understanding of

---

is possible to be sexed as a woman, but to adopt a masculine gender and vice versa'. Charlesworth and Chinkin, 'Editorial Comment', p. 604; emphasis in original.

[367] Charlesworth and Chinkin, *Boundaries of international law*, p. 258.

[368] Charlesworth and Chinkin, 'Editorial Comment', p. 605. 'We do not want to suggest that appeal to ideals of masculinity should be countered simply by giving priority to values associated with femininity. The problem with all types of gendered discourse is that it makes some courses of action impossible to contemplate. Thinking in dichotomous terms limits the ways we can analyze the situation; it confines our perspective to simple either-or propositions; it makes certain actions seem inevitable or nonnegotiable'. See ibid.

[369] See ibid.

[370] See ibid.

[371] Brooks, 'Feminism and International Law', p. 356.

[372] See ibid.

[373] See ibid., p. 357.

[374] Carol Cohn, 'Sex and Death in the Rational World of Defense Intellectuals', 12 (1987) *Signs*, pp. 687–698. Thus, for example, the fact that Madeline Albright was a woman did not stop her from taking the decision for NATO to bomb former Yugoslavia for six weeks.

'national interests' or particular courses of action flowing from it. If as is widely accepted the notion of femininity is socially constructed what needs so to be examined is the life world within which the ideas of women decision makers are shaped. Arguably, their socialization leads them to be more attuned to recognizing particular forms of oppression as against others. Likewise, it may make them more prone to accepting certain kinds of responses more than others. In any case perhaps the key variable is not gender but the ideological lens through which war and peace issues are perceived and policy options filtered. It is interesting in this context to contrast the perspective of a Rosa Luxemburg with that of liberal feminists. The one traces war and violence to universalizing capitalism and the others simply to male domination or the idea of masculinity.[375] To subscribe to the Luxemburg view does not entail underestimating the significance of the greater participation of women in decisions relating to war. If nothing else it will bring about greater awareness that wars, old or new, inevitably mean violence against women (as the International Congress of Women formally pointed out as early as in 1915).[376] In the aftermath of war it may also help ensure that there is active prosecution of cases for violence against women;[377] at present international criminal law is 'aimed only at tinkering with the international legal regime'.[378] The presence of women would also make a difference in thinking about the processes through which a post-conflict society has to be reconstructed. But a Luxemburg would be in a better position to explain the phenomenon of 'imperial feminism'. Socialist feminists would also point out that Charlesworth and Chinkin do not consider the significance of decision makers being drawn from other oppressed groups: those discriminated against on the basis of race or class or disability. After all why would only the greater representation of women in decision making bring about a changed perspective? Once again while Charlesworth and Chinkin acknowledge the existence of different feminisms, their observations tend to be reductionist. Socialist feminism with its focus on social formations, and accompanying social relations, is not only in a better position

---

[375] On the most insightful analysis of the causes of the First World War, see Rosa Luxemburg, *The Crisis in German Social-Democracy: (The 'Junius' Pamphlet)* (New York: The Socialist Publication Society, 1919). See also Rosa Luxemburg, *The Accumulation of Capital* (London: Routledge and Kegan Paul, 1951).

[376] Chinkin and Kaldor note that while it is true that 'sexual violence has been a pervasive feature of all wars throughout history' there are new 'types of gendered violence' in 'new wars'. Chinkin and Kaldor, 'Gender and New Wars', p. 175.

[377] See ibid., p. 179.

[378] Charlesworth and Chinkin, *Boundaries of international law*, p. 335.

to analyse the reasons for wars but also in explaining how the greater representation of all oppressed classes in decision making on use of force could have an important influence over outcomes. Simply put the relationship between 'women and war' is complex even as it may be conceded that as a marginal and oppressed group in society women decision makers are more likely to be sensitive to the situation of others in a subaltern situation.[379]

F.   On Peace Building

Addressing from a feimints perspective the problem of peace building in post-conflict societies Chinkin and Charlesworth advance the following propositions. First, 'there can be no assumption that the violence stops with a formal ceasefire'.[380] Second, 'women typically bear the greatest burden of managing post-conflict relations with war-traumatized children, family members and former fighters'.[381] Third, 'the values that are seen as central to peace-building: human rights, democracy and the rule of law' are 'biased towards male interests'.[382] Fourth, 'the framework for peace-building is colonial in its origin'.with implications for the welfare of women[383] This leads them to ask the question 'can an international legal framework be applied for the empowerment of women in the Third World that is not open to rejection ... as a further form of neo-colonialism?'[384]

The importance of women's participation in peace building has now been recognized in UN Security Council Resolution 1325 on Women, Peace and Security. The resolution calls for the inclusion of a 'gender perspective' in addressing the problem of post-conflict societies, stressing the importance of 'a gender balance of experiences and perspectives to inform and guide the peace process'.[385] The resolution also endorses 'measures

[379] Riley, Mohanty, and Pratt, 'Introduction: feminism and US wars-mapping the ground' in Ronin L. Riley, Chandra Talpade Mohanty and Minnie Bruce Pratt (eds) Feminism and War: Confronting U.S Imperialism' (London: Zed Books, 2008), pp. 1–18 at p. 2. They go on to add that 'few feminist theorists continue to accept the claim that women are natural pacifists, yet there is much debate over how to understand what is in women's interests and how to advance those interests'. See ibid.
[380] Christine Chinkin and Hilary Charlesworth, 'Building Women into Peace: The International Legal Framework', 27 (2006) Third World Quarterly, pp. 937–957 at p. 941.
[381] See ibid.
[382] See ibid., pp. 942–943.
[383] See ibid. See also Charlesworth, Democracy , pp. 112–130.
[384] See ibid., p. 943.
[385] Claudia von Braunmühl, 'A Feminist Analysis of UN Security Council Resolutions on Women, Peace, and Security' in Gulay Caglar, Elisabeth Prugl and Sussane Zwingel(eds.)

that ensure the protection of and respect for human rights of women and girls, particularly as they relate to the constitution, the electoral system, the police and the judiciary'.[386] But in practice the impact of the UNSC resolution has not been substantive.[387] Charlesworth and Chinkin believe that a number of practical steps need to be taken 'to respond to the marginalisation of women in peace-building' which includes the creation of an institutional mechanism to which states would be required to report the steps taken for the implementation of Security Council Resolution 1325.[388] Such a move would have to be accompanied by measures that ensure 'that all involved in peace-building are aware of the international legal obligations with respect to women, have adequate resources for the performance of these obligations, and that responsibility for monitoring compliance is allocated to a person of sufficient seniority, with sanctioning power for failure to do so'.[389]

To their credit, Charlesworth and Chinkin are not averse to making policy suggestions to strengthen the role and rights of women in peace building. But socialist and postcolonial feminists would point out that unless the reasons for the conflicts are understood, as also the context in which international interventions are made, the suggested measures cannot effectively respond to the problems of women in post-conflict societies or to the problem of neo-colonialism.[390] Thus, for instance, Nesiah writes that 'the quest inspired by Resolution 1325 for representation in peace building is often a Trojan horse for far-reaching commitments to global hegemonic economic and political choices'.[391] In her view, 'while Resolution 1325 advocacy presents itself as a transformative expansion of the peace process and a challenge to inherited hierarchies, the resolution

Feminist Strategies in International Governance (London: Routledge, 2013), pp. 163–180 at p. 165.

[386] Chinkin and Charlesworth, 'Building Women', p. 938.

[387] Braunmuhl, 'Feminist Analysis', p. 165; Andrea Scheniker and Jutta Joachim, 'European Countries and the Implementation of UN Security Council Resolution 1325' in Gulay Caglar, Elisabeth Prugl and Sussane Zwingel(eds.) *Feminist Strategies in International Governance* (London: Routledge, 2013), pp. 181–197 at p. 192.

[388] Charlesworth and Chinkin, 'Building Women', p. 953.

[389] See ibid.

[390] See Nesiah, 'Uncomfortable Alliances'. See also B. S. Chimni, 'Post-conflict Peacebuilding and the Return of Refugees: Concepts, Practices, and Institutions' in Edward Newman and Joanne van Selm (eds.) *Refugees and Forced Displacement: International Security, Human Vulnerability, and the State* (Tokyo: United Nations University Press, 2002), pp. 195–211.

[391] Nesiah, 'Uncomfortable Alliances', p. 155.

often works seamlessly with local and global processes that endorse and legitimize dominant ideologies'.[392]

G.   Missing International Economic Law

Two decades ago Saskia Sassen had observed that in the era of global-ization 'two institutional arenas have emerged as new sites for norma-tivity alongside the more traditional normative order represented by the nation-state: the global capital market and the international human rights regime'.[393] While international human rights law has since been exten-sively studied from a feminist perspective, the doings of the global cap-ital market or more broadly global financial, investment and trade law regimes have come to be neglected by feminist scholars. As Kerry Rittich has noted while reviewing the work of Charlesworth and Chinkin, 'eco-nomic issues have not formed a central part of the international women's rights agenda at all'.[394] Charlesworth and Chinkin in particular do not rec-ognize the intimate relationship between the nature of international eco-nomic governance and the status and rights of women. José Alvarej aptly writes of their book *The boundaries of international law*:

> A surprising gap in a book that stresses the economic inequalities between men and women (and presumably the permeable boundaries between public international law and other international rules) is the relative lack of attention to international economic law, including international finan-cial institutions, national development agencies, regional banks, and multinational commercial enterprises – and how these other elements of international civil society relate to the treatment of women.[395]

In a sense it is unfair to complain that the two pioneers of FtAIL have not addressed all aspects of international law. The articulation of FtAIL is after all not an individual but a collective project. Other scholars can readily fill the gaps in their work. The Alvarej critique is however more

[392] See ibid. In her case study of Sri Lanka, Nesiah concludes: 'In Sri Lanka Resolution 1325 has occupied and constrained the landscape of peace and security in ways that have legiti-mated a politics of hegemonic internationalism in the name of women affected by con-flict'. See ibid., p. 156.

[393] Saskia Sassen, 'Toward a Feminist Analytics of the Global Economy', 4 (1996) *Indiana Journal of Global Legal Studies*, pp. 7–41 at p. 32.

[394] Kerry Rittich, 'Book Review', 14 (2001) *Leiden Journal of International Law*, pp. 935–939 at p. 939.

[395] Alvarej, 'Book Review', p. 464. See generally Miranda Das, 'Feminist Approaches to International Law', PhD thesis submitted to the Jawaharlal Nehru University, New Delhi.

fundamental. The absence of any discussion of international economic law suggests that there is no serious connection perceived between structures and practices of international economic governance and the lack of realization of women's social and economic rights. The issue is not simply about neglecting one branch of international law, but the fact that the nature and character of international economic law goes to the heart of the question of the oppression of women. To put it differently, in the absence of a turn to political economy, there is 'growing realization that feminism has lost its emancipatory edge in the era of globalization'.[396] Therefore, socialist feminists would argue that gender analysis of international law be firmly located within international political economy.[397] It is all the more urgent today as 'the concepts drawn from feminism and rights are being used to service the dominant neoliberal economic framework'.[398]

It is therefore not surprising that in recent years there has been increasing 'feminist interventions in the field of international economic governance' including on how different international economic organizations (such as the World Bank and WTO) approach the question of gender.[399] There have emerged networks of feminist economists like 'The International Working Group on Gender, Macroeconomics and International Economics' (GEM-IWG) and the International Gender and Trade Network (IGTN), the latter described as 'the most influential gender advocacy organization in the international trade policy arena'.[400] It is said that IGTN has been 'largely responsible for putting gender on the trade agenda of NGOs, popular movements, governments and multilateral institutions'.[401] It inter alia considers the negative impact of international trade on the livelihood and lives of women.[402] It may explain why

---

[396] Ann Stewart, 'Gender Justice and Law in a Global Market', (2012) CSLG/WP/16 Working Paper Series (New Delhi: Centre for the Study of Law and Governance, Jawaharlal Nehru University), p. 2. See also *Gender Justice and Law in a Global Market* (Cambridge: Cambridge University Press, 2011).

[397] See ibid., p. 3.

[398] See ibid., p. 16.

[399] Gulay Caglar, 'Feminist Strategies and Social Learning in International Economic Governance' in Gulay Caglar, Elisabeth Prugl and Sussane Zwingel(eds.) *Feminist Strategies in International Governance* (London: Routledge, 2013), pp. 249–266 at pp. 249–263.

[400] Mariama Williams, 'A Perspective on Feminist International Organizing from the Bottom Up: The Case of IGTN and the WTO' in Gulay Caglar, Elisabeth Prugl and Sussane Zwingel(eds.) *Feminist Strategies in International Governance* (London: Routledge, 2013), pp. 92–108 at p. 92.

[401] See ibid., p. 100.

[402] See ibid., p. 93.

'women consistently tend to oppose trade more than men'.[403] There is also a range of publications by international organizations on the subject such as UNIFEM's *Women and the New Trade Agenda*.[404] Further, a whole host of issues ranging from 'gender budgeting' to unpaid work by women have been raised.[405] More generally, postcolonial feminists have shown how the liberal idea of development excludes the welfare of women, especially in the third world[406] leading to the feminization of poverty.[407] While some researchers have found support for the claim that economic globalization has improved women's status, the disaggregated results reveal a mixed picture.[408] It is admitted for instance that 'foreign direct investment largely failed to have a reliable impact on women's status'.[409] Socialist feminists have gone further and 'highlighted the similarities between the position of women and that of the Third World in international and national capital accumulation and pointed to the way in which women's labour is devalued and therefore exploited both by men and capital through its association with their role in the social reproductive sphere of the family'.[410]

Yet there are ongoing attempts to normalize the feminist agenda through reframing them. An example is the World Development Report 2012 of the World Bank on 'Gender Equality and Development' which

---

[403] Edward D. Mansfield, Diana C. Mutz and Laura R. Silver, 'Men, Women, Trade and Free Markets', 59 (2015) *International Studies Quarterly*, pp. 1–13 at p. 1. They write that 'in virtually every country that has been analyzed, women are significantly more hostile to trade than men'. See ibid, p. 2. Their study looks at the United States and concludes: 'Taken as a whole, women's protectionist attitudes do not stem from the distributional consequences of trade that most political economy models emphasize, but rather stem from attitudes toward competition, relocation, and foreign involvement.' See ibid, p. 11. But this may not be true of women in the developing world where distributional consequences may matter as well. But this is a subject for empirical investigation.

[404] Susan Joekes and Ann Weston, *Women and the New Trade Agenda* (New York: UNIFEM, 1995).

[405] See generally Caglar et al, 'Feminist Strategies'.

[406] Shirin Rai, 'Gender and Development: Theoretical Perspectives' in Nalini Visvanathan, Lynn Duggan, Nan Wiegersma and Laura Nissonof (eds.) *The Women, Gender and Development Reader* (London: Zed Press, 2011), pp. 28–37. See generally Kerry Rittich, *Recharacterizing Restructuring: Law, Distribution and Gender in Market Reform* (The Hague: Kluwer Law International, 2002).

[407] See generally Valentine M. Moghdam, 'The "Feminization of Poverty" and Women's Human Rights', SHS Papers on Women's Studies/Gender Research (Paris: UNESCO, 2005).

[408] David L. Richards and Ronald Gelleny, 'Women's Status and Economic Globalization', 51 (2007) *International Studies Quarterly*, pp. 855–876 at p. 871. See also Mark M. Gray, Miki Caul Kittlison and Wayne Sandholtz, 'Women and Globalization: A Study of 180 Countries, 1975–2000', 60 (2006) *International Organization*, pp. 293–333.

[409] See ibid., p. 872.

[410] Stewart, 'Gender Justice', pp. 8–9.

attempts to put the liberal feminist agenda on gender equality in the service of neo-liberal globalization. There are two possible views expressed with respect to the report. From a liberal standpoint the report has been described as 'a strategically critical moment for international discourse on development to have the Bank put gender and feminism so high up on its agenda'.[411] The World Bank can be seen to move beyond its 'own earlier dogma that economic growth leads to gender equality and vice versa'.[412] It now acknowledges the role of feminism and women's movements in bringing about social change.[413] But, as Wendy Harcourt points out, the Report suffers from multiple weaknesses. First, it is 'silent on the impact on women's lives of the multiple crises of finance, food, energy, climate, land grabbing and resource extraction'.[414] Second, it does not sufficiently recognize that the reproductive work of women both 'subsidizes productive work in the market' and in times of economic crisis 'the work of the State'.[415] Third, it does not explore 'the complex linkages among finance, trade, economic policy and sexual and reproductive rights and gender based rights'.[416] Fourth, the 'reduction of the complex issue of social protection to conditional cash transfers misses the reality that stop gap measures are not enough to address chronic poverty, and the current crisis is already beginning to reverse gains made on gender equality'.[417] Finally, the report does not address 'the macroeconomic structural gender inequalities' and overlooks that 'the vital importance of social reproduction for markets and the State has to be at the core of economic analysis'.[418] In short, as Rittich has observed, 'to the extent that the pursuit of gender equity conflicts is perceived to conflict with development ideology or practices that are otherwise considered desirable it remains at risk'.[419] She

---

[411] Wendy Harcourt, 'Review Essay: "Beyond Smart Economics": The World Bank 2012 Report on Gender and Equality', 14 (2012) *International Feminist Journal of Politics,* pp. 307–312 at p. 308.

[412] See ibid., p. 309. The official website of the World Bank states that the Report 'focuses on four priority areas for policy going forward: (i) reducing excess female mortality and closing education gaps where they remain (ii) improving access to economic opportunities for women (iii) increasing women's voice and agency in the household and in society and (iv) limiting the reproduction of gender inequality across generations'. www.google.co.in/#psj=1&q=world+bank+report+on+gender+equality+2012

[413] See ibid.

[414] See ibid.

[415] See ibid.

[416] See ibid.

[417] See ibid., pp. 309–310.

[418] See ibid., pp. 310.

[419] Rittich, 'Recharacterizing, Restructuring', p. 244.

therefore rightly laments that 'there is no systematic analysis of the ways in which economic development or market reform policies, *including those which appear to have nothing to do with gender*, might have disparate effects on men and women'.[420] For neo-liberal capitalist globalization has meant among other things the 'feminization of poverty' through transmitting economic crises to the third world and accentuating the negative impact of increasing informal work in very difficult work conditions.

It is, therefore, a serious flaw in the work of Charlesworth and Chinkin that they do not address issues related to international economic governance. It may not be inappropriate to mention here that Charlesworth and Chinkin also do not engage with the impact of neo-liberal capitalist globalization on the global environment and its implications for the life of women, in particular in the Global South.[421] In fact the 'logic of nature' or international environment law finds no place in their work.

H.   On International Institutions

International Institutions (IIs) are today coming to occupy a central role in international politics. But they remain male bastions. The liberal feminist critique of IIs is both about the level of representation and participation of women and the gendered nature of categories and concepts that inform their work. Charlesworth and Chinkin document 'the absence of women at senior levels in international institutions' and argue 'that the invisibility of women at the decision-making levels has affected the treatment not only of "women's" issues, but also the way all international concerns are understood'.[422] While there have been efforts within the UN

---

[420] See ibid., p. 245; emphasis in original.

[421] From a materialist feminist perspective Kirk has argued that 'gender, race, class, imperialism, and the global capitalist economy are connected to ecological destruction'. Gwyn Kirk, 'Standing on Solid Ground: A Materialist Ecological Feminism' in Rosemary Hennessy and Chrysn Ingraham (eds.) *Materialist Feminism: A Reader in Class, Difference, and Women's Lives* (Routledge: London, 1997), pp. 345–363.

[422] Charlesworth and Chinkin, *Boundaries of international law*, p. 171. Grossman describes the importance of women representation in relation to international adjudication which captures the general arguments in favour of enhancing gender representation: 'underrepresentation of one sex affects normative legitimacy because it endangers impartiality and introduces bias when men and women approach judging differently. Even if men and women do not "think differently," a sex unrepresentative bench harms sociological legitimacy for constituencies who believe they think differently nonetheless. For groups traditionally excluded from international lawmaking or historically subjected to discrimination, inclusion likely strengthens sociological legitimacy, while continued exclusion perpetuates conclusions about unfairness. Finally, sex representation is important

system to correct the situation, 'the advancement of women has been glacial'.[423] The lack of serious efforts is reflected in the fact that 'equitable distribution of positions according to nationality continues to have a far greater priority than equitable distribution according to gender'.[424] The under-representation of women is symbolized by the fact that there has been no woman UN Secretary General as yet. Charlesworth and Chinkin have also noted that 'the general silence about women in discussions of UN reform' and thus 'made the issue of sex and gender appear irrelevant to the process'.[425] The 'imbalance' in representation 'raises issues of human rights'.[426] There is also little doubt that the representation of women greatly enhances the legitimacy of IIs and the decisions they take.[427] Charlesworth and Chinkin therefore recommend that women participation should be enhanced in UN and international institutions.[428]

Charlesworth and Chinkin do well to undertake an analysis of IIs from a feminist standpoint as mainstream scholars of international institutions did not take cognizance of the concerns they express.[429] Over the decades, the feminist critique has had an impact, while 'inequality is still pervasive, yet considerations of gender have entered the mainstream of policy-making to a degree previously unimagined'.[430] In 2010, UN Women, the entity for gender equality and the empowerment of women was established, entering into operation on 1 January 2011.[431] Recent writings have

---

to normative legitimacy of international courts because representation is an important democratic value'. Nienke Grossman, 'Sex on the Bench: Do Women Judges Matter to the Legitimacy of International Courts?', 12 (2012) *Chicago Journal of International Law*, pp. 647–684 at p. 676.

[423] See ibid., p. 183. This assessment has recently been reaffirmed in the context of democracy-building in post-conflict societies. Charlesworth, *Democracy*, p. 136.

[424] See ibid., p. 185.

[425] Charlesworth and Chinkin, 'Feminist Analysis', p. 197.

[426] See ibid., p. 189.

[427] See Grossman, 'Sex on the Bench', pp. 647–684.

[428] Charlesworth and Chinkin, 'Feminist Analysis', p. 198.

[429] See for example Jan Klabbers, 'International Institutions' in James Crawford and Martti Koskenniemi (eds.) *The Cambridge Companion to International Law* (Cambridge: Cambridge University Press, 2012), pp. 228–244.

[430] Caglar et al., 'Introducing Feminist Strategies', p. 1.

[431] See UN Women www.unwomen.org/en/about-us/about-un-women 'UN Women incorporates four existing parts of the UN system dealing with women and has been styled as the new UN "gender architecture"'. Hilary Charlesworth and Christine Chinkin, 'The New United Nations "Gender Architecture": A Room with a View?' in A. von Bogdandy, A. Peters and R. Wolfrum (eds.), 17 (2013) *Max Planck Yearbook of United Nations Law*, pp. 1–60 at pp. 3–4.

proposed a substantial agenda for it.[432] However, it is too soon to tell how much difference the entity will make. In fact Charlesworth and Chinkin suggest that 'without a strong normative direction, *UN Women* will do little to change the global *status quo* in which women's inequality is a significant feature'.[433] But they admit that 'the creation of the architecture of *UN Women* may allow the elaboration of, and advocacy for, a richer concept of equality to support women all over the world. This would give *UN Women* a view – a normative direction and a capacity to challenge the boundaries of international law'.[434]

Meanwhile, greater attention needs to be paid to the impact of the policies of international economic institutions (IEIs) on the welfare of women. The key questions that demand a response include:

> What is the role of the World Bank, the IMF, and the WTO in perpetuating gendered economic regimes? How does the international trade regime help construct gender in different countries and different economic sectors? How do transnational corporations, another set of regime agents, participate in gender constructions? What kinds of gender and other status hierarchies operate within international organizations and transnational corporations? To what extent do status hierarchies in these organizations correlate with gender hegemonies reproduced through global economic institutions? Why has the feminist movement had so little success in changing neo-liberal rhetoric and in breaking through organizational glass ceilings? Are institutional strategies in the organizations of economic governance more prone to cooptation than in other organizations?[435]

Charlesworth and Chinkin do not address these questions or sufficiently recognize that IEIs perpetuate 'gendered economic regimes'.[436] This

---

[432] Gulay Caglar, Elizabeth Prugl, and Sussane Zwingel, 'Advancing Feminist Strategies in International Governance' in Gulay Caglar, Elisabeth Prugl and Sussane Zwingel(eds.) *Feminist Strategies in International Governance* (London: Routledge, 2013), pp. 284–294 at pp. 291–294.

[433] Charlesworth and Chinkin, 'The New United Nations', p. 4; emphasis in original. They write that UN Women 'appears as an example of good practice management, merging and consolidating the work of four existing bodies'. See ibid., p. 27.

[434] See ibid. They later observe, 'the creation of *UN Women* is a moment of great promise because of the unprecedented focus on the institutional architecture for the advancement of women'. See ibid., p. 53. However, they again emphasize that *UN Women* should 'play a valuable role in addressing the foundational weaknesses of the normative structure relating to women in international law, which has overall taken a minimalist approach to women's equality and encouraged integration into pre-existing structures'. See ibid., p. 54.

[435] Elisabeth Prugl, 'International Institutions and Feminist Politics', X (2004) *Brown Journal of World Affairs*, pp. 69–84 at p. 81.

[436] See ibid.

is a serious lapse as the policies of IEIs are playing a crucial role in the exploitation and oppression of third world women. Equally significantly, Charlesworth and Chinkin fail to appraise the consequences of the growing role of IIs in global governance. Arguably, IIs are coming to constitute a global imperial state under the influence of an emerging transnational capitalist class.[437] But Charlesworth and Chinkin do not undertake a global intersectional analysis of the policies of IIs, as socialist feminists would do, as a way of characterizing them and assess their current role in global governance. To put it differently, Charlesworth and Chinkin lack a general theory of international institutions that goes beyond the women's question.

I.   Limits of Liberal Reforms

All critical theories of international law have to address the question whether they should encourage, endorse and participate in reform processes that bring about incremental change or pursue strategies that can bring about fundamental changes in systems of national and global governance. As already seen, Charlesworth and Chinkin do not reject the idea of reform; critique is for them not an end in itself. In the words of Charlesworth, 'feminist analysis of international law has two major roles, one deconstructive, the other reconstructive'.[438] Alvarej has therefore rightly observed that Charlesworth and Chinkin are 'reformers, not destroyers'.[439] They describe their vision of the reform process thus:

> In our view, feminists should tackle international law on a number of levels at the same time. We should use existing mechanisms and principles wherever possible to improve women's lives. We should also work to reform the letter of the law so that it more adequately responds to concerns of women. We must insist that the equal participation of women in the international legal system and its institutions is a condition of their legitimacy. Beyond this we can contribute to the Grotian project of redrawing the boundaries of international law by challenging and questioning the 'objectivity' of the international legal system and its hierarchy based on gender.[440]

---

[437] B. S. Chimni, 'International Institutions Today: An Imperial Global State in the Making', 15 (2004) European Journal of International Law, pp. 1–39.
[438] Charlesworth, 'Feminist Critiques', p. 3.
[439] Alvarej, 'Book Review', p. 461.
[440] Charlesworth and Chinkin, Boundaries of international law, p. 336.

The reform initiatives will of course be judged on its merits calling for a continuous review and assessment of existing international laws and institutions. It could mean different evaluation of particular reform initiatives at particular points of time. Thus, for example, reviewing the ensemble of UNSC resolutions on Women, Peace and Security, Otto had early on expressed scepticism about their impact. Her concern had been that the UNSC had 'engaged selectively with feminist ideas, adopting them only in so far as they were useful for promoting its own institutional agenda' promoting 'protective stereotypes'.[441] But she subsequently changed her views as later resolutions showed that the Council 'has managed to build on the footholds created by the earlier resolutions and slowly strengthen the feminist content of this institutional agenda'.[442] In contrast to the GF model she proposes that a distinction be made 'between feminist ideas inside and outside international institutions'.[443] Such a distinction will allow acknowledging when necessary 'the loss of feminist control, which occurs in the process of institutionalization' and stress 'the continuing need to engage critically with those ideas and the purposes to which they are put'.[444] What is called for is a 'critical and persistent engagement ... between the normative projects of feminist activism and the scholarly projects of feminist critique'.[445] In Otto's view, 'feminism will only thrive in the intersections of activism and critique, in the interaction between power and danger. The extraordinary transformation of Security Council resolutions into grass roots feminist organizing tools attests to the productivity of this interplay'.[446] Not everyone may agree with this assessment. It has been seen that Nesiah dissents from the assessment of Otto on the role of UNSC resolutions. The reason is that she brings postcolonial lens to examine the role these resolutions are playing in practice. She exposes the limits of liberal reforms by revealing the ways in which it helps legitimize hegemonic ideologies.

But there is no inherent contradiction in pursuing the dual strategy of critique and reform. It is therefore difficult to agree with Alvarej that Charlesworth and Chinkin do not explain 'how we can both challenge international norms and institutions, and still use them as a basis

[441] Otto, 'Power and Danger', p. 99.
[442] See ibid.
[443] See ibid., p. 120.
[444] See ibid.
[445] See ibid.
[446] See ibid.

for advancing the interests of women'.[447] However, there is genuine fear among feminists that the reform process can provide 'gender legitimacy' to hegemonic international laws and institutions. The danger is not that the reform effort per se will provide 'gender legitimacy' to international law and institutions. The problem is that the reform agenda is pursued by liberal feminists or MFILS without contesting the deep structures that inform the oppression of women and other subaltern groups. Even in the instance of UNSC resolutions, as Nesiah points out, 'sexual violence, rather than more complex sociopolitical analysis of [...] conflicts, emerges as the privileged narrative for international law interventions'.[448]

It is not as if Charlesworth and Chinkin do not have a larger agenda that goes beyond elementary reforms. In fact Charlesworth speaks about the need 'to refocus international law on issues of structural justice that underpin everyday life'.[449] The problem is that Charlesworth and Chinkin wish to realize such justice within a liberal international order. The absence of any talk about the pursuit of serious change in the extant global economic and social order compels the conclusion that Charlesworth and Chinkin do not wish to seriously redraw the boundaries of international law. The question is not merely of pursuing reform or the absence of concern with the fate of other subaltern groups.[450] The issue is a methodological one: liberal feminism does not possess the epistemological tools of socialist feminism to understand and seek fundamental changes in the liberal international order.

[447] Alvarej, 'Book Review', p. 462. Albeit, feminist scholars like Otto who are in favour of reform themselves have self-doubt when they ask 'whether it possible to work for progressive outcomes for women, while also being deeply critical of the same institutions, laws and policies that we expect to produce those outcomes'. Otto, 'Power and Danger', p. 98.

[448] Nesiah, 'Uncomfortable Alliances', p. 153. In the context of her case study of Sri Lanka, Nesiah clarifies that 'sexual violence is undoubtedly a problem in the Lankan context. However, women's experiences of conflict cannot be understood without attention to ethnicity, region, socioeconomic status, and party affiliation, all of which are lost in Resolution 1325's view of gender as a free-standing category'. See ibid.

[449] Hilary Charlesworth, 'International Law: A Discipline of Crisis', 65 (2002) *The Modern Law Review*, pp. 377–392 at p. 391.

[450] Alvarej has queried in the latter context the position of first world liberal feminists: 'Is the goal (as in elevating the level of female participation in international lawmaking) merely to raise women to the exalted position formerly occupied by men – so that both men and women (predominately from the North) can continue to oppress, under the emerging neoliberal rules of globalization, those who are economically disadvantaged in the developing world? Is the goal gender parity or a more fundamental redistribution of power, wealth, and opportunity? If the latter, how exactly will reformist moves correcting gender inequalities accomplish that?' Alvarej, 'Book Review', p. 464. However for an exception see Charlesworth and Chinkin, *Boundaries of international law*, p. 252.

The failings of the liberal method and outlook also explain why Charlesworth and Chinkin do not have a theory of resistance beyond essentialist politics. The problems that it can give rise to can be seen in the feminist critique that the 'Porto Alegre' man of the World Social Forum (WSF) 'constructs a single enemy requiring a single, unified struggle'.[451] In this view, the Porto Alegre man, 'a composite figure, a concatenation of hegemonic and masculinist practices', makes the problematic claims to represent the 'general' cause, rather than 'particular' issues or identities.[452] While there is a point in the criticism it is difficult to see how 'gender' movements alone can cope with unified capital. This question has a bearing on how reform can be brought about in contemporary international law to the advantage of all subaltern groups and classes. Socialist feminism is in a better position to answer the agency question as it moves away from both radical feminism and the traditional left position that privileges the working class as the agent of change. It rests its hope on, to use the words of Slavoz Zizek, an 'explosive combination of different agents'.[453]

V. Conclusion

It is said that capitalism is 'the utopian project of modern patriarchy'.[454] Yet the influential radical feminist approach to law begins not with a critique of capitalism but with that of Marxism. In its view it is the category 'sex' rather than 'class' which captures the central divide in all societies including capitalist societies. In radical feminism it is 'gender' that prevails in the last instance. The enormous impact of radical feminism has meant

---

[451] Janet Conway, 'Analysing Hegemonic Masculinities in the Anti- Globalization Movement(s)', 13 (2011) *International Feminist Journal of Politics*, pp. 225–230 at p. 227.

[452] See ibid. It has been observed: 'Porto Alegre man is a composite figure, a concatenation of hegemonic and masculinist practices clearly apparent in the Forum ... is overwhelmingly gendered male, heterosexual, light-skinned and of the dominant classes. The appearance of Porto Alegre man can be conceived as a form of hegemonic masculinity that has reappeared regularly in many left movements in the West, in agonistic tension with other emancipatory subjectivities associated with the new left'. See ibid, p. 227.

[453] Slavoz Zizek, 'How to Begin From the Beginning', 57 (2009) *New Left Review*, pp. 43–55 at p. 55.

[454] Claudia von Werlhof, 'No Critique of Capitalism without a Critique of Patriarchy! Why the Left Is No Alternative', 18 (2007) *CNS – Capitalism – Nature – Socialism*, pp. 13–27 at p. 13. She writes: 'The capitalist form of patriarchy is the apex of patriarchal development, of the "evolution" that patriarchy itself has invented. It tries to establish a "pure", "complete" and "eternal" patriarchy as a new paradise, bereft of all matriarchal and natural traces. The intention is to go beyond the world as we know it and to reach an allegedly superior one – by a process of metaphysical "birth giving"'. See ibid.

that a strong element of essentialism informs most feminist approaches to law. It is both their strength as well as their weakness. The appeal of feminist approaches is that they never lose sight of the oppression of women. The weakness is that with the exception of socialist and third world feminisms they are not able to take seriously and integrate the concerns and interests of other subaltern groups. While it is true that radical feminists like MacKinnon have in recent years accepted the need for intersectional analysis, and liberal feminists like Charlesworth and Chinkin are sensitive to different basis of oppression, they have yet to take deep structures seriously. As a result, Charlesworth and Chinkin do not appreciate that the 'logic of capital' is a crucial explanation for why 'to date, the longstanding efforts of women's organizations in the international arena have had little effect on the substance and process of international law'.[455] The absence of an analysis of deep structures also does not allow them to effectively challenge the more positive assessment of the state of women's rights by scholars like MacKinnon. Indeed, international political economy receives almost no attention in the work of Charlesworth and Chinkin reflected among other things in the fact that there is no serious discussion in it of international economic law or international economic institutions. A disembedded institution of patriarchy remains the primary explanation for the inability to bring about serious reform in how international law treats the 'woman question'. While an element of essentialism is in an important sense integral to feminism, contemporary international law cannot be recast unless categories such as class and race are also taken seriously. In the absence of a transnational intersectional framework Charlesworth and Chinkin cannot seriously contest the biases of contemporary international law. Therefore, beyond the 'woman question' their critique of international law and institutions remains largely indistinguishable from that of MILS.

It therefore comes as no surprise that their view of critical approaches such as TWAIL is not very different from MILS. To be sure, Charlesworth and Chinkin draw attention to certain similarities between FtAIL and TWAIL such as their views on the sources doctrine. But the latter's central argument with respect to the historic and continuing relationship between imperialism and international law is ignored in the manner of MILS. Therefore, while Charlesworth and Chinkin recognize the concerns of third world feminisms, the need to critique the liberal economic order is not seen as a necessary response to dealing with the unequal

---

[455] Charlesworth and Chinkin, *Boundaries of international law*, p. 16.

status of women in the Global South. Neither is there any recognition that approaches such as TWAIL which undertake the critique of that order complement the feminist approach. There is the absence of understanding that there are ways of being feminist without donning that identity. It is at least one reason for the phenomenon of 'talking to ourselves' as no dialogue is initiated with approaches such as TWAIL to take the feminist analysis forward. Needless to add, any of these cogitations does not excuse the need for critical approaches like TWAIL to directly address the issue of the exploitation and oppression of women.

Despite the limitations of a liberal feminist approach it has to be acknowledged that Charlesworth and Chinkin advance a fundamental and incisive critique of international law. They demonstrate how both the discipline and substance of international law is structurally biased against the life world and interests of women. What is of particular significance is their analysis of the basic categories (such as state) and doctrines of international law (such as the sources doctrine) show how these are embedded in patriarchal institutions and practices. The liberal (eclectic) feminist critique has had on the whole a positive effect. The discourse of international law has become more inclusive with a practical impact on the framing of international law conventions and the working of international institutions. If anything, Charlesworth and Chinkin underestimate its influence. Thus, for instance, in international bodies ranging from from UNSC to the World Bank there is increasing engagement with gender concerns. There is also an effort to invite women to be part of the governance structures of international institutions. The recognition of this change is important in order to be alert to any attempt by such institutions to use the inclusion of gender concerns to gain legitimacy for their oppressive decisions and policies. As Halley and others note, 'governance feminists' have not been sufficiently sensitive to the intricate processes of co-option leading to complicity with power.[456] Radical and liberal feminists in particular can inadvertently come to participate in violence against subaltern peoples which can range from epistemic violence to the use of force. While this is not the case in the instance of Charlesworth and Chinkin, and their assessment of the progress made in realizing women's rights is not inaccurate, the Halley suggestion of taking a 'break from feminism' is not without merit.

---

[456] Some argue that 'feminism of any hue, like other critical projects, is never outside global political violence'. Marysia Zalewski and Anne Sisson Runyan, 'Taking Feminist Violence Seriously in Feminist International Relation', 15 (2013) *International Feminist Journal of Politics*, pp. 293–313 at p. 310.

This is what socialist feminism does at the level of method in as much as it advances an integrationist vision flowing from a critique of deep structures to work towards the emancipation of all exploited and oppressed groups. The fact that socialist feminism is not averse to transnational intersectional analysis rooted in a critique of capitalism and imperialism also promises a more accurate understanding of the role of contemporary international law and international institutions. However, while socialist feminism has the potential to take into account the concerns of third world feminisms, in practice there is tendency among Western socialist feminists to not theoretically account for the experiences of third world women. It is therefore important to rethink socialist feminism in order to accommodate the insights of postcolonial theory.

There still remains a critical gap that marks the theoretical repertoire of both in as much as both socialist and postcolonial feminisms do not articulate a general theory of law or give an adequate account of the history of patriarchy, that is, the ideologies, laws, institutions and practices that constitute it in different social formations over time. This raises the possibility of integrating socialist feminism with a Marxist theory of law and society. While the former can greatly enrich the latter by reframing its method and sociology it cannot replace it. It is important to stress that integration does not mean giving up on feminism in any way or assigning it a secondary place; both the institutions of patriarchy and capitalism deserve to be examined without subordinating the one to the other. The need for integration merely underscores the fact that socialist and postcolonial feminisms do not have a systematic and comprehensive theory of law and society in the manner of Marxism.

7

Towards an Integrated Marxist Approach to International Law (IMAIL)

I.   Introduction

It is hoped that the critical encounter with different contemporary approaches to international law and world order has helped clarify aspects of an Integrated Materialist Approach to International Law (IMAIL). In the previous chapters an attempt was made to elucidate the IMAIL perspective on a whole range of themes and issues, the keywords being capitalism, imperialism, feminism, anarchism, state, law, nature, human nature, power, morality, national interest, indeterminacy, compliance, civil society, development, world community, world court and world state. The present chapter only discusses subjects that are not dealt with in those chapters but which are critical to the elaboration of IMAIL. These include a Marxist theory of law and international law; a sketch of materialist history of international law from 1600 to the present; the specification of principal features of international law in the era of accelerated globalization; the possibility of reform of contemporary international law; an exposition of a materialist theory of interpretation of rules; the clarification of a materialist approach to human rights; and the identification of principles and propositions that should inform any vision of alternative futures. It is therefore worth reiterating that IMAIL emerges from the book as a whole.

The chapter proceeds as follows. Section II attempts to briefly recapitulate the discussions in the different chapters in relation to the three theories – Marxism, socialist feminism and postcolonial theory – and the five logics viz., the 'logic of capital', the 'logic of territory', the 'logic of nature', the 'logic of culture' and the 'logic of law' that constitute the theoretical framework of IMAIL. The objective of this short section is to merely illustrate the distinctiveness of IMAIL.

Section III outlines a Marxist theory of law in the backdrop of the fact that both socialist feminism and postcolonial theory do not advance a general theory of law. While socialist feminism is primarily focused on

INTRODUCTION   441

the legal status of women, postcolonial approaches to law are preoccupied with the Eurocentric nature and character of legal discourse. Both do not offer a systematic account of legal phenomena. A Marxist theory of law on the other hand offers a general theoretical framework in the matrix of which both the socialist feminist and postcolonial approaches to law can be given greater depth even as the materialist theory of law is immensely enriched by drawing on their insights. The section opens with a critical review of the traditional use of the categories base and superstructure to delineate the place and role of law in society. It elaborates in this context the response of Marx and Engels to the charge of economic determinism, as also that of later writers such as Karl Renner and E. P. Thompson. What emerges from this analysis is a rich materialist understanding of the multidimensional role of law in society, including its constitutive role. Any view of the place and role of international law in the international system cannot lose sight of the intricacies of this analysis, which is complicated further on the international plane by the 'logic of territory'. The latter introduces an independent variable that has had a critical bearing on the evolution and development of international law.

Section IV proceeds to discuss the commodity form theory of law advanced by Evgeny Pashukanis in his classic work *General Theory of Law and Marxism*. It is important to examine the commodity form theory for apart from its intrinsic value in understanding a Marxist theory of law it is relied upon by scholars like China Miéville to articulate a distinctive Marxist approach to international law. It will be argued that while it is the lasting contribution of Pashukanis to have identified the *differentia specifica* of law under capitalism, his commodity form theory suffers from several weaknesses. The two principal deficiencies are that Pashukanis did not embed law and legal relations in the sphere of production as against the sphere of circulation (or exchange) and also failed to appreciate the multivalent role of law in capitalist societies.

Section V, however, goes on to show that when it came to international law Pashukanis took a more composite view of its history, nature and functioning. He not only took into account the form and content of international law over time but also the implications of the 'logic of territory'. The section proceeds to argue that instead of consolidating and taking this holistic approach further Miéville offers a reductionist interpretation of Pashukanis that leads him in the final analysis to embrace legal nihilism. Miéville also does not pay sufficient attention to postcolonial theories that highlight the role of 'legal orientalism' in the evolution and development of international law or take cognizance of feminist approaches to

international law. In view of these lapses his commodity form theory of
international law offers an unsatisfactory account of the history, nature,
structure and process of international law.

Section VI sketches a materialist history of international law from 1600
to 1985. It departs from the mainstream telling of the history of international law in as much as it inter alia traces the evolution of international
law to the 'logic of capital' and its mutually constitutive interface with the
'logic of territory'. The phenomena of colonialism and imperialism are
central to this narration of the history of international law. The history of
the period is considered in four different phases: old colonialism (1500–
1760), new colonialism (1760–1875), imperialism (1875–1945) and neo-
colonialism (1945–1985). The section also notes in passing how TWAIL
scholars have relied on postcolonial theory to challenge the Eurocentric
history of international law, a subject already touched upon in the chapter
on New Approaches to International Law (NAIL).[1]

Section VII looks at international law in the era of globalization or what
may be termed the age of 'global imperialism' (1985–). It stresses the need
for characterizing contemporary international law based on an intersectional understanding of the categories 'class', 'gender' and 'race' and taking
into account the limits of 'logic of territory' in the present era. The section also identifies key features of international law in the present period
that manifest the growing influence of an emerging transnational capitalist class (TCC). It then proceeds to discuss the possibility of reform of
contemporary international law and the value of the idea of 'international
rule of law'. It is argued that the reform of imperial international law is
not only possible within defined limits but that it would be irresponsible
to abandon that project. It is submitted that it is important not to dismiss
the gains, admittedly inadequate, that have been made through using the
language of international law in furthering the rights of subaltern groups,
peoples and nations. The fact that a global revolution against capital is
not on the cards means that the complete rejection of the possibility of
its reform disarms the weak against imperialism. While the dualistic
approach of IMAIL, that is of critique and reform, has family resemblance
to other approaches such the intermediate approach of Richard Falk and
the liberal feminist approach of Charlesworth and Chinkin, its diagnosis
of the problems of contemporary international law is based on a radically
different perspective and therefore has a distinct understanding of what
is possible and the agencies through which change is to be brought about.

---

[1] See Chapter 5, pp. 330–333.

Section VIII offers a prolegomena to a materialist theory of interpretation based on the insights of Ludwig Wittgenstein, Hans Georg Gadamer and Jürgen Habermas that can be used to sustain the idea of 'international rule of law'. This section consolidates and takes forward the discussion on legal interpretation in Chapters 3 and 7 in which a critique of the strong indeterminacy thesis of McDougal-Lasswell and Kennedy-Koskenniemi was advanced. It is strongly recommended that this section be read along with earlier cogitations on the subject.

Section IX advances a first take on a Marxist approach to human rights. This is necessitated by among other things the fact that the language of rights has today become central to much progressive discourse on international law. The brief discussion in the section seeks to dispel the impression that Marx or Marxists are opposed to the idea of human rights. In fact it suggests that Marxists recognize that the language of rights, include the right to free and fair elections, has been able to secure real gains for exploited, marginal and oppressed groups. But at the same time Marxists also recognize that at both the domestic and international levels the vocabulary of rights can advance and legitimize the actions of powerful social actors. In other words, international human rights law like international law in general has a dual character, i.e., it helps the weak to bring about progressive change but also advances the interests of the strong. In this light it would be productive to read this section along with the discussion on rights of women in the chapter on feminist approaches to international law.

Section X concludes the chapter and the book by raising the question whether despite the troubling record of 'actually existing socialism' the idea of 'socialism' is still worth preserving. It is proposed that in thinking about alternative futures the human imagination cannot be limited by any particular model. The section instead identifies a set of 'principles' or propositions that must inform any reflection on alternative futures. These principles include a non-negotiable commitment to democratic forms of governance and the tenet of non-violence.

II.   One Theory, Two Others and Five Logics

It is a truism to state that all approaches to international law and world order have a certain explanatory power. Those considered in this volume are no different. However, these approaches either offer a fractional understanding of an increasingly complex world of international law and international politics (and may even valorize that feature) or like the

policy-oriented approach offer a comprehensive theory of international
law and world order without a commensurate explanatory system. It is
believed that in contrast IMAIL has the potential of offering a systematic
and comprehensive account of international law and world order embedded in apposite epistemological and ontological premises and methods.
An integrated approach is articulated on the assumption that Marxists
often tend to assign too much explanatory power to some variables like
the 'logic of capital' and the accompanying category of 'class'. While the
weakness can often be traced to the misinterpretation and misapplication
of Marxism, there are also certain conceptual and theoretical gaps that
can be filled only by turning to other theoretical traditions. But, for such
an eclectic enterprise to be sound, there must be a degree of compatibility
between the different strands of theory brought together. In this context,
IMAIL makes a distinction between simply using insights from different theoretical traditions and literature (as it does in the case of a theory
of meaning) and an integrated eclectic theory that seeks the systematic
incorporation of some central elements of other theoretical traditions. In
the latter instance the compatibility test has to be met. That is the claim
of IMAIL with reference to postcolonial theory and socialist feminism or
more accurately *certain interpretations of both*. It is believed that particular interpretations of these theoretical traditions are sufficiently aligned
with non-dogmatic Marxism to constitute an integrated theory that has
greater salience in explaining and understanding international law.[2] These
traditions allow IMAIL to suitably complement or amend Marxist propositions without abandoning some of its core tenets. But IMAIL is not, it is
worth emphasizing, the result of a merger of these theoretical traditions.
It merely absorbs some central insights of postcolonial theory and socialist feminism that go to enhance the explanatory power of Marxism.

   Thus, for instance, what appeals in postcolonial theory is that it denies
the 'universal status of the European experience'.[3] It makes the uncontest-
able point that it is no longer acceptable to do social sciences in complete
ignorance of non-Western societies and their accumulated experiences.[4]
The significance of postcolonial theory becomes evident when it is

[2] See Chapter 1, pp. 18–30.
[3] Ranajit Guha, 'Introduction' in Ranajit Guha (ed.) *A Subaltern Studies Reader 1986–1995*
   (New Delhi: Oxford University Press, 1997), pp. ix–xxii at p. xxi.
[4] Dipesh Chakrabarty, 'Postcoloniality and the Artifice of History: Who Speaks for "Indian"
   Pasts?' in Ranajit Guha (ed.) *A Subaltern Studies Reader 1986–1995* (New Delhi: Oxford
   University Press, 1997), pp. 263–294 at p. 265.

considered that most of the approaches considered in the volume have, with the possible exception of Richard Falk's WOMP, little to say about the non-Western world or how its experiences bear upon the understanding of the structure and process of international law. Morgenthau and McDougal-Lasswell rarely engaged with the history and concerns of the Global South. While Charlesworth and Chinkin do speak of the need to take on board the insights of third world feminism this sentiment is not adequately reflected in their work. Kennedy and Koskenniemi, at least to begin with, entirely missed out on the central significance of colonialism and imperialism in the evolution and development of international law. Even Marxist scholars like Miéville have little familiarity with or understanding of the non-Western world influencing their understanding of the character of contemporary international law and possibilities of reform. Indeed, it is the coming together of Marxism and postcolonial theory that in a critical way distinguishes IMAIL from other Marxist approaches to international law (MAIL). However, while postcolonial theory is crucial to correct the neglect of the history and experiences of the non-Western world it often overlooks, as was pointed out in Chapter 1, the implications of the fact that the Global North and the Global South have since the sixteenth century been subject to the forces of universalizing capitalism and therefore their histories intersect in significant ways.[5] It is the weakness of postcolonial theory that it does not examine the meaning and implications of the political economy of globalizing capitalism; it remains essentially confined to the 'logic of culture'.[6] To put it differently, while the insights of postcolonial theory are crucial to developing an approach to international law that reflects realities of the Global South it has to be combined with Marxist theory and sociology to escape being one-dimensional.

Insofar as socialist feminism is concerned, it reminds Marxists of the critical and complex relationship between capitalism and patriarchy.[7] The integration of the Marxist and socialist feminist traditions helps understand among other things the ways in which the categories 'gender' and 'class' interface and intersect and thereby explain in a more comprehensive manner the oppressive character of modern international

---

[5] Vivek Chibber, *Post Colonial Theory and the Specter of Capital* (New Delhi: Navayana Publishing Pvt. Ltd, 2013), p. 291; emphasis in original.

[6] See Chapter 1, pp. 27–28.

[7] See generally Johanna Brenner, 'Intersections, Locations, and Capitalist Class Relations: Intersectionality from a Marxist Perspective' in Nancy Holmstrom (ed.) *The Socialist Feminist Project: A Contemporary Reader in Theory and Politics* (Delhi: Aakar, 2011), pp. 336–348.

law. Among the approaches examined in the volume the classical realist approach does not address the issue of gender at all, while the others do so in varying degrees, with individual scholars like Koskenniemi neglecting it altogether. While absorbing the insights of socialist feminism, IMAIL proposes the adoption of a contextual method in understanding its bearing on practice. The recognition that the categories 'gender' and 'class' together allow a superior understanding of different international law regimes or situations goes along with the determination that any one of these may offer greater purchase in particular contexts. A contextual approach to socialist feminism involves, first, the acknowledgement that women's oppression is 'multicausal in origin and mediated through a variety of different structures, mechanism, and levels, which may vary across space and time'.[8] In the circumstances there is no unique way of redressing its diverse expressions. Second, the contextual view employs the insight of Wittgenstein's use theory of meaning to show how in real life situations 'gender' and 'class' oppression can be resisted by avoiding assigning a priori priority to either of them. In the same way as the meaning of a word is its use in the language the role of social categories such as 'class' or 'gender' have to be understood in the context of particular situations which are the subject of specific discursive and material practices.

An essential point that both postcolonialism and socialist feminism make in different ways and IMAIL recognizes is that distinct forms of oppression cannot be subsumed under the single category 'class'. Any such attempt tends to blur their distinctive nature, dynamics and histories. The issue may be illustrated with reference to how Marxists in India tend to equate caste oppression with class oppression. In an essay on the subject, Sudipta Kaviraj draws on postcolonial theory to point out that 'the Marxist error of transposing class for caste' can be traced to the tendency of employing categories 'that resulted from a distillation of the historical experience of the modern West'.[9] The result has been an inability to appreciate the specificities of caste oppression. Kaviraj distinguishes in this context between a theory that deploy categories that are 'contextless-universal' from 'a contextual theory of political persuasion'.[10] In the

---

[8] Maxine Molyneux, 'Conceptualizing Women's Interests' in Nancy Holmstrom (ed.) *The Socialist Feminist Project: A Contemporary Reader in Theory and Politics* (Delhi: Aakar, 2011), pp. 250–257 at p. 250.

[9] Sudipta Kaviraj, 'Marxism in Translation: Critical Reflections on Radical Indian Thought' in Richard Rourke and Raymond Guess (eds.) *Political Judgment: Essays for John Dunn* (Cambridge: Cambridge University Press, 2009), pp. 172–201 at pp. 188–189.

[10] See ibid., p. 178.

latter case 'the persuasiveness of political theory owes something to its alignment with social experience' and is expressive of a case of weak universalism.[11] In his view, while Marx understood the need for turning to specific social experiences Marxists are prone to treat the category 'class' as a catch-all category that captures all oppressive social practices. In the process it is overlooked that Marx used the term category 'class' in different ways to indicate the absence of egalitarian practices.[12] On the other hand, there is a view which represents a mirror image of the dogmatic Marxist view, that is, that caste structure and oppression are unique and cannot be captured in any way by the category 'class'.[13] In order to transcend the binary responses Kaviraj uses the term '*composition* (or *collocation*)' which 'is not exhausted by a simple registration of diversity, which would imply the nonexistence of any broad framework capable of holding the segments together'.[14] The claim of IMAIL is that it can hold the fragments together by enabling a focus on both the particular and the universal and the interrelationship between the two. The specificities of the particular are in this scheme of things the function of contextual social and political theory and judgment.

The international social, political and legal realities that IMAIL seeks to explain and understand also turns on integrating different logics that constitute world order. These are the 'logic of capital', 'logic of territory', 'logic of culture', 'logic of nature' and the 'logic of law'. The different approaches to international law and world order that have been considered in the volume either make no attempt to do so or are not able to adequately conceptualize the relationship between these five logics. It was seen for instance that classical realists like Hans Morgenthau assign primacy to the 'logic of territory' disregarding the 'logic of capital' in understanding international politics and international law. As a result Morgenthau misconstrued, among other things, the meaning and essence of imperialism and its intimate relationship to the evolution and development of international law. In contrast to the realist approach, the New Haven approach potentially takes on board all five logics, but in the matrix of

---

[11] See ibid., pp. 179, 182ff.

[12] See ibid., pp 184ff.

[13] See ibid., p. 193. Kaviraj writes that 'the Marxist tradition had to note the factual existence of caste as social practice, but subsumed it as a relatively minor part of a general class analysis. Ambedkar, the pre-eminent intellectual of caste liberation in modern India, subsumed class into an analysis which asserted the analytical primacy of caste structures'. See ibid., p. 197.

[14] See ibid., p. 194.

a social theory that fails to assign relative primacy to any logic even in particular contexts. It ends up identifying endless variables and collating enormous amounts of information that can easily be manipulated to serve a parochial outlook. Richard Falk's WOMP also addresses all five logics but in the final analysis mistakenly assigns primacy to the 'logic of territory'. Therefore, Falk is unable to sufficiently appreciate that it is the 'logic of capital' and not the state or states system that principally accounts for the different crises that afflict the current world order. The imperative is to consider both together. Hilary Charlesworth and Christine Chinkin ignore the 'logic of capital' altogether leading to a form of gender determinism. Kennedy and Koskenniemi are focused more on aspects of the 'logic of culture', albeit of late they have also addressed the 'logic of capital'. But in the case of Kennedy using methodological individualism which does not permit serious engagement with the essence and workings of global capitalism. It primarily allows the study of political economy of issues in the middle range. On the other hand, Koskenniemi is confined to the historical study of the 'empire of private rights' without considering its implications for the present world order. In contrast to these approaches IMAIL seeks to assimilate the working of all five logics as these intersect and co-constitute each other over time, assigning relative primacy to the 'logic of capital'.

A word may be said on the extent to which the different approaches take into account logics other than the 'logic of capital'. It is not surprising that nearly all the approaches dealt with consider the significance of 'logic of territory' as it is certainly central to any understanding of international law and world order. However, as in the case of the 'logic of capital', different significance is attached to it with Morgenthau and Falk treating the 'logic of territory' as the determining logic in the working of international politics and international law.

The 'logic of culture' also receives the attention of all approaches but these engage with different elements that are also distinctly conceptualized and assigned varying significance. Nearly all the approaches deal with the relationship of language and law. This relationship is most often considered in the context of interpretation of rules but also in terms of how language constructs reality. Yet most of the approaches do not explicitly elaborate theories of language and communication that supports their view of interpretation of rules. The New Haven approach is an exception in this regard using a behaviourial theory of language and communication to advance its approach to interpretation of rules. While NAIL too speaks of theories of language or linguistic theories it does not always explicitly clarify these or the uses to which they are put. On its part IMAIL uses the work of Ludwig Wittgenstein to advance its approach to interpretation supported by insights drawn from the work of Hans Gadamer and Jürgen Habermas.

Finally, most of the approaches, with the honourable exception of WOMP, do not seriously grapple with the 'logic of nature'. This is an important omission as the 'logic of nature' has a significant bearing on the working of all other logics.

In sum, the different approaches examined in the present volume either do not address the different logics at play in the shaping of international politics and international law or do not effectively do so, especially as these treat the 'logic of capital' at best as simply one factor to be taken into account. In contrast, IMAIL not only takes account of all the logics at play but also assigns the 'logic of capital' relative primacy as it critically influences the meaning and working of other logics. It rejects the charge of economic determinism as it proceeds on the assumption that the different logics co-constitute each other, albeit within the boundaries drawn by the 'logic of capital'. IMAIL thus conceives the structure and process of international law 'as a rich totality of many determinations and relations' that flow from the working of the different logics.[15] This view has its roots in materialist theory of law to which the chapter now turns.

III. Towards a Marxist Theory of Law

A. On Base and Superstructure

Marx summed up the materialist conception of history in an oft quoted passage from his preface to *A Contribution to the Critique of Political Economy*:

> In the social production of their existence, men inevitably enter into definite relations, which are independent of their will, namely relations of production appropriate to a given stage in the development of their material forces of production. The totality of these relations of production constitutes the economic structure of society, the real foundation, on which arises a legal and political superstructure and to which correspond definite forms of social consciousness. The mode of production of material life conditions the general process of social, political and intellectual life. It is

---

[15] Karl Marx, *Grundrisse: Introduction to the Critique of Political Economy* Translated with a Foreword by Martin Nicolaus (Hammondsworth: Penguin Books, 1973), p. 100.

not the consciousness of men that determines their existence, but their
social existence that determines their consciousness.[16]

This particular conception of history, with its use of the categories 'economic structure' and 'superstructure' invited even in the lifetime of Marx
and Engels the charge of economic determinism. In response they clarified the limits of a functionalist understanding of the evolution and development of the spheres of ideology, law and state. In a letter to J. Bloch,
Engels explained that:

> According to the materialist conception of history, the ultimately determin-
> ing element in history is the production and reproduction of real life. More
> than this neither Marx nor I have ever asserted. Hence if somebody twists
> this into saying that the economic element is the only determining one, he
> transforms the proposition into a meaningless, abstract, senseless phrase.[17]

He went on to note that base-superstructure imagery captured a static
view of their relationship, eliminating the element of dynamism that characterized lived history.[18]

The substantive points made by Marx and Engels against the charge
of economic determinism in several of their pronouncements on the the
legal sphere deserve some elaboration as these have a crucial bearing on
the articulation and understanding of a Marxist theory of law. First, Marx
pointed out that law is not simply a reflection of the economic structure
of society but is also in many instances constitutive of relations of production. In the very *Preface* in which the categories base and superstructure appear, Marx observes that property relations are the expression in
legal terms of existing relations of production.[19] Thus, according to the
Soviet scholar Evgeny Pashukanis, 'Marx himself emphasizes the fact
that the basic and most deeply set stratum of the legal superstructure –
property relationships – is so closely contiguous with the base that they
are "the same relationships of production expressed in legal language".[20]
The Austro-Marxist Karl Renner went further and noted that 'all economic institutions are at the same time institutions of the law' in the sense

---

[16] Karl Marx, *A Contribution to the Critique of Political Economy* (Moscow: Progress
Publishers, 1984), pp. 20–21.

[17] Karl Marx and Frederick Engels, *Selected Works*, vol. 3 (Moscow: Progress Publishers,
1977), pp. 487 and 488.

[18] See ibid., p. 488.

[19] Marx, *Contribution to the Critique*, p. 21.

[20] *Pashukanis: Selected Writings on Marxism and Law*, Piers Beirne and Robert Sharlet (eds.)
(New York: Academic Press, 1980) translated by Peter B. Maggs, p. 66. Downloaded from
http://libgen.io/book/index.php?md5=FF64C75F8EE84134E07CEE8306C21964.

that these are 'performed within definite legal conditions'.[21] The British Marxist E. P. Thompson has observed that 'productive relations themselves are, in part, only meaningful in terms of their definitions at law'.[22] In other words, it is only in the static conceptual world that production relations *precede* legal relations. In the real world the two often arrive together and are mutually constitutive of the other. Duncan Kennedy goes so far as to observe that in Marx 'legal concepts are built into the base itself'.[23] To be sure, there are contrary voices within the Marxist tradition itself. According to G. A. Cohen, if Marx adopted a legal language it is only because 'ordinary language lacks a developed apparatus for describing production relations in a *rechtsfrei* manner'.[24] But as Steven Lukes points out in response a *rechtsfrei* description may not be possible at all. For instance, as he goes on to explain, 'the performance of contractual obligations is normally described in a vocabulary (paying wages, supplying services, buying and selling, honouring debts) which *already presupposes* the institution of contract and its regulating norms, as well as a whole network of supporting informal norms'.[25] Therefore, 'one cannot identify the powers and constraints embodied in norm-governed economic relationships independently of the norms which, in both senses, govern them'.[26] Thus, production relations and legal relations co-constitute each other.

Second, Marx and Engels made the crucial point that emerging economic structures can use old legal concepts and categories to embed new social relations showing that there need not be a historical correspondence between the two. In this regard, they made reference to Roman law observing that it was in considerable advance of its times allowing the emerging bourgeoisie centuries later to use 'old legal forms and invest

[21] Karl Renner, *The Institutions of Private Law and their Social Functions* (London: Routledge and Kegan Paul, 1976), p. 5. It may be noted that Renner was a positivist. In his view 'a legal institution is a composite of norms'. See ibid., p. 75.

[22] E. P. Thompson, *Whigs and Hunters: The Origin of the Black Act* (London: Penguin Books, 1977), p. 267.

[23] Duncan Kennedy, 'The Role of Law in Economic Thought: Essays on the Fetishism of Commodities', 34 (1985) *The American University Law Review*, pp. 939–1001 at p. 993. Indeed, Kennedy goes on to write that 'if economic determinism is supposed to mean that economics determines society and culture, then to make Marx an economic determinist we have to exclude legal consciousness from culture, since a particular form of legal consciousness is an aspect of the economic base'. See ibid.

[24] G. A. Cohen, *Karl Marx's Theory of History* (Oxford: Clarendon Press, 1978), p. 224. See also pp. 235, 225, 217–218.

[25] Steven Lukes, 'Can the Base be Distinguished from the Superstructure?', 4 (1982) *Analyse and Kritik*, pp. 211–222 at p. 229.

[26] See ibid., p. 230.

(...) them with new commercial content'.[27] Marx even noted the need to explore the methodological implications of this historical development by observing that 'the really difficult point to be discussed here, however, is how the relations of production as relations of law enter into, a disparate development'.[28] As Engels pointed out, this meant that society may retain elements of 'the old feudal laws while giving them a bourgeois content'[29] or draft a new code based on earlier concepts as Western Continental Europe did using Roman law. These developments showed that legal concepts and categories possess a certain independence from the economic structure of society.

Third, Engels emphasized that in the lived world law 'reacts ... upon the economic basis and may, within certain limits, modify it'.[30] This observation can be understood to suggest that law can doubly shape the economic structure of society, that is, by constituting it in the first place and then impacting it in the process of historical interaction. As Engels observed, critics 'often almost deliberately forget that once an historic element has been brought into the world by other, ultimately economic causes, it reacts, can react on its environment and even on the causes that have given rise to it'.[31] He reiterated this view at another place noting that elements of the superstructure 'react upon one another and also upon the economic basis. It is not that the economic situation is *cause, solely active*, while everything is passive effect'.[32] Thus, according to Engels, critics were positing an 'undialectical conception of cause and effect' presenting them

---

[27] Michael E. Tigar and Madeline R. Levy, *Law and the Rise of Capitalism* (New York: Monthly Review Press, 1977), p. 6. Indeed, Engels wrote: 'If the state and public law are determined by economic relations, so, too of course is private law ... The form in which this happens can, however, vary considerably. It is possible, as happened in England, in harmony with the whole national development, to retain in the main the forms of the old feudal laws while giving them a bourgeois content; in fact, directly reading a bourgeois meaning into a feudal name. But, also, as happened in western continental Europe, Roman Law, the first world law of a commodity-producing society, with its unsurpassably fine elaboration of all essential legal relations of simple commodity owners (of buyers and sellers, debtors and creditors, contracts, obligations, etc.), can be taken as the foundation.' Marx and Engels, *Selected Works*, vol. 3, p. 370. See also Marx, *Grundrisse*, pp. 245–246. Karl Marx and Friedrich Engels, *Pre-Capitalist Socio-Economic Formations: A Collection* (Moscow: Progress Publishers, 1979), p. 467.

[28] Cited in *Lloyd's Introduction to Jurisprudence*, 5th edn (London: Stevens and Sons, 1985), p. 1066.

[29] Marx and Engels, *Selected Works*, vol. 3, p. 370.

[30] See ibid., p. 493.

[31] See ibid., p. 497.

[32] See ibid., p. 502; emphasis in original.

'as rigid opposite poles' to the 'the total disregarding of interaction'.[33] Instead, Engels referred readers to those writings of Marx that were concerned with 'history' as opposed to the conceptual scaffold[34] in which the 'interaction' between economic structure and superstructure was seen in full view. These writings include Marx's *Capital* in which 'the section on the working day' shows how legislation 'has such a trenchant effect'[35] on relations of production.

Fourth, Engels made the significant point that 'in a modern state, law must not only correspond to the general economic condition and be its expression, but must also be an *internally coherent* expression which does not, owing to inner contradiction, reduce itself to nought. In order to achieve this, the faithful reflection of economic conditions suffers increasingly'.[36] He went on to explain that this was because 'rarely it happens that a code of law is the blunt, unmitigated, unadulterated expression of the domination of a class – this in itself would offend the "conception of right"'.[37] In fact Engels admitted that in speaking of some elements as that belonging to the superstructure 'we [i.e., he and Marx] neglected the formal side – the ways and means by which these notions, etc., come about – for the sake of the content'.[38] In other words, law has its own form, internal logic, dynamics and integrity, that is, its own laws of motion. Thus, for instance, to secure the legitimacy of judicial determinations these are arrived at on the basis of accepted doctrines and modes of interpretation.

Fifth, Marx and Engels recognized the importance of the legal profession in shaping of laws and the legal system. Since legal norms in capitalist societies tend to have a general and abstract character the legal profession is in a position to influence the application of laws.[39] That is to say, the general and abstract character of laws (relating for instance to contract, property or labour rights) leave sufficient space for creative interpretations,

---

[33] See ibid., p. 497. Engels writes that the critics lack dialectics: 'They always see only here cause, there effect. That this is a hollow abstraction, that such metaphysical polar opposites exist in the real world only during crisis, while the whole vast process goes on in the form of interaction – though of very unequal forces, the economic movement being by far the strongest, most primordial, most decisive – that here everything is relative and nothing absolute – this they never begin to see. As far as they are concerned Hegel never existed'. See ibid., p. 495.

[34] See ibid., p. 487. At another place he observes that 'economic necessity [...]ultimately asserts itself'. See ibid., p. 502.

[35] See ibid., p. 494.

[36] See ibid., p. 492.

[37] See ibid.

[38] See ibid., p. 496.

[39] See ibid., pp. 492ff.

albeit using accepted procedures of interpretation. This view is in accord with the Kennedy observation that at the moment of legal determination 'there is neither a built-in limit to how far concessions can go, nor an inevitable process of unraveling if they go too far'.[40] Therefore, the ecology, tradition and ethics of the legal profession constitute a legal culture that has a significant bearing on the autonomy of the legal system.

Sixth, Marx and Engels not only understood that legal reforms were possible but recognized their importance both in terms of bringing relief to the working class and the functioning of the capitalist system. For instance, in *Capital* Marx recorded the struggles over establishing an eight-hour workday observing that 'the establishment of a normal working-day is the result of centuries of struggle between capitalist and labourer'.[41] The effort he spent on recording the struggle and changes show that Marx never underestimated struggles undertaken to reform the law, albeit he did caution that its outcome had to be carefully assessed.

Despite these observations of Marx and Engels the base-superstructure metaphor continues to be seized by critics even today to contend that Marxism views laws and legal institutions as mere epiphenomena.[42] This could not be farther from truth. Both Marx and Engels assigned a complex role to the legal sphere. Their insights have been further developed by later writers to contend that the legal sphere possesses 'relative autonomy' from the 'economic structure' of society, albeit the meaning and extent of autonomy has been debated. It is useful in this regard to discuss the standpoint of two writers, that is, Karl Renner and E. P. Thompson who went further than others in positing the independence of the legal sphere.

---

[40] See Kennedy, 'Role of Law', p. 998.

[41] Karl Marx, *Capital: A Critique of Political Economy*, vol. 3 (Moscow: Progress Publishers, 1977), p. 257. Marx also wrote: 'For "protection" against "the serpent of their agonies", the labourers must put their heads together, and, as a class, compel the passing of a law, an all-powerful social barrier that shall prevent the very workers from selling, by voluntary contract with capital, themselves and their families into slavery and death. In place of the pompous catalogue of the "inalienable rights of man" comes the modest Magna Carta of a legally limited working-day, which shall make clear when the time which the worker sells is ended, and when his own begins.' See ibid., pp. 285–286.

[42] Geoffrey M. Hodgson, 'The Enforcement of Contracts and Property Rights: Constitutive versus Epiphenomenal Conceptions of Law', 13 (2003) *International Review of Sociology*, pp. 373–389 at p. 373. Others aver that 'there is no Marxist theory of law'. Hugh Collins, *Marxism and Law* (Oxford: Clarendon Press, 1982), p. 9. The interest in law is 'tangential to a predominant focus on the general mode of social organization and the material circumstances in which men are placed'. See ibid. Therefore, 'the nature of legal institutions themselves remains an unexplored terrain'. See ibid.

B. *The Views of Karl Renner*

In the first decades of the twentieth century Renner and his compatri-ots Otto Bauer, Max Adler and Rudolf Hilferding worked out a modified theory of state and law which is subsumed under the name of Austro-Marxism.[43] They pleaded for the development of Marxism under already changed conditions. In a series of articles entitled 'Problems of Marxism' published in 1916 Renner argued that 'capitalist society as Marx experi-enced and described it, no longer exists!'.[44] It had been transformed with the increased concentration of capital and the 'state penetration' of the economy.[45] The growing role of the state in particular had led to the social-ization of the capitalist economy in a manner Marx had not anticipated. Renner wrote that '*laissez faire* capitalism has changed into state capital-ism or is well on the road to doing so'.[46] This transformation took place without introducing a new legal system. Renner believed that this was unnecessary. He made the following three acute observations on the sub-ject of 'base' and 'superstructure' in his well-known work *The Institutions of Private Law and Their Social Functions*. First, Renner clarified that the categories 'substructure and 'superstructure' are mere 'metaphors' which 'serve only to illustrate the connection, not to define it in exact terms'.[47] Second, he noted that 'development by leaps and bounds is unknown in the social substratum, which knows evolution only, not revolution'.[48] It was no different in the case of the legal superstructure. Third, he pointed to the historical experience that 'economic change does not immediately and automatically bring about changes in the law'.[49] The social function of law can therefore undergo change 'unaccompanied by a juridical change of the legal institution'.[50] In other words, 'fundamental changes in society are possible without accompanying alterations of the legal system'.[51] Indeed, Renner described law as an 'empty frame, a vessel without content'.[52] In

[43] See Tom Bottomore and Goode Patrick (eds.), *Austro-Marxism* (Oxford: Clarendon Press, 1978).
[44] Karl Renner, "Problems of Marxism" in Tom Bottomore and Goode Patrick (eds.) *Austro-Marxism* (Oxford: Clarendon Press, 1978), p. 93.
[45] See ibid., p. 96.
[46] See ibid., p. 100.
[47] Renner, *Institutions of Private Law*, p. 55.
[48] Ibid., p. 253; emphasis dropped.
[49] See ibid; emphasis dropped.
[50] See ibid; emphasis dropped.
[51] See ibid., p. 252; emphasis dropped.
[52] See ibid., p. 217.

the context of his times he argued that laws can remain constant and yet a revolution can be brought about.[53] To sustain this view Renner traced the history of the legal institution of private property from simple commodity production to the joint stock company to demonstrate that although the social functions performed by the institution of property had undergone transformation there was no corresponding change in legal norms. In fact, he went on to contend that the construction of a socialist society could be worked out from within the 'neutral frame of law' and a peaceful transition to socialism was distinctly possible. What was needed was, in the words of Tom Bottomore, 'a more constructive extension of the welfare functions of the state and of the rational organization of the economy under a regime of public ownership'.[54]

Renner's view on the autonomy of the legal sphere is important for three reasons. First, he sustains it with historical evidence and draws methodological conclusions that Marx had only hinted at in noting the divergence between economic and legal developments. Renner is able to, in the words of Eugene Kamenka, 'recognize both continuity and change in law and to explain conceptually how this is possible'.[55] Second, Renner demonstrates the possibility of 'a gradual and peaceful transition to socialism'[56] through sustained struggle of the exploited and oppressed classes.[57] The strategy of peaceful transition to 'socialism' is of immense significance as the idea of bringing about social transformation through violent means is increasingly discredited. Third, Renner helps underscore the untenable position of those left critics who reject the prospect of reform of law. Of course, Renner can be the subject of critique from the radical left for having given up the idea of revolution. But the question of revolution, both its necessity and viability, is a matter of historical

---

[53] See ibid., pp. 252ff.
[54] Tom Bottomore, 'Introduction' in Tom Bottomore and Goode Patrick (eds.), *Austro-Marxism* (Oxford: Clarendon Press, 1978), p. 26.
[55] See ibid.
[56] See ibid, p. 28.
[57] He along with his other compatriots: 'argued consistently in favour of peaceful change, brought about with the declared support of a majority of the population and on the basis of a social and economic structure which had already evolved socialism a result of the developmental tendencies of modern capitalism itself and the cumulative effects of the reforms in institutions and policies achieved by the working-class movement. But at the same time they recognised that the class struggle could always erupt in violent forms, because of the extreme readiness of dominant groups and classes to resort to violence in defence of their privileges; and they also insisted, therefore, that the working class had to be prepared, in such conditions, to defend by force its own gains and its prospective attainment of socialism'. See ibid., p. 43.

assessment. What the Austro-Marxists were prescribing was an attractive 'combination of reformist and revolutionary action'.[58] Renner was 'occupying a place precisely between Bolshevism and reformism', a position that has some appeal to sections of the left after the travails of 'actually existing socialism'.[59]

C.   E. P. Thompson and Rule of Law

In more recent times, the intervention of the English historian E. P. Thompson has been significant in thinking about the limits of autonomy of the legal sphere. In his well-known work *Whigs and Hunters*, based on a study of the history of eighteenth-century England, Thompson made a number of observations on law that deserve consideration. First, according to Thompson, law 'has its own characteristics, its own independent history and logic of evolution'.[60] Second, Thompson stressed that 'the essential precondition for the effectiveness of law, in its function as ideology, is that it shall display an independence from gross manipulation and shall seem to be just. It cannot be seen to so without upholding its own logic and criteria of equity; indeed, on occasion by actually *being* just'.[61] In his view, 'if the law is evidently partial and unjust, then it will mask nothing, legitimize nothing, contribute nothing to any class's hegemony'.[62] Third, Thompson noted that the reductionist view 'overlooks ... the immense capital of human struggle ... inherited, in the forms and traditions of the law'.[63] Law 'has not only been imposed *upon* men from above: it has also been a medium within which other social conflicts have been fought out'.[64] Fourth, he pointed out that there is a need to understand the difference 'between extra-legal power and the rule of law'. Thompson exhorted the left to recognize that law imposed serious constraints on the actions of

---

[58] See ibid., p. 38.

[59] See ibid., p. 44.

[60] Thompson, *Whigs and Hunters*, p. 262.

[61] See ibid; emphasis in original.

[62] See ibid., p. 263. In the words of Balbus, 'the autonomy of the Law from the preferences of even the most powerful social actors (the members of the capitalist class) is not an obstacle to, but rather a prerequisite for, the capacity of the Law to contribute to the reproduction of the overall conditions that make capitalism possible, and thus its capacity to serve the interests of capital as a class'. Isaac D. Balbus, 'Commodity Form and Legal Form: An Essay on the "Relative Autonomy" of the Law', 11 (1977) *Law & Society Review*, pp. 577–588 at p. 585.

[63] Thompson, *Whigs and Hunters*, p. 264.

[64] See ibid., p. 267; emphasis in original.

ruling classes, at least in part because the ruling classes themselves came to believe in the rule of law.[65] Fifth, he pointed out that while law 'can be seen to mediate and to legitimise class relations',[66] 'this is not the same thing as saying that the law was no more than those relations translated into other terms, which masked or mystified the reality. This may, quite often, be true but it is *not the whole truth*'.[67] The rule of law is not merely 'another mask for the rule of a class';[68] the relationship is 'a complex and contradictory one'.[69] Therefore it can be said that the idea of 'the regulation and reconciliation of conflicts through the rule of law' is 'a cultural achievement of universal significance'.[70] Thompson concluded that:

> We ought to expose the shams and inequities which may be concealed beneath this law. But the rule of law itself, the imposing of effective inhibitions upon power and the defence of the citizen from power's all-intrusive claims, seems to me to be *an unqualified human good*.[71]

In describing rule of law as 'an unqualified human good' Thompson may have gone too far ignoring the fact that in capitalist societies law and legal ideology justify all forms of violence against the subaltern classes.[72] Law also plays an ideological role in as much as it represents the phenomenal form of actual relations and projects the interests of the capitalist classes as universal interests. But Thompson was entirely right in suggesting that the left should not be dismissive of the idea of rule of law. The truth of this statement can be testified to by millions of people living under authoritarian rule who have no remedy against actions that deprive individuals of their life and liberty. And as will be discussed later in the chapter Marx was never dismissive of the language of rights.[73]

D.   *The Relative Autonomy of Law: Meaning and Limits*

In concluding this section it may be useful to schematically identify the propositions on the autonomy of the legal sphere that emerge from the ruminations of Marx and Engels and others on the categories 'economic

[65] See ibid., p. 263.
[66] See ibid., p. 266.
[67] See ibid., p. 262; emphasis added.
[68] See ibid., p. 259.
[69] See ibid., p. 264.
[70] See ibid., p. 265.
[71] See ibid., p. 266; emphasis added.
[72] Collins, *Marxism and Law*, p. 144.
[73] See infra pp. 534–543.

structure' and 'superstructure'. These are as follows: (i) law can be both constitutive of economic structure of society (i.e., its property relations) and its legal expression; (ii) there is an active and dialectical interaction between the categories 'economic structure' and different elements of the 'superstructure'; (iii) an advanced social formation can use legal categories developed earlier as was the case with concepts and categories of Roman law serving capitalism; (iv) a legal system has its own internal logic and dynamics whose neglect can undermine its coherence and legitimacy; (v) the legal profession, the judiciary and 'legal culture' have an important role to play in the shaping of the law and legal system; (vi) the notion of rule of law represents an important achievement of human society even as the outcomes of its workings is biased against the subordinate groups in class societies; (vii) law and legal institutions can be reformed through peaceful struggles to benefit the exploited and oppressed classes; and (viii) a combination of reformist and revolutionary methods, including using the growing powers of the state and its interventions, can make possible a peaceful transition to 'socialism', a process that does not rule out 'defensive violence'.[74] In sum, the extent of autonomy of the legal sphere from the interest of the ruling classes is determined by a range of factors which include the character of the state, the nature and history of the legal system, the traditions and culture of the legal profession, the particular law or legal institution that is the subject of assessment, and the interrelationship between different dimensions of the superstructure and their combined interaction with the economic structure of society. Further, the moment of autonomy does not arrive only after it has been constituted by the economic structure of society; it is a function of the fact that the economic and legal spheres mutually constitute each other even as these also possess distinct identities and properties. The inelegant term co-constituting captures the relationship between economic structure of society and law.

But critics point out that the term 'relative autonomy' used to describe the nature of independence of the legal system from the economic structure of society lacks specificity. It is not capable of being falsified. That is to say, the extent of autonomy that is possible within a social formation cannot be identified with any precision.[75] But Alan Hunt who

---

[74] Bottomore, 'Introduction', p. 40.
[75] As Alan Hunt observes: 'The theoretical deficiency of the concept relative autonomy is that unless it is capable of being linked to some account which specifies the boundaries or limitation of autonomy it can only be understood as constantly running the danger of lapsing into the assertion of either autonomy or determinism coupled with an expression of faith

makes this point hastens to add that the alternative is not 'a naïve empiricism in which every situation is uniquely the result of the specific causal factors'.[76] While an empirical exercise is unavoidable, it has only to be carried out and evaluated in relation to certain theoretical postulates. There cannot be a formulaic application of the idea of relative autonomy of the legal sphere. Any conclusions can be reached about the meaning and extent of relative autonomy of law only after a complex theoretical and historical exercise in relation to particular social formation and a state. Thus, for instance, in the case of capitalist societies the degree of autonomy of law can be examined 'with reference to a given capitalist state, and to the precise *conjuncture* of the corresponding class struggle (the specific configuration of the power bloc, the degree of hegemony within this bloc, the relations between the bourgeoisie and its different fractions on the one hand and the working classes and supporting classes on the other, etc.)'.[77] The law, like the capitalist state, may be seen 'as the condensate of a relation of power between struggling classes'.[78] If the theoretical-empirical relationship is appropriately conceptualized, the term 'relative autonomy' helps articulate a historically specific non-determinist materialist theory of law.

Such an exercise would thus have to be separately undertaken in the instance of social formations that constituted the world of 'actually existing socialism' to draw appropriate conclusions with respect to the role of law and legal systems in them. If the rule of law did not prevail in socialist societies and human rights were not respected it was at least in part because of a lack of appreciation of the multivalent role of law in society. This point is further elaborated later while considering the commodity form approach of Pashukanis. There was also a distorted understanding of the role of democracy and human rights in building socialism. This matter is considered later in a section that outlines the IMAIL understanding of human rights and its envisaged role in post-capitalist societies. The broad conclusion drawn therein is that democracy and rule of law have to deepen in post-capitalist societies and the human rights of individuals

---

that on the one hand autonomy has determined limitations or, on the other, that determination is tempered or postponed.' Alan Hunt, 'The Theory of Critical Legal Studies', 6 (1986) *Oxford Journal of Legal Studies,* pp. 1–45 reproduced in Costas Douzinas and Colin Perrin (eds.) *Critical Legal Theory* , vol. I (London: Routledge, 2012), pp. 243–286 at p. 266.

[76] See ibid., p. 274.

[77] James Martin (ed.), *The Poulantzas Reader: Marxism, Law and the State* (London: Verso, 2008), pp. 280–281; emphasis in original.

[78] See ibid., p. 283.

firmly protected. The exercise of determining the nature and relative autonomy of law would have to be an independent undertaking also in so far as postcolonial societies are concerned which have to be inter alia looked at through the lens of 'legal orientalism'. In other words, there is no substitute for sustained and detailed historical exercise in determining the nature and role of law in different societies. Any attempt at reductionist derivations can only distort the picture and caricature the Marxist theory of law. Marx spent decades to understand the laws of motion of capitalism and how these play out in real historical social formations. It is well known that he did not have the time to elaborate either a theory of state or a theory of law, leave aside reviewing their historical role over time. What he would have expected of anyone undertaking these tasks is expending the same amount of care as he did in understanding capitalism.

E.   *The Relative Autonomy of International Law: Complicating the Picture*

The articulation of a non-determinist theory of law assumes an even more complex character on the international plane because of several independent factors that include: (i) the coexistence of different social formations (capitalist, socialist and mixed) that constitute the 'world economy' rendering complex the meaning of 'economic structure'; (ii) the phenomenon of universalizing capitalism or imperialism that has critically shaped the nature of world economy and evolution of international law over the last few centuries; (iii) the 'logic of territory' or states system that complicates the process of the adoption, interpretation, adjudication and implementation of international law; (iv) the emergence of a 'legal profession' and a 'legal culture' determined to a great extent by the 'logic of territory' as each nation develops its distinct tradition of international law in response to its historical situation and national interests; (v) the distinctive mode that the 'gender' question or the problem of equality and justice between sexes assumes on the international plane raising a specific set of issues arising inter alia from the response of states with different social character; (vi) the unique nature of transnational class struggle that is seeing today the emergence of a transnational capitalist class on the one hand and a transnational oppressed class on the other. To put it differently, any attempt to transpose on the international plane a frame that assumes a simple parallel between a domestic and international theory of law is problematic as it neglects the peculiar features of international society, especially flowing from the fact of universalizing capitalism and the 'logic of territory'. The absence as yet of a global social formation and a world state prevents such a procedure. However, at the same time, the distinctive nature of international law does not mean the irrelevance of the general Marxist theory of law. It merely implies that a materialist theory of international law must be articulated keeping firmly in view the distinctive characteristics of the world economy and the states system. It in turn means among other things that the insights of postcolonial theory, which brings to the fore the meaning and implications of 'legal orientalism' are taken into account in developing a materialist history of international law. It is the neglect of the insights of postcolonial theory that accounts for why scholars like Miéville mischaracterize contemporary international law and the possibilities of reform in it. While his application of the commodity form theory to international law certainly yields valuable insights, it is unable to capture the intricate and multidimensional nature of contemporary international law. As will be seen presently the distinctiveness of the international legal system had compelled even Pashukanis to make the necessary amendments to commodity form theory when it came to understanding the nature of international law. But at first there is a need to say a few words on the commodity theory of law itself and its strengths and weaknesses.

IV.   The Commodity Form Theory of Law

In the immediate decades after the October revolution there were several attempts made by Soviet scholars to articulate a distinctive materialist approach to international law. A most significant step in this direction was taken by Pashukanis who extended with appropriate modifications his commodity form theory of law to international law[79]. In what follows the commodity form theory of law and international law are briefly analysed. It is followed by a critical review of the work of Miéville who relies on commodity form theory of law to critique contemporary international law.

   Pashukanis is among the most celebrated of Marxist legal theorists. In his book *The General Theory of Law and Marxism* Pashukanis attempted to understand the specific form that law assumes under capitalism, a matter Engels had admitted that he and Marx did not address. Indeed, according to Pashukanis, the *differentia specifica* of law under capitalism is the

---

[79] The subsequent attempts by Soviet scholars like Evgeny Korovin and Grigory Tunkin to advance a Marxist approach to international law were less theoretical exercises and more attempts at justifying Soviet foreign policy in the vocabulary of international law.

particular form it assumes.[80] He therefore emphasized that Marxist theory should investigate not merely the material content of legal regulation in different historical epochs, but also offer a materialistic interpretation of the form legal regulation assumes. In advancing his commodity exchange theory of law Pashukanis attempted to closely follow the observations of Marx in *Capital* and other writings. The distinctive feature of capitalism, as Marx pointed out, is that labour power itself becomes a commodity that can be bought and sold in the market and therefore 'capitalist society is above all a society of commodity owners'.[81] This is the principal reason why under capitalism 'man assumes the quality of a legal subject and

---

[80] In the words of Eugene Kamenka: 'E.B.Pashukanis was concerned with a problem not tackled by Marx or Engels, or by most Marxists: What are the *differentia specifica* of law, what *distinguished* law from other social manifestations, particularly from *other* bodies of rules and commands. The difference, according to Pashukanis, does not lie in the source or function of law, but in its *form*, its formal presupposition of an underlying juridical subject as the bearer of rights and asserter of claims, seen for the purposes of the legal form as autonomous and free, equal and equivalent to all other juridical subjects. Pashukanis sees law not as a command, but as a system of norms and concepts determining claims. In elaborating this view of "formal equality" or presuppositions and implied structures and value in law, Pashukanis had captured an important and central moment in the Western legal tradition that might be said to characterize it.' Eugene Kamenka, 'Marxism, Economics and Law'. Available at: http://biblio.juridicas.unam.mx/libros/3/1014/7.pdf pp. 49–72 at p. 61(accessed on 7 May 2014).

[81] Marx defined capitalism as follows: 'Capitalist production is distinguished from the outset by two characteristic features … *First*. It produces its products as commodities. The fact that it produces commodities does not differentiate it from other modes of production; but rather the fact that being a commodity is the dominant and determining characteristic of its products. This implies, first and foremost, that the labourer himself comes forward merely as a seller of commodities, and thus as a free wage-labourer, so that labour appears in general as wage-labour … The *second* distinctive feature of capitalist mode of production is the production of surplus-value as the direct aim and determining motive of production. Capital produces essentially capital, and does so only to the extent that it produces surplus-value.' Karl Marx, *Capital: A Critique of Political Economy* (Moscow: Progress Publishers, 1959), vol. III, pp. 879–880; emphasis in original. Marx defined labour power as follows: 'By labour-power or capacity for labour is to be understood the aggregate of those mental and physical capabilities existing in a human being, which he exercises whenever he produces a use-value of any description'. Marx, *Capital*, vol. I, p. 164. Marx went on to note that 'labour-power can appear upon the market as a commodity, only if, and so far as, its possessor, the individual labour-power it is, offers it for sale, or sells it, as a commodity'. See ibid., p. 165. In the event 'he and the owner of money meet in the market, and deal with each other as on the basis of equal rights, with this difference alone, that one is buyer, the other seller; both, therefore, equal in the eyes of the law'. See ibid. Further, 'for the conversion of money into capital': 'the owner of money must meet in the market with the free labourer, free in the double sense, that as a free man he can dispose of his labour-power as his own commodity, and that on the other hand he has no other commodity for sale, is short of everything necessary for the realization of his

becomes the bearer of a legal right' and an equal subject in law viz., to participate in the exchange transaction.[82] According to Pashukanis, only when property can be freely disposed off in the market can it become the basis of legal form; the category subject is a general expression of that freedom. Indeed, 'the legal relationship between subjects is only the other side of the relation between the products of labour which have become commodities'.[83] Therefore, 'every legal relation is a relationship between subjects. A subject is the atom of legal theory, the simplest and irreducible element'.[84] It led Pashukanis to conclude that 'contract is one of the central concepts of law'.[85] In sum, 'the social, productive relationship appears simultaneously in two incongruous forms: as the value of a commodity and as the ability of man to be the subject of rights'.[86] Pashukanis pointed out that 'for Marx the analysis of the form of the subject flows directly from the analysis of the form of commodities'.[87] He argued that 'as the wealth of capitalist society assumes the form of an enormous accumulation of commodities, society presents itself as an endless chain of legal relationships'.[88] But as Marx went on to point out, the legal form under capitalism mystified 'a definite relation between men', accounting for 'the fetishism of commodities'.[89]

Despite the fact that Pashukanis attempted to scrupulously rely on the writings of Marx he missed out on critical dimensions of his work in articulating the commodity form theory of law. First, since generalized commodity production only took place under capitalism Pashukanis concluded that the phenomenon of 'law' could not exist in pre-capitalist societies as labour power had yet to become a commodity and man a subject of law.[90] In this view the relations in pre-capitalist societies was regulated

---

labour-power'. See ibid., p. 166. Marx goes on to write that 'the historical conditions of its [i.e., capital's] existence are by no means given with the mere circulation of money and commodities. It can spring into life, only when the owner of the means of production and subsistence meets in the market with the free labourer selling his labour-power. And this one historical condition comprises a world's history. Capital, therefore, announces from its first appearance a new epoch in the process of social production'. See ibid., p. 167.

[82] *Pashukanis*, Beirne and Sharlet (eds.), pp. 76, 82.

[83] See ibid., p. 62.

[84] See ibid., p. 74.

[85] See ibid., p. 82.

[86] See ibid., p. 76.

[87] See ibid., p. 75.

[88] See ibid., p. 62.

[89] Marx, *Capital*, p. 77.

[90] Bill Bowring, *The Degradation of the International Legal Order?: The Rehabilitation of Law and the Possibility of Politics* (Oxford: Routledge-Cavendish, 2008), p. 24.

by customs and other social practices but not by law. Such an understanding prevented Pashukanis to see the elements of continuity and change in the legal system that Marx alluded to in his reference to Roman law, a subject on which Renner later elaborated. Indeed, according to one critic he thereby 'failed to take into account the whole of human pre-capitalist history'.[91]

Second, Pashukanis committed the error of deriving the essence of bourgeois law from the sphere of circulation rather than from relations of production and thus separated the form from the content of the law.[92] In the words of Bob Fine, 'instead of seeing both the content and forms of law as determined by and changing with the development of productive relations, Pashukanis isolated law from its content and reduced quite different forms of law, expressing qualitatively different social relations, to the single, static and illusory "legal form".'[93] Likewise, Warrington has noted that Pashukanis 'ignore(s) the central influence of production on law', that is, the fact that 'capitalism is a process of production, and exchange is merely part of that process'.[94] These critiques are not intended to undermine the distinctive significance of the exchange transaction in the capitalist mode of production, but to stress the fact that the legal form is integrally linked to the dispossession of the majority of people of the means of production. In fact it is only on leaving the sphere of circulation that we see that the society is split into two great classes – the capitalist class and the working class. It is in this sphere that, as Marx observed, the 'free' and 'equal' worker is found chained to the capitalist by myriad of threads. Pashukanis certainly recognized this reality but did not attach sufficient significance to it in advancing his commodity exchange theory of law as he was consumed with the 'formal' side that distinguished bourgeois law from 'law' in all other societies.

Third, as Hans Kelsen pointed out, in Pashukanis there is the 'artificial narrowing of the concept of law'[95] as 'in order to identify law with specific economic relationships, Pashukanis declares that only private law – as a relationship between isolated individuals, subjects of egoistic interest – is

---

[91] See ibid.
[92] Robert Fine, *Democracy and the Rule of Law: Marx's Critique of the Legal Form* (Caldwell, NJ: Blackburn Press, 2002), p. 157.
[93] See ibid., p. 159.
[94] R. Warrington, 'Pashukanis and the Commodity Form Theory' in D. Sugarman (ed.) *Legality, Ideology and the State* (London: Academic Press, 1983), pp. 43–68 at p. 53.
[95] Hans Kelsen, *The Communist Theory of Law* (New York: Frederick A. Praeger, Inc., 1955), p. 92.

law in the true sense of the term'.[96] It prevented him from seeing that law and society intersected in multifarious ways beyond the realm of exchange and the conflicts inherent in it.[97] As Kelsen observed, 'the fact that the law is a social order for the adjustment of conflicts of interests is no sufficient reason for identifying law with private law, and that means, for denying any legal character to that part of the law which is usually called public law'.[98] In his view the underlying assumption 'that the state by its very nature is beyond and above the law' was erroneous.[99]

Fourth, as Paul Hirst has pointed out, Pashukanis even 'reduce(d) the process of legislation to the status of a mere phenomenal form or phantom'.[100] He did not appreciate that legislation and legal institutions needed to be taken seriously and that what called for explanation was the fact that law assumed the form of legislation originating in a specific set of institutions.[101] As Hirst goes on to point out:

> Legislation and legal apparatuses become the points of departure in the analysis of law. It is by being enacted, codified, subjected to dispute and interpretation that laws and the nature of legality are defined and developed. Law is a social practice taking place within particular apparatuses and by means of a particular type of discourse ... Assigning a definitive effectivity to legislation and legal practice means that law can outrun and redefine its discursive and categoric forms.[102]

Poulantzas was likewise critical of Pashukanis as he '*reduce(d)* law and the state to the base' and 'disregard(ed) their specific character as a coherent system of norms and thus completely ignore(d) their relative autonomy'.[103] In response to similar criticisms made in his lifetime, Pashukanis explained that 'if a norm is recognized as the dominant element in all relationships, then, before seeing the legal superstructure, we must assume the presence of a norm-establishing authority, i.e. in other words a political organization. Thus we have to conclude that the legal superstructure derives from the political superstructure'.[104] However, in his

---

[96] See ibid., p. 93.
[97] M. Head, *Evgeny Pashukanis: A Critical Appraisal* (Oxford: Routledge-Cavendish, 2008), p. 91; Fine, *Democracy*, p. 161.
[98] Kelsen, *Communist Theory*, p. 94.
[99] See ibid.
[100] Paul Hirst, *On Law and Ideology* (London: The Macmillan Press Ltd, 1979), p. 110.
[101] See ibid., p. 111.
[102] See ibid.
[103] *The Poulantzas Reader*, p. 28; emphasis in original.
[104] *Pashukanis*, Beirne and Sharlet (eds.), p. 66.

view 'the political superstructure, and in particular the state apparatus, is a secondary, derivative element'.[105] He cited Marx's observation that 'only political superstition forces us to believe that civil society is the creation of the state; on the contrary, the state is the creation of civil society'.[106] In Pashukanis's view, 'state power injects clarity and stability into the legal structure but it does not create its preconditions which are rooted in the material relationships of production'.[107] In saying this Pashukanis denied the constitutive nature of law. He was forgetful that the state with the authority to legislate, and other legal institutions, was already present in the transition from feudalism to capitalism.

In sum, while commodity form is the basis of legal form in capitalist societies, it does not either do away with the constitutive dimensions of law or exhaust the diverse roles it plays in society or establish afresh the necessary legal apparatus and institutions. A capitalist society is comprised of millions of individuals entering into varied forms of social relations that cannot be captured by a singular legal form, i.e., commodity form. In modern society, as Hugh Collins has pointed out, 'legal rules regulate many kinds of social arrangements beyond even the broadest conceptions of relations of production'.[108] These social arrangements are the subject of legislation and other interventions by the State. While these legislations may reflect capitalist relations of production these cannot be given purely functional interpretations. In other words, it would be naïve to suggest that complex modern legal system can all be reduced to the commodity form even as it captures a foundational dimension of it. Thus, for instance, it cannot capture the complex relationship between capitalist legal system and patriarchy. Pashukanis also did not see that other elements of the 'superstructure' (e.g., political superstructure) are regulated by law and do not necessarily reflect the commodity form. While commodity fetishism can be perceived in all social relations it does not colonize them. Further, since Pashukanis was interested in the form of law under capitalism, he did not explore the implications of the coexistence of different modes of production within a social formation (for instance, remnants of the feudal system coexisting with a capitalist system). The commodity form theory of law therefore also neglected the continuity in legal categories and institutions. Finally, unlike Marx, Pashukanis did not fully appreciate that the norm of equality (in the

[105] See ibid., p. 66.
[106] See ibid; emphasis deleted.
[107] See ibid., p. 68.
[108] Collins, *Marxism and Law*, pp. 23–24.

exchange transaction under capitalism) had an intrinsic value even when contrasted with factual inequality. The affirmation of equality was a move towards creating a democratic relationship even though as yet only in form.

In short, the commodity form theory of law did not adequately capture the multidimensional aspects of the form and content of domestic law under capitalism. Since it did not accurately describe the reality of bourgeois law it was unlikely to be able to do so where bourgeois *international* law is concerned given the added complications introduced by universalizing capitalism and the 'logic of territory'.

V.   The Commodity Form Theory of International Law

A.   *Pashukanis on International Law*

Pashukanis however made significant modifications to commodity exchange theory to capture the distinctive nature and character of international law even if he did not adequately address certain issues. He set out his views primarily in a brief, albeit remarkable, essay on 'international law'. He made the following insightful submissions in it on international law:

First, he noted that 'the spread and development of international law occurred on the basis of the spread and development of the capitalist mode of production'.[109] That is to say, 'the victory of the bourgeoisie, in all the European countries, had to lead to the establishment of new rules and new institutions of international law which protected the general and basic interests of the bourgeoisie, i.e., bourgeois property'.[110] But Pashukanis recognized that while 'as a separate force which set itself off from society, the state only finally emerged in the modern capitalist bourgeois period' it by no means followed that 'the contemporary forms of international legal intercourse, and the individual institutions of international law, only arose in the most recent times'.[111] Since exchange relations existed among tribes and communities, international law was prevalent among the earliest ancient legal institutions that existed. In this period international law helped resolve disputes, including territorial disputes, between tribes.[112] In these contexts Pashukanis went on

---

[109] *Pashukanis*, Beirne and Sharlet (eds.), pp. 171-172.
[110] See ibid.
[111] See ibid., p. 175.
[112] See ibid.

to touch upon developments in Greek and Roman law.[113] However, he emphasized that it is only in the capitalist period 'having subordinated itself to the state machine, the bourgeoisie brought the principle of the public nature of authority to its clearest expression', and therefore '*the state only fully becomes the subject of international law as the bourgeois state*'.[114] In the same way as an individual assumed the quality of a legal subject only under capitalism, the state becomes the subject of international law only as a capitalist state.

Second, responding to the eternal question as to whether international law is law, Pashukanis noted that 'bourgeois jurisprudence has devoted a great amount of fruitless effort in solving this contradiction'.[115] According to Pashukanis, the answer to the question whether international law is law lies in – here he anticipates classical realists like Hans Morgenthau – 'the real balance of forces' between bourgeois states.[116] He, of course, recognized that 'within the limit set by a given balance of forces, separate questions may be decided by compromises and by exchange i.e., on the basis of law'.[117] But international law was likely to be disregarded when the interests of a state so demanded.[118] This was especially so in periods of crisis when the balance of forces 'fluctuated seriously' and when 'vital interests' or the 'very existence of a state' was threatened.[119] Pashukanis mentioned in this regard the period of 1914–1918 'during which both sides continuously violated international law'.[120] However, he went on to make the acute observation that 'every state in violating international law also tries to depict the matter as if there has been no violation whatsoever'.[121] The reason is that 'the open denial of international law is politically unprofitable for the bourgeoisie since it exposes them to the masses and thus hinders preparations for new wars. It is much more profitable for the imperialists to act in the guise of pacifism and as the champions of international law'.[122]

Third, Pashukanis rejected technical definitions of international law advanced by bourgeois international lawyers from which 'the class

---

[113] See ibid., pp. 175–176.
[114] See ibid., p. 174; emphasis added.
[115] See ibid., p. 178.
[116] See ibid., p. 179.
[117] See ibid.
[118] See ibid.
[119] See ibid.
[120] See ibid.
[121] See ibid.
[122] See ibid., p. 180.

character of international law' was absent.[123] In his view, 'bourgeois jurisprudence consciously or unconsciously strives to conceal the element
of class'.[124] On his part he noted the links between capitalism and imperialism, and inter-imperialist competition, and observed that the capitalist countries divided the world into civilized and semi-civilized revealing
'*modern international law as the class law of the bourgeoisie*'.[125] According
to Pashukanis, international law of his times was 'the totality of norms
which the capitalist bourgeois states apply in their relations with each
other, while the remainder of the world is considered as a simple object
of their completed transactions'.[126] Pashukanis was certainly right as 'the
real historical content of international law' in this period was 'the struggle
between capitalist states'.[127] In fact international law owed 'its existence to
the fact that the bourgeoisie exercise(d) its domination over the proletariat and over the colonial countries'.[128] It was therefore indeed the class law
of the bourgeoisie.

Fourth, he noted with respect to the assertion of basic or equal rights
of states under international law that 'it is most obvious that we are dealing here with ideas drawn from the sphere of civil law relationships with
a basis in equality between the parties'.[129] He conceded that 'to *a certain
degree* the analogy may be extended. Bourgeois private law assumes that
subjects are formally equal yet simultaneously permits real inequality in
property, while bourgeois international law in principle recognizes that
states have equal rights yet in reality they are unequal in their significance and their power'.[130] Therefore, at the level of political economy there
was only 'a difference in degree' between domestic law and international
law.[131] But he also went on to observe that the 'dubious benefits of formal
equality are not enjoyed at all by those nations which have not developed
capitalist civilization and which engage in international intercourse not as
subjects, but as objects of the imperialist states' colonial policy'.[132] In other
words, he recognized that in the instance of colonized states the analogy
between domestic law and international law collapsed.

[123] See ibid., p. 169.
[124] See ibid; emphasis deleted.
[125] See ibid, p.172; emphasis added.
[126] See ibid..
[127] See ibid., pp. 172, 169.
[128] See ibid., p. 172.
[129] See ibid., p. 177.
[130] See ibid., p. 178; emphasis added.
[131] See ibid., p. 180.
[132] See ibid., p. 178.

Fifth, he criticized Marxist scholars such as Karl Renner for stressing the 'peaceful functions of international law'.[133] Pashukanis pointed out that 'even those agreements between capitalist states which appear to be directed to the general interest are, in fact, for each of the participants a means of jealously protecting their particular interests, preventing the expansion of their rivals' influence, thwarting unilateral conquest, i.e., in another form continuing the same struggle which will exist for as long as capitalist competition exists'.[134] He extended this logic to international organizations and wrote that 'the struggle among imperialist states for domination of the rest of the world is thus a basic factor in defining the nature and fate of the corresponding institutions'.[135]

Sixth, he pointed out that with the emergence of the Soviet Union, international law acquired a different character. It reflected 'the form of a temporary compromise between two antagonistic class systems' and was thus 'international law of the transitional period'.[136] At this historical juncture 'international law becomes *inter-class* law'.[137] In so far as the relationship of socialist states themselves was concerned he wrote:

> international law assumes an entirely different meaning as the inter-state law of the Soviet states. It now ceases to be a form of temporary compromise behind which an intensified struggle for existence is hidden. Because of this the very opposition between international law and the state, so characteristic of the preceding period, disappears. The proletarian states, not having merged formally into one federation or union, must present in their mutual relationships an image of such a close economic, political and military unity, that the measure of 'modern' international law becomes inapplicable to them.[138]

This was the withering away of the law thesis extended to international law.

These were a remarkably rich set of observations on the nature and character of international law. What is of note is that in advancing his understanding of international law Pashukanis did not separate form from content or for that matter the 'logic of capital' from the 'logic of territory'.[139] Insofar as the 'form' of international law is concerned, he

---

[133] See ibid., pp. 169.
[134] See ibid., p. 170.
[135] See ibid., p. 171.
[136] See ibid., p. 172.
[137] See ibid., p. 173; emphasis in original.
[138] See ibid., p. 173.
[139] In lieu of the fact that Miéville ignores the dialectical relationship between form and content, Bill Bowring observes that 'I doubt very much whether his work on the commodity

made four crucial points: the state becomes a subject of international law only as a bourgeois state; there is a theoretical equality of states under bourgeois international law that parallels the equality between commodity owners under civil law; this equality is accompanied, as at the domestic level, by their factual inequality, making compliance with international law the function of 'balance of power'; and that the analogy between domestic and international law collapsed when it came to colonies because these were not treated as equal subjects but rather as objects of international law. Turning to the content of international law, he characterized international law as class law of the bourgeoisie. He identified the key characteristics of bourgeois international law as 'competition between capitalist states' for colonial spoils rooted in the political economy of capitalism and the nature of the bourgeois state. But after the emergence of Soviet Union he characterized international law as inter-class law.

Yet certain weaknesses remained. First, while Pashukanis recognized the intimate relationship between the 'logic of capital' and the production of the 'logic of territory' he did not stress that the relationship between sovereign states is not a simple reproduction of the formal equality of individuals under capitalism. Sovereign states are not individuals selling their labour power leading to the creation of surplus value. While imperialism leads to the exploitation and oppression of other nations and peoples it is not the same thing as extraction of surplus value. Furthermore, the transfer of wealth from the subaltern nations can be simply through the use of force. Likewise, the nature and substance of treaties is much more complex than contracts. In other words, beyond a point the analogy between domestic law and international law is flawed. To be fair, Pashukanis recognized that it holds only to 'a certain degree' but since this qualification was not elaborated it lost its bite. Second, his understanding of the history of international law remained Eurocentric. He did not sufficiently acknowledge the role of 'legal orientalism' in shaping the doctrines and discourse of international law. Pashukanis was also entirely ignorant of the presence of international law in the non-Western world. In both these regards postcolonial theory helps enrich a materialist account of the evolution and development of bourgeois international law. Finally, since it was to be decades before a feminist critique of international law was advanced, early Marxists did not venture in that direction even though the first wave of socialist feminists had already presented a feminist critique of bourgeois society. IMAIL attempts to correct these weaknesses in Pashukanis's approach to international law in the matrix of the complex understanding of the relationship between economic structure of society and law that Marx, Engels, Renner and Thompson articulated.

B.   Miéville and Pashukanis

In recent times, China Miéville has used Pashukanis's commodity form theory of law, and his insights on international law, to advance a more worked out Marxist approach to international law. Indeed, the central objective of Miéville's important book *Between Equal Rights* is 'an attempt to open a black box in the jurisprudence of international law – that of the *legal form itself*.[140] He echoes Pashukanis in stating that hitherto 'the specificity of the legal form' was not taken seriously even by Marxist scholars.[141] Following Pashukanis, Miéville writes a history of international law to demonstrate how international law universalizes the commodity form as political form and comes to be embodied as the principle of sovereign equality of states. He advances two propositions here. The first is that:

> The *legal form* – the form whereby the bearers of abstract rights and commodities confront each other – has existed in various historical conjunctures, but it was only with the rise of the sovereign states that *international law* can be considered to have been born, and it is with the triumph of capitalism and its commodification of all social relations that the legal form universalized and became modern international law.[142]

In a sense the proposition is no different from the routine statement that modern international law originated at Westphalia. But it is different in as much as it establishes a relationship between the 'logic of capital' (i.e., the historical 'triumph of capitalism') and the 'logic of territory'. The second proposition of Miéville is that only when the norm of sovereign equality assumes a universal form in the period after decolonization that international law becomes true to itself:

> the post-War drive to self-determination is not merely a change in the structure or content of international law, but the *culmination of the*

---

theory of law can really serve as the basis for a new theory of international law'. Bowring, *Degradation*, p. 23.

[140] China Miéville, *Between Equal Rights: A Marxist Theory of International Law* (Chicago, IL: Haymarket Books, 2005), p. 2; emphasis in original.

[141] See ibid., pp. 15, 16. He defends Pashukanis against his critics for he did 'have a theory of the political, coercive determination of the content of laws'. See ibid., p. 6. He shows 'the embeddedness of violence in law, and the contingency of an arbitrary sovereign to the legal form, are key to the commodity-form theory'. See ibid., p. 7.

[142] See ibid., p. 161; emphasis in original.

> *universalizing and abstract tendencies in international – legal – capitalism*
> ... the recent conversion of international law to decolonization represents
> the *self-actualization* of international law – the universalisation of the
> abstract juridical equality of its subjects. With the end of formal empire
> comes the apogee of the empire of sovereignty, and of international law.[143]

Thus, according to Miéville, only with decolonization does the element
of formal equality that characterizes capital–wage labour relationship
assume a universal form at the global level.

In transposing Pashukanis's commodity form theory to the international plane, Miéville is aware of the question 'whether in the international realm, where relations between juridical units are relations either
of exchange or administration rather than of wage-labor, a *simpler* form
off Pashukanis's theory might hold'.[144] He explains away the fact by stating that in commodity form theory Pashukanis focuses on private and
not public law: 'for Pashukanis, in the absence of a sovereign authority,
precisely because the coercive violence inherent in the commodity/legal
relationship between abstract equals must inhere in the participant themselves, "public" political relations *are* exchange relations. The public and
private are inextricable here'.[145] He then goes on to advance three conclusions. First, 'for the commodity-form theory, international and domestic
law are two moments of the same form'.[146] Second, Pashukanis's idea of
'real balance of forces' and 'self help' provide answers to the enforcement
dilemma in a decentralized legal system.[147] Third, that 'international law is
a paradoxical form. It is simultaneously a *genuine relation between equals*,
and a form that the weaker states *cannot hope to win*'.[148] In other words, as
Marx had observed, 'between equal rights, force decides'.

Miéville concedes that the relationship between the form and content
of international law remains to be systematically mapped. At the same
time, he emphasizes that for Pashukanis a simple focus on the material
content meant 'having no responsibility towards jurisprudence'.[149] As

---

[143]   See ibid., pp. 267, 268; emphasis in original.
[144]   See ibid., p. 114; emphasis added.
[145]   See ibid., p. 137; emphasis in original. But he does add that 'it is true' that 'private law
is the basis of public law, as we now perceive them from within a state, separated from
each other, but that very distinction is only meaningful as a result of that states's super-
imposition onto the legal form. In its root form – and in international law – the law was
simultaneously abstract and particularistic – "public" and "private"'. See ibid; emphasis in
original.
[146]   See ibid., p. 131.
[147]   See ibid., pp. 128ff.
[148]   See ibid., p. 142; emphasis in original.
[149]   See ibid., p. 117.

he clarifies this did not mean that for Pashukanis the content of law was unimportant or that his theory was '*inimical* to examinations of particular legal contents'.[150] In fact, Pashukanis understood the intimate and dialectical links between form and content. After all Pashukanis was not a bourgeois formalist. He recognized that in the final analysis the commodity form theory was 'relating law to a definite material content – the social relations founded on commodity exchange'.[151] But Miéville admits that when it came to international law 'he left the mechanisms of the relation between form and content [...] unexamined'.[152] Therefore, he observes that 'we need Pashukanis to make sense of international law and the legal form: and we need international law to make better sense of Pashukanis'.[153] He even speaks of the 'mistaken formulations' of Pashukanis.[154]

On his part Miéville claims to have provided 'a systematic, if general, theory of mapping of content into the legal form'.[155] But this claim is difficult to accept. Above all Miéville does not show that like Pashukanis he is aware of the limitations of drawing parallels between wage labour–capital relations with that of the relationship between sovereign states. It may be recalled that Pashukanis had noted that the comparison holds only '*to a certain degree*'.[156] The reason is that the content of the relationship between states in the international arena is multifarious flowing from both the 'logic of capital' and the 'logic of territory'. But Miéville does not attempt to examine the changing content of international law that can be traced to the simultaneous operation of the two logics even as he rightly observes that they come together at a particular moment in history. Instead, he observes that 'international law is a relationship and a process: it is not a fixed set of rules *but a way of deciding the rules*. And the coercion of at least one of the players, or its threat, is necessary as the medium by which particular contents will actualize the broader content of competitive struggle within the legal form'.[157] He is therefore satisfied writing that 'to understand the dynamics by which *specific* international laws are codified we must investigate the power relations between states at those particular moments'.[158] In advancing these propositions Miéville

---

[150] See ibid., p. 118; emphasis in original.
[151] Chris Arthur cited by Miéville, ibid., p. 119.
[152] See ibid., p.118.
[153] See ibid., p. 115.
[154] See ibid.
[155] See ibid., p. 150.
[156] *Pashukanis*, Beirne and Sharlet (eds.), p. 178.
[157] Miéville, *Between Equal Rights*, p.151; emphasis in original.
[158] See ibid., p. 151; emphasis in original.

emphasizes the 'logic of territory' to the exclusion of the 'logic of capital', especially its universalizing nature that produces the phenomenon of imperialism.

In sum, many of the Miéville formulations are not new, that is, the propositions regarding the relationship between capitalism and modern states system, or the balance of forces or self-help (or imperialism) for enforcing international law, or real inequality coexisting with formal equality, or that international law consists of rules about how rules are made. On the other hand, what is missing in Miéville is a concrete analysis of the changing content of international law over time. The fact that Pashukanis derives his commodity form theory primarily from the moment of exchange leads Miéville to privilege form over content and in the final analysis Morgenthau over Marx.[159] He therefore fails to (like Pashukanis) sufficiently appreciate that in historical terms the universalization of the principle of sovereign equality represents important progress; neocolonial international law is less oppressive in crucial ways than colonial international law. He is impatient to arrive at the conclusion that international law is 'fundamentally unreformable'.[160] In fact, Miéville concludes that the danger of looking to international law for bringing about any form of progressive social transformation is that it 'risks ... legitimizing ... the very structure of international law that critical theory has so devastatingly undermined'.[161] In his view, 'the international rule of law is not counter posed to force and imperialism: it is an expression of it'.[162] In coming to this conclusion he fails to recognize the changes brought about in the content of contemporary international law or appreciate the value of the idea of international rule of law. It is no accident that he is extremely critical of E. P. Thompson, and it also comes as no surprise that Karl Renner does not receive a mention in his book.[163] The questions whether the reform of international law is possible, or whether the idea of international rule of law is valuable, are considered later.

Their consideration needs to be preceded by an excursus into the history of international law, 1600–1985 and the identification of the key features of present day international law (1985–). In narrating the history of international law the idea is to argue that the content and character of international law changes over time in response to developments

---

[159] For Miéville's critique of Morgenthau see ibid., pp. 19–23.
[160] Miéville, *Between Equal Rights*, p. 3.
[161] See ibid., p. 299.
[162] See ibid., p. 8.
[163] For Miéville's critique of E. P. Thompson see ibid., pp. 315–316.

in capitalism and while contemporary international law is imperial in character the possibility and benefits of reform should not be ruled out through the struggles of subaltern groups, peoples and nations. Equally the idea of international rule of law should be valued. In short, legal nihilism is the luxury of armchair academics. It cannot inform social and political movements in the real world.

VI.   A Materialist History of International Law (1600–1985): A Sketch

It was seen that Marx and Engels conceived and applied the categories of economic structure and superstructure to locate and understand the domain of law within nations. But in explicating the relationship they (and subsequent Marxist scholars) noted the constitutive, reciprocal, dynamic and multidimensional nature of the relationship. It was further pointed out that at the global level the use of the categories economic structure and superstructure is complicated by the phenomenon of imperialism and the fact that the international system is a sovereign state system. It calls for determining how both the 'logic of capital' and 'logic of territory' have shaped modern international law over time. While the Marxist theory of law and international law can be advanced as a set of abstractions these are 'a product of historic relations, and possess their validity only for and within those relations'.[164] This section and the next therefore review the history of modern international law in the matrix of a general theory of law that among other things emphasizes the relative independence of the legal sphere.

It is a truism to state that the history of *modern* international relations is intimately bound with the history of capitalism and its different phases. As Marx and Engels pointed out, 'the relations of different nations among themselves depend upon the extent to which each has developed its productive forces, the division of labor and internal intercourse'.[165] In nations in which the dominant mode of production was capitalism its universalizing thrust led to a certain relationship with non-capitalist nations. In *The Communist Manifesto* Marx and Engels wrote that 'the need of a constantly expanding market for its products chases the bourgeoisie over the whole surface of the globe. It must nestle everywhere, settle everywhere,

---

[164] Marx, *Grundrisse*, p. 105.
[165] Karl Marx and Frederick Engels, *German Ideology* (Moscow: Progress Publishers, 1976), p. 38.

establish connexions everywhere'.[166] The links that the bourgeoisie establishes all over the world is backed by national States as the interests of
the two intersect and co-constitute each other. The Marxist view is that
a State does not stand above classes and secure the 'national interest' in
the arena of international relations but tends to realize the interests of the
socially and economically dominant classes.[167] However, as Bob Jessop
has pointed out, Marx 'did not offer a theoretical analysis of the capitalist
state to match the scope and rigor of *Das Kapital*. His work on the state
comprises a fragmented and unsystematic series of philosophical reflections, contemporary history, journalism and incidental remarks'.[168] Other
Marxist theorists like Engels, Lenin, Trotsky and Gramsci also did not
advance a systematic theory of state even as they greatly contributed to
understanding its role.[169] The absence of a well-worked-out Marxist theory of state is compounded by the fact that in explaining and understanding international relations the theoretical analysis of the capitalist state
has to be accompanied by a theory of the states system to which Marxist
scholars have not paid sufficient attention. In other words, in telling the
story of international law both the 'logic of capital' and the 'logic of territory' have to be theorized. International legal relations reflect the manner in which societies are internally organized as also the historical state
and character of international relations. It is in the positing of complex
linkages between the internal and the external that IMAIL departs from
approaches like classical realism that only theorize the states system. In
the IMAIL view the logics of capital and territory also interact in distinct
ways in different periods of history to yield a complex map of the history

---

[166] Karl Marx and Frederick Engels, *Selected Works*, vol. 1 (Moscow: Progress Publishers,
1973), p. 112.

[167] Yet the state in capitalist societies does not defend the 'narrowly corporate interests' of the
ruling class but rather the fundamental interest of perpetuating the capitalist system. It
is this fact which inter alia dictates the accommodation of the interests of the subordinate classes, albeit within well-defined boundaries; the moments of reconciliation being
part of that social process which ensures the prevalence of the system and the political
dominance of the propertied classes. In the words of Gramsci, 'the life of the State is
conceived of as a continuous process of formation and superseding of unstable equilibria
(on the juridical plane) between the interests of the fundamental group and those of the
subordinate groups – equilibria in which the interests of the dominant group prevail, but
only up to a certain point, i.e., stopping short of narrowly corporate economic interest'.
Antonio Gramsci, *Selections from the Prison Notebooks* (London: Lawrence and Wishart,
1978), p. 182.

[168] Bob Jessop, 'Recent Theories of the Capitalist State', 1 (1977) *Cambridge Journal of
Economics*, pp. 353–373 at p. 354.

[169] See ibid.

of international relations and international law. International law is thus the outcome of multiple determinations in different periods of history, that include the influence of the 'logic of culture' used to justify the colonial project.

The genesis of capitalism can be traced to the sixteenth century which witnessed the emergence of the 'empire of private rights'. Its materialization was in tandem with a 'world-embracing commerce and a world-embracing market' that saw the birth of colonialism and a nascent modern international law.[170] As capitalism developed in the centres of Europe it began to spread its tentacles and create in its wake 'a universal market', whose integral parts were individual nation states.[171] The universal market functioned on the basis of an international division of labour which defined the relations of the parts (domestic economies/states) to the whole (the world economy). Any change in the division of labour and the structure of the world economy was bound to reflect on the substance of international relations, and eventually the content of international law. In Marx's time the international division of labour had already reached a point that 'large-scale industry, detached from the national soil depended entirely on the world market, on international exchange, on an international division of labor'.[172] It made him observe that 'capitalist production rests on the *value* or the transformation of the labor embodied in the product into social labor. But this is only [possible] on the basis of foreign trade and of the world market. This is at once the precondition and the result of capitalist production'.[173] However, he still considered international economic relations as '*secondary and tertiary phenomena*, in general *derived* and *transmitted* i.e., non-primary, conditions of production'.[174] Marx termed international economic relations as secondary and derivative phenomena in order to underline the logical primacy of internal economic relations. The national economy had an existence which was antecedent in time and space. But it would be erroneous to

---

[170] Marx, *Capital*, vol. 1, p. 145. Marx observed: 'Although we come across the first beginnings of capitalist production as early as the 14th or 15th century, sporadically, in certain towns of the Mediterranean, the capitalistic era dates from the 16th century. Wherever it appears, the abolition of serfdom has long been effected, and the highest development of the middle ages, the existence of sovereign towns, has long been on the wane'. See ibid., p. 669.

[171] See ibid., p. 525.

[172] Quoted by Ya. Pevsner, *State-Monopoly Capitalism and the Labour Theory of Value* (Moscow: Progress Publishers, 1982), p. 344.

[173] See ibid.

[174] Marx, *Contribution to the Critique*, p. 215.

believe, or interpret Marx as saying, that he thus relegated the influence of international economic relations to an eternally secondary status. It is, however, true that Marx never assigned appropriate significance to colonialism for the global development of capitalism. Unlike Rosa Luxemburg later, he did not think of it as a life-and-death issue for the survival of capitalism. Its implications will be considered presently.

Be that as it may, the evolution of the world economy and states system (the 'logic of capital' and the 'logic of territory' respectively) since the sixteenth century has shaped the structure and process of international law. In keeping with the phases of the development of the world economy and the states system, the following periodization and characterization can be delineated:

1. 1500–1760	Old Colonialism: Transition from feudal to bourgeois international law.	
2. 1760–1875	New Colonialism: Bourgeois (colonial) international law.	
3. 1875–1945	Imperialism: Bourgeois (imperialist) international law.	
4. 1945–1985	Neocolonialism: Bourgeois democratic international law.[175]	
5. 1985–	Global imperialism: Global Imperial international law	

The advantage of the periodization and classification adopted is that it underlines the inherent tendency of capital to circumvent the globe and indicates its relationship with and implications for the states system. It captures and portrays the history of international law in tandem with the substratum which gives life to it – the expanding capitalist world economy and the phenomenon of imperialism.[176] The distinct nature of the phases is confirmed by developments within international law with each phase revealing peculiar features.[177] The historical classification also reveals the 'dual' nature and essence of international law – its character when it

---

[175] However, it may be noted that the era of neocolonialism begins differently for different regions as in the case of Latin America where it can be traced back to the nineteenth century.

[176] This sketch does not capture the history of international law from the 'gender' perspective. For a truly integrated history of international law the feminist history of international law has to be read into this sketch. This history is yet to be written.

[177] It is interesting that Ian Brownlie arrived at a similar break-up (of the first four phases) from a study of international legal sources. He mentions the following phases in the evolution of international law: 1648–1750, 1750–1850, 1850–1950 and 1950– revealing that the development of modern international law is inextricably bound with the different phases of global capitalism. Ian Brownlie, 'The Expansion of International Society: The Consequences for the Law of Nations' in Hedley Bull and Adam Watson (eds.) *The Expansion of International Society* (Oxford: Clarendon Press, 1984), pp. 357–370.

governs relationship between the European states *inter se* and its evolving relationship with the non-Western world. This duality is effectively captured by postcolonial narratives that also seek to provincialize the history of European international law. The first dent in the world capitalist economic system was caused by the October Revolution which initiated a process that culminated in the creation of a parallel 'socialist international division of labor'. Even so, two-thirds of mankind formed an integral part of the capitalist international division of labour, determining the character of international law. The decolonization of Asian and Africa since the Second World War saw the universal application of the principles of sovereign equality of states. But it did not mean the end of imperialism which now assumed new forms. The collapse of the 'socialist international division of labor', or 'actually existing socialism', ensured that international law – its structure and content – are shaped by the needs of global capitalism. In the contemporary world, the greater integration of the world economy has deeply impacted international law, even as it has in turn actively contributed to entrenching and promoting the globalization process. It explains the exponential expansion of international law and institutions and their intrusive role in the international life of states. The last phase of 'global imperialism' is dealt with in a separate section as it also addresses the crucial questions relating to the possibilities of reform of international law and the value of international rule of law. It may be noted that a feminist history of international law that describes each of the indicated phases through gender lens is yet to be written.

A. Old Colonialism: 1500–1760

The emergence of the capitalist order in Europe was preceded by a period of primitive accumulation, a process which involved the forcible conversion of immediate producers (principally peasants) into wage labourers and the means of production and money into capital.[178] It had its external dimension as well; wealth (in material and human form) plundered from outside Europe entered metropolitan countries to be turned into capital.

> The discovery of gold and silver in America, the extirpation, enslavement and entombment in mines of the aboriginal population, the beginning

---

[178] In the words of Marx, primitive accumulation 'is nothing else than the historical process of divorcing the producer from the means of production. It appears as primitive, because it forms the pre-historic stage of capital and of the mode of production corresponding with it'. Marx, *Capital*, vol. 1, p. 668.

> of the conquest and looting of the East Indies, the turning of Africa into
> a warren for the commercial hunting of black-skins, signalised the rosy
> dawn of the era of capitalist production.[179]

In fact the establishment of the capitalist order received impetus from the colonial project dating from the sixteenth century, a system that was made possible by the sailing ship in alliance with guns, treachery and deceit. It was also the beginning of attempts by European thinkers to find justification for colonialism. Spain was among the first colonial powers. Therefore, as Anthony Pagden notes, 'from 1511 … until the late seventeenth century, a debate raged in Spain over the legitimacy of the "conquest" of America'.[180] In fact as Antony Anghie argues, 'international law was created out of the unique issues generated by the encounter between the Spanish and the Indians'.[181] The School of Salamanca, that included the Spanish theologian and thinker Francisco de Vitoria (c.1483–1546) and many of his pupils, actively participated in this debate.[182] It is not possible to rehearse here the range of arguments that were advanced to legitimize the colonial project in the Americas.[183] It may merely be noted that since Vitoria was among the first to encounter and deal with the phenomenon of colonialism in Americas, he left a lasting impact on European thinking on the 'right of dependent peoples'. On the one hand, Vitoria was 'a brave champion of the rights of Indians in his time', but on the other hand, he justified their conquest by reference to cultural differences or what Anghie terms the 'dynamic of difference'.[184] These differences were used to assert for the Spanish the right to travel, the carrying on of commerce and wage just war.[185] It can be said that the dualism that characterized the approach of Vitoria continues to the present times.

While Anghie brilliantly captures the encounter between the Salamanca School and colonialism in the Americas it is only a slice of reality of that era. A different encounter between Europe and the non-West took place in India in the same period. It was in the year 1601 that the English East

---

[179] See ibid., p. 703. See in this regard Mark Neocleous, 'International Law as Primitive Accumulation; Or, the secret of Systematic Colonization', 23 (2012) *European Journal of International Law,* pp. 941–962.

[180] Anthony Pagden, 'Conquest and the Just War: The "School of Salamanca" and the "Affair of the Indies" in Sankar Muthu (ed.) *Empire and Modern Political Thought* (Cambridge: Cambridge University Press, 2012), pp. 30–60 at p. 32.

[181] Antony Anghie, *Imperialism, Sovereignty and the Making of International Law* (Cambridge: Cambridge University Press, 2003) p. 15.

[182] Pagden, 'Conquest ', p. 32.

[183] Anghie, *Imperialism*, pp. 13–31.

[184] See ibid., pp. 28 and 4.

[185] See ibid., pp. 23–28.

India Company arrived in India under a Charter from Queen Elizabeth claiming monopoly of right to trade in the East. The vessel that first arrived carried a letter from the Queen 'To the great and mightie King of Achen ... Our loving Brother'.[186] Subsequently, there were attempts to negotiate a treaty with the Mughal kings who ruled large parts of India. The company was granted certain concessions in the second decade of the seventeenth century, including to trade, through 'a *firman* (royal order) issued by Prince Khurram (who later became Emperor Shah Jahan)'.[187] So when Anghie writes that scholars such as C. H. Alexandrowicz 'tend implicitly to treat the colonial encounter as marginal to the discipline', he does not entirely appreciate the different history that Alexandrowicz was recounting.[188] The arrival of the East India Company and its growing presence in India until the Crown formally took over the administration of the colony in 1858 had a different historical trajectory. The crucial point is that *there is no singular encounter between Europe and the non-West* and that the history of each encounter followed a different path. Anghie tends to generalize the story of international law from the history of particular encounters. This has implications for how the role of contemporary international law is theorized; it can either be seen as possessing a singular trajectory or encompassing a set of diverse and plural relationships that create space for progressive interventions even under what is otherwise an imperial international law.

Meanwhile, as Europe evolved, Holland came to possess the 'first fully developed' colonial system and 'in 1648 stood already in the acme of its commercial greatness'.[189] The Dutch philosopher and thinker Hugo Grotius (1583–1645) wrote his work *De Jure Belli ac Pacis* in the years 1623–1624 and is seen as among the founding figures of the discipline of international law. His work *De Jure Belli ac Pacis* has been described as the 'first comprehensive and systematic treatise on international law' which articulated the normative basis of an emerging world order'.[190] Subsequently, the British established their dominance over the fledgling

---

[186] R. P. Anand, *Development of Modern International Law and India* (New Delhi: Indian Society of International Law, 2006), p. 23. On East India Company see generally Nick Robins, *The Corporation That Changed the World: How the East India Company Shaped the Modern Multinational* (Hyderabad: Orient Longman, 2006).

[187] See ibid., p. 24. For details see M. K. Nawaz, 'Some Legal Aspects of the Anglo-Mughal Relations', (1956) *Indian Yearbook of International Affairs*, pp. 70–83.

[188] Anghie, *Imperialism*, p. 36.

[189] Marx, *Capital*, vol. 1, p. 705.

[190] Hersch Lauterpacht, 'The Grotian Tradition in International Law' in Eli Lauterpacht (ed.) *International Law: Collected Papers*, vol. II, Part I (Cambridge: Cambridge University Press, 1975), pp. 307–366 at p. 325.

world economy by means of a powerful merchant marine bolstered by
the Navy and the Navigation Acts of 1651 and 1661. Through these latter acts 'England assumed to herself the monopoly of the colonial trade'
laying down 'that the colonies … should be subordinated to Parliament,
thus making a coherent imperial policy possible; and that trade to the
colonies should be monopolised by English shipping'.[191] The Navigation
Acts laid the basis for British policy over the next century and a half. But
already by the end of the seventeenth century Britain had established
its imperial supremacy. The period saw a debate between Hugo Grotius
and the British writer John Selden on the question of freedom of the
seas; the former defending the idea of 'freedom of the seas' to promote
Dutch trade (in *Mare Liberum*) and the latter 'closed seas' to protect
British interests (in *Mare Clausum*).[192] The Navigation Acts hit the Dutch
hard and war followed in the wake of commercial rivalry. These wars
(1652–1674) broke 'the Dutch hold on trade in tobacco, sugar, furs, slaves
and codfish, and laid the foundation for the establishment of English territorial power in India'.[193] While 'the first Dutch war opened India and
the Far Eastern trade to English merchants; the second Dutch war West
Africa and the slave trade'.[194] The capture of Jamaica in 1655 and the pri-
vateering centre of Dunkirk in France (both annexed in 1661) laid the
foundation of the slave trade which vastly enriched English merchants.
The war of Spanish Succession (1701–1714) obtained for England the
Asiento, the monopoly of supplying slaves to the Spanish American
Empire. With it 'England replaced the Netherlands as the greatest slave-
trading nation in the world'.[195] On the other hand, with the Portuguese
alliance of 1654 'English merchants forced their way into the Portuguese
colonial monopoly in America, Africa and Asia, in return for protection
by English sea-power – something which England had never been strong
enough to offer before'.[196] Finally, the British established their hegemony
through a straightforward policy of prohibiting all manufacturers in the
colonies which could compete with those of the home country. In fact,
as Maurice Dobb has noted, 'measures, not only of coercion applied to

---

[191] Christopher Hill, *Reformation to Industrial Revolution, 1530–1780* (Hammondsworth: Penguin, 1969), p. 155.
[192] See R. P. Anand, *Origin and Development of the Law of the Sea: History of International Law Revisited* (The Hague: Martinus Nijhoff, 1983).
[193] Hill, *Reformation*, p. 156.
[194] See ibid., p. 228.
[195] See ibid.
[196] See ibid., p. 158.

colonial trade in order that it should primarily serve the needs of the parent country, but also to control colonial production, became a special preoccupation of policy at the end of the seventeenth century and the first half of the eighteenth'.[197]

Already by the 1690s an international division of labour was inaugurated in which the colonies (Ireland, Americas and West Indies) were relegated to the position of raw material suppliers to the advantage of the emerging industrial nations. In the words of Marx, the period saw the conversion of 'one part of the globe into a chiefly agricultural field of production, for supplying the other part which remain (ed) a chiefly industrial field'.[198] Thus, a world economy constituted by a 'new world market' came into operation binding together nations in hitherto unknown relationships and forms. Yet, the world economy at this stage is best characterized as being in its infancy both because of the level of integration and the intensity of trade but also in view of the fact that the world market in this phase was not large enough for the simultaneous industrialization of two or more countries on the modern scale.[199] It is well known that British industrialization coincided with its capture of nearly all the world's markets for certain manufactured goods, and the control of most of the world's colonial areas.[200]

It is also in the seventeenth century that the modern states system came to be established, its origins usually traced to the Treaty of Westphalia, 1648. The domestic context of striking a final blow against feudal anarchy was of course the paramount factor in the emergence of the European states system presided over by the absolutist state. With the birth of the absolutist state, the state made its appearance as 'a centralized institution, as the *source of all* "political" *power* inside a *territorial-national* domain'.[201] The notion of state sovereignty gradually came to be accepted. It expressed 'the *exclusive, unique,* institutionalized and strictly *public* dominance over a territorial-national ensemble and the effective exercise of central power without the "extra-political" restrictions of juridical, ecclesiastical or

---

[197] Maurice Dobb, *Studies in the Development of Capitalism* (London: Routledge and Kegan Paul, Ltd., 1947), p. 205.

[198] Marx, *Capital,* vol. 1, p. 425.

[199] E. J. Hobsbawm, 'The General Crisis of the European Economy in the 17th Century – II', 6 (1954) *Past and Present*, pp. 44–65 at p. 55.

[200] See ibid.

[201] Nicos Poulantzas, *Political Power and Social Classes* (London: Verso 1978), p. 162; emphasis in original. The intimate relationship of the latter and mercantile capitalism is well-established; 'the Mercantile System was a system of State-regulated exploitation through trade'. Dobb, *Studies in the Development*, p. 209.

moral order which characterized the feudal state'.[202] An era was inaugurated in which sovereign states entered into relations with each other on
the basis of a secular law of nations. It is perhaps for this reason it is said
that with the Peace of Westphalia 'international law was born'.[203]

The period of old colonialism thus saw the 'logic of capital' and the
'logic of territory' combine and give life to and shape the doctrines of
international law. The idea of a universal law of nations was advanced on
the basis of a 'modern' doctrine of natural law, not seriously challenged
until the nineteenth century when it deflated into, and was replaced by,
the positivist, narrow, Christian law of nations. Thus, the classic tradition 'never conceived a constitutive theory of recognition … nor did it
produce a conception of the family of nations, admission to which was
in the self-determined discretion of any nucleus of Sovereigns'.[204] The
primary problem in these times was the commercial rivalry between the
European nations leading to endemic conflict. It has been calculated that
in the seventeenth century seven years alone passed without major wars
between states. The rivalries were fought out as much on land as on the
oceans. It explains the great amount of attention devoted to the laws of
war and peace in this period along with the problem of freedom of the
seas. It is no accident that much of Grotius's writings were given to the
consideration of these two twin issues.

B.   New Colonialism: 1760–1875

Old colonialism was fuelled by the backwardness of the manufactur-
ing sector in Europe: wealth was accumulated by European merchants
through, inter alia, selling the reputed goods of Asia in Europe. The
essence of new colonialism was a reversal of roles as a consequence of the
imperial policies followed by Britain which had emerged as the leading
metropolitan nation.[205] There was 'a convergence of developments in the
early 1760s' from which dates the phase of new colonialism. Britain's victory over France in the Seven Year War (1756–1763) in which France lost
the whole of its colonial empire inaugurated a new era; the Treaty of Paris

---

[202] See ibid.
[203] John Westlake, *International Law* (Cambridge: Cambridge University Press, 1895), p. 59.
[204] C. H. Alexandrowicz, *An Introduction to the History of the Law of Nations in the East Indies (16th, 17th and 18th centuries)* (Oxford: Clarendon Press, 1967), p. 237.
[205] Thus Hobsbawm has well observed that 'old colonialism did not grow over into new colo-
nialism; it collapsed and was replaced by it'. E. J. Hobsbawm, 'The General Crisis of the
European Economy in the 17th Century – I', 5 (1954) *Past and Present*, pp. 33–53 at p. 46.

(1763) represented a watershed in English colonial policy as 'henceforth greater stress was laid on colonies as markets than as sources of supply'.[206] Underlying this policy departure was the Industrial Revolution. It rendered the mercantile system, along with the old imperial system anomalous, and underlined the need for large colonial markets for its sustenance. The previous closed markets of the plantation and settlement colonies were entirely inadequate in view of the flood of products pouring out of the new factories.[207] The defeat of France paved the way for the conquest of India (through the Battle of Plassey in 1757) and the extension of British settlements in Canada and other areas of the North American continent. In fact, during this period the scope of British global interests broadened dramatically to cover the South Pacific, the Far East, the South Atlantic and the coast of Africa. While the success of the American War of Independence (1775–1783) meant the loss of American colonies it was followed by worldwide expansion: Australia (1788), Sierra Leone (1808), Gambia (1816) and Gold Coast (1821) figured in this expansion. In fact colonial tribute and markets were a significant factor in making Britain a world power. Thus, the scale and speed of capitalist industrialization which Britain witnessed in this period is inconceivable without the loot and plunder of India.[208] A mature world economy was in the process of evolving based upon an international division of labour that linked internal economies in a complex and intricate web of relationships. However, it is good to remember that even at this stage the world economy was built around a single country – Britain. In the middle of the nineteenth century she is said to have been producing two-thirds, of the world coal, perhaps half its iron, five-sevenths of the then supply of steel, about half of the cotton cloth produced and 40 per cent of its hardware.[209]

The peculiar characteristics of international relations in this period influenced the developments within international law. With the firm

---

[206] Hill, *Reformation*, p. 233.

[207] Harry Magdoff, *Imperialism: From the Colonial Age to the Present* (New York: Monthly Review Press, 1978), p. 106.

[208] See Jawaharlal Nehru, *The Discovery of India* (Lucknow: Asia Publishing House, 1961), p. 314; A. K. Bagchi, *Perilous Passage: Mankind and the Global Ascendancy of Capital* (New Delhi: Oxford University Press, 2006); A. K. Bagchi, *Colonialism and Indian Economy* (Oxford: Oxford University Press, 2010); Utsa Patnaik, 'The Free Lunch: Transfers from the Tropical Colonies and Their Role in Capital Formation in Britain during the Industrial Revolution' in K. S. Jomo (ed.), *Globalization under Hegemony: The Changing World* (New Delhi: Oxford University Press, 2006), pp. 30–70.

[209] E. J. Hobsbawm, *Industry and Empire: From 1750 to the Present Day* (London: Penguin, 1968), p. 110.

establishment of the bourgeois world order in Europe, particularly after the French Revolution, sovereignty 'became the central principle in the external policy and the international conduct of all the leading states in the European system'.[210] There was also greater interaction among them leading to increased international legal activity. A fairly large number of treaties were concluded on a wide range of issues, the law of prize was developed, and claims and counter-claims began to be articulated on the basis of international law. Vattel's *Le droit des gens, ou principes de la loi naturelle* (1758) described as 'the first recognizably modern book on international law' 'provided the legal version of the new political understanding of Europe as an international system' and came to be used as a handbook by Foreign Offices.[211] The European law of nations also came to take into account contemporary features of the age. The Congress of Vienna (1815) played an important role in this regard. It adopted a declaration on the abolition of slave trade, gave first expression to the principle of free navigation on international rivers, regulated the rank of diplomatic envoys and introduced the system of perpetual neutrality. However, at the Congress, the British refused any debate over the freedom of the seas. Though later, in view of the fact that 'her naval strength and potential was virtually unchallengeable', and the domination within Britain of free trade mentality, she encouraged the idea of openness of the seas. The famous Navigation Acts, which had contributed so much to the growth and strength of its merchant marine, were repealed in 1849.[212] The British domination however did not prevent European expansion from beginning anew based on the organization and firepower of trained and professional troops matured in the course of internecine conflicts fought between European states in the period 1660–1720.[213] But cooperation among European states also continued. It led to the creation

---

[210] F. H. Hinsley, *Sovereignty*, 2nd edn (Cambridge: Cambridge University Press, 1986), p. 204.

[211] Ibid., pp. 194–195. According to Hinsley: 'The French government was referring to it in the 1760s; by the government of the United States of America it was venerated as being the guide, in the phrase later used by Daniel Webster, "to all those principles, laws and usages which have obtained currency among civilized states", almost from the rime of the American Revolution; and from about that time, during the years between the 1760s and the outbreak of the French Revolution, it came to be regarded in the same light, as is clear from their writings and speeches by British politicians', pp. 200–201.

[212] Paul Kennedy, *The Rise and Fall of British Naval Mastery* (London: The Macmillan Press, 1976), p. 163.

[213] Michael Howard, 'The Military Factor in European Expansion' in Hedley Bull and Adam Watson (eds.) *The Expansion of International Society* (Oxford: Clarendon Press, 1984), pp. 32–42 at p. 36.

of the International Telegraphic Union in 1865 and the Universal Postal Union in 1874.

However, this period also saw international law shrink from a universal law of nations to being a Christian law of nations with colonies becoming objects of international law. The entire law of state responsibility was developed to the disadvantage of the non-European world to meet the growing need to protect economic space for European goods and merchants. The nineteenth century also saw the European powers enforce unequal treaties and capitulation and protectorate regimes in the Levant, Asia and Africa. On the doctrinal plane natural law came to be supplanted by positivism which helped rationalize the use of force against the non-European world.[214] Indeed, the century saw the distinction between civilized/ uncivilized peoples and states become central to modern international law.[215] Of course, the colonial project also posed 'insuperable set of challenges' to positivism that tied itself in contradictions[216] recognizing colonized entities one instance only to de-recognize them the next moment.[217]

C.   Imperialism: 1875–1945

In the last quarter of the nineteenth century, capitalism entered its monopoly phase. It witnessed the tremendous drive towards carving out the still independent sector of the world: nearly all of Africa, a large part of Asia and a number of Pacific islands. In fact,

> the rate of new territorial acquisitions of the new imperialism was almost three times that of the earlier period. Thus, the increase in new territories

---

[214] Anghie, *Imperialism*, pp. 32–114. However, according to one observer, Gerrit Gong, 'the role played by positivist legal doctrines should not be overstated'. That is to say, 'the fact that positivist notions supplanted naturalist doctrines as the fundamental philosophical basis of the European law of nations cannot be held responsible for Europe's increased use of coercive military force against non-European countries. True, this shift may have facilitated the rationalization of the use of force against non-European countries. Positivist legal notions did underscore that "admissibility of war and non-military pressure" were a "prerogative of sovereignty". And, under the positivist conception, a measure of compulsion did not invalidate a treaty. [However,] what changed was not so much the European willingness to use force to impose a standard of "civilization", as the European ability to do so. Gerrit W. Gong, *The Standard of 'Civilisation' in International Society* (Oxford: Oxford University Press, 1984), pp. 42 and 43–44.

[215] A 'central feature of positivism was the distinction it made between civilized and uncivilized states'. Anghie, *Imperialism*, p. 52. Malcolm N. Shaw, *International Law*, 6th edn (Cambridge: Cambridge University Press, 2008), p. 27.

[216] See ibid., p. 38.

[217] See ibid., p. 105.

claimed in the first seventy-five years of the nineteenth century averaged about 83,000 square miles (210,000 square kilometres) a year. As against this, the colonial powers added an average of about 240,000 square miles (620,000 square kilometres) a year between the late 1870s and World War I (1914–1918).[218]

Nations which were not formally colonies were only independent in name, described by V. I. Lenin as semi-colonial countries – Persia, China and Turkey.[219] Postcolonial Latin America was the arena of financial blackmail and armed interventions. A new feature of this age was that the number of nations actively seeking a slice of the colonial pie increased: Germany, the United States, Belgium, Italy, and, for the first time, a non-European power, Japan. Rosa Luxemburg grasped the essence of imperialism in this era in observing that 'imperialism is the political expression of the accumulation of capital in its competitive struggle for what remains still open of the non-capitalist environment'.[220]

Her understanding represented an important step forward for as the Indian Marxist economist Prabhat Patnaik points out Marx's analysis was 'concerned essentially with a "closed" capitalist economy' and 'the interaction between capitalism and the colonies remains an area of silence for Marxist theory' till Luxemburg advanced her thesis on the integral relationship between capitalism and imperialism.[221] As Patnaik observes, 'the problem here is not about what happened in history; indeed, Marxist historians, especially from the Third World, have done invaluable work to throw light on this question. The problem is to incorporate it into the core of Marxist *theory*'.[222] For even Lenin 'did not go into the nature of these colonial relations themselves, and the role they play in the process of reproduction of capital'.[223] Subscribing to a similar view Paul Sweezy has observed:

> Rosa Luxemburg attempted to prove that capital accumulation is impossible in a closed capitalist system. Marx's failure to understand this was due to the unfinished state of his work. She would now supply the missing

---

[218] Magdoff, *Imperialism*, pp. 34–35.
[219] V. I. Lenin, *Selected Works*, vol.1 (Moscow: Progress Publishers, 1975), p. 693.
[220] Rosa Luxemburg, *The Accumulation of Capital* (London: Routledge and Kegan Paul, 1951), p. 28.
[221] See Chapter 2, pp. 61–62.
[222] Prabhat Patnaik, 'The Communist Manifesto after 150 years' in Prakash Karat (ed.) *A World to Win: Essays on The Communist Manifesto* (New Delhi: LeftWord, 1999), p. 7; emphasis in original.
[223] See ibid.

proof, close the most important gap in the Marxian system, and in this way explain the hitherto inexplicable phenomena of modern imperialism.[224]

Other writers have also endorsed this understanding. For instance, David Harvey writes that 'Marx himself never proposed a theory of imperialism ... Marx constructed a theory of accumulation for a capitalist mode of production in a "pure" state without reference to any particular historical situation ... Marx's theory of the capitalist mode of production plainly cannot be used as the basis for deriving a historically specific theory of imperialism in any direct manner'.[225] More recently, Davenport has observed that for Marx and Engels 'international relations presented a practical problem rather than a theoretical one: the contradiction between the national and the international was registered empirically but not penetrated by theory'.[226] In his view:

> imperialism theory, in comparison with the international thought of Marx and Engels, constituted a sustained attempt to link theoretically the dynamics of international politics to the changing structure of capital accumulation – the theorization of imperialism as part of the dynamic of monopoly capitalism.[227]

Apropos Marx's description of the 'international' as being 'secondary and tertiary' Justin Rosenberg writes:

> Marx never returned theoretically to the synoptic level of the *Manifesto* in order to revise the essentially unilinear vision of capitalist development presented there. Had he done so, he might – just might – have reconsidered whether the 'influence ... of international relations' really did belong among the 'secondary and tertiary' dimensions of social reality.[228]

These observations support the contention that Marx thought of capitalism essentially as a closed system even as he extensively wrote on colonialism. Therefore, arguably, it was Rosa Luxemburg who was the first to

---

[224] Paul M. Sweezy, *The Theory of Capitalist Development* (New York: Monthly Review Press, 1968), p. 202. While her thesis may have been criticized at the technical level the broad argument of expansion into non-capitalist spaces remains in place. See ibid., pp. 202ff.

[225] David Harvey, 'The Geography of Capitalist Accumulation: A Reconstruction of Marxist Theory' in Richard Peet (ed.) *Radical Geography: Alternative Viewpoints on Contemporary Social Issues* (London: Methuen & Co Ltd., 1977), pp. 283–284.

[226] Andrew Davenport, 'Marxism in IR: Condemned to a Realist Fate?', 19 (2013) *European Journal of International Relations*, pp. 27–48 at p. 28.

[227] See ibid.

[228] Justin Rosenberg, 'International Relations – The "Higher Bullshit": A Reply to the Globalization Theory Debate', 44 (2007) *International Politics*, pp. 450–482 at p. 480.

posit an internal linkage between the two, i.e., the 'logic of capital' and the 'logic of territory'.

Luxemburg also pointed to emerging inter-imperialist competition, that is, the tendency of imperialist nations to compete with each other for space. The First World War revealed the importance of her insights.[229] In other words, the intensification of colonial policy was not merely a preferred policy but, as Lenin pointed out, a result of the emergence of finance capital as the 'decisive force in all international relations' which founded 'a world system of colonial oppression'.[230] It spread 'its net over all countries of the world' and represented 'a new stage of world concentration of capital and production, incomparably higher than the preceding stages', 'expanding and deepening the further development of capitalism throughout the world'.[231] At the same time, 'a concrete picture of the internal relations of the world economy' disclosed the sharpening of inter-imperialist competition. Rebutting Karl Kautsky's contention of peaceful exploitation of the world by an internationally united finance capital Lenin emphasized that the rule of finance capital increased 'the un-evenness and contradictions inherent in the world economy' and concluded that 'peaceful alliances prepare the ground for wars, and in their turn grow out of wars; the one conditions the other, producing alternating forms of peaceful and non-peaceful struggle on *one and the same* basis of imperialist connections and relations within world economics and world polities'.[232] That Lenin was right and Kautsky wrong is testified to by two world wars.

All these developments – the partitioning of the world, the deepening of international economic relations accompanied by serious crisis, inter-imperialist competition, and uneven world economic growth – left their mark on the body of international law. It would require a separate tome to record the influence of these developments on international law, for it was a period of rapid growth. Only a few general observations may be ventured. First, by the end of the nineteenth century the European law of nations metamorphosed into a law of 'civilized' nations. The doctrine of positivism firmly established itself, later taking a pragmatic turn.[233] Its 'central feature', as noted before, 'was the distinction it

---

[229] See in this context Rosa Luxemburg, *The Crisis in German Social-Democracy: (The "Junius" Pamphlet)* (New York: The Socialist Publication Society, 1919).

[230] Lenin, *Selected Works*, vol. 1, p. 694.

[231] See ibid., pp. 681 and 683.

[232] See ibid., p. 724; emphasis in original.

[233] By late nineteenth century 'positivism decisively replaced naturalism as the principal jurisprudential technique of the discipline of international law'. Anghie, *Imperialism*, p. 33.

made between civilized and uncivilized states'.[234] In this period 'only the practice of European states was decisive and could create international law'.[235] Positivists found various ways to justify the colonial project that included the idea of 'protectorates',[236] 'unequal treaties',[237] 'recognition doctrine',[238] doctrines relating to 'discovery, occupation, conquest and cession'[239] together with the terra nullius doctrine,[240] 'treaties of capitulation',[241] 'quasi-sovereignty', and even partitioning through conferences (e.g., the Berlin Conference 1884–1885).[242] In short, positivist doctrines provided the ideological justification for declaring the barbarous and semi-civilized colonial world outside the pale of the operation of the law of nations. While on the face of it, the standard of civilization principle was often posited as a temporary state of affairs but 'like Sisyphus, the less "civilized" were doomed to work towards an equality which an elastic standard of "civilization" put forever beyond reach'.[243] Imperialist needs, disguised as 'civilization', provided the impetus for rapid developments in the law of state responsibility. Protests in the form of the Calvo and the Drago doctrines advanced in Latin America were nullified through legal manoeuvres.[244] For instance, the Calvo clause was met with the plea that a national could not surrender the rights which vested with the state.[245] On the face of it, the Drago doctrine was accepted at the 1907 Hague Peace Conference.[246] But in actuality it admitted intervention *sub modo* by virtue of the Porter Convention against which Drago himself vainly protested at the Conference.[247] There was sage advice given to those protesting against

---

[234]   See ibid., p. 52.
[235]   See ibid., p. 54.
[236]   See ibid., pp. 87–90.
[237]   See ibid., pp. 72–73.
[238]   See ibid., pp. 75–79, 98–100.
[239]   See ibid., p. 82.
[240]   See ibid., pp. 83–84. See also pp. 91ff, 111.
[241]   See ibid., p. 85.
[242]   See ibid., pp. 90ff.
[243]   See ibid., p. 63.
[244]   The Calvo doctrine 'involved a reaffirmation of the principle of non-intervention coupled with the assertion that aliens were entitled only to such rights as were accorded nationals and thus had to seek redress for grievances exclusively in the domestic arena'. Shaw, *International Law* , p. 824. However, Calvo was not free of other biases. See generally Chapter 5, pp. 350–351.
[245]   See generally Herbert W. Briggs, *The Law of Nations*, 2nd edn (New York: Appleton-Century-Crofts, 1952), pp. 637 ff.
[246]   Luis M. Drago and H. Edward Nettles, 'The Drago Doctrine in International Law and Politics', 8 (1928) *The Hispanic American Historical Review*, pp. 201–233.
[247]   Separate opinion of Judge Ammoun, *Case Concerning the Barcelona Traction, Light and Power Company Limited*, Second Phase, *I. C. J. Reports*, pp. 287–333, at p. 291.

the then law of diplomatic protection: the alternative scenario could be much harsher. The legal institution of diplomatic protection, in the words of Frederick Sherwood Dunn, 'served as a substitute for territorial conquest in bringing the Latin-American states within the orbit of international trade and intercourse, and, while the results obtained were not what these countries might have desired, the probable alternatives would have been far less desirable from their standpoint'.[248]

Second, in the face of imperialist rivalries there were continuous efforts to prevent war and encourage the peaceful settlement of disputes, along with the more realistic attempts to humanize war through developing the laws of war. The Hague Conferences (1899 and 1907) were the first steps in this direction. They foundered on the rock of inter-imperialist competition: no significant progress was made towards disarmament or the peaceful settlement of disputes through arbitration.[249] The victors in the First World War wrote their imperial interests into the Treaty of Versailles, of which the League Covenant was an integral part. It developed the colonial vocabulary further. 'Mandates' was the 'verbal fiction' through which colonialism now came to be legitimized, indeed given juridical sanction.[250] The ideas behind the Mandate System have in many ways shaped 'the operations and character of contemporary international institutions'.[251] More broadly, this period 'represented a number of shifts in the history of international law: from positivism to pragmatism, from law to institutions, from sovereignty to government; from race to economics; from conquest to decolonization; from colonialism to neo-colonialism; from exploitation to development; and from England and France to the United States'.[252]

---

[248] Frederick Sherwood Dunn, *The Protection of Nationals: A Study in the Application of International Law* (Baltimore, MD: Johns Hopkins University Press, 1932), p. 58.

[249] However, for the view that if certain developments in the world of international law had taken place the First World War could have been prevented, see Francis Anthony Boyle, *World Politics and International Law* (Durham, NC: Duke University Press, 1985), p. 43. See for critique B. S. Chimni, 'Peace through Law: Lessons from 1914', 3 (2015) *London Review of International Law*, pp. 245–265 at pp. 256ff.

[250] Ammoun, *Barcelona Traction*, p. 309. For a detailed exposition of the Mandate System see Anghie, *Imperialism*, pp. 115–196. For a trenchant critique of the League of Nations and Mandates System written at the time see Sri Aurobindo, *The Human Cycle, The Ideal of Human Unity, War and Self-Determination*, 2nd edn (Pondicherry: Sri Aurobindo Ashram, 1970), pp. 608–636, 642.

[251] Anghie, *Imperialism*, p. 117.

[252] See ibid., p. 194.

Third, not deterred by the First World War fresh attempts to out-law war through legal means were initiated in the inter-war period, the high point being the Kellogg-Briand Pact (1928). The 'idealistic' think-ing which informed these attempts provoked a sharp realistic critique articulated by E. H. Carr and Hans Morgenthau that these legal develop-ments did not represent any serious progress in preventing war.[253] To be sure, the Kellogg-Briand Pact attempted to purge international law of the Hegelian notion of absolute sovereignty, but the encounter with reality – the political economy of imperialism – could not as yet be put off.[254] The Second World War broke out in 1939, an event the League of Nations, or rather its members, did little to prevent.

Fourth, despite intense political rivalries, the logic of expanding inter-national economic relations necessitated the establishment of inter-national organizations called administrative unions; they emerged in areas where cooperation was necessary and conflicts could be accommodated. Besides ITU and UPU a number of IOs came to be established viz., the International Bureau of Weights and Measures (1875), the International Union of the Protection of Industrial Property (1883), the International Union for the Protection of Literary and Artistic Works (1886), the Anti-Slavery Society for the Protection of Human Rights (1889), the International Union for the Publication of Customs Tariffs (1890), and the Central Office for International Railway Transport (1890). Both private and public international unions proliferated. According to one estimate between 1840 and 1919 something like 400 private permanent associations were established.[255]

Finally, in 1917 the October Revolution took place which had a great impact on international law.[256] However, in telling of the history of inter-national law Western scholarship entirely neglects the contribution of Soviet Union to its progressive development in the Lenin period (1917-1924). Quigley has recently recorded some of the significant contribu-tions of the Soviet Union to the development of international law in the early years. These included the condemnation of all secret treaties (and

---

[253] See Chapter 2. See also E. H. Carr, *The Twenty Years' Crisis: An Introduction to the Study of International Relations*, 2nd edn (New York: Palgrave, 2001).

[254] It is perhaps necessary to clarify that the altered structure of international society allows a more optimistic conclusion today.

[255] D. W. Bowett, *The Law of international Institutions*, 3rd edn (London: Stevens and Sons, 1975), p. 4.

[256] This chapter is not the occasion to record in detail the contribution of former Soviet Union to modern international law.

the publication of 100 odd treaties that 'it found in the tsarist govern-ment archives'),[257] the renunciation of the system of capitulations,[258] the affirmation of the principle of self-determination and the accompanying rejection of the mandate system,[259] the stress on the need for international criminal trials, and the rejection of military intervention.

D.   Neocolonialism: 1945–1985

The end of the Second World War saw the beginnings of the reversal of the expansionist trends of the preceding centuries and the birth of newly independent states. Independence was of course not granted on a platter but achieved through the heroic struggle of the colonial peoples.[260] These struggles rarely receive a mention in the literature on the history of inter-national law. Indeed a conspicuously absent theme, including in critical histories of international law, is that of resistance of subaltern groups, peoples and nations to colonial regimes and later to imperialism in all its forms. For the end of colonialism did not signify the end of imperialism but the beginning of a new phase: imperialism without colonies.

Imperialism, it bears repeating, is just not another word for 'colo-nialism' but refers to a particular stage in the global development of capitalism. This is not an empty distinction. For those who associated imperialism with colonialism, the former phenomenon was extinguished with decolonization or continued only in so far is decolonization was not complete. But 'the identification of imperialism with colonialism obfuscates not only historical variation in colonial-metropolitan rela-tions, but makes it more difficult to evaluate the latest transformation of the capitalist world system, the imperialism of the period of monopoly capitalism'.[261] Faced with the collapse of the colonial system, monopoly

---

[257] John Quigley, *Soviet Legal Innovation and the Law of the Western World* (Cambridge: Cambridge University Press, 2007), pp. 49, 134ff. On the impact of Soviet Union on secret treaties, Quigley cites Oppenheim: 'Widespread dissatisfaction provoked during the World War by the publication of secret treaties [i.e., by Soviet Union] found expression in Article 18 of the Covenant [of the League of Nations'. See ibid., p. 134.

[258] See ibid., pp. 52, 135–137.

[259] See ibid., pp. 137ff. With respect to the principle of self-determination Quigley writes: 'The Soviet challenge was more fundamental than Wilson's. Wilson was calling, in effect, for free competition among the capitalist countries in access to the third world. The implica-tion of the Soviet Decree [i.e., the 1917 Decree on Peace] was that outside powers should keep off'. See ibid., p. 139.

[260] The other major development was the emergence of the socialist bloc.

[261] Magdoff, *Imperialism*, p. 119.

capital devised new means to subordinate the economies of newly independent states. Transnational corporations and banks, unequal exchange, a system of conditionalities prescribed by international financial institutions, and manipulative aid became the chief vehicles of imperialism, backed up by the politics of proxy war, subversion and intervention. The international economic system continued to be structured against the vital interests of the developing nations who bore the brunt of any crisis which afflicted the capitalist world, and manifested in this era in the instability of primary commodity prices and the debt crisis.[262] In fact, the chief characteristic of the post-war world economy was the simultaneous strengthening of contradictory trends – greater and growing interdependence with uneven development. National economies slowly came to be enmeshed in a web of international economic relations and subjected to its internal logic. The world economy began to impose significant limits on the freedom of action of national units in relation to the most sensitive aspects of domestic policy. The negative features of the growing interdependence between states began to manifest themselves.

The complexities and contradictions which marked the decolonization era found their necessary reflection in the sphere of international law and organization. A series of UN General Assembly resolutions reflecting the concerns and aspirations of the developing countries were adopted. These included the Declaration on the Granting of Independence to Colonial Countries and Peoples, 1960, Declaration on Permanent Sovereignty over Natural Resources, 1962, and the Declaration on Principles of International Law concerning Friendly Relations, 1970. The developing countries also took the initiative to establish new institutions such as the United Nations Conference on Trade and Development (UNCTAD) and the United Nations Industrial Development Organization (UNIDO) that would facilitate their development. Further, the developing countries raised and pursued the demand for a new international economic and legal order through adopting the Declaration and Programme of Action on a New International Economic Order, 1974 and the Charter on Economic Rights and Duties of States, 1974. But despite these initiatives the North-South divide continued. In his classic work *Towards a new international economic order* (1979) Mohammed Bedjaoui captured the ways in which international law stood in the way of developing countries

---

[262] B. S. Chimni, *International Commodity Agreements: A Legal Study* (London: Croom Helm, 1986).

in the realization of their development goals. Bedjaoui noted that while imperialism had received 'staggering blows' it showed 'an extraordinary ability to "co-opt", and amazing powers of adjustment'.[263]

Meanwhile, the spatial boundaries of international law were beginning to be redefined to take cognizance of modern developments and concerns, an event proceeding apace with the struggle of the developing countries to metamorphose the content of traditional international law, and to ensure that their societal needs are met through new legal regimes. In the 1960s the two landmark conventions on human rights were adopted viz., the International Covenant on Civil and Political Rights and the International Covenant on Economic, Social and Cultural Right respectively. In the 1970s the negotiation of the law of the sea convention came to receive much attention with the final text being adopted in 1982. While there was some progress in shaping international law to address the problems of peoples of developing countries, it was slow and halting and subject to reversals.

This was, however, a period in which the battle to reshape the international legal order to bring a modicum of welfare to the peoples of developing countries was also accompanied by the challenge of TWAIL scholars to the history of international law as told by Western academia. While the explicit influence of postcolonial theory was yet to be felt in the scholarship, its spirit informed the quest for a narrative that underlined on one side the role of European or imperialist international law in facilitating and legitimizing colonialism and on the other hand acknowledged that international law was present in Asia and Africa in the pre-colonial era which regulated the relationship between many of the states of the regions and European powers. While in this period a feminist approach to international law had yet to be articulated, feminist thinking had already been coming to have an impact as symbolized by the adoption of the Convention on the Elimination of Discrimination against Women, 1979.[264] International law did not simply codify the interests of powerful social forces and states but also responded in some instances to the concerns of marginal and oppressed sections.

---

[263] Mohammed Bedjaoui, *Towards a new international economic order* (Paris: UNESCO, 1979), p. 12.
[264] See Chapter 6, pp. 369–370.

VII.   Nature and Character of Contemporary International Law: The Era of Global Imperialism (1985–)

It is time to turn to analyse the nature and character of international law in the present, i.e., in the era of global imperialism (1985–). This section, however, does not merely attempt to identify the key features of contemporary international law, but also seeks to inject into the narrative theoretical elements that inform the articulation of IMAIL. It proceeds as follows. The section begins with a brief discussion of the relationship of the categories class, gender and race in order to underline the importance of an intersectional and composite approach to characterize contemporary international law, as emphasised in the Chapter on FtAIL. It then stresses the need to take cognizance of both the 'logic of capital' and 'logic of territory' to capture the complex process through which contemporary international law rules are adopted and enforced. This analysis is followed by the identification of key features of international law today. It may be worth noting that these features can be captured and articulated in the technical language of political economy through exploring the process of accumulation of capital on a global scale. However, what is attempted is to identify the social classes that drive the global accumulation process along with those features of international law that facilitate it. To put it differently, the role of universalizing capitalism and states system are dealt with through noting how they manifest in the world of international law.[265] Finally, the significant questions of the possibility of reform of international law and the value of 'international rule of law' to subaltern groups, peoples and nations are discussed.

A.   Integrating Class, Gender, Race

In *The Communist Manifesto* Marx and Engels observed that 'the history of all hitherto existing society is the history of class struggles'.[266] The term 'class' or 'social classes' used by them have been assigned a number of meanings. Some writers have given primacy to the location of social groups in the production system, others to a composite of social practices, and even others to describing how 'classes' are historically constituted,

---

[265] It may however be conceded that particular branches of international law such as international economic law or international trade law could be explained as well through reviewing global production, consumption and relations of distribution.

[266] Marx and Engels, *Selected Works*, vol. 1, p. 108.

and finally to a combination of elements drawn from all these factors. Focusing on the place of a social class in the production process or in the economic sphere Lenin defined classes as follows:

> Classes are large groups of people differing from each other by the place they occupy in a historically determined system of social production, by their relation (in most cases fixed and formulated in law) to the means of production, by their role in the social organization of labor, and, consequently, by the dimensions of the share of social wealth of which they dispose and the mode of acquiring it. Classes are groups of people one of which can appropriate the labor of another owing to the different places they occupy in a definite system of social economy.[267]

Nicos Poulantzas on the other hand identified a 'social class' by its role 'in the ensemble of social practices, i.e., by its place in the social division of labor as a whole' taking into account the political and ideological relations as well.[268] E. P. Thompson rejected the structural understanding of Poulantzas in the preface to his epic *The Making of the English Working Class* and stressed the historical processes through which social classes are formed. He wrote:

> By class I understand a historical phenomenon, unifying a number of disparate and seemingly unconnected events, both in the raw material of experience and in consciousness. I emphasise that it is a historical phenomenon. I do not see class as a 'structure', nor even as a 'category', but as something which in fact happens (and can be shown to have happened) in human relationships.[269]

But even Thompson went on to note that:

> The class experience is largely determined by the productive relations into which men are born – or enter involuntarily. Class-consciousness is the way in which these experiences are handled in cultural terms: embodied in traditions, value-systems, ideas, and institutional forms.[270]

It can be said that each of the formulations accepts the significance of production relations in the constitution of classes in society even as Poulantzas and Thompson stress the significance of structure and history respectively. In other words, while the meaning of 'class' has to take into

---

[267] V. I. Lenin, *Selected Works*, vol. 3 (Moscow: Progress Publishers, 1975), p. 172.

[268] Nicos Poulantzas, *Classes in Contemporary Capitalism* (London: Verso 1978), p. 14.

[269] E. P. Thompson, *The Making of the English Working Class* (Hammondsworth: Penguin, 1963), p. 9.

[270] See ibid., p. 10.

account the place of social groups in the sphere of production, the constitution of classes is a complex historical and cultural process that deeply impacts all aspects of social life. It is usual to divide the capitalist society into two great classes: the capitalist class and the working class. But as Marx noted in his historical writings (e.g., in *The Eighteenth Brumaire*), there are also a number of intermediate classes: the petty bourgeoisie, the lumpen proletariat etc. Marx also spoke of different fractions of the capitalist class that invites separate analysis.[271] In short, the writings of Marx show that the category 'class' has a heterogeneous and multidimensional character.

The class relations in any society also intersect in complex ways with gender, race and caste relations.[272] In fact today the centrality of the category 'class' in determining social relations has been questioned and sought to be displaced by those of 'gender', 'race' and 'caste' depending on the standpoint of the observer. It has inter alia meant the refusal to accept the possibility of an inclusive and composite understanding of 'class' as it is feared that such a move will marginalize the significance of the other fractures in society.[273] But there are others who argue that to altogether dispense with the category 'class' or assign it a subordinate significance would be unfortunate as it represents a fundamental reality of all existing societies. For example, Fredric Jameson cautions that 'it would be great mistake for Marxism to abandon this extraordinarily rich and virtually untouched field of analysis on the ground that class categories were somehow old-fashioned and Stalinist'.[274] He of course recognizes that the category of 'class' 'in its concrete moments is a good deal more complex, internally conflicted, and reflexive than any of the stereotypes'.[275] Jameson's essential point is that the ongoing attempts at foregrounding rival concepts of gender and race can possibly be traced to the fact that they 'are far more adaptable to purely liberal ideal solutions (in other

---

[271] Marx and Engels, *Selected Works*, vol. 1, pp. 464–465.

[272] The theme of intersectional analysis that allows us to capture the complexity of the category 'class' was touched upon in the chapter on Feminist Approaches to International Law. See Chapter 6, pp. 375–378, 398–399.

[273] Speaking of her own experience she concludes that 'class, race, sexuality, gender – and all the other terms with which we categorize and dismiss each other – need to be excavated from the inside'. Dorothy Allison, 'A Question of Class' in Nancy Holstrom (ed.) *The Socialist Feminist Project: A Contemporary Reader in Theory and Politics* (Delhi: Aakar, 2011), pp. 30–45.

[274] Fredric Jameson, *Valences of the Dialectic* (London: Verso, 2009), p. 160.

[275] See ibid.

words, solutions that satisfy the demands of ideology, it being understood that in concrete social life the problems remain equally intractable)'.[276] In the same vein Ellen Meiskins Wood observes in the context of gender oppression:

> Capitalism could survive the eradication of all oppressions specific to women as women – while it would not, by definition, survive the eradication of class exploitation. This does not mean that capitalism has made the liberation of women necessary or inevitable. But it does mean that there is no specific structural necessity for, not even a strong systemic disposition to, gender oppression in capitalism.[277]

While the relationship between capitalism and patriarchy is more complicated than Wood allows for, the fragmentation of theories of exploitation and oppression is not always helpful. Of course there is understandable anxiety that privileging the category 'class' will lead to the creeping expropriation of other categories. A crucial methodological task before Marxists, therefore, is to find a way out of this conundrum. From this perspective one possibility has been articulated by Holstrom:

> in my opinion Marxism's basic theory does not need significant revision in order to take better account of women's oppression. However, I do believe that the theory needs to be supplemented. Feminists are justified in wanting a social theory that gives a fuller picture of production and reproduction than Marx's political economy theory does, that extends the question of democracy not only to the economy but to personal relations. They are also justified in wanting to pay attention to the emotional dimensions of our lives, both to understand how oppression manifests itself in the most intimate aspects of our lives and also most importantly, to give a more complete vision of human emancipation.[278]

However, while such a view of seeing feminism as *supplementing* Marxism may be acceptable to some sections of socialist feminists it would be strongly opposed by others.

Insofar as the relationship between 'class' and 'race' is concerned it has yet to receive the kind of attention it deserves even with reference to domestic legal systems. As Athena Mutua has pointed out in the context

---

[276] See ibid.
[277] Ellen Meiskins Wood, 'Capitalism and Human Emancipation: Race, Gender and Democracy' in Nancy Holmstrom (ed.) *The Socialist Feminist Project: A Contemporary Reader in Theory and Politics* (Delhi: Aakar, 2011), pp. 277–292 at p. 281.
[278] Nancy Holmstrom, 'Introduction' in Nancy Holmstrom (ed.) *The Socialist Feminist Project: A Contemporary Reader in Theory and Politics* (Delhi: Aakar, 2011),pp. 1–13 at pp. 7–8.

of the US legal system, 'a systematic analysis of class, particularly as a product of economic ordering, as well as its relationship to race has not yet emerged, even though critical race scholars have argued for years that the class system in the U.S. mutually constructs race, gender, and other forms of oppression'.[279] But in recent years critical race materialism has moved in the direction of integrating the categories of class and race.[280] The issue at stake is not about assigning a priori priority to a particular category but privileging one or the other depending upon the social context in issue. Such a contextual approach is more promising in formulating an intersectional and composite notion of class as it prevents an arbitrary privileging of class relations irrespective of the social oppression being addressed. The contextual view recognizes that there are multiple social bases for women's oppression or racial oppression and that class oppression is often not its most significant cause. The need for a priori assigning priority to either 'class' or 'gender' or 'race' in explaining such oppression is therefore unnecessary. It is important not to force social experience to fit a privileged category. This point has been made by postcolonial theory as well, as was illustrated earlier by how Indian Marxists have attempted to deal with caste oppression.[281]

Be that as it may, the increasing neglect of the category 'class' cannot be merely traced to the emergence of other categories such as 'gender' and

---

[279] Athena D. Mutua, *The Rise, Development and Future Directions of Critical Race Theory and Related Scholarship*, 84 (2006) *Denver University Law Review,* pp. 329–394 at p. 379.

[280] 'Critical race materialism signifies an approach to interpreting law and society by reading the past to understand how "race" *(in an intersectional, non-essentialized sense)* and economics are deeply constitutive. In this sense, law is reflective of synergistic cultural practices and values that are raced (gendered, sexed) and classed, and identity categories are constructed and reinstantiated by law'. Francisco Valdes and Sumi Cho, 'Critical Race Materialism: Theorizing Justice in the Wake of Global Neoliberalism', 43 (2011) *Connecticut Law Review,* pp. 1513–1572 at p. 1515. They describe international law as follows: 'International law, like domestic law, is the product of local and national elites constructed through race and gender politics reproducing at the trans-national level the same arrangements imposed at the national and sub-national levels: relationships of domination and subordination in the name of goals and values like justice, equality, and dignity'. See ibid., p. 1567; emphasis added. There are at least three recent symposia volumes devoted to the topic of race and class in critical legal scholarship: *Going Back to Class?: The Re-Emergence of Class in Critical Race Theory,* 11(2005) *Michigan Journal of Race and Law; ClassCrits: Toward a Critical Legal Analysis of Economic Inequality,* 56 (2008) *Buffalo Law Review; Critical Race Theory and Marxism,* 1 (2011) *Columbia Journal of Race and Law.* See also Makau Mutua 'Critical Race Theory and International Law: The View of an Insider-Outsider', 45 (2000) *Villanova Law Review,* pp. 841–853; Aoki, 'Space Invaders', pp. 913–958.

[281] See supra pp. 446–447.

'race'. The relevance of the category 'class' has come to be questioned on other grounds that include the absence of an adequately developed map of classes in society, the lack of understanding of their place and role in the ideological and political spheres, its growing irrelevance in the face of the diffusion of capital through the dispersion of stock ownership, and the fact that in the second stage of modernity the advanced capitalist world manifests what Ulrich Beck terms as 'capitalism without classes'.[282] These objections have been addressed in detail elsewhere to argue that the category 'class' retains its salience.[283] But from what has been said it must be clear that in contemporary times a class approach that integrates the gender and race approaches to international law by evolving a composite and contextual approach will have greater traction and attraction. In short, while neither 'class' or 'gender' or 'race' is a master category that explains all international law these together, as they intersect and overlap in real life, provide great explanatory power.

B.   Integrating 'Logic of Territory'

Marxists do not always appreciate the complex process through which international legal rules are adopted. It is not a state but the states system that provides the operative matrix for lawmaking on the international plane. Whereas classical realists disregarded the 'logic of capital' Marxists neglected the 'logic of territory' in understanding the international legal process.[284] However, in some recent Marxist writings on international relations it is conceded that the two logics intersect and influence each other. But as has been aptly observed that 'to assert that the two logics intersect or interact tells us nothing about the relative causal primacy of one over the other'.[285] The question perhaps is not so much of the 'primacy' but of the concurrent influence of both the 'logic of capital' and the 'logic of territory' in different phases of history. Thus, for instance, it can be said that since the *modern* states system evolved and consolidated after the arrival of capitalism it is in a sense a product of it. On the other hand,

---

[282] As Beck puts it, 'for the first time in history, the individual rather than the class is becoming the basic unit of social reproduction'. Ulrich Beck and Johannes Willms, *Conversations with Ulrich Beck* (Cambridge: Polity Press, 2003), p. 101.

[283] B. S. Chimni, 'Prolegomena to a Class Approach to International Law', 21 (2010) *European Journal of International Law*, pp. 57–82.

[284] The implications of the 'logic of territory' were touched upon while reviewing the work of Morgenthau. See Chapter 2, pp. 55–56.

[285] Marx and Engels, *German Ideology*, p. 540.

there is also evidence to support the claim that the birth of the modern states system facilitated the development of capitalism in Europe through, among other things, the elimination of different laws in force in small states of Europe. As Engels wrote:

> The abolition of the motley formal and material legal standards in force in the small states was in itself an urgent requirement for progressive bourgeois development, and this abolition is the chief merit of the new laws – far greater than their content.[286]

However, whatever their mutual influence the two logics of capital and territory do not collapse into each other. In the words of Callinicos:

> the state system is to be understood as a distinct determination (or, rather, set of determinations) within the larger enterprise of developing a satisfactory theory of the capitalist mode of production ... each such determination has specific properties irreducible to those of previously introduced determinations ... the state system has distinctive properties: if it did not, it could not play an explanatory role.[287]

Since the salience of this formulation has not been sufficiently explored by Marxist scholars like Miéville, he does not fully appreciate the progressive dimension of the universal spread of the territorial logic in the wake of decolonization. To be sure, Miéville admits that 'the ending of the era of formal colonialism' was 'a historically progressive moment'.[288] In fact in his view the significance of the wave of decolonization 'should not be underestimated'.[289] But he fails to explain how decolonization is a progressive move other than to observe that it is emancipatory in the same way as wage labour is that over serfdom and slavery.[290] He says little about the ways in which formal equality or territorial logic impact the structure and process of international law. Instead, he goes on to suggest that it is wrong to assume that 'international law can successfully oppose' continuing imperialism as 'it is embedded in the very structures of which international law is an expression and a moment' and further that 'the power dynamics of political imperialism are embedded within the very juridical equality of sovereignty'.[291] In Miéville's view the 'anti-colonial movements

---

[286] Marx and Engels, *Selected Works*, vol. 3, p. 424.
[287] Alex Callinicos, 'Does Capitalism Need the State System?', 20 (2007) *Cambridge Review of International Affairs*, pp.533–549 at p. 542.
[288] Miéville, *Between Equal Rights*, p. 269.
[289] See ibid., p. 270.
[290] See ibid., p. 269.
[291] See ibid., p. 270; emphasis omitted.

became the culmination of the long-term tendency toward universalised juridical sovereignty, and the international law of which sovereign states are the subjects and agents'.[292] Indeed, 'the juridical form of independent sovereignty was one which imperialism itself tended to universalize'.[293] Miéville here comes close to suggesting that the anti-colonial struggles were in some sense unnecessary as imperialism was slowly working towards the grant of independence to create the perfect conditions for imperialist exploitation. He even invokes Pashukanis here: 'Capitalism's tendency is to generalize, and as Pashukanis has made clear, capitalism is *juridical* capitalism. This imperialism of sovereignty is the imperialism of international law, which is the imperialism of juridical relations'.[294] But Pashukanis wrote in the pre-decolonization era and therefore did not deliberate on its significance for the nature and character of international law or for that matter make a distinction between different forms of imperialism. Therefore, to use some of his formulations and to reject as Miéville does the possibility of reform in contemporary international law or be dismissive of the value of international rule of law are deeply problematic propositions. Before turning to examine the Miéville standpoint on these counts it may be useful to look at the key features of contemporary international law.

C.   Key Features of Global Imperialism

In the 1980s the phenomenon of colonialism without colonies began to assume the form of global imperialism, that is, imperialism in the age of accelerated globalization. The period of globalization has seen the emergence of an embryonic global social formation: this formation comprises different modes of production in nation states (in countries of the Global South) but are dominated by the Capitalist Mode of Production (CMP). The global integration process is in fact a multilevel process that implicates national, regional and international spaces. In the early 1980s Ernest Mandel wrote that the 'world-wide capitalist relations of exchange bind together capitalist, semi-capitalist and pro-capitalist relations of production in *an organic unity*'.[295] This understanding can now be cautiously

---

[292] See ibid., p. 266.
[293] See ibid., p. 260.
[294] See ibid; emphasis in original.
[295] Ernest Mandel, 'The Nation-State and Imperialism' in David Held et al. (eds.) *States and Societies* (Oxford: Martin Robertson,1983), pp. 526–539, at p. 527.

extended to the sphere of production what with global production chains becoming the order of the day. The process of global economic integration is facilitated by an emerging 'global law' presided over by a network of global institutions that together constitute a nascent global state.[296] The end aim of global law is to create a borderless global economic space through the adoption and application of uniform legal standards that result in the removal of barriers to the free movement of goods, capital and services. The materialization of a global social formation is also reflected in the rapid development of international human rights law and growing theorization about global cosmopolitanism and constitutionalism. But the global social and political process is a contradictory and conflicting process as it is taking place under the guidance of an ascending transnational capitalist class (TCC) that seeks to unite the world in its image to the disadvantage of the transnational oppressed classes (TOC) who are actively challenging and resisting its vision.

The TCC 'is comprised of the owners of transnational capital, that is, the group that owns the leading worldwide means of production as embodied principally in the transnational corporations and private financial institutions'.[297] It receives the support of the managers of transnational capital and the global middle classes who both share the imagination of TCC and also partake in the profits made by global capital.[298] The segment of TCC from the Global South, especially from BICS (Brazil, India, China and South Africa) countries, is playing an active role in the process. They 'are not the obedient junior partners of the previous imperialist era; rather, they are emerging as independent players and rebalancing global power'.[299] For instance, in the year 2013 FDI outflows from developing countries reached an unanticipated level. According to the UNCTAD Investment Report, 2014 the developing and transition economies together invested $553 billion, or 39 per cent of global FDI outflows, as compared with only 12 per cent at the beginning of the century.[300] The

---

[296] See B. S. Chimni, 'International Institutions Today: An Imperial Global State in the Making, 15 (2004) *European Journal of International Law*, pp. 1–39.
[297] William Robinson and Jeffrey Harris, 'Towards a Global Ruling Class? Globalization and the Transnational Capitalist Class', 64 (2000) *Science and Society*, pp. 11–54 at p. 22.
[298] Leslie Sklair, *Globalization: Capitalism and its Alternatives* (Oxford: Oxford University Press, 2002), p. 99.
[299] Jerry Harris, 'Statist Globalization in China, Russia and the Gulf States', 73 (2009) *Science and Society*, pp. 6–33 at p. 7.
[300] UNCTAD *World Investment Report, 2014 (Overview)* (New York: UN, 2014), p. vii. Available at http://unctad.org/en/PublicationsLibrary/wir2014_overview_en.pdf (accessed on 3 November 2014).

benefits that accrue to TCC are used to 'bribe' the upper strata of the middle classes and segments of the organized working classes to receive their
political support.[301] A global social formation is emerging in which a global class divide overlays the North-South divide. It is a world in which the
richest eighty-five citizens own more wealth than the bottom three and a
half billion people.[302] It is in other words an era of global imperialism, or
imperialism in the era of accelerated globalization.

However, it is important to stress that the concept of TCC should not
be given a reductionist meaning. The emergence of TCC is a complex and
contradictory process.[303] The emergence of a transnational historic bloc,
as William Caroll points out, 'does not eliminate rivalries based in the
objective necessity of capitalist states to influence capital flows to their
own territorial advantage; it only mutes and manages them.'[304] In short,
'as a class-for-itself, the transnational capitalist class is in the making, but
not (yet) made.'[305] In this context Carroll also speaks of 'the detachment
of Southern bourgeoisies, including state-capitalist fractions, from the
elite of network of the North'.[306] This explains the coming together of the
BICS countries (Brazil, India, China and South Africa) or the Shanghai
Cooperation Organization (which includes China, Russia, Kazakhstan,
Kyrgyzstan, Tajikistan and Uzbekistan).[307] It is at least one reason why
despite the commitment of TCC of BICS nations to neo-liberal globalization, international lawmaking at the global level remains in many regards
a contentious process. The other reasons include pressures from that frac-
tion of capital that remains national, the demands of electoral politics,
and the resistance of exploited and oppressed groups. To put it differently,

[301] It offers at least one explanation for why organized sections of the working classes do
not offer resistance to flexible labour policies legislated by the ruling classes, both in the
developed and the developing worlds.
[302] UNCTAD, *Trade and Development Report, 2014: Global Governance and Policy Space for
Development* (New York: UN, 2014), p. 1.
[303] As William Carroll rightly points out there is 'the need to acknowledge complexity in
transnational class formation'. William K. Caroll, *The Making of a Transnational Capitalist
Class: Corporate Power in the 21st Century* (London: Zed Books, 2010), p. 231. Caroll
writes that the 'analyses in this field should resist abstract, polarized characterizations –
as in *either* national *or* transnational capitalist class; *either* an American hegemon bent
on world domination *or* a Washington that acts at the behest of the transnational capitalist class; *either* inter-imperialist rivalry *or* the united rule of global capital'. See ibid.,
emphasis in original.
[304] See ibid., p. 232.
[305] See ibid., p. 233.
[306] See ibid.
[307] See ibid.

the logics of capital and territory do not often coincide in the face of different national histories and trajectories of development. But if the TCC yet plays a significant role in the shaping of international law at least one reason is 'an elite corporate-policy network, part of a transnational historic bloc of capitalists and organic intellectuals that builds consensus and exercises business leadership in the global arena'.[308]

The principal impact of an emerging global law is the loss of policy space for developing countries. As an UNCTAD Report observes, 'the various legal obligations emerging from multilateral, regional and bilateral agreements have reduced national policy autonomy by affecting both the available range and the efficacy of particular policy instruments'.[309] In addition, there is growing international lawmaking by the non-state actor that often assumes the form of soft law but yet constrains policy space available to developing countries.[310] It has made the achievement of the goal of 'development as freedom' difficult in the poor world.[311]

In this backdrop some central developments in the era of global imperialism may be identified that are actively facilitated by global law.[312]

First, global imperialism is marked by the influence and dominance of international finance capital, a hyper mobile capital that can move millions of dollars from one territory to another at the press of a keyboard. The hegemony of finance capital is a function of worldwide liberalization of financial controls encouraged by state and non-state actors and embodied in bilateral, regional and multilateral agreements. Both trade and investment treaties are being used by powerful nations to seek capital account liberalization without appropriate safeguards.[313] On the other

---

[308] See ibid., p. 228.

[309] See ibid., p. viii.

[310] The increasing role of non-state actors in international lawmaking is a trend that is likely to be strengthened in the future. The non-state actors include corporations, international institutions and non- governmental organizations. In the domain of international economic law non-state actors tend to produce regulations and guidelines that ensure the stability of the global capitalist system, especially in the financial and banking sectors. See Jean D'Aspremont (ed.), *Participants in the International Legal System: Multiple Perspectives on Non-State Actors International Law* (London: Routledge, 2011); Lillian Aponte Miranda, 'Indigenous Peoples as International Lawmakers', 32 (2010) *University of Pennsylvania Journal of International Law,* pp. 203–263; Julian Arato, 'Corporations as Lawmakers', 56 (2015)*Harvard International Law Journal,* pp. 229–295.

[311] Amartya Sen, *Development as Freedom* (Delhi: Oxford University Press, 2001).

[312] 'Policy space' 'refers to the freedom and ability of governments to identify and pursue the most appropriate mix of economic and social policies to achieve equitable and sustainable development in their own national contexts, but as constituent parts of an interdependent global economy'. UNCTAD, *Trade and Development,* p. vii.

[313] See ibid.

hand, when the global financial crisis hit the world in 2008 it is those nations that regulated cross-border finance which were the least hit.[314] There is, therefore, a strong opinion that recommends that developing countries should refuse to sign trade and investment treaties that promote capital account liberalization.[315] Even the IMF accepts that capital account liberalization can only be a long-run goal and its viability decided by each sovereign nation.[316] In this respect attention may also be drawn to a European Parliament resolution which states that 'speculative forms of investment' should not be protected in international investment agreements.[317] Further, international financial institutions such as the IMF and the World Bank, non-governmental agencies such as Basel Committee, constituted by governors of central banks of industrialized countries in their independent capacity, and the Financial Stability Board (FSB) are trying to address the regulatory gaps in banking and financial rules to stave off a future financial crisis. But these realizations, recommendations and efforts are unlikely to have the intended impact given the power that international finance capital wields in the corridors of power allowing it to prevent the adoption of hard laws to discourage capital account convertibility.

Second, global imperialism is characterized by the growing protection of the pre-entry, entry, establishment and operational rights of transnational corporations (TNCs). A number of international legal instruments are being used to achieve these objectives. These include hundreds of Bilateral Investment Protection Treaties (BITS), an increasing number of Free Trade Agreements (FTAs) with investment protection provisions, the WTO Agreements on Trade Related Investment Measures (TRIMS) and Trade Related Intellectual Property Rights (TRIPS), and trade in services i.e., the General Agreement on Trade in Trade in Services (GATS), the World Bank Conventions on a Multilateral Investment Guarantee Agency (MIGA) and the Agreement on International Centre for the Settlement of

---

[314] Kevin P. Gallagher, Stephany Griffith-Jones and Jose Antonio Ocampo, 'Historic Moment for the IMF', *Financial Times*, 29 May 2012.

[315] Pardee Center Task Force Report (March 2013) *Capital Account Regulations and the Trading System: A Compatibility Review* (Kevin P. Gallagher and Leonardo E. Stanley Co-Chairs) Boston University, pp. 10–11. See also Jagdish Bhagwati, *In Defense of Globalization* (Oxford: Oxford University Press, 2004), pp. 199–200.

[316] See ibid.

[317] EP (European Parliament) (2011) 'European International Investment Policy', Resolution of 6 April 2011 on the Future of International Investment Policy, Para 11 available at www.europarl.europa.eu/sides/getDoc.do?pubRef=-//EP//TEXT+TA+P7-TA-2011-0141+0+DOC+XML+V0//EN (accessed 7 October 2015).

Investment Disputes (ICSID). On the other hand, few duties are imposed on TNCs vis-à-vis host states. These are either stated in non-binding international codes of conduct (e.g., the 2011 UN Guiding Principles on Business and Human Rights[318]) or are part of voluntary codes adopted by TNCs, used to build the image of responsible and accountable actors.

Third, global imperialism is characterized by what David Harvey has termed 'accumulation by dispossession.'[319] The phenomenon of 'accumulation by dispossession' is inter alia reflected in the global misappropriation of natural resources, including land, mineral, water and biological resources by TNCs. Some examples of such misuse include the overexploitation of groundwater resources, the growing privatization of water resources in cities throughout the world, and the exploitation of tribal land for minerals by corporations. It is no accident that the struggle over land acquisition has become such a contentious issue in third world countries (e.g., in India). Contemporary international economic law facilitates the process of 'accumulation by dispossession'.

Fourth, the era of global imperialism is marked by the unprecedented ascendancy of the doctrine of free trade. The advice to developing countries is to rapidly liberalize international trade. Such recommendation neglects both the history of free trade, which shows that developed countries industrialized behind tariff walls, and also the range of protectionist measures in place even today (e.g., in agricultural commodities).[320] Today trade liberalization is promoted not merely through the WTO but through creating gigantic RTAs such as the Transnational Pacific Partnership (TPP), the Regional Cooperation for Economic Partnership (RCEP) among ten ASEAN countries and India, China, Japan, South Korea, Australia and New Zealand, and the Transatlantic Trade and Investment Partnership

---

[318] UNGA A/HRC/17/31, 21 March 2011: Guiding Principles on Business and Human Rights: Implementing the United Nations 'Protect, Respect, and Remedy' Framework available at www.ohchr.org/Documents/Publications/GuidingPrinciplesBusinessHR_EN.pdf (accessed 6 October 2015).

[319] David Harvey, *The New Imperialism* (New York: Oxford University Press, 2003).

[320] Ha Joon Chang, *Why Developing Countries Need Tariffs* (South Centre, Geneva, 2005) can be accessed at http://allanpatricknet.wdfiles.com/local--files/por-que-nacoes-em-desenvolvimento-devem-adotar-protecoes-lf/WhyDevCountriesNeedTariffsNew.pdf; Vishal Kishore, *Ricardo's Gauntlet: Economic Fiction and the Flawed Case For Free Trade* (London: Anthem Press, 2014); Roberto Mangabeira Unger, *Free Trade Reimagined: The World Division of Labor and the Method of Economics* (Princeton, NJ: Princeton University Press, 2007); B. S. Chimni, 'Developing Countries and the GATT/WTO System: Some Reflections on the Idea of Free Trade and Doha Round Trade Negotiations' in Chantal Thomas and Joel Trachtman (eds.) *Developing Countries in the WTO Legal System* (New York: Oxford University Press, 2009), pp. 21–45.

(TTIP) between the United States and the European Union. Most of the trade liberalization initiatives ignore its consequences for workers, especially in the developing world marked by the absence of adjustment measures. The disconnect between international trade law and ordinary lives is encouraged by the fact that key agreements such as the WTO agreements and FTAs/RTAs are centred on the interests and rights of producers as against consumer interests and rights. As Petersmann has pointed out, 'consumer welfare' 'is nowhere mentioned in the 30,000 pages of WTO law' nor provide 'adequate justification of the one-sided, utilitarian focus on redistributing income in favour of powerful producers interests ('producer welfare')'.[321] In view of the neglect of the working class and consumers, it is not difficult to understand US President Donald Trump's hostility to free trade doctrine at a time of economic crisis.[322]

Fifth, the era of global imperialism is distinguished by the control of advanced capitalist countries over the knowledge economy. Third world industry continues to depend on technology produced in the advanced countries which is protected by a strong global IPR regime constituted of a complex network of bilateral, regional and international agreements.[323] To use this technology the Global South has to pay vast amounts as royalties. Where third world industry has an advantage, as in the pharmaceutical

---

[321] Ernest-Ulrich Petersmann, 'JIEL Debate: Methodological Pluralism and its Critics in International Economic Law Research', 15 (2012) *Journal of International Economic Law*, pp. 921–970 at p. 926.

[322] See generally B. S. Chimni, 'Trans-Pacific Partnership Agreement, Donald Trump and After: A Subaltern Perspective', a paper read at the Conference on Trans-Pacific Partnership Agreement organized by New York University School of Law and United Nations University in Tokyo, Japan from 23–24 November, 2016 (available on request)

[323] On IPRs and TRIPS regime see generally Carlos M. Correa, *Intellectual Property Rights, the WTO and Developing Countries: The TRIPS Agreement and Policy Options* (London: Zed Books, 2000); Peter Drahos and John Braithwate, *Information Feudalism* (London: Earthscan, 2002); Michele Boldrin and David K. Levine, *Against Intellectual Monopoly* (Cambridge: Cambridge University Press, 2008); James Thuo Gathii, 'Construing Intellectual Property Rights and Competition Policy Consistently with Facilitating Access to Affordable Aids Drugs to Low-End Income Consumers', 53 (2001) *Florida Law Review*, p. 727; James Thuo Gathii, 'The Legal Status of the Doha Declaration on TRIPS and Public Health Under the Vienna Convention on the Law of Treaties', 15 (2002)*Harvard Journal of Law and Technology* , pp. 291–317; B. S. Chimni, 'The Political Economy of the Uruguay Round of Negotiations: A Perspective', 29 (1992) *International Studies*, pp. 135–158. A European Parliament (EP) resolution on International Investment Policy, adopted on 6 April 2011, calls on the European Commission 'to include in all future agreements specific clauses laying down the right of parties to the agreement to regulate, inter alia, in the areas of protection of national security, the environment, public health, workers' and consumers' rights, industrial policy and cultural diversity'. EP (European Parliament) (2011) 'European International Investment Policy', Resolution of 6 April 2011 on the Future of International Investment Policy, Para 25.

sector in the supply of generic drugs, TNCs use an aggressive litigation strategy to protect their patent rights to prevent third world pharmaceutical firms from supplying cheap drugs in domestic markets and to the rest of the world. The rationale for a strong IPR regime has increasingly been questioned given its disturbing impact on access to life saving drugs, but with little impact. Instead, the legal regime for the protection of IPRs is being constantly strengthened through what are called TRIPS Plus rules.

Sixth, global imperialism is characterized by the undermining of labour rights, both at the national and the global levels. Labour flexibility has today become the mantra for global capital. In fact, labour dislocation is seen as the necessary accompaniment of a mobile capital. It has resulted in the physical and mental destruction of millions of workers and their families. This is particularly true in third world countries with no form of social security in place. On the other hand, decades of effort by the International Labour Organization (ILO) to create binding standards in the domain of work is today being diluted through the adoption of soft law texts such as the 1998 ILO Declaration on Fundamental Principles and Rights at Work (DFPRW). The DFRPW adopts a minimalist approach by identifying a set of core rights that should have priority, thereby marginalizing other rights and doing even that without putting in place serious enforcement measures.[324] More generally, capitalist imperialism produces great inequality between and within states.[325]

Seventh, the era of global imperialism is characterized by the continued overexploitation of Nature. In this respect the advanced capitalist countries that have been historically responsible for the ecological crises are seeking to get developing countries, in particular BICS countries, to undertake voluntary and legal obligations to address its consequences. The Paris Accord on Climate Change (2015) continues the trend of making developing countries bear the burden of establishing peace with Nature.[326] What is more, the developed countries are attempting to use international law provisions such as the WTO provisions on environment

---

[324] Anke Hassel, 'The Evolution of a Global Labour Governance Regime', 21 (2008) *Governance: An International Journal of Policy, Administration, and Institutions*, pp. 231–251; Philip Alston, '"Core Labor Standards" and the Transformation of the International Labor Regime', 15 (2004) *European Journal of International Law*, pp. 457–521.

[325] Thomas Piketty, *Capital in the Twenty-First Century* (Cambridge, MA: The Belknap Press of Harvard University Press, 2014). Piketty, of course, argues that there are also powerful forces in favour of equality and that appropriate institutions need to be created for the same.

[326] For a Marxist view on climate change see John Bellamy Foster, 'The Great Capitalist Climacteric: Marxism and "System Change Not Climate Change"', 13 (2015) *Analytical Monthly Review*, pp. 1–16.

protection to erect non-tariff barriers against the exports of developing countries undermining further their development prospects.[327]

Eighth, global imperialism is characterized by the displacement of violence to the third world. The peace in the imperialist world has been secured at the expense of the developing world. At the inter-state level, Afghanistan, Iraq, Libya and Syria symbolize this displacement of violence to the third world; there are also a vast number of other ongoing internal conflicts. Yet international criminal tribunals focus on indicting and punishing leaders of the third world with the International Criminal Court having an Africa bias. There are the beginnings of the signs of growing inter-imperialist competition reflected in the relationship between NATO countries and Russia; the annexation of Crimea by Russia simply manifesting one dimension of this relationship.[328]

Ninth, the era of global imperialism is market by efforts of the advanced developed countries to limit legal migration leading to the growth of a global smuggling and trafficking industry. These nations have in particular established a non-entrée regime against asylum seekers and refugees through a range of legal and administrative measures.[329] There is also a rise of controls on voluntary migration. The non-entrée regime consists of a number of measures some more recent than others. These include 'traditional non-entrée' measures like visa controls, carrier sanctions, interdiction on the high seas, mandatory detention etc. and the new generation 'cooperation based non-entrée'.[330] The new generation of *non-entrée* policies include 'reliance on diplomatic relations; the offering of financial incentives; the provision of equipment, machinery, or training; deployment of officials of the sponsoring state; joint or shared enforcement; assumption of a direct migration control role; and the establishment or assignment of international agencies to effect interception'.[331]

[327] B. S. Chimni, 'WTO and Environment: The *Shrimp-Turtle* and *EC-Hormone* cases', (13 May 2000) *Economic and Political Weekly*, pp. 1752–1761; B. S. Chimni, 'WTO and Environment: The Legitimization of Unilateral Trade Sanctions', (12–18 January 2002) *Economic and Political Weekly*, pp. 133–140.

[328] Alex Callinicos, 'Imperial Delusions' Issue 142 (30 March 2014) at www.isj.org.uk/index.php4?id=959&issue=142 (accessed on 4 June 2015).

[329] B. S. Chimni, 'The Geopolitics of Refugee Studies: A View from the South', 11 (1998) *Journal of Refugee Studies*, pp. 350–374; B. S. Chimni, 'The Birth of a "Discipline": From Refugee to Forced Migration Studies', 22 (2009)*Journal of Refugee Studies*, pp. 11–29.

[330] Thomas Gammeltoft-Hansen and James Hathaway, '*Non-Refoulement* in a World of Cooperative Deterrence', 53 (2015) *Columbia Journal of Transnational Law*, pp. 235–284.

[331] See ibid.

Tenth, the era of global imperialism is marked by the rapid growth of international human rights law. There have been a large number of conventions, protocols and declarations adopted on the subject. A number of institutional mechanisms have also been established to review the records of states with respect to voluntarily undertaken human rights obligations. These include various Treaty Bodies and the UN Human Rights Council. These institutional mechanisms have inter alia been entrusted with the task of receiving and scrutinizing periodic reports from States. These bodies make recommendations that States are accepted to take seriously. On the face of it such a global system of oversight of human rights record of States has the potential to promote adherence to human rights law and without doubt achieve this objective to some extent. However, international human rights law also serves to legitimate intrusive interventions in the developing world and in general an unjust world order.

Finally, the era of global imperialism is marked by the ascendance of international institutions established by global law that are coming to constitute a nascent global state. As noted earlier, the developing countries have had to cede critical policy space to international institutions that have the wherewithal to enforce policies and international agreements over which they preside.[332] The international institutions are supported by a network of global cities and experts who provide the material and ideological infrastructure necessary for an imperial global state to function.

In sum, global imperialism is constituted and facilitated by an emerging global law under the influence of TCC that may be characterized as *global imperial international law*. It is responsible for the global spread of alienation, an effect of inhumane social relations that characterize the present era. This alienation can be understood in terms of four kinds of alienation described by Marx in the *Economic and Philosophic Manuscripts*. These are, as Istavan Mészáros points out, the alienation of human beings from nature; the alienation of humans from their own productive activity; the alienation of human beings from their 'species being'; and the alienation of humans from each other.[333] We live in a world that is increasingly devoid of sentiments of solidarity with the deprived

---

[332] Chimni, 'International Institutions', pp. 1-39. Also see Chapter 2, pp. 91–92.
[333] Istvan Mészáros, *Marx's Theory of Alienation*, 3rd edn (Merlin Press, 1972), p. 14. These different forms of alienation have been briefly considered in B. S . Chimni, 'The Past, Present and Future of International Law: A Critical Third World Approach', 8 (2007) *Melbourne Journal of International Law*, pp. 499–515.

and oppressed. The state of affairs is no different when it comes to the fate of even the stateless or refugees who are caught in the interstices of the sovereign state system. The European refugees crisis of 2015–2016 demonstrates this most effectively with hundreds of migrants meeting cold deaths trying to reach Europe. Contemporary international law has not addressed the different forms of alienation that have been universalized in the era of globalization. Indeed, there is a deep alienation of the discipline of international law from individuals that are its subjects. If international law is not merely to serve as a weapon of the global elite, it must find ways to overcome the different forms of alienation on an urgent basis. It must listen to the voice of the TOC that is involved in resisting those rules and regimes of contemporary international law that have a negative impact on their everyday lives. There are ongoing social movements the world over led by a range of forces that include left and democratic parties, civil society organizations, and a coalition of third world states that seek the reform of contemporary international law. It is time that the narrative of resistance is made an integral part of the analysis of international laws and institutions.

It is no accident that this period has seen the arrival of a second generation of third world scholarship (TWAIL II). It has not only demonstrated the continuities between colonial international law and contemporary international law, but also explored the relationship between resistance and legitimacy of international law.[334] TWAIL II has proposed ways of reforming international law in order to inter alia recover policy space so that the concerns of the poor and oppressed can be met. This is also the era in which FtAIL has come to be articulated and there has been relatively greater engagement of international law with the world of women. It was seen in the chapter on FtAIL that while there are differing assessments of the extent to which international law has been able to address the concerns of women there is little doubt that the issue of women's rights has come to stay. In short, both TWAIL and FtAIL are grappling with the issue as to whether and the extent to which international law can be reformed. On the other hand, Marxist scholars like Miéville claiming that reform is impossible and the 'international rule of law' is essentially a euphemism for the complete dominance of imperialist law. In what follows this view is contested. While the arguments are

---

[334] See, for example, Balakrishnan Rajagopal, *International Law from Below: Development, Social Movements, and Third World Resistance* (New York: Cambridge University Press, 2003).

advanced with respect to the views of Miéville, these also apply to positions within TWAIL and FtAIL that do not see the possibility of reform of contemporary international law.

D. Reform or Revolution

Miéville observes that 'I see no prospect of a systematic progressive political project or emancipatory dynamic coming out of international law'.[335] While he does add that 'it would be fatuous to deny that law could ever be put to reformist use',[336] he sees this possibility as being extremely limited. He writes that:

> *States*, not classes or other social forces, are the fundamental contending agents of international law … each with their own class agenda. These internecine battles between the 'warring brothers' of the ruling class make up a great swathe of the international legal structure, and in them there is little purchase for a fundamentally progressive, subversive or radical legal position.[337]

He once again hastens to add 'this is not to foreclose any possibility of "progressive", subversive international legal moment or decisions',[338] but concludes that:

> To fundamentally change the dynamics of the system it would be necessary not to reform the institutions but to *eradicate the forms of law* – which means the fundamental reformulation of the political-economic system of which they are expressions. The project to achieve this is the best hope for global emancipation, and it would mean the end of law.[339]

In interpreting and understanding the views of Miéville it is important to differentiate between two distinct positions. The first is about the claim of continuing imperialist exploitation of third world peoples after the period of decolonization or more broadly the transnational oppressed classes. This is a view that Marxist and TWAIL scholars have long articulated. At times it seems that Miéville holds this position as he is merely stating that a 'systematic progressive political project' through international law is not possible without a fundamental change in the dynamics of global capitalism. However, if that were all then Miéville would have refrained from

---

[335] Miéville, *Between Equal Rights*, p. 316.
[336] See ibid., p. 317.
[337] See ibid; emphasis in original.
[338] See ibid.
[339] See ibid., p. 318; emphasis in original.

accusing the present author of doing 'radicalism with rules'.[340] For the possibility of reform was accompanied by the description of international law as *bourgeois democratic*. The latter characterization captures precisely what Miéville appears to be suggesting in contrasting formal equality and substantial inequality of states. But it appears that Miéville wishes to claim priority with respect to that argument which cannot be done without misrepresenting and dismissing earlier Marxist and TWAIL scholarship. At other times Miéville appears to taking a more radical position of ruling out the possibility of reform. He sustains this position by noting that since it is states and not classes that interact at the international level there is, given the 'logic of territory', much less opportunity of reform of international law through class struggle. In fact the ruling classes of all states converse as 'warring brothers', a view more akin to classical realism than to classical Marxism.

Since Miéville otherwise relies so heavily on the work of Pashukanis to articulate his approach to international law it is best to at first review the latter's positive views on the possibility of reform of international law and legal institutions. In fact one of the characteristics of the work of Miéville is his selective presentation of the work of Pashukanis. He does not refer to those writings that do not sustain his particular view of the role of law and legal institutions in society. As Robert Knox notes:

> Mieville makes very little mention of Pashukanis's later work on the law. Pashukanis's most explicit treatment of the role of law in revolutionary strategy is to be found in 'Lenin and the Problems of Law', which is not mentioned at all in *Between Equal Rights*. What makes this especially puzzling is that the work was written between Pashukanis's *General Theory* and his entry on international law in the *Encyclopaedia of State and Law*. Since Mieville uses both these texts extensively, it would seem difficult to argue that the work was the product of 'Stalinist degeneration'.[341]

The reason Miéville does not refer to the essay 'Lenin and the Problems of Law' is that in it 'Pashukanis castigates those who fail to understand the positive role that legality can play in given concrete circumstances'.[342] In fact, according to Knox, Pashukanis 'envisaged an important role for legal struggle'.[343] The latter observed that it is only 'for the petit bourgeois

---

[340] See ibid., pp. 64–75.
[341] Robert Knox, 'Marxism, International Law, and Political Strategy', 22 (2009) *Leiden Journal of International Law*, pp. 413–436 at p. 429.
[342] See ibid., p. 429.
[343] See ibid.

revolutionary [that] the very denial of legality is turned into a kind of fetish'.[344] On the other hand, 'the revolutionary nature of Leninist tactics never degenerated into the fetishistic denial of legality; this was never a revolutionary phrase'.[345] As Pashukanis noted, Lenin 'firmly appealed to use those "legal opportunities" which the enemy ... was forced to provide'.[346] According to him, 'Lenin knew not only how mercilessly to expose tsarist, bourgeois etc. legality, but also how to use it, where it was necessary and when it was necessary'.[347] Indeed, he was against any approach that 'acknowledged only the "dramatic" methods of struggle'.[348] It is worth noting here that in the context of working towards revolution in Russia Lenin observed that 'it was necessary [...] to work legally in the most reactionary parliaments, in the most reactionary professional, cooperative and similar organizations'.[349] He went on to state that 'revolutionaries who are incapable of combining illegal forms of struggle with *every* form of legal struggle are poor revolutionaries indeed'.[350] Yet if the same thesis is advanced in the sphere of international law it confronts the charge of doing 'radicalism with rules'.[351] In opposition to Miéville, Knox rightly concludes that 'progressive forces can take advantage of "legal opportunities"

---

[344] *Pashukanis*, Beirne and Sharlet (eds.), p. 138.
[345] See ibid.
[346] See ibid.
[347] See ibid. One manifestation of this understanding was 'concluding a treaty with one of the imperialist states (the Peace of Brest)'. See ibid.
[348] See ibid., p. 139.
[349] Cited by Pashukanis, see ibid., p. 139. See Lenin, *Selected Works*, vol. 3, p. 297.
[350] Lenin, *Selected Works*, vol. 3, p. 353.
[351] Lenin was not alone. In her well known essay 'Reform or Revolution' written in 1900 (as a response to a theory propounded by Eduard Bernstein that capitalism will not collapse given its ability to adopt) Rosa Luxemburg wrote: 'The daily struggle for reforms, for the amelioration of the condition of the workers within the framework of the existing social order, and for democratic institutions, offers to the social democracy the only means for engaging in the proletarian class war and working in the direction of the final goals – the conquest of political power and the suppression of wage labor.' *Rosa Luxemburg: Selected Writings* (Kolkata: Search, 2008), p. 23. Luxemburg was a woman, Jew and a Pole. She was a minority in a triple sense. She understood the importance of reforms. The quarrel she had with Bernstein was that in her view social revolution or socialism should remain the final goal. But even as she critiqued bourgeois democracy she wrote: 'If democracy has become superfluous or annoying to the bourgeoisie, it is on the contrary necessary and indispensable to the working class. It is necessary to the working class because it creates the political forms (autonomous administration, electoral rights, etc.) which will serve the proletariat as fulcrums in its task of transforming bourgeois society. Democracy is indispensable to the working class because only through the exercise of its democratic rights, in the struggle for democracy, can the proletariat become aware of its class interests and its historic task.' See ibid., p. 75.

and may successfully realize their aims through international law'.[352] Of course, Knox acknowledges 'the limits of legality'.[353] Yet as he aptly notes, 'progressive forces can – through their economic, ideological, and coercive power – advance their interests through international law'.[354] Susan Marks also reaches the same conclusion. She writes that 'I cannot accept his [i.e. Miéville's] contention that international law has no emancipatory potential'.[355] Marks observes that 'to point to the danger of basing progressive critique on international law is not, of course, to provide reasons for eschewing legal argumentation altogether. We may caution against over-investment in international law while still retaining a sense of its value in critique'.[356]

In keeping with the tendency of not mentioning any work in the Marxist tradition that clashes with his radical conclusions, Miéville does not also mention the writings of Renner who argued that evolution and not revolution characterizes the legal sphere, and that the social function of law can undergo change without accompanying changes in the legal system. In order to sustain his position Miéville, as Knox notes, 'focuses excessively on the role of military violence, the type of violence generally exercised by imperialist states'.[357] But Knox rightly argues that 'more importance should be granted to economic and ideological forms of "force" '.[358] However, Miéville does not engage with international economic institutions such as the World Bank or the International Monetary Fund 'despite their increasing importance and their prominence in a number of Third World critiques of international law'.[359] At least one reason for his neglect of international economic law and institutions is that it

---

[352] Knox, 'Marxism', p. 433.

[353] See ibid., p. 435.

[354] See ibid., p. 436.

[355] Susan Marks, 'International Judicial Activism and the Commodity Form Theory of International Law', 18 (2007) *European Journal of International Law*, pp. 199–211 at p. 202.

[356] See ibid., p. 201.

[357] See ibid., p. 418.

[358] See ibid.

[359] See ibid., p. 425. Hartmann extends this critique to WTO: 'In his empirical studies Mieville himself concentrates on intergovernmental law, where the dimension of "self-help" is evident as it lacks enforcement mechanisms. Surprisingly, his studies do not take into account the constitutionalisation of law, not even in the context of the WTO, whose trade law could profitably be studied by drawing on Pashukanis' analysis of the relation between vendor and buyer.' Eva Hartmann, 'The Difficult Relation between International Law and Politics: The Legal Turn from a Critical IPE Perspective', 16 (2011) *New Political Economy*, pp. 561–584 at p. 567.

would call for assessment of whether the struggles of TOC and coalitions of third world states have been able to secure some reform in them. The other is that Miéville seems to lack familiarity with them.

Finally, as Knox notes, 'Miéville pays insufficient attention to the role of struggle and politics in the constitution of legal subjects',[360] whereas 'through sustained struggle progressive groups might be able to constitute themselves as legal subjects'.[361] According to Knox, 'this can perhaps be observed in the development of human rights law, which has moved away from the state as vindicator for its subjects and towards the direct inter- pellation of individuals as subjects of international law. Most significant, perhaps, is the growing importance of non-governmental organizations and international institutions'.[362] Instead Miéville baldly suggests that 'non-state actors have no impact whatsoever upon the content of inter- national law'.[363] Knox perhaps overestimates the significance of reforms that can be brought about through invoking international human rights law and also underestimates the role of many international institutions in sustaining the imperial project. But that point can be settled through an empirical assessment of what has been possible and what is possible.

Be that as it may, the reference to the writings of Pashukanis, Lenin and Renner and contemporary Marxist critics like Knox and Marks has been made merely to argue that it would be foolhardy to refuse to seek 'reform' of the international legal system at a time when world revolu- tion is a pipe dream. The critics of the international legal system should do what it takes to use it to the benefit of TOC without of course for- getting the limits of what is possible in the existing world order. The present author has repeatedly made the point about the class nature of international law in the postcolonial period and the fact that the prin- ciple of sovereign equality of states in law contrasts with inequality in terms of power and resources. In fact, the reality of inequality underlies many of the initiatives taken by third world countries such as the spe- cial and differential treatment principle both in trade law and environ- mental law. Therefore, the Miéville accusation of doing 'radicalism with rules' not only misrepresents the position but also falsifies the position of Pashukanis (who followed V. I. Lenin in this regard) with respect to the question whether international law should be rejected tout court. The nihilist position Miéville espouses also runs against his own view that

---

[360] Knox, 'Marxism', p. 418.
[361] See ibid.
[362] See ibid., pp. 422–423.
[363] See ibid., p. 427.

decolonization represented a progressive step. For eventually he refuses to distinguish different phases of imperialism. Miéville therefore also ends up offering a flawed history of international law that appears more realist than Marxist. He has a polemical style that is part of a dogmatic Marxist tradition; you trash the work of other scholars, including fellow Marxists.[364] He even goes on to observe that for international lawyers to state that international law cannot be reformed is tantamount to 'biting the hand that feeds them'.[365] The alleviation of the sufferings of the subaltern groups and peoples is not for him to worry about.

E.   *International Rule of Law*

Miéville is therefore also dismissive of the idea of international rule of law. He writes that 'the rule of law is not a self-evident good'[366] and is critical of Thompson for so suggesting.[367] Indeed, he is unwilling to accept that international rule of law matters:

> Of all the insights that the commodity-form approach offers, none is more important than the unapologetic response to those who call for the rule of law. The attempt to replace war and inequality with law is not merely utopian – it is precisely self-defeating. A world structured around international law cannot but be one of imperialist violence ... The chaotic and bloody world around us *is the rule of law*.[368]

It is evident that the Miéville position is almost the antithesis of the Thompson view that 'rule of law' is an unqualified good. While the liberal celebration of international rule of law certainly needs to be critiqued, it is important not to reject the idea itself.[369] In this respect, Miéville

---

[364] John Hazard writes of Pashukanis: 'He was a revolutionary, brought up in the school of "hard knocks where courtesies are unknown and where one attacks to survive". John N. Hazard, 'Foreword' in Piers Beirne and Robert Sharlet (eds.), *Pashukanis: Selected Writings on Marxism and Law* (New York: Academic Press, 1980), pp. xi–xvii at p. xii. Describing his approach to Korovin, Hazard writes that 'he was not content to argue. He made his argument into a personal indictment, as so many other revolutionaries were to do in their attacks upon theoretical positions they opposed'. See ibid. Such is Miéville's admiration for the work of Pashukanis that he has carried even his mode of critique into his book.

[365] Miéville, *Between Equal Rights*, p. 3.

[366] See ibid., p. 315.

[367] See ibid., p. 316.

[368] See ibid., p. 319; emphasis in original.

[369] See B. S. Chimni, 'Legitimating International Rule of Law' in James Crawford and Martti Koskenniemi (eds.) *Cambridge Companion to International Law* (Cambridge: Cambridge University Press, 2012), pp. 290–309.

disregards the remarks of Marx and Engels and others with respect to the relative autonomy of law and the importance of legal struggles. In the context of international law he overlooks several aspects of the functioning of international law. First, in a states system laws do not represent the direct translation of the interests of global capital. In a legal system that functions on the basis of consent of member states concessions have necessarily to be given to weak states. Second, these concessions are in response to demands that have been arrived at by states through an internal process that has to accommodate, at least in democratic societies, the concerns of oppressed and marginal groups. That is to say in international negotiations the state possesses a degree of independence from the proximate interests and activities of the dominant class or class fractions. Third, the idea of international rule of law provides a shield, however fragile, against the use of naked power by powerful states. Thus, for instance, economic institutions such as WTO have created a rule-oriented system in settling disputes between trading states which works to the advantage of weak states. Fourth, there are a range of problems today, such as the ecological crisis, that call for the cooperation of all states in the international community. This cooperation cannot be secured other than by giving concessions to weak states. Fifth, there are the continuous struggles of the transnational oppressed classes to advance their interests in different domains of international law. These struggles both compel powerful states to give concessions to them and prevent them from overriding international laws at will. Finally, if powerful states were to violate international laws at will it would undermine the legitimacy of the international legal system necessary to defend their vital interests.[370]

In sum, despite international law having an imperial character international law is constrained by the 'logic of territory', the collective aspirations of humanity, and the struggles of the transnational oppressed classes.[371] These factors among others give international law a degree of autonomy and the idea of international rule of law meaning. For instance, the principle prohibiting the threat or use of force in international relations reflects the hopes of a vast majority of ordinary peoples for peace. It would be a mistake to be dismissive of this norm merely because it is

---

[370] The attention of the reader here may be drawn to the discussion in Chapter 1 on the reasons for resilience of the positivist approach or mainstream international law scholarship (MILS). See Chapter 1, pp. 12–14.

[371] It is these factors that renew the faith of the invisible college of international lawyers. B. S. Chimni, 'Capitalism, Imperialism and International Law in the Twenty First Century', 14 (2012) *Oregon Review of International Law*, pp. 17–45.

the subject of frequent violation. In other words, it is wrong to conceive of international law in purely instrumental terms as it also expresses common humanity through its vocabulary. The extent to which the aspirations of subaltern classes and nations prevail in particular instances must be a subject of empirical investigation. International law is as Thompson put it 'a complex and contradictory' process. The mistake Miéville makes is not of associating imperialism and international law with violence, but in being entirely dismissive of the idea of international rule of law. He does not see that the idea of international rule of law is being secured through the struggle of millions of peoples who wish to hold states to account. The position on international rule of law advanced here is different from its liberal counterpart as it is advanced along with a deep critique of the functioning of the international legal system. The defence of the idea of international rule of law is not to signal approval of the existing state of affairs but to be respectful of an idea that constrains the open oppression and exploitation of subaltern classes and nations.

VIII.   Towards an IMAIL Theory of Interpretation

The idea of 'international rule of law' presupposes that voluntarily undertaken legal obligations are observed by every international actor in letter and in spirit.[372] This assumes in turn that the meaning of rules is sufficiently determinate as otherwise States and other international actors can represent even an act of violation as being in accord with a rule. But critics have contested this assumption by identifying semantic, structural and strategic sources of indeterminacy that undermine the possibility of arriving at an 'objective' interpretation of rules. In their view it is easy for an international actor to advance interpretations of rules that reflect political preferences masquerading as authentic interpretations of rules. Therefore, what you can hope for at best is that the community of interpreters exercises ethical responsibility to help realize 'common interests' or 'genuine universalism'.

In Chapters 2 to 5 the views of Morgenthau, McDougal-Lasswell-Miller, Falk, and Kennedy-Koskenniemi on indeterminacy of rules were reviewed. It was argued that the effect of strategic, semantic and structural bases of indeterminacy is overstated. In this section a prolegomena to a

---

[372] Article 26 of the Vienna Convention on the Law of Treaties succinctly codifies this understanding: 'Every treaty in force is binding upon the parties to it and must be performed by them in good faith.'

materialist theory of interpretation is offered relying on the insights of Ludwig Wittgenstein, Hans Georg Gadamer and Jürgen Habermas. It is argued, albeit in telegraphic language, that the proponents of the strong indeterminacy thesis misconstrue the process or act of interpretation. In advancing a materialist theory of interpretation, the section proceeds as follows. First, in the backdrop of the insights of Wittgenstein discussed in Chapter 3, it touches on the views of the critical legal scholar Duncan Kennedy who despite subscribing to the indeterminacy thesis concedes that the idea of legal or textual constraint is meaningful (i.e. law is not just politics). However, it is suggested that he does not adequately explain in this regard the thinking process or experience that imposes constraints on a community of interpreters. Second, it turns to the work of Gadamer in order to fill the gap in the Kennedy understanding of 'the real experience' of thinking in the process of interpretation. Gadamer's reflections on 'legal hermeneutics' helpfully explain the process of thinking that informs the interpretation and application of a rule. To begin with Gadamer relies on Wittgenstein's use theory to explain the limits of indeterminacy of a rule. But he supplements it with a dialogic approach to the interpretation of the rule since the application of a rule requires movement between the past (when the rule was adopted) and the present (when the rule is applied). This approach does not neglect the text of the rule or of traditional cannons of interpretation, but in applying the rule calls for a 'fusion of horizons' between the past and the present. While Wittgenstein and Gadamer provide in different ways persuasive answers to claims of semantic and structural sources of indeterminacy of rules they do not offer the resources to effectively critique the content of rules. Therefore, third, the section turns to Habermas to respond to the weaknesses in both Gadamer and Wittgenstein (in the former case being overly deferential to tradition and in the latter not questioning it) and argue that in evaluating the outcomes of rule application there must be a reflexive critique of the rule and its outcomes. But these latter moves are compatible with the idea of international rule of law.

A.   *The Limits of Indeterminacy*

It was argued in Chapters 3 and 5 that contrary to the views of McDougal-Lasswell-Miller on semantic and structural indeterminacy and Koskenniemi on structural indeterminacy, rules are indeterminate only in the weak sense. To sustain this conclusion reliance was placed on two 'rules' of Wittgenstein viz., that the sentence is the minimum unit with which something is said and that the meaning of a word is its use in the language.[373] The weak indeterminacy thesis can be reinforced in the context of adjudication through touching on the views of Duncan Kennedy, who is often (mistakenly in our view) associated with the strong indeterminacy thesis.[374]

To begin with, Kennedy argues that there is only a thin line that divides law and politics in the process of adjudication.[375] He points out that 'there is no quarantined, politics-free zone where adjudication can proceed and, consequently, there is no border to traverse into politics'.[376] This fact accounts for why 'mainstream legal theory' 'devotes itself to discovering strategies to secure the law/politics boundary and to keep political infiltration of legal territory to a minimum (hence, talk of interstices and penumbras, reasoned elaboration of neutral principles, institutional competence, efficiency criteria, representation-reinforcement, coherence and integrity, etc)'.[377] But while Kennedy rejects 'a distinct law/politics divide' in the adjudication process he *does not* take 'the "opposite" position that 'there is no difference between law and politics, that law is just politics, that anything goes'.[378] Karl Klare explains that Kennedy's argument is *not* 'that legal and political discourses are interchangeable'.[379] In logical terms 'the claim that law and politics are inextricably linked does not entail the conclusion that law is *just* politics and nothing else'.[380] Klare conveniently sums up the Kennedy position on 'legal constraint' in the following way:

> Kennedy believes that legal constraint is a meaningful concept (which is why he *explicitly rejects a 'global indeterminacy' thesis* and the view that 'law is just politics'). However, in contrast to the mainstream view, he argues that legal constraint is not a property or an objective knowable quality of legal materials themselves. Rather, legal constraint is *a particular kind of experience a legal actor has* (or may have) in the course of doing legal-interpretive work in the legal medium. Whether and how strongly legal constraint is 'in effect' with respect to any particular legal problem are matters of feeling, belief, controversy, and conviction within the context of a particular discursive community. No neutral decision procedures exist

---

[373] See Chapter 3, pp. 133–138.

[374] Duncan Kennedy, *A Critique of Adjudication: Fin de Siecle* (Cambridge, MA: Harvard University Press, 1997).

[375] Karl Klare, 'The Politics of Duncan Kennedy's Critique', 22 (2001) *Cardozo Law Review*, pp. 1073–1103 at p. 1077.

[376] See ibid., p. 1080.

[377] See ibid., p.1077; footnotes deleted.

[378] See ibid., p. 1078.

[379] See ibid., p. 1081.

[380] See ibid., fn. 25; emphasis in original.

capable of objectively establishing whether a given set of legal materials imposes tight, loose, little, or no constraint on an outcome.[381]

Klare then goes on to add that this means that the text cannot mean whatever we may wish it to mean:

> The legal materials may resist our best efforts to interpret them in a certain way. As an empirical matter (not a result of 'cultural determination'), it frequently happens that trained participants in a particular legal culture reach a consensus that the materials bearing on a particular problem admit of only one outcome or a narrow range of outcomes. The point is that the constraint or bindingness of the legal materials *is an experience or interpretation of them*, not an innate, uninterpreted property of the materials themselves.[382]

The problem however is that Kennedy does not really explain what 'a particular kind of experience a legal actor has' in the process of interpretation that translates into legal constraint. It is submitted that the work of Gadamer provides crucial insights in this regard.

B. Gadamer on Legal Hermeneutics

In his seminal work *Truth and Method* Gadamer offers reflections on 'hermeneutics' by which he principally means 'a theory of *the real experience that thinking is*'.[383] The following features of his description of legal hermeneutics are worth noting. First, Gadamer emphasizes that 'the work of interpretation is *to concretize* the law in each specific case – i.e., it is a work of application'.[384] Speaking of both legal and theological hermeneutics he writes:

> Constitutive for both legal and theological hermeneutics is *the tension* between the fixed text – of the law or of revelation – on the one hand and, on the other hand, the *meaning acquired through its application in the concrete instant of interpretation*, whether in preaching or in the legal judgment ... In both cases, this involves that the text (the law or the message of salvation), if it is to be understood properly, i.e., corresponding to the claim that the text puts forward, *must be understood anew and otherwise at each moment, i.e., in each concrete situation. Understanding is here always application.*[385]

---

[381] See ibid., p. 1083; emphasis added.

[382] See ibid., emphasis added.

[383] Hans-Georg Gadamer, *Truth and Method*, 2nd revised edn (London: Continuum, 2005) 1st South Asian edn, p. xxxiii; emphasis in original.

[384] See ibid., pp. 325–326.

[385] Cited in Jürgen Habermas, 'A Review of Gadamer's Truth and Method' in B. R. Wachterhauser (ed.) *Hermeneutics and Modern Philosophy* (Albany, NY: The SUNY

Second, while the meaning of a text 'is concretized and fully realized only in interpretation [...] the interpretive activity considers itself wholly bound by the meaning of the text. *Neither jurist nor theologian regards the work of application as making free with the text*'.[386] Third, while there is 'a creative legal function that is always accorded to legal decisions, to precedents, or the prevailing administration of the law',[387] there is always a need to return to the text, and here he follows Wittgenstein, for 'every preparation of *a text is already related to interpretation, that is, to its correct, analogous application*'.[388] Fourth, 'application does not mean first understanding a given universal in itself and then afterward applying it to a concrete case'.[389] Instead, a key task of legal hermeneutics is 'mediating between then and now ... which is what we mean by application and which legal hermeneutics also regards as its task'.[390] It means, as Jack Mendelson explains, that 'all acts of interpretation are part of the movement of history in which tradition is preserved and transformed and the horizon of the present constituted'.[391] There is in other words a 'fusion of horizons' of the past and the present or the rule and its application. However, it is crucial to note that for Gadamer the notion of 'tradition' includes 'well-known traditions of ... interpretations'.[392] In fact he identifies several sources of constraint in the process of interpretation. In his view the interpreter 'is *constrained by her pre-understandings, conventions of interpretation and the text itself*'.[393] Fifth, 'it is part of the idea of a rule of law that the judge's judgment *does not proceed from an arbitrary and unpredictable decision, but from the just weighing up of the whole*'.[394] Gadamer goes on to point out that 'anyone who has *immersed himself*

Press, 1986), translated by Fred Dallmayr and Thomas McCarthy, pp. 243–276 at p. 263; emphasis added.

[386] Gadamer, *Truth and Method*, p. 328; emphasis added.

[387] Hans-Georg Gadamer,' Text and Interpretation' in B. R. Wachterhauser (ed.) *Hermeneutics and Modern Philosophy* (Albany: The SUNY Press, 1986) translated by Fred Dallmayr and Thomas McCarthy pp. 377–397 at p. 394.

[388] See ibid; emphasis added.

[389] Gadamer, *Truth and Method*, , p. 336.

[390] See ibid., p. 329.

[391] Jack Mendelson, 'The Habermas-Gadamer Debate', 18 (1979) *New German Critique,* pp. 44–73 at p. 56.

[392] 'A Gadamerian understanding of interpretation would view the canons [i.e. the canons of statutory interpretation] as important dialectical tools'. William N. Eskridge, 'Gadamer/ Statutory Interpretation', 90 (1990) *Columbia Law Review*, pp. 609–681 at pp. 636, 662.

[393] See ibid., p. 672; emphasis added.

[394] Gadamer, *Truth and Method*, p. 326; emphasis added.

in this particular situation is capable of undertaking this just weighing-up. This is why in a state governed by law, *there is legal certainty* – i.e., it is in principle possible to know what the exact situation is. Every law-yer and every counsel is able, in principle, to give correct advice – i.e., he can accurately predict the judge's decision on the basis of the existing laws'.[395] In sum, according to Gadamer, 'interpretation is a search for a common understanding of truth by the text and interpreter, mediated by historical tradition'[396] that includes in the case of legal interpretation well-established traditions of interpretation.

It is true that the Gadamer approach to interpretation 'is not merely an exercise in discovery, but involves a critical approach to the text'.[397] But the meaning of this proposition is not to be misunderstood. Two points may be made in this context. First, that while the act of interpretation involves mediating between then and now or the rule and its present understand-ing, it is a much more constrained process than the one proposed by the New Haven approach that prescribes a comprehensive review of materi-als for discovering the genuine shared expectations of parties. The text retains its significance for Gadamer as for him (following Wittgenstein) the text is already related to interpretation not simply as any interpret-ive outcome but an interpretation that is not free of the text. Where he departs from Wittgenstein is in advancing the notion of 'fusion of hori-zons'. Gadamer contends that in interpreting and applying the rule the interpreter cannot step outside the present. In other words, while the text and its interpretation are internally related, it is not a static but a dynamic world in which the rule is applied. Second, Gadamer (unlike Kennedy) explains the thinking process through which the interaction between the text and the present takes place. The thinking process he describes is an inevitable part of the human condition.

Where Gadamer's method reaches it limits is in assessing the tradition inasmuch as it is constituted by non-linguistic activities. It is worth noting

[395] See ibid; emphasis added. He also observes: 'the judge's decision which has a practical effect on life, aims at being a correct and never an arbitrary application of the law; hence it may rely on a "correct" interpretation, which necessarily includes the mediation between history and the present in the act of understanding itself'. See ibid., p. xxix.

[396] Eskridge, 'Gadamer', pp. 612–613. As Eskridge explains: 'A Gadamerian approach to statu-tory interpretation views the enterprise as a conversation between the current perspective of the interpreter and the textual and historical perspective of the statute. The dialectic of statutory interpretation is neither the imposition of an archaeological or textualist view upon the interpreter, nor the interpreter's substitution of her perspective for that of the statute. Instead, it is the productive dialogue of these perspectives.' See ibid., p. 613.

[397] See ibid. p. 614.

here that in the work of Gadamer the term tradition is used in at least two ways. First, it is made to stand for a rule or traditional cannons of inter-pretation and Gadamer contends that these cannot be ignored. Second, tradition is understood as social institutions. It is in the latter context that he lays 'emphasis on tradition as the starting point and his pessim-ism about the ability to find an objective point from which to criticize tradition from outside the tradition.'[398] In advancing this view Gadamer does not adequately recognize that tradition may embody 'deep structural biases'.[399] It is here that Gadamer's approach is seen to be conservative by critics like Jürgen Habermas.[400] Habermas aptly notes in this regard that 'language is *also* a medium of domination and social power; it serves to legitimate relations of organized force'.[401] In other words language is 'ideological'.[402]

C.   Wittgenstein, Gadamer and Habermas

The failure to understand this goes deeper in the case of Wittgenstein. His theory of meaning does not involve the idea of a critique of non-linguistic tradition through locating it in social structures and institutions or with reference to concepts such as production, ideology, legitimization and power. It remains confined to understanding the meaning of words by locating them in a 'language game' and a 'form of life'.[403] But the 'form of life' or social practices are not themselves the subject of critical attention. This is because from ordinary language philosophy Wittgenstein did not seek to extract, as his interpreters G. P. Baker and P. M. S. Hacker have noted, 'a *theory* about the world, the mind or anything else'.[404] He was simply attempting to clarify the uses of language. Indeed, Wittgenstein claimed that 'we may not advance any kind of theory ... We *must do away*

[398] See ibid., pp. 613–614.
[399] See ibid. p. 630.
[400] See ibid., p. 673.
[401] Habermas, 'Review ', p. 272.
[402] See ibid.
[403] John B. Thompson, *Critical Hermeneutics: A Study in the Thought of Paul Ricoeur and Jurgen Habermas* (Cambridge: Cambridge University Press, 1981), see pp. 115–123, 151–158 and 182–189. Speaking of linguistic philosophy Russell has said that their work was 'completely unintelligible': 'its positive doctrines seem to me trivial and its negative doctrines unfounded. I have not found in Wittgenstein's *Philosophical Investigations* anything that seemed to me interesting and I do not understand why a whole school finds important wisdom in its pages'. Bertrand Russell, *My Philosophical Development* (London: George Allen and Unwin, 1969), p. 216.
[404] See ibid., p. 475; emphasis in original.

with all explanation, and *description alone must take its place*.'[405] The inadequacy of this position, as noted in Chapter 3, was pointed out by the Oxford philosopher J. L. Austin who recognized the necessity of critique (even if in a limited way) by observing that 'ordinary language is *not* the last word: in principle it can everywhere be supplemented and improved upon and superseded'.[406] For 'we are looking again not *merely* at words … but also at the realities we use the words to talk about'.[407]

Wittgenstein, therefore, did not also take into account the possibility of multiple interpretations of rules based on a critique of ordinary language. For Wittgenstein 'to follow a rule means to apply it in the same way'.[408] But while this is a crucial insight into the interpretation process, especially as a point of departure, the suggestion does not dissolve the problem of multiple interpretations. Habermas rightly observes in this regard that:

> Wittgenstein showed how the rules of linguistic communication imply the conditions of possibility of their own application … But Wittgenstein failed to appreciate that the same rules also include the possibility of their interpretation. It is proper to the grammar of a language game not only that it defines a form of life but that it defines a form of life as one's own over against others that are foreign … the dialectical confrontations of what is one's own with what is foreign leads for the most part imperceptibly to revisions.[409]

In other words, Wittgenstein proposed a 'monadological structure' understanding of the 'ordinary language' in which 'the language game congeals to an opaque unity'.[410] In reality 'ordinary languages are incomplete and provide no guarantee for the absence of ambiguity'.[411] It is in these contexts that Gadamer speaks of the 'fusion of horizons'. That is to say, 'hermeneutic understanding is the interpretation of texts, albeit amidst traditions (including legal traditions) in the knowledge of already understood texts'.[412] Unlike Wittgenstein, Gadamer recognizes 'the pluralism of lifeworlds and language games' and therefore anticipates a dialogue.[413] He

---

[405] Ludwig Wittgenstein, *Philosophical Investigations* (Oxford: Blackwell, 1983), rule 109; emphasis added.
[406] J. L. Austin, *Philosophical Papers,* 3rd edn (Oxford: Clarendon Press, 1979), p. 185; emphasis in original.
[407] See ibid., p.182; emphasis in original.
[408] Habermas, 'Review', p. 249.
[409] See ibid., pp. 247–248.
[410] See ibid., p. 249.
[411] See ibid., p. 250.
[412] See ibid., p. 253.
[413] See ibid., p. 254.

notes that 'understanding does not mean merely appropriating customary opinions or acknowledging what tradition has sanctified'.[414]

But Gadamer himself did not go far enough. Indeed, he noted that 'I will not deny, however, that – among all the elements of understanding – I have emphasized the assimilation of what is past and of tradition'.[415] This is where Habermas helps point out that tradition in many an instance facilitates social domination. But it is important to bear in mind, as Christopher Kutz has pointed out, 'the flaw in a system of laws in which systematic bias has an effect is the bias itself, not the indeterminacy of the system ... The minimal ideal of rule of law is served whenever there is an appropriate relation between decision and grounds. Criticism of the political, moral, or social viciousness of the decision is a separate issue altogether'.[416] He goes on to add that 'to the extent that the system of laws serves directly or indirectly to further racial, gender, or class inequalities, it is an appropriate subject for criticism and reform'.[417] But 'the ideal of the rule of law is entirely compatible with such criticism'.[418] In other words, the problem often is not indeterminacy of a rule but its outcome. Or to put it differently, where unacceptable interpretations are advanced these can be dispensed with through the process of communicative action as good argument can come to prevail.

D. Final Reflections

From the preceding discussion it can be said that the problems with a theory of strong indeterminacy thesis are the following: First, as Wittgenstein pointed out the view that to counter the charge of indeterminacy you have to show that a rule is completely transparent, including and prior to its application to facts, which themselves should be completely determinate, yielding a singular interpretive outcome, represents a mistaken understanding of the process of determining the meaning of a rule and its application.[419] The rules are certainly transparent inasmuch as the meaning of words and rules are derived from their use. A key flaw in the argument relating to indeterminacy of international law rules is that its proponents

---

[414] Gadamer, *Truth and Method*, p. xxxiv.

[415] See ibid.

[416] Christopher L. Kutz, 'Just Disagreement: Indeterminacy and Rationality in the Rule of Law', 103 (1994) *The Yale Law Journal*, pp. 997–1030 at p. 1022.

[417] See ibid.

[418] See ibid.

[419] See ibid., p. 1024.

do not recognize that the text is not merely black marks on paper or a view from nowhere but reflects a particular political and historical consensus. This is true both of a rule and its exceptions. Take the instance of Article 2(4) and Article 51 of the UN Charter. It reflected the political and historical consensus in the international community in 1945. It is this understanding of the genesis of rules that leads to the proposition that the rule and interpretation are internally related. The consensus on political and historical judgment embodied in the rule is also the reason that legal texts constrain. It is of course true that a legal rule springs to life only at the moment of application calling for dialogue with the historical text. It has, therefore, to be accepted that the rule and the accepted cannons of interpretation constrain but without dictating singular outcomes. Yet it is also the case that governments understand their obligations on the basis of appreciating the conjuncture in which rules are adopted and the traditions of interpretation that are part of the culture of the international law. The mistake of the proponents of the strong indeterminacy thesis is to neglect altogether the constraints of the historical context of the text and traditions of interpretation on present application. But there are no rules (or concepts) that stand outside history or can be attributed meaning in defiance of canons of interpretation. Thus, for instance, you do not interpret Article 2 (4) and its relationship to Article 51 of the UN Charter, outside the tradition of international law or, which is the same, the history of the 'outlawry of war' in the backdrop of the two world wars. That tradition and the text constrain in terms of attributing meaning to the rules in the present. There is no free play of imagination that allows all interpretations to claim validity. As Gadamer puts it, his aim was to understand *'not what we do or what we ought to do, but what happens to us over and above our wanting and doing'.*[420] But this does not eliminate the possibility of multiple interpretations. At the same time, as Habermas points out, this does not also mean that each interpretation of a rule is as sound as another. The interpretation supported by better arguments, that include acceptable principles of interpretation, prevails. Second, the fact that interpretations tend to favour the powerful (states or classes) is not because rules are indeterminate but because power comes into play in their codification and adoption. This is where the limits of the Wittgenstein-Gadamer approach are made clear by the Habermas critique that language is ideological and a means of domination. But the critique of outcomes that flow from the interpretation of rules is not to be confused with the act of interpretation

---

[420] Gadamer, *Truth and Method*, p. xxvi; emphasis added.

itself. There is a difference between making the claim that a rule is determinate and a rule is just.

IX.   IMAIL and Human Rights

Any approach to international law today has to articulate its perspective
on human rights as their effective protection has come to define the idea
of a good society and polity.[421] IMAIL too cannot avoid its responsibility
in this regard, especially as a prelude to discussing 'alternative futures'.
Indeed, the place of human rights in any imagined future is today a key
to its appeal. To begin with, IMAIL has little quarrel with the McDougal-
Lasswell view that the international community should promote the goal
of 'human dignity'. But it was seen that the policy-oriented approach uses
the term as a shorthand for a bourgeois conception of rights. IMAIL
shares in this regard Richard Falk's critique that the policy-oriented
approach displays unwarranted epistemological confidence in elaborating
its understanding of human rights It also agrees with Hilary Charlesworth
and Christine Chinkin that given the continuing prevalence of patriarchal
structures the language of rights has not been able to adequately address
the concerns of women. IMAIL also concurs with David Kennedy when
he draws attention to the dark side of human rights. However, the IMAIL
critique of human rights discourse goes deeper in as much as it accepts
Marx's critique that there is a tension between the 'logic of capital' and the
'logic of rights'. However, at the same time, it does not agree with the view
that Marx was dismissive of the language of rights or that a Marxist cannot believe in human rights.[422] It is, therefore, important from an IMAIL
perspective to dispel the idea that Marx did not subscribe to the relevance
and power of human rights even as he pointed to the impossibility of their
substantive realization in bourgeois societies.[423]

In a well-known essay Steven Lukes contends that any attempt to
assign salience to human rights runs against 'central doctrines essential
to the Marxist canon'.[424] In this regard, he cites in support many passages

---

[421] For an important take on the reason for this see Samuel Moyn, *The Last Utopia: Human
Rights in History* (Cambridge, MA: The Belknap Press of Harvard University Press, 2010).
[422] Steven Lukes, 'Can a Marxist Believe in Human Rights, 4 (1981) *Praxis International*,
pp. 334–345.
[423] The broader idea of 'democratic socialism' is touched upon in the next section devoted to
the considering the subject of 'alternative futures'.
[424] Lukes, 'Can a Marxist?', p. 335. Others who share the Lukes standpoint include Allan E.
Buchanan, *Marx and Justice: The Radical Critique of Liberalism* (Totowa, NJ: Rowman

from the writings of Marx and Engels. Thus, for instance, in the *German Ideology* Marx and Engels observe that 'as far as *Recht* is concerned we with many others have stressed the opposition of communism to *Recht*, both political and private, as also in its most general form as the rights of man'.[425] Marx's views are apparently no different when it comes to the place of rights in capitalist societies. In an important essay 'On the Jewish Question', Marx writes that in bourgeois society human rights is based 'on the separation of man from man' and that 'the practical application of man's right to liberty is man's right to private property'.[426] Marx goes on to comment that:

> None of the so-called rights of man, therefore, go beyond egoistic man, beyond man as a member of civil society, that is, an individual withdrawn into himself, into the confines of his private interests and private caprice, and separated from the community. In the rights of man, he is far from being conceived as a species-being; on the contrary, species-life itself, society, appears as a framework external to the individuals, as a restriction of their original independence. The sole bond holding them together is natural necessity, need and private interest, the preservation of their property and their egoistic selves.[427]

It would appear from these various observations that Marx was deeply sceptical of the idea and role of human rights. However, such a view would represent a misunderstanding of his position. It is only in the instance of a communist society that he thought that in the absence of social and political conflict the salience of rights would be diminished. In the instance of capitalist societies Marx was merely stressing that 'right can never be higher than the economic structure of society and its cultural development conditioned thereby'.[428] He was in this instance only pointing to the limited potential of realizing human rights in bourgeois societies. But this did not mean that he did not value rights both in terms of the advancement of workers movements or the welfare of subaltern groups. His was a dualist or dialectical view that recognized the significance of human

and Allenheld, 1982), pp. 67–68; Peter Gable, 'Roll Over Beethoven', 36 (1984) *Stanford Law Review*, pp. 1–55 at p. 33. See generally Leszek Kolakowski, 'Marxism and Human Rights', 112 (1983) *Daedalus*, pp. 83–92; and Alice Erh-Soon Tay, 'Marxism, Socialism and Human Rights' in Eugene Kamenka and Alice Erh-Soon Tay (eds.) *Human Rights* (London: Edward Arnold, 1978), pp. 104–113.

[425] See ibid., pp. 337–338.
[426] Karl Marx, 'On the Jewish Question' in Karl Marx and Friedrich Engels, *The Individual and Society* (Moscow: Progress Publishers, 1984), pp. 56–71 at p. 66.
[427] See ibid., p. 67.
[428] Marx and Engels, *Selected Works*, vol. 3, p. 19.

rights even as it pointed to the difficulties of realizing them in capitalist societies. It embodied a historical assessment of the place of rights in
bourgeois societies. Thus, for instance, while Marx celebrated the struggles of the working class to achieve the ten-hour day, he was always aware
that such victories were only a small step in ameliorating the condition of
workers and what is more could even go to legitimize the very system that
the working class was seeking to transform.[429] At a time when progressive
social forces are coming to invest heavily in human rights discourse to
bring about structural changes in society it may be useful to heed Marx's
critique.[430] But this must be done with the clear awareness that he was
speaking of the limits of rights for bringing about transformational social
change. For the rest, he never rejected the idea or significance of rights.[431]
The following further submissions may be considered in this regard.

First, what Marx advanced was a historical critique of the role of civil
and political rights. He argued that categories such as 'equality' or 'freedom' were mistakenly viewed as transhistorical in nature and therefore
realizable in any age. In reality these categories of rights have had a different meaning, significance, and effect in different historical epochs.[432] In
making a historical assessment of the role of rights in capitalist societies
he recognized that it is only under capitalism that the idea of 'equality'
becomes meaningful as labour power itself becomes a commodity. The
individual who offers his labour-power for sale meets the owner of capital in the market and they 'deal with each other as on the basis of equal

---

[429] Amy Bartholomew, 'Should a Marxist Believe in Marx on Rights?', (1990) *Socialist Register*, pp. 244–264 at p. 253.

[430] As Brad Roth observes, 'Marxism retains its relevance in the current period, not as a comprehensive replacement for liberal human rights theories, but as a source of critique that
challenges those theories on the basis of the very values of human freedom and dignity
that they espouse, and as a source of alternative gauges of whether particular policies
advance those values'. Brad R. Roth, 'Retrieving Marx for the Human Rights Project', 17
(2004) *Leiden Journal of International Law*, pp. 31–66 at p. 66.

[431] Bartholomew, 'Should a Marxist?', p. 246.

[432] For instance, the rights of equality and freedom have different content in antiquity, feudalism and capitalism. In the words of Marx: 'Equality and freedom as developed to this
extent [i.e. under capitalism] are exactly the opposite of the freedom and equality in the
world of antiquity, where developed exchange value was not their basis, but where, rather,
the development of that basis destroyed them. Equality and freedom presuppose relations of production as yet unrealized in the ancient world and in the Middle Ages. Direct
forced labour is the foundation of the ancient world; the community rests on this as its
foundation; labour itself as a "privilege", as still particularized, not yet generally producing
exchange values, is the basis of the world of the Middle Ages.' Marx, *Grundrisse*, p. 245.
For the general point see George G. Brenkert, 'Marx and Human Rights', 24 (1986) *Journal
of the History of Philosophy*, pp. 55–77.

rights' and are therefore 'equal in the eyes of the law'.[433] But he also pointed out that capitalism ushers in a world in which in order to survive the worker has no choice but to sell his labour-power to the capitalist. As Marx succinctly put it, 'in reality, the laborer belongs to capital before he has sold himself to capital'.[434] Therefore, Marx concluded that the right to equality was only partially realizable in capitalist societies.[435] This is as true today with the difference that the relationship between the worker and capital assume a myriad forms. These relationships often need to be deconstructed in order to reveal their true essence.

Second, Marx was concerned that the idea of human rights was confined to 'negative liberty' defined in our times by Isaiah Berlin to mean 'the area within which a man can act unobstructed by others'.[436] In this understanding of liberty 'only *deliberate* interference constitutes coercion or deprivation of liberty'.[437] It removes from view impediments to the exercise of liberty arising from the 'lack of equal access to the means of life and the means of labor'.[438] In other words, the idea of negative liberty leaves out of its scope structural coercion arising from institutional arrangements 'made and enforced by a class of owners'; it is not seen as violating the idea of liberty.[439] But it can hardly be denied that the idea of liberty would be severely limited if it did not address the diverse sources of unfreedom. These could be many and varied.

Third, while Marx was critical of confining the idea of rights to negative liberty he was not dismissive of them. He was well aware of their value in the face of attempts by capitalist states to regulate and discipline the lives of ordinary citizens in innumerable ways.[440] Speaking of the French state in *The Eighteenth Brumaire*, Marx observed:

> the state enmeshes, controls, regulates, superintends and tutors civil society from its most comprehensive manifestations of life down to its most

---

[433] Marx, *Capital*, p.165.

[434] See ibid., p. 542.

[435] See ibid., pp. 505–506.

[436] Isaiah Berlin, 'Two Concepts of Liberty' in Michael J. Sandel (ed.) *Liberalism and Its Critics* (Oxford: Oxford University Press, 1984), pp. 15–36 at p. 16.

[437] C. B. Macpherson, *Democratic Theory: Essays in Retrieval* (Oxford: Oxford University Press, 1973), p. 97.

[438] See ibid., p. 96; emphasis in original.

[439] See ibid., p. 98. As Marx wrote in *The Eighteenth Brumaire*, 'so long as the *name* of freedom was respected and only its actual realization prevented, of course in a legal way, the constitutional existence of liberty remained intact, inviolate, however mortal the blows to its existence *in actual life*'. Marx and Engels, *Selected Works*, vol. 1, p. 409; emphasis in original.

[440] Brenkert, 'Marx', p. 72; Bartholomew, 'Should a Marxist?', p. 253.

insignificant stirrings, from its most general modes of being to the most
private existence of individuals; where through the most extraordinary
centralization this parasitic body acquires a ubiquity, an omniscience,
a capacity for accelerated mobility and an elasticity which finds a counterpart only in the helpless dependence, in the loose shapelessness of the
actual body politic.[441]

In view of the parasitic character of the bourgeois state, and its pervasive and invasive presence in the lives of ordinary citizens, Marx understood the value of human rights. Therefore, on several occasions he noted,
for instance, the importance of free speech and free press.[442]

Fourth, if Marx did not see a place for rights in communism it was
because (as noted earlier) he assumed that the need for positive human
rights would disappear with the end of social and political conflict. But
he certainly envisaged their existence under socialism. As Bob Fine has
observed, Marx made it amply clear that bourgeois right was for him 'not
a temporary hangover from capitalist society, to be eradicated as soon as
practicable, but a principle which was to govern socialist society until the
point of its transformation into complete communism'.[443] Or as Phillip
Kain puts it, in Marx's view 'rights are realized first, and only then, in
the second stage of communism, do we pass beyond the "narrow horizons of bourgeois right"'.[444] In other words, Marx had anticipated the view
advanced by scholars like Allen Buchanan, Christine Sypnowich and R. G.
Peffer that till the idealized communist society is reached human rights
are necessary to protect the individual against the state.[445] As Buchanan
has pointed out, the existence of human rights in socialism are absolutely
crucial from several perspectives: as constraints on paternalism, as constraints on what may be done to maximize welfare or other similar good,
as constraints on the use of coercion in provision of public goods, as constraints on democratic procedures to ensure minority rights and equal
participation, and to specify the extent and limits of sacrifices for future

---

[441] Marx and Engels, *Selected Works*, vol. 1, p. 432.
[442] See, for example, Karl Marx, 'Debates on Freedom of the Press' in Karl Marx and Friedrich
       Engels, *The Individual and Society* (Moscow: Progress Publishers, 1984), pp. 27–39. Marx
       speaks of freedom of the press as 'an embodiment of freedom, a positive good' and that
       'press law expresses a right and censorship law a wrong', pp. 29 and 33.
[443] Bob Fine, *Democracy and the Rule of Law: Liberal Ideals and Marxist Critiques*
       (London: Pluto Press, 1984), p. 125.
[444] Phillip J. Kain, *Marx and Ethics* (Oxford: Oxford University Press, 1988), p. 201.
[445] Allen Buchanan, *Marx and Justice: The Radical Critique of Liberalism* (London: Rowman
       and Littlefield, 1982), p. 163; Christine Sypnowich, *The Concept of Socialist Law*
       (Oxford: Oxford University Press, 1990), chapter 5; and R. G. Peffer, *Marxism, Morality
       and Social Justice* (Princeton, NJ: Princeton University Press, 1990), p. 325.

generations.[446] Unfortunately, in Soviet bloc countries (as in China today) the view came to prevail that any petition of rights against the state was a threat to the very project of socialism. It is this practice which gave credence to the view that Marx was against rights per se.

Fifth, Marx had a rich notion of individuality that sits well with the case for human rights.[447] It explains the initiative of the former Soviet Union in the early years to expand the realm of rights. While civil and political rights came to be severely curtailed in the Stalin era and horrific crimes were committed against the Soviet people, the early innovations in the domain of rights can be traced to the theoretical importance attached after Marx to the rights of individuals. In a recent book John Quigley has shown how Soviet legislation in the 1920s was remarkable for its progressive quality. He notes that a most radical set of worker rights were legislated including the right to work, health insurance, disability benefits, old age pensions, free education, paid maternity leave, low cost housing and later annual vacations.[448] The Bolshevik government also rewrote family law to ensure equality between woman and man in contrast to laws that existed in much of the Western world.[449] Quigley contends that while it cannot be proven with 'mathematical precision,'[450] these 'innovations in Soviet law have changed the face of Western law. The inferior legal status of women in Western law, as found in the early twentieth century, has been altered dramatically. Women today enjoy greater legal protection in property, labor, and family relations'.[451] There is in fact little doubt that 'the Soviet legislative innovations of the 1920s provide a remarkable blueprint for legal reforms that entered Western law later in the twentieth century'.[452] The later contempt for human rights and rule of law is not to be traced to Marxism but to the fact of historical neglect of the legal tradition in Russia and a range of other particular factors including the phenomenon of Stalinism.[453]

---

[446] Buchanan, *Marx and Justice*, p. 165.
[447] Bartholomew, 'Should a Marxist?', p. 246.
[448] Quigley, *Soviet Legal*, pp. 11–16.
[449] See ibid., p. 20. Lenin is said to have observed that 'in the course of two years of Soviet power in one of the most backward countries of Europe, more has been done to emancipate woman, to make her the equal of the "strong" sex, than has been done during the past 130 years by all the advanced, enlightened, "democratic" republics of the world taken together'. Cited by Quigley, ibid., p. 26.
[450] See ibid., p. 192.
[451] See ibid., p. 181.
[452] See ibid.
[453] See ibid., p. 60. However, it can be said that the idea of withering away of state and law also contributed to strengthening the negative approach to rights.

Finally, it is worth noting that Marx was not against electoral democracy and explains why later thinkers like Luxemburg were never dismissive of bourgeois parliaments.[454] As in the instance of rights, Marx and Engels merely pointed to the limited role of universal suffrage in bringing about radical social transformation.[455] The general assessment of the strengths and weaknesses of electoral democracy has not changed substantially even today as can be seen from the constant all round talk of deepening democracy through notions like deliberative and participatory democracy.[456]

In short Marx was critical of bourgeois rights but not dismissive of them. As Brad Roth concludes after a critical survey of Marx's position, 'a Marxian approach recommends no sweeping rejection of liberal values and practices, and in the greatest number of real-world instances reaffirms the liberal human rights mission, albeit on a somewhat different rationale'.[457] It also does not treat human rights as dispensable in post-capitalist societies.[458] But Marx did argue that human rights politics is not a replacement for transformative politics. In recent times Boaventura de Sousa Santos has in a similar manner contended that human rights politics can replace the traditional politics of emancipation 'only if a politics of human rights radically different from the hegemonic liberal one is adopted and only if such a politics is conceived as part of a broader constellation of struggles and discourses of resistance and emancipation rather than as the sole politics of resistance against oppression'.[459] Santos goes on to speak of 'inter-cultural post-imperial human rights' that should be based on the right to knowledge ('a new epistemology from the South'), the right to bring historical capitalism to trial in a world tribunal, the right

---

[454] Even as Luxemburg critiqued bourgeois democracy she wrote: 'If democracy has become superfluous or annoying to the bourgeoisie, it is on the contrary necessary and indispensable to the working class. It is necessary to the working class because it creates the political forms (autonomous administration, electoral rights, etc.) which will serve the proletariat as fulcrums in its task of transforming bourgeois society. Democracy is indispensable to the working class because only through the exercise of its democratic rights, in the struggle for democracy, can the proletariat become aware of its class interests and its historic task.' Rosa Luxemburg, 'Reform or Revolution' in *Rosa Luxemburg: Selected Writings* (Kolkata: Search, 2008). p. 75.

[455] Marx and Engels, *Selected Works*, vol. 3, p. 329.

[456] Susan Marks, *The Riddle of all Constitutions* (Oxford: Oxford University Press, 2003).

[457] Roth, 'Retrieving Marx', p. 66.

[458] See ibid., p. 51.

[459] Boaventura de Sousa Santos, 'Human Rights as an Emancipatory Script? Cultural and Political Conditions' in Boaventura de Sousa Santos (ed.) *Another Knowledge is Possible: Beyond Northern Epistemologies* (London: Verso, 2007), pp. 3–41 at p. 3.

to a solidarity-oriented transformation of the right to property, the right to grant rights to entities incapable of bearing duties, namely nature and future generations and the right to democratic self-determination.[460] But such a view of human rights politics is unlikely to find acceptance, especially among mainstream human rights scholars, groups and organizations.

In sketching out an IMAIL perspective on human rights the Marxist perspective today needs to be supplemented by the insights of postcolonial theory and feminism. It must be remembered that Marx articulated his critique of human rights primarily in the domestic context of a capitalist society. He did not sufficiently appreciate that the bourgeois theory of rights was articulated in both the internal and external contexts, the latter context being the colonial project. As Ratna Kapur explains, 'the liberal tradition from which human rights have emerged not only incorporates arguments about freedom and equal worth but ... it also incorporates arguments about civilization, cultural backwardness, racial and religious superiority'.[461] Indeed, the discourse on human rights 'remain(s) structured by this history' which is not alien to it but rather represents the state of its being.[462] In other words, it is no accident that the liberal discourse on human rights was historically used to justify the colonial project for it was articulated in relation to it.[463] Uday Mehta has noted with respect to the idea of liberalism that while it need not necessarily be imperialistic 'the urge is internal to it' as it harbours 'a deep impulse to reform the world'.[464] In other words, integral to the politics of empire is the 'urge to reform and progress –which otherwise so often remains obscured and contested behind a concern with rights and individual freedom, [but now] *becomes virtually determinative and singular*'.[465] The intimate link between liberalism and imperialism means that these can coexist at all times in history. It is useful to recall here that the justly celebrated Universal Declaration of

[460] See ibid., pp. 28ff.
[461] Ratna Kapur, 'Human Rights in the 21st Century: Take a Walk on the Dark Side', 28 (2006) *Sydney Law Review*, pp. 665–687 at p. 674. For an Eurocentric perspective of human rights see Anthony Pagden, 'Human Rights, Natural Rights, and Europe's Imperial Legacy', 31 (2003) *Political Theory*, p. 171.
[462] For a Eurocentric perspective of human rights, see Pagden, 'Human Rights', p. 171.
[463] See generally B. S. Chimni, 'For Epistemological and Prudent Internationalism', *Harvard Human Rights Journal*. Available at http://harvardhrj.com/2012/11/for-epistemological-and-prudent-internationalism/http://harvardhrj.com/2012/11/for-epistemological-and-prudent-internationalism/
[464] Uday Singh Mehta *Liberalism and Empire: India in British Liberal Thought* (Oxford: Oxford University Press, 1999), pp. 20 and 79.
[465] See ibid., p. 80; emphasis added.

Human Rights (UDHR) was adopted with most of Asia and Africa under colonial rule. Today the growing corpus of international human rights law exists side by side with global imperialism. The liberal Western approach to human rights therefore also incorporates a unicivilizational approach to human rights. As Samuel Moyn notes of UDHR, 'it is easy to over-state the global and multicultural origins of the Universal Declaration in light of more contemporary pressures and desires'.[466] What is required is, as Yasuaki Onuma has pointed out, 'the need to supplement and mod-ify the current international instruments of human rights from trans-national and transcivilizational perspectives, in order to identify the most legitimate notion of globally valid human rights'.[467] In operational terms it means that international human rights need 'to be remade in the ver-nacular'.[468] But, as Sally Engle Merry notes, 'the reliance on a transnational legal order makes it more difficult to reinterpret human rights in the vernacular'.[469] Here the hegemony of international law combines with a unicivilizational perspective to exclude other voices and practices. What is required is, without embracing the trap of cultural relativism, the need to take account of the views and experiences of other civilizations.

The link between liberalism and imperialism can also be extended to patriarchy. From a feminist standpoint, Johanna de Groot has pointed out how both women and natives occupied the same position in lib-eral discourse in the nineteenth century. In her words both women and children were:

> portrayed and treated as children in need of the protection and care of male/imperial authority by virtue of their weaknesses, innocence and inadequacy. The use of a parental concept of authority combined a sense of care and involvement with the subordinate sex or race as well as power and control over them, and as such was equally appropriate for the definition of the power of men over women or of dominant over subordinate races.[470]

---

[466] Moyn, *Last Utopia*, p. 66.

[467] Yasuaki Onuma, *A Transcivilizational Perspective on International Law* (Leiden: Martinus Nijhoff, 2010), p. 376.

[468] Sally Engle Merry, *Human Rights & Gender Violence: Translating International Law into Local Justice* (Chicago, IL: The University of Chicago Press, 2006), p. 1.

[469] See ibid., p. 225.

[470] Joanna de Groot, '"Sex" and "race": The Construction of Language and Image in the Nineteenth Century' in Catherine Hall (ed.) *Cultures of Empire: A Reader* (Manchester: Manchester University Press, 2000), pp. 37–61 at pp. 43–44; Mehta, *Liberalism*, p. 31. Mehta notes how 'childhood is a theme that runs through the writings of British liberals in India with unerring constancy. It is the fixed point underlying the various imperial imperatives of education, forms of governance, and the alignment with progress'. See ibid.

This mode of representation must be viewed 'as a process of defining the self and others'.[471] It was constitutive of the self-image of the colonizers. The protective response continues in different forms to the present day leading to the inability of international human rights law to effectively promote the rights of women.

X. Alternative Futures

In much of the book a critique of capitalism, including its relationship with imperialism, has been advanced. But the proponents of capitalism may point out in response that critics overlook the fact that it yet remains the preferred system among peoples and nations of the world.[472] The preference for capitalism is traced by them to certain inherent strengths that it possesses. First, it is argued that capitalism, individual freedom and democracy tend to go hand in hand.[473] Second, it is said that there is no internal or necessary relationship between capitalism and imperialism. Colonialism was an historical aberration and was in any case not entirely without achievement.[474] Furthermore, the advanced capitalist states have taken number of initiatives to advance the welfare of weak nations in the postcolonial world. Third, it is noted that no economic system in history has produced and harnessed inventions and innovations more effectively than capitalism to improve the everyday lives of ordinary citizens. Fourth, while capitalism may be responsible for the ecological crisis it is also able to generate technological innovation and create appropriate social and political institutions to deal with it. Fifth, reference is made to 'the spirit of capitalism' that allows the discrepancy between its normative ideals and the workings of 'actually existing capitalism' to be addressed, thereby helping reduce the 'class', 'gender' and 'race' divides in society.[475] Finally, it

---

[471] Mehta, *Liberalism*, p. 35.

[472] As Boltanski and Chiapello note, despite criticisms capitalism is still seen as 'as an acceptable and even desirable order of things: the only possible order, or the best of all possible orders'. Luc Boltanski and Eve Chiapello, *The New Spirit of Capitalism* (London: Verso, 2005), p. 10.

[473] Milton Friedman, *Capitalism and Freedom* (Chicago, IL: University of Chicago Press, 1962), p. 4.

[474] Peter Berger, *The Capitalist Revolution* (New York: Basic Books Publishers, 1991), pp. 121ff.

[475] Boltanski and Chiapello, *New Spirit*, p. 25. Boltanski and Chiapello define it as 'the set of beliefs associated with the capitalist order that helps to justify this order and, by legitimating them, to sustain the forms of action and predispositions compatible with it'. See ibid., p.10.

is pointed out that the socialist project has been a complete failure causing unspeakable harm to peoples living under socialist regimes. Therefore, it is argued that the way to a better future is to attend to the failings of capitalism rather than make efforts to replace it.

But the exponents of the idea of socialism are unwilling to abandon it even as they condemn past and present models and practices of 'actually existing socialism'. Three types of arguments are advanced to oppose its unambiguous rejection. Firstly, it is argued that capitalism has caused more misery in human history than any other economic and social system. The keywords here are genocide, colonialism, holocaust, world wars, nuclear bomb and neocolonialism. In this telling of the history of capitalism, imperialism is not a thing of the past but an ongoing and palpable reality. There is continuing exploitation of and violence against weak groups, peoples, and nations. Secondly, it is pointed out that 'actually existing socialism' was not entirely without achievement. There were elements of its social policy viz., free education, free health care, free housing, full employment and free vacations that are worth preserving in any society. Indeed, if capitalist societies metamorphosed into welfare societies in the post-Second World War period it was at least in part because of the strong emphasis placed on social and economic rights for citizens in Soviet bloc countries.[476] Thirdly, it is contended that democratic socialism is not only possible, but is the only form deserving of the name 'socialism'.[477] It is recalled that the renowned Marxist theorist Karl Kautsky had made out a powerful case for retaining elements of bourgeois democracy in socialist societies, albeit Lenin had carried the day in his times.[478] The experience of 'actually existing socialism' clearly demonstrates that Kautsky was right in observing that while 'it is possible to have socialized production without democracy' it is inconceivable to think of the liberation

---

[476] It is a critical explanation for why the welfare state came to be dismantled in several advanced capitalist countries the moment the socialist option was discredited.

[477] It is said that the turn to totalitarianism in the Soviet Union was induced by the hostility of the capitalist world to socialism. It was taken advantage of by Stalin and his successors to institute a totalitarian regime. Today, socialism is discredited with reference to the erroneous characterization of the former Cambodian and Albanian regimes and the current North Korean regime as being socialist. These were and are predatory totalitarian regimes seeking to legitimize themselves through invoking the name of socialism. The claim of China being a socialist society is also difficult to sustain as it appears to be pursuing a capitalist path of development under an authoritarian political dispensation.

[478] In his well-known pamphlet 'Renegade Kautsky and Proletarian Revolution' Lenin attempted to demolish the case for bourgeois democracy. V. I. Lenin, *Selected Works*, vol. 3 (Moscow: Progress Publishers, 1975), pp. 17–97.

of the proletariat without democracy.[479] Most contemporary advocates of socialism would also unhesitatingly endorse the Kautsky proposition that 'socialism without democracy is out of question. When we speak of modern socialism we mean not only the organization of production but also the democratic organization of society ... socialism is inseparably linked with democracy. There can be no socialism without democracy.[480] It may be recalled that Kautsky was at pains to explain that when Marx used the expression 'the revolutionary dictatorship of the proletariat' he 'did not mean a dictatorship in the literal sense ... Marx was not talking about a form of government but of a state of affairs which must necessarily arise wherever the proletariat achieves political power.[481] The proletariat did not have to use non-democratic methods for 'a government which knows that the masses are behind it will only use force to protect democracy and not to suppress it.[482] Kautsky reminded his readers that in *The Communist Manifesto* Marx and Engels had noted that 'all previous historical movements were movements of minorities, or in the interests of minorities.[483] In contrast, 'the proletarian movement is the self-conscious independent movement of the immense majority in the interests of the immense majority.[484] There was, therefore, no reason for the proletariat to deprive 'the opposition of their rights.[485]

But despite these contentions the word 'socialism', as Frederic Jameson points out, 'bears the weight of everything oppressive or unproductive associated with the Soviet Union.[486] To use the word 'socialism' is to immediately remind of the terrible crimes committed against Soviet people in its name. The world of 'actually existing socialism' is not seen as a distortion of socialism in the same way as fascism was in the instance of capitalism.[487] Instead, socialism and totalitarianism are seen as bound to each other in myriad ways. In the circumstances Jameson proposes a

---

[479] Karl Kautsky, 'On Political Reform and Socialism (The Dictatorship of the Proletariat)' in Micheline R. Ishay (ed.) *The Human Rights Reader,* 2nd edn (London: Routledge, 2007), pp. 239–246 at p. 240.

[480] See ibid., p. 241.

[481] See ibid., p. 244.

[482] See ibid., p. 246.

[483] Marx and Engels, *Selected Works,* vol. 1, p. 118.

[484] See ibid.

[485] See ibid., p. 245.

[486] Jameson, *Valences,* p.12.

[487] Friedman conceded that you can 'have economic arrangements that are fundamentally capitalist and political arrangements that are not free'. After all, as he noted, 'Fascist Italy and Fascist Spain, Germany at various times ... Japan before World Wars I and II, tsarist

temporary suspension on advancing 'socialism' as an ideal and to think of
a 'third possibility' which employs 'the language of Utopia' without ruling
out 'the eventual return of the vocabulary of socialism'.[488] The 'third possibility' could also mean, as it does for thinkers like Michael Hardt and
Antonio Negri, rejecting the alternatives between capitalism and socialism to open up 'a new space for politics'.[489]

However, it is not enough to simply posit the possibility of a 'third possibility'. The normative principles, institutions and social practices that
would inform it need to be articulated if it has to receive the support of all
sections of society. It is well known that Marx himself did not elaborate 'a
real theory of the destination'.[490] The few remarks that he made leave the
impression that socialism is simply 'the idealized negation of the oppressions of capitalism'.[491] Marx was reluctant to outline in any detail the idea
of socialism as he thought it best to leave it to those who would be engaged
in building a socialist society to find suitable normative and institutional
answers to the problems that were confronted. However, today, in view of
the experience of 'actually existing socialism', the task of developing a normative theory of 'third possibility' cannot be postponed.[492] In fact, there is
an urgent need to clarify to the addressees the basic ideas and principles
that would inform the realization and construction of a 'third possibility'. In undertaking this exercise Marx would have expected the exploited
and oppressed classes to learn from history, especially from the history of
'actually existing socialism'.

While a detailed exposition of the case for 'third possibility' will have to
be left for another occasion it can be said that any conception of it must --
in the backdrop of the analysis and reflections offered in this book-- take
into account the following 'principles' or propositions.

First, the idea of a 'third possibility' should not be thought of as a
once-for-all exercise, some kind of projection of a fixed and frozen

---

Russia in the decades before World War I – are all societies that cannot conceivably be
described as politically free. Yet, in each, private enterprise was the dominant form of economic organization.' Friedman, *Capitalism and Freedom*, p. 10.

[488] Jameson, *Valences*, p.12.

[489] Michael Hardt and Antonio Negri, *Commonwealth* (Cambridge, MA: The Belknap Press
of Harvard University Press, 2009), p. ix.

[490] Michael Burawoy and Erik Olin Wright, 'Sociological Marxism' in Jonathan H. Turner
(ed.) *Handbook of Sociological Theory* (New York: Kluwer Academic/Plenum Publishers,
2002), pp. 459–486 at p. 460.

[491] See ibid., p. 478.

[492] See ibid., p. 463.

utopia.[493] It should be consciously articulated as a set of corrigible and amendable propositions. The depiction of preferred futures in the form of blueprints encourages the use of unacceptable means to shape societal relations as in the instance of 'actually existing socialism'. Peace must therefore be made with the uncertainties and contingencies of history and desired futures made the subject of continuous critical reflection and dialogue.

Second, in imagining and mapping a 'third possibility' the accumulated knowledge and experiences of the non-Western world must be borne in mind. In keeping with the insights of postcolonial theory there must be space for imagining alternative futures in ways that allow the rich diversity of cultures in the non-West to come into play. In the past 'socialism' was proposed as a universal model, even though a degree of diversity was recognized over the years (e.g., 'socialism' with Chinese characteristics). What postcolonial theory envisages is the possibility of departing from whatever Western 'model' of 'third possibility' is advanced. Indeed, there can be no unique or singular version of 'third possibility' that each society must follow.

Third, any conception of 'third possibility' must involve a non-negotiable commitment to the principle of electoral democracy (i.e., to periodic free and fair elections) in a multiparty system and the protection of human rights. However, the system of electoral democracy may be so devised as to minimize the influence of money and power in its working. The 'third possibility' would also seek to institutionalize forms of deliberative and participatory democracy that allows individuals, groups and communities to inter alia participate in decisions relating to production, consumption and distribution of goods and services. The essential idea would be to allow the effective involvement of individuals and communities in decisions that impact their lives and that of Nature.

Fourth, the 'third possibility' should not tolerate in any way the exploitation and oppression of other peoples and nations. Given the historical relationship between 'actually existing capitalism' and imperialism, the

---

[493] Even when different groups and movements are struggling for the same goal such as 'socialism' it is not clear if their understanding of 'socialism' is the same. Thus, for instance, from a socialist feminist perspective it is said that 'while we argue that socialism is in the interest of both men and women, it is not at all clear that we are all fighting for the same kind of "humane socialism", or that we have the same conception of the struggle required to get there, much less that capital alone is responsible for our current oppression'. Heidi L. Hartmann, 'The Unhappy Marriage of Marxism and Feminism: Towards A More Progressive Union, *Capital and Class* pp. 1–33 at p. 5.

'third possibility' must minimally devise a variety of capitalism that renders imperialism unnecessary. It must also reject the idea of subjugation of Nature, promoting instead Peace with Nature. These objectives can be achieved only through introducing substantial changes in the material structures of 'actually existing capitalism'.

Fifth, the 'third possibility' must involve the recognition that there may not be a single answer to the property conundrum. The experience of 'actually existing socialism' has shown that a system founded on socialist property can produce its own forms of inequalities and modes of domination.[494] A 'third possibility' can therefore leave room for the existence of an intricate mix of ownership patterns. As has been noted by one group of researchers with respect to the global commons, there is 'no single type of property regime' that 'works efficiently, fairly, and sustainably in relation to all [common property resources]'.[495] The different types of property regimes that can be considered include open access, group property, individual property and government property.[496] The bottom line is that while wealth creation may be left in the hands of private actors there should be a balance between private and public interests, and the absence of concentration in wealth.

Sixth, the 'third possibility' must not a priori rule out a role for market institutions even as any form of 'market utopia' is rejected.[497] The rationale for retaining a weak role for markets can be traced to its provision of information, the efficient allocation of resources, and the creation of incentives for innovation.[498] A 'third possibility' would accept that there is no formula that can capture the optimal relationship between the State and the market as it is as much a cultural as a material phenomenon. Each society will have to determine on the basis of its historical experience the balance it values between the State and the market.

Seventh, the 'third possibility' should recast 'class', 'gender' and 'race' relations in a manner that promises equality between classes, sexes and

---

[494] Boris Kagarlitsky, *The Twilight of Globalization: Property, State and Capitalism* (London: Pluto Press, 2000), p. 55.

[495] Elinor Ostrom, Joanna Burger, Christopher B. Field, Richard B. Nogaard, David Policansky, Revisiting the Commons: Local Lessons, Global Challenges, 284 (9 April 1999) *Science*, pp. 278–282 at p. 279.

[496] See ibid.

[497] In a market utopia 'if any government or law have a justified part to play, it is solely to enable markets to work properly, to correct market failures, to mimic the market and make up for missing markets'. Michael Taylor, *Rationality and the Ideology of Disconnection* (Cambridge: Cambridge University Press, 2006), p. 59.

[498] See ibid., pp. 59ff.

races. In the imagined 'third possibility' violence in human relationships would be minimized. Each individual will be allowed to develop her full potential through the 'free development and exercise of their physical and mental facilities'.[499]

Eighth, the 'third possibility' should seek to promote democratic modes of global governance. It would envisage the restructuring of regional and international institutions to address the problem of democratic deficit through inter alia promoting deliberative and participatory democracy and adherence to global administrative law. A future world state must in this matrix be envisaged as a confederation or a commonwealth of free peoples.

Ninth, the 'third possibility' should not be seen as realizable by only a particular oppressed group or class. It may be actualized through 'uniting social groups on both a class and non-class basis, the victims of exploitation as well as the victims of social exclusion, of sexual, ethnic, racist and religious discrimination'.[500] The struggles for realizing a 'third possibility' must be based on the principle of non-violence. Its acceptance is crucial as the use of violence only distorts the process of social transformation reproducing an alienated self.[501]

Finally, the 'third possibility' must recognize the close relationship between social and political transformation and self-transformation. It should accept that greater self-knowledge is vital to the creation of a peaceful and just world order. The eventual driving force of the life and work of critical thinkers ranging from Marx to Gandhi, icons of critical thinking, was the spiritual flourishing of humankind. Young Marx explored this theme in secular language in the *Economic and Philosophic Manuscripts* and later developed it in his reflections on alienation in *Capital* and other writings.[502] In the final analysis, Marx hoped that man can be 'freed from chains, not only of economic poverty, but of spiritual poverty created by

---

[499] Marx and Engels, *Selected Works*, vol. 3, p. 149.

[500] Santos, 'Human Rights', p.10.

[501] It is worth clarifying here that even Marx was of the view 'that political force cannot produce anything for which there has been no preparation in the social and political process ... he did not believe in the creative power of force, in the idea of political force of itself could create a new social order'. Erich Fromm, *Marx's Concept of Man* (New York: Ederick Ungar Publishing Co, 1961), pp. 23–24.

[502] Karl Marx, *Economic and Philosophic Manuscripts of 1844*, 5th revised edn (Moscow: Progress Publishers, 1977). According to one scholar, young Marx saw social needs (beyond the political realm of delegated democracy) to include 'recreation, culture, intellectual stimulation, artistic expression, emotional satisfaction, aesthetic pleasure, fulfilling work and meaningful community'. David Leopold *The Young Karl Marx: German*

alienation'.[503] He imagined 'a world in which man is no longer a stranger among strangers, but is in his world, where he is at home'.[504] This view was deeply shared by Gandhi.[505] Marx would have on the other hand readily concurred with Gandhi that to create a world that is not estranged from us anticipates work on the self. In Gandhi's view it involved above all resistance to all forms of oppression and injustice. To help realize the 'third possibility' the community of international lawyers must deploy the language of international law in the spirit of these great masters.

Philosophy, Modern Politics, and Human Flourishing (Cambridge: Cambridge University Press, 2007), p. 296. See also Marx, *Capital*, pp. 76–87.

[503] Fromm, *Marx's Concept*, p. 61.

[504] See ibid., p. 69.

[505] In the words of Akeel Bilgrami, 'the so-called Early Marx who lamented the alienation that afflicted modern capitalist civilization and the Gandhi who thought that India should not embrace the alienated culture of the modern West, were thus intellectual partners in a common theoretical cause'. Akeel Bilgrami, 'Gandhi and Marx', 40 (2012) *Social Scientist* (New Delhi), pp. 3–25 at p. 8.

BIBLIOGRAPHY

Abbott, Kenneth W., 'Modern International Relations Theory: A Prospectus for International Lawyers', 14 (1989) *Yale Journal of International Law,* pp. 335–411.

Abbott, Kenneth W. and Duncan Snidal, 'Law, Legalization, and Politics: An Agenda for the Next Generation of IL/IR Scholars', Jeffrey L. Dunoff and Mark A. Pollack (eds.) *Interdisciplinary Perspectives on International Law and International Relations* (Cambridge: Cambridge University Press, 2013), pp. 33–56.

Allison, Dorothy, 'A Question of Class', in Nancy Holstrom (ed.) *The Socialist Feminist Project: A Contemporary Reader in Theory and Politics* (Delhi: Aakar, 2011), pp. 30–45.

Alvarez, José E., 'Contemporary International Law: An "Empire of Law" or the "Law of Empire"', 24 (2009) *American University International Law Review,* pp. 811–842.

Alvarej, José E., 'Book Review', 95 (2001) *The American Journal of International Law,* pp. 459–464.

Alexandrowicz, C. H., *An Introduction to the History of the Law of Nations in the East Indies (16th, 17th and 18th centuries)* (Oxford: Clarendon Press, 1967).

Ammoun, Judge, Case Concerning the Barcelona Traction, Light and Power Company Limited, Second Phase, I. C. J. Reports, 1970 pp. 287–333.

Amos, Valerie and Pratibha Parmar, 'Challenging Imperial Feminism', 17 (1984) *Feminist Review,* pp. 3–19.

Anand, R. P., 'Attitude of the Asian-African States Toward Certain Provisions of International Law', 15 (1966) *The International and Comparative Law Quarterly,* pp. 55–75.

New States and International Law (Delhi: Vikas Publishing House, 1972).

'Maritime Practice in South-East Asia until 1600 A.D. and the Modern Law of the Sea', 30 (1981) *International and Comparative Law Quarterly, pp.* 440–454.

The Origin and Development of Law of the Sea (The Hague: Martinus Nijhoff, 1983).

Development of Modern International Law and India (New Delhi: Indian Society of International Law, 2006), pp. 24–25.

Anderson, Kenneth, 'The Ottawa Convention Banning Landmines, the Role of International Non-Governmental Organizations and the Idea of International Civil Society', 11 (2000) *European Journal of International Law,* pp. 91–120.

'Squaring the Circle? Reconciling Sovereignty and Global Governance through Global Government Networks', 118 (2005) *Harvard Law Review,* pp. 1255–1312.

'"Accountability" as "Legitimacy": Global Governance, Global Civil Society and the United Nations', 36 (2011) *Brooklyn Journal of International Law,* pp. 841–890.

Anderson, Perry, *Considerations on Western Marxism* (London: New Left Books, 1976).

Arguments with English Marxism (London: Verso, 1980).

In the Tracks of Historical Materialism (London: Verso, 1984).

Anderson, Stanley V., 'A Critique of Professor Myres S. McDougal Doctrine of Interpretation by Major Purposes', 57 (1963) *American Journal of International Law,* pp. 378–383.

Anghie, Antony, 'The Heart of My Home: Colonialism, Environmental Damage and the Nauru Case', 34 (1993) *Harvard International Law Journal,* pp. 445–506.

'Francisco de Vitoria and the Colonial Origins of International Law', 5 (1996) *Social Legal Studies,* pp. 321–336.

'Finding the Peripheries: Sovereignty and Colonialism in Nineteenth Century International Law', 40 (1999) *Harvard International Law Journal,* pp. 1–80.

'Colonialism and the Birth of International Institutions: Sovereignty, Economy and the Mandate System of the League of Nations', 34 (2002) *The New York University Journal of International Law and Politics,* pp. 513–633.

Imperialism, Sovereignty and International Law (Cambridge: Cambridge University Press, 2003).

'TWAIL: Past and Future', 10 (2008) *International Community Law Review,* pp. 479–482.

'Identifying Regions in the History of International Law' in Bardo Fassbender and Anne Peters (eds.), *The Oxford Handbook of the History of International Law* (Oxford: Oxford University Press, 2012), pp. 1058–1081.

Anghie, Antony and B. S. Chimni, 'Third World Approaches to International Law and Individual Responsibility in Internal Conflicts', 2 (2003) *Chinese Journal of International Law,* pp. 77–105.

'Third World Approaches to International Law and Individual Responsibility in Internal Conflict' in Ratner and Slaughter, *Methods of International Law,* pp. 185–211.

Anheier, Helmut K., Marlies Glasius and Mary Kaldor, 'Introducing Global Civil Society', in Helmut K. Anheier, Marlies Glasius and Mary Kaldor (eds.) *Global Civil Society* (Oxford: Oxford University Press, 2001), pp. 3–22.

Aoki, Keith, 'Space Invaders: Critical Geography and the "Third World" in International Law and Critical Race Theory', 45 (2000) *Villanova International Law Review,* pp. 913–958.

Ashcroft, Bill and Pal Ahluwalia, *Edward Said* (London: Routledge, 1999).

Ashcroft, Bill, Gareth Griffiths and Helen Tiffin, *The Post-Colonial Studies Reader* (New York: Routledge, 1995).

Aurobindo, Sri, *The Human Cycle, The Ideal of Human Unity, War and Self-Determination,* 2nd edn (Pondicherry: Sri Aurobindo Ashram, 1970).

Austin, J. L., *Philosophical Papers,* 3rd edn (Oxford: Clarendon Press, 1979).

Badiou, Alain, 'The Communist Idea and the Question of Terror', in Slavoj Zizek (ed.) *The Idea of Communism,* vol. 2 (London: Verso, 2013), pp. 1–13.

Bagchi, A. K., *Perilous Passage: Mankind and the Global Ascendancy of Capital* (New Delhi: Oxford University Press, 2006).

Bagchi, A. K., *Colonialism and Indian Economy* (Oxford: Oxford University Press, 2010).

Baker, G. P. and P. M. S. Hacker, *Language, Sense and Nonsense: A Critical Investigation into Modern Theories of Language* (Oxford: Basil Blackwell, 1984).

  Scepticism, Rules and Language (Oxford: Basil Blackwell, 1984).

Baetens, Freya, 'The Forgotten Peace Conference: The 1915 International Congress for Women', *Max Planck Encyclopedia of Public International Law* (Oxford: Oxford University Press, 2010) available at http://opil.ouplaw.com/home/epil (accessed on 29 June 2015)

Balbus, Isaac D., 'Commodity Form and Legal Form: An Essay on the "Relative Autonomy" of the Law', 11 (1977) *Law & Society Review,* pp. 571–588.

Barnett, Michael and Raymond Duvall, *Power in Global Governance* (Cambridge: Cambridge University Press, 2005).

Barkawi, Tarak, 'Empire and Order in International Relations and Security Studies', in Robert A. Denemark (ed.), *The International Studies Encyclopedia,* Blackwell Publishing, Blackwell reference online; *The International Studies Encyclopedia,* Vol. III (Chichester: Wiley-Blackwell, 2010), pp. 1360–1379 (available online). Available at www.academia.edu/348812/Empire_and_Order_in_International_Relations_and_Security_Studies (accessed 4 June 2015).

Bartholomew, Amy, 'Should a Marxist Believe in Marx on Rights?', (1990) *Socialist Register,* pp. 244–264.

Bartlett, Katherine and Rosanne Kennedy (eds.), *Feminist Legal Theory: Readings in Law and Gender* (Boulder, CO: Westview Press, 1991).

Beck, Ulrich and Johannes Willms, *Conversations with Ulrich Beck* (Cambridge: Polity Press, 2003).

Beckett, Jason A., 'Rebel Without a Cause? Martti Koskenniemi and the Critical Legal Project', 7 (2006) *German Law Journal,* pp. 1045–1088.

'Faith and Resignation: A Journey through International Law', in Matthew Stone, Illan rua Wall and Costas Douzinas (eds.) *New Critical Thinking: Law and the Political* (New York: Routledge, 2012), pp. 145–167.

Bedjaoui, Mohammed, *Towards a new international economic order* (New York: Holmes & Meir Publishers Inc., 1979).

Beitz, Charles R., *Political Theory and International Relations* (Princeton, NJ: Princeton University Press, 1979).

Beneyto, Jose Maria and David Kennedy (eds.), *New Approaches to International Law: The European and the American Experiences* (The Hague: T. M. C. Asser Press, 2013).

Benton, Ted, 'Marxism and Natural Limits: An Ecological Critique and Reconstruction', 178 (1989) *New Left Review*, pp. 51–86.
    'Ecology, Socialism and the Mastery of Nature', 194 (1992) *New Left Review*, pp. 55–72.

Berger, Peter, *The Capitalist Revolution* (New York: Basic Books Publishers, 1991).

Berki, R. N., *On Political Realism* (London: J. M. Dent and Sons, 1981).

Berlin, Isaiah, 'Two Concepts of Liberty', in Michael J. Sandel (ed.) *Liberalism and Its Critics* (Oxford: Oxford University Press, 1984), pp. 15–36.

Berman, Paul Schiff, 'A Pluralist Approach to International Law', 32 (2007) *Yale Journal of International Law*, pp. 301–329.

Bhagwati, Jagdish, *In Defense of Globalization* (Oxford: Oxford University Press, 2004)

Bhargava, Rajeeva, *Individualism in Social Science* (Oxford: Clarendon Press, 1992).
    What is Political Theory and Why Do We Need It? (New Delhi: Oxford University Press 2010), pp. 315–326.

Bhatia, Amar, 'The South of the North: Building on Critical Approaches to International Law with Lessons from the Fourth World', 14 (2012) *Oregon Review of International Law*, pp. 131–176.

Biersteker, Thomas J, Peter J. Spiro, Chandralekha Sriram and Veronica Raffo (eds.), *International Law and International Relations: Bridging theory and practice* (London: Routledge, 2006).

Boldizar, Alexander and Outi Korhonen, 'Ethics, Morals and International Law', 10 (1999) *European Journal of International Law*, pp. 279–311.

Boldrin, Michele and David K. Levine, *Against Intellectual Monopoly* (Cambridge: Cambridge University Press, 2008).

Boltanski, Luc and Eve Chiapello, *The New Spirit of Capitalism* (London: Verso, 2005).

Bottomore, Tom and Goode Patrick (eds.), *Austro-Marxism* (Oxford: Clarendon Press, 1978).

Bourdieu, Pierre, 'The Social Conditions of the International Circulation of Ideas', in Richard Schusterman (ed.) *Bourdieu: A Critical Reader* (Oxford: Blackwell Publishers, 1999), pp. 220–228.

Bourdieu, Pierre, *Masculine Domination* (Cambridge: Polity Press, 2001).

Bourdieu, Pierre and Loïc Wacquant, *An Invitation to Reflexive Sociology* (Cambridge: Polity Press, 1992).

Bourdieu, Pierre, Gisele Sapiro and Brian McHale, 'Fourth Lecture. Universal Corporatism: The Role of Intellectuals in the Modern World', 12 (1991) *Poetics Today*, pp. 655–669.

Bowett, D. W., *The Law of International Institutions*, 3rd edn (London: Stevens and Sons, 1975).

Bowring, Bill, *The Degradation of the International Legal Order?: The Rehabilitation of Law and the Possibility of Politics* (Oxford: Routledge-Cavendish, 2008)

Boyle, Alan and Christine Chinkin, *The Making of International Law* (Oxford: Oxford University Press, 2014).

Boyle, Francis Anthony *World Politics and International Law* (Durham, NC: Duke University Press, 1985).

Brenkert, George G., 'Marx and Human Rights', 24 (1986) *Journal of the History of Philosophy*, pp. 55–77.

Brenner, Johanna, 'Intersections, Locations, and Capitalist Class Relations: Intersectionality from a Marxist Perspective', in Nancy Holmstrom (ed.) *The Socialist Feminist Project: A Contemporary Reader in Theory and Politics* (Delhi: Aakar, 2011), pp. 336–348.

Briggs, Herbert W. *The Law of Nations* (New York: Appleton-Century-Crofts, 1952).

Brilmayer, Lea, 'Realism Revisited: The Moral Priority of Means and Ends in Anarchy', in Ian Shapiro and Lea Brilmayer (eds.) *Global Justice* (New York: New York University Press, 1999), pp. 192–215.

Briskin, Linda, 'Socialist Feminism: From the Standpoint of Practice', 30 (1989) *Studies in Political Economy*, pp. 87–114.

Brooks, Rosa Ehrenreich, 'Feminism and International Law: An Opportunity for Transformation', 14 (2002) *Yale Journal of Law & Feminism*, pp. 345–361.

Brown, Heather, 'Marx on Gender and the Family', (June 2014) *Analytical Monthly Review*, pp. 45–53.

Brownlie, Ian, 'The Expansion of International Society: The Consequences for the Law of Nations', in Hedley Bull and Adam Watson (eds.) *The Expansion of International Society* (Oxford: Clarendon Press, 1984), pp. 357–370.

Principles of Public International Law, 4th edn (Oxford: Clarendon Press, 1990).

Buchanan, Allan E., *Marx and Justice: The Radical Critique of Liberalism* (Totowa, NJ: Rowman and Allenheld, 1982).

Buchanan, Allen E., 'Marx, Morality, and History: An Assessment of Recent Analytical Work on Marx', 98 (1987) *Ethics, pp.* 104–136.

Bull, Hedley, 'The Theory of International Politics 1919–1969', in Brian Potter (ed.) *The Aberystwith Papers: International Politics 1919–1969* (London: Oxford University Press, 1972), pp. 30–55.

'New Directions in the Theory of International Relations', 14 (1975) *International Studies* (New Delhi), pp. 277–286.

The Anarchical Society: A Study of Order in World Politics (New York: Columbia University Press, 1977).

Burawoy, Michael and Erik Olin Wright, 'Sociological Marxism', in Jonathan H. Turner (ed.) *Handbook of Sociological Theory* (New York: Kluwer Academic/ Plenum Publishers, 2002), pp. 459–486.

Burkett, P., 'Some Common Misconceptions About Nature and Marx's Critique of Political Economy', 7 (1996) *Capitalism, Nature, Socialism*, pp. 57–80.

'Nature in Marx Reconsidered', 10 (1997) *Organization and Environment, pp.* 164–83.

Caglar, Gulay, 'Feminist Strategies and Social Learning in International Economic Governance', in Gulay Caglar, Elisabeth Prugl and Sussane Zwingel (eds.) *Feminist Strategies in International Governance* (London: Routledge, 2013), pp. 249–266.

Caglar, Gulay, Elisabeth Prugl and Sussane Zwingel, 'Introducing Feminist Strategies in International Governance', in Gulay Caglar, Elisabeth Prugl and Sussane Zwingel (eds.) *Feminist Strategies in International Governance* (London: Routledge, 2013), pp. 1–18.

Callinicos, Alex, 'Does Capitalism Need the State System?', 20 (2007) *Cambridge Review of International Affairs,* pp. 533–549.

'Imperial Delusions' Issue 142 (30 March 2014) at www.isj.org.uk/index.php4? id=959&issue=142 (accessed on 4 June 2015).

Campbell, A., 'International Law and Primitive Law', 8 (1988) *Oxford Journal of Legal Studies,* pp. 169–196.

Caroll, William K., *The Making of a Transnational Capitalist Class: Corporate Power in the 21st Century* (London: Zed Books, 2010).

Carr, E. H., *Twenty Years Crisis* (London: Macmillan & Co, 1940).

Michael Bakunin (New York: Vintage Books, 1961).

The Twenty Years' Crisis: An Introduction to the Study of International Relations, 2nd edn (New York: Palgrave, 2001).

Carty, Anthony, 'Critical International Law: Recent Trends in the Theory of International Law', 2 (1991) *European Journal of International Law,* pp.1–26.

Cassesse, Antonio, 'Ex iniura ius oritur: Are We Moving Towards International Legitimation of Forcible Countermeasures in the World Community?', 10 (1999) *European Journal of International Law,* pp. 23–30.

Castledine, Jacqueline '"In a Solid Bond of Unity": Anticolonial Feminism in the Cold War Era', 20 (2008) *Journal of Women's History,* pp. 57–81.

Castree, Noel, 'Marxism and the Production of Nature', 72 (2000) *Capital & Class,* pp. 5–36.

Chakrabarty, Dipesh, 'Postcoloniality and the Artifice of History: Who Speaks for "Indian" Pasts?', in Ranajit Guha (ed.) *A Subaltern Studies Reader 1986-1995* (New Delhi: Oxford University Press, 1997), pp. 263–294.

Chakrabarty, Dipesh, Provincializing *Europe,* 2nd edn (Princeton, NJ: Princeton University Press, 2007).

'The Climate of History: Four Theses', 35 (2009) *Critical Inquiry,* pp. 197–222.

Chammalas, Martha, *Introduction to Feminist Legal Theory* (New York: Wolters Kluwer Law & Business, 2013).

Chandhoke, Neera, 'How Global is Global Civil Society?', 11 (2005) *Journal of World-Systems Research,* pp. 355–371.

'"Seeing" the State in India', 40 (2005) *Economic and Political Weekly,* pp. 1033–1039.

Chang, Ha Joon, *Why Developing Countries Need Tariffs* (South Centre, Geneva, 2005) can be accessed at http://allanpatricknet.wdfiles.com/local–files/por-que-nacoes-em-desenvolvimento-devem-adotar-protecoes-lf/WhyDevCountriesNeedTariffsNew.pdf

Charlesworth, Hilary, 'Subversive Trends in the Jurisprudence of International Law', (1992) *ASIL Proceedings,* pp. 125–131.

'Feminist Critiques of International Law and Their Critics', 13 (1995) *Third World Legal Studies-1994, pp.* 1–16.

'Martha Nussbaum's Feminist Internationalism', 111 (2000) *Ethics,* pp. 64–78.

'Author! Author!: A Response to David Kennedy', 15 (2002) *Harvard Human Rights Journal,* pp. 127–131.

'International Law: A Discipline of Crisis', 65 (2002) *The Modern Law Review,* pp. 377–392.

'Feminist Methods in International Law', in Steven R. Ratner and Anne-Marie Slaughter (eds.) *The Methods of International Law* (Washington, DC: The American Society of International Law, 2004).

'Feminist Ambivalence about International Law', 11 (2005) *International Legal Theory,* pp. 1–8.

'Talking to Ourselves: Should International Lawyers Take a Break from Feminism?', in Sari Kouvo and Zoe Pearson (eds.) *Between Resistance and Compliance? Feminist Perspectives on International Law in Era of Anxiety and Terror* (Oxford: Hart, 2011), pp. 17–32.

'Book Review: Catherine A MacKinnon, Are Women Human? And Other International Dialogues', 107 (2013) *American Journal of International Law,* pp. 719–214.

Democracy and International Law (Leiden: Martinus Nijhoff Publishers, 2015).

Charlesworth, Hilary and Christine Chinkin, *The boundaries of international law: a feminist analysis* (Manchester: Manchester University Press, 2000).

'Editorial Comment: Sex, Gender and September 11', 96 (2002) *American Journal of International Law,* pp. 600–605.

'The New United Nations "Gender Architecture": A Room with a View?', in
    A. von Bogdandy, A. Peters and R. Wolfrum (eds.) 17 (2013) *Max Planck
    Yearbook of United Nations Law*, pp. 1–60.

Charlesworth, Hilary, and Emma Larking (eds.), *Human Rights and the Universal
    Periodic Review: Rituals and Ritualism* (Cambridge: Cambridge University
    Press, 2014).

Charlesworth, Hilary, Christine Chinkin and Shelley Wright, "Feminist Approach
    to International Law", 85 (1991) *American Journal of International Law*, pp.
    613–645.

Charnowitz, Steve, 'Nongovernmental Organizations and International Law', 100
    (2006) *American Journal of International Law*, pp. 348–372.

Chatterjee, Partha, 'Introduction: The Wages of Freedom: Fifty Years of Indian
    Nation-State', in Partha Chatterjee (ed.) *Wages of Freedom: Fifty Years
    of Indian Nation-State* (New Delhi: Oxford University Press, 1998),
    pp. 1–20.

The Politics of the Governed: Reflections on Popular Politics in Most of the World
    (Delhi: Permanent Black, 2004).

Chayes, Abram and Antonia Handler Chayes, *The New Sovereignty: Compliance
    with International Regulatory Agreements* (Cambridge: Harvard University
    Press, 1995).

Chibber, Vivek, *Post Colonial Theory and the Specter of Capital* (New Delhi: Navayana
    Publishing Pvt. Ltd, 2013).

'Capitalism, Class and Universalism: Escaping the Cul-de-Sac of Postcolonial
    Theory', (2014) *Socialist Register*, pp. 63–79.

'Confronting Postcolonial Theory-A Response to Critics', 20 (2014) *American
    Sociological Association*, pp. 311–317.

Childs, Peter and R. J. Patrick Williams, 'Introduction: Points of Departure' in Peter
    Childs and R. J. Patrick Williams (eds.) *An Introduction to Post-Colonial
    Theory* (London: Prentice Hall, 1997), pp.1–25.

Chimni, B. S., *International Commodity Agreements: A Legal Study* (London: Croom
    Helm, 1986).

'The Political Economy of the Uruguay Round of Negotiations: A Perspective', 29
    (1992) *International Studies*, pp. 135–158.

'The Geopolitics of Refugee Studies: A View from the South', 11 (1998) *Journal of
    Refugee Studies*, pp. 350–374.

'Globalization, Humanitarianism and the Erosion of Refugee Protection', 13
    (2000) *Journal of Refugee Studies*, pp. 243–264.

'WTO and Environment: The *Shrimp-Turtle* and *EC-Hormone* cases', (13 May
    2000) *Economic and Political Weekly*, pp. 1752–1761.

'Post-conflict Peace-building and the Return of Refugees: Concepts, Practices,
    and Institutions', in Edward Newman and Joanne van Selm (eds.) *Refugees*

and Forced Displacement: International Security, Human Vulnerability, and the State (Tokyo: United Nations University Press, 2002), pp. 195–211.

'Towards a Radical Third World Approach to Contemporary International Law', 5 (2002) *ICCLP Review* (Tokyo University School of Law Publication), pp. 16–30.

'WTO and Environment: The Legitimization of Unilateral Trade Sanctions', (12–18 January 2002) *Economic and Political Weekly*, pp.133–140.

'An Outline of a Marxist Course on Public International Law', 17 (2004) *Leiden Journal of International Law*, pp. 1–30.

'International Institutions Today: An Imperial Global State in the Making', 15 (2004) *European Journal of International Law*, pp. 1–39.

'Cooption and Resistance: Two faces of Global Administrative Law', 37 (2005) *New York University Journal of Law and Politics*, pp. 799–827.

'Developing Countries and the GATT/WTO System: Some Reflections on the Idea of Free Trade and Doha Round Trade Negotiations', in Chantal Thomas and Joel Trachtman (eds.) *Developing Countries in the WTO Legal System* (New York: Oxford University Press, 2009), pp. 21–45.

'The Birth of a "Discipline": From Refugee to Forced Migration Studies', 22 (2009) *Journal of Refugee Studies*, pp. 11–29.

'China, India and the WTO Dispute Settlement System: Towards an Interpretative Strategy', in M. Sornarajah and J. Wang (eds.) *China, India and the International Economic Order* (Cambridge: Cambridge University Press, 2010), pp. 217–250.

'International Law Scholarship in Post Colonial India: Coping With Dualism', 23 (2010) *Leiden Journal of International Law*, pp. 23–51.

'Prolegomena to a Class Approach to International Law', 21 (2010) *European Journal of International Law*, pp. 57–82.

'Sovereignty, Rights and Armed Intervention', in Hilary Charlesworth and Jean-Marc Coicaud (eds.) *Faultlines of International Legitimacy* (Cambridge: Cambridge University Press, 2010), pp. 303–325.

'Capitalism, Imperialism and International Law in the Twenty First Century', 14 (2012) *Oregon Review of International Law*, pp. 17–45.

'For Epistemological and Prudent Internationalism', *Harvard Human Rights Journal*. Available at http://harvardhrj.com/2012/11/for-epistemological-and-prudent-internationalism/

'Legitimating International Rule of Law', in James Crawford and Martti Koskenniemi (eds.) *Cambridge Companion to International Law* (Cambridge: Cambridge University Press, 2012), pp. 290–309.

'The Self, Modern Civilization and International Law: Learning from Mohandas Karmchand Gandhi's *Hind Swaraj*', 23 (2012) *European Journal of International Law*, pp. 1159–1173.

'Peace through Law: Lessons of 1914, 3 (2015) *London Review of International Law*, pp. 245–265.

Chinkin, Christine, 'A Gendered Perspective to the International Use of Force', 11 (1991) *Australian Yearbook of International Law*, pp. 279–293.

'Feminist Interventions into International Law', 19 (1997) *Adelaide Law Review*, pp. 13–24.

'Gender Inequality and International Human Rights Law', in Andrew Hurrell and Ngaire Woods (eds.) *Inequality, Globalization, and World Politics* (Oxford: Oxford University Press, 1999), pp. 95–121.

Chinkin, Christine and Hilary Charlesworth, 'Building Women into Peace: The International Legal Framework', 27 (2006) *Third World Quarterly*, pp. 937–957.

Chinkin, Christine and Mary Kaldor, 'Gender and New Wars', 67 (2013) *Journal of International Affairs*, Fall/Winter pp. 167–187.

Cho, Sumi, Kimberle Williams Crenshaw and Leslie McCall, 'Toward a Field of Intersectionality Studies: Theory, Applications, and Praxis', 38 (2013) *Signs: Journal of Women in Culture and Society*, pp. 785–810.

Chowdhury, Cyra Akila, 'Governance Feminism's Imperial Misadventure: Progress, International Law, and the Security of Afghan Women', FIU Legal Studies Research Paper No.14-04, February 2014 at http://ssrn.com/abstract=2320004

Churchich, Nicholas, *Marxism and Morality: A Critical Examination of Marxist Ethics* (Cambridge: James Clarke & Co, 1994).

Clark, Brett and John Bellamy Foster, 'Marx's Ecology in the 21st Century', 1 (2010) *World Review of Political Economy*, pp. 142–156.

Clark, Grenville and Louis B. Sohn, *World Peace through World Law*, 3rd edn (Cambridge, MA: Harvard University Press, 1966).

Claude Jr, Inis L., *Power and International Relations* (New York: Random House, 1962).

Cohen, G. A., *Karl Marx's Theory of History: A Defence* (Oxford: Oxford University Press, 1978).

Cohen, Marshall, 'Moral Skepticism and International Relations', 13 (1984) *Philosophy and Public Affairs*, pp. 299–346.

Collins, Hugh, *Marxism and Law* (Oxford: Clarendon Press, 1982).

Commission on Global Governance, *Our Global Neighborhood* (Oxford: Oxford University Press, 1995).

Commoner, Barry, *The Closing Circle: Nature, Man, Technology* (New York: Alfred A. Knopf Inc., 1971).

Conaghan, Joanne (ed.), *Feminist Legal Studies: Critical Concepts in Law*, vols. I-IV (London: Routledge, 2009).

Conaghan, Joanne, 'Reassessing the Feminist Theoretical Project in Law', in Costas Douzinas and Colin Perrin (eds.) *Critical Legal Theory: Critical Concepts in Law*, vol. III (London: Routledge, 2012), pp.108–142.

Connolly, William E., *The Fragility of Things: Self-organizing Processes, Neo-liberal Fantasies, and Democratic Activism* (Durham, NC: Duke University Press, 2013).

Conway, Janet, 'Analysing Hegemonic Masculinities in the Anti- Globalization Movement(s)', 13 (2011) *International Feminist Journal of Politics*, pp. 225–230.

Coogan-Gehr, Kelly, *The Geopolitics of the Cold War and Narratives of Inclusion: Excavating a Feminist Archive* (New York: Palgrave Macmillan, 2011).

Correa, Carlos M., *Intellectual Property Rights, the WTO and Developing Countries: The TRIPS Agreement and Policy Options* (London: Zed Books, 2000).

Cox, Robert, 'The "British School" in the Global Context', 14 (2009) *New Political Economy*, pp. 315–328.

Cozette, Muriel, 'Reclaiming the Critical Dimension of Realism: Hans J. Morgenthau on the Ethics of Scholarship', 34 (2008) *Review of International Studies*, pp. 5–27.

Craig, Campbell, *Glimmer of a New Leviathan: Total War in the Realism of Niebuhr, Morgenthau and Waltz* (New York: Columbia University Press, 2003).

Crawford, James, *Chance, Order, Change: The Course of International Law. General Course on Public International Law* (Brill, 2014).

Crenshaw, Kimberle, 'Demarginalizing the Intersection of Race and Sex: A Black Feminist Critique of Antidiscrimination Doctrine, Feminist Theory and Antiracist Politics', (1989) *University of Chicago Legal Forum*, pp. 139–167.

Dakolias, Maria, 'Legal and Judicial Development: The Role of Civil Society in the Reform Process', 24 (2000) *Fordham International Law Journal*, pp. S-26–S55.

Dallmayr, Fred, ' "Self and Other": Gadamer and the Hermeneutics of Difference', 5 (1993) *Yale Journal of Law and the Humanities*, pp. 507–529.

D'Amato, Anthony 'Book Review: Rebecca J. Cook ed., Human Rights of Women: National and International Perspectives', 89 (1995) *American Journal of International Law*, pp.840–844.

'Old Approaches to International Law', 36 (1995) *Harvard International Law Journal*, pp. 509–512.

Darian-Smith, Eve, 'Postcolonial Theories of Law', in Reza Banakar and Max Travers (eds.) *An Introduction to Law and Social Theory*, 2nd edn (Oxford: Hart, 2013), pp. 247–264.

Das, Samir Kumar, 'Introduction: Surveying the Literature on State in Post-Independence India', in, Samir Kumar Das (ed.) *Political Science: The Indian State*, vol. 1 (New Delhi: Oxford University Press, 2013), pp. 1–53.

D'aspremont, Jean, 'Wording in International Law', 25 (2012) *Leiden Journal of International Law*, pp. 575–602.

Davenport, Andrew, 'Marxism in IR: Condemned to a Realist Fate', 19 (2011) *European Journal of International Relations*, pp. 27–48.

Davison, Andrew, Himadeep Muppidi, Freya Irani and Dror Ladin, 'Europe and Its Boundaries: Toward a Global Hermeneutic Political Theory', in Andrew Davison and Himadeep Muppidi (eds.) *Europe and Its Boundaries: Words and Worlds, Within and Beyond* (Lanham, MD: Lexington Books, 2009), pp. 83–111.

de la Rasilla del Moral, Ignacio, 'Martti Koskenniemi and the Spirit of the Beehive in International Law', 10 (2010) *Global Jurist*, pp. 1–53.

Deutsch, Karl and Stanley Hoffman (eds.), *The Relevance of International Law* (New York: Anchor Books, 1971), pp. 34–66.

Dickinson, Laura A., 'Toward a "New" New Haven School of International Law', 32 (2007) *The Yale Journal of International Law*, pp. 547–552.

Dinstein, Yoram, 'International Law as a Primitive Legal System', 19 (1986–87) *New York Journal of International Law and Politics*, pp. 1–32.

Dirlik, Arif, 'The Postcolonial Aura: Third World Criticism in the Age of Global Capitalism', 20 (1994) *Critical Inquiry*, pp. 328–356.

    'Thinking Modernity Historically: Is "Alternative Modernity" the Answer?', 1 (2013) *Asian Review of World Histories*, pp. 5–34.

Dobb, Maurice, *Studies in the Development of Capitalism* (London: Routledge and Kegan Paul, Ltd., 1947).

Donert, Celia, 'Women's Rights in Cold War Europe: Disentangling Feminist Histories', 8 (2013) *Past and Present*, pp. 178–202.

Donnelly, Jack, *Realism and International Relations* (Cambridge: Cambridge University Press, 2000).

Donovan, Josephine, *Feminist Theory: The Intellectual Traditions*, 4th edn, Revised and Expanded (New York: Continuum, 2012).

Drago Luis, M., and H. Edward Nettles, 'The Drago Doctrine in International Law and Politics', 8 (1928) *The Hispanic American Historical Review*, pp. 201–233.

Drahos, Peter, and John Braithwate, *Information Feudalism* (London: Earthscan, 2002).

Duncan, Graeme, *Marx and Mill: Two Views of Social Conflict and Social Harmony* (Cambridge: Cambridge University Press, 1973).

Dunn, Frederick Sherwood, *The Protection of Nationals: A Study in the Application of International Law* (Baltimore, MD: Johns Hopkins Press, 1932).

Dunoff, Jeffrey L., "Engaging the Writings of Martti Koskenniemi: Introduction to the Symposium', 27 (2013) *Temple International & Comparative Law Journal* pp.207–214.

    'From Interdisciplinarity to Counterdisciplinarity: Is There Madness in Martti's Method?', 27 (2013) *Temple International & Comparative Law Quarterly*, pp. 309–338.

Dupuy, Pierre-Marie, 'Some Reflections on Contemporary International Law and the Appeal to Universal Values: A Response to Martti Koskenniemi', 16 (2005) *European Journal of International Law*, pp. 131–137.

Duvall, Raymond and Latha Varadarajan, 'Travelling in Paradox: Edward Said and Critical International Relations', 36 (2007) *Millennium: Journal of International Studies,* pp. 83–99.

Dworkin, Ronald, *Law's Empire* (London: Fontana Press, 1986).

Eagleton, Terry, 'Introduction Part 1', in Terry Eagleton and Drew Milne (eds.) *Marxist Literary Theory: A Reader* (Oxford: Blackwell Publishing, 1996), pp. 1–15.

Eckstein, George, 'Hans Morgenthau: A Personal Memoir', 48 (1981) *Social Research,* pp. 641–652.

Ehrenreich, Barbara, 'What is Socialist Feminism?', (2005) *Monthly Review.* Available at http://monthlyreview.org/2005/07/01/what-is-socialist-feminism (accessed on 21 July 2013). (Originally published in WIN Magazine on 3 June 1976.)

Elliot, Anthony, *Concepts of the Self* (Cambridge: Polity, 2001).

Elster, Jon, 'Marxism, Functionalism and Game Theory: The Case for Methodological Individualism', 11 (1982) *Theory and Society,* pp. 453–482.

Making Sense of Marx (Cambridge: Cambridge University Press, 1985).

Engels, Frederick, *Dialectics of Nature* (Moscow: Progress Publishers, 1954).

The Condition of the Working Class in England (Moscow: Progress Publishers, 1977).

Engle, Karen, 'International Human Rights and Feminisms: When Discourses Keep Meeting', in Doris Buss and Ambreena Manji (eds.) *International Law: Modern Feminist Approaches* (Oxford: Hart Publishing, 2005) pp. 47–66.

'Liberal Internationalism, Feminism, and the Suppression of Critique: Contemporary Approaches to Global Order in the United States', 46 (2005) *Harvard International Law Journal,* pp. 427–439.

Erh-Soon Tay, Alice, 'Marxism, Socialism and Human Rights', in Eugene Kamenka and Alice Erh-Soon Tay (eds.) *Human Rights* (London: Edward Arnold, 1978), pp. 104–113.

Erskine, Toni (ed.), *Can Institutions Have Responsibilities? Collective Moral Agency and International Relations* (Basingstoke: Palgrave Macmillan, 2003).

Eskridge, William N., 'Gadamer/Statutory Interpretation', 90 (1990) *Columbia Law Review,* pp. 609–681.

Falk, Richard, 'International Legal Order: Alwyn V. Freeman vs. Myres S.McDougal', 59 (1965) *American Journal of International Law,* pp. 66–71.

'Shimoda Case: A Legal Appraisal for the Atomic Attacks on Hiroshima and Nagasaki', 59 (1965) *American Journal of International Law,* pp.759–793.

'International Law and the United States Role in the Vietnam War', 75 (1966) *Yale Law Journal,* pp. 1122–1160.

'New Approaches to the Study of International Law', 61 (1967) *The American Journal of International Law,* pp. 477–495.

Legal Order in a Violent World (Princeton, NJ: Princeton University Press, 1968), pp. 60–89.

(ed.), *The Vietnam War and International Law* (Princeton, NJ: Princeton University Press, 1968, 1969, 1972 and 1976).

The Status of Law in International Society (Princeton, NJ: Princeton University Press, 1970).

'What We Should Learn from Vietnam', 1 (1970–71) *Foreign Policy,* pp. 98–144.

This Endangered Planet: Prospects and Proposals for Human Survival (New York: Random House, 1971).

Falk, Richard A., 'Comment I', in John Norton Moore (ed.), *Law and Civil War in the Modern World* (Baltimore, MD: The Johns Hopkins University Press, 1974), pp. 543–545.

Falk, Richard, 'A New Paradigm for International Legal Studies: Prospects and Proposals', 84 (1974–75) *Yale Law Journal,* pp. 969–1021.

A Study of Future Worlds (New Delhi: Orient Longman, 1975).

'The Shaping of World Order Studies: A Response', 42 (1980) *The Review of Politics,* pp. 18–30.

Human Rights and State Sovereignty (New York: Holmes and Meier Publishers, Inc., 1981).

The End of World Order: Essays on Normative International Relations (New York: Holmes and Meier, 1983).

The Promise of World Order: Essays in Normative International Relations (Sussex: Wheatsheaf Books, 1987).

'The World Court's Achievement',) 81 (1987) *American Journal of International Law,* pp.106–112.

'Reflections on Democracy and the Gulf War', 16 (1991) *Alternatives,* pp. 263–274.

'UN being made a tool of US Foreign Policy', *The Guardian Weekly,* 27 January 1991.

Explorations at the Edge of Time: The Prospects for World Order (Philadelphia, PA: Temple University Press, 1992).

'Casting the Spell: The New Haven School of International Law', 104 (1995) *Yale Law Journal,* pp. 1991–2008.

On Humane Governance: Toward a New Global Politics (Philadelphia: Pennsylvania University Press, 1995).

'Nuclear Weapons, International Law and the World Court: A Historic Encounter', 91 (1997) *The American Journal of International Law,* pp. 64–75.

'The Nuclear Weapons Advisory Opinion and the New Jurisprudence of Global Civil Society', 7 (1997) *Transnational Law & Contemporary Problems,* pp. 333–352.

Law in an Emerging Global Village: A Post-Westphalian Perspective (Ardsley, NY: Transnational, 1998).

The Writings of Richard Falk: Towards Humane Global Governance (Delhi: Orient BlackSwan, 2012).

Humanitarian Interventions and Legitimacy Wars: Seeking Peace and Justice in the 21st Century (London: Routledge, 2014).

Palestine: The Legitimacy of Hope (Charlottesville, VA: Just World Books, 2014).

(Re)Imagining Humane Global Governance (Abingdon, Oxon: Routledge, 2014).

'Towards a Legal Regime for Nuclear Weapons', in Richard Falk, Friedrich Kratochwil and Saul H. Mendlovitz (eds.), *International Law: A Contemporary Perspective* (Boulder, CO: Westview, 1985), pp. 453–473.

Falk, Richard, and David Krieger, *The Path to Zero: Dialogues on Nuclear Dangers* (Boulder, CO: Paradigm Publishers, 2012).

Falk, Richard, and Andrew Strauss, *A Global Parliament: Essays and Articles* (Berlin: Committee for a Democratic U.N., 2011).

Falk, Richard, Lee Meyrowitz and Jack Sanderson, 'Nuclear Weapons and International Law', 20 (1980) *Indian Journal of International Law*, pp. 541–595.

Falk, Richard, Friedrich Kratochwil, and Saul H. Mendlovitz, *International Law: A Contemporary Perspective* (Boulder, CO: Westview, 1985).

Falk, Richard A., 'International Law and the United States Role in Vietnam War', 75 (1966) *Yale Law Journal*, pp. 1122–1160.

'The New States and International Legal Order', II (1966) *Recueil Des Cours* (Leyden: A. W. Sijthoff, 1968), pp. 1–102.

'International Law and the United States Role in the Vietnam War: A Reply to Professor Moore', 76 (1967) *Yale Law Journal*, pp. 1095–1158.

'New Approaches to the Study of International Law', 21 (1967) *American Journal of International Law*, pp. 477–495.

'A New Paradigm for International Legal Studies: Prospects and Proposals', 84 (1975) *The Yale Law Journal*, pp. 969–1021.

'The Role of the International Court of Justice', 37 (1984) *Journal of International Affairs*, pp.253–268.

'The ICJ Ruling on Israel's Security Wall', 99 (2005) *The American Journal of International Law*, pp. 42–52.

Falk, Richard A. and Burns H. Weston, 'The Relevance of International Law to Palestinian Rights in the West Bank and Gaza: In Legal Defense of the Intifida', 32 (1991) *Harvard International Law Journal*, pp. 129–157.

Falk, Richard A., Samuel S. Kim and Saul H. Mendlovitz (eds.), *Towards a Just World Order* (Boulder, CO: Westview Press, 1982).

Falk, Richard A., Rosalyn C. Higgins, W. Michael Reisman and Burns H. Weston, 'Myres Smith McDougal (1906–1998)', 92 (1998) *American Journal of International Law*, pp. 729–733.

Farrelly, Colin, "Patriarchy and Historical Materialism", 26 (1) (2011) *Hypatia*, pp. 1–21.

Fassbender, Bardo and Anne Peters (eds.), *The Oxford Handbook of the History of International Law* (Oxford: Oxford University Press, 2012), pp. 862–890.

Fellmeth, Aaron Xavier, 'Feminism and International Law: Theory, Methodology, and Substantive Reform', 22 (2000) *Human Rights Quarterly*, pp. 658–733.

Fine, Bob, *Democracy and the Rule of Law: Liberal Ideals and Marxist Critiques* (London: Pluto Press, 1984).

Fine, Robert, *Democracy and the Rule of Law: Marx's Critique of the Legal Form* (Caldwell, NJ: Blackburn Press, 2002).

Firth, Raymond, *Human Types: An Introduction to Social Anthropology*, revised edn (New York: Mentor, 1958).

Fitzmaurice, Sir Gerald, 'Vae Victis or, Woe to the Negotiators! Your Treaty or our "Interpretation" of it?', 65 (1971) *American Journal of International Law*, pp. 358–373.

Foster, John Bellamy, *Marx's Ecology: Materialism and Nature* (New York: Monthly Review Press, 2000).

'Marx's Ecology in Historical Perspective', 96 (2002) *International Socialism*. Available at www.marxists.org/history/etol/newspape/isj2/2002/isj2-096/foster.htm (accessed on 17 September 2015).

'Ecology and the Transition from Capitalism to Socialism', 60 (2008) *Monthly Review*. Available at http://monthlyreview.org/2008/11/01/ecology-and-the-transition-from-capitalism-to-socialism/ (accessed on 17 September 2015).

'The Epochal Crisis', 65 (2013) *Monthly Review*, pp. 1–12.

Foster, John Bellamy, and Brett Clark, 'Ecological Imperialism: The Curse of Capitalism', (2004) *Socialist Register*, pp. 186–201.

Foster, John Bellamy, Brett Clark and Richard York, *The Ecological Rift: Capitalism's War on Earth* (New York: Monthly Review Press, 2010).

Franck, Thomas M., 'Who Killed Article 2(4)?', 64 (1970) *American Journal of International Law*, pp. 809–837.

Fairness in International Law and Institutions (Oxford: Clarendon Press, 1995).

'Break It, Don't Fake It', (July/August 1999) *Foreign Affairs*, pp. 116–118.

Frank, Jerome, 'A Conflict with Oblivion: Some Observations on the Founders of Legal Pragmatism', (1954) Faculty Scholarship Series. Paper 4092. Accessed at http://digitalcommons.law.yale.edu/cgi/viewcontent.cgi?article=5109&context=fss_papers

Franks, Mary Anne, 'Book Review', 30 (2007) *Harvard Journal of Law & Gender*, pp. 257–267.

Fraser, Arvonne S., 'Becoming Human: The Origins and Development of Women's Human Rights', 21 (1999) *Human Rights Quarterly*, pp. 853–906.

Fraser, Nancy, 'Feminism, Capitalism and the Cunning of History', 56 (2009) *New Left Review*, pp. 97–117.

Freeman, Alwyn, 'Professor McDougal's Law and Minimum World Public Order', 58 (1964) *American Journal of International Law*, pp. 711–716.

Freeman, M., C. Chinkin and B. Rudolf (eds.), *The UN Convention on the Elimination of All Forms of Discrimination against Women: A Commentary* (Oxford: Oxford University Press, 2012).

Frei, Christopher, *Hans J. Morgenthau: An Intellectual Biography* (Baton Rouge: Louisiana State University Press, 2001).

Fricker, Miranda, and Jennifer Hornsby (eds.), *The Cambridge Companion to Feminism in Philosophy* (Cambridge: Cambridge University Press, 2000).

Friedman, Milton, *Capitalism and Freedom* (Chicago, IL: University of Chicago Press, 1962).

Friedmann, Wolfgang, 'Book Review', 64 (1944) *Columbia Law Review*, pp. 606–615.

Gable, Peter, 'Roll Over Beethoven', 36 (1984) *Stanford Law Review*, pp. 1–55.

Gadamer, Hans–Georg, *Truth and Method*, 2nd revised edn (London: Continuum, 2005) First South Asian Edition.

Gallagher, Kevin P., Stephany Griffith-Jones and Jose Antonio Ocampo, 'Historic Moment for the IMF', *Financial Times*, 29 May 2012.

Galtung, Johann, *The True Worlds: A Transnational Perspective* (New York: Free Press, 1980).

Gammeltoft-Hansen, Thomas and James Hathaway, '*Non-Refoulement* in a World of Cooperative Deterrence', 53 (2015) *Columbia Journal of Transnational Law*, pp. 235–284.

Gandhi, Leela, *Postcolonial Theory: A Critical Introduction* (St. Leonards: Allen and Unwin, 1998).

Gathii, James Thuo, 'Neoliberalism, Colonialism and International Governance: Decentering the International Law of Governmental Legitimacy', 98 (2000) *Michigan Law Review*, pp. 1996–2055.

'Construing Intellectual Property Rights and Competition Policy Consistently with Facilitating Access to Affordable Aids Drugs to Low-End Income Consumers', 53 (2001) *Florida Law Review*, pp. 728–788 at p. 727.

'The Legal Status of the Doha Declaration on TRIPS and Public Health Under the Vienna Convention on the Law of Treaties', 15 (2002) *Harvard Journal of Law and Technology* , pp. 291–317.

'How Necessity May Preclude State Responsibility for Compulsory Licensing Under the TRIPS Agreement', 31 (2006) *North Carolina Journal of International Law and Regulation*, pp. 943–970.

'Imperialism, Colonialism, and International Law', 54 (2007) *Buffalo Law Review*, pp. 1013–1066.

'War's Legacy in International Investment Law', 11 (2009) *International Community Law Review*, pp. 353–386.

War, Commerce, and International Law (New York: Oxford University Press, 2010).

Geras, Norman, *Marx and Human Nature: Refutation of a Legend* (London: Verso, 1983).

Gilman, Nils, 'The Cold War as Intellectual Force Field', (First View Article) (2015) *Modern Intellectual History*, pp. 1–17.

Gimenez, Martha E., 'Capitalism and Oppression of Women: Marx Revisited', 69 (2005) *Science & Society*, pp. 11–32.

Glasius, Marlies, *The International Criminal Court: A Global Civil Society Achievement* (London: Routledge, 2005).

  'Does the Involvement of Global Civil Society Make International Decision-Making More Democratic? The Case of the International Criminal Court'. Available at www.orfaleacenter.ucsb.edu/sites/secure.lsit.ucsb.edu .gisp.d7_orfalea-2/files/sitefiles/publications/Glasius_OBii.pdf (accessed on 17 September 2015).

Glennon, M. J., 'The New Interventionism', (May/June 1999) *Foreign Affairs*, pp. 2–7.

Gong, Gerrit W., *The Standard of 'Civilisation' in International Society* (Oxford: Oxford University Press, 1984).

Goodrich, Peter, *Reading the Law: A Critical Introduction to Legal Method and Techniques* (Oxford: Basil Blackwell, 1986).

Gottlieb, Giddon, 'The Conceptual World of the Yale School of International Law', 21 (1968–69) *World Politics*, pp. 108–132.

Gould, Stephen Jay, *The Mismeasure of Man* (Middlesex: Penguin, 1981).

Gouldner, Alvin W., *The Coming Crisis of Western Sociology* (London: Heinemann, 1971).

Gramsci, Antonio, *Selections from the Prison Notebooks* (London: Lawrence and Wishart, 1978).

Gray, Mark M., Miki Caul Kittlison and Wayne Sandholtz, 'Women and Globalization: A Study of 180 Countries, 1975–2000', 60 (2006) International *Organization*, pp. 293–333.

Grewe, Wilhelm, *The Epochs of International Law*, translated and revised by Michael Byers (Berlin: De Gruyter, 2001).

Gross, Leo, 'Treaty Interpretation: The Proper Role of an International Tribunal', (1969) *Proceedings of the American Society of International Law*, pp. 108–122.

  'Hans Kelsen', 67 (1973) *The American Journal of International Law*, pp. 491–501.

  'Problems of International Adjudication and Compliance with International Law: Some Simple Solutions', in Leo Gross, *Essays on International Law and Organization*, vol. 1 (New York: Transnational Publishers, 1984), pp. 399–410.

  'Review of Reviving the World Court', 82 (1988) *American Journal of International Law*, pp. 166–175.

Grundmann, Reiner, 'The Ecological Challenge to Marxism', 187 (1991) *New Left Preview*, pp. 103–121;

  Marxism and Ecology (Oxford: Oxford University Press, 1991).

Guha, Ranajit, 'Introduction' in Ranajit Guha (ed.) *A Subaltern Studies Reader 1986-1995* (New Delhi: Oxford University Press, 1997), pp. ix-xxii.

Guilhot, Nicolas (ed.), *The Invention of International Relations Theory: Realism, The Rockefeller Foundation and the 1954 Conference on Theory* (New York: University of Columbia Press, 2011).

Guzman, Andrew T., 'A Compliance-Based Theory of International Law', 90 (2002) *California Law Review*, pp. 1826–1887.

Habermas, Jürgen, 'A Review of Gadamer's Truth and Method', in B. R. Wachterhauser (ed.), *Hermeneutics and Modern Philosophy* (Albany, NY: The SUNY Press, 1986), pp. 243–276. Translated by Fred Dallmayr and Thomas McCarthy.

Hafner-Burton, Emile M., David G. Victor and Yonatan Lupu, 'Political Science Research on International Law: The State of the Field', 106 (2012) *The American Journal of International Law*, pp. 47–97.

Halley, Janet, *Split Decisions: How and Why to Take a Break from Feminism* (Princeton, NJ: Princeton University Press, 2006).

Governance Feminism: An Introduction (October 2014). On file with author.

Halley, Janet, Prabha Kotiswaran and Hila Shamir, 'From the International to the Local in Feminist Legal Responses to Rape, Prostitution/Sex Work, and Sex Trafficking: Four Studies in Contemporary Governance Feminism', 29 (2006) *Harvard Journal of Law & Gender*, pp. 335–423.

Harcourt, Wendy, 'Review Essay: "Beyond Smart Economics": The World Bank 2012 Report on Gender and Equality', 14 (2012) *International Feminist Journal of Politics*, pp. 307–312.

Hardt, Michael, and Antonio Negri, *Empire* (Cambridge, MA: Harvard University Press, 2000).

Hardt, Michael, and Antonio Negri, *Commonwealth* (Cambridge, MA: The Belknap Press of Harvard University Press, 2009).

Hardt, Michael, and Kethi Weeks (eds.), *The Jameson Reader* (Oxford: Blackwell, 2000).

Harrington, Carol, 'Resolution 1325 and Post-Cold War Feminist Politics', 13 (2011) *International Feminist Journal of Politics*, pp. 557–575.

Harris, Jerry, 'Statist Globalization in China, Russia and the Gulf States', 73 (2009) *Science and Society*, pp. 6–33.

Harris, Roy, *The Language-Maker* (London: Duckworth, 1980).

Hart, H. L. A., *Essays in Jurisprudence and Philosophy* (Oxford: Clarendon Press, 1983).

Hartmann, Eva, 'The Difficult Relation between International Law and Politics: The Legal Turn from a Critical IPE Perspective', 16 (2011) *New Political Economy*, pp. 561–584.

Hartmann, Heidi L, 'The Unhappy Marriage of Marxism and Feminism: Towards A More Progressive Union, 3 (1979) *Capital and Class*, pp. 1–33.

Harstock, Nancy C. M., 'The Feminist Standpoint: Developing the Ground for a Specifically Feminist Historical Materialism', in Sandra Harding and Merrill

B. Hintikka (eds.) *Discovering Reality: Feminist Perspectives on Epistemology, Metaphysics, Methodology, and Philosophy of Science* (Dordrecht: Kluwer Academic Publishers, 1983), pp. 283–310.

Harvey, David, 'The Geography of Capitalist Accumulation: A Reconstruction of Marxist Theory', in Richard Peet (ed.) *Radical Geography: Alternative Viewpoints on Contemporary Social Issues* (London: Methuen & Co Ltd., 1977), pp. 283–284.

Harvey, David, *The New Imperialism* (New York: Oxford University Press, 2003).

Hathaway, Oona, 'Between Power and Principle: An Integrated Theory of International Law', 72 (2005) *The University of Chicago Law Review*, pp. 469–536.

Head, M., *Evgeny Pashukanis: A Critical Appraisal* (Oxford: Routledge-Cavendish, 2008).

Hennessy, Rosemary and Chrys Ingraham, 'Introduction: Reclaiming Anticapitalist Feminism', in Rosemary Hennessy and Chrysn Ingraham (eds.) *Materialist Feminism: A Reader in Class, Difference, and Women's Lives* (Routledge: London, 1997), pp. 1–14.

Hernandez, Gleider I., 'A Reluctant Guardian: the International Court of Justice and the Concept of "International Community"', 83 (2013) *British Yearbook of International Law*, pp. 13–60.

Heyes, Cressida J. (ed.), *Philosophy and Gender: Critical Concepts in Philosophy*, vol. 1 (London: Routledge, 2012).

Higgins, Rosalyn, 'Policy and Impartiality: The Uneasy Relationship in International Law: Legal Order in a Violent World by Richard A. Falk', 23 (1969) *International Organization*, pp. 914–931.

'Integrations of Authority and Control: Trends in the Literature of International Law and International Relations', in Michael W. Reisman and Burns H. Weston (eds.), *Towards World Order and Human Dignity: Essays in Honour of Myres S. McDougal* (New York: The Free Press, 1976), pp. 79–94.

Problems and Process: International Law and How We Use It (Oxford: Clarendon Press, 1994).

'Closing Remarks at the Conference to Honor the Work of Professor Michael Reisman', 34 (2009) *Yale Journal of International Law*, pp. 605–613.

'Ethics and International Law', 23 (2010) *Leiden Journal of International Law*, pp. 277–289.

Hill, Christopher, *Reformation to Industrial Revolution, 1530–1780* (Hammondsworth: Penguin, 1969).

Hinsley, F. H., *Sovereignty*, 2nd edn (Cambridge: Cambridge University Press, 1986).

Hirst, Paul, *On Law and Ideology* (London: The Macmillan Press Ltd, 1979).

Hobsbawm, E. J., 'The General Crisis of the European Economy in the 17th Century – I', 5 (1954) *Past and Present*, pp. 33–53.

Hobsbawm, E. J., 'The General Crisis of the European Economy in the 17th Century – II', 6 (1954) *Past and Present*, pp. 44–65.

Industry and Empire: From 1750 to the Present Day (London: Penguin, 1968).

Hodgson, Geoffrey M., 'The Enforcement of Contracts and Property Rights: Constitutive versus Epiphenomenal Conceptions of Law', 13 (2003) *International Review of Sociology*, pp. 373–389.

Hoffman, Florian, 'An Epilogue on an Epilogue', 7 (2006) *German Law Journal*, pp. 1095–1102.

Hoffman, Stanley, *Contemporary Theories of International Relations* (Englewood Cliffs, NJ: Prentice Hall, 1960).

'Report of the Conference on Conditions of World Order-June 12–19, 1965, Villa Serbelloni, Bellagio, Italy', 95 (Spring 1966) *Daedalus*, pp. 455–478.

Janus and Minerva: Essays in the Theory and Practice of International Politics (Boulder, CO: Westview, 1987).

Holmstrom, Nancy (ed.), *The Socialist Feminist Project: A Contemporary Reader in Theory and Politics* (New Delhi: Aakar Books, 2011).

Howard, Michael, 'The Military Factor in European Expansion', in Hedley Bull and Adam Watson (eds.) *The Expansion of International Society* (Oxford: Clarendon Press, 1984), pp. 32–42.

Howe, Stephen, 'Edward Said: Anxieties of Influence', 67 (2007) *Cultural Critique*, pp. 50–87.

Howse, Robert, and Ruti Teitl, 'Beyond Compliance: Rethinking Why International Law Really Matters', 1 (2010) *Global Policy*, pp. 127–136.

'Does Humanity Law Require (or Imply) a Progressive Theory of History? (And Other Questions for Martti Koskenniemi)', 27 (2013) *Temple International & Comparative Law Journal*, pp. 377–398.

Hunt, Alan, 'The Theory of Critical Legal Studies', 6 (1986) *Oxford Journal of Legal Studies*, pp. 1–45 reproduced in Costas Douzinas and Colin Perrin (eds.) *Critical Legal Theory*, vol. I (London: Routledge, 2012), pp. 243–286.

Hunter, J. F. M. ' "Forms of Life" in Wittgenstein's "Philosophical Investigations" ', 5 (1968) *American Philosophical Quarterly*, pp. 233–243.

Husami, Ziyad, 'Marx on Distributive Justice', 8 (1978) *Philosophy & Public Affairs*, pp. 27–64.

Jacquette, Jane S., 'Feminism and the Challenges of the "Post-Cold War" World', 5 (2003) *International Feminist Journal of Politics*, pp. 331–354.

Jalli, Indira, 'Dalit Feminism and Indian Academics', (2003) *Indian Association for Women Studies Newsletter*.

Jameson, Fredric, *A Singular Modernity: Essay on the Ontology of the Present* (London: Verso, 2002).

Valences of the Dialectic (London: Verso, 2009).

Jayawardena, Kumari, *Feminism and Nationalism in the Third World* (London: Zed, 1986).

Jessop, Bob, 'Recent Theories of the Capitalist State', 1 (1977) *Cambridge Journal of Economics*, pp. 353–373.

State Theory: Putting the Capitalist State in Its Place (Cambridge: Polity, 1990).

'From Micro-powers to Governmentality: Foucault's Work on Statehood, State Formation, Statecraft and State Power', 26 (2007) *Political Geography*, pp. 34–40

Johnson-Odim, Cheryl, '"For their freedoms": The Anti-imperialist and International Feminist Activity of Funmilayo Ransome-Kuti of Nigeria', 32 (2009) *Women's Studies International Forum*, pp. 51–59.

Johnston, Adrian and Catherine Malabou, *Self and Emotional Life: Philosophy, Psychoanalysis, and Neuroscience* (New York: Columbia University Press, 2013).

Jouannet, Emmanuelle, 'Koskenniemi: A Critical Introduction', in Martti Koskenniemi, *The Politics of International Law* (Oxford: Hart Publishing, 2011), pp. 1–32.

The Liberal-Welfarist Law of Nations (Cambridge: Cambridge University Press, 2012).

Jütersonke, Oliver, 'The Image of Law in *Politics among Nations*', in Michael C. Williams (ed.) *Realism Reconsidered: The Legacy of Hans J. Morgenthau in International Relations* (Oxford: Oxford University Press, 2007), pp. 93–117.

Jütersonke, Oliver, *Morgenthau, Law and Realism* (Cambridge: Cambridge University Press, 2010).

Kagarlitsky, Boris, *The Twilight of Globalization: Property, State and Capitalism* (London: Pluto Press, 2000).

Kain, Phillip J., *Marx and Ethics* (Oxford: Oxford University Press, 1988).

Kamenka, Eugene, *Marxism and Ethics* (New York: St. Martin's Press, 1969).

'Marxism, Economics and Law' (accessed on 7 May 2014) http://biblio.juridicas .unam.mx/libros/3/1014/7.pdf, pp.49–72

Kaplan, Morton A. and Nicholas deB Katzenbach, *The Political Foundations of International Law* (New York: Wiley, 1961).

Kapur, Ratna, 'Human Rights in the 21st Century: Take a Walk on the Dark Side', 28 (2006) *Sydney Law Review*, pp. 665–687.

Kautsky, Karl, 'On Political Reform and Socialism (The Dictatorship of the Proletariat)', in Micheline R. Ishay (ed.) *The Human Rights Reader*, 2nd edn (London: Routledge, 2007), pp.239–246.

Kaviraj, Sudipta, 'An Outline of a Revisionist Theory of Modernity', 46 (2005) *European Journal of Sociology*, pp. 497–526.

'Marxism in Translation: Critical Reflections on Radical Indian Thought', in Richard Rourke and Raymond Geuss (eds.) *Political Judgment: Essays for John Dunn* (Cambridge: Cambridge University Press, 2009), pp. 172–201.

Kelman, Mark, *A Guide to Critical Legal Studies* (Cambridge, MA: Harvard University Press, 1977).

Kelsen, Hans, *The Communist Theory of Law* (New York: Frederick A. Praeger, Inc., 1955).

Principles of International Law, 2nd revised edn (New York: Holt, Rinehart and Wilson, 1967).

Kennedy, David, 'Book Review: *How Nations Behave* (2nd edn) by Louis Henkin', New York: Columbia University Press 1979; 21 (1980) *Harvard International Law Journal*, pp. 301–320.

'Theses about International Law Discourse', (1980) *German Yearbook of International Law*, pp. 353–391.

'Primitive Legal Scholarship', 27 (1986) *Harvard International Law Journal*, pp. 1–98.

International Legal Structures (Baden-Baden: *Nomos* Verlagsgesellschaft, 1987).

'The Sources of International Law', 2 (1987) *The American Journal of International Law and Policy*, pp. 1–96.

'Move to Institutions', 8 (1987) *Cardozo Law Review*, pp. 841–988.

'A New Stream of International Law Scholarship', 7 (1988) *Wisconsin International Law Journal*, pp. 1–49.

'Book Review', 31 (1990) *Harvard International Law Journal*, pp. 385–391.

'A New World Order: Yesterday, Today, and Tomorrow', 4 (1994) *Transnational Law & Contemporary Problems*, pp. 330–375.

'International Law and the Nineteenth Century: The History of an Illusion', 17 (1997) *QLR*, pp. 99–136.

'The Disciplines of International Law and Policy', 12 (1999) *Leiden Journal of International Law*, pp. 9–135.

'My Talk at the ASIL: What Is New Thinking in International Law', ASIL Proceedings of the 94th Annual Meeting, April 5–8, 2000, pp. 104–125.

'When Renewal Repeats: Thinking Against the Box', 32 (2000) *New York Journal of International Law and Politics*, p. 335.

'The International Human Rights Movement: Part of the Problem?', 14 (2002) *Harvard Human Rights Journal*, pp. 101–126.

'Tom Franck and the Manhattan School', 35 (2003) *NYU Journal of International Law and Politics*, pp. 397–437.

The Dark Sides of Virtue: Reassessing Humanitarianism (Princeton, NJ: Princeton University Press, 2004).

'Challenging Expert Rule: The Politics of Global Governance', 27 (2005) *Sydney Journal of International Law*, pp. 1–24.

Of War and Law (Princeton, NJ: Princeton University Press, 2006).

'The Last Treatise: Project and Person' (Reflections on Martti Koskenniemi's *Apology to Utopia*)', 7 (2006) *German Law Journal*, p. 982.

'The "Rule of Law," Political Choices, and Development Common Sense', in David M. Trubek and Alvaro Santos (eds.) *The New Law and Economic Development: A Critical Appraisal* (New York: Cambridge University Press, 2006), pp. 95–173.

'One, Two, Three, Many Legal Orders: Legal Pluralism and the Cosmopolitan Dream', 31 (2006–07) *N.Y.U. Review of Law & Social Change*, pp. 641–659.

'Speech: Assessing the Proposal for a Global Parliament: A Skeptics View', XIII (2007) *Widener Law Review*, pp. 395–399.

'The Mystery of Global Governance', in Jeffrey L. Dunoff and Joel P. Trachtman (eds.) *Ruling the World? Constitutionalism, International Law, and Global Governance* (Cambridge: Cambridge University Press, 2009), pp. 37–68.

'Lawfare and Warfare', in James Crawford and Martti Koskenniemi (eds.) *The Cambridge Companion to International Law* (Cambridge: Cambridge University Press, 2012), pp. 158–184.

'Law and the Political Economy of the World', 26 (2013) *Leiden Journal of International Law*, pp. 7–48.

'The International Human Rights Regime: Still Part of the Problem', in Rob Dickinson, Elena Katselli, Colin Murray, and Ole W. Pedersen (eds.) *Examining Critical Perspectives on Human Rights* (Cambridge: Cambridge University Press, 2013), pp. 19–34.

A World of Struggle: How Power, Law, and Expertise Shape Global Political Economy (Princeton, NJ: Princeton University Press, 2016).

'A complete list of publications' at www.law.harvard.edu/faculty/dkennedy/publications/

Kennedy, David, and Christopher Tennant, 'New Approaches to International Law: A Bibliography', 35 (1994) *Harvard International Law Journal*, p. 417.

Kennedy, David, and William W. Fisher III (eds.), *The Canon of American Legal Thought* (Princeton, NJ: Princeton University Press, 2006).

Kennedy, David W., 'A New World Order: Yesterday, Today, and Tomorrow', 4 (1994) *Transnational Law and Contemporary Problems,* pp. 330–375.

Kennedy, Duncan, 'Form and Substance in Private Law Adjudication', 88 (1976) *Harvard Law Review*, p. 1685.

'The Structure of Blackstone's Commentaries', 28 (1979) *Buffalo Law Review*, p. 205.

'The Role of Law in Economic Thought: Essays on the Fetishism of Commodities', 34 (1985) *The American University Law Review*, pp. 939–1001.

A Critique of Adjudication: Fin de Siecle (Cambridge, MA: Harvard University Press, 1997).

Kennedy, Duncan, and Karl Klare, 'A Bibliography of Critical Legal Studies', 94 (1984) *Yale Law Journal*, pp. 461–490.

Kennedy, Paul, *The Rise and Fall of British Naval Mastery* (London: The Macmillan Press, 1976).

Kingsbury, Benedict, 'The Concept of Compliance as a Function of Competing Conceptions of International Law', 19 (1998) *Michigan Journal of International Law*, pp. 345–372.

'Legal Positivism as Normative Politics: International Society, Balance of Power and Lasa Oppenheim's Positive International Law', 13 (2002) *European Journal of International Law,* pp. 401–436.

Kingsbury, Benedict, Nico Krisch and Richard B. Stewart, 'The Emergence of Global Administrative Law', 68 (2005) *Law and Contemporary Problems,* pp. 15–63.

Kirk, Gwyn, 'Standing on Solid Ground: A Materialist Ecological Feminism', in Rosemary Hennessy and Chrysn Ingraham (eds.) *Materialist Feminism: A Reader in Class, Difference, and Women's Lives* (Routledge: London, 1997), pp. 345–363.

Kishore, Vishal, *Ricardo's Gauntlet: Economic Fiction and the Flawed Case For Free Trade* (London: Anthem Press, 2014).

Klabbers, Jan, 'International Institutions', in James Crawford and Martti Koskenniemi (eds.) *The Cambridge Companion to International Law* (Cambridge: Cambridge University Press, 2012), pp. 228–244.

'Towards a Culture of Formalism? Martti Koskenniemi and the Virtues', 27 (2013) *Temple International & Comparative Law Journal*, pp. 417–436.

Klare, Karl E., 'The Politics of Duncan Kennedy's Critique', 22 (2001) *Cardozo Law Review*, pp.1073–1103.

Knox, Robert, 'Marxism, International Law, and Political Strategy', 22 (2009) *Leiden Journal of International Law*, pp. 413–436.

Koh, Harold Hongju,' Why Do Nations Obey International Law?', 106 (1996–97) *Yale Law Journal*, pp. 2599–2659.

'Is There a 'New' New Haven School of International Law', 32 (2007) *Yale Journal of International Law*, pp. 559–573.

'Michael Reisman, Dean of the New Haven School of International Law', 34 (2009) *Yale Journal of International Law*, pp. 501–504.

Kolakowski, Leszek, 'Marxism and Human Rights', 112 (1983) *Daedalus*, pp. 83–92.

Korany, B., 'Strategic Studies and the Third World: A Critical Evaluation', 110 (1986) *International Social Science Journal*, pp. 546–562.

Korhonen, Outi, 'New International Law: Silence, Defence or Deliverance?', 7 (1996) *European Journal of International Law*, pp. 1–29.

Koskenniemi, Martti, *From Apology to Utopia* (Helsinki: Lakimiesliton Kustannus, 1989).

'Comments on chapters 1 and 2', in Michael Byers and Georg Nolte (eds.) *United States Hegemony and the Foundations of International Law* (Cambridge: Cambridge University Press, 2003), pp. 91–100.

'Letter to the Editors of the Symposium', in Steven R. Ratner and Anne-Marie Slaughter (eds.) *The Methods of International Law* (Washington, DC: The American Society of International Law, 2004), pp. 109–126.

The Gentle Civilizer of Nations: the Rise and Fall of International Law 1870–1960 (Cambridge: Cambridge University Press, 2004).

'International Law in Europe: Between Tradition and Renewal', 16 (2005) *European Journal of International Law*, pp. 113–124.

The Gentle Civilizer of Nations: The Rise and Fall of International Law 1870–1960 (Cambridge: Cambridge University Press, 2005).

'The Fate of Public International Law: Between Technique and Politics', 70 (2007) *The Modern Law Review*, pp. 1–30.

'Miserable Comforters: International Relations as New Natural Law', 15 (2009) *European Journal of International Relations,* pp. 395–422.

'The Case for Comparative International Law', 20 (2009) *Finnish Yearbook of International Law,* pp. 1–8.

'Empire and International Law: The Real Spanish Contribution', 61 (2011) *University of Toronto Law Journal,* pp. 1–36.

'Histories of International Law: Significance and Problems for a Critical View', 27 (2013) *Temple International & Comparative Law Journal,* pp. 215–241.

'International Law and the Emergence of Mercantile Capitalism'. Available at www.helsinki.fi/eci/Publications/Koskenniemi/MKMercantileCapitalism .pdf (accessed on 21 January 2014).

Kothari, Rajni, *Footsteps to the Future: Diagnosis of the Present World and a Design for an Alternative* (New York: Free Press, 1974).

Kotiaho, Paavo, 'A Return to Koskenniemi, or the Disconcerting Co-optation of Rupture', 13 (2013) *German Law Journal,* pp. 483–496.

Kotiswaran, Prabha, *Dangerous Sex, Invisible Labor: Sex Work and the Law in India* (New Delhi: Oxford University Press, 2012).

Kovel, J., *The End of Capitalism: The End of Capitalism or the End of the World?* 2nd edn (London: Zed Books, 2007).

Kumar, Pratibha, 'Challenging Imperial Feminism', 17 (1984) *Feminist Review,* pp. 3–19.

Kunz, Josef L., *The Changing Law of Nations: Essays on International Law* (Ohio: Ohio University Press, 1968).

Kutz, Christopher L., 'Just Disagreement: Indeterminacy and Rationality in the Rule of Law', 103 (1994) *The Yale Law Journal,* pp. 997–1030.

Laclau, Ernesto, *Emancipation(s)* (London: Verso, 1996).

Lal, Vinay, *The History of History* (New Delhi: Oxford University Press, 2003).

Lang, Andrew and Susan Marks, 'People with Projects: Writing the Lives of International Lawyers', 27 (2013) *Temple International & Comparative Law Journal,* pp. 437–453.

Lang, Anthony F., *Political Theory and International Affairs: Hans J. Morgenthau on Aristotle's* The Politics (Greenwood, CT: Praeger, 2004).

Lasswell, Harold D., *World Politics and Personal Insecurity* (New York: The Free Press, 1965).

'In Collaboration with McDougal', 1 (1971) *Denver Journal of International Law and Policy,* pp. 17–19.

'Introduction', in W. Michael Reisman and Burns H. Weston (eds.) *Towards World Order and Human Dignity: Essays in Honor of Myres S. McDougal* (New York: The Free Press, 1976), pp. xiii-xviii.

Lasswell, Harold and Abraham Kaplan, *Power and Society* (New Haven, CT: Yale University Press, 1950).

Lasswell, Harold D. and Myres S. McDougal, 'Criteria for a Theory About Law', 44 (1970–71) *Southern California Law Review,* pp. 362–394.

Latour, Bruno, *We have Never Been Modern* (Cambridge, MA: Harvard University Press, 1993). Translated by Catherine Porter.

Reassembling the Social: An Introduction to Actor-Network Theory (Oxford: Oxford University Press, 2002).

'Politics of Nature: East and West Perspectives', 4 (2011) *Ethics and Global Politics*, pp. 1–10.

Lauterpacht, Hersch, *International Law: Collected Papers, vol. 2*, 'The Law of Peace', Part I (Cambridge: Cambridge University Press, 1975).

'The Grotian Tradition in International Law', in Eli Lauterpacht (ed.) *International Law: Collected Papers*, vol. II, Part I (Cambridge: Cambridge University Press, 1975), pp. 307–366.

International Law: Being the Collected Papers of Hersch Lauterpacht, vol. 4 (ed.) E. Lauterpacht (Cambridge: Cambridge University Press, 1978).

Laville, Helen, *Cold War Women: The International Activities of American Women's Organizations* (Manchester: Manchester University Press, 2002).

Legro, Jeffrey W., and Andrew Moravcsik, 'Is Anybody Still a Realist?', 25 (1999) *International Security*, pp. 5–55.

Leiter, Brian, 'Classical Realism', 11 (2001) *Social, Political, and Legal Philosophy*, pp. 244–267.

Lenin, V. I., *Selected Works*, vols 1–3 (Moscow: Progress Publishers, 1975).

On Dialectics (Moscow: Progress Publishers, 1980).

Levine, Andrew, Elliot Sober and Erik Olin Wright, 'Marxism and Methodological Individualism', 162 (1987) *New Left Review*, pp. 67–84.

Levi-Strauss, Claude, *Structural Anthropology*, vol. 2 (Middlesex: Penguin, 1976).

Levitt, Janet Koven, 'Bottom-Up International Law Making: Reflections on the New Haven School of Law Making', 32 (2007) *Yale Journal of International Law*, pp. 393–420.

Levitt, Nancy, and Robert R. M. Verchick, *Feminist Legal Theory: A Primer* (New York: New York University Press, 2006).

Lieber, Keir A. (ed.), *War, Peace, and International Political Realism: Perspectives from The Review of Politics* (Indiana: University of Notre Dame Press, 2009).

Lindner, Kolja, 'Marx's Eurocentrism. Postcolonial Studies and Marx Scholarship', (2010) *Radical Philosophy*, pp. 27–41.

Linklater, Andrew, 'Marxism and International Relations: Antithesis, Reconciliation and Transcendence', in Richard Higgott and J. L. Richardson (eds.) *International Relations: Global and Australian Perspectives on an Evolving Discipline* (Canberra: Australian National University, 1991), pp. 70–91.

Lissitzyn, Oliver J., 'Book Review', 76 (1962–63), *Harvard Law Review*, pp. 668–672.

Little, Richard, *The Balance of Power in International Relations: Metaphors, Myths and Models* (Cambridge: Cambridge University Press, 2007).

Llewellyn, Karl, 'Some Realism about Realism', in *Jurisprudence: Realism in Theory and Practice* (Chicago, IL: The University of Chicago Press, 1962).

Lorca, Arnulf Becker, 'Eurocentrism in the History of International Law', in Bardo Fassbender and Anne Peters (eds.), *The Oxford Handbook of the History of International Law* (Oxford: Oxford University Press, 2012), pp. 1034–1058.

Lord Lloyd of Hampstead and M. D. A. Freeman (eds.), *Lloyd's Introduction to Jurisprudence*, 5th edn (London: Stevens and Sons, 1985).

Logos, G., and H. Godoy, *Revolution in Being: A Latin American View of the Future* (New York: Free Press, 1977).

Loomba, Ania, *Colonialism/Postcolonialism* (London: Routledge, 1998).

Lowy, Michael, 'What is Ecosocialism', 16 (2005) *Capitalism, Nature and Socialism*, pp. 15–24.

Lukes, Steven, 'Can a Marxist Believe in Human Rights, 4 (1981) *Praxis International*, pp. 334–345.

  Marxism and Morality (Oxford: Clarendon Press, 1985).

  Power: A Radical View, 2nd edn (Basingstoke: Palgrave Macmillan, 2005).

Luxemburg, Rosa, *The Crisis in German Social-Democracy: (The 'Junius' Pamphlet)* (New York: The Socialist Publication Society, 1919).

  The Accumulation of Capital (London: Routledge and Kegan Paul, 1951).

  Luxemburg, Rosa: Selected Writings (Kolkata: Search, 2008).

MacKinnon, Catharine A., 'Feminism, Marxism, Method, and the State: An Agenda for Theory', 7 (1982) *Signs*, pp. 515–544.

  'Feminism, Marxism, Method, and the State: Toward Feminist Jurisprudence', 8 (1983) *Signs*, pp. 635–658.

  'Points against PostModernism', 75 (2000) *Chicago-Kent Law Review*, pp. 687–712.

  Are Women Human? And Other International Dialogues (Cambridge, MA: Harvard University Press, 2006).

  'Foreword', in Beverley Baines, Daphne Barak-Erez and Tsvi Kahana (eds.) *Feminist Constitutionalism: Global Perspectives* (Cambridge: Cambridge University Press, 2012).

Macpherson, C. B., *Democratic Theory: Essays in Retrieval* (Oxford: Oxford University Press, 1973).

Magdoff, Fred, and John Bellamy Foster, *What Every Environmentalist Needs to Know About Capitalism: A Citizen's Guide to Capitalism and the Environment* (New York: Monthly Review Press, 2011).

Magdoff, Harry, *Imperialism: From the Colonial Age to the Present* (New York: Monthly Review Press, 1978).

Mandel, Ernest, 'The Nation-State and Imperialism', in D. Held et al. (eds.), *States and Societies* (Oxford: Martin Robertson,1983), pp. 526–539.

Mann, Michael, *States, War and Capitalism: Studies in Political Sociology* (Oxford: Blackwell Publishers, 1988).

Mansfield, Edward D., Diana C. Mutz and Laura R. Silver, 'Men, Women, Trade and Free Markets', 59 (2015) *International Studies Quarterly*, pp. 303–315.

Marcuse, Hebert, 'Marxism and Feminism', 2 (1974) *Women's Studies*, pp. 279–288.

Marks, Susan, *The Riddle of All Constitutions* (Oxford: Oxford University Press, 2003).

(ed.), *International Law on the Left* (Cambridge: Cambridge University Press, 2004).

'International Judicial Activism and the Commodity Form Theory of International Law', 18 (2007) *European Journal of International Law*, pp. 281–307.

'Exploitation as an International Legal Concept', in Susan Marks (ed.) *International Law on the Left* (Cambridge: Cambridge University Press, 2008).

'Human Rights and Root Causes', 74 (2011) *The Modern Law Review*, pp. 57–78.

Marx, Karl, *Grundrisse: Foundations of the Critique of Political Economy (Rough Draft)* Translated with a Foreword by Martin Nicolaus (Middlesex: Pelican Books, 1973).

The Poverty of Philosophy (Moscow: Progress Publishers, 1975).

Capital, vol. I (Moscow: Progress Publishers, 1977).

'Critique of the Gotha Programme', in Karl Marx and Frederick Engels *Selected Works*, vol. 3 (Moscow: Progress Publishers, 1977), pp. 9–30.

A Contribution to the Critique of Political Economy (Moscow: Progress Publishers, 1984).

'On the Jewish Question', in Karl Marx and Friedrich Engels, *The Individual and Society* (Moscow: Progress Publishers, 1984), pp. 56–71.

Marx, Karl, and Frederick Engels, *Selected Works,* vols 1–3 (Moscow: Progress Publishers, 1973).

The German Ideology (Moscow: Progress Publishers, 1977).

Pre-Capitalist Socio-Economic Formations: A Collection (Moscow: Progress Publishers, 1979).

The Individual and Society (Moscow: Progress Publishers, 1984).

Collected Works, vol. 28 (Moscow: Progress Publishers, 1986).

Mazrui, Ali, *World Federation of Cultures: An African Perspective* (New York: Free Press, 1976).

Mazur, Amy G., 'A Feminist Empirical and Integrative Approach in Political Science: Breaking Down the Glass Wall?', in Harold Kincaid (ed.) *The Oxford Handbook of Philosophy of Social Science* (New York: Oxford University Press, 2012), pp. 533–558.

Mazur, G. O. (ed.), *One Hundred Year Commemoration to the Life of Hans Morgenthau (1904–2004)* (New York: Semenenko Foundation, 2004).

McCall, Leslie, 'The Complexity of Intersectionality', 30 (2005) *Signs: Journal of Women in Culture and Society,* pp. 1772–1799.

McCarthy, Helen, 'The Diplomatic History of Global Women's Rights: The British Foreign Office and International Women's Year, 1975', 50 (2015) *Journal of Contemporary History*, pp. 833–853.

McDougal, Myres S., 'The Law School of the Future: From Legal Realism to Policy Science in the World Community', 56 (1946–47) *Yale Law Journal*, pp. 1345–1355.

'Review of Hersch Lauterpacht's International Law and Human Rights (1950)', 60 (1951) *Yale Law Journal*, pp. 1051–1056.

'Law and Power', 46 (1952) *The American Journal of International Law*, pp. 102–114.

'International Law, Power and Policy: A Contemporary Conception', 1 (1953) *Recueil des Cours*, pp. 137–258.

'Remarks on International Concern versus Domestic Jurisdiction', *Proceedings of American Society of International Law*, 1954, p. 120.

'The Realist Theory in Pyrrhic Victory', 49 (1955) *American Journal of International Law*, pp. 376–378.

'The International Law Commission's Draft Articles upon Interpretation: Textuality Redivivus', 61 (1967) *American Journal of International Law*, pp. 992–1000.

'Law and Minimum World Public Order: Armed Conflict in Larger Context', 3 (1984) *Pacific Basin Law Journal*, pp. 21–33.

McDougal, Myres S. and Associates, *Studies in World Public Order* (New Haven, CT: Yale University Press, 1960).

McDougal, Myres S., and Florentino P. Feliciano, *Law and Minimum World Public Order: The Legal Regulation of International Coercion* (New Haven, CT: Yale University Press, 1961).

McDougal, Myres S. and W. Michael Reisman, 'The Changing Structure of International Law: Unchanging Theory for Inquiry', 65 (1965) *Columbia Law Review*, pp. 810–846.

'Harold Dwight Lasswell (1902–1978)', 73 (1979) *American Journal of International Law*, pp. 655–660.

'International Law in Policy Oriented Perspective', in R. St. J. Macdonald and D. M. Johnston (eds.), *The Structure and Process of International Law* (The Hague: Martinus Nijhoff, 1983), pp. 103–129.

McDougal, Myres S., Harold D. Lasswell and Lung-chu Chen, 'Human Rights and World Public Order: A Framework for Policy-Oriented Inquiry', 63 (1969) *The American Journal of International Law*, pp. 237–269.

McDougal, Myres S., Harold D. Lasswell and James C. Miller, *The Interpretation of Agreements and World Public Order: Principles of Content and Procedure* (New Haven, CT: Yale University Press, 1967).

McDougal, Myres S., Harold D. Lasswell and W. Michael Reisman, 'The World Constitutive Process of Authoritative Decision', 19 (1967) *Journal of Legal Education*, pp. 253–300.

'Theories about International Law: Prologue to a Configurative Jurisprudence', 8 (1968) *Virginia Journal of International Law*, pp. 188–299.

'The World Constitutive Process of Authoritative Decision', in Richard A. Falk and C. G. Black (eds.), *The Future of the International Legal Order: Trends and Patterns* (Princeton, NJ: Princeton University Press, 1969), pp. 73–154.

Mearsheimer, John, 'The False Promise of International Institutions', 19 (1994–95) *International Security*, pp. 5–49.

'Hans Morgenthau and the Iraq War: Realism versus Neo-conservatism', Open-Democracy, (19 May 2005), p. 1. Available at: www.opendemocracy.net/democracy-americanpower/morgenthau_2522.jsp (accessed 8 May 2013).

Megret, Frederick, 'From "savages" to "unlawful combatants": A Postcolonial Look at International Humanitarian Law's "other"', in Anne Orford (ed.) *International Law and its Others* (Cambridge: Cambridge University Press, 2006), pp. 265–317.

Mehta, Uday Singh, *Liberalism and Empire: A Study in Nineteenth-Century British Liberal Thought* (Chicago, IL: Chicago University Press, 1999).

Meinecke, Friedrich, *Machiavellism: The Doctrine of Raison d'etat and its Place in Modern History* (Boulder, CO: Westview Press, 1984).

Mendelson, Jack, 'The Habermas-Gadamer Debate', 18 (1979) *New German Critique*, pp. 44–73.

Mendolovitz, Saul H. (ed.), *On the Creation of a Just World Order: Preferred Worlds for the 1990s* (New York: Free Press, 1975).

Merry, Sally Engle, *Human Rights & Gender Violence: Translating International Law into Local Justice* (Chicago, IL: The University of Chicago Press, 2006).

'*Methodological Individualism*' Stanford Encyclopedia of Philosophy. Available at: http://plato.stanford.edu/entries/methodological-individualism/ (accessed on 28 June 2013).

Michalak, Jr., Stanley J., 'Richard Falk's Future World: A Critique of WOMP-USA', 42 (1980) *The Review of Politics*, pp. 3–17.

Mickelson, Karin, 'Taking Stock of TWAIL Histories', 10 (2008) *International Community Law Review*, pp. 355–362.

Mies, Maria, *Patriarchy and Accumulation on a World Scale: Women in the International Division of Labour* (London: Zed Books, 1998).

Miéville, China, *Between Equal Rights: A Marxist Theory of International Law* (Leiden: Brill, 2005).

Miliband, Ralph, *Marxism and Politics* (Oxford: Oxford University Press, 1977).

'State Power and Class Interests', 138 (1983) *New Left Review*, pp. 57–68.

'Class Struggle from Above', in William Outhwaite and Michael Mulkay (eds.) *Social Theory and Social Criticism* (Oxford: Blackwell, 1987), pp. 175–184.

Mishra, Vijay and Bod Hodge, 'What was Postcolonialism?', 36 (2005) *New Literary History* pp. 375–402.

Mitrany, David, *A Working Peace System*, 4th edn (London: National Peace Council, 1946).

Moghdam, Valentine M., 'The "Feminization of Poverty" and Women's Human Rights', *SHS Papers on Women's Studies/Gender Research* (Paris: UNESCO, 2005).

Mohanty, Chandra Talpade, ' "Under Western Eyes" Revisited: Feminist Solidarity through Anticapitalist Struggles', 28 (2003) *Signs,* pp. 495–535.

'Transnational Feminist Crossings: On Neoliberalism and Radical Critique', 38 no. 4 (2013) *Signs: Journal of Women in Culture and Society,* pp. 967–991.

Molyneux, Maxine, 'Conceptualizing Women's Interests', in Nancy Holmstrom (ed.) *The Socialist Feminist Project: A Contemporary Reader in Theory and Politics* (Delhi: Aakar, 2011), pp. 250–257.

Moore, Jason W., 'Environment Crisis and the Metabolic Rift in World-Historical Perspective', 13 (2000) *Organization & Environment,* pp. 123–157.

Moore, John Norton, *Law and the Indo-China War* (Princeton, NJ: Princeton University Press, 1972).

Moore-Gilbert, Bart, 'Marxism and Postcolonialism Reconsidered', 7 (2001) *Hungarian Journal of English and American Studies (HJEAS)* Postcolonial Issues: Theories and Readings, pp. 9–27.

Morgan, Edward M., 'International Law in a Post-Modern Hall of Mirrors: International Legal Structures by David Kennedy', 26 (1988) *Osgoode Hall Law Journal,* pp. 207–233.

Morgenthau, Hans, *The Judicial Function in the International Realm, Its Nature and Its Limits* (Leipzig: Noske, 1929).

'Positivism, Functionalism and International Law', 34 (1940) *American Journal of International Law,* pp. 260–284.

The Decline of Democratic Politics (Chicago, IL: Chicago University Press, 1962).

Scientific Man versus Power Politics (Chicago, IL: University of Chicago Press, 1965).

Politics among Nations: The Struggle for Power and Peace, 4th edn (New York: Alfred A. Knopf, 1967).

Truth and Power: Essays of a Decade, 1960–70 (London: Pall Mall Press, 1970).

'An Intellectual Autobiography', (1978 Jan-Feb) *Society,* pp. 63–68.

In Defense of the National Interest (New York: Knopf, 1981).

Morriss, Peter, 'Steven Lukes on the Concept of Power', in Mark Haugaard and Stewart R. Clegg (ed.) *Power and Politics,* vol. 1 (London: Sage, 2012), pp. 231–242.

Moyn, Samuel, *The Last Utopia: Human Rights in History* (Boston, MA: Harvard University Press, 2010).

Mutua, Athena D., *The Rise, Development and Future Directions of Critical Race Theory and Related Scholarship,* 84 (2006) *Denver University Law Review,* pp. 329–394.

Mutua, Makau, 'Critical Race Theory and International Law: The View of an Insider-Outsider', 45 (2000) *Villanova Law Review,* pp. 841–853.

Nair, Janaki, 'Indian Historiography and its "Resolution" of Feminists' Questions', in Anjan Ghosh, Tapati Guha-Thakurtha and Janaki Nair (eds.), *Theorizing the Present: Essays for Partha Chatterjee* (New Delhi: Oxford University Press, 2011), pp. 35–65.

Nardin, Terry, *Law, Morality and the Relations of States* (Princeton, NJ: Princeton University Press, 1983).

'International Ethics and International Law', 18 (1992) *Review of International Studies*, pp. 19–30.

Nawaz, M. K., 'Some legal aspects of the Anglo-Mughal Relations', (1956) *Indian Yearbook of International Affairs*, pp. 70–83.

Nehru, Jawaharlal, *The Discovery of India* (Lucknow: Asia Publishing House, 1961).

Neocleous, Mark, 'International Law as Primitive Accumulation; Or, the secret of Systematic Colonization', 23 (2012) *European Journal of International Law*, pp. 941–962.

Nesiah, Vasuki, 'Priorities of Feminist Legal Research: A sketch, a draft agenda, a hint of an outline...', 1 (2011) http://journals.kent.ac.uk/index.php/feminist satlaw/article/view/20/83 (accessed 15 June, 2015).

'Uncomfortable Alliances: Women, Peace, and Security in Sri Lanka', in Ania Loomba and Ritty A. Lukose (eds.), *South Asian Feminisms* (New Delhi: Zubaan, 2012), pp. 139–161.

Nielson, Kain, *Marxism and the Moral Point of View: Morality, Ideology, and Historical Materialism* (Boulder, CO: Westview Press, 1989).

Nye, Joseph S., 'Globalization's Democratic Deficit: How to Make International Institutions More Accountable', 80 (2001) *Foreign Affairs*, pp. 2–6.

Obregon, Liliana, 'Completing Civilization: Creole Consciousness and International Law in Nineteenth Century Latin America', in Anne Orford (ed.) *International Law and Its Others* (Cambridge: Cambridge University Press, 2006), pp. 247–265.

O'Connor, James, 'Capitalism, Nature, Socialism: A Theoretical Introduction', 1 (1989) *Capitalism, Nature, Socialism*, pp. 11–38.

'Political Economy and Ecology of Socialism and Capitalism', 3 (1989) *Capitalism, Nature, Socialism*, pp. 93–106.

Offen, Karen, 'Defining Feminism: A Comparative Historical Approach', 14 (1988) *Signs*, pp. 119–157.

Okafor, Chinedu Obiora, 'Newness, Imperialism, and International Legal Reform in Our Time: A TWAIL Perspective', 43 (2005) *Osgoode Hall Law Journal*, pp. 171–191.

'Critical Third World Approaches to International Law (TWAIL): Theory, Methodology, or Both?', 10 (2008) *International Community Law Review*, pp. 371–378.

'Irrigating the Famished Fields: The Impact of Labour-led Struggles on Policy and Action in Nigeria (1999–2007)', 27 (2009) *Journal of Contemporary African Studies*, pp. 159–175.

'Remarkable Returns: On the Influence of a Labour-led Movement on Legislative Reasoning, Process and Action in Nigeria', 47 (2009) *Journal of Modern African Studies*, pp. 241–266.

'Between Elite Interests and Pro-Poor Resistance: The Nigerian Courts and Labour-led Anti-Fuel Price Hike Struggles (1999–2007), 54 (2010) *The Journal of African Law*, pp. 95–118.

Oloka-Onyango, J., and Sylvia Tamale, ' "The Personal is Political", or Why Women's Rights are Indeed Human Rights: An African Perspective on International Feminism', 17 (1995) *Human Rights Quarterly*, pp. 691–731.

Olson, William, and Nicholas Onuf, 'The Growth of a Discipline Reviewed', in Steve Smith (ed.), *International Relations: British and American Perspectives* (Oxford: Oxford University Press, 1985).

Onuf, Nicholas, *International Legal Theory: Essays and Engagements, 1996–2006* (London: Routledge-Cavendish, 2008).

Onuma, Yasuaki, *A Transcivilizational Perspective on International Law* (Leiden: Martinus Nijhoff, 2010).

Orford, Anne, 'Feminism, Imperialism and the Mission of International Law', 71 (2002) *Nordic Journal of International Law*, pp. 275–296.

'The Destiny of International Law', 17 (2004) *Leiden Journal of International Law*, pp. 441–476.

'A Journal of the Voyage from Apology to Utopia', 7 (2005) *German Law Journal*, pp. 994–1010.

'Scientific Reason and the Discipline of International Law', 25 (2014) *European Journal of International Law*, pp. 369–385.

Ostrom, Elinor, Joanna Burger, Christopher B. Field, Richard B. Nogaard and David Policansky, 'Revisiting the Commons: Local Lessons, Global Challenges', 284 (9 April 1999)*Science*, pp. 278–282.

Otto, Dianne, 'Lost in Translation: Re-scripting the Sexed Subjects of International Human Rights Law', in Anne Orford (ed.), *International Law and Its Others* (Cambridge: Cambridge University Press, 2006), pp. 318–356.

'The Gastronomics of TWAIL's Feminist Flavorings: Some Lunch-Time Offerings', 9 (2007) *International Community Law Review*, pp. 345–352.

'The Exile of Inclusion: Reflections on Gender Issues in International Law over the Last Decade', 10 (2009) *Melbourne Journal of International Law*, pp. 11–26.

'Power and Danger: Feminist Engagement with International through the UN Security Council', 32 (2010) *The Australian Feminist Law Journal*, pp. 97–121.

'Prospects for International Gender Norms', 31 (2011) *Pace Law Review*, pp. 873–881.

'Feminist Approaches', in Tony Carty (ed.) *Oxford Bibliographies Online: International Law* (New York: Oxford University Press, 2012). Available at: www.oxfordbibliographies.com/view/document/obo-9780199796953/obo-9780199796953-0055.xml?rskey=eu20uq&result=1&q=

'International Human Rights Law: Towards Rethinking Sex/Gender Dualism', in Margaret Davies and Vanessa Munro (eds.), *A Research Companion to Feminist Legal Theory* (London: Routledge, 2013) pp. 197–215.

Pagden, Anthony (ed.), *The Languages of Political Theory in Early Modern Europe* (Cambridge: Cambridge University Press, 1987).

'Human Rights, Natural Rights, and Europe's Imperial Legacy', 31 (2003) *Political Theory*, p. 171.

'Conquest and the Just War: The "School of Salamanca" and the "Affair of the Indies", in Sankar Muthu (ed.) *Empire and Modern Political Thought* (Cambridge: Cambridge University Press, 2012), pp. 30–60.

Pardee Center Task Force Report (March 2013) *Capital Account Regulations and the Trading System: A Compatibility Review* (Kevin P. Gallagher and Leonardo E. Stanley Co-Chairs) Boston University, pp. 10–11.

Pashukanis: Selected Writings on Marxism and Law, Piers Beirne and Robert Sharlet (ed.) translated by Peter B. Maggs (New York: Academic Press, 1980).

Passmore, John, *A Hundred Years of Philosophy* (Middlesex: Penguin, 1972).

Patil, Vrushali, 'From Patriarchy to Intersectionality: A Transnational Feminist Assessment of How Far We've Really Come', 38 (2013) *Signs*, pp. 847–867.

Patnaik, Prabhat , 'Appreciation: The Other Marx', in Iqbal Hussain (ed.) *Karl Marx on India* (New Delhi: Tulika, 2006), pp. iv–ixviii.

Patnaik, Utsa, 'The Free Lunch: Transfers from the Tropical Colonies and Their Role in Capital Formation in Britain during the Industrial Revolution', in K. S. Jomo (ed.), *Globalization under Hegemony: The Changing World* (New Delhi: Oxford University Press, 2006), pp. 30–70.

Paulus, Andreas L., 'International Law After Postmodernism: Towards Renewal or Decline of International Law?', 14 (2001) *Leiden Journal of International Law,* pp. 727–755.

Pedraza-Farina, Laura, 'Conceptions of Civil Society in International Lawmaking and Implementation: A Theoretical Framework', 34 (2013) *Michigan Journal of International Law,* pp. 606–673.

Peffer, R. G., *Marxism, Morality and Social Justice* (Princeton, NJ: Princeton University Press, 1990).

Perry, Benita, 'Edward Said and Third World Marxism', 40 (2013) *College Literature: A Journal of Critical Literary Studies,* pp. 105–136.

Petersmann, Ernest-Ulrich, 'JIEL Debate: Methodological Pluralism and Its Critics in International Economic Law Research', 15 (2012) *Journal of International Economic Law,* pp.921–970.

Petras, James, and Ken Trachte, 'Liberal, Structural and Radical Approaches to Political Economy: An Assessment and an Alternative', 3 (1979) *Contemporary Crisis,* pp. 109–147.

Pevsner, Ya, *State-Monopoly Capitalism and the Labour Theory of Value* (Moscow: Progress Publishers, 1982).

Pichler, Hans-Karl, 'The Godfathers of "Truth": Max Weber and Carl Schmitt in Morgenthau's Theory of Power Politics', 24 (1998) *Review of International Studies*, pp. 185–200.

Piketty, Thomas, *Capital in the Twenty-First Century* (Cambridge, MA: The Belknap Press of Harvard University Press, 2014).

Pollack, Mark A., 'Is International Relations Corrosive of International Law?: A Reply to Martti Koskenniemi', 27 (2013) *Temple International & Comparative Law Quarterly*, pp. 339–376.

Popa, Raluca, 'Translating Equality between Women and Men Across Cold War Divides: Women Activists from Hungary and Romania and the Creation of International Women's Year', in Shana Penn and Jill Massino (eds.) *Gender Politics and Everyday Life in State Socialist Eastern and Central Europe* (London: Palgrave Macmillan, 2009), pp. 59–74.

Poulantzas, Nicos, *Classes in Contemporary Capitalism* (London: Verso, 1978).
    Political Power and Social Classes (London: Verso, 1978).
The Poulantzas Reader: Marxism, Law and the State James Martin (ed.) (London: Verso, 2008).

President Putin, 'Address by President of the Russian Federation' on 18 March 2014. Available at: http://en.kremlin.ru/events/president/news/20603 (accessed on 27 May 2015).

Prugl, Elisabeth, 'International Institutions and Feminist Politics', X (2004) *Brown Journal of World Affairs*, pp. 69–84.

Purkis, Jonathan, and James Bowen (ed.), *Changing Anarchism: Anarchist Theory and Practice in a Global Age* (Manchester: Manchester University Press, 2004).

Quigley, John, *Soviet Legal Innovation and the Law of the Western World* (Cambridge: Cambridge University Press, 2007).

Rai, Shirin, 'Gender and Development: Theoretical Perspectives', in Nalini Visvanathan, Lynn Duggan, Nan Wiegersma and Laura Nissonof (eds.) *The Women, Gender and Development Reader* (London: Zed Press, 2011), pp. 28–37.

Rajagopal, Balakrishnan, *International Law from Below: Development, Social Movements, and Third World Resistance* (New York: Cambridge University Press, 2003).
    'Martti Koskenniemi's *From Apology to Utopia*: A Reflection', 7(2006) *German Law Journal* , pp. 1089–1094.

Rasulov, Akbar 'New Approaches to International Law: Images of a Genealogy', in Jose Maria Beneyto and David Kennedy (eds.) *New Approaches to International Law: The European and the American Experiences* (The Hague: T. M. C. Asser Press, 2013), pp. 151–191.
    'CLS and Marxism: A History of an Affair', 5 (2015) *Transnational Legal Theory*, pp. 622–639.

Ratner, Steven R., and Anne-Marie Slaughter (eds.), *The Methods of International Law* (Washington, DC: The American Society of International Law, 2004).

Rege, Sharmila, 'Dalit Women Talk Differently: A Critique of "Difference" and towards a Dalit Feminist Standpoint Position', 33 (1998) *Economic and Political Weekly*, Women Studies, pp. 39–46.

Writing Caste, Writing Gender: Reading Dalit Women's Testimonies (New Delhi: Zubaan, 2006).

Rehfield, Andrew, 'Towards a General Theory of Political Representation', 68 (2006) *Journal of Politics*, pp. 1–21.

Reisman, Michael W., 'Coercion and Self-Determination: Construing Charter Article 2(4)', 78 (1984) *American Journal of International Law*, pp. 642–645.

'The View from the New Haven School of International Law', 86 (1992) *American Society of International Law Proceedings*, pp. 118–125.

'Myres S. McDougal: Architect of a Jurisprudence for a Free Society', 66 (1996) *Mississippi Law Journal*, pp. 15–26.

'Theory about Law: Jurisprudence about a Free Society', 108 (1999) *Yale Law Journal*, pp. 935–939.

'Unilateral Action and the Transformations of the World Constitutive Process: The Special Problem of Humanitarian Intervention', 11 (2000) *European Journal of International Law*, pp. 3–18.

Reisman, Michael W., and Burns H. Weston (eds.), *Towards World Order and Human Dignity: Essays in Honour of Myres S. McDougal* (New York: The Free Press, 1976).

Rengger, Nicholas, 'On "Good Governance", Institutional Design, and the Practices of Moral Agency', in Toni Erskine (ed.), *Can Institutions Have Responsibilities? Collective Moral Agency and International Relations* (Basingstoke: Palgrave Macmillan, 2003), pp. 207–218.

Resnick, Stephen A., and Richard D. Wolff (eds.), *New Departures in Marxian Theory* (London: Routledge, 2006).

Rice, Daniel, 'Reinhold Niebuhr and Hans Morgenthau: A Friendship with Contrasting Shades of Realism', 42 (2008) *Journal of American Studies*, pp. 255–291.

Richards, David L., and Ronald Gelleny 'Women's Status and Economic Globalization', 51 (2007) *International Studies Quarterly*, pp. 855–876.

Riley, Ronin L., Chandra Talpade Mohanty and Minnie Bruce Pratt, 'Introduction: Feminism and US Wars – Mapping the Ground', in Ronin L. Riley, Chandra Talpade Mohanty and Minnie Bruce Pratt (eds.) *Feminism and War: Confronting U.S. Imperialism* (London and New York: Zed Books, 2008), pp. 1–18.

Rittich, Kerry, 'Book Review', 14 (2001) *Leiden Journal of International Law*, pp. 935–939.

Recharacterizing Restructuring: Law, Distribution and Gender in Market Reform (The Hague: Kluwer Law International, 2002).

Robins, Nick, *The Corporation That Changed the World: How the East India Company Shaped the Modern Multinational* (Hyderabad: Orient Longman, 2006).

Robinson, William, and Jeffrey Harris, 'Towards a Global Ruling Class? Globalization and the Transnational Capitalist Class', 64 (2000) *Science and Society,* pp. 11–54.

Roling, B. V. A., *International Law in an Expanded World* (Amsterdam: Djambatan, 1960).

Rose, Nikolas, Pat O'Malley, and Mariana Valverde, 'Governmentality', (2006) *Annual Review of Law and Social Science,* pp. 83–104.

Rosenau, James N. et al., 'Of Syllabi, Texts, Students, and Scholarships in International Relations: Some Data and Interpretations on the State of a Burgeoning Field', 29 (1976–77) *World Politics,* pp. 263–340.

Rosenberg, Justin, 'International Relations – The "Higher Bullshit": A Reply to the Globalization Theory Debate', 44 (2007) *International Politics,* pp. 450–482.

Rostow, Eugene V., 'Afterword', in W. Michael Reisman and Burns H. Weston (eds.) *Towards World Order and Human Dignity: Essays in Honor of Myres S. McDougal* (New York: The Free Press, 1976), pp. 562–578.

Roth, Brad R., 'Retrieving Marx for the Human Rights Project', 17 (2004) *Leiden Journal of International Law,* pp. 31–66.

Rowbotham, Sheila, Lynne Segal and Hilary Wainwright, *Beyond the Fragments: Feminism and the Making of Socialism* (Boston MA: Alyson Publications, 1981).

Russell, Bertrand, *My Philosophical Development* (London: George Allen and Unwin, 1969).

Saberi, Hengameh, 'Love it or Hate it, but for the Right Reasons: Pragmatism and the New Haven School's International Law of Human Dignity', 35 (2012) *Boston College International and Comparative Law Review,* pp. 59–144.

'Descendants of Realism? Policy-Oriented International Lawyers as Guardians of Democracy', in Prabhakar Singh and Benoit Mayer (eds.) *Critical International Law: Postrealism, Postcolonialism, and Transnationalism* (Delhi: Oxford University Press, 2014), pp. 29–52.

Sabile, Carol A., 'Feminism and the Ends of Postmodernism', in Rosemary Hennessy and Chrysn Ingraham (eds.) *Materialist Feminism: A Reader in Class, Difference, and Women's Lives* (Routledge: London, 1997), pp. 395–408.

Said, Edward, *The World, the Text and the Critic* (Cambridge, MA: Harvard University Press, 1983).

Culture and Imperialism (London: Chatto & Windus, 1993).

'Response', in Bruce Robbins, Mary Louise Pratt, Jonathan Arac, R. Radhakrishnan, 'Edward Said's Culture and Imperialism: A Symposium', 40 (1994) *Social Text,* pp. 1–24.

Santos, Boaventura de Sousa, 'Human Rights as an Emancipatory Script? Cultural and Political Conditions', in Boaventura de Sousa Santos (ed.) *Another World is Possible: Beyond Northern Epistemologies* (London: Verso, 2007), pp. 3–41.

Epistemologies of the South: Justice against Epistemicide (Boulder, CO: Paradigm Publishers, 2014).

Sassen, Saskia, 'Toward a Feminist Analytics of the Global Economy', 4 (1996) *Indiana Journal of Global Legal Studies*, p. 9. Available at: www.repository .law.indiana.edu/ijgls/vol4/iss1/2

Schacter, Oscar, 'Rhetoric and Law in International Political Organs', in Harold D. Lasswell, D. Lerner and H. Speirer (eds.) *Propaganda and Communication in World History* (Honolulu: University Press of Hawaii, 1980), pp. 446–457.

'The Legality of Pro-Democratic Invasion', 78 (1984) *American Journal of International Law*, pp. 645–650.

Schaffer, Gregory, 'The New Legal Realist Approach to International Law', 28 (2015) *Leiden Journal of International Law*, pp. 189–210.

Schaffer, Gregory and Tom Ginsburg, 'The Empirical Turn in International Legal Scholarship', 106 (2012) *American Journal of International Law*, pp. 1–46.

Scheniker, Andrea, and Jutta Joachim, 'European Countries and the Implementation of UN Security Council Resolution 1325', in Gulay Caglar, Elisabeth Prugl and Sussane Zwingel (eds.) *Feminist Strategies in International Governance* (London: Routledge, 2013), pp. 181–197.

Scheuerman, William E., *Carl Schmitt: The End of Law* (New York: Rowan and Littlefield, 1999).

'Realism and the Left: The Case of Hans J. Morgenthau', 34 (2008) *Review of International Studies*, pp. 29–51.

Schuett, Robert, 'Freudian Roots of Political Realism: The Importance of Sigmund Freud to Hans J. Morgenthau's Theory of International Power Politics', 20 (2007) *History of the Human Sciences*, pp. 53–78.

Sen, Amartya, *Development as Freedom* (Delhi: Oxford University Press, 2001).

The Argumentative Indian (London: Penguin Books, 2005).

Shaw, Malcolm N., *International Law*, 6th edn (Cambridge: Cambridge University Press, 2008).

Shaw, Martin, 'War, Imperialism and the States System: A Critique of Orthodox Marxism for the 1980s', in Martin Shaw (ed.) *War, State and Society* (London: Macmillan, 1984), pp. 64–68.

Simma, Bruno and Andreas L. Paulus, 'The Responsibility of Individuals for Human Rights Abuses in Internal Conflicts: A Positivist View', in Steven R. Ratner and Anne-Marie Slaughter (eds.) *The Methods of International Law* (Washington, DC: The American Society of International Law, 2004), pp. 23–47.

Simpson, Gerry, 'Dueling Agendas: International Relations and International Law (Again)', 1 (2004-2005) *Journal of International Relations & International Law*, pp. 61-75.

Singh, Narinder, *Economics and the Crisis of Ecology* (New Delhi: Oxford University Press, 1976).

Skinner, Quentin, 'On Encountering the Past', (2001), p. 44. Available at: www .jyu.fi/yhtfil/redescriptions/Yearbook%202002/Skinner_Interview_2002.pdf (accessed on 25 May 2015).

    Visions of Politics Volume I: Regarding Method (Cambridge: Cambridge University Press, 2002).

Sklair, Leslie, *Globalization: Capitalism and its Alternatives* (Oxford: Oxford University Press, 2002).

Skouteris, Thomas, 'New Approaches to International Law', Oxford Bibliographies. Available at: www.oxfordbibliographies.com/obo/page/international-law (accessed 5 February 2015).

Slaughter, Anne Marie, 'Sovereignty and Power in a Networked World Order', 40 (2004) *Stanford Journal of International Law*, pp. 283-327.

    'Filling Power Vacuums in the New Global Legal Order', (2013) *Boston College International & Comparative Law Review* (Symposium Issue), pp. 920-936.

Slaughter, Anne Marie, Andrew S. Tulumello and Stepan Wood, 'International Law and International Relations Theory: A New Generation of Interdisciplinary Scholarship, 92 (1998) *The American Journal of International Law*, pp. 367-397.

Slaughter Burley, Anne-Marie, 'International Law and International Relations Theory: A Dual Agenda', 87 (1993) *The American Journal of International Law*, pp. 205-239.

Smith, Neil, *Uneven Development: Nature, Capital and the Production of Space* (Oxford: Blackwell, 1990).

    'The Production of Nature', in G. Robertson and M. Mash (eds.) *FutureNatural* (London: Routledge, 1996), pp. 35-54.

Spivak, Gayatri Chakravarti, 'Three Women's Texts and a Critique of Imperialism', 12 (1985) *Critical Inquiry*, pp. 243-261.

    'Can the Subaltern Speak?', in C. Nelson and L. Grossberg (eds.) *Marxism and the Interpretation of Culture* (Basingstoke: Macmillan Education, 1988), pp. 271-313.

Stewart, Ann, *Gender Justice and Law in a Global Market* (Cambridge: Cambridge University Press, 2011).

Stewart, Ann *Gender Justice and Law in a Global Market*, (2012) CSLG/WP/16 Working Paper Series (New Delhi: Centre for the Study of Law and Governance, Jawaharlal Nehru University).

Stone, Julius, *Legal System and Lawyer's Reasonings* (London: Stevens and Sons Ltd., 1964).

'Approaches to the Notion of International Justice', in Richard A. Falk and C. G. Black (eds.) *The Future of the International Legal Order: Trends and Patterns* (Princeton, NJ: Princeton University Press, 1969), pp. 372–462.

'A Sociological Perspective on International Law', in R. St. J. Macdonald and D. M. Johnston (eds.) *The Structure and Process of International Law* (The Hague: Martinus Nijhoff, 1983), pp.263–303.

Visions of World Order; Between State Power and Human Justice (Baltimore, MD: The Johns Hopkins University Press, 1984).

Suleri, Sara, 'Woman Skin Deep: Feminism and the Postcolonial Condition', 18 (1992) *Critical Inquiry,* pp. 756–769.

Sutherland, Kate, 'Marx and MacKinnon: The Promise and Perils of Marxism for Feminist Legal Theory', 69 (2005) *Science and Society,* pp. 113–132.

Suzuki, Eisuke, 'The New Haven School of International Law: An Invitation to a Policy Oriented Jurisprudence', 1 (1974) *Yale Studies in World Public Order,* pp. 1–48.

Sypnowich, Christine, *The Concept of Socialist Law* (Oxford: Oxford University Press, 1990).

Tanesini, Alessandra, *An Introduction to Feminist Epistemologies* (Oxford: Blackwell, 1999).

Taylor, Charles, *Philosophy and the Human Sciences,* vol. II (Cambridge: Cambridge University Press, 1985).

Thompson, E. P., *The Making of the English Working Class* (Hammondsworth: Penguin, 1963).

Whigs and Hunters: The Origin of the Black Act (London: Penguin Books, 1977).

Thompson, John B., *Critical Hermeneutics: A Study in the Thought of Paul Ricoeur and Jurgen Habermas* (Cambridge: Cambridge University Press, 1981).

Tickner, J. Ann, 'Hans Morgenthau's Principles of Political Realism: A Feminist Reformulation', 17 (1988) *Millennium – Journal of International Studies,* pp. 429–440.

Gender in International Relations: Feminist Perspectives on Achieving Global Security (Columbia, NY: Columbia University Press, 1992).

Tigar, Michael E. (with the assistance of Madeleine R. Levy), *Law & the Rise of Capitalism* (New York: Monthly Review Press, 1977).

Tomkins, Emilya and Keith (eds.), *The Essential Kropotkin* (London: Macmillan, 1976).

Topper, Keith, *The Disorder of Political Inquiry* (Cambridge, MA: Harvard University Press, 2005).

Trimble, Phillip R., 'International Law, World Order, and Critical Legal Studies', 42 (1990) *Stanford Law Review,* pp. 811–845.

Tully, James, *Strange Multiplicity: Constitutionalism in the Age of Diversity* (Cambridge: Cambridge University Press, 1995).

Turner, Stephen and George Mazur, 'Morgenthau as a Weberian Methodologist', 15 (2009) *European Journal of International Relations,* pp. 477–504.

Twining, W., 'The Significance of Realism', in Lord Lloyd of Hampstead and M. D. A. Freeman (eds.) *Lloyd's Introduction to Jurisprudence*, 5th edn (London: Stevens and Sons 1985), pp. 777–783.

Udehn, Lars, 'The Changing Face of Methodological Individualism', 28 (2002) *Annual Review of Sociology*, pp. 479–507.

UNCTAD, *Trade and Development Report, 2014: Global Governance and Policy Space for Development* (New York: UN, 2014).

 World Investment Report, 2014 (New York: UN, 2014).

UNGA A/HRC/17/31, 21 March 2011: Guiding Principles on Business and Human Rights: Implementing the United Nations 'Protect, Respect, and Remedy' Framework.

Unger, Roberto Mangabeira, 'The Critical Legal Studies Movement', 96 (1983) *Harvard Law Review*, p. 561.

 The Critical Legal Studies Movement (Cambridge, MA: Harvard University Press, 1986).

Urbinati, Nadia, and Mark E. Warren, 'The Concept of Representation in Contemporary Political Theory', 11 (2008) *Annual Review of Political Science*, pp. 387–412.

Valdes, Francisco, and Sumi Cho, 'Critical Race Materialism: Theorizing Justice in the Wake of Global Neoliberalism', 43 (2011) *Connecticut Law Review*, pp. 1513–1572.

Valverde, Mariana, 'The Rescaling of Feminist Analyses of Law and State Power: From (Domestic) Subjectivity to (Transnational) Governance Networks', 14 (2014) *UC Irvine Law Review*, pp. 325–352.

Von Wright, Georg Henrik, *Philosophical Logic* (Oxford: Basil Blackwell, 1983).

Waltz, Kenneth N., *Man, the State and War: A Theoretical Analysis* (New York: Columbia University Press, 1959)

Wang, Zhihe, Huili He, and Meijun Fan, 'The Ecological Civilization Debate in China: The Role of Ecological Marxism and Constructive Postmodernism – Beyond the Predicament of Legislation', (November 2014) *Analytical Monthly Review*, pp. 35–56.

Warrington, R., 'Pashukanis and the Commodity Form Theory', in D. Sugarman (ed.) *Legality, Ideology and the State* (London: Academic Press, 1983), pp. 43–68.

Weber, Max, *Economy and Society*, Guenther Roth and Claus Wittich, (eds.) (Berkeley: University of California Press, 1968).

Wells, Catherine P., 'Legal Innovation within the Wider Intellectual Tradition: The Pragmatism of Oliver Wendell Holmes, Jr', 82 (1988) *Northwestern University Law Review*, pp. 541–595.

Werlhof, Claudia von, 'No Critique of Capitalism without a Critique of Patriarchy! Why the Left Is No Alternative', 18 (2007) *CNS – Capitalism – Nature – Socialism*, pp. 13–27.

West, Cornel, *The Ethical Dimensions of Marxist Thought* (New York: Monthly Review Press, 1991).

Westlake, John, *International Law* (Cambridge: Cambridge University Press, 1895).

Wiessner, Siegfried, 'Law as a Means to a Public Order of Human Dignity: The Jurisprudence of Michael Reisman', 34 (2009) *Yale Journal of International Law*, pp. 525–532.

Wiessner, Siegfried, and Andrew R. Willard, 'Policy-Oriented Jurisprudence and Human Rights Abuses in Internal Conflict: Toward a World Public Order of Human Dignity', in Steven R. Ratner and Anne-Marie Slaughter (eds.) *The Methods of International Law* (Washington, DC: The American Society of International Law, 2004), pp. 47–79.

Williams, Glanville, 'Language and the Law', 61–62 (1945–46) *The Law Quarterly Review*, pp. 71–86, 179–95, 293–303, 337–406.

Williams, Mariama, 'A Perspective on Feminist Organizing from Bottom Up: The Case of IGTN and the WTO', in Gulay Caglar, Elisabeth Prugl and Sussane Zwingel (eds.) *Feminist Strategies in International Governance* (London: Routledge, 2013), pp. 92–108.

Williams, Michael C., (ed.) *Realism Reconsidered: The Legacy of Hans J. Morgenthau in International Relations* (New York: Oxford University Press, 2007)

'Why Ideas Matter in International Relations: Hans Morgenthau, Classical Realism, and the Moral Construction of Power Politics', 58 (2004) *International Organization,* pp. 633–665.

The Realist Tradition and the Limits of International Relations (Cambridge: Cambridge University Press, 2005).

Williams, Raymond, 'The New Metropolis', in Hamza Alavi and Teodor Shanin, (eds.) *Introduction to the Sociology of Developing Societies* (London: Macmillan, 1982), pp. 363–365.

Wittgenstein, Ludwig, *Philosophical Investigations* (Oxford: Blackwell, 1958).

Wood, Allen, 'Marx on Right and Justice: A Reply to Husami', 8 (1979) *Philosophy & Public Affairs,* pp. 267–295.

Wood, Ellen Meiskins, 'Capitalism and Human Emancipation: Race, Gender and Democracy', in Nancy Holstrom (ed.) *The Socialist Feminist Project: A Contemporary Reader in Theory and Politics* (Delhi: Aakar, 2011), pp. 277–292.

Woodward, Barbara K., *Global Civil Society in International Law Making and Global Governance: Theory and Practice* (Leiden: Brill, 2010).

Wright, Quincy, *The Strengthening of International Law* (Leyden: A. W. Sijthoff, 1960).

Xavier, Sujith, 'Theorizing Global Governance Inside Out: A Response to Professor Ladeur', 3 (2012) *Transnational Legal Theory*, pp. 268–284.

Young, Brigitte, 'Structural Power and the Gender Biases of Technocratic Network Governance in Finance', in Gulay Caglar, Elisabeth Prugl and Sussane Zwingel (eds.) *Feminist Strategies in International Governance* (London: Routledge, 2013), pp. 267–282.

Youngs, Gillian, 'Feminist International Relations: A Contradiction in Terms? Or; Why Women and Gender Are Essential to the World We Live In', 80 (2004) *International Affairs,* pp. 75–87.

Young, Oran R., 'International Law and Social Science: The Contributions of Myres S. McDougal', 66 (1972) *American Journal of International Law,* pp. 60–76.

'Compliance in the International System', in Richard Falk, Friedrich Kratochwil and Saul H. Mendlovitz (eds.) *International Law: A Contemporary Perspective* (Boulder CO: Westview Press, Inc., 1985), pp. 99–111.

Zalewski, Marysia, and Anne Sisson Runyan, 'Taking Feminist Violence Seriously in Feminist International Relation', 15 (2013) *International Feminist Journal of Politics,* pp. 293–313.

Zambernardi, Lorenzo, 'The Impotence of Power: Morgenthau's Critique of American Intervention in Vietnam', 37 (2011) *Review of International Studies,* pp. 1335–1356.

Zizek, Slavoz, 'How to Begin From the Beginning', 57 (2009) *New Left Review,* pp. 43–55.

Zoglin, Kathryn, 'United Nations Action against Slavery: A Critical Evaluation', 8 (1986) *Human Rights Quarterly,* p. 315.

INDEX

Abbott, Kenneth W., 37, 93, 98, 120
Abi-Saab, Georges, 15, 306, 344–45
Accumulation
  global imperialism, accumulation by
    dispossession in, 511
  Marx on, 481n178
The Accumulation of Capital
  (Luxemburg), 61
"Actually existing socialism"
  generally, 18, 19, 20n65, 443
  collapse of, 149, 481
  environmental crisis and, 202
  McDougal on, 153, 176
  "third possibility" versus, 544–46
  women and, 375, 375n76, 402
Adler, Max, 455
Administrative unions, 495
Afghanistan War, 39, 83, 232, 514
Africa, imperialism and, 489–90
Agreement on Trade Related
    Intellectual Property Rights
    (TRIPS), 347n513, 510–11, 513
Agreement on Trade Related
    Investment Measures
    (TRIMS), 510–11
Alavi, Hamza, 2n5
Albania, socialism in, 544n477
Albright, Madeline, 422n374
Alexandrowicz, C.H., 234–35,
  329n431, 483
Algiers Declaration on the Rights of
  Peoples, 228
Alienation
  in global imperialism, 515–16
  Marx on, 550n505
Allison, Dorothy, 501n273

Al Qaeda, 422
Alvarej, José, 426, 433, 434–35, 435n450
Ambedkar, B.R., 447n13
American Indians, colonialism
  and, 267–68
*American Journal of International
  Law,* 248
American legal realism
  fields of origin and, 7
  Lasswell on, 116n58, 118n67
  McDougal on, 116n58, 118n67,
    119n69
  policy-oriented approach critique
    of, 116–20
    authority and control in, 118–19,
      119n69
    common interests versus special
      interests, 117–18, 117n63
    law versus policy, 119–20
    scholarship distinguished from
      decision-making process, 120
  Reisman on, 116–17
American War of Independence, 487
Amin, Samir, 234
Amos, Valerie, 402n244
Anand, R.P.
  generally, 9, 15
  David Kennedy and, 257, 306,
    320n391
  Falk on, 235n324
  Koskenniemi and, 326–27,
    329n431, 344–45
  policy-oriented approach and,
    145n183
  WOMP approach and, 234–35,
    235n324

Peace building, liberal feminism
on, 424–26
Peffer, R.G., 538–39
Petersmann, Ernest-Ulrich, 512
Philosophical Investigations
(Wittgenstein), 530n403
Pierce, C.S., 114n44
Policy-oriented approach to
international law
overview, 104–11, 174–78
American legal realism, critique
of, 116–20
authority and control in, 118–19,
119n69
common interests versus special
interests, 117–18, 117n63
law versus policy, 119–20
scholarship distinguished from
decision-making process, 120
capital, logic of, 110–11
capitalism and, 148–49
Charlesworth on, 143–44, 534
Chinkin on, 534
classical realist approach versus, 39,
69, 112–13
coercion and, 111, 171–74
Cold War and, 108n24
comprehensive nature of, 174–75
Critical Legal Studies versus, 141,
304n317
culture, logic of, 448–49
David Kennedy on, 177–78, 534
decision-making process in
overview, 111, 157–61, 170–71
analytical framework of, 158–59
base values of, 167–69
complexity of, 160–61
hegemony and, 164
individual and, 165–66
multi-national corporations
and, 163–64
outcomes of, 169–70
participants in, 161–66
perspectives on, 166–67
power, conceptualization
of, 159–60
scholarship distinguished, 120
state and, 161–62

strategies in, 167–69
systematic approach, importance
of, 159
economic determinism versus,
110–11, 153
Falk on, 104n2, 107, 109, 143, 145–
46, 145n183, 177, 178, 534
fields of origin and, 6–7, 9
five logics, integration of,
110–11, 448–47
FtAIL versus, 143–44, 176
historical background, 105
history and, 151–52
human rights and, 147–50, 534
IMAIL, critical examination from
perspective of, 3, 110
indeterminacy of rules and
overview, 110, 123
contextuality, 128n108
function of sentence, 129–33
goals of interpretation, 128–29
importance of rules, 122n88
ordinary meaning rule, 125 (*See
also* Ordinary meaning rule)
semantic indeterminacy, 124–25
structural indeterminacy, 138–40
surrogationalism, 131n117
textuality, 128n108
use theory of meaning, 133–38
VCLT, critique of, 125–29
influence of, 9n26
intellectual tasks of jurisprudence in
overview, 110–11, 140–42
alternatives, 155–57
clarification of goal values, 147–50
conditioning factors,
identification of, 152–53
future trends, projection
of, 153–55
observational standpoint, 142–47
past trends, description of, 150–52
IR-IL compared, 120
law versus policy, 120–23, 175–76
lawyers, role of, 156–57
liberal feminism versus, 418
Marxism versus, 149
MILS, critique of, 12
NAIL versus, 4, 177–78, 256–57

Responsibility to protect, 165–66
Revolution
Lenin on, 518–19
Luxemburg on, 519n351
Miéville on, 517–22
morality and, 82
reform versus, 517–22
Rice, Daniel, 42n28
Richards, I.A., 130–32, 130n115, 135,
136–37, 136n146
Riles, Annelise, 320n391
Riley, Ronin L., 424n379
Rio Earth Summit, 202
Rittich, Kerry, 359, 367n36,
426, 429–30
Rodney, Walter, 2n6
Rome Statute of the International
Criminal Court, 217n211, 220,
228, 380
Rosenau, James N., 38n5
Rosenberg, Justin, 491
Rostow, Eugene, 107n23
Roth, Brad, 540
Rule of experts, 272–82, 288–94
generally, 273n156, 274n158,
280n194, 281n197
capitalism versus, 273–75, 280–82
complexity of global governance
and, 272–73
constraints on experts, 288–94
imperialism versus, 273–75, 280–82
inequality and injustice and, 289
institutional individualism, 277n184
institutions and, 280n196
methodological individualism,
276–77, 276n180, 277n182,
277n184, 280–82, 290
microfoundations, 278–79
radical holism, 277
social forces, 279–80
Rule of law
"culture of formalism" versus,
336–37, 347n510
global imperialism and, 522–24
Marxist theory of law and, 457–58
Miéville on, 522–24
Thompson on, 457–58, 522–24
Russell, Bertrand, 530n403

Russia, annexation of Crimea by,
227, 227n282, 514. *See also*
Soviet Union

Saberi, Hengameh, 106–07, 141,
160n261, 161, 161n263
Said, Edward
generally, 2n6, 6n13, 27n98
on imperialism, 25n87, 27, 27n97, 63
on secular criticism, 5, 5n11, 180
Salamanca School, 482
Santos, Boaventura de Sousa, 16n49,
157, 357, 540–41
Sarkar, Tanika, 397
Sassen, Saskia, 426
Sathirathai, Surakiart, 306
Scelle, George, 185
Schaffer, Gregory, 95n351, 96n358,
305n318
Scheuerman, William E., 88n307,
90n326
Schmitt, Carl, 42n28
Schuett, Robert, 50–51
Schumacher, E.F., 200
Scientific Man vs. Power Politics
(Morgenthau), 50
Secular criticism, 5
Security Council, 92
Selden, John, 266, 484
Self-determination, liberal feminism
and, 415–16
Self-help, 75n251
Semantic indeterminacy, 110, 124–25
Sen, Amartya, 399
Sentence, function of, 129–33
Seven Years War, 486–87
Sexual subordination, radical feminism
and, 372–73
Shalakny, Amr, 257–58, 307n330
Shamir, Hila, 382
Shanghai Cooperation
Organization, 508
Signs (journal), 247–48
Silver, Laura R., 428n403
Simma, Bruno, 10–12, 122
Singh, Nagendra, 15, 320n391,
329n431
Singh, Sahib, 355n554

CPSIA information can be obtained
at www.ICGtesting.com
Printed in the USA
LVHW050522301118
598764LV00020B/1530/P